Educating Negotiators for a Connected World
Volume 4 in the Rethinking Negotiation Teaching Series

Published by DRI Press, an imprint of the
Dispute Resolution Institute at Hamline University School of Law,
with the generous financial support of the JAMS Foundation.

Dispute Resolution Institute
Hamline University School of Law
1536 Hewitt Avenue
Saint Paul, MN 55104
www.hamline.edu/law/adr

Library of Congress Control Number: 2012955231

ISBN 978-0-9827946-3-0

For bulk orders, contact the Hamline University School of Law Bookstore,
1536 Hewitt Avenue, Saint Paul, MN 55104. (651) 523-2369. For reprint
inquiries, contact the DRI program administrator, (651) 523-2946.

Educating Negotiators for a Connected World

Volume 4 in the Rethinking Negotiation Teaching Series

Christopher Honeyman
James Coben
Andrew Wei-Min Lee

Editors

DRI PRESS
SAINT PAUL, MINNESOTA

TABLE OF CONTENTS

III. New Topics, New Techniques for the Global Classroom

IV. Teaching About Wicked Problems

V. New Frontiers

VI. Epilogue

ACKNOWLEDGEMENTS

More colleagues than we can possibly name deserve our warm thanks here. First and foremost, of course, are the contributing writers in this volume. Less obviously, this book does not stand alone, but is part of a complex strategy: the contributors' work here builds on that of the forty-three contributors to 2009's *Rethinking Negotiation Teaching* and the parallel special section of eight articles in Negotiation Journal (April 2009), the thirty-seven contributors to 2010's *Venturing Beyond the Classroom*, the twenty-three contributors to 2012's *Assessing Our Students, Assessing Ourselves*, and the contributors to 谈判 *Tán Pàn: The Chinese-English Journal on Negotiation*.

None of this would have happened without Giuseppe de Palo, who together with Chris and Jim created the project and served as co-editor for volumes one and two in the series. Volume 3 co-editor Noam Ebner deserves special praise for recognizing that a book specifically dedicated to assessment was both sorely needed, and possible. Also key to this effort have been our steering committee members: it would be impossible to imagine a more perceptive or more incisive team of advisers than Jay Folberg, Roy Lewicki, Carrie Menkel-Meadow, Sharon Press, Frank Sander, Andrea Schneider, Richard Shell, and Michael Wheeler. Thanks also to Kitty Atkins, the Dispute Resolution Institute associate director, for tireless commitment to solve any and all problems. Also essential at Hamline has been Jessica Kuchta-Miller, whose thoughtful edits and careful proofreading helped ensure a quality product, and Debra Berghoff (a/k/a "Magical Hands"), whose mastery of software and graphics once again has made all our lives much simpler.

Separately, this book, like its predecessors, would have been impossible without the support of the JAMS Foundation. The Foundation's early commitment to the project was instrumental to its successful launch, and the Foundation's continued support helps to extend the project's global impact.

Finally, Chris and Jim would be remiss not to offer special thanks to Andrew Wei-Min Lee and Vivian Feng Ying Yu, who through adroit negotiation and sheer determination managed to get us all to Beijing for the conference that inspired the content you find here. We cannot conceive of more inspiring and gracious hosts.

To follow future developments of the project, please visit http://law.hamline.edu/rethinkingnegotiation.html. There you will find the latest project updates, lists of participating scholars, and all book chapters generated to date in downloadable pdf formats (at no charge), as well as a link to issues of 谈判 *Tán Pàn*, to be published in Hong Kong as a joint project of the Dispute Resolution Institute at Hamline University School of Law and the International Institute for Conflict Engagement and Resolution (IICER) in the Department of Law and Business at Hong Kong Shue Yan University.

ᖇ 1 ᖇ

Introduction: What Have We Learned?

*Christopher Honeyman, James Coben & Andrew Wei-Min Lee**

Background: The 4th of 4

It is time to bring a rather unusual project to a close, and as this book is the final volume in the Rethinking Negotiation Teaching (RNT) project, we will try here to sum up the effort as a whole.

We have been fortunate to work with more than a hundred of the field's leading teachers and thinkers, from more than two dozen countries. As a result of their insights, the project evolved from its original design.

At the project's beginning in 2007, the organizing team (originally Christopher Honeyman, James Coben and Giuseppe De Palo) proposed to revamp the teaching of basic negotiation to take account of recent discoveries, while continuing an assumption that there was such a thing as a typical basic course. At the time, that seemed unexceptionable. Certainly, our experiences with courses taught in many countries supported the notion that a common set of concepts, materials and methods had evolved. Indeed, one of the concerns which drove the project was the perception that the concepts, materials, methods and, even more important, the underlying values of all of

* **Christopher Honeyman** is managing partner of Convenor Conflict Management, a consulting firm based in Washington, DC and Madison, Wisconsin. He has directed a 20-year series of major research-and-development projects in conflict management, including as co-director of the Rethinking Negotiation Teaching project. His email address is honeyman@convenor.com. **James Coben** is a professor of law and senior fellow in the Dispute Resolution Institute at Hamline University School of Law, and co-director of the Rethinking Negotiation Teaching project. His email address is jcoben@hamline.edu. **Andrew Wei-Min Lee** is the founder and president of the Leading Negotiation Institute, founded in 2007 and based in Shanghai. The Leading Negotiation Institute's mission is to develop dispute resolution pedagogy and practice in China. The Institute partners with leading universities and dispute resolution institutions both within China and around the world to provide opportunities to exchange personnel, ideas and opportunities in the field of negotiation and dispute resolution. His email address is andrewlee008@gmail.com.

these were primarily American in origin, and perhaps less transferable to other cultures than many teachers assumed. The introductions to *Rethinking Negotiating Teaching* and *Venturing Beyond the Classroom* (volumes 1 and 2 in the RNT series) discussed our subsequent findings in some detail, and we will have more to say on this score below.

During the project's five-year run, however, our colleagues have taught us (as well as each other) a great deal, and we have attempted to be responsive. This meant that the project itself evolved in new directions. We think they have, for the most part, been highly productive. But the new directions do make it a bit more complicated to describe what has happened since this project was conceived. The best demonstration, of course, is a review of the project's overall written output. That speaks for itself; but at some considerable length. So we will try to be concise here.

When the project began, the organizing team had recently concluded a predecessor effort: an international six-university consortium had set out to design better-aligned teaching of negotiation, mediation and arbitration as between U.S. and European graduate teaching environments. The team was also able to draw on a related predecessor project, which had produced a large reference volume, *The Negotiator's Fieldbook* (Schneider and Honeyman 2006) published by the American Bar Association. That inquiry had found almost thirty disciplines' research and practical experiences to be relevant, at a sophisticated level, to an understanding of how negotiation works.

Partly for logistical reasons, the team elected to focus on what seemed a manageable environment for discussions that would involve heavy travel by most of the participants. We set out to create a learning laboratory in which the common "executive" course in basic negotiation would be the unit of experimentation and analysis. Three conferences over several years were initially envisioned, moving (for reasons noted in *Rethinking Negotiation Teaching*) from West to East, and with the venues to be Rome, Istanbul and (originally) Delhi. Products then anticipated included three books and three special issues of journals; by the standards of most projects, ambitious enough.

In the end, our three conferences took place in Rome, Istanbul and Beijing; and in addition to four books, the project produced special issues of two journals,[1] plus a wholly new bilingual journal of negotiation, 谈判 *Tán Pàn* (see www.negotiationchina.com), to be published in Hong Kong as a joint project of the Dispute Resolution Institute at Hamline University School of Law and the International Institute for Conflict Engagement and Resolution (IICER) in the Department of Law and Business at Hong Kong Shue Yan University. So far, so good.

In the first year, the team faithfully followed the original design, and the fifty scholars in attendance at our first meeting closely studied our "benchmark" two-day executive course. (This, surely, created for the hand-picked instructors one of the more intimidating professional environments they had encountered, with thirty Italian and Middle Eastern adult students in the front of the room – and fifty professional peers of the instructors in the back. We continue to owe them a debt.)

But even by the second conference, we found ourselves modifying the original design. Instead of updating the two-day course, the team shrank the formal student/instructional time to a single day, while most of the scholars attending the Istanbul meeting actually used most of that day for project purposes other than sitting in on the course. By the third meeting, in Beijing, there was a further shift in the project's relationship to current students, as the meeting was timed to coincide with the annual all-China English language negotiation competition for law schools. Instead of mounting a laboratory course at all, faculty involvement with the students in Beijing took the form of judging successive rounds of the competition. Still, in a larger sense the conferences continued to be learning laboratories – and effective ones, if the enthusiasm of our scholars for subsequent writing is any measure.

Each of these changes, in our judgment, took place for good and sufficient reason. In essence, we felt there was more to learn both from and for our faculty, after the first year, in environments other than the classroom. This was even reflected in the title of volume 2 in the RNT series, *Venturing Beyond the Classroom.* Yet the changes also reflect something which needs emphasizing here: The effort to rethink negotiation teaching has clearly *itself* required rethinking, as we have moved forward. This has shown up in a succession of different themes, which might be capsulated thus:

- Centrality of culture in virtually all topics, with the paradoxical result that "culture" *cannot* be taught effectively as a topic in and of itself;
- Version 1.0 versus 2.0 imagery, and other failed metaphors;
- Value of short executive courses, versus skepticism about them;
- Value of time in-class at all, as opposed to in more "authentic" environments;
- Extent to which fundamental expectations of the discipline of "negotiation" are tied to Western and even U.S.-specific values;
- Increasing interest in and emphasis on nonverbal, non-rational forms of intelligence;

- Recognition of a class of problems that initially seem impossible to negotiate, partly because any effort to define "the problem" creates new ones. And a beginning towards developing techniques to handle this.

With such an array of new ways of thinking about teaching in our field, it would be strange indeed if we had stuck to our original design. We are not so modest as to believe that the shift of topics or of emphasis represents failure. Yet certainly there is one outright failure, which we should acknowledge: the project initially set out to create a concrete new course structure for a "version 2.0" standard executive course. Plainly, we have not done so. Some will be disappointed, regardless of any protestation that the reason is essentially that we have changed our minds as to the wisdom of such a proposition.

This has implications for the expanding teaching "industry" within our larger field. It seems inescapable that an increasing proportion of teaching of negotiation, as of other subjects in degree-granting institutions, is performed by adjunct or other poorly-compensated teachers. We will have more to say about this in the Epilogue to this volume. For now, these often-overburdened professionals could be forgiven some dismay at what this project has, in essence, concluded:

- Courses should be redesigned for every new audience, even though this will require an advance investigation of the nature of each new audience, which most teachers and trainers currently do not undertake;
- Authentic exercises should be used instead of much of the current reliance on role-plays, even though, especially for traveling teachers/trainers whose environments keep changing, this requires much more design time;
- Assessment has been shown to be frequently a mishmash of illogic and intellectual laziness, and doing it properly is going to be a whole lot more work;
- Some of what is being discovered under the heading of "wicked problems" can no longer be safely left to experts in "intractable" conflict, because it is turning out to be relevant in more routine environments; and most significantly,
- Our field now has new frontiers in all directions: inward within the individual negotiator, toward an integration of the mental with the physical, and toward a "mathematics of emotions"; outward, toward the engineering of more sophisticated tools for handling major public disputes; toward professionalization, with a new appreciation of the value of decades of prior work experience in a "new" professional negotiator; and simultaneously, toward broader dissemination

of skills, with a new appreciation of the fact that virtually everyone *will* negotiate (even in the boxing ring!) but most *will not* ever take a course in the subject.

Daunting as some of these conclusions may be at least to some, we believe that is a price worth paying for the intellectual ferment that is so plainly under way. Our field may be getting visibly more complicated to understand, let alone manage; but it sure ain't getting boring.

For these reasons, despite our expressed intent to use this book to try to wrap up the project as a whole, there will be many loose ends visible to the reader. Again, we think this is merely a sign of the vitality of a field which, by comparison with some other professional disciplines, is still in the first flush of youth. In the introduction to *Rethinking Negotiation Teaching*, we compared the state of the modern field of negotiation and conflict management and their teaching today (or at least, three or four years ago) to medicine, a hundred years ago. The comparison still seems apt to us. Again, we will have more to say about this in the Epilogue.

The Making of This Book

In the following section, we will describe briefly each chapter's role in this book. First, however, we will briefly describe the last meeting of the project, and how it relates to where we think the field stands today.

The Beijing (2011) meeting included a follow-up to the Istanbul (2009) meeting's focus on "adventure learning," though one somewhat constrained geographically by Peking University's institutional concern about liability, if something adverse were to happen while a student was in the company of our faculty outside the university grounds. We opted to have groups of faculty meet with students informally *within* the grounds, but all over campus, and with a set series of questions designed to foster discussion (an "oblique" exercise, in terms of adventure learning theory examined in *Venturing Beyond the Classroom*). Equally valuable was a half-day spent actually in class with students, analyzing their reactions to what they were learning, and two days during which different combinations of our faculty members served part-time as judges in the All-China English Language Negotiation Competition. All of these experiences fed into parts of this book, in various ways.

In view of the tight time available, formal presentations of new teaching material were restricted to three, with each presented twice, in order to answer earlier concerns about scholars having had to miss several other important presentations in order to attend any given one. The selection of the three was therefore critical; in the end, each one inspired a theme that became a section of this book.

We chose topics most likely to enlarge the scope of everyone's thinking:

- A session on the role of physical movement in fostering mental creativity in negotiation (see *Embodied Conflict Resolution*, chapter 22, which anchors the "New Frontiers" section in this volume);
- A session on the rapidly emerging specialty in "wicked problems" (see chapters 17-21 in this volume);
- And, in an effort to help our Western scholars understand something of the conditions under which negotiation is taught in Asia, a session on Pacific Rim adaptations to existing teaching topics and methods, this last given by professors from China, South Korea, Japan and Singapore (see "Lessons from the Global Classroom," chapters 5-10 in this volume).

As was by then customary, significant time on the last two days was set aside for formation of new writing teams and discussion within them.

The results of those discussions in this volume will be addressed in brief in the next section; but the reader should also review the more specialized and equally adventurous discussion of *assessment*. This drew so much enthusiasm and dedication that what had been planned as short sub-papers within a single chapter developed into seventeen chapters, requiring a book of their own (*Assessing Our Students, Assessing Ourselves*, volume 3 in the RNT series).

The Big Picture
What does it mean to "rethink" a field? These three chapters offer both theoretical and highly practical takes on the subject.

Principles for Designing Negotiation Instruction
John Lande, Ximena Bustamante, Jay Folberg & Joel Lee
In this chapter, the authors make coherent a sweeping range of topics treated in the RNT project's first two volumes. (*A personal note: The editors continue to believe that the chapter authors have been too kind about what we see as the project's numerous errors.*) Nevertheless, this chapter is the right starting place for any teacher who, upon seeing four volumes that purport to help him or her redesign a course, knows that the course is bound to be too short to incorporate most of the material. So, where to begin? Well – here.

Of Babies and Bathwater
Howard Gadlin, Ian Macduff & Andrea Kupfer Schneider
The authors admit a strong preference for preservation of the baby. They present a cogent argument that contrary to the imagery some-

times used in the RNT project, there has been no sharp 1.0 to 2.0 divide, no sudden shift in our collective thinking about what our field contains or should teach. Rather, they point out, the teachings of the field have evolved steadily and gradually over several decades, with at least the better courses regularly incorporating aspects of the new research. The whole "Negotiation 2.0" concept, they argue, thus runs the risk of undermining that continuity, and implying instead that some of the core concepts that have proven to be widely applicable around the field and around the world are now to be distrusted. The authors also object cogently to a second potential consequence of this imagery: that the hard-won learning of many generations in older societies about how people should deal with each other is now to be distrusted, seen as out of fashion, and even replaced entirely by a set of imported concepts that may be largely unsuited to the culture importing them.

Venturing Home: Implementing Lessons from the
Rethinking Negotiation Teaching Project
Ken Fox & Sharon Press
In 2011, the authors set out to create from scratch the first fully-realized course to take advantage of everything that had been learned up till then in the course of the RNT project. For 2012, they have already revamped the course, to respond to their own initial critiques as well as to some of the latest writings, in this volume and the parallel volume 3. The result is the closest educational venture that yet exists to the project's original intent to create a "Negotiation 2.0" course. Fortunately, the length of the course series the authors designed is significantly greater than a typical compressed "executive" course. That has allowed room for a significant degree of depth, subtlety and experimentation.

Lessons from the Global Classroom
Inspired by the Beijing conference's focus on the necessity of adaptation, these five chapters offer diverse perspectives on how our field as a whole might best educate negotiators for a connected world.

As We See It
Bee Chen Goh, Habib Chamoun-Nicolas, Ellen E. Deason, Jay Folberg
& Sukhsimranjit Singh
Developing further the "adventure learning" experiments conducted by the project in Istanbul and reported on in *Venturing Beyond the Classroom*, the authors tried new negotiation experiments in the markets of Beijing. Comparing their experiences from their respectively Chinese-Malaysian, Mexican, North American and Indian cultural

perspectives, they conclude that *self-awareness* must be a central re-quirement in cross-cultural negotiation training, and that up to now, it has been far too commonly taken for granted.

How Different Is "Different"?
Teaching Persons to Negotiate Cross-Culturally
Joseph B. Stulberg, Janice Kwon & Khory McCormick
The authors note with appreciation the rising volume of research dis-cussing cross-cultural negotiations; but they find its application to teaching and training often arid, simplistic and unpersuasive. They argue for a richer and more complex treatment of culture in negotia-tion, to give a more accurate impression of two salient circumstances in particular: the degree to which factors believed to be culturally distinct operate in "intra-cultural" negotiating contexts as well as in cross-cultural ones, and the degree to which negotiating dimensions, concepts, strategies and tactics may be similar across cultures, such that a belief that a completely different approach is required as soon as one is negotiating with someone from another culture is as likely to provoke error as a belief that one can safely behave exactly as one would at home.

Innovations and Pitfalls in Chinese ADR Pedagogy:
Experiences from the Field
Shahla Ali, Kang Rong, Alonzo Emery, Tai-Wei Chao & David Matz,
with an Appendix by San Tianyu
How well do "traditional" (i.e., 1980-2010 era) Western approaches to teaching negotiation translate, in a supposedly "traditional" soci-ety that is now undergoing ultra-rapid change? Between them, the authors have extensive experience teaching negotiation in China. Here, they assess that experience in a cross-comparison of five differ-ent Chinese law and business teaching environments. One common factor, they find, is that the postmodern innovation of having stu-dents participate in every aspect of a course, including course design and the selection of topics for discussion, and explicitly incorporat-ing Chinese historical and philosophical sources, has proved useful in helping the students perceive the universality at the core of principled negotiation.

Muntu Meets Mencius: Can Ancient Principles Guide Modern
Negotiations on the Export of Africa's Natural Resources to China?
Phyllis Bernard, with a commentary by Stephanie Mitchell
Discussions of negotiating relationships across cultures tend to start with the assumption that one of the cultures will be American, or at least European. In this chapter, Bernard and then Mitchell start with

a completely different environment: the rapidly expanding relationships, commercial and otherwise, between China and sub-Saharan Africa. They find much of the negotiating pattern, unfortunately, to be anything but sensitive to the real cultural and economic needs, particularly of Africa. Bernard's text proposes, and Mitchell's commentary assesses, a possible shift based on teaching negotiators in key settings some shared cultural elements, represented by similar proverbs in Chinese culture and a wide variety of African cultures. The authors also discuss some differences that may be an enduring source of trouble.

Beyond "Negotiation 2.0": Teaching Negotiation in the Multi-Stakeholder, Multi-Level, and Multi-Process World of Public Policy
Masahiro Matsuura, Boyd Fuller, Sanda Kaufman,
Dong-Young Kim & Kenshi Baba
The authors assess the prospects for teaching public policy negotiation and mediation across Asia. They find that the doctrines they were presented with as embedded elements of teaching materials presume a number of factors that are associated strongly with Western culture, but which are hard to find in public policy dispute management in Japan, Singapore, or Korea. Yet contrary to the perhaps-expected response that the training and teachings must now be thoroughly modified to respond to the context, the authors find themselves concluding, in part at least, that their societies would benefit if targeted ways can be found to use the Western insights to help open up public policy processes in their societies.

Ethics in Legal Negotiation: A Cross-Cultural Perspective
Andrea Kupfer Schneider, Ellen Deason, Dawn Chen & Zhouxh Xiahong
From Chinese and American perspectives, the authors consider a Chinese negotiation class, when presented with an ethical problem or two, as a lens. They examine the implications of the students' decisions for Chinese negotiations, particularly in an environment of law practice. In turn they use these as the basis for an analysis of the larger implications of a rapid and disorienting series of recent changes in Chinese law and legal practice.

New Topics, New Techniques for the Global Classroom
The six chapters in this section are as diverse as any in the RNT series, but they have one thing in common: they all address topics or techniques that are just beginning to be discussed, in classrooms anywhere. Ruminations on "the utility of beauty" and the "golden rule" are followed by analyses of how to get students to *understand* whatever they just did or saw, both inside and outside the classroom. The

section ends with a chapter that proposes a radically new environment for teaching, and one that takes the concept that "everyone negotiates, everywhere" to its logical extreme: the ring, in professional boxing.

Redefining Beauty: Negotiating Consumption and Conservation
of Natural Environments
Charles A. Lawry, Sanda Kaufman & Anita D. Bhappu
Many people who are learning cross-cultural negotiation are studying the subject for utilitarian reasons, because they expect to negotiate commercial, industrial, or governmental issues across cultures. They may not immediately perceive the relevance of aesthetics. But to a significant extent, any of these kinds of negotiations is likely to have an environmental component, even when the presenting issues in the negotiation do not appear to be primarily "environmental" in content. Thus it becomes germane to a surprisingly large range of people that perceptions of what is appropriate environmentally have a consumption-versus-conservation element that is, at some fundamental level, about differing cultural perceptions of what is useful – and what is beautiful. The authors analyze some of the implications, including the perception that better cross-cultural training and wider travel is helping many people to appreciate others' views of beauty. That leads to a degree of aesthetic and social "convergence" that will be needed in future, for very practical purposes.

Following the Golden Rule and Finding Gold:
Generosity and Success in Negotiation
Lela P. Love and Sukhsimranjit Singh
This chapter picks up where *The Psychology of Giving and Its Effect on Negotiation* (Chamoun and Hazlett 2009), *Finding Common Ground in the Soil of Culture* (Bernard 2009), and *Re-Orienting the Trainer to Navigate – Not Negotiate – Islamic Cultural Values* (Bernard 2010) left off earlier in the RNT series. The authors argue that principles of generosity are strongly supported by principles common to all the world's major religions, and that it follows that precepts that are widely shared (in theory) might yet be taught to be actually followed in negotiation practice. This, they contend, would have major effects not only on the general level of cooperation vs. competition, but on the specific, material as well as spiritual, well-being of the negotiators as individuals. There is a paradox, though: the spiritual benefit inures to you only if you *don't* strategize to achieve it.

Debriefing the Debrief
Ellen E. Deason, Yael Efron, Ranse Howell, Sanda Kaufman,
Joel Lee & Sharon Press
An afterthought; a rushed invitation for general comments; some PowerPoint slides flashed at the end of an exercise; a pre-prepared reading list of "take away lessons" . . . . do these sound familiar? The authors argue that all too often, good intentions for thorough debriefing of negotiation exercises degenerate into something disappointing, or even pointless. They contend that debriefing is too critical an element in overall learning to be defensibly treated this way. In a thorough analysis that should also be read in conjunction with the same authors' treatment of debriefing adventure learning specifically (chapter 14 in this volume), they first outline a choice of goals; then analyze the characteristics of good debriefing work, and discuss some general approaches; and then outline predictable challenges and some tactics for handling them. As is appropriate for the project's increasing focus on the differences between student groups (see Lewicki and Schneider, *Instructors Heed the Who*, chapter 3 in *Venturing Beyond the Classroom*), the authors end by discussing how debriefing might be tailored for specific audiences.

Debriefing Negotiation Adventure Learning
Ellen E. Deason, Yael Efron, Ranse Howell, Sanda Kaufman,
Joel Lee & Sharon Press
This chapter (which should be read in conjunction with the same authors' *Debriefing the Debrief*, chapter 13 in this volume) addresses the special conditions which attach to efforts to debrief adventure learning. The same real-world authenticity that is the most attractive feature of adventure learning, they point out, introduces predictable problems – beginning but not ending with the mundane failure of negotiating groups to return to class at the same time, when the debrief has been scheduled. But it gets worse than that, in ways the authors cheerfully outline. The authors follow with a number of suggestions, which collectively should help students get the most out of the exercise – and help the teacher sleep better the night *before* the exercise.

Bringing the Street to the Classroom and the Student to the Street: Guided Forays into Street-Wise Negotiations
Habib Chamoun-Nicolas, Boyd Fuller, David Benitez & Randy Hazlett
Many writings in this series have argued for greater authenticity in training and teaching, including getting students out of the classroom. No greater authenticity in negotiation teaching settings is likely to be found than in the authors' experiments with teaching students who are actually at work negotiating, while they really are *at* work.

The authors argue that two key attributes of authenticity are served by this technique: repeated engagement, as distinct from isolated role-plays, and expanded stakes, where the student stands to gain or lose in an immediate career sense. Not only is the training, at least in part, actually performed at work, but the students are observed closely by people who are associated with management. The authors report on early experiments in a multinational business setting (in Mexico and the United States), and a public policy setting in Singapore.

Negotiation in Professional Boxing
Habib Chamoun-Nicolas, Randy D. Hazlett, Russell Mora,
Gilberto Mendoza & Michael L. Welsh
In this groundbreaking piece, a group of authors with unimpeach-able expertise in one of the least likely environments ever considered for negotiation analyze what is actually going on in the professional boxing ring. Their surprising conclusions take the facile claim of our field that "everybody negotiates" to a whole new level. Not only does this chapter serve as a kind of extreme-case demonstration of why students should consider learning negotiation to be central to *any* oc-cupation they may take up in future; it might well serve as inspiration for some new studies in other fields in which negotiation may previ-ously have been thought irrelevant.

Teaching About Wicked Problems
Building on chapters 24-27 in *Venturing Beyond the Classroom*, the chap-ters that follow explore how educators can take on the challenge to address "wicked" problems in negotiation courses.

Adapting to the Adaptive:
How Can We Teach Negotiation for Wicked Problems?
Jayne Seminare Docherty & Leonard L. Lira
This chapter picks up where the "wicked problems team" left off in *Venturing Beyond the Classroom*: with the need to formulate effective teaching strategies for an exceptionally important area of inquiry, in which our understanding is, as yet, far short of perfection. Docherty and Lira are examples of professionals whose students cannot wait for anything close to perfection: both in peacebuilding and in the military, a professional must work with the understanding that is available. It is significant that in their very different environments, Docherty and Lira have been learning from each other, adapting ideas from the mili-tary into peacebuilding and vice versa, in order to formulate teaching programs that can work even within the single perspective of either discipline. Their experiments are groundbreaking, and of importance to many other professional fields.

Making it Up as You Go:
Educating Military and Theater Practitioners in "Design"
Leonard L. Lira & Rachel Parish
Following directly from the preceding chapter, Lira and Parish lay out a potential example of a training course for "wicked problems," finding unexpected parallels in two completely different professional environments: the theater and the military. The authors demonstrate how an elective "Design" course in the U.S. Army Command and General Staff College parallels the development of theater professionals. This matches the insights of Jayne Docherty, a professor of peacebuilding, in the previous chapter and the one which follows.

Teaching Three-Dimensional Negotiation to Graduate Students
Jayne Seminare Docherty, with Calvin Chrustie
In a conscious parallel to the preceding chapter, Docherty describes an initial experiment, developed largely from Chrustie's practical experience, with teaching "wicked problems" to graduate students in peacemaking at a Mennonite university. The collaboration between a professor of peacebuilding on the one hand, and a highly experienced police officer and peacekeeper on the other, is as significant to the development of our field as the flow of information, experiments and ideas back and forth between the peacebuilding professional environment and the Command and General Staff College of the U.S. Army, discussed in chapter 17 in this volume, and further amplified in this chapter.

Playing the Percentages in Wicked Problems: On the Relationship between Broccoli, Peacekeeping, and Peter Coleman's *The Five Percent*
Howard Gadlin, David Matz & Calvin Chrustie
In the initial joint effort of the RNT's "wicked problems" team (Chrustie et al., *Five Stories*, chapter 25 in *Venturing Beyond the Classroom*), the authors began with the more dramatic, international and violent settings, and worked from there to demonstrate how these problems also operate within less violent environments, such as city politics and the internal doings of a large organization. Here, in an effort to assess for teaching purposes a major new work in the field (*The Five Percent*, by Peter Coleman 2011), the authors begin in the opposite order, and scale up their discussion from the most modest of beginnings – a vegetable – to conclude with analysis of one of the most contentious and unstable disputing environments: peacekeeping.

Teaching Wickedness to Students:
Planning and Public Policy, Business, and Law
Roy Lewicki, Sanda Kaufman & James Coben
Many readers of this book, and this series, may start out thinking that of all the problems and all the issues and all the techniques they need to engage with as teachers of negotiation, at least they can leave "wicked problems" to specialists in international, environmental, race relations and other "intractable" conflict. Howard Gadlin's analysis in chapter 20 of the role of wicked problems inside any large organization should be enough to give pause to that complacency. This chapter's three authors normally encounter students who are more "typical," recent-graduate-level, and classroom-oriented than the midcareer military professionals discussed by Leonard Lira and Rachel Parish in chapter 18, or the often middle-aged, returning students in the graduate program in peacemaking described by Jayne Docherty and Calvin Chrustie in chapter 19. The authors candidly assess barriers and offer up a series of practical recommendations for teaching "wicked problems" in planning and public policy, business, and law programs.

New Frontiers

Predicting the future is a notoriously chancy business. That said, these concluding chapters in the RNT series challenge all of us to think in new directions. We are prepared to predict that at least some of the new directions will be far-reaching.

Embodied Negotiation:
Resurrecting Roleplay-Based Curricula Through Dance
Nadja Alexander and Michelle LeBaron
Moving on from the same authors' seminal 2009 critique of the overuse of role-plays in negotiation teaching, *Death of the Role-Play* (chapter 13 in *Rethinking Negotiation Teaching*), Alexander and LeBaron have taken the rapidly increasing enthusiasm for experiential learning in a new direction: multiple intelligences. Their particular interest is in a use of experiential learning that focuses on *kinesthetic intelligence*, employing actual physical movement, particularly dance, to unlock creativity in other mental domains, as well as to encourage authentic participation by people whose skills are not primarily verbal or mathematical. Those who may be inclined to be skeptical should note that this work is receiving increased attention among people whose dominant skills are definitely verbal: this chapter serves as a brief introduction to a project whose longer work is to be published soon by the American Bar Association.

The Influence of Emotion in Negotiation: A Game Theory Framework
Habib Chamoun-Nicolas & Randy Hazlett
Perhaps the "other side of the coin" of the preceding chapter, this chapter's authors review what has been learned about long-term relationships from the insights of game theory. They note that game theory's presumption of "rational," interest-maximizing negotiators is a significant limitation, in a world in which is increasingly accepted that we all think from the starting point of our emotions (see Patera and Gamm, *Emotions – A Blind Spot in Negotiation Training*, chapter 19 in *Venturing Beyond the Classroom*). Evolutionary game theory, they argue, provides a basis to learn from repeated interactions, which could be adapted by introducing emotional bias into the game theory framework. This would allow game theory to be used in analysis of altruism, empathy, reputation and other phenomena which are becoming more and more important in teaching negotiation. Their analysis also challenges us all to absorb more via a kind of intelligence most negotiators rather desperately avoid exercising: the mathematical.

A Game Of Negotiation: The "Deliberation Engine"
Christopher Honeyman, Peter S. Adler, Colin Rule, Noam Ebner,
Roger Strelow, & Chittu Nagarajan
This chapter envisions a negotiation game which can promote learning, as well as fact-finding on any hot-button issue. The authors outline a particular form of online game, in variants separately designed to work with formal education, working professionals, and the general public. The game, as conceived here, is designed to address a mounting problem in negotiations of the largest scale, public issues: an apparently increasing tendency of people and parties to make up their own facts. Global climate change is considered as a test case. A related chapter in this volume, *The Education of Non-Students*, assesses the prospects for a related new strategy, using theater, film and games to begin to provide informal negotiation education for the vast majority of the public who will never take any kind of course on negotiation.

Negotiation Stands Alone
Alexandra Crampton & Michael Tsur
Yes, the authors concede, "everybody" negotiates: but that's like saying "everybody drives," and then watching aghast when "everybody" climbs into a racing car, or an eighteen-wheeled tractor-trailer. The authors draw from Tsur's experience teaching Israeli hostage negotiators and in other high-pressure environments to argue for an entirely distinct concept of a professional negotiator, one that starts with a

rather experienced "student" and builds a sharply different training regimen from there.

The Education of Non-Students
Eric Blanchot, Noam Ebner, Christopher Honeyman,
Sanda Kaufman & Rachel Parish
Most people do not take courses – yet they learn new things and change their attitudes and behavior all the time. So far, with some exceptions, our field has taken little advantage of informal avenues for education. This concluding chapter explores how we might foster social change toward better attitudes in negotiation, using various media far outside the classroom setting (electronic games, film and other visual materials, and theater) that can serve as platforms for informal negotiation education. The authors believe our field needs not one or two, but an array of such approaches.

Epilogue: The Biz
Christopher Honeyman & James Coben
Collectively, the scholarship produced in the RNT project significantly "ups the ante" for what teachers ought to provide (and students and institutions ought to *demand*) in quality negotiation education. But can these higher aspirations be reconciled with the rapidly changing economics of higher education and the "entertrainment" tendencies of the executive training field?

The View from Here
We have no right to dictate goals for anyone but ourselves. We can, however, make some predictions as to the likely next directions of at least some of our colleagues in this effort. The dance/multiple intelligences inquiry, represented in this volume by chapter 22, is already producing an entire new book (*Making Movement Matter*), to be published in the near future by the American Bar Association (LeBaron, MacLeod, and Acland 2013 forthcoming). We have rarely seen so much enthusiasm and outright fun being shown by distinguished professors with any new topic, and we predict a bold future with rapidly rising interest in many quarters. (For those who may find this hard to believe, we suggest that they reflect on the history over the past fifteen years of *mindfulness meditation* in relation to our field: that line of skill development has gone from a single pioneering scholar, Leonard Riskin (2002 and 2006), starting to investigate, to training programs being offered in a wide variety of venues and to a wide variety of professional audiences, with some supposedly starchy law firms among the most enthusiastic adopters.)

We have similar hopes for the "informal education" inquiry which concludes this volume: while by definition it does not draw on the skills of professional educators in as predictable a way as their customary duties, informal education serves the social goals of the field better, perhaps, than any other strategy we could collectively adopt. Its inherent economy also seems responsive to the growing concerns about the rising unaffordability of higher education in the West. Similarly, we hope that if the original team is unable for any reason to develop the concept of the "deliberation engine" (chapter 24 in this volume), others will find a viable way: we can hardly overemphasize the many indications that public debates and policy disputes are often badly handled in the United States, despite its claim to be a "city on a hill." Clearly, new tools and new strategies for pursuing public negotiations over policy are going to be needed.

We should not neglect our own next directions, both as examples of what we hope others will develop, and because we seek others' input into our own efforts. Although technically this volume concludes the RNT project, it leaves in a successor's role a brand-new and continuing venture, our 谈判 *Tán Pàn: The Chinese-English Journal on Negotiation*. We hope for a continuing relationship with the scholars who have made up the core of this project. Even more, we hope that this project's conspicuous openness to scholars from many disciplinary traditions and nations will draw matching interest from scholars of many disciplines in China, as well as elsewhere in Asia. We believe their ideas about negotiation may often not have been heard in our field (as yet) largely because they were previously identified with other fields entirely – and now, the connections to our own field are ready to be drawn, with a specially-designed venue organized.

Finally, we have great hopes for the future in the all-important area of "wicked problems" (chapters 24-27 in *Venturing Beyond the Classroom* and chapters 17-21 in this volume). If this project has been effective at anything, it has been effective at demonstrating the intellectual richness and rising complexity of our field, including the widespread relevance of a succession of topics once thought to be of only specialized interest. The latest writing on wicked problems, for example (see particularly Howard Gadlin's discussion in *Playing the Percentages in Wicked Problems*, chapter 20 in this volume) should make it plain that what no one even identified as a sub-field of negotiation a few years ago has increasing applicability to a host of organizational, political, community and other "everyday" problems – and not just to the range of extraordinary issues our team started by considering.

There is now every reason to believe that Social Security, Afghanistan, health care and other huge public issues in the United

States, not to mention their counterparts elsewhere, cannot and will not be addressed with anything resembling success until the key protagonists understand something of what is being learned about these problems *as a class*. But it is increasingly becoming apparent that our field has, if anything, over-specialized and under-recognized this new avenue of inquiry. In future, we believe that it stands to influence disputes and transactions in many more settings than even our exceptionally perceptive team originally thought. Between their efforts in theorizing, teaching and practice and (we should acknowledge) the distinguished parallel efforts of Peter Coleman and his colleagues based at Columbia University, we believe the stage is set for a next phase of broader and more rapid development of ideas and methods, by a still larger array of talented people.

We will be particularly pleased if this project is someday seen as having contributed to that.

Notes

[1] Honeyman, C., J. Coben, and G. De Palo (guest eds). 2009. Special section of eight articles: Second generation global negotiation education. *Negotiation Journal* 25(2): 141-266; Rethinking negotiation teaching project: May 2008 Rome and October 2009 Istanbul conference. 2010. *Hamline Journal of Public Law & Policy* 31(2): i-vii; 367-568.

References

Bernard, P. 2009. Finding common ground in the soil of culture. In *Rethinking negotiation teaching: Innovations for context and culture*, edited by C. Honeyman, J. Coben, and G. De Palo. St. Paul, MN: DRI Press.

Bernard, P. 2010. Re-orienting the trainer to navigate – not negotiate – Islamic cultural values. In *Venturing beyond the classroom: Volume 2 in the rethinking negotiation teaching series*, edited by C. Honeyman, J. Coben, and G. De Palo. St. Paul, MN: DRI Press.

Chamoun, H. and R. Hazlett. 2009. The psychology of giving and its effect on negotiation. In *Rethinking negotiation teaching: Innovations for context and culture*, edited by C. Honeyman, J. Coben, and G. De Palo. St. Paul, MN: DRI Press.

Chrustie, C., J. S. Docherty, L. Lira, J. Mahuad, H. Gadlin, and C. Honeyman. 2010. Negotiating wicked problems: Five stories. In *Venturing beyond the classroom: Volume 2 in the rethinking negotiation teaching series*, edited by C. Honeyman, J. Coben, and G. De Palo. St. Paul, MN: DRI Press.

Coleman, P. 2011. *The five percent: Finding solutions to seemingly impossible conflicts*. New York: Perseus Books.

Ebner, N., J. Coben, and C. Honeyman (eds). 2012. *Assessing our students, assessing ourselves: Volume 3 in the rethinking negotiation teaching series*. St. Paul, MN: DRI Press.

Honeyman, C., J. Coben, and G. De Palo (eds). 2009. *Rethinking negotiation teaching: Innovations for context and culture.* St. Paul, MN: DRI Press.

Honeyman, C., J. Coben, and G. De Palo (eds). 2010. *Venturing beyond the classroom: Volume 2 in the rethinking negotiation teaching series.* St. Paul, MN: DRI Press.

LeBaron, M., C. MacLeod, and A. Acland (eds). 2013 forthcoming. *Making movement matter: Conflict, dance and neuroscience* (working title). Chicago, IL: American Bar Association.

Lewicki, R. J. and A. K. Schneider. 2010. Instructors heed the who: Designing negotiation training with the learner in mind. In *Venturing beyond the classroom: Volume 2 in the rethinking negotiation teaching series*, edited by C. Honeyman, J. Coben, and G. De Palo. St. Paul, MN: DRI Press.

Riskin, L. L. 2002. The contemplative lawyer: On the potential contributions of mindfulness meditation to law students, lawyers, and their clients. *Harvard Negotiation Law Review* 7:3-66.

Riskin, L. L. 2006. Knowing yourself: Mindfulness. In *The negotiator's fieldbook: The desk reference for the experienced negotiator*, edited by A. K. Schneider and C. Honeyman. Washington, DC: American Bar Association.

Schneider, A. K. and C. Honeyman (eds). 2006. *The negotiator's fieldbook: The desk reference for the experienced negotiator*. Washington, DC: American Bar Association.

☙ 2 ❧

Principles for Designing Negotiation Instruction

John Lande, Ximena Bustamante, Jay Folberg & Joel Lee*

Editors' Note: In this chapter, the authors make coherent a sweeping range of topics treated in the RNT project's first two volumes. (A personal note: The editors continue to believe that the chapter authors have been too kind about what we see as the project's numerous errors.) Nevertheless, this chapter is the right starting place for any teacher who, upon seeing four volumes that purport to help him or her redesign a course, knows that the course is bound to be too short to incorporate most of the material. So, where to begin? Well – here.

Introduction

What's a negotiation instructor to do? So much to teach and so little time. Most instructors can't shoehorn into a traditional negotiation course[1] all the things they would like to do. Participants in the Rethinking Negotiation Teaching[2] (RNT) conferences have identified many additional subjects and instructional methods, which increases opportunities to provide the best possible instruction but also increases the challenges in doing so. Instructors' dilemmas are compounded when teaching negotiation outside of their home instructional environment. In any case, they should consider the many variations in audiences, settings, and goals of the negotiation instruction. The RNT

* **John Lande** is Isidor Loeb Professor and former director of the LL.M. Program in Dispute Resolution at the University of Missouri School of Law. His email address is landej@missouri.edu. **Ximena Bustamante** is a legal research fellow at the law firm of Girardi & Keese; previously she was a Weinstein International Fellow of the JAMS Foundation. Her email address is ximena.c.bustamente@gmail.com. **Jay Folberg** is professor emeritus at the University of San Francisco School of Law and executive director of the JAMS Foundation, as well as a mediator with JAMS. His email address is jfolberg@jamsadr.com. **Joel Lee** is an associate professor at the faculty of law, National University of Singapore. His email address is joellee@nus.edu.

project calls on instructors not to "over-rely on 'canned' material of little relevance to students" (Honeyman and Coben 2010a: 2).

Since instructors cannot teach everything about negotiation in a single course, this chapter suggests some general principles for instructors to make decisions for their courses, whether they teach them internationally and/or domestically. It incorporates many of the ideas suggested in the three RNT conferences as well as the predecessor efforts reflected in a symposium in the Marquette Law Review (Special Issue 2004), Negotiation Journal (Special Section 2009), and the Negotiator's Fieldbook (Schneider and Honeyman 2006). Indeed, this article is intended to serve as an index to these publications, helping readers follow up particular issues by identifying readings on point.

There is no one right or best way to teach negotiation, so instructors should select approaches most suitable to their situations. The following ideas include some general suggestions that should be applicable in most situations as well as a menu of ideas that instructors can choose from.

General Principles for Instructional Design

Instructors should carefully develop instructional goals and objectives, which should generally drive their decisions (Abramson 2009; Cohn et al. 2009; McAdoo and Manwaring 2009; Nelken, McAdoo, and Manwaring 2009; Wade 2009). Some common goals are for students to 1) increase their understanding of different negotiation approaches and perspectives, 2) become more careful observers of negotiation process, goals, tactics, and effects, 3) enhance negotiation skills, 4) change their attitudes about particular negotiation approaches, 5) understand policy issues about negotiation, and 6) learn to learn (or "metacognition") (Moffitt and Peppet 2004; Alexander and LeBaron 2009; McAdoo and Manwaring 2009; Nelken, McAdoo, and Manwaring 2009). Courses using case studies of actual negotiations may emphasize goals of gaining a realistic understanding of what actually happens in negotiation and appreciating the multiplicity of variables and complexity of interactions between actors (Matz 2009). Obviously, these are very general goals and instructors are likely to have particular versions of their goals relating to the specific knowledge and skills they want their students to develop.

Instructors must decide how much to incorporate standard modules from prior courses and how much to tailor the course to the expected class. Generally, instructors should increase the amount they modify the material in proportion to the extent to which the class population is likely to differ from prior classes who took the course. Instructors should consider possible differences in the student population (e.g., university students vs. practitioners); instructional format; or educational, practice, or national culture. When instructors have previously taught the course to a similar set of students in the same culture and it worked well, there is less need to modify the course (other than to incorporate new developments since the prior offering). On the other hand, if there are significant differences, instructors should change their plans accordingly. Although it might be easier to use standard repeatable modules for all courses, students are likely to be more motivated to learn if instructors tailor the courses to fit the students' circumstances (LeBaron and Patera 2009; Nelken, McAdoo, and Manwaring 2009; Lewicki and Schneider 2010).

Beyond customizing the course to increase knowledge and skills that are relevant to students' national or ethnic cultures (Abramson 2009; Kovach 2009; Bernard 2010; Lewicki and Schneider 2010), instructors should also consider the students' *educational* cultures. For example, negotiation courses in law schools and business schools are embedded in cultures with norms and expectations about how courses are taught, what students are expected to do in the courses, and how the material is relevant to negotiations that students are likely to engage in during their careers. Similarly, negotiation trainings for business executives and lawyers have particular (and usually different) norms and expectations. Instructors should be sensitive to students' technological culture as well. Increasingly, students will be oriented to technologically sophisticated environments and instructors should consider how they can best work with their students in their technological environment. Moreover, when students participate in the instruction as members of an organization, the instruction should be tailored to be most effective within the organizational culture (Cohn et al. 2009).

The tailoring of a negotiation course should be oriented to the assumptions, ideas, and values that students bring into the classroom, as they will have to integrate new ideas and experiences into their initial mindsets (Abramson 2009; LeBaron and Patera 2009; Nelken, McAdoo, and Manwaring 2009). For example, students normally start with certain orientations about competition and cooperation that are likely to affect how they respond to course material. Ideally, before a course begins, instructors would get a sense of what ideas students bring to the course (Bhappu et al. 2009; Cohn et al. 2009) but even if not, instructors can certainly elicit it early in the course (Abramson 2009). They should also consider students' comfort levels with and openness to challenge and ambiguity (Kamp 2010).

Instructors should not necessarily conform to students' educational norms and expectations; but they should pay attention to them. This is not to suggest that instructors should necessarily try to agree with students' predispositions; actually instructors may want to challenge students to re-examine their preconceptions. Indeed, an important part of learning involves transformation of the mental "schemas" that students bring into the course about the subject and teaching methods (McAdoo and Manwaring 2009). Instructors who deviate from accepted norms may encounter student resistance, which can divert attention and interfere with the learning process. If instructors decide that they can best achieve their goals by deviating from educational norms in some way, it is useful to be especially clear about the learning objectives and rationale, as this is likely to lead students to respond better and learn more. For example, instructors should be particularly clear about the rationale and expectations for adventure learning assignments, since many students are not familiar with them.[3] The RNT project documented educational risks as well as benefits in adventure learning, suggesting the need for particular care when incorporating such activities in negotiation instruction.[4] Instructors should also clearly explain the rationale even for more familiar methods such as simulations (Ebner and Kovach 2010), which can be problematic if not well planned and implemented (Alexander and LeBaron 2009). This principle applies for topics as well as teaching methods, such that instructors should be especially explicit about the rationale for covering topics that students would not immediately expect to be included in negotiation courses, such as mindfulness, curiosity, generosity, and even emotions (Nelken 1996).

Instructors should design their courses to promote students' motivation to engage in the course activities productively. Although it would be ideal if all students were highly-motivated and responsible throughout a course, some start with less-than-optimal motivation and may not respond well to particular course activities and assignments. Students predictably (and sometimes legitimately) do not respond well if they believe that the course activities are not valuable for them.

Engaging students in developing their goals and activities may help motivate them to work harder and learn more (Nelken 2009; Nelken, McAdoo, and Manwaring 2009). There is evidence that requiring students to *design* simulations, for example, may be a particularly good teaching strategy (Druckman 2006; Druckman and Ebner 2010; Ebner and Druckman 2012). The extent that instructors should engage students in designing the instruction, if at all, is a function of various factors including the students' level of motivation, experience, judgment, and maturity as well as cultural norms about roles of students and instructors.

Furthermore, engaging students in designing some aspects of a course can help instructors focus the course at an appropriate level of challenge for the students in the class (Nelken, McAdoo, and Manwaring 2009). Students are likely to learn most if they find the course is neither too easy nor too hard. If it is too easy, they miss some opportunities for learning and may lose motivation to engage in the course. On the other hand, if they find the course too hard, they may get discouraged and also fail to learn as much as possible. Of course, a class may be composed of students at different levels of ability so that what may be too easy for some students may be appropriate or too hard for others. Thus, instructors should consider if there is likely to be a substantial range of student abilities and, if so, design the course to provide learning opportunities at an appropriate level of challenge for as many students as possible. Moreover, students have different learning styles (such as being more active or reflective) that affect how well they respond (Kovach 2009). Instructors need to take special care when the instruction is not in the native language of some or all of the students (Abramson 2009; Stulberg, Canedo, and Potockova 2009).

A Canon of Negotiation

We believe that there is significant value in both having a common body of instruction and also tailoring instruction to the particular circumstances of each course. Without a shared "canon" of negotiation instruction (Honeyman and Schneider 2004), people essentially talk different "languages," making it hard to be as effective as possible. When most instructors include major elements of the canon in their courses, it can help students and practitioners communicate and work with each other more effectively as part of a common professional community. This is not to advocate an orthodox canon or a single, unassailable approach to instruction. Instead, we believe that the canon is (and should be) a general set of issues and understandings that is always subject to question and improvement. The RNT project challenges the community of negotiation instructors to consider broadening the canon by including additional perspectives, topics for instruction, and teaching methods.

In fact, there has been a general canon of negotiation instruction, sometimes called "Negotiation 1.0" in RNT terminology. We believe that the terms "Negotiation 1.0" and, as the reader will encounter later, Negotiation 2.0 may have had developmental value in assisting us to think about the distinctions between "what we have always done" and "what we could possibly do." That said, we think that this terminology oversimplifies and creates a misimpression that Negotiation

2.0 is necessarily superior to Negotiation 1.0. We will say more about this at the end of this chapter.

In 1999-2000, the Harvard Program on Negotiation conducted a study involving interviews with prominent negotiation instructors in law, business, public policy and planning, and international relations programs. The study found some common themes as well as variations within and between the four types of programs. Some of the variations reflected differences in emphasis on particular elements (such as instruction in theory and practical skills).

In general, the courses normally provided an intellectual framework for negotiation analysis such as assessing parties' interests and options, identifying reservation points and bargaining ranges, gathering necessary information, and considering various factors that might affect negotiation. The courses also shared common methods including use of simulations and debriefings, opportunities for student reflection, and requirements for self-assessment and evaluation (Fortgang 2000; Cobb 2000).

Similarly, Christopher Honeyman and Andrea Kupfer Schneider (2004) reported that experts at a 2003 symposium on negotiation instruction identified six topics that are most commonly part of negotiation teaching: 1) personal strategy, 2) communication skills, 3) integrative and distributive negotiation, 4) bargaining zones, alternatives to negotiated agreements, and reservation prices, 5) generating options, and 6) preparation for negotiation.

A review of law school syllabi of negotiation courses posted on the website of the ADR Section of the Association of American Law Schools suggests a similar congruity. The courses covered various negotiation theories, typically including interest-based and positional negotiation, as well as others such as game theory and procedural justice theory. Courses covered stages of negotiation and legal and ethical issues related to negotiation, and included instruction in relevant skills such as self-reflection, communication, interviewing, counseling, using assertiveness and empathy, preparation, and dealing with differences in power and culture. As one would expect, not all courses include all of these issues.

Several RNT authors have highlighted the importance of including negotiation ethics as part of the canon (Gibson 2004; Gibson 2006; Menkel-Meadow 2006; Nolan-Haley and Gmurzynska 2009; Schneider et al., *Ethics in Legal Negotiation*, in this volume). Similarly, we believe that laws governing negotiation should be part of the canon, at least when the negotiation is subject to legal regulation (Korobkin, Moffitt, and Welsh 2004).

Instructional Enhancements

The RNT project is designed to improve negotiation instruction, at least partly by increasing the range of subjects and teaching methods that instructors might include. In RNT parlance, the new instructional approach is called "Negotiation 2.0." In the past, some instructors have certainly included some of these enhancements in their teaching, though they have probably not been included in most courses. Since instructors have a hard time cramming in everything they want from Negotiation 1.0, the challenge is even greater with the enlarged menu of options offered by Negotiation 2.0.[5] This section summarizes some of the additional choices that instructors may consider.[6]

Perspectives, Theories, and Assumptions

Instructors must make explicit or implicit decisions about their overall perspectives in teaching their courses. For example, this may involve a broad perspective based on theories about social construction of conflict, relationship systems, identity and culture, or particular disciplines such as psychology or neurobiology. A cross-cutting framework involves learning theories and the most appropriate teaching methodology (Hughes 2004; Yarn and Jones 2006; LeBaron and Patera 2009).

All instruction has some theoretical frameworks and assumptions. Even if instructors do not consciously and explicitly decide to present such perspectives, they effectively choose some perspective. When these decisions are implicit, they reflect what some call the "hidden curriculum" (LeBaron and Patera 2009). Specific descriptive and prescriptive assumptions involve:

- Whether knowledge has independent existence and/or is socially created (Fox 2009);
- The level of stability of the context or social structures surrounding negotiations (Docherty 2006);
- Whether negotiation is oriented to resolution of immediate disputes, dealing with underlying or protracted conflicts, and/or promoting systemic change (Avruch 2006; Coleman et al. 2006; Docherty 2006; Hauss 2006; Ricigliano 2006; Mayer 2009);
- The extent to which people have independent agency in making their decisions as opposed to being directed or constrained by social forces (Gold 2009; LeBaron and Patera 2009);
- The extent to which people act based on conscious, calculating, and competitive self-interest as opposed to less-conscious and cooperative motivations (Docherty 2006; Fox 2009; Gold 2009; LeBaron and Patera 2009; Fox, Schonewille, and Çuhadar-Gürkaynak 2010);

- The roles of culture, relationships, identity, and emotion in negotiation, and whether they are discrete variables in negotiation that represent potential problems to overcome, or are parts of people's general worldviews (Docherty 2004a; Goh 2006; Kelly 2006; Abramson 2009; Bernard 2009a; Bernard 2009b; Fox 2009; Gold 2009; Volpe and Cambria 2009; Ebner and Kamp 2010; Fox, Schonewille, and Çuhadar-Gürkaynak 2010; Nelken, Schneider, and Mahuad 2010; Patera and Gamm 2010);
- The role of justice and fairness in negotiation (Welsh 2004; Ryan 2006; Wade-Benzoni 2006);
- Whether power is conceived as a function of resources, constraints on action, or in other ways (Cobb 2000; Docherty 2004c; Honeyman 2004; Korobkin 2004; Bernard 2006);
- The extent to which people think of time in terms of linear or other sequences (Bernard 2009a);
- Whether explicit communication and direct confrontation are generally desirable (Gold 2009; LeBaron and Patera 2009);
- When interest-based negotiation can be useful (Chamoun-Nicolas, Folberg, and Hazlett 2010; Roberge and Lewicki 2010) and whether it is universally applicable (Abramson 2009; Gold 2009; LeBaron and Patera 2009);
- The appropriate goals for negotiation and measures of success, and particularly whether reaching agreement should be a predominant goal (LeBaron and Patera 2009, Ebner and Efron 2009);
- What norms are relevant and appropriate in negotiation, e.g., legal, religious, moral, and ethical norms (Seul 2006; Abramson 2009; Fox, Schonewille, and Çuhadar-Gürkaynak 2010).

Topics for Instruction

Most negotiation courses include instruction in a combination of theory and practical skills, though the proportions of each vary depending on the instructional goals and students' needs in each course. Where there are differing philosophies about particular issues, instructors need to decide whether to advocate some philosophies over others (or possibly whether to present only a preferred view), or merely to present the differing views (Adler 2006). Ron Fortgang (2000) describes this issue as whether to "proselytize" or use an approach like a "world religions" course. In particular, many negotiation instructors favor interest-based negotiation and disfavor positional negotiation (Ebner and Efron 2009). RNT-oriented instructors may advocate certain other perspectives. In general, we recommend that instructors provide accurate, realistic, and respectful portrayals of various approaches, including advantages and disadvantages. Instructors should prepare students for negotiations that they are likely to encounter in real-life practice. This not only includes respectful treatment of positional negotiation but also "ordinary legal negotiation" in which lawyers exchange information to work out what they consider to be an appropriate result primarily based on the norms in their legal practice community (Lande 2012). Presenting a realistic portrait of negotiation need not preclude instructors from advocating their preferred views about contested issues, while encouraging students to develop their own views.

Good instructional design requires balancing the depth and breadth of coverage of particular issues. On one extreme, instructors may try to cover such a wide range of issues that students do not learn or retain much knowledge. On the other extreme, instructors may focus on a few issues or perspectives in such depth that students do not learn enough different subjects or perspectives. In general, instructors should strive to find a happy medium in their courses.

Almost inevitably, instructors will cover some topics that are not in the standard canon, which should include matters that best advance the instructional goals in their particular courses. Some of these topics may be embedded in the canon, but may deserve their own listing in the syllabus. These topics might include:

- When negotiation is or is not appropriate (Bingham 2006; Blum and Mnookin 2006; Morash 2006; Mnookin 2010);
- How to get others to agree to negotiate (Hawkins, Hyman and Honeyman 2006; Lande 2011; Zartman 2006b);
- Procedures that can improve or complement negotiation (Brown et al. 2004; Mayer 2006);
- Effect of parties' abilities and disabilities (Jeglic and Jeglic 2006; Larson 2010);
- Communication patterns (Kolb 2006; Putnam 2006);
- Effect of participation of agents in negotiation (such as tensions in lawyer-client relationships) (Docherty and Campbell 2004; Mnookin, Peppet, and Tulumello 2000; Brazil 2006; Nolan-Haley 2006; Macfarlane 2006; Macfarlane 2008; Lande 2011);
- Planned early negotiation such as Collaborative, Cooperative, and Settlement Counsel processes (Lande 2011);
- Two-level negotiation (i.e., negotiation both within and between negotiation teams) (Fortgang 2000; Sally and O'Connor 2004; Bellman 2006; Matz 2006; Sally and O'Connor 2006; Honeyman et al., The "Deliberation Engine," in this volume);

- Timing and rhythm in negotiation (Ricigliano 2006; Zartman 2006a; Zartman 2006b);
- Aspirations (Schneider 2004; Guthrie and Sally 2006);
- Gender issues (Kolb and Putnam 2006; Tinsley et al. 2009a; Tinsley et al. 2009b; Schneider, Cheldelin, and Kolb 2010);
- How identity issues affect negotiation (Shapiro 2004b);
- Emotions (Shapiro 2004a; Nelken, Schneider, and Mahuad 2010; Patera and Gamm 2010; Chamoun-Nicolas and Hazlett, *Influence of Emotion*, in this volume);
- Partisan perceptual biases (Brown 2009);
- Prosocial preferences (Sally 2004a; Wade-Benzoni 2006);
- Ceremony, generosity, and developing rapport (Williams 1996; Nadler 2004; Bernard 2009a; Bernard 2009b; Chamoun and Hazlett 2009; Bernard 2010; Love and Singh, *Following the Golden Rule*, in this volume);
- Curiosity and creativity (Brown 2004a; LeBaron and Honeyman 2006; Guthrie 2009; Alexander and LeBaron, *Embodied Negotiation*, in this volume; Honeyman, et al., *Education of Non-Students*, in this volume);
- Framing of issues and use of metaphors (Campbell and Docherty 2004; Docherty 2004b: Gadlin, Schneider, and Honeyman 2006; Miller and Dingwall 2006);
- The role of information and learning before and during negotiation (Moffitt and Peppet 2004; Kirschner 2006; Sally 2004b);
- Mindfulness, perceptions, heuristics, neuroscience, persuasion and other psychological issues (Guthrie 2004; Guthrie and Sally 2004; Korobkin and Guthrie 2004; Sally 2004a; Sally 2004b; Deutsch 2006; Heen and Stone 2006; Riskin 2006; Shestowsky 2006; Freshman and Guthrie 2009; LeBaron and Patera 2009; Birke 2010; Fox, Schonewille, and Çuhadar-Gürkaynak 2010);
- Risk, decision analysis, uncertainty, and ambiguity (Hoffer 1996; Senger 2004; Moffitt 2004; Honeyman 2006b; Senger 2006);
- Trust (Bernard 2010; Roberge and Lewicki 2010);
- Effect of reputations (Tinsley, Cambria, and Schneider 2006);
- Apology and forgiveness (Brown 2004b; Waldman and Luskin 2006);
- Negotiation by email or other electronic means (Bhappu and Barsness 2006; Ebner et al. 2009; Matz and Ebner 2010
- Use of experts, interpreters, mediators, and other professionals (Abramson 2006; Kaufman 2006; Honeyman 2006a; Love and Stulberg 2006; Wade 2006c; Lande 2011);

- Overcoming apparent impasse and using "negotiation nimbleness" (Wade 2006b; Wade and Honeyman 2006; Volpe and Cambria 2009);
- Dealing with negotiators' constituencies (Wade 2006a);
- Wicked problems (i.e., some problems that are unique, complex, and ill-defined) (Lira 2006; Taylor and Donohue 2006; Volpe et al. 2006; Chrustie et al. 2010; Docherty 2010; Honeyman and Coben 2010b; Chrustie et al. 2010b; Lira 2010; Docherty and Lira, *Adapting to the Adaptive*, in this volume; Lira and Parish, *Making it up as You Go*, in this volume; Docherty and Chrustie, *Teaching Three-Dimensional Negotiation*, in this volume; Gadline, Matz, and Chrustie, *Playing the Percentages in Wicked Problems*, in this volume; Lewicki, Kaufman, and Coben, *Teaching Wickedness to Students*, in this volume).

The conflicts and settings that instructors address in a course convey important information to students (Abramson 2009). To a large extent, these decisions follow naturally from the disciplinary setting as instructors are likely to choose examples that seem particularly relevant to their students. Even so, there are significant variations within disciplines, so that law school instructors may choose between negotiations of disputes or transactions, various types of cases (e.g., contract, tort or family), and cases involving varying degrees of salient legal issues. Similarly, international relations instructors may focus on negotiation in diplomatic relations, treaty negotiation, crisis intervention, and/or trade disputes. An important and hoped-for development is the pending introduction, using a sophisticated Internet-based platform, of practical tools to create *multidisciplinary* student teams. These will have the edifying experience of negotiating within a (generally multinational) team as well as with their opposite-number team, in simulations that will draw their problem sets from all disciplines represented (Honeyman et al., *The "Deliberation Engine*," in this volume).

Teaching Methods and Related Issues

Instructors should consider what roles are most appropriate for themselves and the students. Instructors may be in the role of an expert or a "co-learner" with the students or some combination (LeBaron and Patera 2009; Nelken, McAdoo, and Manwaring 2009; Chamoun-Nicolas et al., *Bringing the Street to the Classroom*, in this volume). A related issue is the extent to which instructors present planned material and/or elicit students' learning of whatever actually occurs in the class (Fox, Schonewille, and Çuhadar-Gürkaynak 2010).

Negotiation courses vary in the types of activities involved. These may include case simulations, real-life negotiation (as a participant or observer) or similar activities, dance, movement, and exercise, among others (Alexander and LeBaron 2009; LeBaron and Patera 2009; Howell and Cohn 2010; Honeyman and Parish 2012; Alexander and LeBaron, *Embodied Negotiation,* in this volume). Activities vary in whether they are designed to teach one or more points (Fox, Schonewille, and Çuhadar-Gürkaynak 2010). Instructors may organize different activities to be done by the entire class together, in small groups, and/or by individual students. Thoughtful planning of logistics of activities is important, especially for adventurous activities that have critical aspects beyond the instructors' control (Coben, Honeyman, and Press 2010; Larson 2010; Panga and Grecia-de Vera 2010), online simulations (Ebner et al. 2009; Matz and Ebner 2010; Honeyman et al., *The "Deliberation Engine,"* in this volume), and also for more traditional activities like face-to-face simulations (Alexander and LeBaron 2009; Ebner and Kovach 2010). Debriefing is critically important because students are not likely to fully appreciate the significance of their experiences without careful reflection (see Deason et al., *Debriefing the Debrief,* in this volume).

Written assignments may include journals, self-assessment tools, academic papers, creation of simulations, creative works like plays or short stories reflecting negotiation insights, and exams (Fortgang 2000). The dizzying array of teaching topics and methods creates significant challenges in giving students appropriate evaluations; volume three in the RNT series contains eighteen chapters on this subject alone (Ebner, Coben, and Honeyman 2012. See also Cohn et al. 2009; McAdoo and Manwaring 2009).

Many instructors consider that students' systematic instruction is completed at the end of the course, though courses produce greater value if they provide guidance for students to continue learning and practicing key skills (Bhappu et al. 2009; Cohn et al. 2009; LeBaron and Patera 2009; Lande 2011). Moreover, the instructors' own learning should not end when a course is over as they should conduct evaluations to identify what worked well and what might be improved in future courses (Abramson 2009; Cohn et al. 2009).

Conclusion

The RNT project makes a major contribution to teaching of negotiation and dispute resolution more generally. It embodies an adventurous spirit of questioning accepted beliefs and even its own theories and assumptions. Rather than confidently asserting dogmatic positions, it promotes experimentation and continuous innovation. Although it is impossible to know the specific effects of this work, there should be no doubt that the RNT project will lead to substantial improvements in teaching and learning of negotiation around the world. We believe that there is substantial value in maintaining a general canon of negotiation while incorporating instruction of a wide range of additional perspectives, topics, and teaching methods. We hope that the RNT project will help the community of negotiation instructors refine and possibly expand the canon to some extent.

The terms Negotiation "1.0" and "2.0" reflect the infectious spirit of innovation in RNT. While there may have been some developmental value in the 1.0/2.0 terminology, continued usage may be confusing as these terms do not have clear, shared, and helpful meanings. This framework oversimplifies the characterization of various instructional approaches into two discrete and uniform models. Obviously, there is variation in both models. Courses that some might consider as "1.0" actually embody some "2.0" features and presumably some "2.0" courses include "1.0" features. Rather than choosing between two coherent models, instructors face a profusion of difficult choices in theoretical frameworks, topics, and teaching methods, as this chapter demonstrates. Moreover, this terminology implies that "1.0" is inherently inferior and "2.0" is superior when, in fact, there are valuable and problematic aspects of both "models." In particular, there is real benefit to teaching a shared canon and it would be unwise to throw out valuable parts of the "1.0" baby with the bathwater of problematic elements of some instruction (Gadlin et al., *Of Babies and Bathwater*, in this volume). It may be particularly important to retain important elements of "1.0" for negotiation principals and professionals in settings with poorly developed negotiation cultures (Grecia-de Vera 2010) while also incorporating important elements of negotiation cultures that do exist (Lee 2010). Although it may not make sense to continue using this terminology, the RNT project has stimulated productive reflection and concrete ideas about how best to advance negotiation teaching, as this chapter demonstrates.

Notes

[1] Negotiation is typically taught in training programs and university courses, among other formats. Compared with courses, training programs are often in shorter and more concentrated periods of time and typically do not require students to do substantial reading or writing assignments. So instructors encounter greater constraints in training programs than in courses. Even so, course instructors have a daunting set of decisions to make in designing their instruction. The principles described in this chapter apply to various instructional formats, though instructors would necessarily apply them differently in different formats. For convenience, this chapter generally refers to course instruction but can be applied in various formats. Similarly, the chapter generally refers to students rather than trainees. This usage differs from Kevin Avruch's (2009) thoughtful discussion of distinctions between training and education, which focuses on whether the instruction involves supposedly undisputed canonical knowledge (i.e., training) as opposed to

matters that are subject to critique and revision (i.e., education). This is similar to Ron Fortgang's (2000) distinction between "proselytizing" and a pluralistic "world religions" approach to instruction.

[2] Hamline University School of Law has conducted the Rethinking Negotiation Teaching (RNT) project in cooperation with the JAMS Foundation, Convenor Conflict Management and ADR Center Foundation (Italy). The project's goals are to "critique contemporary negotiation pedagogy and create new training designs." The project has published four volumes of publications as well as a special issue of the *Negotiation Journal* and one of the *Hamline Journal of Public Law & Policy* based on conferences of negotiation instructors and other experts. The project has also launched *Tan Pan, the Chinese-English Journal of Negotiation*. The conferences took place in Rome, Italy (May 2008), Istanbul, Turkey (October 2009), and Beijing, China (May 2011). The chapters from the four volumes (including the one in which this chapter appears) can be downloaded from the project's website, http://law.hamline.edu/rethinking-negotiation.html.

[3] Some chapters in prior RNT publications focus on achieving a goal of "authenticity" in student activities (e.g., LeBaron and Patera 2009). We think that it is more useful to focus on goals of relevance and promoting learning. Authenticity in a course activity can be useful but, in itself, it does not necessarily lead to students finding that the activities are relevant to them, or that they promote important learning (Manwaring, McAdoo, and Cheldelin 2010; Panga and Grecia-de Vera 2010).

[4] There are so many chapters about adventure learning in the two prior RNT volumes that we do not list them all. Two chapters were particularly helpful in providing systematic analysis and advice in planning and conducting adventure learning activities (Manwaring, McAdoo, and Cheldelin 2010; Press and Honeyman 2010). Some hybrid activities may combine the benefits of simulations and adventure learning activities (Cohn and Ebner 2010).

[5] This is somewhat reminiscent of our meals in Beijing where our gracious hosts provided an overwhelming assortment of dishes. Some of us used strategies of trying a little of everything. Others favored the tried and true. Still others were especially attracted to unfamiliar dishes. In any case, we all had to choose. We didn't notice anyone who tried to fill up on all the dishes, but even that would have been a choice.

[6] The Program on Negotiation study of negotiation pedagogy identified many issues arising in the RNT project. It found differences:

1) between a focus on skills and a focus on analytic or theoretical competence;
2) between a commitment to the practice of reflection and a commitment to analytic writing;
3) between a focus on structural and strategic analysis and a focus on managing relational processes;
4) between an essentialized view of culture and a view of culture as emergent normative frames for interaction;
5) between a view of negotiation power as a function of resources and a view of power as the structural and discursive constraint on action;
6) between a preference for scorable games/structured simulations and a preference for the inductive use of cases/role plays to surface core issues in negotiation;

7) between courses that offer multiple frames for understanding and those that advocate a particular frame;
8) between courses that accent two-party negotiations and those that presume multi-party;
9) between professors/institutions that have resources to use videotape and multiple teaching assistants and those who must rely on individualized meetings with students in order to provide feedback;
10) between courses that address gender and those that do not;
11) between courses that problematize the role of the agent in multi-party disputes (as neutral or as advocate) and those that do not;
12) between courses that focus on emotion and identity as contexts for negotiation and those that focus on emotion and identity as barriers to the negotiation process (Cobb 2000: 5-6).

References

Abramson, H. 2006. The culturally suitable mediator. In *The negotiator's fieldbook: The desk reference for the experienced negotiator*, edited by A. K. Schneider and C. Honeyman. Washington, DC: American Bar Association.

Abramson, H. 2009. Outward bound to other cultures: Seven guidelines. In *Rethinking negotiation teaching: Innovations for context and culture*, edited by C. Honeyman, J. Coben, and G. De Palo. St. Paul, MN: DRI Press.

Adler, P. S. 2006. Protean negotiation. In *The negotiator's fieldbook: The desk reference for the experienced negotiator*, edited by A. K. Schneider and C. Honeyman. Washington, DC: American Bar Association.

Alexander, N. and M. LeBaron. 2009. Death of the role-play. In *Rethinking negotiation teaching: Innovations for context and culture*, edited by C. Honeyman, J. Coben, and G. De Palo.St. Paul, MN: DRI Press.

Avruch, K. 2006. The poverty of buyer and seller. In *The negotiator's fieldbook: The desk reference for the experienced negotiator*, edited by A. K. Schneider and C. Honeyman. Washington, DC: American Bar Association.

Avruch, K. 2009. What is training all about? *Negotiation Journal* 25(2): 161-169.

Bellman, H. S. 2006. Internal conflicts of the team. In *The negotiator's fieldbook: The desk reference for the experienced negotiator*, edited by A. K. Schneider and C. Honeyman. Washington, DC: American Bar Association.

Bernard, P. E. 2006. Power, powerlessness, and process. In *The negotiator's fieldbook: The desk reference for the experienced negotiator*, edited by A. K. Schneider and C. Honeyman. Washington, DC: American Bar Association.

Bernard, P. E. 2009a. Bringing soul to international negotiation. *Negotiation Journal* 25(2): 147-159.

Bernard, P. E. 2009b. Finding common ground in the soil of culture. In *Rethinking negotiation teaching: Innovations for context and culture*, edited by C. Honeyman, J. Coben, and G. De Palo. St. Paul, MN: DRI Press.

Bernard. P. E. 2010. Re-orienting the trainer to navigate not negotiate Islamic cultural values. In *Venturing beyond the classroom: Volume 2 in the rethinking negotiation teaching series*, edited by C. Honeyman, J. Coben, and G. De Palo. St. Paul, MN: DRI Press.

Bhappu, A. D. and Z. I. Barsness. 2006. Risks of e-mail. In *The negotiator's field-book: The desk reference for the experienced negotiator*, edited by A. K. Schneider and C. Honeyman. Washington, DC: American Bar Association.

Bhappu, A. D., N. Ebner, S. Kaufman, and N. Welsh. 2009. Online communication technology and relational development. In *Rethinking negotiation teaching: Innovations for context and culture*, edited by C. Honeyman, J. Coben, and G. De Palo. St. Paul, MN: DRI Press.

Bingham, L. B. 2006. Avoiding negotiating. In *The negotiator's fieldbook: The desk reference for the experienced negotiator*, edited by A. K. Schneider and C. Honeyman. Washington, DC: American Bar Association.

Birke, R. 2010. Neuroscience and settlement: An examination of scientific innovations and practical applications. *Ohio State Journal on Dispute Resolution* 25(2): 477-529.

Blum, G. and R. H. Mnookin. 2006. When *not* to negotiate. In *The negotiator's fieldbook: The desk reference for the experienced negotiator*, edited by A. K. Schneider and C. Honeyman. Washington, DC: American Bar Association.

Brazil, W. 2006. Professionalism and misguided negotiation. In *The negotiator's fieldbook: The desk reference for the experienced negotiator*, edited by A. K. Schneider and C. Honeyman. Washington, DC: American Bar Association.

Brown, J. G. 2004a. Creativity and problem-solving. *Marquette Law Review* 87(4): 697-709.

Brown, J. G. 2004b. The role of apology in negotiation. *Marquette Law Review* 87(4): 665-673.

Brown, J. G. 2009. Addressing partisan perceptions. In *Rethinking negotiation teaching: Innovations for context and culture*, edited by C. Honeyman, J. Coben, and G. De Palo. St. Paul, MN: DRI Press.

Brown, J. G., M. C. Campbell, J. S. Docherty, and N. Welsh. 2004. Negotiation as one among many tools. *Marquette Law Review* 87(4): 853-860.

Campbell, M. C. and J. S. Docherty. 2004. What's in a frame? (That which we call a rose by any other name would smell as sweet). *Marquette Law Review* 87(4): 769-781.

Chamoun, H. and R. Hazlett. 2009. The psychology of giving and its effect on negotiation. In *Rethinking negotiation teaching: Innovations for context and culture*, edited by C. Honeyman, J. Coben, and G. De Palo. St. Paul, MN: DRI Press.

Chamoun-Nicolas, H., J. Folberg, and R. Hazlett. 2010. Bazaar dynamics: Teaching integrative negotiation within a distributive environment. In *Venturing beyond the classroom: Volume 2 in the rethinking negotiation teaching series*, edited by C. Honeyman, J. Coben, and G. De Palo. St. Paul, MN: DRI Press.

Chrustie, C., J. S. Docherty, L. Lira, J. Mahuad, H. Gadlin, and C. Honeyman. 2010. Negotiating wicked problems: Five stories. In *Venturing beyond the classroom: Volume 2 in the rethinking negotiation teaching series*, edited by C. Honeyman, J. Coben, and G. De Palo. St. Paul, MN: DRI Press.

Cobb, S. 2000. *Negotiation pedagogy: A research survey of four disciplines*. Cambridge, MA: PON Books.

Coben, J., C. Honeyman, and S. Press. 2010. Straight off the deep end in adventure learning. In *Venturing beyond the classroom: Volume 2 in the rethinking negotiation teaching series,* edited by C. Honeyman, J. Coben, and G. De Palo. St. Paul, MN: DRI Press.

Cohn, L. P. and N. Ebner. 2010. Bringing negotiation teaching to life: From the classroom to the campus to the community. In *Venturing beyond the classroom: Volume 2 in the rethinking negotiation teaching series*, edited by C. Honeyman, J. Coben, and G. De Palo. St. Paul, MN: DRI Press.

Cohn, L., R. Howell, K. K. Kovach, A. Lee, and H. de Backer. 2009. We came, we trained, but did it matter? In *Rethinking negotiation teaching: Innovations for context and culture*, edited by C. Honeyman, J. Coben, and G. De Palo. St. Paul, MN: DRI Press.

Coleman, P. T., L. Bui-Wrzosinska, R. R. Vallacher, and A. Nowak. 2006. Protracted conflicts as dynamical systems. In *The negotiator's fieldbook: The desk reference for the experienced negotiator*, edited by A. K. Schneider and C. Honeyman. Washington, DC: American Bar Association.

Deason, E., S. Press, R. Howell, S. Kaufman, J. Lee and Y. Efron. 2012. Debriefing the debrief. In *Assessing our students, Assessing ourselves: Volume 3 in the rethinking negotiation teaching series*, edited by C. Honeyman, J. Coben, and A. W. Lee. St. Paul, MN: DRI Press.

Deutsch, M. 2006. Internal and external conflict. In *The negotiator's fieldbook: The desk reference for the experienced negotiator*, edited by A. K. Schneider and C. Honeyman. Washington, DC: American Bar Association.

Docherty, J. S. 2004a. Culture and negotiation: Symmetrical anthropology for negotiators. *Marquette Law Review* 87(4): 711-722.

Docherty, J. S. 2004b. Narratives, metaphors, and negotiation. *Marquette Law Review* 87(4): 847-851.

Docherty, J. S. 2004c. Power in the social/political realm. *Marquette Law Review* 87(4): 862-866.

Docherty, J. S. 2006. The unstated models in our minds. In *The negotiator's fieldbook: The desk reference for the experienced negotiator*, edited by A. K. Schneider and C. Honeyman. Washington, DC: American Bar Association.

Docherty, J. S. 2010. "Adaptive" negotiation: Practice and teaching. In *Venturing beyond the classroom: Volume 2 in the rethinking negotiation teaching series*, edited by C. Honeyman, J. Coben, and G. De Palo. St. Paul, MN: DRI Press.

Docherty, J. S. and M. C. Campbell. 2004. Teaching negotiators to analyze conflict structure and anticipate the consequences of principal-agent relationships. *Marquette Law Review* 87(4): 655-664.

Druckman, D. 2006. Uses of a marathon exercise. In *The negotiator's fieldbook: The desk reference for the experienced negotiator*, edited by A. K. Schneider and C. Honeyman. Washington, DC: American Bar Association.

Druckman, D. and N. Ebner. 2010. Enhancing concept learning: The simulation design experience. In *Venturing beyond the classroom: Volume 2 in the rethinking negotiation teaching series*, edited by C. Honeyman, J. Coben, and G. De Palo. St. Paul, MN: DRI Press.

Ebner, N., A. D. Bhappu, J. G. Brown, K. K. Kovach, and A. K. Schneider. 2009. You've got agreement: Negoti@ting via email. In *Rethinking negotiation teaching: Innovations for context and culture*, edited by C. Honeyman, J. Coben, and G. De Palo. St. Paul, MN: DRI Press.

Ebner, N., J. Coben, and C. Honeyman (eds). 2012. *Assessing our students, assessing ourselves: Volume 3 in the rethinking negotiation teaching series.* St. Paul, MN: DRI Press.

Ebner, N. and D. Druckman. 2012. Designing simulations as classroom learning tools. In *Assessing negotiation students: Volume 3 in the rethinking negotiation teaching series*, edited by N. Ebner, J. Coben, and C. Honeyman. St. Paul, MN: DRI Press.

Ebner, N. and Y. Efron. 2009. Moving up: Positional bargaining revisited. In *Rethinking negotiation teaching: Innovations for context and culture*, edited by C. Honeyman, J. Coben, and G. De Palo. St. Paul, MN: DRI Press.

Ebner, N. and A. Kamp. 2010. Relationship 2.0. In *Venturing beyond the classroom: Volume 2 in the rethinking negotiation teaching series*, edited by C. Honeyman, J. Coben, and G. De Palo. St. Paul, MN: DRI Press.

Ebner, N. and K. K. Kovach. 2010. Simulation 2.0: The resurrection. In *Venturing beyond the classroom: Volume 2 in the rethinking negotiation teaching series*, edited by C. Honeyman, J. Coben, and G. De Palo. St. Paul, MN: DRI Press.

Fortgang, R. S. 2000. Taking stock: An analysis of negotiation pedagogy across four professional fields. *Negotiation Journal* 16(4): 325-338.

Fox, K. H. 2009. Negotiation as a post-modern process. In *Rethinking negotiation teaching: Innovations for context and culture*, edited by C. Honeyman, J. Coben, and G. De Palo. St. Paul, MN: DRI Press.

Fox, K. H., M. A. Schonewille, and E. Çuhadar-Gürkaynak. 2010. Lessons from the field: First impressions from second generational negotiation teaching. In *Venturing beyond the classroom: Volume 2 in the rethinking negotiation teaching series,* edited by C. Honeyman, J. Coben, and G. De Palo. St. Paul, MN: DRI Press.

Freshman, C. and C. Guthrie. 2009. Managing the goal-setting paradox: How to get better results from high goals and be happy. *Negotiation Journal* 25(2): 217-231.

Gadlin, H., A. K. Schneider, and C. Honeyman. 2006. The road to hell is paved with metaphors. In *The negotiator's fieldbook: The desk reference for the experienced negotiator*, edited by A. K. Schneider and C. Honeyman. Washington, DC: American Bar Association.

Gibson, K. 2004. The new canon of negotiation ethics. *Marquette Law Review* 87(4): 747-752.

Gibson, K. 2006. Ethics and morality in negotiation. In *The negotiator's fieldbook: The desk reference for the experienced negotiator*, edited by A. K. Schneider and C. Honeyman. Washington, DC: American Bar Association.

Goh, B. C. 2006. Typical errors of Westerners. In *The negotiator's fieldbook: The desk reference for the experienced negotiator*, edited by A. K. Schneider and C. Honeyman. Washington, DC: American Bar Association.

Gold, J. A. 2009. Cultural baggage when you "win as much as you can." In *Rethinking negotiation teaching: Innovations for context and culture*, edited by C. Honeyman, J. Coben, and G. De Palo. St. Paul, MN: DRI Press.

Grecia-de Vera, G. W. 2010. Can we engineer comprehensiveness in "negotiation"education? In *Venturing beyond the classroom: Volume 2 in the rethinking negotiation teaching series*, edited by C. Honeyman, J. Coben, and G. De Palo. St. Paul, MN: DRI Press.

Guthrie, C. 2004. Principles of influence in negotiation. *Marquette Law Review* 87(4): 829-837.

Guthrie, C. 2009. I'm curious: Can we teach curiosity? In *Rethinking negotiation teaching: Innovations for context and culture*, edited by C. Honeyman, J. Coben, and G. De Palo. St. Paul, MN: DRI Press.

Guthrie, C. and D. Sally. 2004. The impact of impact bias on negotiation. *Marquette Law Review* 87(4): 817-828.

Guthrie, C. and D. F. Sally. 2006. Miswanting. In *The negotiator's fieldbook: The desk reference for the experienced negotiator*, edited by A. K. Schneider and C. Honeyman. Washington, DC: American Bar Association.

Hauss, C. 2006. Retraining ourselves for conflict transformation. In *The negotiator's fieldbook: The desk reference for the experienced negotiator*, edited by A. K. Schneider and C. Honeyman. Washington, DC: American Bar Association.

Hawkins, A., C. S. Hyman, and C. Honeyman. 2006. Negotiating access. In *The negotiator's fieldbook: The desk reference for the experienced negotiator*, edited by A. K. Schneider and C. Honeyman. Washington, DC: American Bar Association.

Heen, S. and D. Stone. 2006. Perceptions and stories. In *The negotiator's fieldbook: The desk reference for the experienced negotiator*, edited by A. K. Schneider and C. Honeyman. Washington, DC: American Bar Association.

Hoffer, D. P. 1996. Decision analysis as a mediator's tool. *Harvard Negotiation Law Review* 1(1) 113-137.

Honeyman, C. 2004. The physics of power. *Marquette Law Review* 87(4): 872-874.

Honeyman, C. 2006a. Understanding mediators. In *The negotiator's fieldbook: The desk reference for the experienced negotiator*, edited by A. K. Schneider and C. Honeyman. Washington, DC: American Bar Association.

Honeyman, C. 2006b. Using ambiguity. In *The negotiator's fieldbook: The desk reference for the experienced negotiator*, edited by A. K. Schneider and C. Honeyman. Washington, DC: American Bar Association.

Honeyman, C. and J. Coben. 2010a. Introduction: Half-way to a second generation. In *Venturing beyond the classroom: Volume 2 in the rethinking negotiation teaching series,* edited by C. Honeyman, J. Coben, and G. De Palo. St. Paul, MN: DRI Press.

Honeyman, C. and J. Coben. 2010b. Navigating wickedness: A new frontier in teaching negotiation. In *Venturing beyond the classroom: Volume 2 in the rethinking negotiation teaching series,* edited by C. Honeyman, J. Coben, and G. De Palo. St. Paul, MN: DRI Press.

Honeyman, C. and R. Parish. 2013 (forthcoming). Make a move. In *Making movement matter: Conflict, dance and neuroscience,* edited by M. LeBaron, C. MacLeod, and A. Acland. Chicago: American Bar Association.

Honeyman, C. and A. K. Schneider. 2004. Catching up with the major-general: The need for a "canon of negotiation." *Marquette Law Review* 87(4): 637-648.

Howell, R. and L. P. Cohn. 2010. Epilogue: Two to tango. In *Venturing beyond the classroom: Volume 2 in the rethinking negotiation teaching series,* edited by C. Honeyman, J. Coben, and G. De Palo. St. Paul, MN: DRI Press.

Hughes, S. H. 2004. Understanding conflict in a postmodern world. *Marquette Law Review* 87(4): 681-690.

Jeglic, E. L. and A. A. Jeglic. 2006. Negotiating with disordered people. In *The negotiator's fieldbook: The desk reference for the experienced negotiator,* edited by A. K. Schneider and C. Honeyman. Washington, DC: American Bar Association.

Kamp, A. 2010. Is what's good for the gander good for the goose? A "semi-student" perspective. In *Venturing beyond the classroom: Volume 2 in the rethinking negotiation teaching series,* edited by C. Honeyman, J. Coben, and G. De Palo. St. Paul, MN: DRI Press.

Kaufman, S. 2006. The interpreter as intervener. In *The negotiator's fieldbook: The desk reference for the experienced negotiator,* edited by A. K. Schneider and C. Honeyman. Washington, DC: American Bar Association.

Kelly, L. 2006. Indigenous experiences in negotiation. In *The negotiator's fieldbook: The desk reference for the experienced negotiator,* edited by A. K. Schneider and C. Honeyman. Washington, DC: American Bar Association.

Kirschner, S. M. 2006. Training a captive audience. In *The negotiator's fieldbook: The desk reference for the experienced negotiator,* edited by A. K. Schneider and C. Honeyman. Washington, DC: American Bar Association.

Kolb, D. M. 2006. Strategic moves and turns. In *The negotiator's fieldbook: The desk reference for the experienced negotiator,* edited by A. K. Schneider and C. Honeyman. Washington, DC: American Bar Association.

Kolb, D. M. and L. Putnam. 2006. Gender is more than who we are. In *The negotiator's fieldbook: The desk reference for the experienced negotiator,* edited by A. K. Schneider and C. Honeyman. Washington, DC: American Bar Association.

Korobkin, R. 2004. Bargaining power as threat of impasse. *Marquette Law Review* 87(4): 867-871.

Korobkin, R. and C. Guthrie. 2004. Heuristics and biases at the negotiation table. *Marquette Law Review* 87(4): 785-808.

Korobkin, R., M. Moffitt, and N. Welsh. 2004. The law of bargaining. *Marquette Law Review* 87(4): 839-845.

Kovach, K. K. 2009. Culture, cognition and learning preferences. In *Rethinking negotiation teaching: Innovations for context and culture,* edited by C. Honeyman, J. Coben, and G. De Palo. St. Paul, MN: DRI Press.

Lande, J. 2011. *Lawyering with planned early negotiation: How you can get good results for clients and make money.* Washington, DC: American Bar Association.

Lande, J. 2012. Teaching students to negotiate like a lawyer. *Washington University Journal of Law and Policy* 39(1): 109-144.

Larson, D. A. 2010. Adventure learning: Not everyone gets to play. In *Venturing beyond the classroom: Volume 2 in the rethinking negotiation teaching series,* edited by C. Honeyman, J. Coben, and G. De Palo. St. Paul, MN: DRI Press.

LeBaron, M. and C. Honeyman. 2006. Using the creative arts. In *The negotiator's fieldbook: The desk reference for the experienced negotiator,* edited by A. K. Schneider and C. Honeyman. Washington, DC: American Bar Association.

LeBaron, M. and M Patera. 2009. Reflective practice in the new millennium. In *Rethinking negotiation teaching: Innovations for context and culture,* edited by C. Honeyman, J. Coben, and G. De Palo. St. Paul, MN: DRI Press.

Lee, A. W. 2010. Ancient wisdom for the modern negotiator: What Chinese characters have to offer negotiation pedagogy. In *Venturing beyond the classroom: Volume 2 in the rethinking negotiation teaching series,* edited by C. Honeyman, J. Coben, and G. De Palo. St. Paul, MN: DRI Press.

Lewicki, R. J. and A. K. Schneider. 2010. Instructors heed the who: Designing negotiation training with the learner in mind. In *Venturing beyond the classroom: Volume 2 in the rethinking negotiation teaching series,* edited by C. Honeyman, J. Coben, and G. De Palo. St. Paul, MN: DRI Press.

Lira, L. L. 2006. The military learns to negotiate. In *The negotiator's fieldbook: The desk reference for the experienced negotiator,* edited by A. K. Schneider and C. Honeyman. Washington, DC: American Bar Association.

Lira, L. 2010. Design: The U.S. Army's approach to negotiating wicked problems. In *Venturing beyond the classroom: Volume 2 in the rethinking negotiation teaching series,* edited by C. Honeyman, J. Coben, and G. De Palo. St. Paul, MN: DRI Press.

Love, L. P. and J. B. Stulberg. 2006. The uses of mediation. In *The negotiator's fieldbook: The desk reference for the experienced negotiator,* edited by A. K. Schneider and C. Honeyman. Washington, DC: American Bar Association.

Macfarlane. J. 2006. The new advocacy. In *The negotiator's fieldbook: The desk reference for the experienced negotiator,* edited by A. K. Schneider and C. Honeyman. Washington, DC: American Bar Association.

Macfarlane, J. 2008. *The new lawyer: How settlement is transforming the practice of law.* Vancouver, British Columbia: University of British Colombia Press.

Manwaring, M., B. McAdoo, and S. Cheldelin. 2010. Orientation and disorientation: Two approaches to designing "authentic" negotiation learning activities. In *Venturing beyond the classroom: Volume 2 in the rethinking negotiation teaching series,* edited by C. Honeyman, J. Coben, and G. De Palo. St. Paul, MN: DRI Press.

Matz, D. 2006. Intra-team miscommunication. In *The negotiator's fieldbook: The desk reference for the experienced negotiator,* edited by A. K. Schneider and C. Honeyman. Washington, DC: American Bar Association.

Matz, D. 2009. What really happened in the negotiation? In *Rethinking negotiation teaching: Innovations for context and culture,* edited by C. Honeyman, J. Coben, and G. De Palo. St. Paul, MN: DRI Press.

Matz, D. and N. Ebner. 2010. Using role-play in online negotiation teaching. In *Venturing beyond the classroom: Volume 2 in the rethinking negotiation teaching series,* edited by C. Honeyman, J. Coben, and G. De Palo. St. Paul, MN: DRI Press.

Mayer, B. 2006. Allies in negotiation. In *The negotiator's fieldbook: The desk reference for the experienced negotiator*, edited by A. K. Schneider and C. Honeyman. Washington, DC: American Bar Association.

Mayer, B. 2009. *Staying with conflict: A strategic approach to ongoing disputes.* San Francisco: Jossey-Bass.

McAdoo, B. and M. Manwaring. 2009. Teaching for implementation: Designing negotiation curricula to maximize long-term learning. *Negotiation Journal* 25(2): 195-215.

Menkel-Meadow, C. 2006. The ethics of compromise. In *The negotiator's fieldbook: The desk reference for the experienced negotiator*, edited by A. K. Schneider and C. Honeyman. Washington, DC: American Bar Association.

Miller, G. and R. Dingwall, 2006. When the play's in the wrong theater. In *The negotiator's fieldbook: The desk reference for the experienced negotiator*, edited by A. K. Schneider and C. Honeyman. Washington, DC: American Bar Association.

Mnookin, R. 2010. *Bargaining with the devil: When to negotiate, when to fight.* New York: Simon and Schuster.

Mnookin, R. H., S. R. Peppet, and A. S. Tulumello. 2000. *Beyond winning: Negotiating to create value in deals and disputes.* Cambridge, MA: Belknap Press.

Morash, S. 2006. Nonevents and avoiding reality. In *The negotiator's fieldbook: The desk reference for the experienced negotiator*, edited by A. K. Schneider and C. Honeyman. Washington, DC: American Bar Association.

Moffitt, M. 2004. Contingent agreements: Agreeing to disagree about the future. *Marquette Law Review* 87(4): 691-696.

Moffitt, M. and S. R. Peppet. 2004. Action science and negotiation. *Marquette Law Review* 87(4): 649-654.

Nadler, J. 2004. Rapport in negotiation and conflict resolution. *Marquette Law Review* 87(4): 875-882.

Nelken, M. 1996. Negotiation and psychoanalysis: If I'd wanted to learn about feelings, I wouldn't have gone to law school. *Journal of Legal Education* 46: 420-429.

Nelken, M. L. 2009. Negotiating classroom process: Lessons from adult learning. *Negotiation Journal* 25(2): 181-194.

Nelken, M., B. McAdoo, and M. Manwaring. 2009. Negotiating learning environments. In *Rethinking negotiation teaching: Innovations for context and culture*, edited by C. Honeyman, J. Coben, and G. De Palo. St. Paul, MN: DRI Press.

Nelken, M., A. K. Schneider, and J. Mahuad. 2010. If I'd wanted to teach about feelings I wouldn't have become a law professor. In *Venturing beyond the classroom: Volume 2 in the rethinking negotiation teaching series,* edited by C. Honeyman, J. Coben, and G. De Palo. St. Paul, MN: DRI Press.

Nolan-Haley, J. 2006. Agents and informed consent. In *The negotiator's fieldbook: The desk reference for the experienced negotiator*, edited by A. K. Schneider and C. Honeyman. Washington, DC: American Bar Association.

Nolan-Haley, J. and E. Gmurzynska. 2009. Culture: The body/soul connector in negotiation ethics. In *Rethinking negotiation teaching: Innovations for context and culture*, edited by C. Honeyman, J. Coben, and G. De Palo. St. Paul, MN: DRI Press.

Panga, S. S. and G. B. Grecia-de Vera. 2010. A look at a negotiation 2.0 classroom: Using adventure learning modules to supplement negotiation simulations. In *Venturing beyond the classroom: Volume 2 in the rethinking negotiation teaching series,* edited by C. Honeyman, J. Coben, and G. De Palo. St. Paul, MN: DRI Press.

Patera, M. and U. Gamm. 2010. Emotions: A blind spot in negotiation training? In *Venturing beyond the classroom: Volume 2 in the rethinking negotiation teaching series,* edited by C. Honeyman, J. Coben, and G. De Palo. St. Paul, MN: DRI Press.

Press, S. and C. Honeyman. 2010. A second dive into adventure learning. In *Venturing beyond the classroom: Volume 2 in the rethinking negotiation teaching series,* edited by C. Honeyman, J. Coben, and G. De Palo. St. Paul, MN: DRI Press.

Putnam, L. L. 2006. Communication and interaction process. In *The negotiator's fieldbook: The desk reference for the experienced negotiator,* edited by A. K. Schneider and C. Honeyman. Washington, DC: American Bar Association.

Ricigliano, R. 2006. A three-dimensional analysis of negotiation. In *The negotiator's fieldbook: The desk reference for the experienced negotiator,* edited by A. K. Schneider and C. Honeyman. Washington, DC: American Bar Association.

Riskin, L. L. 2006. Knowing yourself: Mindfulness. In *The negotiator's fieldbook: The desk reference for the experienced negotiator,* edited by A. K. Schneider and C. Honeyman. Washington, DC: American Bar Association.

Roberge, J. and R. J. Lewicki. 2010. Should we trust grand bazaar carpet sellers (and vice versa)? In *Venturing beyond the classroom: Volume 2 in the rethinking negotiation teaching series,* edited by C. Honeyman, J. Coben, and G. De Palo. St. Paul, MN: DRI Press.

Ryan, C. 2006. Rawls on negotiating justice. In *The negotiator's fieldbook: The desk reference for the experienced negotiator,* edited by A. K. Schneider and C. Honeyman. Washington, DC: American Bar Association.

Sally, D. 2004a. Game theory behaves. *Marquette Law Review* 87(4): 783-793.

Sally, D. 2004b. Social maneuvers and theory of mind. *Marquette Law Review* 87(4): 893-902.

Sally D. and K. O'Connor. 2004. Team negotiations. *Marquette Law Review* 87(4): 883-892.

Sally, D. F., and K. M. O'Connor. 2006. Team negotiations. In *The negotiator's fieldbook: The desk reference for the experienced negotiator,* edited by A. K. Schneider and C. Honeyman. Washington, DC: American Bar Association.

Schneider, A. K. 2004. Aspirations in negotiation. *Marquette Law Review* 87(4): 675-680.

Schneider, A. K., S. Cheldelin, and D. Kolb. 2010. What travels: Teaching gender in cross-cultural negotiation classrooms. In *Venturing beyond the classroom: Volume 2 in the rethinking negotiation teaching series,* edited by C. Honeyman, J. Coben, and G. De Palo. St. Paul, MN: DRI Press.

Schneider, A. K. and C. Honeyman (eds). 2006. *The negotiator's fieldbook: The desk reference for the experienced negotiator.* Washington, DC: American Bar Association.

Senger, J. M. 2004. Decision analysis in negotiation. *Marquette Law Review* 87(4): 723-735.

Senger, J. M. 2006. Assessing risk. In *The negotiator's fieldbook: The desk reference for the experienced negotiator*, edited by A. K. Schneider and C. Honeyman. Washington, DC: American Bar Association.

Seul, J. R. 2006. Religion and conflict. In *The negotiator's fieldbook: The desk reference for the experienced negotiator*, edited by A. K. Schneider and C. Honeyman. Washington, DC: American Bar Association.

Shapiro, D. L. 2004a. Emotions in negotiation: Peril or promise? *Marquette Law Review* 87(4): 737-745.

Shapiro, D. L. 2004b. Identity is more than meets the "I": The power of identity in shaping negotiation behavior. *Marquette Law Review* 87(4): 809-816.

Shestowsky. D. 2006. Psychology and persuasion. In *The negotiator's fieldbook: The desk reference for the experienced negotiator*, edited by A. K. Schneider and C. Honeyman. Washington, DC: American Bar Association.

Special Issue 2004. Catching up with the major-general: The need for a "canon" of negotiation. *Marquette Law Review* 87(4): 637-902.

Special Section 2009. Second generation global negotiation education. *Negotiation Journal* 25(2): 141-266.

Stulberg, J. B., M. P. Canedo Arrillaga, and D. Potockova. 2009. Minimizing communication barriers. In *Rethinking negotiation teaching: Innovations for context and culture*, edited by C. Honeyman, J. Coben, and G. De Palo. St. Paul, MN: DRI Press.

Taylor, P. J. and W. Donohue. 2006. Hostage negotiation opens up. In *The negotiator's fieldbook: The desk reference for the experienced negotiator*, edited by A. K. Schneider and C. Honeyman. Washington, DC: American Bar Association.

Tinsley, C. H., J. J. Cambria, and A. K. Schneider. 2006. Reputations in negotiation. In *The negotiator's fieldbook: The desk reference for the experienced negotiator*, edited by A. K. Schneider and C. Honeyman. Washington, DC: American Bar Association.

Tinsley, C. H., S. I. Cheldelin, A. K. Schneider, and E. T. Amanatullah. 2009a. Women at the bargaining table: Pitfalls and prospects. *Negotiation Journal* 25(2): 233-248.

Tinsley, C. H., S. I. Cheldelin, A. K. Schneider, and E. T. Amanatullah. 2009b. Negotiating your public identity: Women's path to power. In *Rethinking negotiation teaching: Innovations for context and culture*, edited by C. Honeyman, J. Coben, and G. De Palo. St. Paul, MN: DRI Press.

Volpe, M., J. J. Cambria, H. McGowan, and C. Honeyman. 2006. Negotiating with the unknown. In *The negotiator's fieldbook: The desk reference for the experienced negotiator*, edited by A. K. Schneider and C. Honeyman. Washington, DC: American Bar Association.

Volpe, M. and J. J. Cambria. 2009. Negotiation nimbleness when cultural differences are unidentified. In *Rethinking negotiation teaching: Innovations for context and culture*, edited by C. Honeyman, J. Coben, and G. De Palo. St. Paul, MN: DRI Press.

Wade, J. H. 2006a. Bargaining in the shadow of the tribe. In *The negotiator's fieldbook: The desk reference for the experienced negotiator*, edited by A. K. Schneider and C. Honeyman. Washington, DC: American Bar Association.

Wade, J. H. 2006b. Crossing the last gap. In *The negotiator's fieldbook: The desk reference for the experienced negotiator*, edited by A. K. Schneider and C. Honeyman. Washington, DC: American Bar Association.

Wade, J. H. 2006c. Dueling experts. In *The negotiator's fieldbook: The desk reference for the experienced negotiator*, edited by A. K. Schneider and C. Honeyman. Washington, DC: American Bar Association.

Wade, J. H. 2009. Defining success in negotiation and other dispute resolution training. *Negotiation Journal* 25(2): 171-179.

Wade, J. H. and C. Honeyman. 2006. A lasting agreement. In *The negotiator's fieldbook: The desk reference for the experienced negotiator*, edited by A. K. Schneider and C. Honeyman. Washington, DC: American Bar Association.

Wade-Benzoni, K. A. 2006. Giving future generations a voice. In *The negotiator's fieldbook: The desk reference for the experienced negotiator*, edited by A. K. Schneider and C. Honeyman. Washington, DC: American Bar Association.

Waldman, E. and F. Luskin. 2006. Unforgiven: Anger and forgiveness. In *The negotiator's fieldbook: The desk reference for the experienced negotiator*, edited by A. K. Schneider and C. Honeyman. Washington, DC: American Bar Association.

Welsh, N. A. 2004. Perceptions of fairness in negotiation. *Marquette Law Review* 87(4): 753-767.

Williams, G. R. 1996. Negotiation as a healing process. *Journal of Dispute Resolution* 1996(1): 1-65.

Yarn, D. H. and G. T. Jones. 2006. In our bones (or brains): Behavioral biology. In *The negotiator's fieldbook: The desk reference for the experienced negotiator*, edited by A. K. Schneider and C. Honeyman. Washington, DC: American Bar Association.

Zartman, I. W. 2006a. Process and stages. In *The negotiator's fieldbook: The desk reference for the experienced negotiator*, edited by A. K. Schneider and C. Honeyman. Washington, DC: American Bar Association.

Zartman, I. W. 2006b. Timing and ripeness. In *The negotiator's fieldbook: The desk reference for the experienced negotiator*, edited by A. K. Schneider and C. Honeyman. Washington, DC: American Bar Association.

೮ 3 ೞ

Of Babies and Bathwater

Howard Gadlin, Ian Macduff & Andrea Kupfer Schneider[*]

Editors' Note: The authors admit a strong preference for preservation of the baby. They present a cogent argument that contrary to the imagery sometimes used in the RNT project, there has been no sharp 1.0 to 2.0 divide, no sudden shift in our collective thinking about what our field contains or should teach. Rather, they point out, the teachings of the field have evolved steadily and gradually over several decades, with at least the better courses regularly incorporating aspects of the new research. The whole "Negotiation 2.0" concept, they argue, thus runs the risk of undermining that continuity, and implying instead that some of the core concepts that have proven to be widely applicable around the field and around the world are now to be distrusted. The authors also object cogently to a second potential consequence of this imagery: that the hard-won learning of many generations in older societies about how people should deal with each other is now to be distrusted, seen as out of fashion, and even replaced entirely by a set of imported concepts that may be largely unsuited to the culture importing them.

> We shall not cease from exploration
> And the end of all our exploring
> Will be to arrive where we started
> And know the place for the first time.
> (T.S. Eliot – "Little Gidding," the last of the "Four Quartets")

[*] **Howard Gadlin** is the ombudsman and director of the Center for Cooperative Resolution at the National Institutes of Health. His email address is gadlinh@od.nih.gov. **Ian Macduff** is the director of the Center for Dispute Resolution, School of Law, Singapore Management University. His email address is ianmacduff@smu.edu.sg. **Andrea Kupfer Schneider** is a professor of law and director of the dispute resolution program at Marquette University Law School in Milwaukee, Wisconsin. Her email address is andrea.schneider@marquette.edu.

Introduction

In their 2003 book, *The Innovator's Solution*, Clayton Christensen and Michael Raynor extend Christensen's notion of disruptive technologies to describe two basic types of innovation – sustaining and disruptive. Disruptive innovation refers to a product or service that overturns, or leads to the overturning of, a technology or business model that has dominated and defined an area. Personal computers, CDs, and digital cameras are all examples of innovations that were disruptive when they were introduced. CDs are a good example of a disruptive innovation that was itself disrupted by a later innovation, downloadable digital media. Sustaining innovation, meanwhile, refines and improves an already established technology or service. The various improvements over the years in automobile or laptop computers would be an example of sustaining technologies.

Marketing being what it is, we are all familiar with the efforts of manufacturers to convince us that a new product model represents a revolutionary breakthrough that renders obsolete all earlier models. The intent of these marketing campaigns is to create a desire for an alleged innovation – a model that, just by virtue of being new, surpasses the old model. One aspect of these marketing campaigns is to downplay the degree of continuity between new models and those they seek to replace. The denial of continuity is also apparent in some of the professional worlds, where practitioners, researchers and theorists sometimes make claims about innovative ideas, practices or techniques, and promote them like products competing in the market. This tendency is especially prevalent among those who, concerned that extant approaches are not adequate to address fully the complex social, political, or scientific policy problems we face, impatiently blame current theories or practices and set out to create "totally new" approaches. We have three primary critiques of this approach: 1) branding and ambiguity; 2) exclusion and history; and 3) culture and complexity.

Branding and Ambiguity

It is interesting that "Negotiation 2.0" has been taken as the battle cry for the Rethinking Negotiation Teaching (RNT) project. This labeling is a misapplication of a marketing model, which conveys the idea that "Negotiation 1.0" is obsolete while selling "Negotiation 2.0" as a superior and wholly new innovation. This model assumes that negotiation is a commodity, that negotiation training involves selling or marketing something new, and that 2.0 has to be better in every way than 1.0. This assumption then leads to the assumption that 1.0 is flawed and out of date – that no one would want to or need to buy the original model – and that we can throw our old model out.

The implication of the claim embedded in the "2.0" model number is that this next step is both wholly new (as Web 2.0 is said to be fundamentally different from Web 1.0) and, at the same time, wholly familiar (in the way than the iPad 2 is a souped-up version of the iPad 1 that you may have come to know and love, and the "new" version is even more of the same). The marketing implication is that there is a superior quality to and a significant shift involved in buying the new version – but you are not actually changing brands.

For those committed to this model, we have prepared a flyer, suitable for framing, to be used in the advertising campaign for "Negotiation 2.0."

The ironic risk is that the "Negotiation 2.0" label both expresses a false disruptive innovation claim and contains the possibility that the power of a "2.0" model will be diminished because of the perceived nature of such modern marketing claims. The power of the claim as to innovation and exclusiveness in dispute resolution can be seen in one further ironic way in at least some parts of Asia – for example Singapore – where mediation is a wholly traditional and embedded form of community dispute resolution, in varying forms, in the three main ethnic communities, Chinese, Malay and Indian. And yet, in professional conversations the impression is also conveyed that negotiation and mediation are somehow "new" to the region; this novelty and importation dates roughly from the arrival on those shores of the "Harvard model." The irony is twofold: first, because the modern "alternative" dispute resolution movement owes much of its origins and form to comparative research on non-litigious forms of dispute resolution in China, Japan, India and the Philippines; and second, the impact of the "new" product has been to render at least less visible and probably less desirable the traditional processes, which have at least a 5000-year heritage behind them. There is, in effect, a disabling impact of this marketing, in that those who once knew what negotiation and mediation involved no longer trust that knowledge or experience, as it has been displaced by the new product.

This also indicates one other aspect of the signifying power of labels, whether intentional or unintentional: to claim that a product or process, now in its second iteration, is "new," and that its foundations lay in the newly branded version "1.0," is to imply that there was nothing that came before. This might well be claimed, say, for Web 1.0 and 2.0, in that this is a wholly new world of communication and information management; but it seems less plausible in the case of the ancient and culturally-rich practices of negotiation and mediation. Again, the power of this claim to and label of innovation is that it disempowers those who may now discount the foundations of their own negotiation traditions.

We prefer a different stance toward efforts to develop and enhance negotiation training, one that acknowledges the ways in which new negotiation theories are built on previous theories and traditional practices, and provides continuity with ongoing negotiation training and teaching. This would be an evolutionary model, one in which even critical revisions of earlier notions acknowledge the value of earlier contributions as steps in development, and avoids claiming that the new is better because it is new, or that the old is inferior and should be discarded.

Exclusion and History

One consequence of the "branding" thinking is that it reinforces an image of the necessity, uniqueness and primacy of a mode of doing things. That has the effect of excluding those who dance to a different drummer, or whose expertise is grounded in a different ethos, culture and practice. Practitioners, trainers and scholars will be familiar with the experience of those perhaps less imaginative and flexible trainees who take a more prescriptive view of the "model" of mediation or negotiation that they encounter: the risk is that some will learn only too well the steps and sequences to be followed, thereby losing much of the beauty and flexibility of the dance of negotiation. On the other hand, the risk is that training the providers and – perhaps worse – the gatekeepers of professional standards will result in some of the less wise among these taking the model or the process not merely as indicative but rather as normative (see Avruch 2009).

One example of this was encountered by one of the authors at an arbitrators' and mediators' conference at which leading lights in the sponsoring professional body sought to delineate the core steps in mediation "which we will all agree on." The lively and in the end divisive conversation that followed made the points very clearly that: first, this descriptive exercise (if it could be settled) was designed to be normative, so that all mediators would be evaluated according to the degree to which they actually did all of those things; and second and more important, that exercise in setting standards had the precise effect of excluding from professional recognition those who had been working in the field long before the professional body was created and the standards set. Moreover, those most likely to be excluded, to be "defined out" of the field of mediation, were senior indigenous practitioners who had earned their stripes through experience, wisdom and seniority – and had, for the most part, never heard of the new conventions.

The converse of Groucho Marx's "I wouldn't join a club that would have me as a member" must then be the risk that we define that standards of membership in such a way that those who *were* members of the club (of mediators *or* negotiators) find that they no longer meet the standards.

Perhaps a brief history of negotiation teaching would be helpful in terms of understanding why a market structure of comparing "Negotiation 1.0" to "Negotiation 2.0" is so frustrating. One of the blessings of negotiation teaching, at least from the late 1980s onward, was the interdisciplinary mix of readings and concepts provided. In fact, one could start even earlier, with either Mary Parker Follett in the 1920s (Follett 1924) or Richard Walton and Robert McKersie in the 1960s (Walton and McKersie 1965), to consider early writing on negotiation strategy in the business or labor markets. But we will start in the late 1980s, as negotiation classes become stand-alone classes at many law and business schools. A more robust curriculum was developed, and while this was concurrent with the development of alternative dispute resolution (ADR) as a field, it was not necessarily the same thing, nor was it fueled by the same goals.

Early negotiation classes included a diverse set of readings ranging from law – both the more integrative approach (Fisher, Ury, and Patton 1981; Menkel-Meadow, 1984) and the more competitive approach (White 1967) – to business (Raiffa 1982; Lax and Sebenius 1986) – to international relations (Axelrod 1984) – to classic game theory (Schelling 1980). In other words, this class was already quite interdisciplinary, and decidedly *not* narrow-minded.

Through the 1990s, more elements were added to the training mix. Cognitive barriers highlighted by one particular group, primarily composed of psychologists and economists, located at Stanford (e.g. Kenneth Arrow, Daniel Kahneman, Amos Tversky, and Lee Ross), were first compiled in *Barriers to Conflict Resolution* (Arrow, Mnookin, and Tversky 1995), and then widely translated into shorter applications and experiments through their students' efforts (e.g., Korobkin and Guthrie 2006) as well as the work of other psychologists who focused, e.g., on the elements of persuasion (Cialdini 1993). Adaptation and development also took place in the business school environment; for example, Max Bazerman and Margaret Neale's (1994) writing focused on the psychological barriers, as well as irrational mistakes that negotiators make. A sharpened focus on internal negotiations and emotions also occurred, as the well-known "interpersonal skills exercise" from the Program on Negotiation – developed with trained psychologists – led to rethinking about what makes negotiations difficult (Stone, Patton, and Heen 1999), as well as new consideration of mood (Freshman, Hayes and Feldman 2002) and emotions (Nelken 1996; Fisher and Shapiro 2005; Nelken, Schneider, and Mahuad, 2010). Similarly, experts from the education field were also consulted about adult learning, how to teach skills that stick, and other pedagogical tools (summarized in McAdoo and Manwaring 2009; Manwaring, McAdoo, and Cheldelin 2010).

By the early 2000s, negotiation training was expanding again, this time to include hard sciences (summarized in Yarn and Jones 2006), complex adaptive systems (Jones 2003), a larger array of types of psychology (Shestowsky 2006), and more from anthropology, particularly in terms of thinking about cultural differences (LeBaron 2003). In most negotiation courses today, and in those textbooks, students could well be reading the classics listed above plus an array of game theory (Brams 2003), cognitive psychology (Gladwell 2000; Levitt and Dubner 2006; Thaler and Sunstein 2009), neuroscience (Ariely 2010), emotion (Goleman 1995; Fisher and Shapiro 2005), anthropology, and more.

If one examines the evolution of negotiation courses and the negotiation textbooks that accompany them, it is clear that even defining Negotiation 1.0 should be challenging. What is "1.0"? Do we stop with the revolutionary change to a primary focus on problem-solving, as outlined in *Getting to Yes* (Fisher, Ury, and Patton 1991), *The Manager as Negotiator* (Lax and Sebenius 1986), and *The Structure of Problem-Solving* (Menkel-Meadow 1984)? Or, after that, what do you include? What do you not include?

When Christopher Honeyman and Andrea Schneider wrote about a "canon of negotiation" almost ten years ago (Honeyman and Schneider 2004), would *that* be Negotiation 1.0? The starting point for that inquiry already included items such as a personal style (Williams 1983; Schneider 2002), the use of communication skills (Putnam 2006), the idea of integrative v. distributive negotiations (Raiffa 1982; Fisher, Ury, and Patton 1991), the concept of a bargaining zone and best alternative to a negotiated agreement (BATNA) (Fisher, Ury, and Patton 1991), the use of brainstorming, and the importance of preparation. But the idea of a "canon," as it stood at the time, only referred to the sharply limited list of items then taught across *all* negotiation classes. Logically enough, each field in which negotiation was being taught already used much more material developed within its own discipline; it just was not the same material across fields.

So we come back to the definitional problem – if we cannot even agree on what Negotiation 1.0 is, how can we define Negotiation 2.0? And, more important, what makes us think that Negotiation 2.0 will be better?

The majority of negotiation textbooks are comprised of excerpts that have morphed and grown over the last twenty years as more and more material is taught while still including the classic readings. Our argument is that the designation "2.0" makes it sound like there is little valuable from 1.0 that needs to be salvaged. In fact, however one defines 1.0, it is clear that the path of negotiation training is more evolutionary than revolutionary. There is not a dramatic shift in what one teaches – and has not been since problem-solving came on the scene – even as we add more diverse, and more nuanced material to such courses.

Culture and Complexity

As indicated earlier in this chapter, we recognize that we have borrowed much of what we do from a global supermarket of negotiation styles. What this adds to our thinking, practice and pedagogy is an obligation to "thicken" the way we practice and prescribe negotiation. The "simple" version of this is the need now to recognize cultural variation in negotiation and mediation practice. But the more nuanced version – which is obscured by the implications of the "1.0/2.0" labels – is that we are caught in a complex of narratives about the nature of disputes, relationships, process values, and acceptable outcomes. This is not the place to revisit the complex and unresolved question as to what we mean by "culture": the answer to that question is less important than realizing that the very nature of the debate, and the heat that it raises, are themselves indications of the complexity of the issue and the degree to which "adding" culture to our concepts of negotiation is far more than a merely additive process.

Hence one of the significant shifts involved in the move from first to second generation negotiation practice and pedagogy lies in the acknowledgement that diversity both enriches and complicates the way in which we must see and do things. "Global best practice" is now clearly a far more complex concept than it might have been even a couple of decades ago. This is hardly new – and indeed the central claimed virtues of non-litigation-based forms of dispute resolution lay in part, at least, in their flexibility. If we return to early foundations, we can be reminded of the shift in the 1970s in the United States, at which time the arguments began to emerge for process pluralism, multi-door courthouses, and eventually, "fitting the forum to the fuss" (Sander and Goldberg 1994). These arguments, we suspect, were grounded less in cultural considerations than in perceptions of the constraints on and within the system of adjudication, and the arguments were then at least neutral as to the cultural or identity issues about access.

The question then is whether there is the same degree of enthusiasm for pluralism when the claims for it are made less in the name of system efficiencies and generic access to justice than in the interests of identity politics and cultural autonomy in decision-making. If, however, the generic principle of "fitting the forum" is persuasive, then we need to think about why it might *not* be persuasive if given a multi-cultural slant. What starts out and develops as a case-management idea takes on a different coloration – as it were – when the same arguments for pluralism are advanced in the name of multiculturalism (Sander and Goldberg 1994; Lande and Herman 2004).

This is not, at the same time, an uncritical acceptance of the "cultural defense" as the reason for changing processes. One argument expressing caution about distinct, culturally specific dispute processes derives from the same line of argument raised in relation to ADR and civil justice: the importance of public norms, or shared norms. This argument – framed by, among others, Richard Abel (1981), Owen Fiss (1982), David Luban (1988), and Simon Roberts (1998) – is typically raised in a secular and jurisprudential context, raising a concern about the "erosion" of the public realm. The same argument might well apply where the claims for procedural distinctiveness are based on ethnicity or faith. This is not the place to explore the implications of multiculturalism and the "claims of culture"; our concern here is merely to acknowledge that it is the recognition of difference that – in part at least – lays behind the laudable shifts to new thinking in negotiation pedagogy. We do note, in support of the "complexity" point, that even the recognition of those claims of culture necessarily raises a range of policy and practical questions about the impact of such recognition. For example, one cannot neglect either the problems of the impact of multicultural accommodation on the "claimant" group itself – especially risks of group recognition as a "license for in-group subordination" – or the impact of individual rights on minority communities (Shachar 2001).

The point made by Seyla Benhabib (2002: vii-viii), specifically in relation to the political "claims of culture" is that:

> . . . our contemporary condition is marked by the emergence of new forms of identity politics all around the globe. These new forms complicate and increase centuries-old tensions between the universalistic principles ushered in by the American and French Revolutions and the particularities of nationality, ethnicity, gender, "race," and language. Such identity-driven struggles are taking place not only at the thresholds and borders of new nation-states. . . [but] are also occurring within the boundaries of older liberal democracies.

The single, though hardly simple, point for our current purposes is that the epistemic and ontological shift brought about by the recognition – in a political, policy and process sense – of the fact of diversity also necessarily adds complexity. And that complexity is likely not to be captured in a rebranding of negotiation practice; nor are those whose acknowledged and included lives enrich our cosmopolitan mix likely to see themselves necessarily included in the new product line.

The development of negotiation practice and pedagogy takes place against this rich and complex backdrop of diversity and at times contentious pluralism. While that practice is enriched by the recognition of diversity, it also treads a tricky path between assimilation ("add culture and mix") and the fetishism of cultural difference. The risk, as Terence Turner suggests, lies in the use of "culture" as a property of an ethnic group or race; the reification of cultures as separate entities; the overstatement of internal homogeneity; the use of culture to legitimize "repressive demands for cultural conformity"; and the use of culture to fetishize claims and "put them beyond the reach of critical analysis" (1993: 412). But that is a matter for another paper. The point here is that the same shift in thinking and perception that underpin the recognition of difference and the adaptation of the first iteration of negotiation pedagogy also complicates the picture: what we have added is not merely more colors and styles, but rather the normative and existential complexity of difference. And that, we suspect, is not captured by the "2.0" label – even though the intent of the shift in branding is to mark the shift in practice.

Conclusion

The idea that 2.0 can replace 1.0 thus misses the history of negotiation teaching, and collapses what has been a long and interesting development into a snapshot in time–into a straw man–that one can then attack as outdated and outmoded. Negotiation teaching is ready for the next challenge, ready for new material, and can adapt to new structures. It is its ability to add new disciplines and new information, while building on the classics, which makes negotiation teaching so interesting in the first place.

Let's not throw out the baby with the bathwater.

References

Abel, R. 1981. *Politics of informal justice: The American experience.* Waltham, MA: Academic Press.

Ariely, D. 2010. *The upside of irrationality: The unexpected benefits of defying logic at work and at home.* New York: Harper.

Arrow, K., R. H. Mnookin, and A. Tversky (eds). 1995. *Barriers to conflict resolution.* New York: W.W. Norton.

Avruch, K. 2009. What is training all about? *Negotiation Journal* 25(2): 161-169.

Axelrod, R. 1984. *The evolution of cooperation.* New York: Basic Books.

Bazerman, M. and M. Neale. 1994. *Negotiating rationally.* New York: Free Press.

Behabib, S. 2002. *The claims of culture: Equality and diversity in the global era.* Princeton, NJ: Princeton University Press.

Brams, S. J. 2003. *Negotiation games: Applying game theory to bargaining and arbitration,* rev. edn. New York: Routledge.

Christensen, C. and M. Raynor. 2003. *The innovator's solution: Creating and sustaining successful growth.* Cambridge, MA: Harvard Business School Publishing Group.

Cialdini, R. B. 1993. *Influence: The psychology of persuasion.* New York: William Morrow.

Fisher, R. and D. Shapiro. 2005. *Beyond reason: Using emotions as you negotiate.* New York: Penguin.

Fisher, R., W. Ury, and B. Patton 1991. *Getting to yes. Negotiating agreement without giving in,* 2nd edn. New York: Penguin.

Fiss, O. M. 1984. Against settlement. *Yale Law Journal* 93: 1073-1086.

Follett, M. P. 1924. *Creative experience.* New York: Longmans, Green and Company.

Freshman, C., A. Hayes, and G. Feldman. 2002. The lawyer-negotiator as mood scientist: What we know and don't know about how mood relates to successful negotiation. *Journal of Dispute Resolution* 2002(1): 1-79.

Gladwell, M. 2000. *The tipping point: How little things can make a big difference.* New York: Little Brown.

Goleman, D. 1995. *Emotional intelligence: Why it can matter more than IQ.* New York: Bantam Books.

Honeyman, C. and A. K. Schneider. 2004. Catching up with the major-general: The need for a "canon of negotiation." *Marquette Law Review* 87(4): 637-647.

Jones, W. 2003. Complex adaptive systems. In *Beyond intractability* edited by G. Burgess and H. Burgess. Boulder, CO: University of Colorado Conflict Research Consortium. Available at http://www.beyondintractability.org/essay/complex_adaptive_systems (last accessed March 1, 2013).

Korobkin, R. and C. Guthrie. 2006. Heuristics and biases at the bargaining table. In *The negotiator's fieldbook: The desk reference for the experienced negotiator*, edited by A. K. Schneider and C. Honeyman. Washington, DC: American Bar Association.

Lande, J. and G. Herman. 2004. Fitting the forum to the family fuss: Choosing mediation, collaborative law, or cooperative law for negotiating divorce cases. *Family Court Review* 42(2): 280-288.

Lax, D. A. and J. K. Sebenius 1986. *The manager as negotiator*. New York: Free Press.

LeBaron, M. 2003. *Bridging cultural conflicts: A new approach for a changing world*. San Francisco: Jossey Bass.

Levitt, S. D. and S. J. Dubner. 2006. *Freakonomics: A rogue economist explores the hidden side of everything*. New York: William Morrow.

Luban, D. 1988. *Lawyers and justice: An ethical study*. Princeton, NJ: Princeton University Press.

Manwaring, M., B. McAdoo, and S. Cheldelin. 2010. Orientation and disorientation: Two approaches to designing "authentic" negotiation learning activities. In *Venturing beyond the classroom: Volume 2 in the rethinking negotiation teaching series*, edited by C. Honeyman, J. Coben, and G. De Palo. St. Paul, MN: DRI Press.

McAdoo, B. and M. Manwaring. 2009. Teaching for implementation: Designing negotiation curricula to maximize long-term learning. *Negotiation Journal* 25(2): 195-215.

Menkel-Meadow, C. 1984. Toward another view of legal negotiation: The structure of problem solving. *UCLA Law Review* 31: 754-842.

Nelken, M. 1996. Negotiation and Psychoanalysis: If I'd wanted to learn about feelings, I wouldn't have gone to law school. *Journal of Legal Education* 46(3): 420-429.

Nelken, M., A. K. Schneider, and J. Mahaud. 2010. If I'd wanted to teach about feelings I wouldn't have become a law professor. In *Venturing beyond the classroom: Volume 2 in the rethinking negotiation teaching series*, edited by C. Honeyman, J. Coben, and G. De Palo. St. Paul, MN: DRI Press.

Putnum, L. L. 2006. Communication and interaction patterns. In *The negotiator's fieldbook: The desk reference for the experienced negotiator*, edited by A. K. Schneider and C. Honeyman. Washington, DC: American Bar Association.

Raiffa, H. 1982. *The art and science of negotiation*. Cambridge, MA: Belknap Press.

Roberts, Simon, 1998. Against legal pluralism: Some reflections on the contemporary enlargement of the legal domain. *Journal of Legal Pluralism* 42: 95-106.

Sander, F. and S. Goldberg. 1994. Fitting the forum to the fuss: A user-friendly guide to selecting an ADR procedure. *Negotiation Journal* 10(1): 49-68.

Schelling, T. C. 1980. The strategy of conflict. Cambridge, MA: Harvard University Press.

Schneider, A. K. 2002. Shattering negotiation myths: Empirical evidence on the effectiveness of negotiation style. *Harvard Negotiation Law Review* 7: 143-233.

Schneider, A. K. and C. Honeyman (eds). 2006. *The negotiator's fieldbook: The desk reference for the experienced negotiator*. Washington, DC: American Bar Association.

Shachar, A. 2001. Two critiques of multiculturalism. *Cardozo Law Review* 23(1): 253-297.

Shestowsky, D. 2006. Psychology and persuasion. In *The negotiator's fieldbook: The desk reference for the experienced negotiator*, edited by A. K. Schneider and C. Honeyman. Washington, DC: American Bar Association.

Stone, D., B. Patton, and S. Heen. 1999. *Difficult conversations: How to discuss what matters most*. New York: Viking Penguin.

Thaler, R. H. and C. R. Sunstein. 2009. *Nudge: Improving decisions about health, wealth, and happiness*. New York: Penguin Books.

Turner, T. 1993. Anthropology and multiculturalism: What is anthropology that multiculturalists should be mindful of?" *Cultural Anthropology* 8(4): 411-429.

Walton, R. E. and R. B. McKersie. 1965. *A behavioral theory of labor negotiations: An analysis of a social interaction system*. New York: McGrawHill.

White, J. J. 1967. The lawyer as negotiator: An adventure in understanding and teaching the art of negotiation. *Journal of Legal Education* 19: 337-354.

Williams, G. R. 1983. *Legal negotiation and settlement*. St. Paul, MN: West Publishing.

Yarn, D. H. and G. T. Jones. 2006. In our bones (or brains): Behavioral biology. In *The negotiator's fieldbook: The desk reference for the experienced negotiator*, edited by A. K. Schneider and C. Honeyman. Washington, DC: American Bar Association.

⚛ 4 ⚛

Venturing Home: Implementing Lessons from the Rethinking Negotiation Project

*Kenneth H. Fox & Sharon Press**

Editors' Note: In 2011, the authors set out to create from scratch the first fully-realized course to take advantage of everything that had been learned up till then in the course of the RNT project. For 2012, they have already revamped the course, to respond to their own initial critiques as well as to some of the latest writings, in this volume and the parallel volume 3. The result is the closest educational venture that yet exists to the project's original intent to create a "Negotiation 2.0" course. Fortunately, the length of the course series the authors designed is significantly greater than a typical compressed "executive" course. That has allowed room for a significant degree of depth, subtlety and experimentation.

> "Roads go ever ever on, over rock and under tree ... Roads go ever ever on under cloud and under star, [y]et feet that wandering have gone [t]urn at last to home afar. . . . Look at last on meadows green [a]nd trees and hills they long have known." (Tolkien 1937: 252-253)

Introduction

At the end of his long journey to Lonely Mountain, Bilbo Baggins realizes that he, like most, must venture home again. Yet, when returning

* **Kenneth Fox** is a professor of business and director of conflict studies at Hamline University, and a senior fellow in the Dispute Resolution Institute at Hamline University School of Law in St. Paul, Minnesota. His email address is kenfox@hamline.edu. **Sharon Press** is an associate professor of law and director of the Dispute Resolution Institute at Hamline University School of Law in St. Paul, Minnesota. Her email address is spress01@hamline.edu.

to the trees and hills of a shire he has long known, he realizes he has changed – he is not the same hobbit who ventured forth so long ago and his dear shire no longer looks the same.

So, too, has been the journey for many of us who participated in the multi-year Rethinking Negotiation Teaching ("RNT") project. After venturing "over rock and under tree" – to Rome, Istanbul, and finally Beijing – farther and farther from our geographic, cultural and ideological "meadows green," it is time to come home. It is time to see what we have learned and how we have changed as negotiation teachers and scholars.

The RNT project has focused on a rich and broad range of themes related to negotiation and negotiation teaching. In this chapter, we focus on what we (in this instance, the authors of this chapter in particular) have taken from the past four years, and how we have incorporated those insights into classroom practice. Specifically, we address three themes:

1) The big picture – what we believe to be our most important conceptual shift toward a new generation of negotiation thinking.

2) Practical Implications – how we translated our emerging conceptual framework into classroom teaching practices. In this section, we describe a new six credit international business negotiation certificate program and the ways in which we incorporated various themes from the RNT project.

3) The Connected World – finally, we draw several conclusions about the ways in which the project fundamentally changed the way we think about, and teach, negotiation in our ever more connected world.

The Big Picture:
Plus ça change, plus c'est la même chose?

As the French critic Alphonse Karr once quipped, "the more things change, the more they stay the same" (Karr 1849). We wanted to test this epigram in relation to the RNT project. Put differently, after four years of journeying, looking, thinking and writing, is anything really new about our understanding of negotiation and negotiation teaching? We think so, although not in ways we had originally expected.

At the outset of the RNT project, participants were reminded of Jeffrey Rubin's observation that " . . . the field of dispute settlement is so broad, encompassing so many forms of theory and practice, that no one of us knows the full contours of the terrain" (Honeyman, Coben, and De Palo 2010: 2). Our experience bore out this admonition. We learned a great deal simply by working with new colleagues from broadly different academic disciplines and professional settings. They introduced us to a rich variety of ideas and insights that illuminated more "contours of the terrain." But this was a reflection of our own individual learning and not an evolution in the negotiation *terrain* itself. In order for the RNT project to truly advance the field, there would need to be more.

We believe there was. The project's real impact came at a deeper level, where we observed and experienced a shift in the very conception of how negotiators can understand themselves, interact with one another, and recognize the larger context within which negotiation interactions occur. As a consequence, we also saw a shift in the ways one can teach negotiation. As we discuss below, these shifts are both deeply philosophical and very practical – impacting how we now understand the negotiation process and how we have since designed and delivered new negotiation teaching strategies in the classroom. We suggest these deeper shifts are where one can find the true heart of "Negotiation 2.0."

A Philosophical Shift

In the first volume of the RNT series, Ken suggested that

> [d]espite the multitude of worldviews we experience in [negotiation] practice, . . . our knowledge about the field arises, primarily and ironically, from a single worldview. . . . We are only beginning to examine conflict and negotiation from the perspective that I refer to as post-modern scholarship. I suggest it is precisely here that fundamentally new ways of thinking about negotiation can flourish. By stepping outside the current paradigm, we may find new and interesting insights that were previously invisible" (Fox 2009: 19).

The "current paradigm" to which Ken refers rests on a set of assumptions about negotiators as separate and autonomous entities who come together for the purpose of claiming or creating maximum value to satisfy the negotiator's (or her principal's) self-interest. Others made similar observations during the RNT project. For example, Michelle LeBaron and Mario Patera observed that

> the tendency of first-generation negotiation trainers to base negotiation training on the tried-and-true principles of *Getting to Yes* (Fisher and Ury 1981) has kept our collective attention riveted on material, instrumental aspects of negotiation. We contend, along with Peter Adler (2006), that second generation negotiation scholarship and teaching must be protean

– it must equip people to adapt, shape-shift and create new synergies in the moment (LeBaron and Patera 2009: 58-59).

Ran Kuttner made a similar observation about current negotiation thinking, arguing that current negotiation theory is based on

> a view of human nature that emphasizes separateness, autonomy, individuality, and self-interestedness. According to this view, human beings are engaged primarily with themselves and with satisfying their own needs, while others are viewed as instruments in service of reaching that satisfaction (Kuttner 2010: 939).

This "current paradigm"[1] leads to a particular (first generation) understanding of human nature, interaction and negotiation.

As part of the RNT Project, a number of scholars stepped outside this current paradigm. One example of a new paradigm for understanding negotiation is seen in the examination of "wicked problems."[2] An entire section of the second volume of the RNT series was devoted to such negotiation situations, which arise

> . . . when technical problems meet conditions of political, social, and institutional uncertainty or when established ways of doing business are incapable of addressing the presenting problems (Docherty 2010: 482)." Wicked problems "cannot be separated from the surrounding context; any engagement with a wicked problem has its own implications for the larger societal, political, and cultural order (Chrustie et al. 2010: 453).

These "wicked" negotiation situations highlight the interconnections between the "content" of the negotiation and the complex and ever-changing context in which the content itself is embedded. As Chris Honeyman and Jim Coben wrote, to resolve wicked problems "we must be creative; we need to adopt a stance of openness that facilitates continued learning and revision of our understanding of the problem and possible outcomes. We also need to monitor the ways our own actions reshape the problem and its contexts" (Honeyman and Coben 2010: 440).

Honeyman's and Coben's observation marks an important shift in the way negotiators view themselves in relation to their counterparts and to the "problem." Wicked situations strip away any sense of certainty and stability in negotiation. These situations put into question the very concept of a shared set of truths and assumptions (see Anderson 1995:

6, making even broader claims about shared truths in our increasingly complex and diverse "post-modern" world). As Jayne Docherty writes,

> [a]ddressing these types of problems requires a post-modernist theoretical foundation that incorporates two levels of analysis: "social constructionism, which posits that meaning is embedded in society through patterns of social interaction" and "relational or dialogic theories," which focus on the ways we co-create meaning through our specific interpersonal and social interactions [internal references omitted] (2010: 482).

The Project's study of "wicked problems" highlights an important understanding of negotiation that applies well beyond "wicked" situations. It can (and, we argue, should) be part of all negotiation teaching and practice.

Other scholars also have focused on how negotiation thinking changes when looking at embedded meaning in social interaction. For example, Kuttner has examined negotiation from a Buddhist-oriented, relational, view of the "self" – a view very similar to the "post-modern" view that challenges the most basic philosophic tenets of Western thinking about how we understand humans, interaction and, as a consequence, negotiation. Specifically, Kuttner examines the recent move in the conflict field to question the idea of "self" as a separate, independent and fixed entity, an idea that is central to "first generation" negotiation thinking (Kuttner 2010: 932).

In turn, Kuttner finds that Baruch Bush and Joseph Folger, John Winslade and Gerald Monk, Leonard Riskin, and others all question, though in different ways, this dimension of first generation thinking (see, e.g., Berger and Luckmann 1966; Lyotard 1979; Gergen 1999; McNamee and Gergen 1999; Pearce 2007). Bush and Folger, who articulated the transformative model of mediation, describe a relational worldview where "[i]ndividuals are seen as both separate and connected, both individuated and similar. They are viewed as being to some degree autonomous, self-aware, and self-interested, but also to some degree connected, sensitive, and responsive to others" (Bush and Folger 1994: 242). In this regard "we should read the emphases of the relational worldview from within a different framework, with different governing values than those of the individualistic worldview" (Kuttner 2010: 944). The "relational worldview" described by Bush and Folger changes the way we understand humans, human interaction, conflict, and, in our context, even negotiation.

Winslade and Monk, who articulate the narrative model of mediation, similarly criticize the idea of "self" as possessing a "separate, permanent inner core" and, in its place, articulate an alternative set of "governing values" that speaks of the "self" as being "relationally constructed" (Kuttner 2010: 932). "Through [this] . . . postmodern lens, a problem is seen not as a personal deficit of the person but as constructed within a pattern of relationships . . . From this perspective, identity is not fixed, nor is it carried around by the individual largely unchanged from one context to another" (Winslade and Monk 2000: 44-45).

Riskin offers a mindfulness-based approach to negotiation that also questions the individualistic mindset, particularly in the practice of law (2002). Referring to what he calls "the Lawyer's Standard Philosophical Map," Riskin states

> [t]he traditional mind-set provides a constricted vision of legal problems and human relations that rests on separation and autonomy, on rights and rules. Thus, it contrasts with mind-sets grounded on connection, relationship, and duty. And mind-sets can affect a lawyer's understanding and performance in virtually any task (2002:16).

Riskin's observation is consistent with what we have described so far: the current (first generation) negotiation thinking is grounded in a conception about human relations that centers on individualism, separation and autonomy. This view shapes the way we think about negotiation and, as a result, negotiation teaching. In contrast, a second generation, relational, view of humans is gaining currency in the conflict field, and is changing the way we think about negotiation.[3]

This view of negotiation not only reflects what scholars have written, but also fits with conversations we had with colleagues at each of the three RNT working conferences. In particular, we noticed how colleagues who come from, or understand, "high context cultures" recognize how meaning not only comes from the words a negotiator says, but also – and more importantly – from the myriad contextual elements that surround those words. Further, the contextual elements that surround those words are not static, but instead are emergent, fluid, and dynamic. Over these past four years of the RNT project, we have come to embrace this different, relational, way of viewing humans and the practice of negotiation. Moreover, we have come to see this view as more than revealing hidden contours of the existing negotiation "terrain." Instead, we see it as changing the very landscape on which negotiation stands.

After venturing "over rock and under tree" it was time to come home. It was time for us to see how our "shire" had changed and how to put this new way of thinking into practice in the classroom.

Practical Implications – Part One
(A Framework for Teaching)

The re-imagining of "self" that we describe in the section above re-flects a paradigm shift in how we conceive of negotiation. But this philosophical re-imagining also has very practical implications for ne-gotiators and negotiation teachers. These implications reveal them-selves in two important ways.

First, the way that negotiators imagine themselves and their counterparts begins to change. This "re-imagining" of the negotiator herself, in turn, has an impact on the way negotiators see the very process of negotiation. Put differently, this "re-imagining" occurs in three dimensions: a different and fuller "awareness of self;" a dif-ferent and greater "awareness of other;" and a different and greater "awareness of context." We take each in turn.

Awareness of Self

At a fundamental level, a relational understanding of negotiation be-gins with a very intentional focus on the negotiator herself. It begins with self-awareness in two dimensions: *mindfulness* and *critical self-reflection*.

Mindfulness is a concept that is well examined in the conflict field (Riskin 2002; Freshman, Hayes, and Feldman 2002; Riskin 2004; Rock 2005) and gaining attention in the corporate and business world as well (Gardiner 2012). At its simplest level, mindfulness involves "cul-tivating an awareness of what exists in the present moment, without objective, ambition or judgment" (Rock 2005: 350). Mindfulness is achieved through a variety of practices, including meditation. Riskin states that this practice "can produce important insights as well as practical benefits. Just as practice drills help basketball players hone their jump-shots which they can use in games, mindfulness medita-tion can help people develop an ability to pay attention, calmly, in each moment, which they can apply to everyday life" (2002: 26).

Closely related to mindfulness is an awareness of our emo-tional selves, often referred to as "emotional intelligence" (Solovey and Mayer 1989; Goleman 1997; Mayer, Solovey, and Caruso 2008). Emotional intelligence relates to one's ability to perceive, under-stand, regulate and use emotional information as one experiences it (Solovey et.al 2008: 533). As part of the RNT project, several col-leagues examined the role of emotion in negotiation and its im-portance in negotiation teaching (Patera and Gamm 2010; Nelken, Schneider, and Mahuad 2010). We agree that a deeper understanding of one's emotional experiences is an important part of "awareness of self" and, as Solovey writes, is "fundamental to social intelligence"

(Solovey et al. 2008: 533-34). Mindfulness and emotional intelligence are increasingly recognized as mainstream concepts and "teachable" practices. They are also an essential element in developing the awareness necessary to engage meaningfully in the process of "co-arising" in negotiation.

The second dimension of self-awareness focuses on critical self-reflection. Critical self-reflection involves a close examination of the framework on which our beliefs are built – the ways in which we make sense of our experiences. This, in turn, has two dimensions: First, it involves a greater awareness of how our understanding of events (including negotiation situations) is shaped by our worldviews and ideologies (or, as Jeffrey Nealon and Searls Giroux (2003) describe it, what each of us will even "count as knowledge"; see also Fox 2009: 19). For example, concepts like "democracy," "communism," or even "respect" or "cooperation" can hold deeply different meanings to different people depending on the way they experience and make sense of, their world. We return to this specific example when we discuss the negotiation program we designed.

In addition to understanding how our worldviews shape the meaning we "construct" from our experiences, second generation thinking also calls on us to recognize how our own worldview is not necessarily normative. By this we mean that our way of thinking (and seeing the world) is not the "gold standard" against which other negotiators' perspectives should be measured. This is particularly important as we increasingly engage in trans-national and cross-cultural negotiation interactions.[4] In order to see such differences among negotiators, we need to develop a greater awareness of what we, ourselves, hold to be "true" about the world, what is valuable or important to us, how we see things organized, and how we believe we should act in given situations. (Docherty 2001:51).

The process of critical self-reflection is different than the practice of mindfulness. While mindfulness involves a shift in our way of "being present" in the moment (including a presence with our emotional selves), critical self-reflection involves more deeply examining the attitudes, beliefs and assumptions we carry with us into negotiation settings. In the context of mediation, Ken Cloke writes

[T]he roles we play in mediation are largely defined by our own attitudes, expectations and styles. These roles, in turn, depend on a set of assumptions about human nature, the nature of conflict, and the nature of change that have reverberated throughout Western political and philosophical thought for centuries, resulting in radically different definitions of mediation (2001: 9).

The same can be said of negotiation. The assumptions on which we stand regarding human nature (for example, the individual or the relational "self;" the nature of "things") lays the groundwork for fundamentally different views of negotiation (Kuttner 2010: 935). As a result, we see the development of self-awareness as a critical element in second generation negotiation training.

Awareness of Other

In the same way that negotiators need to develop a greater awareness of themselves, they must also know how to develop a greater awareness of their counterpart. From a second generation perspective, awareness of one's counterpart goes beyond doing research on the person's reputation, background, company or culture. It also involves a way of focusing and "tuning in" to their counterpart at the negotiation table. We believe that, to the degree negotiators can develop their awareness of self, they enhance their ability to develop this "awareness" of their counterpart. Put differently, a negotiator's ability to be critically self-reflective opens up the possibility to more fully recognize and deeply understand the worldview and presence of the negotiator sitting across the table.

In addition to the qualities discussed in relation to self-awareness, awareness of other also involves a sense of curiosity – a genuine desire to learn about and from one's counterpart. In the first volume of the RNT series, Chris Guthrie wrote about the importance of curiosity:

> To understand one's counterpart, a negotiator needs to be curious about what her counterpart has to say. In other words, a negotiator should cultivate a "stance of curiosity" or develop "relentless curiosity about what is really motivating the other side" [internal citations omitted] (Guthrie 2009: 63).

We agree. When viewed in conjunction with developing greater self-awareness, this awareness of other is consistent with "relational or dialogic theories," which focus on the ways we co-create meaning through our specific interpersonal and social interactions. It is also consistent with broader second generation principles that recognize that the "action" is in the "interaction," which requires a keen awareness of the negotiation interactions as they unfold.

Awareness of Context

Finally, we believe negotiators need to attend to the larger context that surrounds and informs (and, in turn, is influenced by) a particular set of negotiation interactions. By "context," we mean developing a greater awareness of how specific negotiation events are part of larger situational and social contexts in three dimensions: the practical and social surroundings in which the negotiation is imbedded; the dialogic interplay between the specific negotiation interactions and the surrounding context as the negotiation unfolds; and the different theoretical principles available to negotiators to make sense of, and navigate, the negotiation process.

This understanding of "context" is consistent with what Docherty suggests about a constructionist view of negotiation, namely that "meaning is embedded in society through patterns of social interaction" (Docherty 2010: 482). It is also consistent with what Honeyman and Coben write in the context of wicked problems: negotiators "need to monitor the ways our own actions reshape the problem and its contexts" (Honeyman and Coben 2010: 440). By recognizing how negotiation events are part of, and also reshape, larger patterns of social interaction, negotiators are better able to adapt and engage in purposeful negotiation.

We see these three dimensions of awareness – of self, other, and context – as central elements to second generation negotiation thinking. They reveal new and different ways to understand negotiation. They also change how we think about negotiation teaching. And if we believe that these three levels of awareness are central to effective negotiation, then these three levels of awareness must also be central elements in the negotiation classroom.

The second implication of this philosophical re-imagining is that the distinction between negotiation "content" and "process" begins to disappear. First generation negotiation teaching includes the study of strategic negotiation steps and stages. These make perfect sense if one views individuals as autonomous and rational actors who respond to stable external stimuli (Fox 2009). However, from a second generation point of view, negotiation interactions take on a more fluid, emergent and dynamic character (the character of "co-arising" selves). This shift becomes evident as we think about the nature and connections between "self," "other," and "context," particularly in the ways they interact. From this different perspective, social context and patterns of interaction become central to, if not the essence of, meaning-making. In other words, it is in the *interactions themselves* where we find the "negotiation action" consistent with the relational practice described by Bush and Folger (2005) in the context of transformative mediation. It becomes clear that negotiators need to develop a different and greater awareness of the emergent and dynamic ways in which the negotiation process unfolds.

One concrete result of this shift in focus (from the individual actor to the interaction) is that negotiators must re-orient themselves to become more aware of "what" they focus on and, at the same time, to "how" they understand the very process of unfolding negotiation interaction. As we discuss below, this shift in focus has important practical implications for negotiation teaching and course design.

The challenge we faced was how to translate this set of abstract principles into concrete practice. In the following section, we describe how we designed a six-credit negotiation certificate program around these principles. We also discuss additional lessons we incorporated from the RNT project that we believe reflect important "second generation" negotiation teaching.

Practical Implications – Part Two (Application: The International Business Negotiation Certificate Program)

A first attempt to design and deliver "second generation" negotiation teaching took place in Istanbul in October, 2010, as part of the RNT project's second working conference. The second volume of the RNT series includes a description of that pilot one-day executive training (Fox, Schonewille, and Çuhadar-Gürkaynak 2010). In the training, we tested the idea of focusing on three overarching principles that were similar to, but less developed than, the levels of awareness described above: increasing self-awareness; cultivating curiosity; and the over-arching importance of worldview (Fox, Schonewille, and Çuhadar-Gürkaynak 2010: 16). After this pilot course, we reported:

> Further work is needed to develop and clarify what distinguishes first from second generation negotiation principles. While we understood these concepts in isolation from a training setting, once in the classroom, we found ourselves interacting with students in ways quite similar to previous trainings (Fox, Schonewille, and Çuhadar-Gürkaynak 2010: 29).

After that one-day pilot training in 2010, the authors, together with a group of advisors[5] undertook to refine the design and content and to deliver a full academic negotiation certificate program built on the lessons from the entire RNT project. The result was a two-course, six-credit law-school program in international business negotiation (IBN). During the summer of 2011, we offered the first IBN certificate program and enrolled a diverse group of law and other graduate students at Hamline University in Minnesota. The program fully implemented the conceptual framework which had been developing since Istanbul and also provided a platform to pilot new methods for interaction via distance technology. In 2012, we partnered with RNT project colleague Nadja Alexander at Hong Kong Shue Yan University International Institute of Conflict Engagement and Resolution (IICER) to launch the completed program, which combined a more fully refined conceptual framework and a fully implemented distance learning component with an international group of participants. The course attracted law and business students from throughout the United States, including several who were born and raised outside the United States, as well as lawyers, business professionals, and students from Hong Kong, the Netherlands, the United Kingdom, Germany, and Mainland China.

What follows is a description of an integrated two-course program. We include some discussion of refinements that were made between the first year of implementing the program in 2011and the full implementation in 2012, as well as revisions we made based on the continued evolution of the RNT project. We conclude with a list of features we believe to be most important to integrate into a "second generation" negotiation program.

A Strong Focus on Students' Own Lived Experience

IBN is designed to draw, as much as possible, on students' own lived experiences. This puts into concrete practice the exploration of such abstract notions as "self," "other," and "context." It also reflects insights that grew directly from the RNT project and that called for greater student empowerment (Nelken, McAdoo, and Manwaring 2009), that critically examined the use of role-plays in student learning (Alexander and LeBaron 2009; Ebner and Kovach 2010; Matz and Ebner 2010), and that explored "adventure learning" in negotiation teaching (see chapters 7-14 in volume 2 of the RNT series [Honeyman, Coben, and DePalo 2010]).

We drew on students' lived experiences in several ways: First, the course is organized thematically more than based on a set structure. That is, we moved away from discrete "modules" or teaching units and instead organized the program as a matrix. Looking longitudinally (across time), in the first class meeting we introduced the three levels of awareness – self, other and context (which included an explicit examination of culture), and then carried the themes forward through the entire two-course program, returning to them regularly. As the courses progressed, we then introduced more discrete topics (for example, positions, interests, competition, cooperation, and so forth). This created natural conversational intersections between the on-going themes and the more discrete topics. As we introduced students to the various discrete topics, we would return to the ongoing themes, inviting students to reflect on the discrete topics based on their own experiences and in the context of the three themes. We also designed activities that invited students, first, to connect their own experiences with the concepts being examined, and second, to interact with and teach one another about how they understood the concepts from their respective worldviews. The result was an ongoing class conversation with multiple threads that remained grounded in the students' own experiences while increasing in depth and complexity as the course progressed.

Second, we developed experiential activities that drew as much as possible on real experience, rather than assigned roles. One of the on-going debates in the RNT project has been whether to abandon the use of role plays. We tried to avoid this "sucker's choice." Instead, we adopted the philosophy that experiential activities can be designed to sit at any point along a continuum, from raw and completely unscripted lived experience to contrived and artificial play-acting. We designed each activity with a particular learning objective in mind, and then looked for ways to minimize artificiality and maximize eliciting from students their own experiences as they interacted with one another in the activities.

By way of example, none of the negotiation activities included assigning names or, to the extent possible, specific "roles" to play. We avoided instructions that included information such as lists of a party's interests or secret objectives. Instead, we described negotiation situations we believed students could relate to (and that were representative of what they would actually encounter in real international business negotiation situations) and assigned tasks where the students could draw on their own experience to flesh them out. Furthermore, we also did not use isolated, one-off activities. Instead, we designed a series of negotiation interactions that were inter-related and that evolved logically over time. Specifically, because ours is an international business negotiation program, we formed two companies, based on actual publicly listed companies – an American high technology start-up and a Chinese technology manufacturing company – where students could research the real organizations and related issues as the course progressed. The students were assigned to, and stayed with, their company throughout the entire program. This enabled the students to work together (within their given company) over time, developing their own corporate culture and making decisions based on an increasingly rich and complex identity and history of decisions.

In addition, our negotiation activities built on one another and followed a natural business progression: business formation, facility site selection and government approvals, internal negotiations related to hiring, product development or manufacture, intra- and inter-team negotiations and business strategy, external negotiations (related to supplies and later, an exclusive manufacturing agreement between the two companies), conflict anticipation and dispute response. Making particularly good use of the iPad technology each student had at their disposal, each activity included hyperlinks to actual internet resources. In this way, students drew upon real research about real companies and developed depth over time as they made a range of increasingly inter-related individual and collective decisions involving their company.

When the program shifted from two parallel in-residence courses (one in Minnesota and the other in Hong Kong) to an integrated distance learning course, the participants were faced with another layer of challenges in how to negotiate or otherwise work with someone whom they had not met or with whom they had no prior relationship, who was in a time-zone thirteen hours away, and who did not share the same mother tongue or life-experience. Even arranging when and by what means they were to negotiate surfaced very real practical and conceptual challenges. The "realness" of this shift deepened the degree to which the students had to engage their real selves in the negotiation activities and put in clear relief the importance of self, other and context awareness.

Third, in addition to regular negotiation activities, students participated in an adventure learning activity that took them outside the classroom and into their local business districts as they worked through intra- and cross-team negotiations. The activity asked teams of students to inspect a selection of downtown office buildings that might be suitable as their company's regional headquarters. They were provided with real commercial building market information, links to each building's leasing web-site, and company-specific selection criteria (such as overall space needs, private vs. shared office lay-outs, and so on). The buildings represented a range of strategic choices (for example, a "Class A" high-rise as compared with a historic or a low-cost efficiency building). This required the teams to develop and examine their own company's identity, financial priorities and business needs. While some of this information was contrived, the overall activity called on the students to engage in a range of very real interactions and decisions.

Fourth, as instructors, we were intentionally elicitive rather than didactic in our classroom interactions. Rather than presenting material and concepts from the standpoint of "all-knowing" professors, we identified topics to explore together. For example, when we had a focused discussion of culture (in addition to an ongoing conversation thread), in addition to select readings, we asked each student to complete their own culture survey. We then aggregated the information and distributed this to the entire class as a basis for an online discussion. The activity led to a deep, rich, nuanced and insightful conversation about what "culture" is (and is not) that could never have come from readings or lectures alone and that went well beyond what we, as instructors, could imagine. The activity also illustrated the generative process of "co-created" meaning making – where the students' own lived experiences contributed substantially to the "content" of the course. We discuss our roles as instructors further below. We also discuss how this process contributed to a change in how we viewed "content" and "process" in the class.

Finally, we incorporated into the classroom various physical "movement" activities that drew upon other dimensions of the students' own "ways of knowing." The idea of "kinesthetic" learning is an emerging area of study in the conflict field that complements cognitive and emotional "knowledge." At its most basic, experiencing physical movement can unlock different dimensions of understanding and can inform how we think. Examples include the adventure learning activity described above, and asking students to participate in a "human thermometer" (a single line where students organize themselves along a continuum in response to instructor prompts, described in detail in Fox, Schonewille, and Çuhadar-Gürkaynak 2010), as well as a range of other additional activities drawn from Michelle LeBaron's work (see, for instance, Alexander and LeBaron, *Embodied Negotiation*, in this volume).

Taken together, the four elements we discuss here represent a focus on inviting students to bring the richness and value their lived experience offers into the learning environment.

A Fundamental Re-Thinking of the Role of the Instructor in Relationship to the Student

Perhaps the biggest shift in course design was how we reconceptualized our roles as instructors in relation to our students. During our planning discussions related to keeping the IBN course "real," we had an "aha" moment about how the project had contributed to our way of thinking about teaching negotiation. In order to make a space in the class environment for students' own real and lived experiences, we had to let go of our "first generation" definition of what it means to be an "instructor." Put differently, we had to make a fundamental shift from an "individualist" to a "relational" paradigm in how we experienced the classroom environment and how we related to our students. This took our abstract understanding of the philosophic shift we describe in section one, above, and caused us to rethink in concrete terms how to design course elements and interact with students at every moment of the program.

In volume two of the RNT series, Roy Lewicki and Andrea Schneider argued that while the negotiation field has paid attention to theory development (the "what") and to pedagogy (the "how"), the field has neglected the "who" – gaining a better understanding of the particular students who are in a given classroom or training (Lewicki and Schneider 2010). They offered a three-level guide to "market segmentation" to help instructors determine the degree to which a given negotiation course or training should be commoditized or customized (Lewicki and Schneider 2010: 50-51). We agree that instructors need to focus more on "who" is in the classroom. At the same time, the "who" they describe is a "first order" shift in thinking – a way to more accurately categorize and segment the negotiation teaching market for purposes of course design. While this is a valuable contribution to our understanding of negotiation teaching, our experience with IBN suggests yet a different paradigm.

The "shift" we experienced with the IBN program and describe here is, we believe, a "second order" shift in the "who" in the classroom – that is, a deeper and more fundamental re-imagining of the nature of the relationship – and way of interacting – among instructors and students. Put differently, the quality and manner in which instructors interact with students in the classroom (the "how") *is itself* an essential "content" element of a course (the "what") that cannot be realized without a relational connection along the lines we describe in section one of our essay above (the "who"). Once you accept a different role for the instructor in relation to the students and recognize how knowledge and insights "co-arise" through the process of discourse, the "who" shifts from a static category of *students* to become *real people* whose lived experiences add to and enrich every aspect of their (and the instructor's) learning.

We submit that this "second order" shift is a major contribution of the RNT project. We further submit that the inseparability of the "what," the "how," and the "who" of teaching is wholly consistent with the relational principles discussed above that inform second generation negotiation thinking.

An additional concrete way in which the "what," the "how," and the "who" all came together was in our decisions related to instructors. Given our commitment to honoring "lived experience," the course instructors were intentionally drawn from a mix of backgrounds. During the first year of IBN, Ken (business school professor from the United States) was the primary instructor for the basic negotiation course with some assistance from Sharon (law school professor from the United States). For the advanced business negotiation course, Andrew Wei-Min Lee (Australian negotiation consultant and adjunct law professor now living in mainland China) and Vivian Feng Ying Yu (mainland Chinese practitioner and adjunct law professor) joined the faculty. The following year, Ken taught the basic negotiation course in Hong Kong, while Sharon and Andrew taught the same class in Minnesota. For the distance portion (the advanced international business negotiation course), Ken and Sharon co-taught the combined class. The advantages of having instructors from different backgrounds were many, but one example for illustrative purposes may be helpful.

In the U.S.-based course, rather than having a discussion of the importance of recognizing different perspectives, we had a discussion of the one-child policy in China, which surfaced different views on this controversial topic (in addition to Andrew as co-instructor, the U.S. class included two Mainland Chinese students). The rich conversation confronted participants with different worldviews, and led to interesting and profound insights about the implications for negotiation. Similarly, in the Hong Kong-based course, Ken engaged with the class in a discussion about the different conceptions of "communism" and "capitalism." The diverse mix of students (Mainland China, Hong Kong, Western Europe and North America), combined with Hong Kong's changing status from a British colony to a "Special Administrative Region" within China, led to a similarly rich conversation, with unexpected insights about what various students took to be "true," "right," and "just," and how these differences impact the ways one approaches negotiation.

Throughout the program, all the instructors looked for ways to bring out differences in perspectives naturally and to engage the participants in self-discovered learning. Thus, we considered not only "who" the students/participants in the course were, but also "who" *we*, the instructors, were (intentionally looking for instructors whose cultural and professional backgrounds differed in important ways from one another and from the students).[6] In so doing, the "who," the "what" and the "how" became intertwined.

Additional Second Generation Implications
In addition to the important paradigm shift we experienced and put into practice as described above, we also incorporated a number of other valuable "second generation" lessons into the IBN program. Among these were:

Incorporation of Distance and Other Technology into the Course Design and Delivery

In contemplating and developing a distance component to the program, we were committed to having it provide, at a minimum, equivalent learning quality to an in-residence course. For a variety of reasons described below, we believe that the distance portion of the program was not only an equivalent learning format to an in-residence class, but actually enhanced student learning as we integrated the lessons from the RNT project.

Recognizing that international business negotiations frequently take place across great distances, we integrated various types of distance technology and activities into the course design and delivery. Each student received an iPad with a proprietary "app" designed for the program. The app, along with other uploaded software programs, provided students with virtually all the materials and technology needed for the entire program (including readings, video content, access to the internet, and communications software). Assignments and course activities were stored in the "cloud" and included hyperlinks connected to appropriate internet sites. During the distance portion of the fully implemented program, the U.S. and Hong Kong groups were deliberately intermixed, even though they had never met or otherwise worked together before. Students in both locations worked on course project teams, participated in online discussions and conducted a series of negotiations with their counterparts across the world.[7] The result was that students encountered very real limitations and advantages to working with technology and distance. For example, they experienced how synchronous (e.g., Skype) and asynchronous (e.g., email) technology were relatively more or less effective for group projects, class assignments and negotiation activities when their classmates and counterparts are in a time zone thirteen hours away.

Selecting Appropriate Course Materials.

One challenge we faced was identifying a text and other course materials for the program. To the extent possible, we wanted the readings to promote critical discussion related to our key themes (awareness of self, other and context) and which would encourage, rather than interfere with, reflection on students' lived experience. There is no limit to the number of books on negotiation.[8] However, many of the books we reviewed, while excellently written, were prescriptive in nature. Because of our approach to teaching, and the program's international business focus, we ultimately decided to utilize *Negotiating Globally* (2nd edition) by Jeanne Brett, supplemented by a number of readings drawn from a variety of sources (the course syllabus is attached as an Appendix). In addition, we took advantage of the multi-media capabilities of the iPad by incorporating websites and apps into the course, such as Culture GPS and TEDTalks. We also produced a series of video interviews with business and legal practitioners and negotiation scholars. These interviews allowed students to "sit in" on conversations about real life negotiation experiences by a diverse group of professionals who work, negotiate and teach internationally.

Designing Assessments

A final area where we focused on incorporating a "2.0" frame to the IBN program was in assessment. We agree with the many contributors to Volume 3 of the RNT series who suggest that assessment is not merely a static, end of course, grading tool. Rather, "as we have already observed but cannot stress too highly, [assessment] is at the heart of our teaching. It is always under way, at least by implication, affecting relationships, communication, motivation and learning" (Ebner, Coben, and Honeyman 2012: 5). We found this particularly true with regard to the distance portion of the IBN program.

We believe that careful attention to the assignments and the assessments in the distance portion of the IBN program resulted in a distance learning experience that was not merely comparable to, but actually exceeded, the possibilities for integrating the lessons of the RNT project in an in-residence environment. Before commenting further, a brief description of our assessment methods in the distance portion, both formative and summative, may be helpful:

Negotiation reports

At the conclusion of each assigned negotiation, the students completed an individual and a collective report (jointly completed by all participants in the negotiation activity). The individual reflection reports contained the following questions:

1) *What was your strategy and how well did it work in relation to the outcome of this negotiation?*

2) *If you were to do this negotiation again tomorrow, what specifically would you do the same? What specifically would you do differently? Why?*

3) *In relation to the primary negotiation content area associated with this activity, what new insights have you gained in relation to awareness of self, other, and negotiation process/theory/context?*

4) *What new insights have you gained from this activity about the use of distance technology when conducting negotiation activities? How, if at all, will you use technology differently the next time you participate in a distance negotiation?*

> 5) *What, if any, ethical issues arose in this negotiation and how did you address them?*

The questions were specifically designed to encourage the students to reflect on the negotiation, particularly drawing their attention to the concepts of awareness of self, other and context and to connect their "lived experience" with negotiation theory. Even though the reports were not graded, they were considered as part of the assessment of the student's program participation and, more important, served the valuable function of focusing the student's attention on the experience of the negotiation, what the student learned from the negotiation, and what, if anything, she would do differently in the future. In addition to individual reports, the students also had to work as a group to complete a collective report for their negotiation. This provided an additional opportunity for the students to negotiate a real set of issues: who would write it, what it would contain, and how it would be approved before submission. Finally, the reports gave us a window into how the negotiations were unfolding, even though we could not observe them directly.

Reading/video reports

In addition to reporting on negotiation activities, students completed a Reading/Video Report for each group of readings (or videos) due on any particular day. Unlike some distance learning programs, we were directive in when the students were to complete the supplemental material (readings and videos) which we assigned. For each due date, the students completed a Report Form on the material which was to have been completed. Since each due-date included several readings or videos, the students were called upon to synthesize the material rather than simply summarize an individual reading.[9] These reports focused their attention on the most important elements to the readings/videos, provided some level of accountability for completing required readings, and often gave us an on-going indication of what material was clear and what material might warrant added attention.

Online discussions

During the roughly two-week distance portion of the program, the students participated in four separate online asynchronous discussion threads.[10] The forty-two students (from both the United States and Hong Kong locations) were divided into four mixed sub-groups for each discussion thread, and were then re-assigned to different subgroups for each subsequent thread, thereby enabling each student to have in-depth interaction with a variety of different students and perspectives. The first discussion focused on ethics, the second on ethics implications for international business, the third on negotiation context and framing, and the fourth on culture. Each of the discussions included a thought-question prompt to which each student posted a substantial response, and at least one follow-up comment to other students' postings, after having read the initial postings of their colleagues. As instructors, we were able to pull out each student's initial posting and subsequent response(s) and, using a scoring matrix, measure the level of their participation in the discussion and the depth and quality of their insights and understanding of the theme. The students' engagement in these discussions was extremely thoughtful, and reflected a truly generative process of "co-arising," understanding where powerful insights emerged from the unfolding conversations.

Reputation index

Incorporating an idea from Nancy Welsh (2012), we used a "reputation index" assessment tool twice during the program (once at the end of course one, and again at the end of the distance course). A "reputation index" is a means by which students (and, if desired, instructors) can provide feedback to one another about their reputation as negotiators and contributors to class learning. Using the index twice enabled us to do both formative and summative assessment over time. At the end of the first class, the students were asked to identify up to six other students with whom they had direct negotiation experience and who they thought had "developed a positive reputation as a negotiator,"[11] up to another six students who they thought had "developed a negative reputation as a negotiator,"[12] and up to six other students who "contributed substantially to your learning in this course through good feedback, insightful participation or other actions (intended or otherwise) that have helped you learn." For each person identified as having a positive or negative reputation, the students were instructed to provide a concrete narrative explanation for that assessment. We aggregated the responses and explanations and each student received a confidential (and anonymous) summary of the reputation they earned. For this part of the program the students were not graded based upon the reputation they had earned from others, but solely based on their own "thoughtful completion" of the index about others.

At the conclusion of the second distance course, the students were again asked to complete a reputation index that included all students from both the United States and Hong Kong groups. This second time, students were graded on their "thoughtful completion" of their own form as well as the reputation they had earned from others in the combined class.

In both cases, we were impressed by the care with which the students completed the index and the thoughtful comments they provided to their colleagues. Even more significantly, we found that students took the comments received in the first class to heart and acted upon those items about which they received negative feedback. For example, one student who had received negative comments from the first course actually reached out to fellow students during the second course to redress what they had reported experiencing. As instructors, we found it useful to have an indication of how the students perceived each other. We also found that this nearly "360°" feedback loop was much richer and more impactful than could have been achieved by our feedback alone. We found it to be a powerful example of how assessment can function "at the heart of our teaching."

Group presentation

After having been divided into cross-national sub-groups of ten or eleven students each, the students engaged in multi-party negotiations to choose partners and topics for five team research presentations to their sub-group.[13] After researching and preparing their team presentations, the sub-groups convened over Skype with the instructors and made their presentations to one another. The students were not directly evaluated on the team and topic selection negotiation itself (although they did complete individual and collective reports on the negotiation), but they were assessed on their actual presentation to their sub-group based on criteria they knew in advance. The presentation assessments included factors that could only be successfully achieved through effective teamwork and use of technology. As a result, students received feedback on more than the content of their presentation, but also on their ability to work as a team across significant distance.

Final paper

At the conclusion of the program, each student selected a topic for a final paper. They could choose to write an analytical paper, or to conduct an in-depth interview with an experienced negotiator and write a paper based on what they learned from the interview. As part of the process, the students had one-on-one consultations with the instructors (via Skype, phone, or in one case in-person) to discuss the topic and research plan in depth. This allowed the instructors to provide formative feedback to each student as they progressed on their final assignment. In addition to substantive criteria, the students were also assessed on the degree to which they meaningfully participated in the consultation.

While any of these assessment practices might be found in existing courses, we believe that taken as a whole they moved assessment to the heart of student learning, and reflect important insights from the RNT project.

"The Connected World" – How the RNT Project Changed our Paradigm

The use of the "2.0" imagery dropped out of favor with many project participants because it (wrongly in our view) was considered to be an attempt to discard old negotiation ideas and develop something entirely new and different. From our view, this is not the case. As computer users might recall, when you get the next version of software, it often looks a whole lot like the prior version. It includes the same functionality that has served you well. Yet, as you use it, you begin to see new features and, more importantly, different capabilities that are only possible because of its deeper design changes. In the same way, we believe the IBN program is a negotiation 2.0 version. The fundamentals of negotiation teaching as previously performed are all still there. Yet, because of the deeper shift in how we conceptualize negotiation, we believe those fundamentals take on a different and even richer meaning for students. Moreover, reflecting on the RNT project as a whole and on our own lived experience teaching the IBN program, we find that in addition to a changed conception of negotiation, *we* too have changed. We approached our students' learning from a very different standpoint. We incorporated different ideas and interacted with them in a qualitatively different way. We had to test our ideas in a genuinely global setting, with students from across the world working and learning together.

Looking back, we see the following as essential elements to teaching negotiation 2.0 for a connected world:

1) The process of negotiation takes on a very different complexion when experienced from a "relational" standpoint. By developing a greater awareness of "self," "other," and "context," and by appreciating the nature of how meaning is "co-arising," negotiators are able to see and work with previously invisible negotiation dynamics.

2) From this "relational" standpoint, the instructor's role is significantly different. She elicits and facilitates an emergent conversation, rather than lecturing and delivering a set body of information. She must be sufficiently knowledgeable and comfortable with negotiation as to follow the ebb and flow of class conversations as they emerge in order to seize on important teachable moments.

3) Learning is enhanced by focusing on lived experience. There are many ways that lived experience can be mined, and a negotiation course should take advantage of all of them, from the design of activities, to the use of adventure learning and movement, to structured opportunities for discussion among the students. Some students will have prior experience that they will be able to draw from and some will draw from the experience they have in the class – all of these lived experiences are valuable. Moreover, by drawing on students' (and instructors') lived experiences, students are better tuned into, and prepared for, interactions across cultures and worldviews.

4) Distance learning adds intrinsic value. Learning outside of the traditional classroom opens up many opportunities to teach and engage students in different ways. By its very nature, distance learning calls upon students to be more responsible for their learning and, if the program is structured well, to be more reflective. Given the importance of awareness (of self, other, and context), this makes distance learning an ideal platform for delivery of portions of a 2.0 negotiation course.

5) Assessments are central to student learning. Since we know that students learn in a variety of ways, assessments should include a range of methods. Thoughtful use of assessment will provide the students with opportunities to learn while at the same time providing instructors the opportunity to evaluate student learning more precisely.

Conclusion

On reflection, we are convinced that the RNT project did not simply uncover formerly hidden "contours of the existing [negotiation] terrain." The project added to the landscape.

Getting to this point was a long philosophical and practical journey "over rock and under tree." In the same way that Bilbo Baggins returned home from his long journey, we, too, have had to venture home to our classrooms. And like Bilbo's return to the shire, our return to the classroom revealed that while everything appeared familiar, at the same time, our negotiation classroom was ever changed.

Notes

[1] This paradigm goes back at least as far as the Enlightenment (see Pearce 2007: 173, writing of Thomas Hobbes *Leviathan*, where the primary entity is the "solitary man").

[2] As described elsewhere (see Honeyman, Coben, and De Palo 2010: 439), the term "wicked problems" was first articulated in the context of public

planning. We find the use of this term in the context of negotiation both helpful and confusing. It is helpful to the extent that it signals a qualitatively different set of factors that change the very nature of what negotiation can be about. It is confusing to the extent that literature from fields outside of negotiation often describe "wicked problems" in ways that obscure or misdirect us away from what we consider to be the heart of what makes them so "wicked": the realization that some situations require negotiators to engage with fundamental questions of meaning and "truth."

[3] Kuttner goes further still than Honeyman and Coben, Bush and Folger, Winslade and Monk and Riskin, suggesting that by looking to Buddhist teachings, we can more fully understand the "relationally constructed self" and the nature of "things." In turn, understanding these Buddhist teachings, he suggests, will give us a very different understanding of negotiation. According to Kuttner, a key concept in the Buddhist worldview is "dependent co-arising" – that is, the notion that no "thing" (including the "self," "interests" and so on) can exist as independent and separate. Rather, a "thing's" "existence" only arises in relation to other "things" (Kuttner 2010: 950). The notion of "co-arising" is similar to, but goes deeper than, the idea of "co-constructed" meaning. From a communication perspective, meaning is "co-constructed" or "co-created" through the process of communication interaction as it unfolds between people (and not through the words themselves) (Fox 2009: 21). "Co-arising" goes even deeper than the *meaning we give* to things, suggesting that the true *nature* of things "demands the realization of relationality – a realization that all things are always dependent on other things – in other words, whatever we believe to exist, exists only in relation to other things (Kuttner 2010: 950). These post-modern claims stand in stark contrast to a worldview that favors individuality, autonomy and separateness. Honeyman and Coben's, Bush and Folger's, Winslade and Monk's, Riskin's, and Kuttner's critiques all illuminate a fundamental re-imagining of "self" and "other." They also mirror what was first noticed in the first RNT conference in Rome. And, by re-imagining the "self" in relational terms, it becomes possible to re-imagine negotiation as well – a profoundly different orientation toward our field of study. This deeper exploration of the "self" and "other" warrants even further examination as second generation scholarship evolves.

[4] Here, we do not limit "cross-cultural" interactions to international negotiations. In our increasingly diverse communities, and professions, we encounter "cross-cultural" interactions at home more often than we might imagine. See, for instance, Volpe and Cambria (2009).

[5] We gratefully acknowledge Professors James Coben and Bobbi McAdoo, for their comments during the development of the program. We also gratefully acknowledge Andrew Lee and Vivian Feng, for offering their advice and for co-teaching in the program.

[6] We also included a set of video-taped interviews with negotiation experts and scholars from Israel and Italy as well as from multi-national corporations who regularly negotiate across the globe.

[7] At the same time the students were engaging in the use of technology, they were reading appropriate materials – including essays from the RNT project – that challenged them to develop greater awareness of "self," "other" and "context."

[8] A quick search of Amazon.com for books with a title that included "negotiation" yielded over 16,000 results.

[9] The Reading/Video Report included the following questions:

- Discuss the key insights/"take-away" points you learned from the various assignments due today. This question calls for critical thinking and synthesis. Think in terms of how the material informs your awareness of self, other, and international business negotiation. Be sure to include some discussion from each individual article, book chapter and/or video.
- What, if any, new questions arise from this assignment that you would like to explore further?
- In what ways were these readings/videos helpful/not helpful to your understanding of international business negotiation? Why or why not?

[10] The students also conducted one on-line discussion during the first (in-residence) course so as to have practice with the online technology before dispersing to their distant homes.

[11] The instructions included the following additional information: "Positive reputations as negotiators are gained by displaying competence, effectiveness, trustworthiness, integrity and so on."

[12] The instruction included the following additional information: "Negative reputations as negotiators are gained by displaying – or being perceived as displaying – dishonesty, incompetence, ineffectiveness, lack of trustworthiness, lack of integrity, lack of preparation, and so on."

[13] For the sake of some consistency and also to provide every student with information on some important topics, the students could select from the following topics: negotiation and technology; culture and negotiation; creativity and negotiation; and "wicked problems."

References

Adler, P. S. 2006. Protean negotiation. In *The negotiator's fieldbook: The desk reference for the experienced negotiator*, edited by A.K. Schneider and C. Honeyman. Washington, DC: American Bar Association.

Alexander, N. and M. LeBaron. 2009. Death of the role-play. In *Rethinking negotiation teaching: Innovations for Context and Culture*, edited by C. Honeyman, J. Coben, and G. De Palo. St. Paul, MN: DRI Press.

Anderson, W. T. 1995. *The truth about the truth: De-confusing and re-constructing the post-modern world*. New York: Penguin Group.

Berger, P. and T. Luckmann. 1966. *The Social construction of reality: A Treatise in the sociology of knowledge*. New York: Anchor Books.

Bernard, P. 2009. Finding common ground in the soil of culture. In *Rethinking negotiation teaching: Innovations for Context and Culture*, edited by C. Honeyman, J. Coben, and G. De Palo. St. Paul, MN: DRI Press.

Bush, R. A. B. and J. Folger. 2005. *The promise of mediation: The transformative approach to conflict*, rev. edn. San Francisco: Jossey-Bass.

Chrustie, C., J. S. Docherty, L. Lira, J. Mahuad, H. Gadlin, and C. Honeyman. 2010. Negotiating wicked problems: Five stories. In *Venturing beyond the classroom: Volume 2 in the rethinking negotiation teaching series*, edited by C. Honeyman, J. Coben, and G. De Palo. St. Paul, MN: DRI Press.

Cloke, K. 2001. Mediating dangerously: The frontiers of conflict resolution. San Francisco: Jossey-Bass.

Docherty, J. S. 2001. *Learning lessons from Waco: When the parties bring their Gods to the negotiation table.* Syracuse: Syracuse University Press.

Docherty, J. S. 2010. "Adaptive" negotiation: Practice and teaching. In *Venturing beyond the classroom: Volume 2 in the rethinking negotiation teaching series,* edited by C. Honeyman, J. Coben, and G. De Palo. St. Paul, MN: DRI Press.

Ebner, N., J. Coben, and C. Honeyman. 2012. Introduction: Assessment as mirror. In *Assessing our students, assessing ourselves: Volume 3 in the rethinking negotiation teaching series,* edited by N. Ebner, J. Coben, and C. Honeyman. St. Paul, MN: DRI Press.

Ebner, N. and K. Kovach. 2010. Simulation 2.0: The resurrection. In *Venturing beyond the classroom: Volume 2 in the rethinking negotiation teaching series,* edited by C. Honeyman, J. Coben, and G. De Palo. St. Paul, MN: DRI Press.

Fisher, R. and W. Ury, 1981 *Getting to yes: Negotiating agreement without giving in.* New York: Houghton Mifflin.

Fox, K. 2009. Negotiation as a post-modern process. In *Rethinking negotiation teaching,* edited by C. Honeyman, J. Coben, and G. De Palo. St. Paul, MN: DRI Press.

Fox, K., M. Schonewille, and E. Cuhadar-Gurkaynak. 2010. Lessons from the field: First impressions from second generation negotiation teaching. In *Venturing beyond the classroom: Volume 2 in the rethinking negotiation teaching series,* edited by C. Honeyman, J. Coben, and G. De Palo. St. Paul, MN: DRI Press.

Freshman, C., A. Hayes, and G. Feldman. 2002. Adapting meditation to promote negotiation success: A guide to varieties and scientific support. *Harvard Negotiation Law Review* 17: 67-82.

Gardiner, B. 2012. Business skills and Buddhist mindfulness. *Wall Street Journal,* April 4th.

Gergen, K. 1999. *An invitation to social construction.* Thousand Oaks, CA: Sage.

Goleman, D. 1997. *Emotional intelligence: Why it can matter more than IQ.* New York: Bantam.

Guthrie, C. 2009. I'm curious: Can we teach curiosity? In *Rethinking negotiation teaching: Innovations for context and culture,* edited by C. Honeyman, J. Coben, and G. De Palo. St. Paul, MN: DRI Press.

Honeyman, C., J. Coben, and G. De Palo (eds). 2010. *Venturing beyond the classroom: Volume 2 in the rethinking negotiation teaching series.* St. Paul, MN: DRI Press.

Karr, A. 1849 (January). Les Guêpes.

Kuttner, R. 2010. From adversity to relationality: A Buddhist-oriented relational view of integrative negotiation and mediation. *Ohio State Journal on Dispute Resolution* 25(4): 931-974.

LeBaron, M. and M. Patera. 2009. Reflective practice in the new millenium. In *Rethinking negotiation teaching: Innovations for context and culture,* edited by C. Honeyman, J. Coben, and G. De Palo. St. Paul, MN: DRI Press.

Lewicki, R. J. and A. Schneider. 2010. Instructors heed the who: Designing negotiation training with the learner in mind. In *Venturing beyond the classroom: Volume 2 in the rethinking negotiation teaching series*, edited by C. Honeyman, J. Coben, and G. De Palo. St. Paul, MN: DRI Press.

Lyotard, J-F. 1979. *The postmodern condition: A report on knowledge*. Minneapolis, MN: University of Minnesota Press.

Matz, D. and N. Ebner. 2010. Using role-play in on-line negotiation teaching. In *Venturing beyond the classroom: Volume 2 in the rethinking negotiation teaching series*, edited by C. Honeyman, J. Coben, and G. De Palo. St. Paul, MN: DRI Press.

Mayer, J., P. Solovey, and D. Caruso. 2008. Emotional intelligence: New ability or eclectic traits. *The American Psychologist* 63(6): 503-517.

McNamee, S. and K. Gergen. 1999. *Relational responsibility: Resources for sustainable dialogue*. Thousand Oaks, CA: Sage.

Nealon, J. and S. Giroux. 2003. *The theory toolbox: Critical concepts for the humanities, arts & social sciences*. Lanhaj: Rowman & Littlefield.

Nelken, M., B. McAdoo, and M. Manwaring. 2009. Negotiating learning environments. In *Rethinking negotiation teaching: Innovations for context and culture*, edited by C. Honeyman, J. Coben, and G. De Palo. St. Paul, MN: DRI Press.

Nelken, M., A. Schneider, and J. Mahuad. 2010. If I'd wanted to teach about feelings I wouldn't have become a law professor. In *Venturing beyond the classroom: Volume 2 in the rethinking negotiation teaching series*, edited by C. Honeyman, J. Coben, and G. De Palo. St. Paul, MN: DRI Press.

Patera, M. and U. Gamm. 2010. Emotions – A blind spot in negotiation training? In *Venturing beyond the classroom: Volume 2 in the rethinking negotiation teaching series*, edited by C. Honeyman, J. Coben, and G. De Palo. St. Paul, MN: DRI Press.

Pearce, W. B. 2007. *Making social worlds: A communication perspective*. Oxford: Blackwell.

Riskin, L. 1982. Mediation and lawyers. *Ohio State Journal on Dispute Resolution* 43: 29-60.

Riskin, L. 2002. The contemplative lawyer: On the potential contributions of mindfulness meditation to law students, lawyers and their clients. *Harvard Negotiation Law Review* 17: 1-66.

Riskin, L. 2004. Mindfulness: Foundational training for dispute resolution. *Journal of Legal Education* 54: 79-91.

Rock, E. 2005. Mindfulness mediation: The cultivation of awareness, mediator neutrality, and the possibility of justice. *Cardozo Journal of Conflict Resolution* 6: 347-365.

Shell, R. 2006. *Bargaining for advantage: Negotiation strategies for reasonable people*, 2nd edn. New York: Penguin.

Solovey, P., B. Detweiler-Bedell, J. Detweiller-Bedell and J. Mayer. 2008. Emotional intelligence. In *Handbook of Emotions*, 3rd edn., edited by M. Lewis, J. M. Haviland-Jones, and L. F. Barrett. New York: Guilford Press.

Solovey, P. and J. Mayer. 1989-90. Emotional intelligence. *Imagination, Cognition and Personality* 9(3): 185-211.

Stone, D., B. Patton, and S. Heen. 1999. *Difficult conversations: How to discuss what matters most*. New York: Viking Penguin.

Tolkien, J. R. R. 1937. *The hobbit*. New York: Houghton Mifflin.

Volpe, M. and J. Cambria. 2009. Negotiation nimbleness when cultural differences are unidentified. In *Rethinking negotiation teaching: Innovations for context and culture*, edited by C. Honeyman, J. Coben, and G. De Palo. St. Paul, MN: DRI Press.

Welsh, N. 2012. Making reputation salient: Using the reputation index with law students. In *Assessing our students, assessing ourselves: Volume 3 in the rethinking negotiation teaching series*, edited by N. Ebner, J. Coben, and C. Honeyman. St. Paul, MN: DRI Press.

Winslade, J. and G. Monk. 2000. *Narrative mediation: A new approach to conflict resolution*. San Francisco: Jossey-Bass.

Appendix

CERTIFICATE IN INTERNATIONAL
BUSINESS NEGOTIATION
July 5 – July 27, 2012

Professor Kenneth Fox, Hamline University School of Business
Professor Andrew Wei-Min Lee, Peking University
Associate Professor Sharon Press, Hamline University School of Law

The DRI Certificate in Business Negotiation is an integrated two (2) course, six (6) credit program that is designed to prepare law, business and other graduate students and professionals to negotiate effectively in a wide range of dynamic, complex, multi-cultural, and international settings and environments. This document includes the syllabi for both courses.

Overall Learning Objectives
By the end of the certificate program, students will:
1) Understand and be able to effectively apply key principles that underlie the negotiation process in a variety of complex business, legal and other professional settings. (course one)
2) Know themselves as negotiators and professionals who work in a range of cultural and professional contexts. (course one)
3) Know how to adapt to, and work effectively in, diverse and complex negotiation situations, including individual, group, team and organizational settings, internal and external negotiation interactions, trans-national and multi-cultural situations and with emerging and changing communication technologies. (course two)
4) Have developed the capacity to recognize, understand and incorporate changing insights and trends in negotiation. (course two)

Requirements for Both Courses
Technology Requirements
This certificate program requires regular use of various technology-based equipment, platforms, programs, and processes. As a result, every student is required to have and use the provided iPad 2 tablet computers. Students will pick up their iPad at the Pre-Class Technology Orientation on July 5.

Attendance and Participation in Certificate Program
Students registered for the certificate program are expected to attend and actively participate in all sessions and activities of both courses. Students are not permitted to register for, or participate in, only a single of the two courses, regardless of prior coursework or experience with negotiation. There are no exceptions.

Some activities may be scheduled to accommodate time-zone differences with other students and/or faculty who participate in the program from a distance. While course instructors will provide as much notice as possible for such activities, students are expected to remain available and flexible so as to respond to outside scheduling needs.

Each student contributes to class discussions in his or her own way. The instructors will assess each student's willingness to seriously engage the topics under consideration, as well as the quality and thoughtfulness of your contributions and insights. In other words, it is primarily the quality (and not necessarily the quantity) of your contributions to discussions and exercises that matter. Effective and thoughtful comments demonstrate your recognition of the key concepts we are studying and add your unique (but relevant) perspective to discussions, for the enrichment of all.

This certificate program evolved from Hamline University School of Law's work leading a four year international project to examine what is taught in negotiation and how it is taught. The project put special emphasis on how best to "translate" teaching methodology to succeed with diverse, global audiences. Results of this project, including links to its multiple publications, can be found at http://law.hamline.edu/rethinkingNegotiation.html. The instructors wish to acknowledge the sponsors, leaders and contributors to this four year project for the vision, insights and scholarship that informed the design of this certificate program.

Negotiation
(2 credits)

Course Description:
This course introduces students to the skills, constraints, and dynamics of the negotiation process in the context of international business transactions. Through readings and highly interactive exercises, students will learn the fundamental skills of systematic and thorough negotiation preparation, the ongoing management of a negotiation process, and the identification and achievement of optimal agreements. Legal and ethical constraints of negotiation will also be considered as students in intentionally diverse teams participate in negotiations typically encountered in the formation of a business. Course content is drawn from the fields of law, psychology, business, and communication. This course will serve as the foundation for Advanced International Business Negotiation and must be completed in the same summer as Advanced International Business Negotiation is completed.

Specific Course 1 Learning Outcomes:
By the end of course one, students will:
- Understand and be able to effectively apply key principles that underlie the negotiation process in a variety of business, legal and other professional settings.
- Prepare effectively for most any negotiation;
- Understand when a particular negotiation approach is appropriate;
- Employ appropriate and effective negotiation skills and techniques.
- Know themselves as negotiators and professionals who work in a range of cultural and professional contexts.

- Appreciate the importance of curiosity and creativity in the negotiation process;
- Build emotional intelligence as a negotiator in a range of contexts;
- Recognize the relationship between culture, worldview and negotiation interaction.

Course 1 Readings:
Specific reading assignments are listed with their corresponding class day. We will use one (1) primary required text in course 1 plus one optional text. In addition, we have collected a number of articles you will be reading that are part of a course reader, which will be uploaded to your iPad. The texts are:

> **Required:** *Negotiating Globally* (second edition) by Jeanne M. Brett (hereafter NG)
> **Optional:** *Getting to Yes: Negotiating Agreement without Giving In* by Roger Fisher and William Ury (hereafter "GTY"- this text has not been uploaded and can be purchased separately)
> A number of additional readings are from the following three books, which are referenced accordingly in the syllabus: *Rethinking Negotiation Teaching: Innovations for Context and Culture*, Christopher Honeyman, James Coben and Giuseppe de Palo, Eds. (hereafter "Rethinking")
>
> *The Negotiator's Fieldbook: The Desk Reference for the Experienced Negotiator,* Andrea Kupfer Schneider and Christopher Honeyman, Eds. (hereafter "Fieldbook")
>
> *Venturing Beyond the Classroom: Volume 2 in the Rethinking Negotiation Teaching Series,* Christopher Honeyman, James Coben and Giuseppe de Palo, Eds. (hereafter, "Venturing")

Negotiation Course Assignments and Grading:

On-line Discussion (10%)
July 7 – July 10 (by noon) – You will participate in one (1) on-line discussion during the first course, which will comprise 10% of your grade. The topic will be distributed in class. Specific grading criteria are found at appendix one, at the end of this course packet. You are expected to participate in the forum as follows:

> Between Saturday, July 7 at 4:30pm and Tuesday, July 10 at noon, you are to post one substantial original posting in response to question prompts in the discussion portion of the class app on your iPad. Specific instructions will be distributed in advance of July 7.

Reflective Journal (20%)
You will write one reflective journal, which will be due on July 14 by 23:59 GMT. The specific journal topic and instructions will be distributed at the beginning of the course.

Final paper (50%)
Due July 14 – You will complete a take-home paper for course one that will be due by July 14 by 23:59 GMT. Specific instructions will be distributed in class.

Participation (10%)
Ten percent of your course grade will be based upon your participation. We expect that all students will actively participate in the course. Exceptional participation can raise your course grade. Uneven or poor participation can lower your course grade.

Reputation Index (10%)
Ten percent of your course grade will be based on your thoughtful completion of a reputation index instrument which will be due on July 14 by 23:59 GMT. Specific instructions will be distributed in class.

Course 1 – Detailed Schedule

Pre-course preparation – No later than Tuesday, July 3

Preparation for course beginning
Confirm that you have completed and returned your "Pre-certificate Questionnaire Form" electronically

Class Day I – Thursday, July 5
2:00 – 4:00 Pre-class Technology Orientation
Check in for class, pick up iPad, orientation to technology.

4:30 – 9:15
Focus
Introduction and overview, including a variety of self-awareness and group activities designed to open up a deeper conversation about how individuals, companies and cultures make sense of, and approach negotiation; Conversation about course and course design. Negotiation in the larger context of worldview, culture and conflict. Introduction to negotiation theory and key concepts.

Preparation for today's class
Read NG, chapters 1 and 2 (pps. 1 – 52) (R1-1)
Read Riskin, Knowing Yourself: Mindfulness (Fieldbook 27) (R1-2)**Class Day 2 – Friday July 6 – 4:30 – 9:15**
Focus
Formation of initial company teams. Understanding the tension between claiming and creating values with a focus on the distributive (claiming) mindset. Power and Influence.

Preparation for today's class
NG Chapters 1 and 2, continued;
Read Nealon & Giroux, *Ideology* (R1-3);
<u>*Read*</u> Bernard, *Finding Common Ground In the Soil of Culture* ("Rethinking")
(R1-4)
Read Birke, Neuroscience and Settlement: An Examination of Scientific
Innovations and Practical Applications (R1-5)
[Activities: Cray Computer (N1-1)]

Class Day 3 – Saturday, July 7 – 9:00 – 12:30 (class) 12:30 – 4:30
Adventure Learning
Focus
Understanding the integrative (value-creating) mindset. The tension be-
tween empathy and assertiveness; Emotion in negotiation; Set-up for
adventure learning
[Activities: Hiring Negotiation (in class)(N1-2); Headquarters
Identification (adventure)(N1-3); Interest Framing Activity (N1-4)]

Preparation for today's class
Read NG chapter 3 (R1-6);
Read Chamoun, *Bazaar Dynamics* ("Venturing") (R1-7)

Note
On-line discussion (D1-1 *Comparison of Negotiation Models*) opens today at
4:30 pm. Your original posting is due by Tuesday, July 10 at noon (central).

Class Day 4 – Monday, July 9 – 4:30 -9:15
Focus
Debrief Adventure Learning; Executing negotiation strategy. A close
look at integrative negotiation; Psychological barriers; listening skills;
Decision analysis
[Activities: Equipment purchasing negotiation (in class)(N1-5)]

Preparation for today's class
Read NG chapter 4 (R1-8). Additional optional reading: GTY.
Planning for exclusive manufacturing agreement begins (N1-6) and con-
tinues through July 15, 2012

Class Day 5 – Tuesday, July 10 – 4:30 - 9:15
Focus
Negotiation planning; Ethical issues in transnational business negotiations

Preparation for today
Read Ebner, Bhappu, Brown, et al, "You've Got Agreement: Negoti@ting
via e-mail" (R1-9) (Rethinking); Model Rule 4.1, Rules of Professional
Conduct (US) (R1-10)

Note
Your original on-line posting (D1-1) is due at noon today.
- Your final take-home paper will be distributed at the end of class today. It is due Saturday, July 14 by 23:59 GMT.
- Discussion D2-1 (ethics) begins – original response due Tuesday, July 16, 23:59 GMT.
- Voice Thread and Linked In profile due July 14 by 23:59 GMT. Reputation Index and Reflective Journal due July 14, by 23:59 GMT.

Advanced International Business Negotiation (4 credits)

Course description: Building on the basic negotiation principles introduced in "Negotiation," this course will critically examine advanced concepts, skills, constraints and dynamics of the negotiation process in the context of international business transactions and dispute settlement. Designed to attract an international and interdisciplinary mix of students, it draws upon and incorporates key theoretical and pedagogical lessons from Hamline University School of Law's "Rethinking Negotiation Teaching" project. Students will receive an overview of legal and institutional principles that impact international business, examine and experience how worldviews shape negotiation as it unfolds and engage in a series of applied and coached activities that require translation of negotiation theory into practice. The course design enables students to gain experience in negotiating across national boundaries and to make effective use of emerging communication technologies. Special focus will be given to negotiation challenges that arise during the process of business formation, internal management, sales and transactions, joint ventures, and responding to internal and external disputes.

Course 2 learning outcomes: In addition to more deeply examining learning objectives one and two which were considered in the negotiation course, this course has the following specific additional objectives:

1. Know how to adapt to, and work effectively in, diverse and complex negotiation situations, including:
   a. individual, group, team and organizational settings;
   b. internal and external negotiation interactions;
   c. trans-national and multi-cultural situations;
   d. emerging and changing communication technologies; and
   e. Conflict anticipation and dispute response situations

2. Develop the capacity to recognize, understand and incorporate changing insights and trends in negotiation

Course 2 Readings and Videos

Readings and videos are assigned in connection with activities and discussions. For each set of assigned readings and videos you will submit the following:

- The name of the reading or video(s)
- The key take away points
- Two questions you have about the application of the reading or video(s) to international business negotiation
- A statement as to whether the reading or video(s) was helpful to your understanding of international business negotiation and why or why not

Each reading or video should be completed prior to your participation in the activity or discussion for which it is most relevant (date will be provided on the syllabus). Your statement about the reading or video assignment is to be submitted after you have completed the activity or discussion in order to allow you to reflect on its relevance. We will continue to work with the primary text, Negotiating Globally (Second Edition) as well as using readings from other related chapters and articles and videos. Internet site references are also listed with appropriate class days.

The following readings must be completed prior to the start of the Advanced International Business Negotiation Course:

- Chapters 1 – 4, NG (R1-1, R1-6,R1-8)
- Riskin, Knowing Yourself: Mindfulness (Fieldbook 27) (R1-2)
- Nealon & Giroux, *Ideology*; (R1-3)
- Bernard, *Finding Common Ground In the Soil of Culture* ("Rethinking") (R1-4)
- Birke, Neuroscience and Settlement: An Examination of Scientific Innovations and Practical Applications (R1-5)
- Chamoun, *Bazaar Dynamics* ("Venturing") (R1-7)
- Ebner, Bhappu, Brown, et al, "You've Got Agreement: Negoti@ting via e-mail" (Rethinking) (R1-9)
- Model Rule 4.1, Rules of Professional Conduct (US) (R1-10)

Advanced International Business Negotiation
Course Assignments and Grading

Discussions (30%)
You will participate in four (4) graded on-line discussions during the second course, as follows:

> **Discussion 2-1 (ethics):** *On Tuesday, July 10, a discussion prompt will be posted. Between July 10 and July 16 (23:59 GMT), you are to make an original post to this prompt. On July 16, a new prompt will be added which calls on you to reflect on the initial posts in discussions D1- 1 (models) and 2-1 (ethics). A minimum of two responsive postings that build on this prompt and on the postings of your classmates are required by July 19, 23:59 GMT. Specific instructions will be distributed in advance of July 10.*

> **Discussion 2-2 (implications for international business):** *Between July 16 and July 19, you will participate in a discussion. Your original post to the prompt will be due by July 17, 23:59 GMT and one responsive post will be due by July 19, 23:59 GMT.*

> **Discussion 2-3 (Context and Framing):** *Between July 18 and July 20, you will participate in a discussion. You original post to the prompt will be due by July 20, 23:59 GMT and one responsive post will be due by July 22, 23:59 GMT.*

> **Discussion 2-4 (Culture):** *After reviewing the culture app on July 18, you will post, by July 19 23:59 GMT, an original post relating to the app and your own lived experience. Between July 19 and July 21, review a minimum of five other posts and you will post one responsive post. Details will be provided.*

All students are expected to actively participate in the course discussions.

Reputation Index Part II (10%)
Ten percent of your course grade will be based on your thoughtful completion of a reputation index instrument which will be due on July 27 by 23:59 GMT. Specific instructions will be distributed in class.

Group Presentation (15%)
Each student will participate in a team on-line presentation. All students on the team will receive the same grade. Specific instructions will be distributed in class. Presentations will take place on July 26 – 27.

Final Analytical Paper (45%)
Due Friday, August 10 at 23:59 GMT – You will write a substantial analytical paper on a topic to be selected during course two. Preparation for the paper will include one on-line consultation with one of the course instructors. Additional information will be distributed in class.

Participation

We expect that all students will actively participate in the course. Reading and video reports will be considered in assessing student participation. Exceptional participation can raise your course grade. Uneven or poor participation can lower your course grade. As a distance education course, you should anticipate spending approximately 4 hours per day for the entire period of this course (including weekends).

Detailed Course Assignments

The distance portion of the program is organized in layers. We will introduce new areas of focus as described on the daily schedule while continuing to work with previously introduced topics and areas of focus. As a result, you will see multiple topics and ideas being covered at the same time. Pay close attention to the new and continuing assignments in addition to the dates when assignments are due. **Posting after the assignment due date will result in an automatic one grade deduction for the assignment.**

Saturday, July 14
Focus Area:
> Context and groundwork for international negotiating (differences between public vs. private negotiations in international settings, including negotiating with bureaucracies, government entities); Institutional context (such as impact of differences in regulatory, legal and economic systems); Social dilemmas

New Assignments:
> Complete chart on international settings from the perspective of your own national identity - due July 15, 2012
> Presentation Topics and Clusters Posted N2-2- due July 18, 2012
> Complete the following prior to engaging in this negotiation:
> > - NG Chapters 8 and 9 (reading report form due July 19, 2012) (R2-1)
> Review Ebner, Bhappu, Brown, et al, "You've Got Agreement: Negoti@ting via e-mail" (Rethinking) (R1-9)

Continuing Assignments:
> Exclusive Manufacturing Contract Planning (N2-1) – due July 15, 2012
> Discussion (D2-1) – original post due July 16

Assignments Due:
> Reflective Journal (course 1) due
> Final Paper (course 1) due
> Reputation Index I due
> VoiceThread and/or Linked In Profile posted

Sunday, July 15
Focus Area:
Negotiating within teams/workgroups; deal design (while continuously returning to the reflective work on the theme of worldview and meaning-making)

New Assignments:
Multi-party negotiation for topics and partners begins (N2-2) - due July 18, 2012
Exclusive Manufacturing Negotiation Results (N2-1) - due July 20, 2012
Complete the following prior to engaging in this negotiation:
- NG Chapter 7 (R2-2) (reading report form due July 19)
- Read Matz, *"Intra-team communication"* (Fieldbook 63) (R2-3) (reading report form due July 19, 2012)

Assignments Due:
Chart on international settings due to professors by 23:59 GMT
Exclusive Manufacturing Agreement Planning Summary Document (N2-1) submitted to professors by 23:59 GMT
Monday, July 16
Focus Area:
Multi-party complex negotiation; timing and ripeness

Monday, July 16
Focus Area:
Multi-party complex negotiations; timing and ripeness

New Assignments:
Review posted chart on context and worldview and begin discussion D2-2 (implications for international business negotiation) - original post due by July 17; one responsive post due by July 19
Discussion D2-1 (models and ethics) additional prompt added – minimum 2 responsive posts due by July 19
Complete the following readings before completing negotiation 2-2 (readings report due July 20)
- Caton Campbell and Docherty, "What's In a Frame" (Fieldbook 5) (R2-4);
- Money and Allred, An Exploration of a Model of Social Networks and Multilateral Negotiations, <u>Negotiation Journal</u> (R2-5);
- Zartman, Timing and Ripeness (Fieldbook 17) (R2-6);
- Lax and Sebenius, 3D Negotiation: Playing the Whole Game (R2-7)

Assignments Due:
Discussion 2-1 (ethics) original post by 23:59 GMT

Tuesday, July 17
Focus:
Multi-party complex negotiations, continued

New Assignments:
No new assignment

Assignments Due:
Discussion D2-2 (implications for international business negotiation) original post due by 23:59 GMT

Wednesday, July 18
Focus:
Culture

New Assignments:
Discussion D2-3 (context and framing) begins – initial post due July 20; minimum 1 responsive post due July 22
Review Culture App for own culture of origin post original comment in Discussion D2-4 (culture) about the consistency of the app with your own lived experience due July 19, 2012
Complete culture survey due July 18, 2012
Review chapter 2 & 3 NG (no reading report required) (R1-1, R1-6)
Presentation pairs begin researching and preparing presentations to be made to all participants of their cluster on July 26 or July 27, 2012

Assignments Due:
Multi-party negotiation for topics and partners (N2-2) results posted by 23:59 GMT
Culture survey submitted by 23:59 GMT

Thursday, July 19
Focus:
Perspectives on International Business Negotiation Part I

New Assignments:
View video interviews with business leaders (group one) (R2-8) – video report form due July 22, 2012 *(Note: You are only required to view two – you may choose any two to view)*
Discussion D2-4 Review minimum of 5 postings, responsive post due July 21, 2012

Assignments Due:
Discussion D2-1 (models and ethics) minimum 2 responsive posts by 23:59 GMT
Discussion D2-2 (implications for international business negotiation) one responsive post due by 23:59 GMT
Post comment in Discussion D2-4 about the consistency of the culture

app with your own lived experience due 23:59 GMT
Reading reports for NG Chapters 7, 8, 9 and Fieldbook 63 due

Friday, July 20
Focus:
Perspectives on International Business Negotiation Part II

New Assignments:
N2-3 Information - International ADR Providers/Processes posted – located in *Zigg 2012/Activities Course 2 and Shenzhen/Negotiation Activities – Review in preparation for N2-3 which opens on July 22*
N2-2 Continues for Presentation Times – See Instruction for Paired Presentations in the Zigg and Shenzhen folders – **no negotiation reports required**

Assignments Due:
Discussion D2-3 (context and framing) initial post due 23:59 GMT
Exclusive Manufacturing Negotiation (N2-1) Results due 23:59 GMT
Reading report for:
- Caton Campbell and Docherty, "What's In a Frame" (Fieldbook 5);
- Money and Allred, An Exploration of a Model of Social Networks and Multilateral Negotiations, Negotiation Journal
- Zartman, Timing and Ripeness (Fieldbook 17)
- Lax and Sebenius, 3D Negotiation: Playing the Whole Game

Saturday, July 21
New Focus:
Deal Drafting and conflict anticipation

New Assignments:
Complete the following before negotiation N2-3
- NG Chapters 5 and 6 (R2-10) – reading report form due July 25, 2012
- Honeyman et al, "The Next Frontier is Anticipation" (R2-11) – report form due July 25, 2012
- Holland, "Drafting a Dispute Resolution Provision in International Commercial Contracts" (R2-12)– Reading report due July 25, 2012

Assignments Due:
Discussion D2-4 (culture) responsive post due 23:59 GMT

Sunday, July 22
New Focus:
Deal saving/deal breaking

New Assignments:
> Negotiation N2-3 on ADR Provider and Clause begins due July 24, 2012
> View 2 video interviews (group 2) – OPTIONAL

> *Optional additional reading:*
> a. chapter 2, "Reasons for Choosing Alternative Dispute Resolution;" (R2-13)
> b. chapter 7, "The Roles of Dispute Settlement in ODR;" (R2-14)
> c. chapter 8, "Legal Issues Raised by ADR;" (R2-15)and
> d. chapter 11, "ADR Under the ICC ADR Rules;" (R2-16)
> e. (See also *"Venturing"* chapters 25-27) (R2-17)

Assignments Due:
> Discussion D2-3 (context and framing) minimum 1 responsive post due 23:59 GMT
> Video report forms for business leaders due 23:59 GMT

Monday, July 23
Focus:
> Deal saving/deal breaking

New Assignments:
> Discussion Forum Opens to Select Group Presentation Time (23:59 GMT)

Assignments Due:
> Presentation Time Discussion Opens at 22:00 GMT

Tuesday, July 24
Focus:
> Deal breaking

New Assignments:
> Contract breach negotiation (assume no ADR clause) N2-4 due July 27, 2012

Assignments Due:
> Negotiation N2-3 on ADR Provider and Clause Reports (individual and collective) due 23:59 GMT

Wednesday, July 25
Focus:
> Contract breach, continued

New Assignments:
> NG Chapter 10 (R2-18) – report form due July 27, 2012

Assignments Due:
> NG Chapters 5 and 6; Honeyman et al., "The Next Frontier is Anticipation"

(R2-11) and Holland, "Drafting a Dispute Resolution Provision in International Commercial Contracts" (R2-12) – report form due 23:59 GMT

Thursday, July 26
Focus:
Synthesis

New Assignments:
Sign up for individual consultations between July 28 and August 10 by July 27, 2012
Reputation Index II due July 27, 2012

Assignments Due:
First set of presentations – time to be determined

Friday, July 27
Focus:
Synthesis

New Assignments:
View mediation of contract breach video (R2-19) – report form due July 30, 2012

Assignments Due:
Second set of presentations – time to be determined
NG Chapter 10 report form submitted by 23:59 GMT
Reputation Index II by 23:59 GMT
Contract breach negotiation N2-4 reports (individual and collective) due 23:59 GMT

Between July 28 and August 10
Students will each have one scheduled conference (by phone, Skype or other technology) to review progress toward final paper.

Monday, July 30
Mediation of contract breach video report form due by 23:59 GMT

Friday, August 10
Final papers due. Specific instructions for submission will be distributed.

०ঃ 5 ৵

As We See It

*Bee Chen Goh, Habib Chamoun-Nicolas, Ellen E. Deason, Jay Folberg & Sukhsimranjit Singh**

Editors' Note: Developing further the "adventure learning" ex-periments conducted by the project in Istanbul and reported on in Venturing Beyond the Classroom, the authors tried new negotiation experiments in the markets of Beijing. Comparing their experiences from their respectively Chinese-Malaysian, Mexican, North American and Indian cultural perspectives, they conclude that self-awareness must be a central requirement in cross-cultural negotiation training, and that up to now, it has been far too commonly taken for granted.

"Know yourself, know the other, victory is guaranteed." (Sun Tzu)

Introduction

Cross-cultural negotiation, in the ethnological sense, is a fascinating engagement. Quite naturally, participants tend to think, when they begin to embark upon cross-cultural negotiation, that they are ex-

* **Bee Chen Goh** is professor and co-director, Centre for Peace and Social Justice, Southern Cross University School of Law and Justice in Australia. Her email address is beechen.goh@scu.edu.au. **Habib Chamoun-Nicolas** is an honorary professor at Catholic University of Santiago Guayaquil-Ecuador and an adjunct professor and member of the executive board at the Cameron School of Business at University of St. Thomas in Houston. His email address is hchamoun@keyne-gotiations.com. **Ellen E. Deason** is the Joanne Wharton Murphy/Classes of 1965 and 1973 Professor of law at The Ohio State University Moritz College of Law in Columbus, Ohio. Her email address is deason.2@osu.edu. **Jay Folberg** is a professor emeritus and former dean of the University of San Francisco School of Law and now a mediator with JAMS. His email address is jfolberg@jamsadr.com. **Sukhsimranjit Singh** is associate director and lecturer in law at the Center for Dispute Resolution, Willamette University College of Law in Salem, Oregon. His email address is singhs@willamette.edu.

ploring the other, and that they are getting to understand the other culture better, and that, at the end of the exercise, they will be a little more enlightened about the habitual know-how of the other. Yet, for those who have been involved in cross-cultural work, the reverse is true. The more one engages in cross-cultural experiences, the more one gets to understand oneself (Goh 1996). There is an apparent inherent irony, a paradox, which easily eludes one who is untrained in cross-cultural ways. As such, Sun Tzu's timeless wisdom, "know yourself, know the other, victory is guaranteed" applies equally well in the negotiation context as on the battlefield.

This collaborative chapter reflects five contributors' respective cultural backgrounds and how each uses his or her own cultural yardstick to define "the other" – in a common setting, Chinese markets in Beijing. As culture operates in the unconscious (Hall 1959), it is quite natural that one's expectations and assumptions are derived from what one is familiar with. This chapter examines how one tests such expectations and assumptions when transposed to the cultural setting of the other.

The lesson for negotiation teaching to be obtained from our collective experiences is to emphasize the importance of self-awareness as the ground rule in cross-cultural understanding. Self-awareness has been acknowledged as an important perceptual tool (Augsburger 1992). However, its usefulness in cross-cultural negotiation teaching has, thus far, perhaps been taken for granted, or assumed. A well-designed curriculum in cross-cultural negotiation teaching embedding and commencing with "Cross-Cultural Self-Awareness Skill" will add considerably to this field, a point raised again later.

Below is a summary of the relevant account of the respective contributors' experiences in a common setting, Chineses market in Beijing in May 2011, and how each of us, in our own ways, brought to bear our own cultural baggage to interpret the same cultural environment. It also demonstrates that a particular deal's "success" can be attributed to the individual contributor's cultural self-perception and self-inferential behaviour. "Beauty is in the eye of the beholder"; indeed, the same may be said of culture. Our perceptual world is largely shaped by our inner lens. If there is concord with what we see and what we perceive, there is great beauty before us, and the cross-cultural experience becomes rewarding. Conversely, if what we see runs counter to our perceptions, our world is turned upside-down or inside-out, and we face confusion and chaos. There is frustration as to why things do not work.

Negotiating in Beijing

Bee Chen Goh

My Chinese ancestry[1] and facility with Mandarin[2] made me feel like a "returnee"[3] on this conference trip to Beijing. For our purpose here, my negotiation and shopping venue was the Hong Qiao Pearl Market, right across from the Temple of Heaven. Contrary to expectations of a normal market, this market is very modern, clean and well laid-out with merchandise neatly categorized by floor. It is also much more than just a pearl market, with a splash of sundry electronic goods, personal accessories, household ornaments, Chinese paintings and so on. What was interesting for me was how I would be perceived by the stall-holders as a potential buyer. Like everyone else, I walked in with the intention to purchase and leave with a "local" bargain. I was in an advantageous position, given my ethnic Chinese appearance and Mandarin fluency (Chen 2001). So, let us see where those self-perceived cultural advantages took me.

I was on an assignment to buy high quality leather belts for my husband. Using my intuition as my GPS, I found myself in front of a leather-belt specialty stall. My interested posture in examining the leather belts inside a glass counter drew the stall-owner to me in seconds. I observed him examining "me" – perhaps trying to make out if I was a local or only looked local (Goh 1996; Chen 2001).[4] In China, as they say, there are Chinese prices and foreigners' prices. Overseas Chinese are a little in between. Unless you are adept in negotiating, you deal at lower than foreigners' prices but higher than local Chinese prices.

After the initial silent seconds, albeit with an exchange of friendly smiles between us, and before I decided to open my mouth to ask for a good price, the stall-owner voluntarily reduced the opening price displayed in writing as 460 yuan to 280 yuan. I knew at once that the voluntary reduction without any effort on my part to negotiate was an acknowledgment of my Chinese-ness and implicit in that, giving me face as a fellow Chinese, or at the very least, Chinese-looking person (Goh 1996; Chen 2001). I must add, at this juncture, that China being such a vast country, Mandarin as spoken would differ according to regional accents. Beijingers, being Northern Chinese, speak with a distinctive northern accent. The reason I decided to take my time to look at the belts rather than communicate verbally right in the beginning was to minimize my exposure as a non-local Chinese. The stall-owner was still second-guessing my origin when he took the price down but he was prepared for further bargaining as locals would. I examined the belts and recognized their high quality. Inasmuch as I wanted to walk away with a very low price, I was more conscious of buying at a fair price, especially for a high-quality good. So, I started my pricing at 100 yuan, with room to move upwards. I reckoned that if I could buy the belt at 150 yuan, it would have been a good and fair purchase. The stall-owner, of course, said it was impossible to sell such a high-quality belt at 100 yuan. Besides, he said, he had given me a Chinese price with the original discount. By this time of verbal exchanges, he inquired whether I was from Hong Kong.

Although I can speak Cantonese, I politely said I was not. From my perspective, I knew that I wanted to buy from this shop. I had surveyed other shops and their belt quality was inferior. With this in mind, I needed to handle the negotiation in this stall strategically and successfully. I also felt that I could approach this negotiation confidently without the walk-away exercise, relying on our largely familiar and common cultural backdrop. The usual tactic is to create a "bulk" purchase, which stall-owners are used to. They are accustomed to lowering their price with the promise of volume, based on present or the likelihood of future repeat transactions. As it turned out, I was keen on buying two belts – though not quite the bulk he was looking for, the fact that it was more than one was giving him some "face."

The stall-owner eventually agreed at 300 yuan for both (which matched my expectation of 150 yuan each). Interestingly, at this deal-closing time, there was an unsolicited interjection from a Peking University student who was with my group. She further bargained the price to 280 yuan for both. The stall-owner first rejected this interference by saying that the deal was already struck. She then said that her mother ran a business in a Chinese province and she would recommend bulk purchases. The stall-owner finally agreed to my buying at 280 yuan for two belts, happily slipping a couple of business cards into the shopping bag in the hope of repeat business.

In this case, although prices had been lowered, and there was a clear process of bargaining, what I perceived as a notably good outcome was that there was no appearance of being upset on the stall-owner's part (unlike most of what my fellow delegates had experienced in markets). As for myself, I paid what I considered to be a fair rather than a low price. I attribute this outcome to our Chinese cultural congruency. That is, we operated on the same cultural platform, and intuitively sensed and matched each other's expectations by being on the same cultural wavelength.

I had another interesting encounter at the accessories section. On that shopping day, I happened to wear a Peking University T-shirt, which I had bought from a campus store just the day before. While I was browsing, the lady stall-owner spotted me with the university

T-shirt and spoke to me right away in Mandarin, translated to mean: "Wow, you're an academic from Peking University! You must be very highly-educated. It is a reputable university. We are very honored to serve you. You will get local prices from us. We call these 'friendship' prices." As I did not intend to buy anything from her stall, I smiled and said that I was visiting the university. I thanked her politely for her face-giving remarks and gestures. Later, I commented to a fellow delegate that even my T-shirt did some bargaining for me!

What were the lessons learned from shopping and negotiating at the Pearl Market? Overall, I experienced near-complete ease negotiating in Beijing. I attribute this comfort to my cultural parity. Negotiating with the Chinese in successful and rewarding ways must mean one thing: Chinese cultural competency (Goh 1996; Chen 2001). In my case, looking ethnically Chinese was an apparent asset. It was also advantageous for me to be able to converse in Mandarin. I thought and acted like a local Chinese person. I upheld the fundamentally Chinese cultural values in my conduct with the stall-holders – being polite and friendly, smiling a great deal, always gentle in demeanour, using culturally-nuanced language in negotiating, confident with estimates of local Chinese pricing and being patient and unfussed at all times.

Habib Chamoun-Nicolas

My first experience negotiating in a Beijing market was very frustrating. Almost every store at the Beijing Night Market displayed a sign in Chinese and English that read, "No Bargaining." One store even had a sign that read, "I refuse to bargain." English was generally spoken as a second language by many of the young store owners and employees. Very few spoke other foreign languages. At least on the night we went out, we noticed the public at the Night Market was mostly foreigners and well-to-do young Chinese. The prevailing attitude at the thirty or so stores attended by young Chinese vendors was "if you don't buy, that is your problem." There was no eagerness to sell.

When we tried to bargain, some of the store owners got mad at us. In fact, there was a store in which, after attempting to bargain, we noticed the store owners and others making fun of us. Bargaining in the Beijing Night Market was forbidden as a form of bad manners. We associated this behavior with the fact that some young Chinese boys were buying gifts in this market for young Chinese girls. They had an evident sense of pride in purchasing expensive items in the market. They had the money and appeared to be looking to buy prestige. Someone receiving a gift purchased at this market would, it seemed, know it to be a good, expensive, prestigious gift. Knowing this, the young boys did not dare bargain for something in this market. From the owner's perspective, the boys were buying quality items in a prestigious place. They were expected not to try to bargain, just like in any other prestigious marketplace (such as at Tiffany's in New York). Also, it seemed as if the Chinese store owners had adopted a collective strategy of not allowing the prices to be lowered under any circumstances. As a buyer, you could lose face by bargaining in such as store, whereas, of course, in Chinese society, "giving and keeping face" is important (Wibbeke 2009: 25).

Our experiences at the Silk and Pearl Market in Beijing were completely opposite to those at the Night Market. The moment we entered the Night Market, store employees tried to persuade us to enter their stores. They anchored with very high first offers, and asked how much we would pay for the merchandise. They tried to speak several languages: French, Spanish, and English; however, it was obvious that they knew only a few words, not enough to make a conversation. They relied heavily on calculators to deliver prices to customers, perhaps to avoid confusion.

If we compare the Istanbul Grand Bazaar sellers (see Chamoun-Nicolas, Folberg, and Hazlett 2010; Docherty 2010; Cohen, Honeyman, and Press 2010) with the Beijing Silk and Pearl Market, we can see that the Istanbul sellers were more prepared to interact with foreigners, with some speaking as many as twelve different languages. The Chinese sellers we encountered could use just a few select words in different languages as conversation starters. In contrast, the Istanbul sellers greeted potential customers with tea, and even if you did not purchase anything from their store, they politely ushered you out of the store, hoping that perhaps you would come back. At the Beijing Silk and Pearl Markets, forceful shopkeepers gave us a price, but then started unilaterally reducing the price when we failed to make a counter-offer. Failure to make a sale made them conspicuously angry. When we made ridiculous counter-offers, they acted offended. But we did not know if the offense was feigned or real. In some cases, we noticed they would rather not sell and let the buyer go. Others expressed annoyance, giving buyers the opportunity to change their mind to mitigate the situation.

Developing empathy in such an environment is difficult. The aggressive opening tactics created distance, and the store owners appeared to follow a sales strategy of offering a big price "reduction" rather than focusing on product quality. To counter this, there were signs at the market entrance to vendors, reading "Protect intellectual property rights. Be law-abiding vendors" and to customers, reading "Shop with Confidence" with a telephone number for quality control. It is not known if this is a negotiated, enforced pact or simply a tactic to try to entice consumers to lower their guard.

My preconceived notion of Chinese as poker-faced negotiators of few words was shattered. Instead, I experienced Chinese people showing their emotions, yelling, and getting angry at "hard bargainers." Even our plan to assemble a caravan of taxis in order to get to the market as a group of twenty created problems. Refusing to wait for other taxis, our driver got out and started yelling at our group of five to get out. Only when we decided not to wait did he agree to transport us.

The stereotype of Chinese as "good hagglers" from previous negotiation experiences, such as negotiating in Chinese communities in Mexico or in the United States, was called sharply into question in this Beijing market environment. Instead, my impression was that the Chinese really did not like to haggle unless it was essential. In the Night Market, a rule against haggling was explicitly stated, yet the market appeared successful. In the Silk and Pearl Markets, haggling appeared to be just a pricing tactic, initiated by the seller rather than the buyer. It seemed as if the Chinese sellers looked for uniformity in deal making: the shopkeepers took few risks and followed apparently set procedures. This forestalled any real communication from developing – or perhaps this is a natural result of language difficulties (Goh 1994).

As a specific example, at the Pearl Market, I negotiated for a pearl bracelet for my wife. I spoke French to my friend and English to the Chinese jewelry store manager. A Chinese lady showed us a beautiful pearl bracelet for 850 yuan; I offered 85 yuan. She was, or at least appeared, offended. My friend told her in English that it was a fake pearl. She started yelling at both of us and (apparently) got so mad that she put things away. We returned to the store to find out if the pearls were genuine. This time, the same sales person got a small knife and started scratching the surface of a pearl. (If it is real, some powder will be emitted. Also, a real pearl will not be affected by heat.) After being shown that the pearls were real, we started haggling. I got an agreement at 200 yuan. Was the seller really angry? Was this a tactic? Was 200 yuan a fair price? I believed that a truly good price would have been 100 yuan. However, 200 was good enough for me, for a real pearl bracelet.

The Chinese jewelry store manager getting mad and yelling could have been either a negotiation tactic, or a sign that we had offended her. If this was a negotiation tactic used on foreigners who are hard bargainers, it could be because Chinese negotiators fully understand that foreigners are culturally different (Goh 1994). However, if this was not the case, then it may be explained by the five dimensions of Hofstede: with a low assertiveness orientation, Chinese value face-saving and have a negative view of aggression (Wibbeke 2009). Respect and tolerance are two Phoenician principles of doing business cross-culturally (Chamoun and Hazlett 2007). Perhaps the same principles apply in China, such that if the owner was really angry, it was because we had crossed a line of respect and tolerance that we should not have.

Ellen E. Deason

I came to Beijing uncomfortable with bargaining; I am probably typical of many Americans in that regard.[5] When there is haggling to be done – in buying a house or car or at a flea market – my husband does the bargaining. As a negotiation teacher, I am familiar with some of the tactics of the haggling style, but I am a reluctant participant and certainly do not seek out the process. In addition, unlike many Americans, I am not a "shopper." I avoid most shopping, including window shopping, as much as possible.

I went with a group to the Night Market described by Habib Chamoun-Nicolas. The "no bargaining" signs surprised us, and several experienced bargainers in the group tested the waters, but to no avail. Even for goods with no marked price, the sellers seemed unwilling to play the game.

I wanted to buy some tea. In one shop a small block of pressed tea was labelled thirty yuan, but I was interested in an attractively wrapped round disc with no price indicated. I inquired and was told the price was 100 yuan. When I expressed surprise at the difference, the young saleswoman indicated that the disc was not only larger, but it was aged tea – five years old. Part of me wanted to make an offer, but I felt I needed to "psych up" to do it. I decided to compare the prices in other shops and think about the purchase. After walking the entire street I discovered that this was the only tea shop and decided to take the plunge. The salesperson, this time an older man, again quoted a price of 100 yuan, but he said the disc was four years old. I politely refrained from pointing out the discrepancy and offered eighty yuan, thinking I should try lower, but somehow was unable to do so. He accepted immediately, and I just as immediately concluded that I should have offered a lesser amount. But it felt like a triumph to have bargained at all. I have no idea if I got a reasonable price. In a later tea shop visit I bought loose tea, but did not ask the price of a similar pressed disc. Perhaps I did not want to dampen my good feelings about the first transaction with an unfavorable comparison.

Later, I visited the Pearl Market described by Bee Chen Goh, but with another group. This time I was determined to stretch my comfort zone and bargain *hard*. And, after an unsatisfactory experience with a taxi driver in Beijing, it was important to me to feel I was not being "taken advantage of" as a foreigner. The atmosphere was very different from the Night Market. From my perspective, it was chaotic, with (mostly) women calling out from stalls, "Lady, look at this . . . " On some level I realized that, as discussed by Chamoun-Nicolas and colleagues (2010), this was merely an eager attempt to attract my attention as the first step in building a relationship, however limited and short-term. But I felt somewhat assaulted.

I tried hard bargaining for some wallets – a purchase I was not committed to make, so I felt some detachment from the process. I offered one-tenth the asking price, as recommended in the guidebook and by some of my colleagues, purposely taking on the mindset of a game to test myself. I kept my moves (indicated on a calculator) small and tried for a quantity discount. The bargaining eventually stalled at her demand of 100 yuan and my offer of fifty for three wallets. The atmosphere shifted. The seller protested that she could not make money at the price I wanted and the message of her tone and body language (as I understood it) was that I was being unreasonable, even abusing her. Eventually we settled at eighty yuan. I'm sure she would not have made the sale without earning some profit. I felt, however, that the interaction had soured and that she was glad to be done with me. My "success" brought me the satisfaction of accomplishing what I had set out to do, but very little pleasure with the purchase. I later concluded that I had forfeited a pleasant relationship for a few dollars.

In contrast, a third bargaining transaction was characterized by a congenial relationship throughout the interaction. When the group went into a jewelry stall, the proprietress did not call us in and did not initially say anything other than welcome. We admired the strands of semi-precious stones and beads and she answered questions. It felt less hard-sell than many small stores in the United States. I found a necklace I really wanted, so I was not as disengaged as with my previous purchase. I asked the price and was told 100 yuan. I almost offered eighty but, remembering the tea transaction, I decided to try a little lower and offered seventy yuan. The seller accepted immediately, but I did not feel (as I had with the tea) that I should have opened lower. Everyone in the group made purchases, mostly with very little bargaining because the asking prices seemed so reasonable. We parted as satisfied customers with smiles and thanks. She gave us each her card, and mentioned that the shop sells online. We all agreed that we were much more comfortable with this more relaxed, low-key style of interaction and that the value of our purchases – in comparison to prices in dollars at home – was very good.

As I reflected on my different reactions to these experiences I thought about the role of trust in my perception of the fairness of the price and the way in which that trust operated in each situation, based on my own cultural perspective. In my experience, the epitome of a trusting, satisfying relationship in a market setting is found at my local farmers' market, where I typically bring repeat business to particular stands, stimulated by reliable quality and value from the seller. The interactions at the tourist markets in Beijing were, in contrast, one-shot deals with no expectation of a lasting relationship (although the possibility of additional purchases was introduced in the jewelry store by the mention of online sales). In that way, the setting was similar to visits to small retail stores in the United States. There, however, unlike in Beijing, my trust in the fairness of the price is linked to the impersonal convention that everyone will pay the same posted price, and on my ability to easily compare those posted prices among vendors.

The convention of posting fixed prices can be seen as a framework that provides a form of "institutional trust." Such trust is "present when one has confidence in predicting behavior because external safeguards are in place" (Deason 2006: 1403). It can encourage a transaction or activity to proceed even in the absence of a personal relationship between partners of the type that Roberge and Lewicki (2010) theorize is built on calculus-based or identity-based trust. (See also Lewicki 2006.) Institutional mechanisms that can substitute for relationship-based trust include both formal safeguards, such as contracts or guarantees, and informal shared understandings, such as procedures that the participants expect each other to follow.[6] Within the context of a market, the convention of fixed and posted prices fills this institutional role. They mean that one can be confident that everyone will pay the same price, at least until an item goes on sale. And they make it easy for shoppers to compare prices of goods offered at other stores, especially given online information.[7]

With prices that are not fixed and often not posted, the markets in China did not offer this comfortable mechanism to ensure that the seller would not take advantage of my lack of preparation and knowledge. The challenge for me was that, based on all reports, I had every expectation that prices quoted to a foreign tourist would be highly inflated. This meant that I could not "trust" the quoted price. Yet I would not feel good about my purchases if I thought I had been "taken advantage of" and paid an excessive amount, so I felt vulnerable.

I dealt with the challenge of that vulnerability differently in each case. With the tea, I applied a different standard and did not worry about whether the price was "fair." Although I did not engage fully in a bargaining interaction with the seller, I was content with merely having made an offer, especially in a context where many merchants were refusing to bargain at all.

With the wallets, my trust in the vendor was low and my distrust of the situation was high (see Lewicki 2006). Despite the fact that bargaining was for me an experiment in the nature of a role-play, I was struck by the intensity of the personal interaction and by the sense that I was dealing with an adversary. Yet the haggling process acted as an institutional mechanism that provided me with confidence in the outcome, and allowed me to go forward with the purchase despite the absence of any trust based on a personal relationship with the seller. Because I played the bargaining game I do not feel that I was "taken" or exploited. If anything, I regret that I was not more generous with the seller (see Love and Singh, *Following the Golden Rule*, in this volume; Chamoun and Hazlett 2009).

With the necklace, I was content with very soft bargaining. Perhaps I was pulling back from my hard-bargaining experience. Certainly I did not feel the need to prove to myself that I could do it. And after my sense of being an adversary, I think I was willing to pay a premium for the pleasant shopping experience. But more than that, in the time we spent in her shop, we formed a comfortable relationship with the proprietress. I felt a level of trust and goodwill based on this relationship which, coupled with some sense of prices for comparable items in the United States, lessened the need to use bargaining as a way to give me confidence that the price was reasonable.

Jay Folberg

Markets or bazaars and the bargaining associated with them have always intrigued me. Maybe it is because I grew up in our family's pawnshop, and associated shopping with bargaining. As I discovered during our adventure learning, which was part of the Rethinking Negotiation Teaching conferences in Istanbul and Beijing, market bargaining behavior is not the same in all cultures, even though there are similarities (see generally Chamoun-Nicolas, Folberg, and Hazlett 2010). I will share here some of the differences observed from an addicted bargainer's perspective, along with some lessons learned.

My quest for silk scarves as gifts will serve as a base of comparison between my bargaining experience in a Turkish bazaar and several Chinese markets. In each setting I first walked about to survey the merchandise and narrow my selection. In both countries market stalls do not display prices (see Deason 2006), except for occasional "bargain bins," so I approached vendors to inquire about prices for a few selected scarves. With this market research, I collected "intelligence" on quality, price and availability in order to formulate a best alternative to a negotiated agreement (BATNA) for bargaining.

In both Istanbul and Beijing, my look at their merchandise usually resulted in a vendor approaching me to pursue a sale. In Beijing, the vendors, mostly women, seemed more aggressive in approaching me as I came close to their stalls. No "small talk" or inquiries were made before commencing bargaining, other than occasional comments about the high quality of the scarves and other goods for sale. This may have been a function of language differences, as much as custom, compared to the Turkish merchants, most of whom had a better command of English to help this monolingual American. The Chinese merchants carried hand-held digital calculators to display prices and facilitate bargaining in numbers rather than words. They began with initial prices as much as ten times higher than the final bargained sale price. If the initial price was rejected with a laugh or a firm "no," a lower price would be offered and when rejected often followed up with a still lower price. Not all Chinese merchants in market stalls started with outrageously high prices and then bargained against themselves, but a surprising number did. Although some of the Chinese merchants did return smiles and attempted to engage in "selling" their scarves, most stuck to an exchange of numbers, handing the calculator to me to enter counter offers. Perhaps because language was more of a barrier and it was more difficult to engage, beyond the numbers, I had to walk away from several merchants before finding the price that I had reason to think was at the lowest end of the bargaining range or zone of possible agreement (ZOPA) for the type of scarf I had chosen.

I came upon this price when walking away from one merchant. A neighboring vendor offered to sell an identical scarf at my walk-away price, which she had overheard. (Either the two vendors were in cahoots, or not on very good terms with one another.) Those I walked away from sometimes grumbled something in Chinese that I thought I understood, even though I do not speak the language. After discovering what appeared to be close to a bottom line seller's price, I could display to other merchants what I purchased at that price and get a begrudging match for a similar scarf.

Upon reflection, I have a positive memory of bargaining in the bazaars of Istanbul and a less positive feeling about bargaining in Beijing. The engagement I experienced with the Istanbul merchants provided satisfaction in filling my interests in obtaining scarves I could give to friends at home, knowing that I obtained them at a reasonable price, and with a good story to boot. In Beijing I focused on obtaining scarves at the lowest possible price, while losing sight of the value of my time, the relatively insignificant difference a dollar or two might mean for me in the way I felt about my experience, and the impression I created. I was so focused on testing my bargaining theories and skills to get the lowest possible price, I probably came across as a hard-bargaining, rude American tourist (to put it nicely). This has weighed upon me. The principal lesson learned from this experience is the importance of prioritizing my own interests in negotiation, including how I might feel about the interaction afterwards and distinguishing short-term from long-term benefits.

There are other lessons that might be learned or confirmed from my comparative experiences in Turkey and China:

- The value of personal engagement, whether it be showing interest or curiosity about a bargaining partner, or just demonstrating your humanity, in order to build even a minimal level of rapport and trust before bargaining;
- Anchoring through self-serving first offers can be a powerful factor, but first offers should not be so extreme that the receiving party walks away;
- Bargaining against yourself is usually counterproductive;
- Bargaining with a smile is usually effective and feels better than sternness;
- Sensitivity to cultural differences and traditions can be important;
- Language can be a barrier, and can create false impressions.

As a result of my experience bargaining in Chinese market stalls and with the benefit of reading the insights of my co-authors, my teaching will now include more on the need for self-awareness, particularly in cross-cultural settings. There might also be something to this concept of considering the role of generosity as an interest in negotiation (see Love and Singh, *Following the Golden Rule*, in this volume).

Sukhsimranjit Singh

Negotiating at the Rethinking Negotiation Teaching Conference in Beijing was a great and humbling experience. Overall, I became more self-aware of the importance of being humble after negotiating with different salesmen and service providers in Beijing. From my departing negotiation – with the taxi driver at Beijing International Airport – to one of my initial ones, with a street vendor at the Great Wall, I could not help but notice the cultural differences between the bargaining behaviors of the Chinese and Americans, as well as cultural similarities between the bargaining behaviors of the Chinese and the Indians. In this section, I present my observations of the bargaining culture, with a few take-away points on self-awareness.

Allow me to focus on cultural similarities. Many scholars have put India close to China in terms of national culture (Douglas 1973; Hofstede 2001). They both are collectivists; they pursue harmony despite being heavily populated; both possess thousands of years of history; and both value saving face (see Singh 2009; Goh 1996). Recalling my life in India, I cherish the days I went to do street shopping in New Delhi, where my father taught me the tough skills of bargaining. "First, you should look disinterested in goods, second you must do market research, and third, if needed, walk away from a shop" were some of his suggestions. Personally, I could never measure up to my father's bargaining ability, perhaps due to my accommodating nature, yet as part of the Rethinking Negotiation Teaching series in Beijing, when we were told to go out and "try" bargaining, in the spirit of the game, I tried.

Awareness about quick judgments

As a new father, I was keen to shop for my daughter. As soon as I got the opportunity to do so at the Great Wall, I bargained. After a few initial offers, "we" settled for about 1/10th of the asking price. I walked away from the shop with a feeling that I had "won." However, my next purchase was at a government-owned shop (inside a museum). The seller proudly announced, "this is a fixed-price shop so please select (goods) accordingly." I bought an item at full price. It reminded me of the Himachal emporium shops located in Shimla, India, which are also government-owned with fixed-prices. My family used to shop at the Himachal emporium to buy authentic yet reasonably priced gifts because the shops are known for their quality products.

Interestingly, if we look through a different lens, the above-mentioned negotiations (at the Great Wall and the museum) represent a distinct culture in themselves: the culture of "fixed-price shops" versus that of "shops that ask for heavy bargaining." This piece will focus on the latter. In developing and emerging economies, the practice of hard bargaining is attached to a sub-culture of a market, mostly to an informal and un-regulated market (Henderson 2002). I too, experienced the shouting, displays of instant emotion, from pleasure to dismay, when I accepted a vendor's offer, or convinced her to accept mine. From my own cultural background, I expected that style of negotiation. I sought shops and chose markets that allowed for such bargaining to take place. For example, when I tried my luck in an authorized Nikon DSLR Camera shop for a high-end DSLR camera in the digital market at Beijing, there was no discount or bargaining. Small vendors, green and gray markets that allow for bargaining, are more prevalent in India and China than in the U.S. Perhaps then, the bigger question to ask is: How does the "national culture" of China or India allow for such a "bargaining culture" to prevail?

Personally, the first element of awareness while visiting China was to avoid judging this practice of bargaining. Secondly, I was determined not to over-generalize the experiences. For example, if one were to surmise that the Chinese bargain very hard based on just a few bargaining experiences, I would respectfully disagree (and so would a number of scholars on the subject). The assessment of a national culture should constitute a more rigorous exercise, with study of bargaining tendencies of Chinese citizens in a wide variety of settings within and outside of China (Goh 1996; Henderson 2002; Hofstede 2006).

I have noticed casually, however, that Chinese and Indian salespeople are comfortable with the notion of bargaining. It is not a big deal for them; however, even this is changing. As culture evolves and changes over a period of time, so does national culture (Hall 1984). Comparing my living in India in 2005 to my visit in the summer of 2011, I noticed the dominance of fixed-price shops and the fact that people did not bargain much, if at all. I was disappointed since I was looking for the old bargaining experience; the establishment of new shops like the new Wal-Mart (in collaboration with a local corporation) in my parents' village did not allow this.

Awareness of our roles in the negotiations

Another question is: What does a tourist from the West bring to the table? A currency that is highly valued over a local currency, a willingness to spend money, and perhaps a naivety about the local market. The bargaining tactics that my father tried to teach me were bargaining for necessity, since we (in India) were living as a common middle-class family without the luxuries of shopping at the more expensive, fixed-price shops. In Beijing, just like New Delhi, some of the sellers were trying to make money off us, visitors – out of necessity – and perhaps, others tried to rip us off, out of our naivety. However, as long as the goods I bought from Beijing were of a certain value to me, there could not be any rip-off. For my family and friends, they carried a symbolic value, which was more important than monetary value.

So does national culture play a role in local bargaining? National cultures like those of China or India allow for bargaining practices to prevail. They prevail in gray markets and un-regulated markets as they have for hundreds of years. Such practices might be a necessity for a large nation with a large population, but they could also be product of a society that is governed by societal norms and not by legal norms as in the West (Nisbett 2003).

Awareness of differing roles in the negotiation process is important. For example, in our case the role of an American tourist is, let us say, to bargain for the sake of bargaining. The role of a Chinese (or Indian) salesperson could easily be to sell one product to make the minimum wage for the day. There is no cause for concern for the purchaser (I would not get fired from my job just because I did not buy a gift for my wife); but theoretically, a young salesperson at a local market could lose her job if she did not make enough money for the day, as she practices in a market where competition is huge, margins are minimal, and visitors are a rare commodity.

Awareness of our own limitations

Language can lead to misunderstandings, especially when communication takes place between a high-context and a low-context culture (Hall 1982).

When I took a taxi back to the Beijing International Airport, I negotiated my last deal in Beijing for the Rethinking Negotiation Teaching trip. Perhaps the best lesson I learned from the trip was in this taxi. Before my wife and I entered the taxi, we agreed to pay 225 yuan for the taxi services, excluding the tip. This was arranged with the help of a hotel guide, who could speak both Mandarin and English. About halfway through our ride, the taxi driver asked me something in Mandarin. I replied in English, saying, "I don't understand you." After a couple of failed attempts at communication, he hand-gestured what looked like a three to me. He is trying to re-negotiate his taxi price, I thought to myself. I said "NO!" He looked helpless; so no doubt did I. Then my wife guessed that perhaps he was trying to ask us about something else. Did he know which terminal we were supposed to arrive at? I knew it was terminal 3 and as soon as I showed him the number 3 written on a piece of scrap paper, we settled our "dispute." All he wished to know was "at which terminal, 2 or 3, should I drop you off?"

Looking back, I realize that I was not self-aware of my limitations, and hence was making assumptions based upon my limited knowledge at the time of communication (Hall 1984; 1989). I learned that communication across cultures, especially when language is a barrier to communication, is difficult (Hall 1989). In my case, the driver was thinking of saving us time by driving my family to the proper terminal, and I was thinking that he was trying to exploit my situation by re-negotiating his price.

The importance of self-awareness

In summary, through my negotiation experiences in Beijing, in addition to my awareness about not making quick judgments, about our roles in negotiation, and about our limitations, I learned about the importance of preparation. This includes having a working knowledge of the local language and the importance of knowing that even after tremendous preparation, one should always stay open to new learning by remaining humble before, during, and after the negotiations. I close by quoting Ting-Toomey and Chang (2005: 131):

> There should be zeal to learn about new culture. There should be an honest non-judgmental approach to learning the new culture. Take it this way. A new culture will only adopt you if you are willing to accept that culture without inhibitions.

Self-awareness as a Negotiation Teaching Tool

As alluded to above, the field of negotiation teaching can benefit greatly from designing a curriculum that embeds "cultural self-awareness," particularly in cross-cultural situations. The five respective experiences in a common setting (Beijing market) with a common theme (bargaining) invariably reveal hidden expectations and assumptions, typical of human behavior, yet are quite telling in cross-cultural settings. Quite noticeably, we brought our respective self-inferential cultural behavior to the idea of bargaining, with interesting results on analysis. For instance, Goh attempted to negotiate like a Chinese; Chamoun-Nicolas felt frustrated at not being able to negotiate at the Beijing Night Market; Deason came to Beijing uncomfortable with haggling; Folberg associated shopping with bargaining; and Singh likened the Chinese way of bargaining to that of the Indians.

Indeed, when one thinks of cross-cultural negotiation, one both expects to unearth differences about the other culture and hopes to gain cultural competency in the ways of the other. Our experiences validate the point that, in fact, understanding the other is an inverse exercise: in the end, it is understanding *oneself* that enables any meaningful cross-cultural experience to occur.

As Jayne Docherty (2010) emphasizes, in order to prepare students for complex, adaptive problems, teaching self-awareness needs to extend beyond a focus on abilities in using skills to an "awareness of self in relation to a socially negotiated context" (Docherty 2010: 502). She suggests that teachers help students consider questions such as "Who am I in society, and how does that shape the way I negotiate with others? . . . How can I use my negotiation skills or other conflict transformation skills to change social systems that I do not like or that I consider unfair or unjust?" (Docherty 2010: 502) These questions not only help prepare a student to engage in "symmetrical anthropology," which includes discovering their own culture of negotiation, but also underline ways in which that self-discovery can show that "the very domain of our work – social conflict – is culturally constructed" (Docherty 2004: 716).

As one example of a teaching technique, in a mediation course that Goh teaches in Australia, the first student assessment item deals with a "Cultural Awareness Case Study." Not surprisingly, the majority of her Australian students of Anglo-Saxon background are at a loss, and confused initially at what is expected of them. It is mind-boggling for these students: "It is *their* culture I am interested in, not *mine*!" or, "You mean, I have a 'culture'? What culture?" On the other hand, the extremely positive feedback received once the assessment task is done is testament to their deep learning experience and cross-cultural engagement, with a realization that the so-called other enables one to learn about oneself first, which is needed for any cross-cultural difference of the other to be interpreted intelligently. Our respective cross-cultural experiences recounted in the common ground of the Beijing market highlight this point about self-awareness as a requisite step towards acquiring competence in cross-cultural negotiation.

Students often have difficulty articulating their own cultural predilections, because they take them for granted and because these behaviors are controlled by parts of the brain that are not concerned with speech (Hall 1989:153). One way to start a conversation is to assign Rubin's and Sander's (1991) work on stereotypes in negotiation, and then use stereotypes as a starting point to help students consider their own, more authentic, cultural traits. Deason has tried a modified version of Rubin's and Sander's exercise on stereotypes, in which they grouped participants by national origin and asked them to characterize their national negotiating style as seen by others. In small group discussions, U.S. students can readily identify stereotypes about how Americans interact and negotiate. These stereotypes can then provoke reactions about students' cultural and personal approaches that contrast with (or perhaps confirm to some degree) the stereotypical expectations.

Because we are generally oblivious to our own culture, self-awareness must be organized, and teachers must facilitate a process of self-discovery. As an authentic process that allows this discovery, adventure learning is a powerful tool for fostering cultural self-awareness in negotiation. For example, this was apparent in some of the students' adventure learning reflections in Sandra Cheldelin's course (Manwaring, McAdoo, and Cheldelin 2010), which included observations about cultural constraints on their negotiation, associated with students' own attitudes. This theme could be developed further in an adventure learning experience by making self-awareness of attitudes toward negotiation an explicit goal of the exercise, and devoting some of the debriefing to the topic. (On the importance of debriefing adventure learning, see Deason and colleagues, *Debriefing Adventure Learning*, in this volume.) The opportunities for reflection on one's own culture are sharpened in a setting such as Istanbul or Beijing, or in a class with a diverse group of nationalities, because of the potential for contrasts. But many metropolitan areas offer cross-cultural negotiation possibilities, and perhaps even an experience that does not involve participants from different backgrounds could be designed to serve as a vehicle to increase cultural self-awareness.

Conclusion

Cross-cultural experiences can be life-enhancing. Hopefully, they add value to our personal growth as human beings. Our defining moments as human beings are when we show we have the ability to exhibit tolerance, mutual respect and empathy to our fellow human beings, when we can be non-judgmental, and when we can promote mutual understanding. This is not a tall order. However, it requires that we recognize "where we are coming from" culturally as well as physically. We need to be honest with ourselves in self-reflection, and generate positive self-awareness, as steps along the way to cross-cultural enlightenment. It is in this light that we offer our experiences for an emergent pedagogy in cross-cultural negotiation teaching and learning.

Notes

We would like to thank Dr. Eileen Wibbeke for her helpful feedback on the draft.

[1] My paternal grandparents emigrated to Malaysia (then known as Malaya) in the late nineteenth century from the Southern Chinese province of Fujian.

[2] I was raised in a typical Chinese village in Malaysia with a strong Confucian ethic and traditional Chinese values. My father was the local Chinese school principal and my mother taught in the same school. Naturally, my parents had all us children educated in Mandarin in our primary school years. We then switched to English-medium or Malay-medium schools when it came to secondary schooling.

[3] A term commonly referring to one being able to identify with mother-country on account of ethnicity or nationality.

[4] It is important to note that, in Chinese-style negotiation, often the "person" matters more than the deal.

[5] As described by Panga and Grecia-de Vera (2010: 178), my sense that many Americans are hesitant to bargain is supported by the expert observations of a seller at the Istnabul bazaar.

[6] For conceptual convenience, I refer to institutional trust as a substitute for trust, although scholars debate whether institutional trust is a "real" form of trust or a functional substitute (Rousseau et al. 1998). It is not necessary to

resolve that debate to accept an important role for this form of trust. Another debate that is particularly relevant in the cross-cultural setting of this chapter concerns the interaction between institutional trust and interpersonal trust built on relationships. One line of research suggests that external controls that substitute for trust are likely to undermine the development of interpersonal trust and generate a need for even more legalistic rules to govern the interaction (Sitkin 1995). Another view is that institutional substitutes for trust can create an environment that supports the development of interpersonal trust (Sitkin 1995; Rousseau et al. 1998).

[7] That potential for comparison makes me confident that economic incentives exert some control; if prices are too far out of line the establishment will not stay in business.

References

Augsburger, D. 1992. *Conflict mediation across cultures*. Westminster: John Knox Press.

Chamoun, H. and R. Hazlett. 2007. *Negotiate like a Phoenician*. Houston, TX: KeyNegotiations.

Chamoun, H. and R. Hazlett. 2009. The psychology of giving and its effect on negotiation. In *Rethinking negotiation teaching: Innovations for context and culture*, edited by C. Honeyman, J. Coben, and G. De Palo. St. Paul, MN: DRI Press.

Chamoun, H. and P. Linzoain. 2005. *Deal-guidelines for a flawless negotiation*. Houston, TX: Key Negotiations.

Chamoun-Nicolas, H., J. Folberg, and R. Hazlett. 2010. Bazaar dynamics: Teaching integrative negotiation within a distributive environment. In *Venturing beyond the classroom: Volume 2 in the rethinking negotiation teaching series*, edited by C. Honeyman, J. Coben, and G. De Palo. St. Paul, MN: DRI Press.

Chen, M. J. 2001. *Inside Chinese business*. Boston, MA: Harvard Business Press.

Coben, J., C. Honeyman, and S. Press. 2010. Straight off the deep end in adventure learning. In *Venturing beyond the classroom: Volume 2 in the rethinking negotiation teaching series*, edited by C. Honeyman, J. Coben, and G. De Palo. St. Paul, MN: DRI Press.

Deason, E. E. 2006. The need for trust as a justification for confidentiality in mediation: A cross-disciplinary approach. *The University of Kansas Law Review* 54(5): 1387-1418.

Docherty, J. S. 2004. Culture and negotiation: Symmetrical anthropology for negotiators. *Marquette Law Review* 87(4): 711-722.

Docherty, J. S. 2010. "Adaptive" negotiation: Practice and teaching. In *Venturing beyond the classroom: Volume 2 in the rethinking negotiation teaching series*, edited by C. Honeyman, J. Coben, and G. De Palo. St Paul, MN: DRI Press.

Douglas, M. 1973. *Rules and meanings: The anthropology of everyday knowledge*. Selected readings. Harmondsworth, Middlesex: Penguin.

Goh, B. C. 1994. Cross-cultural perspectives on Sino-Western negotiation. *Australian Dispute Resolution Journal* 5: 268-284.

Goh, B. C. 1996. *Negotiating with the Chinese*. Aldershot, UK: Dartmouth Publishing Company.

Goh, B. C. 2006. Typical errors of Westerners. In *The negotiator's fieldbook: The desk reference for the experienced negotiator*, edited by A. K. Schneider and C. Honeyman. Washington, DC: American Bar Association.

Hall, E. T. 1959. *The silent language*. Westport: Greenwood Press.

Hall, E. T. 1982. *The hidden dimension*. New York: Anchor Books.

Hall, E. T. 1984. *The dance of life: The other dimension of time*. New York: Anchor Books.

Hall, E. T. 1989. *Beyond culture*. Garden City, NY: Anchor Press.

Harper, D. 2001. *Online etymology dictionary*. Available at http://www.etymonline.com/ (last accessed April 4, 2012).

Henderson, C. 2002. *Cultures and customs of India*. Westport, CT: Greenport Press.

Hewstone, M. and R. Brown. 1986. Contact is not enough: An intergroup perspective on the "contact hypotheis." In *Contact and conflict in intergroup encounters*, edited by M. Hewstone and R. J. Brown. London: Blackwell.

Hofstede, G. 1994. *Cultures and organizations: Software of the mind: Intercultural cooperation and its importance of survival*. London: HarperCollins.

Hofstede, G. 2001. *Culture consequences*. London: Sage Publications.

Hofstede, G. 2006. What did GLOBE really measure? Researchers' minds versus respondents' minds. *Journal of International Business Studies* 37(7): 882-896.

Hofstede, G. 2011. Geert Hofstede website. Available at http://www.geert-hofstede.com/ (last accessed April 4, 2012).

Johnston, L. and C. N. Macrae. 1994. Changing social stereotypes: The case of the information seeker. *European Journal of Social Psychology* 24(5): 581-592.

Lewicki, R. J. 2006. Trust and distrust. In *The negotiator's fieldbook: The desk reference for the experienced negotiator*, edited by A. K. Schneider and C. Honeyman. Washington, DC: American Bar Association.

Lewicki, P. 1985. Nonconscious biasing effects of single instances on subsequent judgments. *Journal of Personality and Social Psychology* 48(3): 563-574.

Manwaring, M., B. McAdoo, and S. Cheldelin. 2010. Orientation and disorientation: Two approaches to designing "authentic" negotiation learning activities. In *Venturing beyond the classroom: Volume 2 in the rethinking negotiation teaching series*, edited by C. Honeyman, J. Coben, and G. De Palo. St. Paul, MN: DRI Press.

McDougall, W. 1920. *The group mind*. Cambridge, UK: Cambridge University Press.

Nisbett, R. 2003. *The geography of thought*. New York: The Free Press.

Panga, Jr., S. S. and G. B. Grecia-de Vera, 2010. A look at a negotiation 2.0 classroom: Using adventure learning modules to supplement negotiation simulations. In *Venturing beyond the classroom: Volume 2 in the rethinking negotiation teaching series*, edited by C. Honeyman, J. Coben, and G. De Palo. St. Paul, MN: DRI Press.

Roberge, J. and R. J. Lewicki. 2010. Should we trust grand bazaar carpet sellers (and vice versa)? In *Venturing beyond the classroom: Volume 2 in the rethinking negotiation teaching series*, edited by C. Honeyman, J. Coben, and G. De Palo. St. Paul, MN: DRI Press.

Rousseau, D., S. Stikin, R. Burt, and C. Camerer. 1998. Not so different after all: A cross-discipline view of trust. *The Academy of Management Review* 23(4): 393-404.

Rubin, J. and F. E. A. Sander. 1991. Culture, negotiation, and the eye of the beholder. *Negotiation Journal* 7(3): 249.

Salacuse, J. 1991. *Making global deals: What every executive should know about negotiating abroad*. New York: Times Business.

Singh, S. 2009. *Sikhs, India and The Indian Constitution in the UNITED SIKHS Annual Sikh Civil Rights Report*, New York.

Sitkin, S. B. 1995. On the positive effect of legalization on trust. In *Research on Negotiation in Organizations,* edited by R. J. Bies, R. J. Lewicki, and B. H. Sheppard. Greenwich, CT: JAI Press.

Snyder, M. 1981. On the self-perpetuating nature of social stereotypes. In *Cognitive processes in stereotyping and intergroup behavior*, edited by D. L. Hamilton. Hillsdale, NJ: Erlbaum.

Steele, C. M. 1988. The psychology of self-affirmation: Sustaining the integrity of the self. *Advances in Experimental Social Psychology* 21: 261-302.

Storti, C. 2007. *Speaking of India: Bridging the communication gap when working with Indians*. Boston, MA: Intercultural Press.

Ting-Toomey, S. and Chung, L. 2005. *Understanding intercultural communication*. New York: Oxford University Press.

Wibbeke, E. S. 2009. *Global business leadership*. Oxford, UK: Elsevier.

❀ 6 ❧

How Different Is "Different"?
Teaching Persons to Negotiate Cross-Culturally

*Joseph B. Stulberg, Janice Kwon & Khory McCormick**

Editors' Note: The authors note with appreciation the rising volume of research discussing cross-cultural negotiations; but they find its application to teaching and training often arid, simplistic and unpersuasive. They argue for a richer and more complex treatment of culture in negotiation, to give a more accurate impression of two salient circumstances in particular: the degree to which factors believed to be culturally distinct operate in "intra-cultural" negotiating contexts as well as in cross-cultural ones, and the degree to which negotiating dimensions, concepts, strategies and tactics may be similar across cultures, such that a belief that a completely different approach is required as soon as one is negotiating with someone from another culture is as likely to provoke error as a belief that one can safely behave exactly as one would at home.

Introduction

To those interested in conducting and teaching negotiation, a dominant question, stated very generally, is: Does or should one's approach to bargaining differ if one's negotiating counterpart is from a "different culture"?[1]

The answer seems obviously simple: "of course." Failure to appreciate differences can easily lead to misinterpretation of communications and missed settlement opportunities. There is a burgeoning

* **Joseph B. Stulberg** is the Michael E. Moritz Chair in Alternative Dispute Resolution at The Ohio State University Moritz College of Law in Columbus, Ohio and a 2012 Ikerbasque Research Professor (IKERBASQUE, Basque Foundation for Science). His email address is stulberg.2@osu.edu. **Janice Kwon** is an attorney at IBM. Her email address is jkwon@us.ibm.com. **Khory McCormick** is a partner in Minter Ellison Lawyers in Brisbane, Australia. His email address is khory.mccormick@minterellison.com.

social science literature that tries to identify such differences (see, e.g., Brett and Okumura 1998; Brett 2001; Hall 1976; and Hofstede 1980).

In our judgment, this response is simplistic. While the differences often cited – such as the role of hierarchy in decision-making (see, e.g., Ridgeway and Erickson 2000), or high-context or low-context communication styles (see, e.g., Hofstede 1980) – are important, those concepts apply across and within multiple cultures. Furthermore, such analyses, by emphasizing differences, neglect to identify concepts, strategies and tactics that are similar across negotiating settings.

A different approach is warranted. We set out below three hypothetical stories; they build off – but do not reproduce – several interviews conducted with real world participants. From these hypothetical situations, we highlight salient negotiating concepts, strategies and skills that are exhibited in these accounts. Given these dimensions, we suggest how the insights from the first generation of social science literature that examines cross-cultural negotiation falls short of addressing the salient negotiating dynamics illustrated in the hypothetical stories. We conclude with suggestions as to how one might approach the design of teaching materials and pedagogy to prepare a student to be an effective negotiating participant in the global context.

Conducting Negotiations Cross-culturally: Three Stories

Case 1: The Lawyer

"I am an international lawyer. I focus on representing clients in international ADR proceedings – mostly, arbitration. I love my work – well, at least my clients. I love defending them because they often do business with persons and lawyers who are shameless in their conduct. I enjoy defending and securing my client's interests.

Here is a typical case. I was asked to represent a South American businessman who had been an investor with a business that was organized and operated by a partner from another South American country. The business relationship collapsed. The lawyers representing the other client were both French and South American. I am a U.S.-trained lawyer operating from our firm's Paris office.

I immediately arranged to meet with my client. I do not – and never would – handle these initial conversations by telephone. I needed to meet him, to get to know his needs. I had to understand and appreciate the way in which his country's values and life-styles shaped his business viewpoint; how he viewed his business counterpart; and how his business counterpart dealt with him.

At that first meeting I learned that our business counterpart was tapping my client's phones and had surreptitiously intercepted my client's internal and external email messages. Rotten stuff. We immediately took steps to secure the integrity and privacy of our communications. I cannot, and usually do not try to change that kind of behavior by our adversary. I try to work around it.

One immense challenge in working in the international arbitration context is that lawyers come from two traditions: the common law tradition and the civil law tradition. In case you didn't know it, all lawyers – and their training – are not "the same."

For example, there are striking differences between common law and civil law traditions regarding discovery practice. In the civil law tradition, there is no concept of disclosure. Can you believe that? A civil law trained lawyer will not disclose documents that contain information damaging to her client's legal case. By contrast, those of us trained in the common law tradition view the discovery process, from exchanging interrogatories to conducting witness depositions, as central to effective case preparation.

How can I get the other side to share information? Work like mad. One positive and recent development in international arbitration is that the International Bar Association developed and recommends guidelines for handling discovery requests (IBA 2010).[2] The Redfern Schedule[3] enables me to develop a proposed order for the arbitration panel in which I identify the requested documents, indicate why they are important to the case, and explain why producing them does not impose a disproportionate burden on the adversary. Of course, opposing counsel can object to any, or all, such requests. The arbitration panel then renders a decision establishing the parameters with regard to the document request and a general schedule for exchange, if there is to be one. I might not persuade the panel to provide me everything that I seek (after all, some of the panel members, too, are civil law trained) but having this procedural avenue available helps me to deal with opponents whom, I say charitably, might never disclose adverse information.

I have learned from experience not to be forthcoming, at least initially. It actually goes against both my training and my professional values; I would much rather share relevant information. But I have a greater duty to protect my client. Until I see some reciprocity of openness from my opponent, I remain cautious. Every lawyer, or her firm, in this small community has a reputation for how either she, or her firm, approaches her representation role. I, or my partners, can quickly learn the "good" and the "bad" about their approach(es) and adapt our own conduct accordingly. In an ideal world, perhaps, there would be a uniform code of professional conduct governing lawyers across jurisdictions. Having that would, at the least, establish a common basis for going forward. Put differently, it would create an institutional platform for establishing minimal standards for what constitutes professional conduct and integrity.

I do not settle many cases just before an arbitration hearing – or, as my American friends who litigate like to say, "on the courthouse steps." I am not opposed to settling cases. If my client thinks it best to settle, we will. Yet what is the incentive? First, I spent a lot of time negotiating with the other side which rules will govern matters such as the arbitral situs, the choice of law, the language of the hearing, and the institutional rules. With that investment, I'm reasonably confident about the process, so that I would not hesitate to use it. Second, arbitration is private; I would not need to settle the case in order for my client to keep matters out of the public eye. Third, international arbitrators, for better or for worse, do not often render decisions that are clear "win/lose" outcomes. Depending on the case, it may be that the arbitrators provide my client with what we would have sought in a negotiated settlement."

Case 2: The Chief Executive Officer (CEO)

"I love being in business – and helping to lead a company. When I had a chance to become the CEO of a well-known luxury goods company, I jumped at it.

I knew – and told people before I became CEO – that the future of our business was in China, both in terms of a customer market and in terms of manufacturing operations. We had no presence there when I started; I was determined, without jeopardizing the company, to get there.

I knew two important things about China. It had a manufacturing infrastructure that was efficient, reliable, and capable (just look at Nike if you don't believe it). Second, the business people in China – at least those I interacted with – "got" capitalism. I don't know how they learned it – maybe because many had been trained at business schools in the West. However they got it, they certainly embraced it; and that made it easy to deal with them.

I think leadership requires clarity, both internally and externally. Through our publications and website, we publicly signaled three things to potential partners. First, we wanted a manufacturing collaboration with an independent Chinese company; we did not want to establish our own operations and then hire local nationals to operate it. Second, we would partner only with a company that would commit to us that it would neither knowingly engage in human rights abuses nor violate child labor laws. Third, we had to be certain that any arrangement would in no way compromise our company's unimpeachable, long-standing reputation for quality products.

We went looking. When we found a partner, we embraced him – brought him and his people inside our organization to see and learn our product design process. Once they understood that, we gave them test samples to produce for us. We evaluated their ability to produce the item timely and with perfect quality. We also worked at, and reflected on, our collective capacity to work together. As everyone's confidence level grew, we moved toward a more substantial collaboration.

What did that more substantial collaboration look like? Operationally, we provided our partner with a significant order. We had developed our own staff presence at the partner's work site (ultimately, all of whom were Chinese). These people – our employees – were physically present at the plant on a daily basis. Their responsibilities were to provide operational support to our partner and monitor work processes, quality control measures and human rights compliance. These people were not "moles"; our partners knew they were there both as a resource for them, and for us. Look, our goal is to make money. If they succeeded, we succeeded. So if something in the manufacturing process was not working correctly, we wanted – had to – be able to identify it quickly and fix it. We talk to each other; that's what business partners do. If it could be fixed and not repeated, terrific; if we could not fix it, it was clear that we would terminate the relationship.

We would never sacrifice our reputation for quality; that meant that we would insist that the partner use the materials that we provided. No choice there.

We put very few things in writing. What we did put in writing was explicit: our principles for engagement; our demand for quality; and a contractual exit strategy. But we never developed a formal written contract regarding such matters as order terms or capital investments. Our Chinese partner made its own decisions and financial investments regarding equipment purchases, production facilities ("factories") for our product, staffing size, and, beyond a minimum, compensation levels.

Of course we had company concerns that influenced how we did business and how our partners would concretely display their understanding of our concerns. We wanted their employees to be loyal to our brand and not use their idle time to produce "counterfeit" knockoffs of our product. We needed to protect trade secrets. If our manufacturing partner did not have enough business from us to keep his work force fully employed on our products, then he clearly had the right to strike manufacturing deals with others – and possibly hurt us in the ways I just cited.

So what did we do? After some months, our partner established a separate, dedicated manufacturing facility to produce only our products; I wanted him to know how much that was appreciated, so we increased our order size – not to ensure 100 percent production capacity but to support his commitment. He got it. But none of that was required or put in writing.

I was confident and proud of our Company engagement principles; I do not want to do business with people who knowingly employ young children or who require employees to work abominably long hours. I don't want that type of partner anywhere. Beyond that, with one exception, I did not want to change or mess with the way that company conducts its business. I did insist, though, on one other matter: I required that our partner pay his employees a fair wage – not by my standards, but to pay them a wage that would enable his employees to meet their basic human needs. Why? Because there is no way that I could live with myself if I knew that I was able to live like I do – in comparative luxury – while persons working in factories with whom I had authority to structure relationships were earning a wage that would not enable them to meet basic human needs. We were making those factory owners very wealthy people; it would be reprehensible of me not to insist that their employees benefit at a tolerable level.

The approach has worked. Within a few years, we are manufacturing almost all of our company products in China. How did we unwind the relationships with those companies in other parts of the world who had previously produced our products? How much time do you have? That was a whole other set of crucial, complex, simultaneous conversations."

Case 3. U.S. College Administrator in Charge of Foreign Study Programs

"I administer foreign study programs for our College.

We have a lot of them: some are semester or year-long programs; some are summer programs; others are concentrated, intensive short courses. Faculty members and the provost, of course, design the academic dimensions and teach some of the courses, but I participate actively in their discussions about program design – both with our College people and our potential collaborators. This is because my job is to make the program work on the ground.

Why have such programs? Pretty obvious: we live in a global society; we need to understand and learn how to get along. Our educational task is to provide rich, distinctive educational experiences for our students – if we can enhance their education about a global society by providing them something they could not get at our home institution, then why not do it? Our partners – particularly where we have students enrolled in classes taught by their faculty – clearly understand that goal.

Every program must operate within certain parameters. For instance, the academic program must be in compliance with our accrediting agency's rules and guidelines – that's a no-brainer. We need to be clear for students about how their participation impacts their academic credit and financial needs: Do the courses count toward satisfying the requirements of their major field of study or a certificate program? Does studying abroad adversely impact a college's minimum residency requirement? Can student loans be used for study abroad initiatives? Another, perhaps less obvious, matter about program design is that the budgets must work. We cannot price the program beyond the financial capacity of our students. A final dimension is that while part of the international experience is to have students adopt a lifestyle that is different from their home orientation, we have to be concerned that the program facilities meet the needs of the students. We need functional classrooms; the housing arrangements must meet minimum comfort levels. If we do not meet these, then as the administrator, I will be fielding complaints from faculty and students throughout the program. It is not worth it.

No program, obviously, moves forward without our physically meeting with our potential partners, inspecting the facilities, and the like. Our potential partners clearly want the same. Communicating by phone and email is nice. But we have to work together – we have to know one another before we start.

I have been doing this a long time. I know that new personnel who want to put their stamp on "innovative" programs do not like to hear this, but I now approach every discussion about creating a new foreign study program with one dominant thought: there are always endless alternatives to working with this proposed partner, including having no program at all – so we should never say "yes" to going forward just because someone thinks that our potential partner is irreplaceable.

That does not mean I am a "naysayer" and always try to find reasons for why something cannot be done. I'm not that type of person. I just care too much about doing it correctly – and doing it correctly for each program that we operate. We did one program with partners who thought that not only was every item negotiable, but also that every settled item was renegotiable. Of course, nothing was ever put in writing that resembled a "contract." From an administrative standpoint, I never felt confident that significant matters were stable. That was a challenge.

I understand formalities and structure. They exist everywhere; their formats differ. In some settings, for instance, the professor is highly esteemed and no one will do anything without her endorsement. In other settings, it's the university administrator – Provost or Dean – to whom that deference is displayed.

Those formalities spill over into decision-making procedures. For some matters, our Dean makes the decision; on others, she defers to me and states to our counterparts: "I will do whatever my colleague (me) thinks is best." How people on the other side of the table make their decision is just something we have to learn as we proceed – it typically differs from our own.

I can get along with almost anyone. But I will not compromise basic human values: for example, I do not like, or tolerate, arrogance. I respect roles. But when an arrogant person uses the authority of her role to treat people in dismissive, demeaning ways, I do not kowtow to it – wherever I am. I try to deal with it by letting others talk, or proposing program implementation strategies that divorce me from interacting with that individual. But if none of those efforts work, I will make it clear to my supervisor and colleagues that the relationship will be difficult and we should seek a different partner. I do not think that arrogance must be tolerated."

Lessons Learned
These vignettes illustrate multiple elements that shape one's vision and conduct during negotiations. What are they?

1) Conceptual
These theoretical elements laced the party's conduct.

a) Values operate at multiple levels, and they matter.
Values shape conduct. Values are held by individual organizational leaders conducting conversations, as well as by their organizations.

There are multiple categories of values – normative claims – that significantly play out in a negotiation. They include the following:
- *Ethical values.* The lawyer recognized that her client's counterpart engaged in improper tactics – tapping telephone calls – that might put her client at a disadvantage. She did not reciprocate. When she learned that the reputation of her lawyer counterpart (or their firm) was unprofessional, she did

not reciprocate. The University administrator affirmed that no one needs to tolerate the contempt with which an arrogant individual treats others. And the business person insisted that his business counterpart pay its employees an appropriately-based living wage for two ethical reasons: first, he knew they had capacity to do so, because he was central to making them wealthy individuals; and second, he would not be able to enjoy his own comfortable lifestyle knowing that he was in a position to do something effectively about how his business enterprise and operations treated its people – in a phrase, he felt ethically responsible.

- *Human values that govern organizational or professional conduct.* Reputation and integrity count. The business committed itself to be a certain type of participant in a global economy: it would not earn a profit for some at the expense of human rights abuses involving child labor or insufferable working conditions. The lawyer would not mirror the unprofessional conduct of her counterpart by deliberately misrepresenting the existence or content of a damaging document.

- *Enterprise values.* Partners' values regarding the goals and elements of various enterprises are shared – or, at least, significantly overlap. The people in the business enterprises shared a philosophy regarding the appropriate economic goals for business in a global environment. In the words of the CEO, "my partner 'got' capitalism." That shared perspective shaped collaborative understanding about production processes, sales strategies, and human resource protocols that promoted efficiency and quality. For the college, there was – importantly – a shared sense of what constitutes an "educational enterprise." The lawyer, intriguingly, raised a crucial question: Do members of the legal profession across borders share a common set of professional values?

b) Power is always at play. Power comes in multiple forms and does not reside exclusively with one party.

Power – the capacity to make another do what one wants – is real. To ignore it is irresponsible and unwise. But there are multiple sources of power – and it is wrong to believe that "all power" in a given negotiation or transaction resides completely with only one participant.

Relevant examples are many.

The U.S. company derived enormous power from its market share and reputation for quality. It could, in many ways, dictate terms to a potential partner. But its partner also had significant power: crucially, the manufacturing infrastructure to produce these products at a cost that would enable the U.S. company to remain competitive – and the possibility of penetrating the far eastern consumer market.

The U.S. college wanted to create opportunities for its students to gain an "international experience" as part of their education. Its power resided in its capacity to create an academic and study program that would serve its students' multiple interests and the College's ability to motivate, recruit and admit persons to the program. But that capacity is useless without the presence and willingness of a credible educational partner located outside the U.S. While one party might try to resolve legal controversies by using aggressive or unethical business or advocate practices, its counterpart can, to some extent, meet that assault by assertive, effective use of the procedures governing their mutually-adopted dispute resolution forum.

Although each party brings her own training and skills to a negotiation, in practical terms in a cross-cultural context the situation is never determined exclusively by adoption of and adherence to one party's preferred paradigm.

c) One must manage multiple negotiations simultaneously.
Human conduct does not operate in a vacuum; it is rarely "dyadic."

When negotiating with one's bargaining counterpart, there are often conversations and negotiations occurring simultaneously with one's client, co-workers, or business collaborators.

The litigator must always converse with – and persuade – her client about the appropriate course of conduct; the administrator must develop a shared understanding with her supervisors and co-workers about how a particular program will operate and how that impacts the performance of their other job tasks; and the CEO, minimally, must figure out how to terminate current manufacturing operations without the exit sabotaging future company activity in that region of the world.

d) Human interaction is complex.
The circumstances of any negotiation or transaction are multi-layered and unique, but the way in which any individual brings her corporate, shared or personal values and her power to bear in any given circumstances, though culturally influenced, is idiosyncratic.

2) Strategic
Negotiating strategies and tactics abound. Common elements of negotiation techniques include the following:

a) Decisions are made in multiple ways.

People, groups and institutions make decisions in multiple ways: some can be made "at the table" with those negotiators or parties who are there participating; some require further consultation and approval by other entities such as a board of directors, a union membership, or a council of elders. Some decisions are made only by the person with the requisite title or role in the hierarchy; other such "persons" might delegate that decision-making authority to colleagues who might know the most.

These types of differences affect not only what information direct actors are willing to share with one another, but also the timeframe within which decisions are made. Quite obviously, the decision making apparatus and timeframe for one party need not be identical to that of its negotiating counterpart.

b) Trust cements relationships but must be built over time.

If one has reason to believe that her bargaining counterpart will not do what she represents she will do – and one's own business or personal interests are impacted by that conduct – then one proceeds cautiously in order to protect oneself. That is understandable. The lawyer was cautious, initially, with what she was willing to share with her counterpart. The company sought a partner and brought it into its operational environment; but there were a series of benchmark evaluations – tests – regarding the timely, quality production of products, and these constituted the building blocks for more extensive engagement. And when one college participant experienced that its counterpart viewed not only every item as negotiable but every settled item as renegotiable, confidence in each other's reliability eroded.

c) Party interests dovetail and shape possibilities.

There is a reason why persons can "do business" with one another: someone else is in a position to do something for you that you want. Whether or not one embraces the provocative rhetoric of "interests",[4] the three stories illustrate what shapes deal-making. The Chinese partner can manufacture the product in a way that generates economic savings and profits; only a non-U.S. university can provide the U.S. student with that international learning experience. It is such differences that make agreement possible.[5]

d) Being firm does not mean being rigid, inflexible or a cultural imperialist.

Foreign counterparties are often criticized for attempting to impose their own values and practices on others. But does being firm in a negotiation mean being imperialistic in that derogatory sense? That seriously misreads – and wrongly evaluates – the situation. The educator asserts: we cannot discuss a program that will not meet the standards of our accrediting agency. Is that imperialistic? The Company asserts: we cannot compromise our reputation for manufacturing and selling quality, luxury products. Is that imperialistic? These principles shape their enterprises. They ground their mission and define their institutional integrity. They establish their bargaining priorities on such issues as course design or product materials. They "blend" the conventional difference between "interests" and "positions" because one's interest, for example, in offering an accredited educational program may allow no flexibility in the school's "position" on such matters as length of the class session. Of course, it is easy to misrepresent such principles and constraints, but some of them are central to the enterprise.

e) Communications take many forms.

Communicating effectively with another person is an extraordinarily challenging human activity. It is pedestrian to note that there are multiple ways to communicate – through language or through non-verbal conduct; that levels of communicating can purposefully range from being precise to being deliberately vague; and that understanding and acknowledging a counterpart's communication can be signaled in ways that differ from the way in which that original message was transmitted. The lesson of experience is that we need to remain open to the possibilities of the subtlety, richness and elegance of the human capacity for communicating.

How do these general observations play out in a negotiating environment? Clearly, the effectiveness of negotiation strategies and tactics is a subject best left to separate discussion.[6]

However, these observations are capable of transcending cultural barriers.

The business person wanted to protect the company's trade secrets; when his partner built a factory dedicated exclusively to his product, he increased the size of his order. This was not a contractual deal. They communicated indirectly but very concretely through their conduct. However, if there were problems with quality control in the production process, did one or another charge a breach of contract? No – "we do what business partners do: talk it out and fix the problem."

By contrast, the lawyer communicated clearly to her counterpart: in writing, she requested document production pursuant to the procedural rules. She had no reason to trust the other side to produce it otherwise.

f) BÁTNAs (best alternatives to a negotiated agreement) are genuine.

In the real world, options to reaching a negotiated agreement vary significantly according to context.

The lawyer's best option, particularly when dealing with a former business partner whom you are accusing of absconding with corporate funds, was to have an international tribunal arbitrate the case rather than try to settle it through direct negotiations. The College administrator who accurately assesses that his school would be better off "with no international program" rather than adopt the one being proposed enjoys, at one level, a very strong BATNA.

But the strength and robustness of one's BATNA, like power in negotiation, varies over time. The options one party has when developing a business relationship with a counterpart, for instance, might differ considerably from his available options when implementing a partnership.[7] In the case of our businessperson, he might not enter into a contractual relationship with a potential partner – and feel comfortable about doing so – if that potential partner does not agree to commit itself to cooperate with the company's engagement principles regarding child labor laws; but once the parties are engaged, that option – of "not sustaining the relationship" – might remain viable, but not represent the "best" alternative. Things change.

Implications For Teaching Negotiation

What implications do these cases and observations about bargaining have for teaching negotiation to persons interested in "cross-cultural" negotiation?

1) First Generation Efforts

We might hope for guidance from recent social science studies, but would be somewhat disappointed.

There is a body of first generation "social science" scholarship that analyzes negotiating behavior among participants from different cultures. Those efforts have triggered engaging observations and insights for scholars and practitioners alike.

Early entries, primarily analyzing international business transactions, developed conceptual categories designed to improve the understanding of business persons conducting activity in cultures (often meaning countries) different from their own. Edward Hall pioneered the insight of the difference between "high-context" and "low-context" communication, while Geert Hofstede's studies on cross-cultural differences contributed the vocabulary and insights of the Power Distance Index, individualism v. collectivism, masculinity v. feminin-

ity, uncertainty avoidance index, and long-term v. short-term orientation (Hofstede 1980).[8]

More recent studies target how culture influences one's psychological processes regarding a person's motives, or information processing practices that, in turn, help shape the way in which that individual
conducts negotiations. Michele Gelfand and Naomi Dyer invite us to
examine whether bargaining heuristics vary by culture, and whether
that, in turn, leads to different bargaining behavior. Lynn Imai and
Michele Gelfand pursue the intriguing question of whether a person's
level of "cultural intelligence" (CQ) influences her approach to negotiation, with the hypothesis that the higher one's cultural intelligence, the more "integrative" a negotiator will be (2010).

These insights provide thoughtful guidance for understanding negotiating conduct, but they fall short in three distinct ways: a) the definition of "culture" contains no principle for determining an appropriate
"grouping" of persons;[9] b) the salient differences that are identified are
significant to negotiations both "intra-culture" and "cross-culture";[10]
and c) the bargaining simulations and teaching materials from which
the insights are drawn have significant limitations for generalizing.[11]

We suggest a different approach.

2) What We Learn From the Hypothetical Stories about Teaching Bargaining

The multiple bargaining elements illustrated in the recited cases target core components for developing and enriching our teaching materials and pedagogical techniques.

Those components include the following:

a) Values play a central role in conducting a negotiation.

Participant values must be identified, highlighted and discussed. The
teaching goal is not to convert a participant to embrace a particular
perspective (e.g., that an unrestricted capitalistic economic system is
desirable, or that common-law norms governing disclosure should be
preferred) but to make these matters explicit.

The teaching materials should reflect, particularly in simulations, information regarding participant individual ethical values, the role of professional norms, and the central values that
lace the organizational or institutional settings in which they operate. Doing so will highlight more vividly the ways in which persons and organizations have shared or dovetailing norms that
support the possibility of constructive engagement, as well as
highlight how values anchor or preclude possible relationships.[12]

b) Power dynamics influence and structure negotiations.
Power sources are far more diverse and dynamic than the monolithic image of financial power often suggests. Many current negotiation simulations are graded predominantly on the scale of financial pay-offs; doing so systematically skews the capacity for participants to deploy, measure and appreciate multiple power resources. Simulation materials must be sufficiently rich to enable students to experience how power operates. Additionally, as affirmed in the case of the international lawyer, the simulation material should make the possibility of non-agreement much more probable – and *valued* – than is assumed in the traditional dyadic negotiation simulation.

c) Simultaneous or satellite negotiations require a consideration of multiple strategic and practical matters.
"Dyad negotiations" fail to invite both the execution and analysis of how these multiple tensions impact negotiator planning, communication, and conduct.

d) The utility of stereotyping as an analytical tool depends on the context of its use.
References to "high context"/"low context" cultural characterization, which have the potential to morph into stereotypes, may serve as a trigger for context or reality checking. While it is useful to introduce students to generalizing concepts, such perspectives should not be allowed to blur the student's awareness of the commonality of elements in cross-cultural negotiation strategies and tactics, nor blur the need to create "open mind" unprejudiced thinking about those factors which motivate counterparties.

The teaching materials ought to challenge the student to consider the value of approaching cross-cultural negotiations with an acceptance that they do not know, or need to know, everything they could know about their counterparty's cultural drivers. However, the absence of the need to possess a complete cross-cultural knowledge base does not prevent one from understanding a counterparty's needs and wants. This focus on the uniqueness of any given negotiation context increases the utility of thoughtful listening by parties. The context level (high, low or otherwise) of any given cultural context may only affect the *extent* to which the opportunity for such thoughtful listening occurs, independently of the listener's own actions. Teaching tools must focus on developing skills related to remaining sensitive to the dynamics of a particular negotiating context regardless of the cultural background of the parties such as those just mentioned.

e) Teaching materials.

Lectures, short exercises, or simulations must systematically target both enhancing participants' analytical abilities to recognize strategic behaviors, and sharpening their performance skills in executing them. For example, every negotiator must sharpen her linguistic ability both to communicate proposals clearly and to discern counterproposals accurately. Richard Walton and Robert McKersie's (1991) remarkable analysis of how a negotiator communicates or interprets the degree of commitment to a proposal – that is, how firm or how flexible is it – or Fisher, Ury and Patton's (1991) thoughtful analysis of "negotiation jujitsu" offer crucial insights regarding such matters. This can be accomplished independently of the apparent desire of many instructors to proselytize for a particular bargaining theory.

Conclusion

It is commonplace to note that everyone negotiates. (See Chamoun et al., *Negotiation in Professional Boxing*, in this volume, for an extreme example.) As our individual lives and activities become increasingly linked globally, gaining a heightened understanding as to how differences in a person's background, culture and personality shape bargaining interactions is more and more central to effective efforts to develop global partnerships or resolve conflicts.

We believe, though, that scholar and practitioner insights that accord heightened salience to targeted negotiating elements in cross-cultural negotiations, such as decision-making procedures or communication styles, have inadvertently created two misleading impressions: first, they understate the degree to which those same features operate in "intra-cultural" negotiating contexts; second, they neglect the extent to which other negotiating dimensions, concepts, strategies and tactics are similar across cultures. We suggest that it is important to restore the equilibrium. When such rebalancing occurs, multiple bargaining elements, as suggested in our case stories, become crystallized, and command attention. Those elements include the way in which personal and organizational values shape bargaining frameworks and negotiator flexibility, and the manner in which power dynamics relate to personal and organizational values and govern bargaining possibilities. And when these dynamics become incorporated into teaching materials, learners will become more effectively attuned to the complexities, possibilities, and limitations of the bargaining process.

Notes

[1] There is, of course, a threshold inquiry: When we claim that people from different "cultures" are "negotiating" with one another, are we asserting that they are engaged in – participating in – the "same" activity? We presume that they are, but that is a conclusion that needs justification, not simply assertion. Here is a brief attempt.

If persons believe that "culture" is so specific – so relativistic – that each "culture" has its own epistemology, then we might be mistaken when we speak about persons "negotiating" cross-culturally. "Negotiating" to one participant might be a different activity for the other, much like the English word, "football" denotes distinctly different sports in the United States and in England (or the rest of the world).

This dramatic "cultural relativity" seems implausible. At least for real actors who operate in the contexts of trying to resolve cross-boundary litigation, conducting commercial business transactions, or establishing educational exchange programs, they appear to be, and believe they are, engaged in the "same" activity of trying to reach a mutually acceptable outcome. There appears to be some shared understanding that when parties "negotiate" with one another, they are, in philosopher Ludwig Wittgenstein's words, acting in an activity that bears a "family resemblance" with one another.

This is significant because it enables one to: a) offer a definition of the negotiation process that can describe – or guide – conduct of persons from differing cultures; and b) examine where and in what ways bargaining concepts, strategies or tactics "should differ" – i.e., be adjusted to one's operating environment so as to minimize miscommunication and missed settlement opportunities.

[2] The Arbitration Committee of the International Bar Association's Legal Practice Division has more than 2,300 members from over 90 countries. The Committee has standing sub-committees to address specific issues relating to the use and effectiveness of the arbitration of transnational disputes, including the Rules of Evidence Subcommittee. In 1999, that Subcommittee developed and issued *The IBA Rules on the Taking of Evidence in International Arbitration*. The IBA describes these Rules "… as a resource to parties and to arbitrators to provide an efficient, economical, and fair process for the taking of evidence in international arbitration. The Rules provide mechanisms for the presentation of documents, witnesses of fact and expert witnesses, inspections, as well as the conduct of the evidentiary hearings. The Rules are designed to be used in conjunction with, and adopted together with, institutional, ad hoc or other rules or procedures governing international arbitrations. The IBA Rules reflect procedures in use in many different legal systems, and they may be particularly useful when the parties come from different legal cultures." The Rules were revised and adopted in their current version in May 2010 (IBA 2010).

[3] The "Redfern Schedule" is a six-column chart that organizes information regarding advocate requests for document production in an arbitration of a transnational dispute. Devised by Alan Redfern, an established arbitrator of international business controversies, the chart displays each party's request(s) for document production, the moving party's arguments for the document's relevance, the Respondent's objections (if any) to production, the Claimant's replies, and the Tribunal's decision. *Techniques for Controlling*

Time and Costs in Arbitration: Report from the ICC Commission on Arbitration. International Chamber of Commerce, 2007.

[4] The term as used in negotiation literature and practice is typically ascribed to Roger Fisher and William Ury (1991).

[5] David Lax and James Sebenius (1986) crystallize this crucial observation.

[6] Bargaining strategies and tactics are often best understood as flowing from a theoretical framework. For instance, if one embraces a competitive bargaining theory, then a negotiator prepares her opening proposal shaped by that theory's support of the notion that a negotiator's task is to maximize self-gain. While each of the elements of negotiating strategy that we identify and examine is presented independent of a particular theoretical bearing, we recognize that each major current theory of negotiation does attempt to account for them.

[7] This distinction resembles, but is not identical, to that made by Robert Mnookin and colleagues (2000) between negotiating "disputes" (claims of right) and "deals."

[8] To the negotiator, the application of these general categories is presumptively straightforward and has been wonderfully sketched by John Barkai (2008).

[9] Jeanne Brett and Tetsushi Okumura offer the following thoughtful definition of "culture:" "society's characteristic profile with respect to values, norms, and institutions. It is a socially shared knowledge structure or schema, giving meaning to incoming stimuli and channeling outgoing reactions" (1998: 496). The weakness of this definition is straightforward: the word "society" does not sharply delineate a grouping that identifies a "fundamental" culture that eliminates other groupings. The definition, therefore, applies with comparable insight to the "culture" of multiple groupings, ranging from a "family" or "community" to particular institutions (the "culture of Fox News") to professions ("the culture of the profession of nurses.") While authors such as Michele Gelfand and Namoi Dyer caution readers not to equate "culture" with "geographic location" (2000), no current definition we have found offers distinctive principles for connecting "culture" to a unique grouping.

[10] The important concepts proposed regarding culture – "high/low communication," "individualistic/collectivist" – apply to conducting a negotiation in both "intra-group" and "cross-group" settings. Any savvy negotiator knows that it is important to learn whether her negotiating counterpart has authority to make decisions on her own or must operate within her "organizational hierarchy." Additionally, the skilled negotiator knows that there are multiple ways to communicate a message – the image that "American style is direct" is, even if sensible, a gross exaggeration (see, e.g., Walton and McKersie 1991).

[11] Many findings about "cross-cultural negotiations" are based on simulated negotiation exercises executed by persons of various ages who are engaged in an educational activity. As thoughtfully noted by those designing the studies, these factors significantly limit the capacity to generalize. Three limitations in particular stand out: the simulated exercises are typically buyer/seller of goods or services; the exercise involves "dyads;" and the only measure of success or failure is a pay-off structure. To the extent these elements do not reflect the actual world in which persons bargain, the ability to generalize is limited (see, e.g., Avruch 2006).

[12] The instructor, for example, from the U.S. perspective might introduce readings, discussion and simulations involving various provisions of the *Foreign Corrupt Practices Act*. For more on blending substantive and process content in teaching negotiation in a global context, see Salacuse 2010.

References

Avruch, K. 2006. The poverty of buyer and seller. In *The negotiator's fieldbook: The desk reference for the experienced negotiator*, edited by A. K. Schneider and C. Honeyman. Washington, DC: American Bar Association.

Barkai, J. 2008. Cultural dimension interests, the dance of negotiation, and weather forecasting: A perspective on cross-cultural negotiation and dispute resolution. *Pepperdine Dispute Resolution Law Journal* 8(3): 403-446.

Brett, J. M. 2001. *Negotiating globally: How to negotiate deals, resolve disputes, and make decisions across borders.* San Francisco: Jossey-Bass.

Brett, J. M. and T. Okumura. 1998. Inter- and intracultural negotiation: U.S. and Japanese negotiators. *Academy of Management Journal* 41(5): 495-510.

Fisher, R., W. Ury, and B. Patton. 1991. *Getting to yes: Negotiating agreement without giving in*, 2nd edn. New York: Penguin.

Gelfand, M. J. and N. Dyer. 2000. A cultural perspective on negotiation: Progress, pitfalls, and prospects. *Applied psychology: An International Review* 49(1): 62-99.

Hall, E. T. 1976. *Beyond culture*. New York: Anchor Press.

Hofstede, G. 1980. *Culture's consequences: International differences in work-related values*. Beverly Hills, CA: Sage.

Imai, L. and M. J. Gelfand. 2010. The culturally intelligent negotiator: The impact of cultural intelligence (CQ). *Organizational Behavior and Human Decision Processes* 112(2): 83-98.

International Bar Association. 2010. *IBA rules on the taking of evidence in international arbitration.* Available at http://www.ibanet.org/Publications/publications_IBA_guides_and_free_materials.aspx#takingevidence (last accessed March 20, 2012).

Lax, D. A. and J. K. Sebenius. 1986. *The manager as negotiator.* New York: Free Press.

Mnookin, R., S. Peppet, and A. Tulumello. 2000. *Beyond winning: Negotiating to create value in deals and disputes.* Cambridge, MA: Belknap Press.

Ridgeway, C. L. and K. G. Erickson. 2000. Creating and spreading status beliefs. *American Journal of Sociology* 106(3): 579-615.

Salacuse, J. 2010. Teaching international business negotiation: Reflections on three decades of experience. *International Negotiation* 15(2): 187-228.

Walton, R. E. and R. B. McKersie. 1991. *A behavioral theory of labor negotiations: An analysis of a social interaction system*, 2nd edn. Ithaca, NY: Cornell University Press.

℘7℘

Innovations and Pitfalls in Chinese ADR Pedagogy: Experiences from the Field

*Shahla Ali, Kang Rong, Alonzo Emery, Ta-Wei Chao, & David Matz, with an Appendix by San Tianyu**

Editors' Note: How well do "traditional" (i.e., 1980-2010 era) Western approaches to teaching negotiation translate, in a supposedly "traditional" society that is now undergoing ultra-rapid change? Between them, the authors have extensive experience teaching negotiation in China. Here, they assess that experience in a cross-comparison of five different Chinese law and business teaching environments. One common factor, they find, is that the postmodern innovation of having students participate in every aspect of a course, including course design and the selection of topics for discussion, and explicitly incorporating Chinese historical and philosophical sources, has proved useful in helping the students perceive the universality at the core of principled negotiation.

Introduction

This chapter examines negotiation skills pedagogy in the People's Republic of China (PRC) from five different perspectives. By reflect-

* **Shahla Ali** is an assistant professor of law at the University of Hong Kong. Her email address is sali@hku.hk. **Kang Rong** is a professor at Northwest University School of Economics and Management in Xi'an, China. Her email address is kangrong@nwu.edu.cn. **Alonzo Emery** is an assistant professor at Renmin University Law School in Beijing, China. His email address is alonzo. emery@gmail.com. **Ta-Wei Chao** is the executive director of ESSEC IRENE ASIA (Asian Branch of the Institute for Research and Education on Negotiation, ESSEC Business School) in Singapore. His email address is chao@essec.fr. **David Matz** is a professor in the Graduate Programs in Dispute Resolution at the University of Massachusetts/Boston in Boston, Massachusetts and principal at The Mediation Group in Brookline, Massachusetts. His email address is davidematz@gmail. com. **San Tianyu** is an attorney in Shanghai and formerly was a student at Jilin University Law School. Her email address is san1986@126.com.

ing on their varied experiences teaching in the PRC, the contributors analyze what teaching strategies proved beneficial and what methods could use improvement. Each analysis concludes with teaching and research recommendations of use to instructors in China and elsewhere. The theme linking the five narratives focuses on how the specific cultural context of China provides both challenges and opportunities for negotiation pedagogy and research.

First, Shahla Ali offers a historical overview of dispute resolution in China and how classroom discussions grounded in such a historical and cultural context can prove most effective. Second, Kang Rong compares her Fulbright research into negotiation pedagogy conducted in the United States to her teaching of negotiation skills in China. Third, Alonzo Emery discusses how empowering students to write their own simulations enabled them to embrace negotiation skills teaching more fully. Fourth, Ta-Wei Chao draws from his experience training business students in China to highlight the role that culture plays in negotiation teaching. Fifth, David Matz analyzes his experience teaching negotiation at Jilin University Law School, with a focus on how controversial topics can teach both students and instructors about cultural differences and similarities in negotiation practice. Together, these five narratives suggest that although many of the principles taught in normative negotiation skills classes seem universally transferable, distancing negotiation skills training from the specific cultural context likely will limit the effectiveness of any course. In the Appendix, former student San Tianyu reflects on her experience in the Jilin University law school class.

Five Narratives

1) History Underpinning Negotiation Skills Teaching in Hong Kong (Shahla Ali)

In recent years, negotiation scholars have developed a number of useful insights into the field of negotiation teaching. Many of these insights have direct relevance for negotiation teaching throughout the world, including in Hong Kong. Among these insights have included the importance of taking negotiation training outside of the classroom (see generally Coben, Honeyman, and Press 2010; Cohn and Ebner 2010), the involvement of students in course design (see generally Nelken, McAdoo, and Manwaring 2009) and the need for awareness of issues involving subjectivity, kinship and awareness of cultural ties (see generally LeBaron and Patera 2009; Bernard 2009).

First, in applying insights regarding the importance of taking negotiation learning outside the classroom (Coben, Honeyman, and

Press 2010), in recent years, students in negotiation courses taught both at the graduate and undergraduate levels within a law school in Hong Kong have been encouraged to apply the skills learned during the given course (e.g., identifying common ground, effective information gathering, the use of external standards) to a personal life situation during that same week. Time is allotted at the beginning of the following class to discuss what worked well, what was effective and what was not so effective from the student's perspective. A number of useful insights have been gained through this process and most importantly, this practice has reinforced the notion that negotiation is a skill that can be learned through practice rather than an innate capability.

Second, student involvement in course design (Nelken, McAdoo, and Manwaring 2009) has made a significant contribution to course development. At the mid-point of the course students are invited to share anonymous feedback regarding those aspects of the course they find effective and those aspects where they suggest improvement through a "stop" "start" "continue" feedback sheet. In addition, student groups are invited, at the outset of the course, to share their course expectations. Feedback at the beginning, mid-point and end of class has led to some significant adjustments to course structure, design and content including greater integration of negotiation skill demonstrations and examples. Experience gleaned both from student feedback and course delivery for two and a half years sheds light on what teaching methods work well and which might be adjusted or improved, thus offering suggestions for future development.

Third, insights regarding the need to pay special attention to issues involving subjectivity, kinship and awareness of cultural ties has likewise had direct impact on course teaching. The class composition is generally quite international, with students representing a diverse array of cultural and professional backgrounds, with a significant number of students of Chinese descent.

Connecting selected elements of problem-solving negotiation with ancient Confucian texts provides a sense of context and connection between ancient wisdom and contemporary practice (see generally Lee 2010). Increasingly, the link between our societies' visions of social order and the development of systems of dispute resolution has been made explicit. For example, Lawrence Friedman writes that systems of justice stand closely associated with the ideas, aims, and purposes of society (see generally Friedman 1975). Sun Li Bo adds that "differing thought processes have led to differences in the understanding of the concept of justice and the way to put this ideal into practice" (1996: 58).

In the negotiation course we discuss how in traditional China, justice was seen as the achievement of harmony. According to Sun Li Bo, the concept of justice was "based on morality, from which one . . . brings harmony to a family, and skillfully administers a country" (1996: 58). During the period surrounding the Warring States, Confucius saw the Chinese empire plagued by interstate war, rebellion, intrigue and immorality, and faced with the challenge of providing sustenance to a significantly large population on a very limited percentage of arable land.

Inspired by the great teachings of the past, Confucius sought to contribute to harmony through promulgating principles of virtue and forgiveness (Sun Li Bo 1996: 62). These principles became integrated into China's unique system of dispute prevention and resolution, called *tiaojie*, meaning to "reunite" or "bind together." For centuries, *tiaojie* was used to resolve the majority of all civil disputes in China.

Emphasizing harmony among the collective, for centuries *tiaojie* was the preferred method of dispute resolution, and considered superior to adjudication (Lubman 1967: 1290). Some have considered *tiaojie* to resemble mediation with elements of arbitration. When broken down into its literal meaning, *tiao* meant "to mix or stir" and *jie* meant "solution." Therefore, *tiaojie* denoted a means by which individuals could restore harmony by means of compromise (through the mixing of views) and forgiveness, resulting ultimately in a solution.

In practice, *tiaojie* focused on resolving disputes through a network of local peacemakers charged with assisting disputing parties. These peacemakers intervened in conflict situations and encouraged disputing parties to yield, forgive, or compromise for the sake of harmony – even in the face of "unreasonable disputants":

> If one gets into fights with others, one should look into oneself to find the blame. It is better to be wronged than to wrong others ... Even if the other party is unbearably unreasonable, one should contemplate the fact that the ancient sages had to endure much more. If one remains tolerant and forgiving, one will be able to curb the other party's violence (Akigoro 1993: 604-608).

The following conclusions, from a case study recorded in Shandong province, give a sense of the primacy of harmony in the context of *tiaojie*. In particular, we see how peacemakers worked to encourage parties to "meet half way," "admit their own mistake," and eventually "share the expenses equally" regardless of fault.[1]

First, the invited or self-appointed village leaders come to the involved parties to find out the real issues at stake, and also to collect opinions from other villagers concerning the background of the matter. Then they evaluate the case according to their past experience and propose a solution. In bringing the two parties to accept the proposal, the peacemakers have to go back and forth until the opponents are willing to meet half way. Then a formal party is held either in the village or in the market town, to which are invited the mediators, the village leaders, clan heads, and the heads of the two disputing families. The main feature of the party is a feast. While it is in progress, the talk may concern anything except the conflict ... If the controversy is settled in a form of "negotiated peace," that is both parties admit their mistakes, the expenses will be equally shared ... thus the conflict is resolved (Yang: 1945: 134).

In discussions in class, we examine the differences and similarities between a problem-solving negotiation approach and *tiaojie*. While many students acknowledge the importance of understanding historical approaches to negotiation, most also recognize the vast changes that have taken place in contemporary society. In discussing the concept of culture, our starting point is that genetics and biology confirm that we are all one human species and that recent insights into culture view it as a "relatively fluid and variable between populations" (Karlberg 2004) and not necessarily associated with a particular ethnicity. Therefore, through travel, education and exposure we pick up particular habits and approaches that influence our overall approach to negotiation. Based on the insights arising from both the commonality of human origin and the enriching contribution of diverse cultures, we discuss a number of guidelines for working with culture in the negotiation process, including the importance of a learning orientation, empathy and reflexivity, openness to complexity, and a focus on the individual rather than the culture while adapting flexibly to cultural dimensions. Such discussions provide an opportunity to reflect on underlying assumptions regarding the negotiation process.

Recommendations for the future

In looking toward the future of these courses, it seems that one area of potential development is the further expansion of the course assignment requiring students to engage in experiential learning through the attempt at resolving some real-life existing problems that the students face, either in the workplace or dormitory environment or the community at large. This hands-on applied element of the negotiation course would include multiple environments, cultural contexts and learning styles, and would aim to integrate theoretical learning into practical application. (For examples, see Chamoun et al., *Bringing the Street to the Classroom*, in this volume.)

2) Both Pedagogy and Culture Matter (Kang Rong)

In 2001, I started teaching international business negotiation at Northwest University of China. As with other negotiation skills courses taught at other universities, students welcomed the pedagogy and also found it extremely different from other courses. From 2009-2010, I conducted research on the composition of negotiation cases and their use in teaching as a Fulbright Scholar at the University of Southern California (USC), where I took part in two courses: Negotiation and Deal-making; and Cross-cultural Negotiation. During my research tenure, I had the opportunity to see how my American counterparts teach negotiation. In this section, I focus on three issues: a) the methodology of simulation teaching; b) the impact of culture on cases used; and c) case comparison assignments.

Methodology of simulation teaching

First, I would like to discuss the most popular way to teach negotiation: simulation or role-play.

I first learned about the role-play or simulation- based method of teaching negotiation in 2000 when taking part in a "train the trainers" session at Peking University geared toward teachers from the western part of China (this training was responding to the fact that in the years leading up to 2000, China's MBA programs had become extremely popular, but seriously lacked professional instructors who could teach management courses, especially in western China). Ron Anton, an alumnus from the Kellogg School of Management at Northwestern University, taught a negotiation course in the Beijing International MBA program (BiMBA) offered by the China Economy Research Center. Our group of teachers from western China joined in along with the MBA students. Although the course was only six sessions, it was well organized. It was the first time students had been given differing fact-patterns of the same case and asked to engage in live negotiation. Even the method of pairing students for negotiation was carefully designed so that during the whole session, nobody knew in what way his partner would be chosen. The course was interesting and different, because in all other courses, although case studies are used, students got the exact same material to analyze.

This new way of teaching through simulations seemed to reflect well the characteristics of real-life negotiation (traditional Chinese pedagogy in higher education institutions is characterized by the axiom: "teachers talk, students take notes"). Later through research, I realized that simulations and role-play comprise the most popular way of teaching negotiation in many universities all over the world. I started to experiment with this method in my own classes, while observing what happened throughout the entire process. For students who never used the simulation-based method, and even for those who have used simulations where both parties receive the *exact same* information, I found that simulations where there are multiple, slightly tweaked fact patterns given to the opposing parties present the most interesting way of learning from simulations. It is easy for students to realize and agree that real life is full of instances where information is neither equal nor symmetrical. Due to the fact that asymmetric information reflects real life, students can learn more readily from their own behavior and experience.

In using simulations, I arrived at some findings which interested me greatly, some of which far exceeded my expectations. The effect of simulation teaching depends on how seriously students treat the simulation, or how they feel about the reality of such "games." The more engaged the students are, the more they learn from the experience. Some problems arise from this level of interest, however. For example, some students are always able to "get the jump on" the simulation case, always thinking about how to get to know the other side's information. Sometimes they put the two opposing sets of confidential instructions together, and compare the various hidden points. If I spot this, I always stop them, and tell their partners that letting the other side know their confidential information may result in their losing ground. But it must be admitted that such kinds of people do exist in real life: in real negotiations, these individuals do not follow the routine or even, necessarily, the rules of society, but rather employ more "creative" methods. Thus, to find a student going beyond the scope of the simulation is not always a pure negative.

Another example concerns an auditor in the last class I taught. He was very active at the beginning, but after several weeks when he had chances to negotiate with other partners, he came to me and asked me whether I should put forward the following rule: an agreement must be reached by the end of class, or alternatively, finalized agreements will get a prize, or additional credit in the class. I asked why he made such a suggestion, and he told me that without this rule, some partners continue to push, without worrying about the time issue, because an outcome of "no agreement" does not result in punishment or "failure." Although I do believe it is not a good idea to give students who reach an agreement more credit, I continue to wonder what would be a good way to evaluate students' performance, especially when the class session has limited time (see Ebner, Coben, and Honeyman 2012 for a comprehensive examination of assessment alternatives).

Cultural impact on cases used

The second obvious impression when I teach in China and compare that experience to observing negotiation teaching in the United States is that culture influences many elements in negotiation and negotiation teaching (see, e.g., Bernard 2009; Gold 2009; Kovach 2009; LeBaron and Patera 2009; Bernard 2010; Docherty 2010; Lee 2010). In my experience and in speaking to my colleagues in China and abroad, I find that Chinese students do not ask questions as often as Western students. First of all, they take what teachers say for granted, and even if they have questions, they generally do not ask them openly. I had encountered a very different situation at USC. I attended the negotiation class, sometimes joining in as a negotiator, sometimes as a teacher. One day, when I joined in as a member of a group, which had gotten the assignment the week before, one young woman questioned my presence and asked the professor why there was a change of team members. In China, I have never met such a reaction. No matter how the team is formed, Chinese students generally do not ask "why?" Also, in reviewing the negotiation syllabi of many U.S. universities, one rule is impressive: the professors ask students to report one day earlier if they cannot be present. I do not employ such a rule in my class, so I cannot decide before the class who should negotiate with whom: matching students is done randomly during the actual day of class.

Another issue on culture relates to the cases chosen. From my experience, some cases are great just because they help students understand another way of living and another set of rules of society; but if the difference lies in the roots of the culture, things may become complex. I still remember how in the BiMBA course, among the six cases used, one case, a negotiation between brothers, stood out as very different from the others. In that negotiation, the father died recently, and the question of which brother should live with their mother and other related monetary issues had to be decided, as well as matters related to their father's inheritance. Many Chinese students felt this was difficult, and in the Chinese context, a particularly sensitive topic. Thus, that class ended quickly – because each side gave in very quickly. The traditional family network or relationship is often regarded in China, as elsewhere, as the most important foundation of society. Thus, issues related to the family naturally are seen as quite different from business issues. Many students regarded family issues, such as the negotiation between brothers in the case, as unworthy of negotiation. Giving in quickly was seen as being more appropriate.

During the negotiation competition held at Peking University in May 2011, cases about family members were used. In evaluating the students' performance, my deepest impression was that they were *not* truly representing family members, but rather were using negotiation strategy as they would in the business world. This seemed highly unrealistic and forced. That experience made one question come to the fore: What cases should be used in the classroom? I believe there are several rules of thumb to follow: First, if the training purpose is to help students develop good negotiation habits, simple cases should be used, no matter whether there is cultural shock or not. Second, if the training purpose is on cross-cultural issues, cases written in foreign languages about what happened in other countries should be chosen (with a translation available), because cases originally written in another language may force students to understand more deeply the different language and culture, as the two remain intimately linked. Third, to explain the theory of negotiation, cases composed on the basis of local events are better, because it must be admitted that not only are languages different, many physical items are different. These things are difficult to comprehend, especially for students without much experience living or studying abroad. A well-chosen case may help students understand not only popular negotiation topics, but the underlying conflict structures, and even the cultural roots of the conflict. For understanding theory, cases based in other societies can be referred to as supporting stories, but do not work well as simulation materials.

Case comparison assignment

In terms of teaching method, I would like to mention a teaching process of comparing two negotiations, wherein students are asked to collect data and information about two negotiations, and then compare and write an analysis of the negotiations.

I have found patterns of topic choice a very interesting point of difference between Chinese and American students. For students majoring in international trade and world economy, it would seem natural for them to choose business merger cases to compare. But, in fact, they did not choose business-oriented cases, but rather they chose diplomatic issues, such as border conflicts. This was quite different from what I had seen at USC. The students there chose negotiation cases mainly from the domain of *sports*. I believe this difference exists because when sports negotiations occur in the United States, there is major media coverage of such negotiations. Although I have used the case-comparison analysis only once to date, I believe it is a very good technique. I will continue to use it in the future because it teaches students to think comprehensively. Through comparison, they may identify the structure of conflicts, as well as solutions to the various conflicts, and especially, what could have been done better. This deeper understanding, I hope, will allow them to reach better results in future negotiations of their own.

3) The Impact of Empowering Students to Write Simulations (Alonzo Emery)

From November 2010 to April 2011, I taught two quarter-length negotiation skills courses to Masters degree candidates at Renmin University Law School in Beijing. My reflection focuses on both the challenges faced introducing these skills and the strategies used to overcome obstacles. I conclude by proposing a path for ongoing research and pedagogical tools development.

In weekly journal reflections and anonymous course evaluations, students expressed enthusiasm about negotiation in general and the interactive nature of our courses in particular. The opportunity for students to speak at length in class remains a rarity in an educational system where class size can balloon into the hundreds and where professors traditionally lecture and students sit and listen. Like many universities in China, Renmin University Law School is reforming parts of its educational system by hiring more faculty and developing courses focused on skills and clinical practice to supplement courses teaching rules and regulations.

While students in my skills-based courses seemed to embrace a process of learning centered around simulations and discussions, some students still questioned the courses' content. Students often asked about the applicability of the curriculum to the "real-world" challenges they would face living and working in the People's Republic of China. For example, one student cautioned us to deploy active listening skills – particularly the prong of inquiry – with extreme care when operating within highly hierarchical structures, suggesting that even well-intentioned and carefully phrased questions could seem insulting to an individual unaccustomed to inquiries coming from perceived inferiors. During the unit on creating value, other students suggested that invitations to "expand the pie" seemed artificial and risked destroying hard-won deals if not introduced carefully. In response to both comments I noted that in all of my previous negotiation courses, my fellow classmates or, later, pupils – whose backgrounds ranged from environmental lawyers in China's Hubei Province to community leaders in the Mississippi Delta to students in the Harvard Law School Negotiation Workshop – raised similar questions. Thus, hesitance to embrace some concepts of principled negotiation seems fairly universal. In my courses at Renmin University, I explained to students that we spend class time devoted to practicing value creation and active listening precisely because the deployment of these skills often feels unnatural and needs time to become integrated into practice. Although this answer registered as satisfactory enough to move class forward, I failed to answer directly the tougher, underlying questions regarding cultural specificity and universal applicability, in part because I believe there exists no "cookie-cutter" answer: case-specific context will always exert some influence on how skills are deployed.

In both of my courses at Renmin University, some students commented that the simulations were too far removed from their lives and future practice. During the first class, and throughout the term, I reminded students that I chose simulations carefully in order to encourage students to focus on *skills* rather than the substantive minutiae of the law. Still, students thought that operatic divas (ala *Sally Soprano*)[2] and mythical diseases (ala *DONS*)[3] would not loom large in their future. The foreign nature of the simulations, in terms of content and context, made it difficult for some students to take the exercises seriously.

After engaging students in an environmental-impact simulation during the first term,[4] I attempted to target the issue of applicability by anchoring our debrief discussion in reality. I asked students to think about some contemporary environmental-impact cases from around the world and, particularly, to consider what alternatives to a negotiated agreement seemed plausible in those cases. One student noted that an alternative such as "parading" through the streets remains undesirable or impossible in certain political or cultural contexts. Students suggested that principled negotiation might not prove helpful in situations where the legality or *de facto* operability of certain alternatives remains questionable.

In the end, I attempted to surpass the cognitive roadblock created by our specific social, legal, political and cultural context by assigning students the task of researching *real* China-based negotiations and adapting their fact-patterns into simulations that we could run in class. The results were impressive in so far as students were able to focus the simulations on critical skills while also imbuing the fact patterns with details resonating in China's highly specific cultural and professional climate.[5] As many of my students planned to enroll in the Disability Law Clinic I offered the next term, the simulations they returned with focused primarily on the nexus of disability, education and the law. In our courses, students had already seen simulations that addressed issues of accessibility and inclusive education in the

American context as written by Professor Ruth Colker for her accessibility studies course at Ohio State University's College of Law. In my course, students now presented simulations reflecting their own national reality. Each of their simulations focused on developing a particular skill (active listening in one case, creating value in another, client interviewing in a third), but they all related to a more familiar story about disability in the specific cultural and legal context of China. The enthusiasm for the project encouraged some students to go beyond the call of duty by later adapting their simulations into video recordings of a "bad-take," or "non-skillful," version followed by a "good-take," more skillful, version of the negotiation.

One project in Renmin University's Disability Law Clinic the following semester charged students with developing a one-day negotiation skills training for disabled university students, the parents of disabled children and special and inclusive education teachers from the area. After much debate about whether or not to use a translated version of *Sally Soprano*, students decided to run one of their own simulations to demonstrate the usefulness of value creation. The passion that the training's participants invested in their roles suggested that the students' decision to use their own simulation was appropriate (see Druckman and Ebner 2010).

I think that even if some of the simulations the students authored ultimately prove unsuitable for wider distribution, the practice of researching real-world negotiations and then translating these negotiations into skills-based simulations helped my students embrace a model of learning that relies on simulations. The act of independently identifying the skills used and tensions felt in real negotiations proved more powerful than any story I could have told or newspaper article I could have produced as proof that these types of negotiations actually exist and that the skills we practice might actually work.

Based on my experience teaching negotiation skills in China, it seems that the exercise of researching and writing a reality-based simulation early in a longer negotiation skills course (or as a mid-term assignment, for example) could go a long way toward extinguishing recurring doubt about the applicability of negotiation skills in the real world. As a result, I will continue to work with my colleagues in China to develop an endogenous bank of simulations aimed at honing the same traditional skills of principled negotiation, but in a vernacular and context more familiar to my students. Making these skills culturally specific and relevant remains perhaps the greatest task for negotiation pedagogy as it expands its influence beyond western classrooms. The issue of cultural relativity figures as one of the most intriguing, and yet woefully underexplored, frontiers of negotiation scholarship.

4) *The Impact of Culture on Negotiation Skills Training (Ta-Wei Chao)*

In 2011, I taught a course on negotiation skills over two days to thirty-six MBA students from one of China's most prestigious universities. The students' ages ranged from twenty-five to forty; most students had significant working experience. In total, there were four sessions of three and one half hours each that employed a mix of simulations (translated into Chinese from the simulation banks at Harvard, ESSEC IRENE, and the Kellogg School of Business), debriefing sessions, discussion and lecture. I focused on skills and concepts traditionally used in trainings modeled after the Harvard Program on Negotiation workshop, including the three tensions in negotiation: preparation; value creation; and alternatives and anchoring. However, in the fourth session, I focused on cross-cultural negotiation issues, as most of the students planned to work for multi-national corporations or Chinese companies planning to "go global" and I wanted to target the types of cross-cultural issues they would face in their future practice.

What teaching methods worked well

In the beginning, I was concerned that the students would not talk a lot and could not really engage fully in the role-play, since this kind of pedagogy was new for them and is not aligned with the classical Chinese lecture-oriented teaching style. Instead, students embraced it and performed very well. I did not find that any of them experienced difficulty in engaging in simulation-based learning. (Anecdotally, when I taught in Europe, I occasionally met students who could not accept role-play or did not know how to immerse themselves in the simulations' characters.) During the discussion, my Chinese students also participated enthusiastically and posed many interesting questions.

If we try to explore why this kind of highly interactive and discussion-intensive pedagogy can work so well for Chinese students (when it is not 100 percent aligned with our expectation in the beginning), I would like to offer some possible reasons:

    a) Chinese as the teaching language makes students less nervous, so that they can perform better.

    b) When I led the debriefing session, I tried to contextualize the whole discussion as much as I could. I think this made it easier for students to participate in the discussion since some unfamiliar concepts became more concrete to them. "Contextualize" means that I tried to use Chinese examples or propose real cases in China, and asked them to comment on these examples in order to illustrate the concepts I would like to share with them.

c) We successfully created an atmosphere of open discussion. In many Chinese students' eyes, images of teachers are usually related to "serious," "stiff," "conservative" types, so that students often come to the, perhaps therefore reasonable, assumption that it is better not to discuss things openly with their teachers for who would like to discuss issues with people who *will not* change their minds? Students' assumptions may not be based in reality; but the assumption concerning teachers implies that instructors need to make a concerted effort to change Chinese students' bias against engaging with them, if they would like to create an atmosphere of open discussion. So, I used small interactive games, brain-teasers, jokes and anecdotes about personal experiences to make students understand that I am not a "traditional" Chinese teacher, but rather someone who actually likes to interact with them and is open to sharing or receiving ideas. I believe this allowed them to set their minds at ease and try something new with me.

What teaching methods might be done differently/adjusted

In terms of training content, the ideas on negotiation theory and practice from the Western world are very insightful and are something new for Chinese negotiators. Chinese negotiators can definitely learn a lot from them. Yet Chinese culture is highly context-specific and extremely subtle in its nuances, so that knowing how to read between the lines or say an indirect "no" remain important. Although it may seem like a cliché, the reality is that relationship (guanxi) significantly impacts negotiation results in the Chinese context. Leading Western ideas on negotiation (with the exception of certain writings in the current series; see e.g., Bernard 2009; LeBaron and Patera 2009 in volume 1; Bernard 2010; Docherty 2010, in volume 2) do not seem to take into account sufficiently the above-mentioned factors.

Scholars must discuss these two topics in greater detail, along with the classical issues on negotiation as taught in "version 1.0" of the field, if we are to teach Chinese participants in a way that better reflects the reality of their daily experience.

Recommendations for the future

I would summarize my recommendations for adapting negotiation pedagogy for use in China as follows:

a) Contextualize the discussion and lectures;
b) Put extra effort into thinking about how to create an atmosphere of open discussion;
c) Be sensitive to the issue of language of instruction;
d) Talk more about specific negotiation challenges in Chinese society (e.g., "Guanxiology," the art of reading between lines, etc.).

I believe that by contextualizing the content and delivery of negotiation teachings, Chinese students – and perhaps students everywhere (see generally Lewicki and Schneider 2010) – can more easily embrace what are often universal truths about negotiation, and furthermore, create their own solutions to deal with the culture-specific issues.

5) Class Discussion as a Springboard to Cultural Comparison (David Matz)

In the Spring of 2010, I taught a twenty-eight hour negotiation course to students of the Jilin Law School in Changchun, China. The course was in English; students were screened in advance for their language skills and academic flexibility. Screening was necessary since the course would be "interactive," not the traditional academic experience for Chinese students. Except for a recently launched Juris Master (JM) program offered by many schools and modeled after the American Juris Doctor (JD) program, law school in China generally comes immediately after high school, so the average age of students was twenty years old. Jilin University, in the northeast corner of the country, is home to a top law school in China (one ranking puts it at fifth in the country); national competition for entry to this and similar schools is intense, and starts when the students are very young.

The syllabus and reading list for this course looked much like the one I teach at UMass/Boston in the Graduate Program in Conflict Resolution: readings, discussion, and role-plays built around the Richard Walton and Robert McKersie (1965) theme of competition and collaboration, with the David Lax and James Sebenius (1986) version of the negotiator's dilemma at the heart; this is followed by a session on two ethical issues. Techniques, attitudes, conundrums, and goals are woven throughout, surrounded by occasional insights from social psychology and game theory.

When preparing, I received the standard warning that Chinese students in class do not interact with teachers: they take notes and look at their shoes. I planned the class prepared to work at changing that attitude; it took about five minutes. For the balance of the course their behavior and comments were largely indistinguishable from students in the United States. I used one role-play in which a real estate developer negotiates with a state government. In monitoring their negotiations, I heard much of what I would hear at home. After the debrief I asked, as I did for each role-play, whether anything in the role-play was different or difficult because it was set in the United States. Half the hands in the room went up:

"In China, we don't negotiate with government. We go around it, we use *guanxi* ("networking, pull"), and we use pressure. We don't negotiate."

"But you were negotiating with government in this role-play," I said.

"Sure. That was the assignment and that is what you do in America."

Flexibility was not their problem.

Differences, of course, did arise. Halfway through the course one young man asked for the opportunity to "say something to the class." He delivered an obviously heartfelt and thought-out speech of about ten minutes. He is the son of a high-ranking military father and, as a result, had seen much of China. His experience negotiating with women in the class worried him. About three-quarters of the class was female. He had great respect for "these lovely girls" but expressed his conviction that China is run by men and would continue to be so. He felt that a course like this could give the women in the class the expectation that after they left university, they would be on an equal footing with men. While that might be true at lower levels of government, party, or military, he felt that it would never be true in the middle or higher levels.

As he spoke I focused on the women in the class, expecting an explosion of scorn, derision, or worse. When he finished, there was silence. I asked for reactions. One woman said matter-of-factly that she thought the male speaker was probably wrong, that China is changing, and so would the gender roles. Another said, with apparent calm, that it would have to change because half the students in law schools and medical schools today are female, so they would be needed, if only to fill the leadership positions of the future. And another woman pointed out that she had just negotiated with the male speaker and that there had been no problem at all. No one mentioned justice, fairness, or practice in the West.

I asked if the women spoke amongst themselves about the future of women in leadership, about a glass ceiling, etc. "No. Not really." I asked the male speaker if he had any response to the women's comments, and he said that "they are not taking account of the Chinese way, of Chinese history and Chinese culture. Women-in-power is a Western idea. We will never do that."

I asked the speaker if he himself had any special issue negotiating with women in the class. He said no, but that he had not given it his full energy because "that would not be fair." Making it personal did produce a modest explosion; several women told him, in Chinese while I begged that they translate, that he was just making an excuse for not doing better in the negotiation.

This was not the only occasion when a Chinese student's view clashed sharply with my own. (I also taught a course in human rights; such clashes came up predictably and often.) When this happens in the United States, I do what I did in Jilin: I look for differences among the students to open up value assumptions, the implications for their different lines of thought, and how those differences fit with other things we have discussed. In the United States, when this discussion ends, I will usually offer my view, including which arguments I find persuasive, which I do not, and why. In China I did not take this last step. I expected that they would ask about the role of women in the United States or the West; they did not, and I did not volunteer on this. There is a centuries-old tension in China between a deep loyalty to the Chinese way of doing things, on the one hand, and being open to the ways of the West, on the other. This tension is no less present today. Though we tend to see dramatic demonstrations of openness to learning from Western thought, I found many occasions where even students drew boundaries. My practice was to respect those boundaries, and when the students did not ask me about the role of women in the West and focused instead on what women's changing roles meant for the development of China, I chose not to volunteer anything about this.

Student enthusiasm and participation in the course was widespread. One student, San Tianyu, said toward the end that she wanted to write a book about her experience. (I suggested she start with an essay, which she did. It is presented here as the Appendix.) In the essay she describes how initially she had decided against taking the course, because she imagined a fast-talking American laying out rigid rules. She overcame this expectation because she "was attracted by the selection process: only those who were going to pass the interview were eligible to attend the training. For me, giving up or escaping means cowardice."

San Tianyu's competitive motivation was of course also demonstrated in her work in the role-plays. Near the end of the course I gave them *Pepulator*[6] (a prisoner's dilemma variant). In round eleven, her opposing negotiator made a quite rational-sounding promise to let her side "win" that round in return for the reverse in round twelve, thus maximizing their joint gains. Then he defected. He had lied. His lie became the subject of intense discussion in the debriefing, and in the next role-play, the same person was unable to persuade anyone to trust him, and his negotiation result suffered. "This role-play helped me understand the sentence 'history never goes away.' Even today I am still obsessed with it." Her paper spells out that obsession. The class discussion began with a focus on competitiveness and truth telling, but the students soon took it to questions of the kind of society they wanted for China, where they saw the country headed, and where they thought they could fit in. If their classroom comments reflect their feelings, they are not happy.

China's mercurial history, recent and distant, and rocketing rate of contemporary change leaves students unsettled. Though getting a good job is of course their most common conversation, very close to the surface are the interwoven questions of national and personal identity. Seen from the outside, China is full of energy and optimism, but these students, who seem inevitably to be among the country's leaders in the next generation, were troubled and perplexed. A negotiation course was not a bad framework for students to explore these questions.

Conclusion

In negotiation pedagogy, as elsewhere, context and participation remain key. The introduction of foreign concepts to China has suffered a fraught history due largely to a failure to appreciate the importance of cultural context and the participation of the recipients in the discourse surrounding these concepts. As the historian Jonathan Spence (1980) writes in his landmark book *To Change China: Western Advisers in China*, ideas and individuals from the West have tried to influence Chinese thought from the Ming Dynasty (1368-1644) onward, and yet most of those attempts proved futile, meeting active resistance at worst or selective assimilation at best. The authors here have shown how student participation in all aspects of a course – from course design to discussion topic selection – can help reveal the universality inherent in many of principled negotiation's core concepts. Specifically, looking to Chinese historical and philosophical sources to underpin theoretical teachings highlights this universality and therefore demonstrates how these concepts are not necessarily "foreign." Also essential to fostering engagement is centering discussions on contextually relevant case studies that resonate with students. The academic institutions described here, and others across China, should coordinate to establish a bank of Chinese-language (or multilingual) simulations that can be shared freely across schools – an endeavor not yet undertaken in a systematic way. To ensure a future for negotiation studies in the PRC, students and the professoriate in China should continue to engage in discussions they find relevant, design curricula and simulations reflecting their reality, and add further to the discourse on negotiation through academic research and writing translated to reach a broader audience. In so doing, Chinese students and scholars can continue to explore issues related to negotiation while their counterparts from around the world can learn from them in this specific academic domain.

Notes

[1] During this time, the concept of "gain" was understood as the happiness of the majority (Lieberthal 1995: 16).

[2] Authored by Wayne Davis, Mark N. Gordon, and Bruce Patton, *Sally Soprano Part I* is a simulation focused on negotiating the employment terms of an operatic diva. Available from the Harvard Law School Program on Negotiation at http://www.pon.harvard.edu/shop/sally-soprano-i/ (last accessed June 15, 2012).

[3] Authored by Robert Bordone and Jonathan Cohen (adapted from *PONS Negotiation* by Nevan Elam and Whitney Fox), *DONS* is a simulation negotiating potential damages for willful infection of a disease. Available from the Harvard Law School Program on Negotiation at http://www.pon.harvard.edu/shop/dons-negotiation/ (last accessed June 15, 2012).

[4] Authored by Denise Madigan, Thomas Weeks, and Lawrence Susskind, *Harborco* is a multi-party, multi-issue scoreable negotiation over a proposal to build a new deep-water port. Available from the Harvard Law School Program on Negotiation at http://www.pon.harvard.edu/shop/harborco/ (last accessed June 15, 2012).

[5] In a chapter in volume two of this teaching series, Daniel Druckman and Noam Ebner (2010) also noted that students who designed simulations learned more than students who simply participated in them. Druckman and Ebner conclude that class role-play exercises should therefore be supplemented by simulation design exercises.

[6] Authored by Mark Drooks and Mark Gordon, *Pepulator* is a scoreable, multiple round negotiation between companies over the monthly price of a product. Available from the Harvard Law School Program on Negotiation at http://www.pon.harvard.edu/shop/pepulator-pricing-exercise/ (last accessed June 15, 2012).

References

Akigoro, T. 1993. Sofuku no kenkyu. In *Chinese civilization: A sourcebook*, edited by P. Ebrey. New York: The Free Press.

Bernard, P. 2009. Finding common ground in the soil of culture. In *Rethinking negotiation teaching: Innovations for context and culture*, edited by C. Honeyman, J. Coben, and G. De Palo. St. Paul, MN: DRI Press.

Bernard, P. 2010. Re-orienting the trainer to navigate – not negotiate – Islamic cultural values. In *Venturing beyond the classroom: Volume 2 in the rethinking negotiation teaching series*, edited by C. Honeyman, J. Coben, and G. De Palo. St. Paul, MN: DRI Press.

Coben, J., C. Honeyman, and S. Press. 2010. Straight off the deep end in adventure learning. In *Venturing beyond the classroom: Volume 2 in the rethinking negotiation teaching series*, edited by C. Honeyman, J. Coben, and G. De Palo. St. Paul, MN: DRI Press.

Cohn, L. and N. Ebner 2010. Bringing negotiation teaching to life: From the classroom to the campus to the community. In *Venturing beyond the classroom: Volume 2 in the rethinking negotiation teaching series*, edited by C. Honeyman, J. Coben, and G. De Palo. St. Paul, MN: DRI Press.

Docherty, J. S. 2010. "Adaptive" negotiation: Practice and teaching. In *Venturing beyond the classroom: Volume 2 in the rethinking negotiation teaching series*, edited by C. Honeyman, J. Coben, and G. De Palo. St. Paul, MN: DRI Press.

Druckman, D. and N. Ebner. 2010. Enhancing concept learning: The simulation design experience. In *Venturing beyond the classroom: Volume 2 in the rethinking negotiation teaching series*, edited by C. Honeyman, J. Coben, and G. De Palo. St. Paul, MN: DRI Press.

Ebner, N., J. Coben and C. Honeyman (eds). 2012. *Assessing our students, assessing ourselves: Volume 3 in the rethinking negotiation teaching series.* St. Paul, MN: DRI Press.

Friedman, L. M. 1975. *The legal system: A social science perspective.* New York: Russell Sage Foundation.

Gold, J. 2009. Cultural baggage when you "win as much as you can." In *Rethinking negotiation teaching: Innovations for context and culture*, edited by C. Honeyman, J. Coben, and G. De Palo. St. Paul, MN: DRI Press.

Karlberg, M. 2004. *Beyond the culture of contest.* Oxford, UK: George Ronald Publisher.

Kovach, K. K. 2009. Culture, cognition and learning preferences. In *Rethinking negotiation teaching: Innovations for context and culture*, edited by C. Honeyman, J. Coben, and G. De Palo. St. Paul, MN: DRI Press.

Lax, D. A. and J. K. Sebenius. 1986. *The manager as negotiator.* New York: Free Press.

LeBaron, M. and M. Patera. 2009. Reflective practice in the new millennium. In *Rethinking negotiation teaching: Innovations for context and culture*, edited by C. Honeyman, J. Coben, and G. De Palo. St. Paul, MN: DRI Press.

Lee, A. W. 2010. Ancient wisdom for the modern negotiator: What Chinese characters have to offer negotiation pedagogy. In *Venturing beyond the classroom: Volume 2 in the rethinking negotiation teaching series*, edited by C. Honeyman, J. Coben, and G. De Palo. St. Paul, MN: DRI Press.

Lewicki, R. J. and A. K. Schneider. 2010. Instructors heed the who: Designing negotiation training with the learner in mind. In *Venturing beyond the classroom: Volume 2 in the rethinking negotiation teaching series*, edited by C. Honeyman, J. Coben, and G. De Palo. St. Paul, MN: DRI Press.

Lubman, S. 1967. Mao and mediation: Politics and dispute resolution in communist China. *California Law Review* 55(5): 1284-1359.

Lieberthal, K. 1995. *Governing China.* New York: W. W. Norton.

Nelken, M., B. McAdoo, and M. Manwaring. 2009. Negotiating learning environments. In *Rethinking negotiation teaching: Innovations for context and culture*, edited by C. Honeyman, J. Coben, and G. De Palo. St. Paul, MN: DRI Press.

Spence, J. D. 1980. *To change China: Western advisers in China*. New York: Penguin Books.

Sun Li Bo. 1996. Morality, law and religion: A comparison of three concepts of justice. In *Towards the most great justice*, edited by C. O. Lerche. Wilmette, IL: The Bahá'í Publishing Trust.

Walton, R. E. and R. B. McKersie. 1965. *A behavioral theory of labor negotiations: An analysis of a social interaction system*. New York: McGrawHill.

Yang, M. 1945. *A Chinese village: Taitou, Shantung Province*. New York: Columbia University Press.

Appendix

Real Feeling in a Role- Play

*San Tianyu**

June 21-30 in the year 2010 were the best ten days that I have ever had.

On June 6, while I was attending my sister's wedding, I received a message from a classmate: our law school (Jilin Faculty of Law) was going to organize a negotiation course, to be given by an American professor (David Matz from the University of Massachusetts/Boston). An interview was required for selecting students to attend the training.

Since students were required to attend the class seven days, full time, and were not allowed to be absent, my first reaction was not to attend to avoid the rigid schedule. However, I was attracted by the "interview selection": only those who were going to pass the interview were eligible to attend the training. For me, giving up or escaping would mean cowardice. So I registered immediately. Half a month later, I was proud of my slight desire for competition, although it looked a little naïve.

Before I attended the course, when I thought of "negotiation skills" two scenarios came to mind: in one, the party with the most power won; in the other a weaker party, through eloquence, quick thinking, or some ability to detect the other's weakness turned the tables. He would be like a leading actor in a movie who saved the heroine in a dangerous situation, and won the applause afterwards. The winner seemed to be endowed with talents I would be unable to duplicate. Such an endowment could not be taught to ordinary people, just as it was impossible to teach a student how to write an inspiring poem.

I also worried about how to deal with the opposite party's lies. Should we expose his lies or make up our own to respond? Should we treat the opposite party sincerely in an effort to build up mutual trust, or should we deal with him cautiously, as if we were playing chess? How could we tell his real needs from his lies? How should we view the relations with the opposite party? Should we keep fighting until the opposite party was squished like a bug on a windshield, or should we save his face while getting what we want?

As it turned out, if the class had focused only on theories, I wouldn't have regarded it as the best class I have ever had. It was the role-plays which were held almost every day that were really unforgettable. One striking thing about the role-plays was that nobody regarded them as a game. All of us were devoted to our roles. Those who failed to reach agreement frowned and complained that their opposite party was asking for too much. One student who needed to receive $700,000 for his result, opened by asking for $3,000,000. When, in the debriefing, we laughed at him for his greed, David said "every-

---

* Editors' note: The author and her "opponent" are now "life partners" living in Shanghai. This essay is edited down from the original. Translation assistance came from Kun-Xu.

thing in the role play is fake: materials, roles, money and consequences. You won't get one more cent in your pocket. But one thing is real, and that will follow you after this course. Do you know what that is?" We answered: time, knowledge, connections. Then David asked us to consider reputation. Our real characteristics were reflected in our role-playing, and the reputation we developed would last a long time.

What David said was soon confirmed. During the second half of the training, after we had already learned a lot about negotiating skills, a role-play featuring a commercial war between two companies was presented. Even today, I am still obsessed with it.

Though the instructions were simple, the game was complex. Two companies made the same product, and made money according to the amount they charged for that product each month. The goal of each side was simple: make the most money you can make. They could sell their goods at 10 yuan, 20 yuan or 30 yuan. If their quoted prices each month were the same, they would share the market evenly. If one side's price was higher than the other side's, the company that set the higher price would lose market share, while the other, with its lower price, would win a larger market share. And if both companies set the lowest price (i.e., 10), each would receive only a minimal profit. A result of 30-30 would mean that each company made the same profit *and* did well. But if one priced at 30 and the other at less (10 or 20) the one with less would make the most that could be made in one round by one company, and the one with 30 would do poorly. Thus each company was reluctant to take the risk of charging 30 in any one round. There were eight rounds and profits were reported for each round.

During the first round, neither company trusted the other but neither were we too unfriendly. So my team set the price of 20 yuan. We were excited and eager to learn the price from the opposite party. When the professor's assistant wrote down the prices on the black board, we felt ashamed when we saw that our opponents offered a very friendly price of 30. So we planned to offer 30 as well during the second round. Thus the role-play started smoothly. I naively believed that both sides would report 30-30 for the following rounds, trust each other, and share the market evenly.

At the fourth round, David added a new regulation: each side would choose a representative to negotiate with the other side. Moreover, the profit during this round would be doubled. After negotiating we reached an agreement that we would both report 30-30 for the fourth, sixth, seventh, and eighth rounds, and during the fifth round we would let them offer 20 and we would report 30 to give them a chance to offset their loss during the first round. We were very afraid that the doubled profit would make them become very profit-driven, but we still chose to trust them. When I saw the result 30-30 during the fourth round, we were very happy and started to absolutely trust them.

But in the sixth round, the other side did not keep to its commitment, and the prices were again 20-30. David then announced that another negotiation was allowed before the seventh round, and profit was fourfold. Although, again, we reached a negotiated agreement of 30-30, our trust in the other team's willingness to keep its word had collapsed as a result of their behavior in the sixth round (20-30). As a consequence, the prices during the seventh (and eighth) rounds were 10-10. These, of course, were lose-lose results.

At the end of the eighth round, the teams came back to the classroom. We looked at our opponent with anger. David said: "It is difficult to build up trust, but easy to destroy it. A single number can convey a good-will gesture, or greed." He taught us the value of forgiveness in building trust, and how to convey friendly information in order to enhance mutual trust. Yet, after telling us how to reach a win-win result, he said "History never goes away". And then he asked, with what we had learned so far, to do another four rounds.

We and our opponents collaborated during rounds nine and ten with 30-20 and 20-30. Then new regulations were again added. Profit quintupled for the last two rounds, *unless* both sides reported the same price in the same round. Only when each side set a different price in each round would the party reporting the lower price receive the fivefold profit. Negotiation before the eleventh round was allowed.

The results of that negotiation were encouraging. The opposite team swore to keep to their commitment, promising that during the eleventh round, they were going to offer 30 and let us offer 20 so that we could earn the profit first. And in the twelfth round we would reverse the offers. I imbued my teammates with the "be forgiving" approach, and we chose to trust the opposite party again. The opposite party, however, embraced the approach of "history never goes away". They believed that we would not forgive their history of going against a negotiated agreement early in the role-play, and thus we would seek revenge in the twelfth round. With that assumption, they took a preemptive step by setting the price of 10 against our price of 20 during the eleventh round.

When I saw the number "10" on the bulletin board, my heart almost stopped working. I couldn't believe there were people who lied again and again. The result, of course, was 10-10 in the twelfth round, and nobody won the fivefold profit.

The game was over. We were back in the classroom again. Our teammates rushed to the opponents and questioned them. Sitting alone, I was too sad to look at them. Was it ridiculous? Apparently, everything was fake. It was a mock commercial war. It was just a game. The so-called "perfidy" was part of the game and the game rules allowed such perfidy. But my heart was broken. I didn't want to speak a word. Looking back, I had encouraged my teammates to make our company grow fast by treating our partners sincerely. But two bad moves made our scores drop steeply. Among the four teams playing (in two parallel games), my team, known now for being "naïve and sincere," ranked last. Thus the opponent beat us, though they did not make the most money they could.

In the debriefing, David raised a puzzling question. One set of teams used the hallway to make decisions, while the other group stayed in the classroom. As it was the height of summer and sweltering, the front and back doors of the classroom had been kept open during the first eight rounds to increase air circulation. During the last four rounds, however, someone was continually closing (and David was continually re-opening) the two doors. When David asked "who closed the doors?" nobody answered. The classroom suddenly became quiet, as if a pair of intangible and cold hands froze the moment. During the role-play, there had been more and more mistrust, so various students, fearing suddenly that their deliberations could be overheard, had shut the opened doors again and again. We were all devoted to the game and had unconsciously kept away from our close friends and classmates. A pretend commercial war had built up a wall between two teams that until then had had no ill feeling toward each other.

I then began to realize that what I experienced was not only the implementation of a negotiation theory, but a real society where you needed to have survival skills. Being sincere was not enough for self-defense. It was a society in which no chance was given to you to peacefully co-exist with others.

I was shocked that morning. Something I had believed for a long time was questioned. I took our scores down from the bulletin board and kept them. Every time I looked at the numbers, I felt as if I was looking at my scar. In my eyes, the numbers looked like little guys: Our little guys were naïve and simple; their little guys were shrewd. I couldn't even find an appropriate word to denounce them. And yet, in spite of all this disappointment about the result, I still viewed the morning as the "best morning ever." And then, on the last day of the course, even the feeling of being hurt was cured.

The role-play of the last day dealt with sharing snow-plowing expenses. Each negotiating team had five people. They came from different backgrounds and the size of their houses varied. Before an upcoming snowstorm, they negotiated the share of the expense to support the snow-plowing fund. Each person had a budget limit and all wanted to contribute as little as possible. The negotiation was supposed to be tough but in fact went smoothly. All of us were devoted to our roles, and agreement was eventually reached. When the results were disclosed, we found that all five of us had contributed his/her maximum budget. We shook hands afterwards as if it were a real case. I was very happy and thought the other (parallel) negotiations had reached the same result. But one of them turned out very differently. One team consisted of my former teammates plus their former opponent who had failed to keep his promise during the commercial war. This time he played the role of the poor single mother, and even when he claimed that he had already given his maximum budget, nobody trusted him. He was finally forced to contribute more than his budget limit and ended up with additional obligations helping neighbors with housework, taking care of children, and taking dogs for a walk. People made fun of him and his result during a group discussion. We finally got back at him.

This set of role-plays gave me a better understanding about the sentence "history never goes away." And, finally, at the end of the training, I regained my faith. I believed that kindness, sincerity and mutual help were necessary and powerful; they could not only help us realize our own negotiating goals, but they also might keep us happy.

୧୫ 8 ୫ଏ

Muntu Meets Mencius:
Can Ancient Principles Guide Modern
Negotiations on the Export of Africa's Natural
Resources to China?

Phyllis E. Bernard
*Commentary by Stephanie J. Mitchell**

Editors' Note: Discussions of negotiating relationships across cultures tend to start with the assumption that one of the cultures will be American, or at least European. In this chapter, Bernard and then Mitchell start with a completely different environment: the rapidly expanding relationships, commercial and otherwise, between China and sub-Saharan Africa. They find much of the negotiating pattern, unfortunately, to be anything but sensitive to the real cultural and economic needs, particularly of Africa. Bernard's text proposes, and Mitchell's commentary assesses, a possible shift based on teaching negotiators in key settings some shared cultural elements, represented by similar proverbs in Chinese culture and a wide variety of African cultures. The authors also discuss some differences that may be an enduring source of trouble.

* **Phyllis E. Bernard** is a professor of law and director of the Center on Alternative Dispute Resolution at the Oklahoma City University School of Law. Bernard is an honorary member of FIDA, Rivers State, Nigeria, and has been welcomed as a Daughter of the Soil in Nigeria's Delta Region. Her email address is phyllis@phyllisbernard.com. **Stephanie J. Mitchell** is deputy head of the Entrepreneurship Unit, European Commission Directorate General of Enterprise & Industry. A former associate professor of law at Oklahoma City University School of Law, her private and public sector experience has included opening the Beijing office of an American law firm, and extensive negotiating experience in Asia, Europe and North America. She lived and worked for ten years in greater China, and speaks Mandarin. Mitchell's commentary reflects her personal experience and views and should not be taken as representing the views of the European Commission. Her email address is stephanie.mitchell@telenet.be.

"Those who sacrifice their conscience to ambition
burn a painting to obtain ashes." – Chinese Proverb

"Who digs the well should not be refused water." –
Swahii Swahili(Kenya) Proverb

Introduction

Beyond Game Theory to Geopolitical Reality and the Morality of Alternative Dispute Resolution Training Models

Once upon a time, the West saw China as a sleeping dragon. The dragon has now awakened, with a voracious appetite for the raw materials needed to build the world's leading economy. The modern People's Republic of China consumes vast and ever-increasing quantities of oil, timber, minerals, ore – even arable land to grow food for China. The nations of Black Africa, generally south of the Sahara Desert (known as Sub-Saharan Africa or "SSA") possess in abundance the natural resources China requires. China is, in fact, now Africa's largest trading partner.

Trade agreements between China and SSA nations have been in place for many years. But SSA nations are beginning to ask whether they should sell; and if so, on what terms? As many reputable observers from SSA frame the problem: "China is undermining the lessons" African nations have learned about "the importance of transparency, social justice and environmental sustainability" (Lemos and Ribiero 2007: 64). Extraction contracts all too frequently shore up African governments and elites with funds used not to improve the lives of the populace generally, but rather to "avoid local and international pressure to clean up corruption" (Ibid).

More pointedly: At the 2009 conference of the African Union's New Partnership for Africa's Development ("NEPAD") China signed an agreement to abide by the environmental laws of SSA nations where they operate. Are these principles migrating from the public signing ceremony into private negotiations? Or do they remain inchoate? If so, how can we bring them from theory into practice?

Challenging as they may seem, these issues are only the ones more easily tracked and catalogued by scholars and the media. What is rarely given due attention is the less visible but even more important dynamic: that to the indigenous people who live in and around the subject land, the extraction process itself is an abomination, in the harshest theological and social sense of the word.

To understand how this deeply held belief can impact a negotiation's success, consider the following, which a translation will not or cannot adequately convey. The earth of Africa is sacred; so much so that when the oil-producing region of Nigeria is poisoned by that oil, the languages of the indigenous people make a direct connection between harm to the land and harm to the soul of the people. Among the Ogoni ethnic group, one word for "land" is *ogoni*. Among the Igbo (the tribe of my family heritage), one word for "land" – *ala* – is the same as for the Divine Feminine, the embodiment of God as mother to the tribe, the source of all sustenance.

Under most first generation negotiation models, the issues identified above might be "off the table." Western-oriented negotiation models rarely pursue law, ethics, identity and surely not the metaphysical. The standard commercial negotiation's prime directive has been to reach an agreement at least minimally acceptable to the parties inside the room, on whatever terms. What happened outside the closed doors did not concern the negotiators.

For second generation negotiators, the scope is broader, the questions are deeper. The approach, therefore, is substantially different. This chapter describes a more Afro-centric and Sino-centric approach that holds promise for creating arrangements with "embedded sustainability" – derived from awareness of cultural dynamics now often shunted to the sidelines. This approach changes the role of the negotiator, requiring reconsideration of the philosophy, methods and morality of standard commercial negotiations and negotiation training.

Lifting the "Curse" from Africa's Resource Wealth

Among some sectors of SSA, current distrust of natural resource contracts carries a residue of negative associations from an earlier era when the International Monetary Fund ("IMF") funded vast infrastructure projects with often dubious outcomes. True or not, the common perception was that foreign investments propped up abusive rulers in the 1990s, such as Kenya's Daniel Arap Moi. The press bluntly encapsulated this bitterness in a headline: "Welcome to Kenya, the IMF's little colony" (Smith 2008: 35).

This chapter offers second generation negotiators approaches that may facilitate the formation of resource contracts aligned with the pragmatic idealism of the current "African renaissance." This approach acknowledges traditions that undergird SSA societies, while not becoming mired in superstition that has held back progress. At the same time, this approach does not enshrine Western models as the ultimate sign of modernity. Just as Africa's energetic emerging professional and middle class – known as the "Cheetahs" – has found a balance that embraces African tradition along with Western knowledge, this chapter proposes a way to negotiate that incorporates principles from both worlds.

For successful implementation, the African Cheetahs must find Chinese counterparts. I have written this chapter with an eye to such individuals who might come from the People's Republic of China itself. However, better prospects might be found among the expanding network of Chinese and ethnic Chinese already living in Africa, particularly those engaged in cultural outreach to neighboring African communities. The Confucius Institute in Kigali, Rwanda offers an example (though note Stephanie's reservations below concerning some other Confucius Institutes).

With appropriate support and training, second generation negotiators might understand that below the surface level, stakeholders may harbor concerns that cannot be monetized or lightly bargained away. Concerns of communities impacted by the mining, logging, or drilling of resources are shaped by norms that highly value interrelationships, mutual support, and a sacred connection with the land. When extractive industries shred the social fabric of communities, anxieties can emerge as fears of witchcraft, and/or as political violence aimed at competing communities, resident Chinese, foreign businesses, or government leaders seen as supporting the degradation of land and of people.

Why do feelings of frustration or anxiety among SSA villagers matter when negotiating a contract of resource extraction? Because as Joseph Folger and Robert Baruch Bush have explained: "there are facts in the feelings" (1996: 271). Among some Kenyans feelings that the IMF enabled Moi's harsh regime became fact. That "fact" became articulated as a "widespread view that the World Bank and the IMF were false fronts for the transnational corporation known as the Satanic Church . . . dedicated to undermining national economies" (Smith 2008: 35).

In the past decade, the World Bank has made great strides toward changing such passionately negative perceptions. The International Finance Corporation's ("IFC") Office of the Compliance Advisor ("CAO") for a decade has provided mediation and ombudsman services to reduce and resolve societal stress engendered by oil, gas, mining and agribusiness. Both CAO and the World Bank's Extractive Industries Transparency Initiative ("EITI") promote a "participative multistakeholder approach" where local communities and extractive industries "are actively involved in governing the process" (Caspary and Seiler 2011: 2).[1]

The next stage in the evolution of extractive resource contracts must bring stakeholder input at the earliest stages of negotiation, not after contracts have largely been completed and implemented. Furthermore, the processes for dialogue need to adopt paradigms that connect to the cultures of the indigenous peoples who bear the great-est burden of Africa's "resource curse."

This chapter presents an approach to negotiation that is struc-tured around themes drawn from ancient traditions of African and Chinese cultures. These themes have the capacity to transcend re-sistance to Western-oriented legal codes and governance standards – while still honoring the underlying purposes of those laws and stan-dards. The time is right for such changes, because initial enthusiasm that Sino-SSA partnerships could develop a distinctive non-Western modern future has, in many places, yielded to caution. In particu-lar, civil societies that have sacrificed much to bring democracy and human rights to SSA voice concerns that deals struck behind closed doors bring gains only to African elites, while "the African poor may suffer as a result of job losses, greater corruption, and political repres-sion" (Obiorah, Kew, and Tanko 2008: 292).

The record of "wins" and "losses" is not linear; it varies up and down, among nations and sub-regions within nations. One constant remains, however: not only are conditions for resource extraction vi-tal for the internal politics and social stability of SSA nations; but un-rest threatens maritime transport of energy and raw materials in both East and West Africa (Huang 2008: 308). Perceived repression can breed armed resistance, resulting in asymmetrical guerrilla warfare, riots, work stoppages, and coups d'etat.

Indeed, the overarching framework for these negotiations may bear closer resemblance to "conceptual planning" by the military than to standard commercial deal-making. (See Lira and Parish, *Making it up as You Go*; Docherty and Lira, *Adapting to the Adaptive*, in this vol-ume.) These negotiations require constantly evolving awareness of socio-political factors. In SSA, negotiations for extractive industries have historically been forged in the presence of the ultimate lever-age in bargaining: armed force, situated in the foreground or back-ground. Such life and death power exists not only in national and local police who use the criminal justice system to stifle opposing voices, but also in formal military and informal militia; private "secu-rity" forces; child soldiers, both "active duty" and "veterans still ad-dicted to the Kalashnikov lifestyle" (Meredith 2011: 358); organized street gangs; broad, relatively spontaneous communal violence; and targeted attacks (typically machete or arson) summoned for political ends (Meredith 2009: 580-585). Add to this negotiation context a per-sistent pattern of assaults, kidnappings, arson and murders targeted against foreign companies and their personnel. Lately, kidnappings have "gone local" in the Niger Delta, killing African employees of

African banks, and attacking and holding hostage innocent children and elders of elected African officials (Najibo and Nwiline 2009: 86-89).

For negotiators of resource extraction agreements, the stakes for the stakeholders could not be higher.

"*Muntu*" and "Mencius" as Symbolic Language

I have, perhaps brashly, synthesized the ancient and diverse civilizations of SSA and China, by using the titles "*Muntu*" and "Mencius" as icons, or symbols of much larger philosophical concepts. I apologize to these great traditions for encapsulating their grandeur this way. The terms serve as markers for rivers of learning and living that stretch back millennia; they are gathered together here only in summary form, and as conceptual tools.

In the West, the term *muntu* may largely be familiar only to scholars of primal religions, African philosophy, culture and social anthropology. The Kenyan theologian John S. Mbiti has produced the most in-depth exegesis on the hierarchy of traditional African cosmology and its ordering of heaven and earth, life and the afterlife. His complex deconstruction of *muntu* could be simplified as: "The principle of cosmic unity . . . . a holistic conception of life . . . [which] entails a connection between God, ancestors, animals, plants and inanimate objects, and everything that is created" (Mbiti 1991: 38).

Because *muntu* is pre-eminent it is always a factor – especially regarding the removal and harvesting of Africa's natural resources; directing the energies of Africa's people; and all acts that destroy or disrupt the ecological balance. Commercial negotiators may not be accustomed to thinking of their work within a context of sacredness; but the results of their work can indeed be perceived as sacrilege.

Need multinational corporations be concerned with such matters? Insofar as blindness to these issues affects levels of productivity, stability in the supply chain and long-term profits – yes, it matters, even in the most restrictive interpretation of a multinational corporation's role in the world.

Consider the fundamental misalignment between the traditional African understanding of work and the standard view under Western capitalism. Because:

1) All being is an expression of *muntu*; and
2) The individual exists as a part of the energy of their family and community; and
3) The value of one's life is measured by the generosity and quality of energy – life force – shared with one's family and community; then

4) Work has value as an expression of community solidarity; not merely as a way for an individual to make money.

Before I dig deeper into this bedrock concept, exploring how it might shift the entire conceptualization of resource extraction projects, let me offer one way this understanding of *muntu* can be incorporated into negotiations. Traditionally, work provides occasions to strengthen the bonds of family and friendship. Thus, labor was imbued with a rich heritage of songs for mutual support. At lunch, workers rested with their family members, eating home-cooked food. These practices did not decrease productivity, but rather increased it; for the social context conferred dignity on the back-breaking labor. Reviving some of these traditional ways of working may also return a sense of personhood. When that has been stripped away, when humans become – in commonly used terminology – "animals," humanity will resist and find expression through violence within the workplace (e.g., the Konkola copper mine riots – see, e.g., Reuters 2009) or increased assaults against individual Chinese (a rising tide in cities in South Africa and Zambia).

This is, obviously, a very non-Western perspective; but one worth acknowledging, at least among multinational corporations seeking access to the natural wealth of Sub-Saharan Africa.

Refining Terminology: Why *Muntu*?

Southern African ethicists have often argued for the use of *ubuntu* when discussing emerging norms for corporate social responsibility, particularly in reference to Africa. *Ubuntu* can be seen as a more readily accessible interpretation of the higher concept *muntu*. In some contexts, *ubuntu* translates the ineffable, transcendent *muntu* into understandable social norms that reinforce the bonds of the life force among community members.

I have chosen to use the more expansive term *muntu* to skirt some of the politically charged connotations that emerged when *ubuntu* was cited as a key rationale for the South African Truth and Reconciliation Commission (TRC). While the TRC is highly regarded by most Westerners, it is not without controversy within South Africa. The troubling question was whether the communal values of *ubuntu* – reconciliation – were placed above the need for truth (Richardson 2008).

Similar preferences underlay the decision not to employ the term *harambee*, meaning "coming together" or "togetherness." In many places – both in Africa (particularly Tanzania) and in America during the Black Power era – *harambee* entered the dialectic of socialist revolution, nationalization of foreign investments and redistribution of wealth. Whether accurate or not, again, the connotations may lead in directions not intended for this particular analysis.

By invoking *muntu*, I seek to rise above heavily laden political discourse that already has a momentum and political dialectic all its own. Yes, *muntu* has many nuanced, subtle translations. Nevertheless, it remains a fairly consistent and widely shared worldview among black Africans both on the continent and in the diaspora. Concepts that transcend temporal politics may have greater likelihood of connecting with other cultures, especially if, as in China, there is a similar sense of transcendent life force, which finds expression in duties to the family and community.[2]

Mencius as Symbol of Syncretic Chinese Philosophy

The reasons just stated might seem somewhat out of step with the choice of "Mencius" as an icon to represent a traditional Chinese worldview. Remembering that the objective is to find shared principles and common ground, I do not purport to seek nor achieve parity in positions. Instead, I look for underlying interests where Sino-SSA negotiators may find overlapping principles on which they can build greater trust and more durable business arrangements. In this approach, I ask the reader to look beyond Master Mencius, the philosopher and sage, and a successor to Confucius (Kongzi). I refer to Mencius as the symbol of a syncretic Neo-Confucian tradition which assimilated aspects of Buddhism and Taoism, and which continues to adapt to "changing circumstances and times."

As with *muntu* in SSA, the age-old customs deriving from the teachings of Mencius may have much greater power among contemporary Chinese folk culture, usually in rural areas; much less among the sophisticates of Shanghai or Beijing. But where these folk traditions retain deep roots, they serve many functions analogous to the vitality of SSA folk customs: the weakness of civil society and governmental structures make reliance upon the extended network of family a necessity. Those bonds are reinforced by reference to ancient – not modern – beliefs.

As General Sun Yat-Sen described the spiritual rationale for the 1911 Chinese Revolution: "Our three *min* principles [nationalization, citizen rights and the welfare of human beings] originate from Mencius . . . Mencius is really the ancestor of our democratic ideas" (Jacques 2009: 219). The concept of the Mandate of Heaven provided that if the emperor failed to rule the nation in a "virtuous and benign way" according to the ethical guidelines for conduct, the people had the right to rebel. This philosophy of mutual duties, with some reciprocity, permeated the concept of traditional Chinese hierarchy in its ideal form. Prosperity depended upon mutuality, support of and for the community, and most of all – upon the family.

The parallels to SSA social construction and cosmology offer a substantial base to build precepts of corporate social responsibility deriving from principles that pre-date modern Western civilization.

In the contemporary revival of Neo-Confucianism as a model for global business ethics, one may find more references to Mencius than to the founder of Confucianism. This movement plays a role in China's ever-increasing "soft power" "charm offensive" (Kurlantzick 2007). Traditional Confucianism long ago ossified into social principles that left little room for modern sensibilities of mutuality, equality, fairness or compassion. The writings of Mencius, on the other hand, do; for Mencius significantly loosens the tight restraints of Confucian norms that seemed often to conflate harmony and honor, even when they might be at odds with each other.

Nevertheless, the idea of Confucianism – particularly its latter modifications following the softening, humanizing interpretations and additions by Mencius – evolved into conventions that bound together the diverse peoples and distant provinces of China. The *spirit* behind the customs – an ineffable sense of how the cosmos fits together and man's role in that energetic order – surpassed the *letter* that codified the custom. It is that spirit which communicates through the modern Confucius Institutes (at least sometimes, when they are at their best); which influences Westerners sometimes to view China with more optimism than some Chinese; and which overlaps just enough with traditional African worldviews to make viable the negotiation approach I propose.

Rhetorical Style, in This Writing and in the Negotiation Approach

This chapter does not purport to have all the answers. I seek merely to add threads to on-going, difficult conversations. Some of those conversations utilize the insightful rhetoric of proverbs, quotations and a storytelling approach widely known and used in Africa and China. Examples of this communication style are woven throughout the discussion that follows, partly as scholarly reference points and partly as examples of pedagogy that can be used in second generation training. Since 2000, I have used indigenous proverbs, parables, riddles and stories as primary teaching methods in alternative dispute resolution (ADR) training workshops in Africa. The effectiveness of this approach is that it brings into modern contexts aspects of the oral traditions that are a source of pride in SSA cultures. Moreover, this rhetoric serves vital purposes in business discourse, as demonstrated in the section that follows.

Why should Western-oriented business people and negotiators care about proverbs? Because some degree of ambiguity is often necessary in order to reach agreement; yet, at the same time, there must be enough clarity that all involved understand that there has been the necessary "meeting of the minds" (Honeyman 2006: 404). Proverbs allow the speaker to address "awkward home truths" in an indirect way that allows probing or boundary-setting "with a minimum of embarrassment." Thus, it is said, "when truth is missing, proverbs are used to uncover it." They are "horses for solving problems." Indeed, among the Yoruba (Nigeria) it is said: "He who knows proverbs can settle disputes."

Can these communication methods work if all parties in the dispute resolution – or dispute prevention – process do not share the same cultural context? I suggest a qualified "yes." Rhetorical methods can indeed reveal common ground. Yet if the areas of overlap are illusory, the agreements will not last. I have sought to capture the essence – although not the details – of ancient traditions from China and from Africa, overlaying fundamental values to show how parties can embed sustainability into their operations.

Looking from the broader framework, more must be considered before considering how to meet the spirit, if not the letter, of EITI principles. The Chinese and African companies must elect to negotiate contracts that serve the broader public interest. I believe the rationale must be some version of the concept that it is in the multinational corporation's best interest to seek prosperity to many and stability to all. For that to occur, corporate cultures must shift their orientation concerning short-term versus long-term profits. This change begins in the boardroom and moves downward throughout the business organization (see IFC 2011). Only then will delegates of the companies have the authority and incentive to negotiate using anything other than standard bargaining tactics, which have often sown the seeds of widespread conflict.

Negotiating Corporate Social Responsibility in a Profit-Driven World

If Your Majesty says, "How can I profit my state?" the Chief Counselors will say, "How can I profit my clan?" and the nobles and commoners will say, "How can I profit my self?" Superiors and subordinates will seize profit from each other, and the state will be endangered." Mencius (Mengzi)

The above quote from Mencius is the primary reference point for the modern neo-Confucianism movement in Chinese business ethics. This passage confused contemporary rulers in the fourth century B.C.E. It continues to puzzle us today. The paradox was explained later in the dialogues: "if one is single-mindedly focused on profit, then it leads to harm." On the other hand, if there is compassion or sympathy for others, "then one will not seek profit, but one will never fail to profit" (Van Norden 2008: 2).

This approach to commercial transactions is not a stranger in the West, nor in Africa (see generally, Love and Singh, *Following the Golden Rule*, in this volume). It could be denominated as Quaker Capitalism or Islamic business ethics (see Bernard 2010; but see also Rose 2006.) Its ripples are seen in current efforts to bring accountability and integrity to corporate governance. But it simply is not widely espoused in standard commercial negotiation training.

For the sake of clarity, consider the following fundamental and widely shared assumption: if the delegate for a multinational company entered negotiations with a foreign entity on the stated rationale of "benevolence," surely the other side would see this as a sign of fatal weakness, and seize upon it to manipulate all terms to their benefit, and to the detriment of the company which sees itself as "benevolent."

Is this cynical, or merely realistic? Indeed, does this describe realpolitik in action at the bargaining table? Probably. However, that is not the end of the analysis. For a second generation approach does not ignore the hard realities of the world. Instead, this approach embraces those difficulties as the only way to develop a long-term business plan that is sustainable and self-enforcing.

The initial steps may sound similar to standard negotiations. It is the ambiguity of the situation, including the elusive but central dynamic of identity, that makes the process challenging. The realpolitik of these negotiations requires us to identify:

1) who the parties are in fact;
2) their authority to represent the interests of stakeholders not at the table; and
3) the negotiators' "bandwidth" of discretion to engage in problem-solving and long-term business planning (see IFC 2011; Honeyman et al. 2007).

That being said, the success of a relationship approach versus a pure profit approach hinges upon the policies and perspectives of the companies' leadership. A negotiator trained in second generation methods is unlikely to have an opportunity to apply them unless their business's hierarchy concurs in the goals and methods. (See Matsuura et al., *Beyond "Negotiation 2.0,"* in this volume.) This is especially true when the "wicked problems" embedded in the commercial deal implicate issues of corporate social responsibility regarding the environment, human rights and transparency.

To address such issues in a meaningful, lasting manner the governing body of each company in the negotiations must evidence some level of commitment to such values. That commitment must be explicit and institutionalized, from the top down. Company delegates sent to bargain must know that a long-term strategy designed to produce stable, self-enforcing arrangements is not only acceptable; indeed, it will be viewed favorably.

Ostensibly, this should not be difficult for some SSA nations, like South Africa, which has enshrined in its constitution *ubuntu*, the principle of compassion and justice. Another translation of *ubuntu* is "humanness" – one of the great Confucian virtues (*"ren"*) elaborated upon by Mencius, also called "benevolence" (Haegert 2000). Nevertheless, neither *ubuntu* nor *ren* has a predetermined place in the corporate ledger that calculates profit, loss, and share value. Arguably, negotiating according to these virtues could even bring into question the soundness of company management.

Hence, this approach urges the inclusion of educational workshops with corporate directors and officers before or in tandem with training workshops for negotiators. This approach to resource contracts will undoubtedly require (and with luck inspire) a change in corporate culture. Particularly since most organizations fear change, rather than embracing it, the in-house preparation for negotiation should provide additional workshops, demonstrations and informal events that reach from the top of corporate governance structures throughout the rest of company operations. This can include hospitality and entertainment, showcasing music, art and history in ways that allow indirect, non-pedantic learning – laying the groundwork to support change. Again, Confucian Institutes already established in SSA nations should provide vital support for this expanded version of Chinese commercial negotiation. Both Chinese and African business people routinely engage in such socializing in order to assess the degree of trust to be accorded in the business relationship. As the Ambede of Gabon and Congo say: "If you want to lean on a tree, first make sure it can hold you." Sino-SSA negotiators seek to evaluate their potential partner's integrity and capacity before committing to a contract. This echoes the advice of the Mandingo proverb: "Before killing the chicken [to serve as part of hospitality], carefully observe the character of your guest."

I suggest that these occasions can also teach and thereby influence change in an organization's culture – without explicit "teaching" (see Blanchot et al., *Education of Non-Students*, in this volume). A multinational corporation may find merit in extending the scope of these informal learning opportunities to include supervisors and officers not directly engaged in the negotiations or operation of the prospective venture. In fact, in some situations silent but essential stakeholders behind the scenes should also be included, to alleviate external pressures to maintain the "profits only" approach to negotiation of resource contracts.

Overcoming Internal Corporate Resistance

Both Chinese and SSA companies may encounter resistance among their internal and external constituencies. For some stakeholders, it may be sufficient to assimilate the Muslim proverb: "We will water the thorn for the sake of the rose." That is to say, we will patiently wait for the returns on our investment. For others, the greater incentive for patience and long-term vision rests in the Ethiopian cautionary proverb: "To his hosts the incoming stranger first appeared like gold, then turned to silver, and eventually ended up as crude iron" (Ayele 1998). Still others may concur in the logic of the Ghanaian proverb: "If you collect peppers one by one, the plant grows well; but if you break the stem, it dies."

In hierarchical Sino-SSA societies, this more than "single-focus-on-profit" philosophy needs the support of all key persons in the chain of authority. This is the first and most important step in making it possible for negotiators and business units to take the risk of pursuing the ancient ways of Mencius or *muntu*. For example, company delegates who reach agreements where resources are collected "one by one" rather than "breaking the stem" must be rewarded through compensation and career advancement.

Muntu and Mencius as Icons with Cross-Cultural Convergence

Readers of popular authors Chinua Achebe and Amy Tan have probably noticed similarities between African and Chinese cosmology. Their novels describe a primal world of emanate energy that fills a fluid existence and time. All being is a manifestation of *muntu* in Africa or the *Dao* in traditional Chinese religion. In both metaphysical systems, beings embody a meeting of biological life and spiritual life. While the biological life may cease, the spiritual life does not. Death does not end a human's existence; this occurs when the family no longer remembers, honors or calls upon this ancestor. Ancestors exist in the spirit realm to watch over their loved ones and to serve as intercessors with the larger forces of the universe, gods and spirits.

For negotiators, this shared conceptualization of respect for elders and ancestors provides a common frame of reference for understanding ethical conduct. It provides a rational basis for focusing upon long-term, broadly distributed gains, where success is measured in terms of the legacy left behind. This more culturally-oriented rationale sets a vastly different trajectory for deal-making than using the measurement of quarterly profits.

Similarly, Sino-SSA negotiators may share a common understanding about the essentialism of family; that existence cut off from one's family is nearly incomprehensible. These values, again, can significantly impact the range of acceptable and understandable options, including the capacity to see certain components of the strategic plan by nearly standing in the shoes of the other party or stakeholders.

But sadly, both SSA nations and the Chinese also share a bloody history of internecine violence, much of it led by warlords of various descriptions. Cultural norms of close family connections can be a two-edged sword: it can bring protection, it can also create vulnerabilities.

The ultimate loss is to be cut off from one's family, to have no progeny, to have no one left to mourn or pray for you. This belief has implications for understanding some of the dynamics that infuse African politics with magic and mayhem. Dictators, "strong men," ambitious businessmen and athletic teams alike are reputed to use various forms of traditional religion, or magic, to enhance their power. Or, at any rate, the rituals of secret societies linked to sorcery and cannibalism are used to create and solidify a public image of invincibility. Tragically, there is a logic behind carnage that kills men, women, children, babes in arms, and elders. The purpose is to wipe out the entire family line, thus ending existence in this world and the next.

Mitigation for this darkness is found in the more prevalent message of honoring relationship, particularly by blood. This is not facile sentimentality. It reflects the nature of a world in which personal welfare depends more upon family than government. As the Umbundu (Congo) proverb states: "Relatives are a better defense than a fortress." As expressed often in this chapter, tradition requires the development of sharing energy, substance and opportunity with extended family and community. This is how one becomes fully human and worthy of veneration after death.

Can Negotiators Appeal to Traditional Ideals of Ethical Authority?

According to the pragmatic idealism championed in this negotiation approach, both parties to a negotiation over resource extraction would be encouraged to remain alert for the way even a much-feared "strong man" prefers to be seen. Is it as a bloodthirsty hooligan? Or as a beneficent yet firm leader? Appeals to a self-image that leads in the direction of progress *are* possible. An example is given below.

Mencius applies this energetic ethic to leadership. His philosophy encourages disciplined, rational optimism about human nature. The "capacity for virtue is innate in humans, but it must be cultivated ("filled out") in order for us to become fully virtuous" (Van Norden 2008: 47). When that capacity is cultivated in kings, so that they were "not unfeeling toward others," they put into practice "governments that were not unfeeling toward others." In this way, it is possible to bring "order to the whole world" (Ibid: 46).

To put it in the words of a Tumbuka proverb: "Authority is in generosity." The challenge, then, is to move the negotiations toward principles of generosity toward the workforce and surrounding villages, *as a demonstration of traditional authority* in a modern world. This might be one of the highest iterations of the concept of "face" in either culture. (For more on the value to a commercial negotiator of engaging in more than token generosity, see Love and Singh, *Following the Golden Rule*, in this volume, and Chamoun and Hazlett 2009.)

The Strong Shares Power with the Weak – Why?

The approach suggested here moves the interests of the workers from the background to the foreground, to be negotiated with maximum feasible breadth and transparency. This concept may challenge the worldview of many Chinese and African elites, for the cultures socialize them to believe such deference is unnecessary. At this layer of the multi-tiered approach to negotiation, an Ethiopian proverb may address the "awkward home truth" at issue: "When the webs of the spider join, they can trap a lion." While any single village or villager may seem insignificant, their combined power can turn the resource extraction contract to dust.

The most painful and persistent example of how a small number of determined, desperate people can stymie the plans of multinational corporations is found in the oil-producing region of Nigeria, the Niger Delta. For two decades teenagers under the guidance of a few adults have wrought havoc with drilling rigs and refineries, kidnapping and holding for ransom (foreign) employees of the companies. The bona fides of the money demands might be open to question. Are these merely acts of hooliganism? Or are they acts of revolutionary resistance? Do the funds companies pay benefit the communities, as the kidnappers claim? Or has what originated as asymmetrical warfare degenerated into mere banditry?

The same region can also provide an example of a less violent, and probably far more effective form of resistance. In the 1990s, instead of young males attacking oil company facilities with weapons, mothers and grandmothers demonstrated and ultimately seized control over an entire refinery, occupying it for days. Their "weapons" were the dignity with which they conducted themselves, stemming from the inherent authority of mothers and grandmothers in the tribal tradition. Local police attempted to rout the women, but failed when the women announced that they would engage in the ultimate act of shaming the men into better conduct: they threatened to take off their blouses and to bare their breasts in public. This was an honored, historical method used in demonstrations by market women that had helped turn the tide in the emancipation of Nigeria from British colonial rule.

These were small victories for the "weak" in a longer war against the "strong" as represented by multinational corporations. Of course, contemporary multinational corporations prefer to avoid even the perception of being at war with any segment of their market or supply chain. It is simply bad for business, especially in a global economy where an incident in one village in SSA can be broadcast through social media around the world, and in less than two hours, gather momentum and credibility as a bona fide news event – and within a seventy-two hour period, result in a drop in stock market value.

Even if disputes or disappointments cannot be wholly prevented, their impact can at least be mitigated if the multinational corporations have prepared the way by building trust in advance among affected stakeholders.

The Value of Contemporaneous Communication Beyond the Circle of Direct Parties

Keeping the local community informed and involved helps build trust and cooperation. Ideally, a habit of communication between the villagers and company representatives will enhance the capacity to control rumors and disaffection that can erupt in attacks against the foreign investors, their African associates, and the host government itself. A Mongo (Democratic Republic of Congo) proverb explains the dynamic well: "Roots do not know what a leaf has in mind." Therefore, make sure the "roots" (the locals who must perform the work of resource extraction) and "leaves" (the companies and elites who benefit from the contract) stay in communication, even if their relative social status is unlikely to change.

The work begins with identifying village and clan leaders, both formal and informal. We follow the Akan (Ghana) proverb: "It is better for a person to make friends first before he or she gets into trouble."

This brings the discussion to a point where law and negotiation's standard law-free (if not lawless) conventions might collide. It might be more useful to conceptualize this as a place where negotiators could explore various pre-litigation prevention strategies. Again, introducing these ideas into the negotiation will be greatly aided by use of the rhetoric of proverbs, storytelling and quotations. Consider the following: Nigerian environmental laws allow for the community to provide comments on resource agreements; but they do not provide for further participation. Nor do the laws provide for *contemporaneous* sharing of information, which is considered a hallmark of transparency. The locales ripe for resource extraction include areas critical not only for local economies but for the global ecology. The Niger Delta is often spoken of in terms of its oil-producing abundance. However, little comment is made – beyond the local inhabitants – that the Niger Delta is Africa's largest consistent wetland, and the third largest wetland in the world. It is, thus, a critical source of habitat for aquatic life, and of water for farming and for drinking. Hence, the interest in and apprehensions of the people who live in the Delta have cause; their very existence is at risk.

Of course, the negotiating parties may determine it worthwhile to comply with the threshold mandates of the national laws. But, as many consensus-building efforts in America have discovered, when it comes to environmental damage – which is always reasonably foreseeable – it helps to engage likely victims well in advance. By bringing potentially affected communities in as participants, not merely commenters on the sidelines, companies can achieve a clearer understanding of how land, land use, waterways, water use, and social context interrelate. Informed stakeholders can contribute ideas usually far more efficiently and effectively than technical engineers alone, operating in a vacuum.

Must these community members be physically present in the negotiations? Not necessarily. If contemporaneous participation is not feasible, continual communication, albeit asynchronous, can achieve some of the same objectives. Low-tech and high-tech options abound: texting via mobile phone; announcements, news stories and interviews on the radio; and postings on the walls of community centers, to name a few.

In many settings, negotiations that include some of the above processes will help the "roots" to know what the "leaves" are planning. This buys for the extractive industries a modicum of trust, which is essential for future long-term success. Without trust, founded on demonstrable cause, extractive industries may be fueling the development of much more vigorous enforcement of existing laws, and/or the watchdog non-governmental organizations (NGOs) eager to bring "naming and shaming" to bear, targeting the share value of companies unwilling to shoulder the burden of socially responsible self-governance.

Voluntary compliance can be achieved, I believe, through appeal to Sino-SSA traditions that honor work within the context of family, neighborhood and community. This is, as described earlier in this chapter, not merely a matter of money, but of virtue.

Commerce and Community

As in China, Black Africa holds as a central tenet the idea that cooperation, trust and mutual aid lead to great accomplishments. Working in harmony creates success for all. Consider:

"A village united in fraternity is prosperous" – Bayaka
"A single hand (of a person) cannot cover the sky" – Akan (Ghana)
"Wherever [a] Burundi [person] points a finger, a house is built [by his neighbors]" - Burundi
"Who mistrusts everybody is the real enemy of the village" – Nilotic (Sudan)

Thus, tradition extols the virtue and practice of bringing a community together in a business venture, to share in the work and the rewards. Compare this with an approach that arranges peoples' lives without consultation or engagement, and without public, visible signs of respect.

Respect – preserving "face" – is an essential feature of both Chinese and African cultures. In many ways, the primary goal of negotiations with the local producers of a natural resource has respect – perceptions of fair treatment and justice – as its bottom line. This does not prohibit hard bargaining. Consider an Umbundu (Angola) compliment for a businessman, describing him as "a person of pleasant and agreeable appearance, but close and exacting, a driver of hard bargains." Difference is acceptable; disrespect is not. As the Muslim proverb states: "Where there are poor, there are rich. But where there is justice, they are all brothers." At a minimum, there must be the appearance of justice.

Further, in some way or another, parties must assure that the Kuria (Tanzania and Kenya) principle is followed: "You should never forget your neighbor when you invite people to the feast." The challenge is to know which "neighbors" to invite. Consider first readily identifiable, formal leaders designated by public institutions to wield authority. But also consider less easy to recognize – but often even more powerful – leaders who lead by influence of status, integrity and respect. The village chief, tribal elders and local government officials fall into the first category. The latter category includes leaders of secret societies, women's groups within clans, and religious leaders (both mainstream and traditional).

Special mention should be made of another influence that can prove determinative: the area "strong man" or warlord. Particularly in regions where the institutions of civil justice and law enforcement are ineffectual, whoever can direct armed contingents of "guards," "restive youths" or thugs holds the power of realpolitik. At such a person's command, a wave of violence or individualized attacks can be unleashed – or quelled. Resource extraction ventures need their support, or at least their non-intervention.

Recognize, however, that engaging this particular element of the community brings its own special hazards. To quote the Bahunde (Democratic Republic of Congo) caution: "A knife does not recognize its owner." That is to say, the same warlord who at one time seemed to support the venture may also turn against it, and against the people who brought the extraction work to the village. This may present the unseen tip of the ultimate "wicked problem."

Tackling these complex interactions may demand of the negotiators fewer external, verbal skills and greater internal capacity and self-discipline. The companies may also confront tensions within their organizations, requiring sensitive leadership to support their negotiator teams. (See the discussion by Calvin Chrustie in Gadlin, Matz, and Chrustie, *Playing the Percentages in Wicked Problems*, in this volume.)

Peace in the Negotiator's Heart and Peace in the Supply Chain Depend Upon Peace in the Negotiator's Company

More than most commercial negotiations, SSA resource extraction agreements may benefit from an especially thoughtful selection of negotiators, looking to factors somewhat outside the ordinary. Ideally the multinational companies will identify similar special qualities among directors, officers and managers within their organization, so they can provide high-level support and guidance for the company's delegates, in line with evolving corporate policies.

The chief quality sought is empathy. I refer here not to the externalities taught as part of active listening techniques. This is not a "charm offensive." I speak of authentic empathy derived from shared experience, providing a solid rationale for SSA communities to trust that the companies do in fact hear and understand. The companies

who are negotiating need at least one person in the field and someone in the executive suite with a capacity for discernment and appreciation when confronted with profound ethnic, class and political
tensions, since they can erupt into violence if these potentialities are
glossed over or minimized. To be able to say one has been briefed on
the community's history, or has studied it in school is a far – and insufficient – cry from being able to relate to the subjective experience,
including the lack of that trust that is essential to maintain day-to-
day operations once the agreement has been struck. (For other elements likely to be needed in a negotiator at this level, see Crampton
and Tsur, *Negotiation Stands Alone*, in this volume.)

This may, in fact, be the most challenging factor in the entire negotiation approach presented here. For the very people within the
Chinese corporation who may be most useful in these negotiations are
likely the very people whom Han-dominated hierarchies have marginalized. The idea that an ethnic minority member from Southern
China could be a worthy representative of the company calls for a true
paradigm shift – a change in corporate culture starting at the top, and
flowing throughout the organization.

The Chinese companies that choose this route to long-term
success can expect a trajectory much like the initial experiences of
American companies when they brought black Americans and wom-
en into the upper levels of management and into the board room. A
change in corporate culture, where an ethnic minority member and/or
woman – whether in China, Africa or America – becomes a respected,
contributing member of the team does not occur due to government
fiat. This change takes place because the corporation realizes that this
person they may have long disdained can actually be the key to making money for their business. Period. Full stop.

Until recently, it was assumed that superficial analogies between
the historically colonized Chinese and Africans would be sufficient to
create shared perceptions and goals. As business ventures, Chinese
investment, and immigration of Chinese workers have increased
penetration into African societies and economies, it is becoming ever
more clear that the basis for harmonious business relationships must
emerge from something deeper. Multinational corporations that seek
to thrive in the twenty-first century must secure a 360-degree view,
which includes the view of the historically vanquished. This is how
negotiators will understand not only what is said, but what is not
said, within the indigenous communities who bear the burdens of the
production process.

Relying largely or solely upon the assurances of African elites determined to benefit themselves at the expense of their country has

not proven to be a long-term recipe for success. Although China has, itself, a long history of preferring the "strong man" over the consensus-builder, recently Africa has shown a trend which suggests that contracts with an oligarchy – at the expense of the populace – have a negative prognosis. Despots fall, and seamy business deals fall with them. The experience of Samuel Doe and Charles Taylor in Liberia stand out as bitter examples, sweetened only by the recent implementation of EITI standards designed to assure disclosure, transparency, fairness and to protect human rights for workers.

Yet the "strong man" is a fact of life in many of the countries I am concerned with here. If he exists, he *will* be a factor. Candidly, outside negotiators will have much less impact on him than the constituencies he deals with day in and day out. Nevertheless, the African custom – like the Chinese – is to make the rounds of courtesy calls to receive the permission, even the blessing, of local personages whose cooperation affects the viability of a new venture.

How do you engage the man who pulls the strings above the stage? Is there any way to have dealings with such a person and retain your sense of morality, of the larger purpose of your work? This is a fraught question, but to avoid it is to avoid dealing with much of the real Africa – not to mention some other parts of our real world. My own answer may not be for everyone: it is both tentative and personal. It draws me toward the view that who the negotiator is makes a real difference, on a level that may persuade even the "strong man" to behave according to a deeper self-conception of who *he* is than his usual reputation would suggest.

Making a Courtesy Call on a Nigerian Strong Man

How does this part of the revised "job description" play out in commercial negotiations? Despite the need for shared experience between the negotiator(s), shared experience – standing alone – may not be enough. Empathy must be balanced with the capacity to step back from the situation and separate the negotiator's past from the present. The role calls for some measure of personal, individual peace and reconciliation. I can offer a personal example, in a storytelling mode and in a style of negotiation training and commercial negotiations attuned to Sub-Saharan Africa.

> *My work in Nigeria has focused on the Niger Delta, the oil-producing region typically described in the media as "strife-torn." It technically qualifies as "post-conflict" if one measures the "conflict" as the Biafra War (Nigerian Civil War) of the 1960s. The short-lived Biafra Confederation consisted of many tribal groups which anthropologists*

might categorize as off-shoots of the dominant Igbo tribe. Britain and the multinational oil companies generally did not back the secessionist Biafra republic. Ultimately, long-standing tensions among the many ethnic groups that formed Biafra shattered the alliance. The western faction split and an embargo was instituted at Port Harcourt, resulting in the death by starvation of one million Igbos.

In the highlands of Jamaica, my grandfather's people were able to retain much of their tribal identity, unlike most Africans in the diaspora. We were River Igbo, and the deeper I traveled into Igboland along the Niger River, the more the residents looked like my blood relatives. Everywhere I could see the faces of my uncles, aunties, cousins. The person who looked like he could have been one of the two boys my grandmother had miscarried – if they had lived – turned out to be the local strong man.

He was an arms dealer, whose very name filled most people with dread, especially those from westward areas that had seceded. I, however, saw our host differently, in great part because of familiarity. His looks, the timbre of his voice, the accent, the intelligence and – yes, benevolence – of his gaze; they all resonated with positive associations.

My only (internal) question was: Did he sell arms only to one side in the civil war, or to both? For me, the answer mattered. David, my first husband, was a photojournalist behind the Biafran lines for the entire war who ultimately died due to after-effects of the starvation. Our living room mantel used to display a mortar shell that David kept from those days. I tried hard to remember the markings on the ordnance. Had the mortar come from the British arsenals, paid for by the oil companies? If not, then I might be looking at the man who had helped David come home, along with the former colonel who later drove a taxi cab in Washington, DC and was David's designated substitute just in case he was out of town when the baby came.

Such are the thoughts and feelings of one who was on the losing side of an ethnic conflict, when confronted with a person otherwise labeled as a warlord. Such is the reality behind the saying: "One man's terrorist is another man's freedom fighter."

What Value Does Empathy Derived from Shared Memory Add to Negotiations?

The specific purposes and results of the particular interaction above are beyond the scope of this chapter. But at this point we see a human connection at a deep, intuitive level which can move interactions to a new level of understanding. Yet this is not sufficient in and of itself. The negotiator must have enough skill and self-awareness to move beyond his/her own experience, and in turn through that next level of problem-solving, by exercising detachment. This is the paradox. The more intense the memories that create the common ground – which may be essential to grasp the nuances of risk assessment and option-seeking – the more the negotiator may need to have moved past their personal pain towards reconciliation with the forces that caused their pain.

With the insights thus provided, a negotiator can see the person as something more than merely "the other." He becomes a person who may be open to a variety of options to achieve "buy-in" – other than mere cash pay-offs or bribes. To the extent that a sense of protectiveness for his community remains alive, or that he feels national pride, or concern for his clan, negotiations can seek ways to nurture his stature as a patriarch by supporting the success of the resource extraction project.

Stature based upon perceived character, benevolence and pursuit of harmony to improve the lives of the community retains value in rural areas where the natural resources China desires are located. Traditionally, prestige derives from positive, supportive energy shared with others in the community, because that energy increases connections to *muntu*. Money alone does not lend true prestige – which becomes an increasing concern even for warlords, as they age. (Everyone wishes to be deemed worthy of veneration in the afterlife.)

That being said, respect can be enhanced through good works – which might be achieved in cooperation with Chinese investors. Illustrations include building, staffing and supplying schools, hospitals and clinics, or improving roads and other infrastructure.

If – and this is a major qualifier – the negotiated agreements contain terms to assure that these in-kind projects are completed in a timely manner and with high quality, durable materials, they can in fact become good works that bring honor to those who support the arrangement. On the other hand, local supporters/stakeholders *lose* face if schools, hospitals or clinics promised in the negotiations are never staffed according to plan, or do not offer career opportunities to local residents as teachers, health care providers, managers or administrators. The former, however, leads to peace in the village – with ripple effects that contribute to a robust, uninterrupted supply chain.

China's Role in Africa:
Views from Different Sides of the Table

The positive view of China's commercial role in Africa is summarized in the following quote:

Whether oil in Angola, timber in Mozambique or copper in Zambia, China is breathing new life into these African economies. All over Africa today you will see Chinese construction firms building railroads, highways, telecoms, enormous dams, even presidential palaces (Alden and Davies 2006: 91, quoting Elizabeth Economy).

Numerous sources applaud the "strategic partnership, based on mutual political trust" between China and Africa (see, e.g., Xiao 2010). This is not, however, the only view.

China was expected to serve as a positive role model for SSA nations, showing how to lift the masses from poverty to agricultural and industrial success, preferably without reliance upon foreign aid from the West (see Ravallion 2008). However, the conduct of China's oil companies in Sudan, Nigeria and Angola has seemed indistinguishable from the bloody patterns of European powers. While billions have been spent to rebuild transportation infrastructure shattered during warfare, Beijing has also supported the sale of arms in the Niger Delta and, on the other coast of the continent, for Khartoum to use against the south in Darfur (Alden and Davies 2006: 92).

Chinese ventures in other industries – such as telecommunications and textiles – have a less militaristic shadow. Still, the influx of cheap Chinese manufactured goods has decimated the livelihoods of local individuals and small businesses – especially market women – in South Africa, Lesotho, Kenya, Nigeria and Cameroon (Jacques 2009: 327). Ineluctably, the corrosion of economic stability also threatens civil society, since Africa's market women have long been key to political power at the grassroots level.

Why should this concern commercial negotiations about, say, oil and gas production? *Because the capacity of African mothers to exercise control over their adolescent sons was essential to reduce electoral and communal violence in the Niger Delta.* Their authority within their families derives in no small measure from their capacity to contribute financially to the household. The mothers' influence over "restive youths" contributed to the truce reached with the Movement for the Emancipation of the Niger Delta (MEND) and similar groups, reducing attacks on oil companies in the region – activities that exert significant influence on the availability and price of oil worldwide (Bernard 2009a). To the extent that major oil importers, like the United States, consider such supplies essential to national security, the ripple effect can be profound, contributing to armed conflict not only in the Niger Delta but throughout Nigeria, Africa as a whole, and the Middle East (Chua 2003.)

In the Niger Delta, which provides all of the oil and virtually all of the foreign exchange that benefits the Nigerian economy, the harshest burden of resource extraction has fallen upon the Southern region formerly known as the Republic of Biafra, including the River Igbo, the Ijaw, and the Ogoni. Earlier in this chapter I indicated the sacred closeness between the people and the land, referring to terminology that does not effectively translate into the language of commerce. Multinational corporations can gain credibility while fulfilling legal obligations to protect their business investment; however, when a company enters into real dialogue with persons affected by the extractive project, area farmers and fishermen can suggest economical, low-maintenance, low-cost ways to increase safety measures and mitigate damage. Given that the Niger Delta experiences oil spills on a weekly basis, and other extractive industries have similar records, it is only rational to plan in advance for systems to contain, clean up and the restore the environment after damage has occurred. (See the discussion of "thinking ahead" about inevitable conflict in the IFC Toolkit 2011 (vol. 2): 1-5.) If the multinational corporation includes local African businesses as contractors in the cleanup, and hires area parents in the work, the multinational corporation can gain much value for relatively little expense. As much as anything else, the multinational corporation gains support from the villagers because the project has already demonstrated respect for their knowledge and abilities.

In mediation, the third-party neutral might rightly eschew making such suggestions directly. But in negotiations, the party representatives have greater latitude to be more forthcoming with solutions, using strategic planning scenarios. This would be an extremely appropriate time to employ the rhetoric of proverbs to introduce the proposals and solutions indirectly, so neither party or stakeholder feels unduly pressured to make a commitment – while at the same time the negotiators probe feasibility.

Summary: How African Value Orientation Overlaps with Chinese Value Orientation

It is possible to summarize many of the concepts presented within this chapter by reference to a useful analytical tool developed by a team of West African scholars of business management (Spralls, Okonkwo, and Akan 2011: 11-14). They focus primarily upon how consciousness of *muntu* can shape negotiating behavior among the Igbo – widely regarded as the dominant entrepreneurs in Nigeria. I have excerpted from their matrix of African values and beliefs those which most closely relate to the themes of this chapter (Ibid: 13):

Value	Belief
1	View the world as an integrated whole in which all events are traceable to one source.
2	Ground practical/common-sense thinking in proverbs.
3	Root theoretical thinking in mysticism.
4	View truth as depending on one's relationship with or the status of its source.
5	Fully trust relatives but not strangers.

These authors have synthesized the "Nigerian cultural dimensions and influence on negotiations" – creating a summary of interests and styles highly similar to Chinese commercial negotiation. (For more on Chinese commercial negotiation, see other chapters in this volume, including Goh et al., *As We See It*; Ali et al., *Innovations and Pitfalls*; Lawry, Kaufman, and Bhappu, *Redefining Beauty*; and Schneider et al. *Ethics in Legal Negotiation*.) Whether grounded in *Muntu* or Mencius, one finds:

- The preferred negotiation approach is integrative, rather than distributive, because it allows collective gains in complex arrangements designed to address multiple needs of multiple stakeholders.
- Relationships in business and personal life are inseparable. Commercial contracts are matters of relationship, not legal theory. Trust comes slowly, initiated through introductions by family members.
- Elders are respected as having wisdom and knowledge vital to assuring success, and ensuring that the interests of the group will be protected.
- Hierarchy is valued; hence formal protocol indicates respect, while informality indicates disrespect. Sending the wrong person to negotiate – someone too young or with insufficient status in the organization – can be a "deal killer."
- Communication styles favor indirectness, non-verbal cues, and emotion; proverbs and adages are used to persuade. Mastering this rhetorical skill enhances the chances of mastering the business deal.

(Spralls, Okonkwo, and Akan 2011: 19-20).

Corporations, Communities and Countries:
From Holistic Communication to Shared Prosperity

Optimism about the capacity to change current practices regarding the negotiation of resource extraction agreements often shrivels in the light of widely disseminated images of African elites engaged in ostentatious displays of wealth. Such perceptions of excess add to the reality that a select few tend to receive vast sums of money in the short term, while the many receive few, if any, lasting long-term benefits. Even the promises of infrastructure in return for natural resources have lost their glow: for in an increasing number of cases, the highways constructed in lieu of royalties to the government for the general benefit of the population are found to be poorly engineered, and unable to withstand the stresses of tropical climates. Similar fates have befallen stadiums, schools and hospitals promised by Chinese corporations. Those who negotiated such contracts – behind closed doors and with no input from the community stakeholders – become vulnerable to violent backlash.

Building the African Side of the "Bridge"

If the holistic approach suggested here is to work, connections may need to be forged with a different segment of African professionals in the emerging economies of the twenty-first century. I refer to the Western-educated professionals who have returned to their homelands. They form a rising bourgeoisie with a social consciousness that renders them a more likely "bridge" to future fairness in extraction agreements. They are quietly but determinedly building SSA nations into the "Cheetahs" – the African version of the Asian entrepreneurs who helped their countries' economies become known as "Tigers."

As seen in the United States, South Africa and other places where societies were restructured to achieve justice, the leaders typically are neither the downtrodden nor the dominators. Rather, the change agents are a highly educated and motivated upper middle class, as described in the classic but critical study, *The Black Bourgeoisie* by E. Franklin Frazier (1957). The strategic, long-range leaders of the American civil rights movement were established, high-status members of that Black Bourgeoisie: e.g., Martin Luther King, Jr., Ralph Bunche, Sadie T.M. Alexander, Adam Clayton Powell, Jr., Thurgood Marshall, and Dorothy Height. Their privileged positions as professionals did not diminish their passionate commitment to the advancement of all Negro people of their era – including all, irrespective of color or class. For they lived in and related to "both worlds," black and white.

In the same spirit, a new generation of pragmatic-idealist, activist-intellectual professionals is rapidly rising in Africa. Their comfort in spanning "both worlds" – in behavior and in long-term objectives – embody what some Western observers might perceive as a paradox. Yet for Africans on the continent and in the diaspora, their status as what I call "bridge people" demonstrates the wholeness of personal integration, not splitting off or personal disintegration.

Consider the following description, familiar to those who spend time in the personal spheres of activity for such professionals, entrepreneurs and (quiet) leaders. At work, this Princeton-educated lawyer wears an Armani suit, and a multi-course client lunch is held at a posh restaurant featuring French *nouvelle cuisine*. When he returns home, he exchanges the Western suit for flowing robes. He eats with his hand, shaping starchy *fufu* in the traditional way to scoop tasty local stew with his fingers. As described in a massive modern history of Africa:

> There is a growing realization that you do not have to be either African or European or even half and half. You can be both, two cultures integrated and whole. Their very success as global professionals generates the confidence to assert their Africanness. . . . This generation is open to the world and part of the global movement, enabling their economies to expand (Dowden 2009: 541-542).

How would such global Africanness manifest itself in the negotiation approach put forth in this chapter? One of the best examples I can offer is the negotiation training methods that I initiated with chapters of the International Federation of Women Lawyers (FIDA) in the Niger Delta, and which they took to its apotheosis.

The Rhetoric of African Oral Traditions Applied in Negotiation Training

The concerns and successes of the FIDA model for village women to negotiate peace in their families, neighborhoods and larger communities began as a project funded in 2000 by the Shell Petroleum Development Corporation – the only entity at the time willing to underwrite my travel to Port Harcourt and the workshops to train the trainers in an adaptation of tribal peacemaking "Oklahoma style," which FIDA had asked me to bring to Nigeria. Shell's desire had been to train cadres of women to send in as crisis negotiators when oil facilities had been shut down by protestors, or oil company facilities had been sabotaged, or foreign workers had been kidnapped. This seemed a set-up for failure.

Hence, we refocused the model to address issues where women had natural authority, and built outwards from there. Dialogues with FIDA revealed that most of the communal violence that later erupted into clashes over distribution of oil revenues, fair allocation and siting of neighborhood improvements, etc. were actually an outgrowth of long-simmering disputes within extended families. The village women heartily embraced the Confucian model for building peace in the world, beginning with peace in the home, and peace in one's own heart. These were matters within their sphere of influence – directly and through traditional women's tribal organizations, working with analogous men's groups.

Their successes over the years multiplied, to bring a modicum of peace in the wider region. Where that was not fully achievable, their efforts at least lessened or mitigated violence. As ever, the environmental damage inflicted by oil companies – poisoning the land, fishing and water upon which existence survived – was the primary factor that stressed social relations throughout the Delta, feeding communal strife and political violence. Over time, the intransigence of companies such as Shell (notwithstanding its later willingness to fund the training discussed here) gave rise to a growing sentiment among the local peoples that the indifference to their situation was not only "environmental racism" but "environmental genocide."

In 2002, the Bayelsa Mediation Exchange, sponsored by FIDA, the American Bar Association, and the U.S. State Department brought a high-ranking delegation from the Niger Delta to Oklahoma City to expand this training to include inter-tribal and inter-religious conflict prevention and resolution.

The delegation consisted of elected officials, more accurately described as statesmen, not mere politicians. While trained in law at Oxford and Cambridge, these attorneys and lawmakers were also members of families with hereditary titles and wide spans of public and private influence. Their personal conduct and the conduct of their work were in the tradition of servant leadership and the traditional values of *muntu*. These leaders saw their first obligation as protecting and enriching the well-being of their community. Their success was measured not by personal gain, but by helping to build peace as the foundation for widely shared prosperity.

The delegation returned to Nigeria with my husband and me to coach workshops utilizing the methods honed in Oklahoma. The audience was mixed: officials side by side with village women who had never left home, and who had traveled days through a gauntlet of river pirates to attend this workshop. They wanted to learn more about how to bring harmony to their homes, in order to end communal warfare.

My presentations already syncretized abstract ADR theory from American scholars with potent symbols from the natural world in which our village peacemakers lived. My simple line drawings of fish traps, growing plants, gestation and birth – these had connected with the hundreds of women trained since 2000 to become "midwives of peace." This time I had the privilege to observe in awe the flowing, elegant, earthy transformation of our high status dignitaries into animated, soulful *griots* – traditional keepers of wisdom and wit; storytellers supreme.

Their deep knowledge of the oral traditions of Nigeria raised my work to a higher level (which I transferred to similar trainings in Rwanda and Liberia). Yes, I included a number of proverbs and much storytelling. But their animated, vibrant translation and elaboration turned these teaching methods into performance art; which is, indeed, the SSA oral tradition. Most striking was how the traveling delegation – comprised of global professionals operating at some of the highest levels of society – took the training developed in Oklahoma and made it authentically Nigerian.

With the self-confident grace of the Cheetahs, they flowed seamlessly between the Western theories of ADR and the everyday language of everyday people – Pidgin (also known as "Special English"). With call-and-response, song and rhythmic clapping, a Minister of Justice, a First Lady, a Senator Pro Tempore and a future Justice of the Court of the African Union built a bridge between law and culture, between upper class and lower class, between the modern, urban West and traditional, rural Africa.

This group of lawyers lived on these cultural bridges every day; this was their own global reality. "Bridge people" such as these may offer the best chance to negotiate community-focused, ground-up extraction agreements. Their work may prove the most effective way to embed a culture of compliance with practices designed to assure sustainability.

Building the Chinese Side of the Bridge

Will such SSA "bridge people" find counterparts in high-level decision-making roles in Chinese multinational companies? Will the only likely candidates be found among Africa's resident Chinese, already involved in cultural outreach activities?

In fairness, I should expand that question: Will even American-based or European-based multinationals have among their boards of directors or corporate officers ethnic minority members who can authentically relate to the issues raised in cross-cultural negotiations as described here?

The word "authentic" perhaps misleads, although this qualifier probably occurs immediately in the mind of most Western readers. Earlier in this chapter I suggested that at least one person on the negotiation team should, ideally, possess the capacity for genuine empathy with the concerns of the community where the natural resources are located. Note, however, I did not require that all members of the team, or even all decision-makers in the corporate hierarchy, share those empathic qualities. They do, however, need to respect the economic value that derives from this inclusive approach. Corporations cannot "feel" empathy; but individuals can and must show respect.

Respect in these contexts is measured by external behaviors: rituals, rhetoric and right conduct congruent with relevant traditions. Belief – as an internal, ineffable acceptance of certain values – is not necessarily part of the dynamic. Generally speaking, only conduct in accordance with those values matters. Those values can intersect across cultures – Chinese and Sub-Saharan African – when expressed with appropriate ambiguity that permits the exercise of discretion for creative problem-solving as the extractive project is implemented day-to-day.

This approach to negotiation builds lines for holistic communication – not theological conversion. To an extent, "conversion" is irrelevant when addressing SSA-Sino worldviews, symbolized here by *muntu* and Mencius. When viewed through the standard theoretical construct used in theology, the sociology of religion and comparative religion, both Chinese and SSA traditions are "orthopraxic" not "orthodoxic." What matters in orthopraxic cultures is whether externalized, observable behaviors conform to communal norms. Unlike in orthodoxy (most Western religions), inquiries (inquisitions) to plumb the private depths of an individual's "true" and subjective "belief" in the credo have no place among the laity, the general population. This sociological congruence between China and SSA, in and of itself, lays the foundation for pragmatic solutions, guided by transcendent ideals of interrelationship and perceived integrity. This meets the test of most negotiations as taught in both first and second generation approaches: focus on outward, observable behaviors, conduct, and goals to mark progress; avoid indefinable subjectivity.

Conclusion

Most Anglo-Americans and persons steeped in or attuned to a fairly linear, logic-only, somewhat limited brand of Western education may find the approach and methods suggested in this chapter challenging. Others, whose complex modern-traditional-private-public lives have long bridged the cultural norms described, may find encouragement here. Second generation models of negotiation training can not only acknowledge, but embrace, non-Western cultural values and bargaining styles. Admittedly, it will require effort for most Westerners to shift to the next level of discourse, using proverbs and parables that can immediately change the paradigm of negotiation. Instead of being a Western deal-making win-lose, short-term wrestling event, it becomes an introduction to long-term, lasting relationships that can prevent and survive missteps and miscommunication. The holistic style of communication presented here – both as an approach and as an example demonstrated through much of the chapter – engages parties and stakeholders. It offers more than a simple nod of respect to the culture; which, of course, is worthwhile. But more, with thoughtful usage, this rhetorical method can reveal hidden difficulties that may otherwise impair the success of the venture.

The broader description of the preferred negotiator profile represents a significant break from standard methods. If followed, the negotiation team – even decision-makers within the corporation – will bring to the forefront individuals usually ignored or dismissed. These are situations where the very ethnic heritage that made minorities disfavored in the past can serve pragmatic goals for the multinational corporation: they can help increase productivity and profit. Particularly in cultural settings loaded with indirect and implicit messages, non-verbal cues, and a need to build relationships that blend personal trust with business success, standard, American-based models of commercial negotiation – whether applied by Americans or, ironically, by Chinese negotiators – hold little promise for achieving the deeper, long-range goals of sustainable resource development through sustainable agreements.

I have written elsewhere in the Rethinking Negotiation Teaching series about the complex worldview and sensibilities that shape the structuring of commercial contracts involving persons whose lives bridge modern and traditional cultures (Bernard 2009b; Bernard 2010). This chapter has elaborated upon those perspectives, offering deeper insights into the methods I have used in grassroots ADR training models ranging from the tribal peoples of Oklahoma to ethnic communities in Africa. The most significant difference in this iteration is to urge multinational companies to include in negotiation training, workshops and informal cultural education events their own boards of directors, officers and supervisors in the affected chain of command (see IFC Toolkit 2011). I make so bold as to suggest that multinational companies consider diversifying their own boards of directors if they are to thrive in the global arena, dealing routinely with populations whose cooperation at the grassroots level is, ultimately, vital to stable production and global security.

This call for diversity on corporate boards might be scoffed at as mere "tokenism." However, as a Sufi former finance minister for Iran explained to me:

When it comes to corporate social responsibility, do not discount the value of a 'token.' Yes, something good might begin as a token gesture, not given great support, initially. However, over time, people continue doing things that way, and twenty years in the future, people only know that 'this is the way we do things.' They don't see it as a token. It is now part of an institution – but has lifted the principles and practices.

This is a goal worth negotiating for. Even if the immediate results appear small, they are never insignificant. Time will tell.

Commentary: *Stephanie J Mitchell*

Is Mencius in the Meeting?

Introduction

Muntu Meets Mencius raises important questions for those involved in Africa-China resource negotiations. This commentary elaborates on several aspects of Phyllis's discussion, with a view to developing still further its useful analytical and practical framework. An introductory discussion of terminology is followed by reflections on Chinese traditional values with respect to nature, Chinese negotiating style and practice, and a concluding analysis of challenges and opportunities for future work in this area.

Terminology: Who *is* Mencius?

As Phyllis states, *"Muntu"* and "Mencius" here are used as shorthand, as icons, and should not be read in the same way as they would be understood by, say, philosophers or historians.

This usage was difficult for me as there is, as might be expected, a wide body of literature and active debate on the role played throughout Chinese history, politics and culture by various strands of (neo-) Confucianism. Those debates are very much alive today, and inform serious discussion of a far-ranging set of legal and governance issues. There is also the temptation to query the choice of neo-Confucianism as a "model" at all, given the rich role played in Chinese culture throughout history by Daoism and Buddhism, and by the classic claim that Confucianism falls not so much in the Western typology of "religion," but rather among approaches to "government."

In pedantic mode I might have suggested, instead of "Mencius," a reference to "Chinese traditional culture and values" as the wellsprings which we seek to tap in this endeavor – but that would admittedly be far more cumbersome. Such an approach would, however, have the merit of avoiding confusion when invoking Daoist practice or anecdote, for example, for the two traditions may be seen to be quite diametrically opposed in many ways. Daoism, while co-existing with Confucianism and other traditions in China, most emphatically is not Confucianism. The mention of the Dao is an example of why I am uncomfortable with the "Mencius" and "(neo-)Confucian" terminology throughout the article. Daoism and mystical thought are at odds with Confucianism and more particularly with the neo-Confucian revival. This is not to say that the two do not co-exist within Chinese culture and society: very clearly they do. Even very recent history is replete with examples – or rumors – of Chinese leaders seeking mystical Daoist help to live and reign longer. But this is the very reason why I argue that semantically it would make far more sense to talk about "traditional Chinese culture," which is a vessel that can hold all these mutually contradictory notions.

I was also leery of the appearance of embracing (neo-) Confucianism in an appeal to values, as the label is often used in the kind of "bumper sticker" or "slogan" way which Phyllis rightly decries elsewhere in the article. "Confucian" thought includes much which might today be anathema to many, in China or elsewhere, as well as much which might appeal. Most notably, Confucianism in its essence is built around a series of hierarchical relationships – the ruler and the ruled, the elder brother and the younger, the husband and the wife. These relationships are meant to imply duties and obligations in both directions; but in traditional Chinese society, a widow would effectively be subject to another male member of the family, even to her own son. In such a society it would be hard to imagine much sympathy for or understanding of the African situation of powerful matriarchy Phyllis describes. On the other hand, a sense of the value of hierarchy may be very useful to negotiators on both African and Chinese sides of the negotiating table: knowing when "the man who can take decisions" is actually present and when "the man with the key" is out of the building is a vital element of negotiating knowledge in the Chinese context.

In the practical context of this volume and this chapter in particular, however, the larger philosophical questions above should be set aside, however appealing they might otherwise be. And beyond my concern with terminological clarity, however, there is much of value here. The matrix of traditional African values, for example, would be recognizable in at least half its items to anyone familiar with "Chinese traditional culture and values," particularly regarding the value attached to the land. This leads naturally to my second point – the nature of values, and the value attached to nature in China. Finally, it is as true in modern China as in the African examples that Phyllis cites about deciding not to use "harambee" or "ubuntu," that terminology is highly politicized in China. Confucius has been reviled as recently as the 1970s "Down with Lin Biao, Down with Confucius" campaign and his apparent "revival" is extremely recent and clearly also being used for modern-day political ends. China has an exceedingly long and deep tradition of playing contemporary politics with references to the past; in fact, one could say that doing so is almost a tradition in itself!

Cultures and Values: The Real and the Ideal

In any discussion focusing on values and culture anywhere, one must always remain alert to the difference between the ideal – the values openly espoused, or which are felt to be correct or acceptable or honorable or virtuous to espouse – and the real – those which one perceives in operation through more objective measurement or observation. This divergence is a common problem in comparative law studies and a veritable mainstay in related debates.

Any cross-cultural survey will tell us that the Chinese place a high value on harmony with nature – but those surveys will also show variations among Chinese from various backgrounds (mainland, Hong Kong, Taiwan, Singapore, etc). Even more important is the necessity of unpacking what is meant by the survey questions and the way in which the questions are understood. (See Lawry, Kaufman, and Bhappu, *Redefining Beauty*, in this volume.)

By way of example, I remember a cross-cultural management training seminar in Hong Kong in the mid-1990s during which one such survey purported to show greater value attached to "nature" by, among others, Chinese and French managers than by their American counterparts. A Frenchwoman there found this perfectly self-explanatory: "Look at those horrible perfect lawns Americans insist on, wasting water and using so many chemicals!" An American student countered that those lawns ended at driveways full of recycling bins . . . and so on.

A student of Chinese history might wonder about which conception of "nature" was evoked by the question to begin with. After all, there have been thousands of years of Chinese attempts to control, divert, connect and dam some of the world's greatest rivers, to fight drought, floods, and famine, and to demarcate the land and impose the marks of its rulers on its mountains. To this day, in fact, natural disasters may be seen as a sign that a dynasty – or a regime – is on its last legs, a warning from Heaven of displeasure with Man's intermediaries.

An artist or art historian of China might also pose questions. Take, for example, the artifice involved in importing "strange stones" to scholars' gardens to create – at great price – the illusion of "naturalness." Almost any tourist to China risks raising a camera to capture a scene of natural beauty and hearing "*That's* not the view, the *real* view [that is, the one to which poetry and literature have referred over centuries as beautiful] is over here!"

In the legal context, Chinese scholars have been known to retort that American ideals are no more real. One commonly heard – if overtly political – argument is that social "rights" and "freedom" are effectively meaningless if people still live in poverty.

With a single, logical conclusion elusive as to any of these issues, it becomes more functional to treat the real and the ideal in the context of rights in resource negotiations (and elsewhere) as a sort of feedback loop. In the example of the traditional Chinese view of nature, the ruler is expected to control – and honor – nature in the correct manner so as to enable the people to live peaceably and well. Is a natural disaster a sign that the ruler has done too much, or not enough? Is this a philosophy of honoring nature, respecting it, or something else? It is, at the very least, a philosophy which acknowledges an intimate relationship between people and their natural environment, and it may be the *existence* of this relationship, rather than its details, that should be acknowledged as a point of departure in resource negotiations.

Chinese Negotiating Style and Practice

Several aspects of Chinese negotiating style and practice can add texture to Phyllis's recommendations. One is Chinese negotiators' approach – mentioned above – of starting from first principles. Western negotiators frequently either neglect this aspect of negotiations, sometimes to their later regret, or overemphasize it, imagining that an agreement on principles constitutes a fully enforceable contract, rather than a first step in a negotiating process. A common misstep might be to imagine that a statement of principle respecting "equality and mutual benefit" is mere boilerplate. That might appear to be the case only until questions of valuation or contributions to a venture arise – at which point a lack of attention to the agreed principle of "equality" could be quite dangerous.

In its rightful place, beginning a negotiation with agreement on guiding principles can serve as a useful tool for all involved in a negotiation. There is no reason why appreciation for some common principles, such as those evoked by Phyllis, should not occupy a place in this part of the process, and then in the corresponding texts developed.

But a disconcerting feature of Chinese negotiations, on however large or small a scale, parallels the "lack of direction" mentioned by Phyllis as an African characteristic. A Western negotiator may often be left with the feeling that a negotiation in China "wasn't about what it was [supposed to be] about." A classic example of this phenomenon, dating back to the earliest days of China's "opening up" in the early 1980s, would be a process something like this:

Western negotiator (W): We understand there's a new law offering attractive provisions on [e.g., tax incentives for investment in a particular sector]. We think our proposal falls in that category.
Chinese negotiator (C): You are misinformed, there is no such law.

Next meeting:

W: Here is a copy of the law, it seems to offer hope for our investment proposal.
C: This is not a public document, how have you obtained confidential documents?

And later:

W: We've obtained a public copy of the law, and checking the English version, we think our position is correct.
C: This is not an official translation, your understanding is not correct.

And so on . . .

What is it "really about"? In the Chinese case it may really be about identifying the real sources of power, who may very well not be in the room. It may also be about other offers pending, or about playing various parties off against each other. Undoubtedly African negotiators today are faced with the dynasties-old Chinese tactic of reminding the "barbarians at the gate" that the next set of barbarians – whose price and terms may very well be lower and better – are in the next meeting room, just waiting their turn for a bite at the prized Chinese apple.[3]

All of the elliptical strategy and puzzling tactics may, in fact, be "all about" the price, pure and simple. Negotiations about technology and services often stall when confronted with a Chinese view that only those offerings which "can be dropped on your foot" – i.e., the tangible parts of a deal – have real value. In this context it can be difficult to obtain a proper price or valuation for services, for peripherals, replacement parts, instruction or maintenance, etc. In the simplest retail context, the Chinese concept that "only price matters" can play out in an amusing fashion for a Western shopper. But this apocryphal story is offered as a hint of a broader cultural phenomenon Westerners should be trained to expect:

The scene: a clothes shop in Beijing
> W: I like the style of that shirt, do you have it in blue?
> C: (takes down the white shirt to show the customer) It's 110 RMB.
> W: Hmm, yes, nice, do you have it in blue?
> C: OK, OK, for you 80 RMB.
> W: No, you don't understand, it's to go with a blue suit, I already have plenty of white shirts, I really need blue. Does it come in blue?
> C: Fine, fine, 50 RMB.
> W: (Looks around in desperation, sees no blue shirts, apologizes, shrugs, walks out of shop)
> C: (turning to colleague) I don't understand, 50 is a **really** good price, why did he leave?!

It is important to note in this context that the interest-based model of negotiating does not commonly make an appearance in Chinese negotiations. It is not only Westerners or Africans who would benefit from the training Phyllis advocates. If, in fact, it is "all about the price," then all the other discussions – whatever they are nominally "about" – are really dedicated to finding out if the other side has really, actually reached its true, final, bottom line. It is thus very important for any negotiator to "know thyself" before even arriving at the negotiating room. I would argue that this is even more important than knowing anything about one's Chinese opposite number.

Is Mencius in the Meeting – and Does Mencius have a Heart?

And so we get to the heart of the matter. Phyllis argues for training negotiators with heart, with empathy, and with an understanding of the common principles she finds in both SSA and China. It is easy enough to envisage the more desirable results that could be wrought if such an approach is achievable. But surely there is the nub of the matter: is such a change truly achievable?

Let us begin by asking who is "in the meeting" – that is to say, who are the negotiators? Phyllis refers to representatives of African governments, elites, and, ultimately, communities and other sources of power. She also refers to representatives of multinationals. But there is no mention of the most likely representatives on the Chinese side of the table. Most resource investments or similar large-scale projects will be undertaken by Chinese businesses which are *state-affiliated*, although this is by no means the only or even the most prevalent (depending on which measure one uses) form of Chinese business today. Even for those large Chinese businesses which are not state-owned (e.g., such firms as Lenovo or Huawei) the question of "who controls" the negotiation will remain apposite.

In the putative search for the right Chinese negotiators, I would find it more persuasive if we simply left it at – "the African Cheetahs must find Chinese counterparts" without citing the Confucius Institutes. There are a number of reasons for this. Most importantly, teachers of Chinese language and culture are not likely to occupy the same socio-economic "bridge" status as the Cheetahs. There *are* Chinese middle classes and upper-middle classes, who now form a substantial portion of urban Chinese society, but there is no particular reason for supposing that employees of the Confucius Institute fit that characterization. I would postulate that such counterparts are far more likely to be found within the ranks of the rising executives within a Chinese corporation, its home-grown legal or financial advisers and staff, and similar personnel. These are the people most likely to be able to move between cultures, which Phyllis notes is the useful quality offered by the Cheetahs.

In addition, the Confucius Institutes are not immune from controversy of various sorts; there is no need to recapitulate the various claims and counterclaims about them, but the key point is that they are not present outside China in order to understand non-Chinese: they are there to teach Chinese. Among accusations leveled at them are that they co-opt institutions with which they are affiliated, away from even scholarly discussion of topics which may be critical of or offensive to the Chinese government, and that they offer a "plastic" watered-down version of Chinese culture, of the "song and dance" variety. Whether these accusations are true in individual cases or not, they may be seen to be roughly the cultural equivalent of the economic and social arguments against foreign firms in the resource extraction sphere.

Finally, perhaps it is not for us to be prescriptive and hazard guesses at where we think useful Chinese counterparts to the Cheetahs may be found, but rather to content ourselves with specifying the sorts of characteristics they will need to use a new approach to resource extraction agreements between China and African nations. Those characteristics are presumably the very same as those of the Cheetahs, the characteristics of "human bridges" so well described in the Dowden quote.

And more encouragingly, it is clear, as Phyllis notes, that it is possible for negotiators to be trained in a fashion which will address the many possible sources of power, community legitimacy, and stability. It is equally clear that the last of these factors, stability, is of great and growing concern to Chinese leaders, whether with regard to matters abroad or at home. Abroad, it has undoubtedly been a shock to the leadership to find Chinese personnel taken hostage or otherwise treated in the same fashion – unwanted, resented – as former colonial overlords. It has also undoubtedly been worrying to realize that the projects they undertake – whether resource extraction or infrastructure, etc. – can be threatened, even purely in budgetary and completion terms, by social problems.

This sort of problem, however, is far from alien to the Chinese government. In fact, it exists on a large scale *within* China. The environmental degradation which is sometimes cast as the "price" of enormous economic development over the past three decades has given rise to much social unrest within China, even if only a small percentage of such events are reported widely outside the country. Since the introduction of the Administrative Litigation Law in the early 1990s, there has also been a surge of lawsuits against functionaries of the Chinese government, whether for police abuse of those detained, for improper handling of land disputes, or for other perceived failings. Public protests, demonstrations, and ultimately even violence are far from unknown within China.

Like people everywhere, Chinese individuals and communities expect more and better from their governments. There is a long-seated tradition in China of the "righteous official" who combats corruption from within and who stands up for the wronged party, however low on the social scale the innocent victim may be. And at a practical rather than abstract level the government is well aware that its legitimacy depends on "serving the people," even if that Mao-era slogan would go unrecognized or even scoffed at by the man on the Chinese street today. The Chinese government is also aware that it needs to learn to listen more and better in its foreign dealings, as the recent case of Burma has underlined. In canceling a $3.6 billion dam being built there by Chinese state-owned enterprises, the Burmese government abruptly drew the attention of the Chinese government to the fact that its efforts were not universally perceived as well-connected to the needs of the local people or even of the local regime. The Chinese government has, according to recent reports, made the connection between the Burma experience and Africa, and is now urging businesses to "be more respectful of local customs and people, and to invest more in . . . corporate social responsibility" (Economist 2012; see also Yu, Chen, and Yang 2012).

But to get back to the question at the start of this section: who are the Chinese representatives in the negotiating room, whether government or corporate, and who or what do they really represent? Are they personally and professionally susceptible to Phyllis's call for "heart" and empathy, or is it "about what it's about" – only the price? I think the mention of minorities here is misdirected. I find it very difficult to imagine that, say, a Miao or Yi employee would make a better negotiator than a Han Chinese. If such a person has made it to a level of reasonable responsibility in a Chinese business or administration, then he or she has been educated entirely in Mandarin and may have little remaining connection with any other culture – perhaps no more than the opportunity to wear different clothes for celebrations, or possibly certain privileges with respect to the one-child policy. I suspect the issue is a red herring, as the issue of multinationals diversifying their boards and their staffing seems to have been conflated with the issue of who might be useful interlocutors on the Chinese side of SSA resource negotiations. It may well be true that diversity is beneficial for corporations and administrations – but that is not the same issue as the one we are discussing here; the argument paints with too broad a brush in my view.

I would in fact make the opposite argument – that what we should keep our eyes open for might be an "ueber-Chinese": someone so well established in their home culture and business that they can afford to be "strong enough to be seen to be weak." Of course for "weak" we should read "different," "magnanimous," "open-minded" or simply "taking a different approach to negotiations." To borrow the ancient Vulcan proverb offered by Spock in *Star Trek VI: The Undiscovered Country*, "only Nixon could go to China." Someone whose leadership is unquestioned in the Chinese context could well afford to take a more holistic view of negotiation; someone more marginal would have much greater difficulty obtaining sufficient negotiating authority to follow a new approach.

From the fact that Chinese organizations *are* building schools, highways, and other civic infrastructure in Africa, one may conclude that at some level, at least a "thin" awareness of the importance of community interests beyond the dollars-and-cents (or renminbi) bottom line does exist. And yet, what will happen if those projects are plagued by the same penny wise, pound foolish approach that has become known within China as "building with tofu" (bean curd) instead of with concrete?[4] Is there any reason to hope for better results outside China than inside?

I agree with Phyllis that if there is to be any hope for better results, the change must start at the top of whichever organization is on the Chinese side of the negotiation, as it must in Africa or within multinationals. It is a management truism that "what gets measured, gets done," and this certainly proves true in the Chinese government environment. Officials at various levels of the Chinese government are known to be measured on various indicators. One could reasonably assume that if, say, water quality in the official's locality were one of the measured indicators, dictating not only the local budget but also local prospects for promotion, then water quality might at least be *reported* to have improved – and the need for reports that will not immediately become an object of ridicule becomes a real, if partial, constraint on bad behavior. As it is, indicators for, say, criminal convictions during anti-crime campaigns are clearly seen to spike.

It would thus be tremendously interesting to know to what measurements the Chinese negotiators for resource extraction contracts are held, and how and by whom they are measured. As a subject for future research, getting this information out into public view could be influential. Is the only standard whether the "price is right"? And if so, is the standard destined to remain that way? Or, as Phyllis suggests, is there a way to measure the social sustainability and acceptability of a project, and begin to reward its negotiators accordingly? Such a measurement could be seen as a measure of likely "investment success"; and it would presume an interest in at least medium-term success. If it could be ascertained and reliably reported – all big "ifs," admittedly – then such a system could benefit the Chinese people as well. For it would surely be equally applicable both at home and away.

Recent events give some hope that the right negotiators – the "opposite numbers" to the Cheetahs of Phyllis's description – are already beginning to appear, and to have some influence both within China and in her overseas ventures. In 2011 a group of members of Chinese non-governmental organizations visited Burma, where China has long exercised great influence and where recent large-scale infrastructure projects had evidently been assumed by the Chinese government to constitute evidence of neighborly interest and support.

But that was not necessarily the case. What the Chinese NGO representatives found was that there was little or no attention to interests of local inhabitants near the site of the Chinese-built Myitsone Dam; in their report they expressly noted that other countries working in Burma were better at maintaining good relationships with local people and not only with the government. They further noted that Chinese actions in ignoring environmental impact requirements would have violated China's own laws, had they taken place in China. They made an express comparison to investment risk in Libya. The dam project itself was shortly thereafter shut down by the Burmese government.

The NGO representatives recommended much greater attention to what Phyllis and I might describe as "listening skills" on the part of Chinese state representatives. Without going into extensive detail on other cases, both inside and outside China, and on the evolution of civil society-government relations there, these developments suggest that the message that "attention must be paid" is getting through to the top levels of Chinese government. (See *Economist* 2012 and Yu, Chen, and Yang 2012. Further support is found in a recent New York Times/International Herald Tribune article, on an announcement by the Chinese government that in future a "social risk assessment" will be required for all major projects *within* China. See Bradsher 2012.)

If that is the case, then we have not one, but multifarious nominees for the "Cheetahs" to look forward to on the other side of the negotiating table – or at least, and to begin with, over meals or at cultural events. First there are the senior level government representatives who, according to the *Economist* report, have already given orders that Chinese projects overseas must pay greater attention to the sorts of factors we have been discussing here. Second, there is an even more interesting pool of people in the sort of civil society representatives who visited Burma and investigated conditions there, in itself an impressively proactive effort. I have met some such people in China, beginning more than a decade ago, and they are as remarkable as their counterparts elsewhere in the world – all the more so if one considers the difficult legal and regulatory environment they have to negotiate. They are retired professors, teachers and judges, idealistic young people, experts on environmental and technical issues, and as many other kinds of people from as many different walks of life as you might find doing this sort of work elsewhere. Their devotion, knowledge and creativity may be one of China's greatest assets in tackling the sorts of issues Phyllis describes. It would not be at all surprising if they also become skilled second generation negotiators.

Notes

[1] After a fourteen-year civil war funded by diamonds, disputing rights to exploit timber and other natural resources, Liberia was the first African nation to be designated EITI Compliant as of October 2009. EITI awarded Liberia the Implementing Country Award in 2009, "based on Liberia's rapid progress and trend-setting performance" (Caspary and Seiler 2011: 2).

[2] As noted by Augustine Shutte, "[t]he fundamental norm in the ethics of traditional African thought is human nature itself: it is the living *muntu* who, by divine will, is the norm of either ontological or natural law" (2001: 129). Shutte also notes "[i]t is, in fact, a natural law kind of ethics. And, as this nature is understood in terms of *seriti* of vital force, so the moral life in all its individual, social and political ramifications is understood in terms of the

struggle to increase this [life] force … It is the ideal which animates the life of the *muntu*, the only thing which he [or she][the individual] is ready to suffer and to sacrifice himself [or herself] " (2001: 175).

[3] It is more than worth underlining, for those "barbarians" considering caving in at the thought of the other barbarians in the next tent, that there is no convincing evidence that offering cut prices or other "introductory" discounts has ever been a route to commercial success in dealing with China. It almost invariably seems to lead simply to a demand for further discounts on the next piece of business.

[4] This turn of phrase was common after the Sichuan earthquakes, when it was discovered that public buildings – notably schools, where so many children died – had been built with inferior materials and techniques, as compared to other structures which offered the promise of turning a profit and remained standing after the quake.

References

Alden, C. and M. Davies 2006. A profile of the operations of Chinese multinationals in Africa. *South African Journal of International Affairs* 13(1): 83-96.

Ayele, N. 1998. *Wit and wisdom in Ethiopia*. Los Angeles, CA: Tsehai Publishers.

Bernard, P. E. 2009a. Eliminationist discourse in a conflicted society: Lessons for America from Africa? Marquette Law Review 93: 173-207.

Bernard, P. E. 2009b. Finding common ground in the soil of culture. In *Rethinking negotiation teaching: Innovations for context and culture*, edited by C. Honeyman, J. Coben, and G. De Palo. St. Paul, MN: DRI Press.

Bernard, P. E. 2010. Re-Orienting the trainer to navigate - not negotiate - Islamic cultural values. In *Venturing beyond the classroom: Volume 2 in the rethinking negotiation teaching series*, edited by C. Honeyman, J. Coben, and G. De Palo. St. Paul, MN: DRI Press.

Bradsher, K. 2012. Social risk test ordered by China for big projects. *New York Times, Nov. 13, 2012.* Available online at www.nytimes.com/2012/11/13/world/asia/china-mandates-social-risk-reviews-for-big-projects.html (last accessed December 3, 2012).

Caspary, G. and V. Seiler. January 2011. Extractive industries transparency initiative: Combatting the resource curse in fragile and conflict-afflicted countries. *Smart Lessons*. International Finance Corp./World Bank Group.

Chamoun, H. and R. Hazlett. 2009. The psychology of giving and its effect on negotiation. In *Rethinking negotiation teaching: Innovations for context and culture*, edited by C. Honeyman, J. Coben, and G. De Palo. St. Paul, MN: DRI Press.

Chua, A. 2003. *World on fire: How exporting free market democracy breeds ethnic hatred and global instability*. New York: Doubleday.

Dowden, R. 2009. Africa: Altered states, ordinary miracles. New York: Public Affairs.

Economist. 2012. Relations with Myanmar: Less thunder out of China.Oct 6th.

Ethiopian Proverbs, Teybyan Website. www.tebyan.net dated 2/18/2007

Folger, J. and R. A. B. Bush. 1996. Transformative mediation and third-party intervention: Ten hallmarks of a transformative approach to practice. *Mediation Quarterly* 13(4): 263-278.

Frazier, E. F. 1957. *The black bourgeoisie: The book that brought the shock of self-revelation to middle-class blacks in America.* New York: Free Press.

Haegert, S. 2000. An African ethic for nursing? *Nursing Ethics* 7(6): 492-502.

Honeyman, C. 2006. Using ambiguity. In *The negotiator's fieldbook: The desk reference for the experienced negotiator*, edited by A. K. Schneider and C. Honeyman. Washington, DC: American Bar Association.

Honeyman, C., J. Macfarlane, B. Mayer, A. K. Schneider, and J. Seul. 2007. The next frontier is anticipation: Thinking ahead about conflict to help clients find constructive ways to engage issues in advance. *Alternatives* 25(6): 99-103.

Huang, C. 2008. China's renews partnership with Africa: Implications for the United States. In *China into Africa: Trade, aid and influence*, edited by R. Rotberg. Washington, DC: Brookings Institution Press.

International Finance Corp. (IFC). 2011. *Toolkit 4: Resolving corporate governance disputes.* Global Corporate Governance Forum. User guide and 3 volumes available at http://www.gcgf.org/wps/wcm/connect/topics_ext_content/ifc_external_corporate_site/global+corporate+governance+forum/publications/toolkits+and+manuals/adr_toolkit (last accessed December 3, 2012).

Jacques, M. 2009. *When China rules the world: The end of the western world and the birth of a new global order.* New York: Penguin Press.

Kurlantzick, J. 2007. *Charm offensive: How China's soft power is transforming the world.* New Haven, CT: Yale University Press.

Lemos, A. and D. Ribiero. 2007. China's investment in Sudan: Displacing villages and destroying communities. In *African Perspectives on China in Africa*, edited by F. Manji and S. Marks. Oxford: Fahamu Books.

Mbiti, J. 1990. *African religions and philosophy*, 2nd edn. Portsmouth, NH: Heinemann.

Meredith, M. 2009. From political mercenarism to militias: The political origin of the Niger Delta militia. In *Fresh dimensions on the Niger Delta crisis in Nigeria*, edited by V. Ojakorotu. Delray Beach, FL: JAPSS Press.

Meredith, M. 2011. *The fate of Africa: A history of the continent since independence.* New York: Public Affairs.

Najibo, N. and B. Nwiline. 2009. Relative deprivation and hostage taking in Nigeria's Niger-Delta region, 1987-89. In *Fresh dimensions on the Niger Delta crisis in Nigeria*, edited by V. Ojakorotu. Delray Beach, FL: JAPSS Press.

Obiorah, N., D. Kew, and Y. Tanko. 2008. "Peaceful rise" and human rights: China's expanding relations with Nigeria. In *China into Africa: Trade, aid and influence*, edited by R. Rotberg. Washington, DC: Brookings Institution Press.

Ravallion, M. 2008. *Are there lessons for Africa from China's success against poverty?* World Bank Policy Research Working Paper No. 4463 (January 2008).

Reuters. 2009. Update: *2-pay strike hits Zambia's Konkola cooper mine.* Nov. 11.

Richardson, B. 2008. Reflections on reconciliation and *ubuntu.* In *Persons in community: African ethics in a global culture*, edited by R. Nicolson. Scottsville, South Africa: University of KawZulu-Natal Press.

Rose, D. 2006. Ulysses and business negotiation. In *The negotiator's fieldbook: The desk reference for the experienced negotiator*, edited by A. K. Schneider and C. Honeyman. Washington, DC: American Bar Association.

Rotberg, R. (ed). 2008. *China into Africa: Trade, aid and influence*. Washington, DC: Brookings Institution Press.

Shutte, A. *Ubuntu: An ethic for a new South Africa*. Pietermaritzburg, South Africa: Cluster Publications.

Smith, J. 2008. *Bewitching development: Witchcraft and the reinvention of development in neoliberal Kenya*. Chicago, IL: University of Chicago Press.

Spralls, S. A., P. Okonkwo, and O. H. Akan. 2011. A traveler to distant places should make no enemies: Toward understanding Nigerian negotiating style. *Journal of Applied Business and Economics* 12(3): 11-25.

Van Norden, B. (Trans.) 2008. *Mengzi with selections from traditional commentaries*. Cambridge, MA: Hackett Publishing Co.

Xiao, J. 2010. China-Africa relations: progress, challenge and prospect. *Fudan Journal of the Humanities and Social Sciences* 3(1): 55-89.

Yu, X., Y. Chen, and Y. Yang. 2012. Chinese NGOs travel to Myanmar. *China Development Brief No. 53*, Spring 2012.

ೞ 9 ೬

Beyond "Negotiation 2.0": Teaching Negotiation in the Multi-Stakeholder, Multi-Level, and Multi-Processes World of Public Policy

Masahiro Matsuura, Boyd Fuller, Sanda Kaufman, Dong-Young Kim & Kenshi Baba*

Editors' Note: *The authors assess the prospects for teaching public policy negotiation and mediation across Asia. They find that the doctrines they were presented with as embedded elements of teaching materials presume a number of factors that are associated strongly with Western culture, but which are hard to find in public policy dispute management in Japan, Singapore, or Korea. Yet contrary to the perhaps-expected response that the training and teachings must now be thoroughly modified to respond to the context, the authors find themselves concluding, in part at least, that their societies would benefit if targeted ways can be found to use the Western insights to help open up public policy processes in their societies.*

Introduction
The Trip from Negotiation 1.0 to 2.0[1]
Using our experience teaching public sector negotiation and mediation, we argue here that "Negotiation 2.0" is still making two naïve

* **Masahiro Matsuura** is associate professor at the Graduate School of Public Policy, University of Tokyo. His email address is matsuura@pp.u-tokyo.ac.jp. **Boyd Fuller** is assistant professor at the Lee Kuan Yew School of Public Policy, National University of Singapore. His email address is boyd.fuller@nus.edu.sg. **Sanda Kaufman** is professor of Planning, Public Policy and Administration at Cleveland State University's Levin College of Urban Affairs. Her email address is s.kaufman@csuohio.edu. **Dong-Young Kim** is associate professor at the Korea Development Institute School of Public Policy and Management. His email address is dykim@kdischool.ac.kr. **Kenshi Baba** is visiting researcher at the Graduate School of Public Policy, University of Tokyo. His email address is kbaba@pp.u-tokyo.ac.jp.

assumptions that underlie "Negotiation 1.0," namely: a) the negotia tion starts when the parties first sit at the table; and b) the negotiations at the table are the most important ones.

"Negotiation 2.0" was the catchy term initially used by the Rethinking Negotiation Teaching (RNT) project to represent an effort to revitalize negotiation pedagogy by developing more nuanced tools and concepts that can apply to the various challenges faced by today's negotiation professionals.[2] To date, the project has looked extensively at psychological, technological, and "wicked" aspects of real-life negotiation (more about "wickedness" later). We argue, however, that these aspects, together with the complexity and uncertainty of multiparty, public sector negotiations, make it necessary for us to teach students both: a) how to negotiate the negotiation process and structure that will be used – including who will negotiate, how the negotiators communicate with interested parties not at the table, etc.; and b) how to manage a multi-party process – who may/should be at the table, away from it, or both, and who may be interacting in multiple ways, in various groupings, in multiple forums besides the visible one for which the negotiation is being designed and in which it is conducted by the facilitator or mediator.

Simply put, context – including antecedents of the situation, contemporaneous political and economic related issues, culture, and other dimensions as well as the parties not present at the table – matters! Context shapes and can be shaped before and during the official negotiations. To teach students context awareness and related negotiation skills, we need to introduce them both conceptually and experientially to complex, real-like and real-life situations, while emphasizing that no design or skill is one-size-fits all. Each negotiated decision process may require an interactive pre-negotiation, to identify and get the necessary parties to the table, negotiate (design jointly) the process those parties will follow, and obtain the support necessary to make process implementation possible and worthwhile.

To demonstrate, we will discuss in this chapter our experiences of teaching negotiation to public-sector professionals and graduate-level students, most of whom will work in the public sector. We analyze the gaps that remain unaddressed even with the innovations introduced in Negotiation 2.0. We describe some of the changes we have made in our teaching to advance and improve our pedagogy. Some of the approaches and devices we use can transfer to other fields in which negotiation is taught. Moreover, people from these other fields – lawyers, business people, mediators and other interveners – may have to take part in public disputes and need to be equipped to do so.

To begin this discussion, we briefly introduce the current journey from Negotiation 1.0 to 2.0. Then some of the gaps we believe to be in need of attention will be described by two of the chapter authors, who have extensive experience teaching negotiation in South Korea and Japan. In the next three sections we discuss some innovative solutions, including the use of very real, complex cases analyzed over several class sessions, and then the use of real-life projects to introduce students to different aspects of convening stakeholders, including process design, which we believe to be in pressing need for a place in every classroom.

Theories of negotiation have evolved from contributions of multiple disciplines and have applied to a wide variety of fields and scales, ranging from family disputes to diplomatic negotiations. The main benefit of participating in typical negotiation seminars lies in the applicability of lessons to many different settings. Instructors often go beyond their own professional backgrounds and deliver training programs and lectures for audiences in fields different from their own. One consequence of this custom is the gradual standardization of negotiation pedagogy. In the classroom, most instructors talk about the same descriptive issues, such as the disadvantages of "lose-lose" negotiation, and offer the same prescriptions, such as distinguishing between positions and interests and focusing on the latter, and seeking mutual gains by trading among issues. Another consequence, perhaps more fraught with real risks, is that the instructors have persuaded themselves that the wisdom they are conveying is universally applicable, hence the pervasive lack of attention to context specifics and to what they might entail for these prescriptions. Our trainees can emerge ill-equipped for context awareness and lacking adaptive skills.

Even though many instructors do tailor their lectures to some extent to different audiences, the main content components and teaching materials are repeatedly used in different settings. We see this standardized training practice as the main characteristic (see Lewicki and Schneider 2010), and one of the weaknesses, of first generation of negotiation teaching, which the project editors initially called "Negotiation 1.0."

While key principles of a de-contextualized version of negotiation pedagogy apply to many different fields and have the advantage of saving time and resources in preparing training materials, the authors of this chapter have found a need to address some issues specific to the public decisions field.[3] We have developed and used some tools and concepts that account for the process complexity, multiple stakeholders, the intractability to be expected in values-laden disputes, and other elements of negotiation common to public affairs settings. Portions of Negotiation 1.0 – especially basic principles of integrative negotiations some have taken to calling the *Harvard model* – stand the test of time and even "travel" well across scales, space, cultures and institutional structures. We see the challenges for Negotiation 2.0 as the sorting out and preservation of the components that travel, while innovating in the areas that need contextual adaptations, such as designing negotiation processes, adapting to cultural specifics, and crafting implementable agreements.

Before we proceed, we must introduce the public policy context and what distinguishes it from other negotiated decision contexts. Public decision situations often pose "wicked problems" and occur within complex and uncertain environments. Wicked problems have already been discussed extensively in volume two of the Rethinking Negotiation Teaching series, and several additional writings on the subject appear as chapters 17-21 in this volume.[4] On the other hand, process and contextual complexity have received little or no attention. Some of the key dimensions of process complexity and uncertainty are:

1) numerous stakeholders with differing interests and perceptions of the shared reality, which can manifest at the table, within constituencies, and between constituencies and their representatives;

2) a mix of formal and informal deliberations and decision processes that can unfold in multiple forums over long time periods (more than a year is not unusual);

3) uncertain and contested knowledge, coming from multiple sources (technical, academic, political, and "local") whose methods, validation, and presentation differ and whose legitimacy is often poorly understood and questioned by proponents of other knowledges (Ozawa 1991; Fuller 2011);

4) low feedback about decision consequences because they accrue slowly, at times beyond the lifetime of the decision makers (Susskind and Cruikshank 1987; Shmueli, Kaufman, and Ozawa 2008; Kaufman 2011); and

5) imbalance of sociopolitical power among stakeholders, especially in developing countries.

The challenges posed by the wicked and complex nature of public disputes require that mediators especially, but also negotiators, pay more than the usual attention to certain aspects of the process, including *when and how the process is convened* and negotiated, and *how communication is managed among the many parties at and away from the table during the process*. These are the two contributions to Negotiation 2.0 pedagogy that we wish to make in this chapter.

Two Contributions to Negotiation 2.0:
"Convening the Table" and Managing Many Parties

Understanding the challenges and strategies for convening and for multi-party process design, we argue, is an essential set of ideas and skills for today's students of public policy as well as law, business, and other disciplines. The Arab Spring is just one of many recent political developments that demonstrate the need for business leaders, legal experts and other stakeholders to have the capacity to engage each other to handle complex problems in the public arena that exceed the scope of problems governments can handle by themselves. Getting the parties and process "right" is a key skill for handling wicked and complex problems.

Challenges of Convening the Table

Negotiation 1.0 typically assumes (and reflects this assumption in classroom simulations) that the parties to a conflict are obvious, willing to participate, and capable of doing so. These presumptions are a luxury in the world of public affairs disputes. How do we identify the parties that should be at the table? How should we choose the stakeholders who will participate, and in what capacities (party, observer, expert, etc.)? How can we get the appropriate representatives for each stakeholding group to come to the table? How can we maintain the legitimacy of the process while doing so? These are only a fraction of the questions with which the mediators/facilitators, who design and manage such processes, have to deal.

Stakeholders, including governments and their agencies, are often reluctant to negotiate because of their previous, and often quite acrimonious, experiences with each other. They may feel that the other side is selfish, irrational, and perhaps even an enemy determined to eliminate its opponents' way of life (Mnookin 2010). Such parties make poor negotiating partners, but they are a fact of life in the public decisions context. Therefore, we need to equip students with both awareness and some tools for contending with these challenges.

The reluctance to negotiate in the public arena increases when the parties take into account the multiple forums that they have for pursuing their interests. Public policy negotiations are necessarily embedded within a system of existing formal policy and planning processes, in which multiple venues exist for defining problems, generating solutions, and making decisions (e.g., legislatures, courtrooms, and public consultations). Parties may perceive that some or all of these are preferable to an ad-hoc forum for negotiation outside such formal venues, especially if the problem is wicked and their counterparts are seen as unreasonable.

In practice, many experts in consensus building in the field of public policy recommend investing significant time and resources in a *pre-negotiation phase* to get the right parties to the table, negotiating the right set of issues, in the right conditions, and at the right time. In other words, it is better to go slow in setting up the negotiation so that the group can go fast when the negotiations get underway. There is widespread agreement about the importance of preparing for negotiations and therefore of teaching students about it. Even within the Negotiation 1.0 framework, we typically teach individual preparation [e.g., figuring out interests and best alternatives to a negotiated agreement (BATNAs)]. Negotiating the public negotiation process before engaging in it in a multi-party situation parallels the individual preparation stage, is as necessary, and is as important to teach.

One portion of the preparation to negotiate public disputes is called *convening*. This pre-negotiation process can be initiated by a process sponsor. (For example, the U.S. Environmental Protection Agency is a frequent convener in environmental disputes.) As in the case of individual preparation, there are tricks of the trade for public decisions. For example, to make headway in protracted, stalled conflicts, conveners may choose to involve new parties – such as engineers or business people – to change the agenda and open up new opportunities for cooperation.[5] Conveners and managers of negotiations also need to ensure that their negotiations comply with existing laws and regulations[6] and that there is some visible linkage between the negotiated outcome and the related policies and programs that government agencies, or occasionally other parties, choose to implement.

Public dispute resolution interveners agree that *conflict assessment* is a crucial step towards convening the negotiation table (Susskind and Cruikshank 2006; Kim 2007). Conflict assessments are generally conducted by an intervener who begins by identifying potential stakeholders, including both the known vocal parties and others whose interests may be affected by the decision at hand, but who have not yet manifested their interest. Then the intervener conducts a series of in-depth interviews with each party to identify their interests and willingness to participate in the proposed decision (which could be a disputed project or an initiative for change). The conveners' preliminary analysis results in their assessment of whether the negotiation should proceed,[7] which representatives should be at the negotiation table, what approach seems most suitable, and what logistics and resources are needed. A conflict assessment also helps the broader convening process, since the interviews (and the report of responses, shared with all interviewees) also allow the stakeholders to probe the proposed process, influence its shape, and learn more about the intentions and competence of the conflict assessor, the process, and the convener.

Multi-party Conflicts and Process Design

Our second contribution revolves around the oft-unrecognized, multi-party nature of most negotiations. Negotiations are multi-party if there are more than two entities – individuals, groups, organizations – whose interests are at stake in the negotiation, whether or not they are at the table. Public affairs usually involve not only multiple negotiating stakeholders but also multiple levels within some of the parties, and several levels of negotiations. The direct negotiating parties usually represent constituencies that often comprise several organizations with similar interests. Even seemingly hierarchical organizations may have several decision-makers and factions. Some stakeholders, such as legislators, may be involved in negotiations indirectly, especially if the decision under consideration impacts their constituencies or requires a change in laws or regulations. The staffs of government agencies, while not at the table, may have to be consulted if the options being considered impact elements under their purview. Wise representatives spend as much time communicating with, and helping their constituents keep up with the negotiation as they do seeking solutions amongst themselves (Cutcher-Gershenfeld and Watkins 1999; Susskind 1999).

Once convened, the public negotiation process requires careful design so that the scale (number of parties, issues, relationships, etc.) and complexity of the real world (coalitions, parties with different roles and responsibilities, involving constituencies and the broader public effectively, managing the media, etc.) are represented and managed effectively. The number of representatives may have to be limited in order to provide sufficient space for dialogue and negotiation, though some public decision processes have managed to enable meaningful dialogue with high numbers of participants. Mediators often hold meetings with those not at the table to inform them about the process's activities and development and to discuss strategies with those representing their interests. The legitimacy of public decision processes hinges on keeping constituencies informed.

Process decisions create and distribute opportunities and burdens among the parties. Multi-party negotiations in the public sector carry a large management and adaptation burden compared to negotiations between a few private individuals or businesses. One reason is the absence of an overarching organizational structure, and of procedural rules and shared vocabularies. Although interdependent, the parties in public disputes are often laterally rather than hierarchically related. They conduct the negotiations according to a process designed ad hoc for their particular situation, down to the selection of decision rules (e.g., whether the support of two-thirds of the participants carries a decision, or whether consensus is sought). The choice of decision rule affects the power balance among parties. For example, when the decision rule requires unanimity, some parties can log-roll (i.e., trade their yes vote with others to protect their important interests). With a majority decision rule, weaker parties have to form coalitions to advance their interests.[8] Their ability to do so will likely depend on their own resources, as well as on whether the process encourages or impedes communication away from the table among representatives. Then unless the communication within the decision process is managed, the participants run the risk of spending more time building and maintaining coalitions (usually around a negotiated and thus inflexible position) than in understanding and defining the problem appropriately and seeking creative solutions.

Other process challenges involve managing the logistics of multi-stakeholder meetings, sustaining the participation commitment, investing genuine meaning in the representation, learning about technical issues (e.g., scientific, legal, and economic), co-constructing the information base to be used for the decisions, and helping stakeholders produce implementable decisions.

Can/Should Negotiation 1.0 or 2.0 Training Address the Convening and Process Design Challenges?

Conventional negotiation training programs, especially short ones, rarely articulate such procedural aspects. Reasons for this omission include the lack of time in a course with a negotiation teaching agenda that is already quite ambitious, instructors who may have mastered the theory but sometimes have no practice experience, and lack of adequate tools to enable students to practice some of these skills. Simulations typically capture the negotiation moment itself (one face-to-face round), with stakeholders and issues already identified. This is very different from real public negotiation processes. These processes involve a number of face-to-face and away-from-the-table rounds among painstakingly identified parties who develop the issue mix, the timeline, and the decision rules and logistics as part of the negotiation process. Similarly, current role-play negotiation simulations are mostly designed for few stakeholders, with roughly equal power.

Neither convening nor multi-party process design is specifically addressed in most simulation materials and case studies. Public dispute simulations and cases are more difficult to design if they are to reflect even a fraction of their real complexity. (Two such simulations, *Francilienne* and *Silver County*, are described later in this chapter; see also Druckman 2006.) Therefore, fewer of these are available relative to the plethora of few-party simpler negotiations in other contexts, and very few of them model the multi-level nature of public policy negotiations. Nor do simulations address how the negotiation fits in and interacts with broader policy-making efforts. In fact, even public dispute role-plays represent an underlying assumption that most of the action occurs in a few face-to-face negotiation encounters embedded in an already designed process (see Miller and Dingwall 2006). And they also fail to provide any insights about process convening and management, since the simulated negotiation moment happens when all the necessary information has been collected and structured for the benefit of the role-playing students.

Inexperienced mediators have to develop some of the necessary convening and process management skills through trial and error, in the early years of practice as a junior facilitator or mediator, or by apprenticeship – the old-fashioned hands-on way. Negotiation 1.0 and 2.0 may be useful for some aspects of collaborative public decision processes; however, neither addresses adequately the convening challenge that precedes such dialogues. We believe that – even if these skills cannot be honed through coursework alone – we owe students at least awareness of these challenges, as well as some tools to help them acquire the skills. In the following section, we detail some of the challenges in teaching negotiation for public affairs professionals and discuss how Negotiation 2.0 could be improved to address these challenges.

Reports From the Field of Teaching Negotiation
For Public Policy Students

We present briefly the contexts – universities and professional education in Japan, Korea, Singapore and the United States – in which the chapter's authors teach public negotiation, and we describe some of the challenges and solutions in each context. To some extent, the similarities and differences tell of the importance of context (culture, governmental structure and institutions, etc.) not only for the negotiation process but also for its pedagogy. Our similarities and differences also point to the fact that many of the field's insights travel well, but some do not.

Institutional Tuning is as Important as Interpersonal Negotiation Skills (Dong-Young Kim, Korea)

I have taught negotiation and dispute resolution in the public sphere for diverse groups of participants in various venues and occasions in Korea since 2006. In general, the scope and depth of the content and the pedagogical methods vary depending on the time allotted and the contexts in which the trainees will practice. I teach three regular (semester-length) graduate-level courses at the Korea Development Institute (KDI) School of Public Policy and Management: Participatory Governance, Introductory Negotiation Skills in Public Dispute Resolution, and Advanced Topics for Multiparty Negotiations.

All my courses are conducted in English to accommodate the diverse composition of the student body. Half of the students come from developing countries around the world. Most students are junior or mid-career government officials, while a few come from the private sector, including various types of industry, non-government organizations, and media companies. Occasionally, I have designed and provided, through the Center for Conflict Resolution and Negotiation at the KDI School, short-term (two- to three- day) training programs in the Korean language, mainly for Korean government officials. I also lecture in two- or three-hour special sessions within one- or two-day-long workshops for certain organizations.

I began by offering a semester-length negotiation course at KDI, in which students are introduced to the so-called Harvard model for successful negotiation, first proposed by Roger Fisher, William Ury, and Bruce Patton in *Getting to Yes* (1991). Students in this course learn how to conduct interest-based negotiation in order to build consensus on an agreement which is better than their BATNA and consists of one of the options they generate. They also learn how to balance value creation and value claiming through communication with other parties in ways that separate the people from the problem. They improve their negotiating skills and get to understand this prescriptive model by participating in simulation games and through the debriefings designed for specific take-home lessons. Satisfaction with this course seems very high, judging by the high evaluation scores for the course, which is very popular at my institution.

Based on communications with my students and their feedback at the end of the course, I hypothesize that their satisfaction derives mostly from their perceptions that: 1) their interpersonal skills in dealing with angry people and understanding their interests are improved and may prevent worst-case scenarios; and 2) learning methodologies are interesting and stimulating compared to other courses which are mainly in lecture format. They often report that they feel empowered when they perceive that their new skills really worked in negotiation simulations in the classroom and in real (if relatively inconsequential) personal situations outside the classroom. However, the students' answers to the question I pose during the final class of the course greatly intrigue me. I ask them whether they are ready to face reality in typical kinds of public disputes in Korea and their respective home countries, and to change the world. They do not answer my question positively.

The big discrepancy between the high satisfaction level and feelings of empowerment in the classroom and the lack of confidence in facing reality outside the classroom troubles me. How to make my teaching transcend the barriers between classroom-level enlightenment and genuine capacity building in reality has become my key challenge. Several reasons for the discrepancy are expressed in students' comments and in their sharing past and current experience in real public disputes. In reality they rarely get the chance to utilize their skills to create value by inventing options together, because they are much influenced by powerful external forces they feel they cannot control.

For example, in government or public organizations in many developing countries, senior officers are not interested in negotiating or talking with citizens who are perceived as angry and "irrationally demanding," or intent on delaying decision-making and implementation of projects or programs. The incentive system within public organizations is based on a quest for efficiency, which prompts people to go fast first in order to go faster later. This assumption, criticized as false efficiency in many advanced democracies, is not false from their perspective. They perceive other stakeholders, usually powerless citizens, or civil society, to lack the countervailing power to create uncertainties around their unilateral actions.

This perception of government immunity to public challenges stems from a lack of legal foundation which people might use to challenge or sue the government. It is also due to a lack of democratic political battlegrounds where people might shore up their power by building coalitions. In such a context, the powerful party in a conflict dismisses the potential costs of not talking with the less powerful parties. This in turn eliminates the incentives for the less powerful citizenry to come to the negotiation table – a prerequisite for any negotiation. The concept of ripeness (Zartman 2006) applies, though the society cannot wait until a powerless group can accumulate some degree of countervailing power to shake up the current power balance, which may take too long with respect to pressing decision needs.

In accounting for their perceived inadequacy to tackle public disputes, students who have been associated with civil society in developing countries also claim that negotiating with powerful governments is meaningless. Government is so powerful that their voices cannot be heard. Rather than taking a interest-based approach – sit around the table with powerful government agents and talk as partners – they see their only chance at attaining their goals in fighting physically (a power-based approach) to create tangible costs, or other negative consequences such as casualties, for the otherwise unresponsive government. For people who perceive themselves as powerless, the alternative to physical violence is accommodation: accepting the terms set by powerful parties. Then there are no overt disputes or conflicts. For example, millions of rural and indigenous people have been forced to evacuate from their hometowns to make room for the construction of large dams near their town, without any meaningful compensation from companies or governments (Schneider 2005).

Note that these assumptions offered by the students who deal with powerful and powerless groups about the barriers to effective negotiation remain at the personal discourse level. Government officials, for their part, criticize adversarial non-governmental organizations (NGOs) and belligerent residents, accusing them of being irrational, lacking civility, or not having effective negotiation and communication skills. In turn, non-governmental parties blame government officials for being hard-nosed, inflexible, and ineffective negotiators. Perhaps the solution for breaking the barriers to effective negotiation resides in building capacity at both the individual and institutional levels.

Admittedly, my classroom negotiation message about the solution – that personal-level skill sets and mindset changes can solve or prevent public disputes in Korea and other developing countries – is based on an assumption that may not correspond entirely with reality. However, I also came to understand quickly a key reason why the classroom lessons do not match serious, real situations. The classroom negotiation skills are designed to work in situations that fit the institutional, cultural and power balance context of the countries with a tradition of practicing deliberative democracy. For example, in such contexts (which are by no means perfect but much closer to the conditions required for negotiating public decisions) there exist opportunities for parties to improve their BATNAs in various ways, as we recommend in class. But this is not yet the reality of many developing countries. Teaching interpersonal negotiation skills to students who will practice their professions in such situations has inherently limited applicability.

Perhaps negotiation pedagogy should go beyond personal-level skills and should not regard the problematic contexts as set and immutable. If negotiation teaching continues to ignore the real external forces or institutional settings that make students less effective negotiators, and instead keeps promising that with just their negotiating skills they can prevail under such circumstances, soon enough the students become frustrated by the discrepancy between the teaching and the harsh realities created by their interaction with unfamiliar settings they believe they cannot control. Therefore, to go beyond Negotiation 1.0 we should help students look beyond specific personal negotiating behaviors. They should seek to understand their own and the others' behaviors. Then instead of giving up, they can try to change a context inauspicious to negotiation from the inside, as well as from the outside, through informed discourse.

For example, we might teach students about conflict management systems design (e.g., Ury, Brett, and Goldberg 1988; Costantino and Merchant 1996) for the public sphere, although so far it has been applied mainly within organizations. Equipped with such knowledge, students in a public setting may reach a deeper understanding of conflict situations, with more systematic views about the relations between institutional settings, motivation, people's behaviors and skill sets, and resources in organizations and societies. This knowledge is unlikely to go to waste even if we must warn students that as young professionals they will undoubtedly encounter difficulty in seeking to apply this knowledge in the near future, before the social context has changed.

Teaching Innovative Policy Process in the Face of Institutional Inertia (Kenshi Baba, Japan)

My teaching experience derives from organizing a training program of public involvement skills for professionals in charge of facility siting in electric utility companies. In Japan, we have ten electric power companies, which are quasi-monopolies in their respective regions. Electricity facility siting issues have two facets: private companies' decision making, and public policy which affects many stakeholders. These critical issues differentiate my experience with utility industry professionals from other stories involving mostly university students in academic settings.

The training program for facility siting professionals was held in 2003. I prepared a Japanese edition of a public participation guidebook for electric facility siting issues and invited a famous lecturer from the United States who was an author of the guidebook. We designed a one-day program, with material usually delivered over three days. Therefore, the content was limited to basic components and did not have any applied components such as role plays. In their feedback session, the training participants expressed their skepticism about the proposed participatory methods. They expressed doubts about people acting rationally and anticipated difficulties in information disclosure. They expressed their uncertainty about the ability to bring about desired outcomes. Interestingly, the negotiation literature of twenty-five years ago reports that professionals in the United States shared most of these concerns, except for the skepticism about the methodology (Ducsik 1986). Japanese professionals were very reluctant to apply the lessons learned, while the U.S. professionals were more concerned about how to apply them.

By reflecting on my hands-on experience, I have come to think that the Japanese professionals were "locked-in" to their own conventional practices of trying to persuade the local stakeholders to accept their siting proposals. For instance, they adhered to *nemawashi* (caucus with politically powerful individuals) and *annmoku-no-ryou-kai* (getting implicit understandings), techniques that have long been practiced in Japan.

Far from discrediting the effectiveness of participatory negotiation processes for public decisions, my experience suggests that we have to pay attention to the cultural context in which they will be applied, including institutional structures. For instance, in Japan, the legally-mandated Environment Impact Assessment (EIA) system was put in place as recently as in 1999. Even though the training participants had experience with EIAs under a Cabinet guideline, public participation had not been mandatory and information disclosure had been limited in the earlier EIA system. Such institutional arrangements allowed the siting professional to be trapped in the inertia of conventional practices.

The context is changing, however. First, the structure of Japanese rural communities has been changing. Political figures are no longer powerful enough to persuade community members through the traditional approaches. Second, newly introduced procedures require extensive public participation. For instance, the amended EIA law of 2011 requires a Strategic Environmental Assessment for major power projects. Therefore, siting professionals will inevitably be faced with the need to deal with the new context in the near future.

In such an environment, one would expect the siting professionals to see the need to explore and acquire new negotiation skills. However, they continue to adhere to seemingly obsolete and impractical negotiation tactics in the changing environment. My experience with a training session in 2003 confirms this trend.

This incongruity suggests that the conventional practice of persuading local communities is embedded in the organizational culture of the utilities industry. There is a strong inertia among the corporate workers to adhere to the conventional practice, rather than to try a new approach. Therefore, a new model of corporate training has to be introduced. For instance, negotiation training can be embedded in a longer-term organizational change effort, such as Kurt Lewin's (1947) unfreeze-change-freeze steps, especially if corporate members follow particular processes despite their ineffectiveness in the current environment–which is something they may be reluctant to admit.

Teaching Stakeholder Analysis and Process Design
(Sanda Kaufman, United States)
I teach at the Levin College of Urban Affairs (Cleveland State University), which offers undergraduate and graduate degrees in public administration, public management, planning, environmental studies, and nonprofit administration. I have designed and teach the only negotiation course (offered in each of two semesters, and cross-listed for both undergraduate and master's degree students). This course is elective for graduate students, but it is part of the core requirements for some undergraduate degrees, such as public safety. Only a small proportion of my audience, however, is "captive," suggesting that many students recognize the professional need to acquire negotiation and conflict management skills. Usually each of my classes has a mix of students working towards all the degrees offered. I also teach an environmental dispute resolution semester-long course for environmental professionals, and several executive-style negotiation workshops in one- or three-day formats for elected officials and government agency staff from the Northeast Ohio region.

The college courses face several challenges, driven only in part by class makeup and the need to pack a great deal of information and skills practice into a single course. Chief among the challenges is the students' acculturation (from other courses and from their public service orientation) to a perspective on public issues that makes it difficult for them to entertain perspectives different from their own. In role-plays that are the stock-in-trade of negotiation classes they have difficulty in representing credibly some of the roles (such as industry representatives, or lawyers). In debriefs, students in "bad guy" roles as they tend to define them (again, the industry reps and the lawyers) acknowledge their difficulties and the fact that they readily saw the need to concede in order to serve communities or protect the environment. In that sense, we face the same effects as when mono-cultural students are asked to represent negotiators from other (unfamiliar) cultures: what emerges in role-plays are the students' stereotypes of these other cultures. Their skills are not advanced, and indeed their stereotypes may be reinforced.

The same professional acculturation seems to communicate rather too effectively the notion that cooperation is a virtue, rather than a conscious choice of strategy based on the specifics of a situation that has genuine alternatives. This undermines the development of persuasion skills, since they are rarely needed. In the spirit of Richard Shell (2000), I find myself too often having to remind students that agreements are not good in themselves, and can even be detrimental if they do not serve the interests of the stakeholders they represent better than the alternatives.

The challenges that I probably share with many of my colleagues who teach negotiations for public decisions relate to the scarcity of materials for effective teaching of process-related negotiation skills. Even if a few of us may have developed some helpful devices and experiences, these are not nearly as widely known and available as the usual one-shot, face-to-face, equal-power simulations we all tend to use. Granted: the single-course model may be inadequate for accommodating all that students should ideally master in order to be effective at representing stakeholders in public decisions; skills such as selecting stakeholding representatives for direct participation, negotiating the issue mix, or the effect of external events that may change the stances of participants are difficult to simulate in the classroom. Nevertheless, we are arguably shortchanging our students when we do not convey to them a full picture of the reality with which they will contend as professionals, and when we do not equip them with process design tools. Thus, despite all contextual differences among public decision settings, this view parallels the conclusion Dong-Young Kim reached based on his teaching in Korea. This is an example of principles that travel well across continents though the details of how they apply differ (and the devil is in the details!). We have made a similar claim about the negotiation principles we all teach.

The few notable exceptions to the paucity of rich, reality-like simulations illustrate well the obstacles we face in producing more of the rich materials that address process design issues. The two I present here briefly – the *Francilienne* and *Silver County* – are far from perfect, but they are helpful in representing facets of the reality of public domain negotiations we rarely capture with the more usual simulations (see also Druckman 2006).

The *Francilienne* (De Carlo 2009) is a multi-media set of materials delivered (at the time of its production) on a (rather costly) CD-ROM, containing information – in the form of numerous official documents, press and TV clips, interviews with stakeholders, news-like filmed public protests – about the site selection and other issues related to the real project to build the Francilienne peripheral highway around

Paris to alleviate traffic problems. Students are provided with various negotiation theory materials, and then are asked to study a portion of the materials, reflect, propose and discuss next steps and other negotiation issues, after which they are progressively served other chunks of the material as they occur in time. The *Francilienne* illustrates very effectively the complexity of public decisions, the diversity of perspectives driven by divergent interests, power issues, and institutional arrangements, along with the obstacles they present to negotiated agreements, the difficulties in evaluating highly technical information, aspects of the public participation process – not to mention the information overload that any stakeholder may experience in similar situations. The very fact that this simulation (in French) has not made inroads to become one of our staple classroom materials illustrates one of the key points of this chapter – that culture and institutional arrangements differ enough that the more realistic a simulation is, the less it can travel.

Silver County draws on many real conflicts, some played out in Colorado, which is the model (Elliott et al. 2002). It uses (fictitious) web-based press clips, agency documents, organization websites, maps and plans of an imaginary county sharing many characteristics with the real Colorado situations on which it draws. It can be used in several ways depending on instructional needs. For example, it can be delivered in installments along a semester to communicate the duration of such public decision making, the many venues in which stakeholders attempt to protect their interests, and the lack of a "script," making it necessary to negotiate the decision process itself. It illustrates well many of the characteristics of public decisions reflected in the *Francilienne*. Students can be asked to understand and represent some of the parties, and propose a negotiation process for addressing some or all the conflicts (including population and economic growth issues, land conservation, environmental justice, industrial pollution cleanup, and protection of an endangered frog species). Since there is no classroom negotiation table, students can engage in coalition building and negotiations in different venues, including or excluding other participants. I often urge students to use their confidential role instructions in the usual (one-shot) simulations as models for how they should prepare for real negotiations. With *Silver County* they can use the available materials and assemble them in role formats, and even practice being constituents who must give instructions to their representative. This simulation too was rather labor-intensive, though perhaps less than its French counterpart.

These two examples suggest that with a different approach to simulations, we may yet bring into the classroom the reality of public decision processes. Neither of the two directly helps teach process design, but instructors can use such materials along a semester to drive home some of the basics, certainly better than with the simulations built around one face-to-face negotiation session with pre-digested marching orders for each role.

In the environmental dispute resolution course I have used a different strategy for bringing to the classroom some of the complexities of the convening process. I have asked groups of three to four students to find local cases of environmental disputes, to conduct a stakeholder analysis using only publicly accessible information (meeting documents, websites, etc.), and to propose a process design, or critique the decision process actually used. Though this semester-long exercise lacks the reality check that would be afforded by stakeholder interviews, it does help students to confront real complexities and attempt to understand perspectives different from their own, as well as the difficulties of process design.

On a continuum of classroom experiences from the simplest role-plays to complex simulations, to documenting and analyzing real cases, to adventure learning (as described in other chapters), to practicing convening and process design in the context of real cases with real stakeholders, it seems apparent that the latter may be considered a "gold standard," because there is no substitute for pitting students against the richness of reality. However, such experiences are not easily afforded in all situations. For example, in communities such as Northeast Ohio (with a considerably smaller population than Tokyo, Seoul or Singapore), where only a handful of stakeholding representatives are likely to take part in most public decision deliberations, sending forty students every semester to interview them would quickly give rise to stakeholder fatigue. We have the responsibility of protecting stakeholders' limited time for meaningful participation. Soliciting interviews as practice for the students would only be possible on rare occasions. Therefore, our challenge remains to produce more of the complex simulations that are rich, realistic, and institutional context-specific, and to make them broadly available.

Experiential Convening Training Through Practicum (Masahiro Matsuura, Japan)

The Graduate School of Public Policy (GraSPP) at the University of Tokyo was established in 2004 as a unique program for training public policy professionals. Following national educational system reforms, the school offers a new kind of master's degree that certifies professional skills for policy-making. Its curriculum includes many practicum courses that involve students in actual policy-making efforts and develops their skills through direct experience.

While conventional negotiation training is an integral part of cultivating students' ability to assess the situation and develop an effective negotiating strategy in the public policy field, students benefit enormously from additional training opportunities that encourage them to reflect on negotiation in the context of policy making. A number of factors, not only cultural but also institutional and legal, affect negotiation in the public policy field (Matsuura 2007). Students must acquire the practical knowledge that will help them design deliberative policy processes to negotiate effectively. Kim's account of his students' difficulties in applying negotiation skills to the field in developing nations supports this point.

Since 2007, I have been offering a semester-long course called "Public Policy Process Management" with two other instructors at the GraSPP. In real settings, groups of three to five students are asked to conduct a stakeholder analysis as if they were nonpartisan interveners. While the topics for their analysis are proposed by instructors, students explore the issue with real government officials or civil society activists, design interview protocols, conduct interviews, and analyze the key issues and interests of stakeholders. Each instructor is assigned to one of the student groups and provides mentoring and advice for their interviews and analysis. This is in fact a semi-simulated opportunity for the students to obtain practical skills (including ways of conducting effective interviews with real stakeholders). Our course offers a safe environment for them to engage in experiential learning.

For instance, in summer 2011 my students explored the effect of global climate change in the agriculture sector in a particular subregion of a prefecture. The students identified the stakeholders and explored how they could design a dialogue for devising a better climate change policy in the agricultural sector. After I facilitated the development of necessary rapport between the students and a few key local government officials, students conducted interviews with farmers, seed growers, and retailers. I set up an email list for the student group in order to monitor the communication among them, as well as their correspondence with stakeholders.

The group produced a list of key stakeholders to be included in the discussion about the effect of climate change on agriculture in that particular area. Their analysis was enlightening to the community of climate change researchers; it found that most stakeholders in the agricultural sector are not much worried about global climate change. Stakeholders were concerned about short-term issues, such as the fluctuating national trade policy, the lack of successors, and the price tag of anti-climate change measures.[9] The students presented their findings in class and in a written report. They also presented their findings to the local farmer community, as well as to a nation-ally-commissioned research group exploring possible climate change adaptation policy.

This course has been popular since its start and has enrolled the maximum number of students for our supervising capacity. While I offer another semester-long Negotiation 1.0 course in a relatively con-ventional format, this kind of practicum has to become an integral part of training professionals under the Negotiation 2.0 pedagogy. Every professional field has its own professional norms and standards of practice, so the lessons from Negotiation 1.0 courses have to be tailored to each student's professional setting. Students can improve their own theory-in-use by reflecting on their practice through the lens of negotiation theories. Based on my experience, however, it seems more effective for a trainer to offer a course or session in which trainees can apply their knowledge to practice, in a relatively safe set-ting.

The Challenge of Convening (Boyd Fuller, Singapore)

The class taught by Masahiro Matsuura on stakeholder analysis fo-cuses the students on one of the key activities of convening consen-sus-building processes for public disputes. I focus here on convening as a whole. Convening plays an important role in bringing parties to the negotiation table in public disputes. I believe this topic has received too little attention in the Negotiation 2.0 project, given that most negotiating professionals are likely to become stakeholders in a public decision process sometime during their careers.

In my research around Asia and the United States, getting parties to the table ready, willing and able to negotiate is often one of the big-gest challenges for negotiation, in many contexts. Even in the United States, with its relatively long history of public participation, negoti-ated rule-making, mediated settlements of environmental litigation, and other forms of public dispute resolution, parties often choose to negotiate only when they come to believe that all other options (which they tend to prefer) will fail to yield acceptable results.

In Asia, the challenges are greater, in large part because there is little experience with deliberative processes. As Dong-Young Kim re-ports for the Korean case and Kenshi Baba observes in the Japanese case, decision makers are often unused to, uncertain about, and re-luctant to increase the involvement of non-traditional parties in deci-sion-making. They may worry about getting attacked and losing face in front of hostile stakeholders. They may worry about the lack of expertise of some stakeholders (e.g., civil society, the public) and how that might distort policy-making. Their traditional negotiation counterparts, such as domestic and international big business and other government agencies, may not want to negotiate with new partners, or change what is for them a known and often seemingly favorable agenda. They may worry about how negotiating with new players might impact their own benefits. Finally, the new parties are greater in number, unfamiliar, and sometimes positioned lower in the social hierarchy.

Accompanying the various apprehensions about negotiating public decisions, there is a cultural tendency in some Asian countries to avoid conflict and to emphasize harmony. A T-shirt that I have often seen in Malaysian tourist shops illustrates this point well. It shows the facial expressions for each mood – e.g., sad, angry, happy, etc. On the shirt, each mood is accompanied by the same happy face, to indicate how the Malaysians often hide their true feelings behind polite smiles. Stakeholders often delay discussing their disagreements openly until it very late, or even too late. When the disagreement does surface, some of the parties are still unwilling to negotiate, often because they feel injured by the other party(-ies) and believe that negotiation will yield nothing.

And yet, the pressure to involve civil society organizations and citizens in policy-making is increasing in several democratic Asian countries. The key challenge for proponents of consensus building and other forms of multi-stakeholder processes and negotiations is how to help governments and other stakeholders convene processes that not only produce effective and legitimate results but also create the skills and desire to use negotiations for addressing other issues. In this context, I see one of my roles as a teacher of negotiation and public dispute resolution at the Lee Kuan Yew School of Public Policy as preparing people to take on the task of getting the *process* right. The students who take my advanced negotiation course on convening and facilitating policy dialogues represent possible proponents (change agents) who are working or will work in public sector entities, and will seek to advance the use of negotiated decision processes.[10]

The most applied project in my course is a policy dialogue. Students are required to convene and facilitate such a dialogue (usually no longer than one day long) involving stakeholders other than themselves on an issue around which there is noticeable debate and disagreement. During the course of the semester, students have to identify a topic and then go through the process of convening their proposed dialogue. They have to do research beforehand to identify potential stakeholders and their interests, and the issues about which they disagree. From that point on, the students usually plan and conduct a conflict assessment. The interviews they conduct help the group learn more about the content of the disagreement, the interests of particular stakeholders, and their willingness to participate in the proposed dialogue. The interviews also help the stakeholders to learn more about the students – e.g., how serious and knowledgeable they are – as well as the proposed purpose and product of the dialogue.

As the students conduct their conflict assessment, they also discover some of the factors that can block some parties from participating or even meeting with the class representative. In one case, for example, some government stakeholders refused to talk with students because of the sensitivity of the issues, and of ongoing negotiations on the same issue taking place behind the scenes. As students work through these challenges, they can discover more about the considerations of stakeholders, how their classroom process can have real political implications, and also about some of the levers they can pull to get reluctant parties to meet them or participate.

Process design is another aspect of convening. Initial design ideas have to be shared with stakeholders during the conflict assessment interviews. As the conflict assessment concludes and the class is better informed about the issues and stakeholders, the students usually prepare a more detailed design to send with their official invitations to the potential participants.

Lastly, students need to understand and practice how to create the necessary political legitimacy and support for the dialogue. As the students discuss the proposed process with those they interview, those stakeholders often ask them what the dialogue hopes to accomplish, what agency or actor is supporting it, and whether it is linked with any official process. Devising answers for these questions and preparing them ahead of meetings with stakeholders becomes part of the students' tool kit.

The Singaporean and Japanese cases propose teaching innovations that are similar, in that both teach, through a combination of real situations and simulated convening, the importance of the conflict assessment stage, and of understanding the interests of multiple parties before negotiation starts. In both instances, students take on the role of a process designer or process manager rather than that of a stakeholding negotiator. Both cases suggest complementing Negotiation 1.0 teaching with hands-on experience in areas that have not been effectively simulated in the classroom.

Implications of Our Experience for the Journey to Negotiation 2.0

Context Matters: Integrating Public Policy Elements in the Pedagogy

Our reports from the field converge on the need to tailor negotiation training to the public policy context. Matsuura and Fuller highlight the need to give enough attention to the difficulties of convening, which we have already discussed in the introduction of this chapter. Kim and Baba discuss the effect of institutional barriers and inertia, which together limit the application of Negotiation 1.0 in many real public policy settings. Kaufman focuses on the lack of teaching materials that orient students in the complexities of public policy disputes.

None of the authors, however, dismisses the utility of training public policy students with the conventional Negotiation 1.0 pedagogy. In fact, we all continue to teach basic negotiation courses even while we are alert to the discrepancy from the complex settings of actual public policy negotiations. What we argue for is the need to develop additional components for the Negotiation 1.0 curriculum that address unique features of negotiation and disputes in each field of practice. We also propose that far from being useful only to public policy students, public decision negotiation skills should be taught more broadly, because professionals in all fields of practice may become parties to a public decision.

Experiential Learning: Embedding Students in Real Settings

In the introduction, we stressed the significance in the public domain of the convening process in negotiation decisions. Matsuura and Fuller offer similar semester-long courses to their students at their public policy schools, in which they teach convening explicitly. The former asks his students to conduct a stakeholder analysis (i.e., assessment of issues and key stakeholders), and the latter asks them to bring actual stakeholders to the table and manage a constructive dialogue among them.

Such a course, which requires students to engage in real issues, often called a practicum, has long been in place in the public policy and planning schools. In conventional negotiation pedagogy, however, most instructors have relied on in-class simulated negotiation. As Kaufman points out, most simulation materials provide only a simplified negotiation framework, and omit the complexities with which real negotiators have to deal. Considering the complex nature of the real transactions and the difficulty of simulating them satisfactorily for teaching purposes, it seems likely that students would learn much more from going out of the classroom and engaging in real negotiation.

At graduate schools, a practicum could be designed as an opportunity for action research. Students could identify real decision situations, involve key stakeholders, and practice their negotiation process design skills to help communities. Since the whole process could take several years, depending on the magnitude of the issue, an instructor could involve students only in some parts of the whole action research process. Professors can team up with consultants and professionals to design such a practicum. Although its application might have to be limited to full-time students rather than executive training (because of the time and resources required), a negotiation practicum could be a major contribution to the journey to Negotiation 2.0.

Institutional Aspects: Changing the System
Reflecting on feedback from his students, Kim discussed the difficulties of applying the lessons from Negotiation 1.0 lectures to the real situations in Korea and in certain developing countries due to power distance. A similar issue was raised by Baba's frustrating experience with the introduction of participatory processes to the "locked-in" utility industry. Kaufman also discusses the effect of students' professional acculturation and its effect on learning to negotiate on behalf of constituencies.

In response, Kim suggests that negotiation pedagogy should include lessons from dispute resolution systems design, and expand them to the extra-organizational domain, in order to cultivate students' thinking in terms of systems. Baba quotes Kurt Lewin's organizational change process as a strategy for introducing a new participatory planning process. These are areas that should probably be addressed in Negotiation 2.0. Conventional negotiation training has focused on how the self and the others can maximize their joint benefit, without addressing the specific context. The focus is on the negotiating parties, as if process and outcomes depended only on their choices. This framing of negotiation obscures the significant influence of institutions (e.g., regulations, organizations, and norms) and professional cultures on negotiation.

Negotiation 2.0 should give more attention to the interaction between the institutions and individual negotiation, and encourage students to consider how one can change the institutional structures in ways that bring about the mutual gains that have been featured in the Negotiation 1.0 framework.

Conclusion

Four of the five co-authors of this chapter practice and teach negotiations in Asian countries. There are important and real institutional, organizational, and cultural differences between the North American and the Asian settings that affect considerably how decisions are made in the public domain. These differences pose an added layer of difficulty to the teaching of public dispute negotiations.

Historically, practice, research, and teaching dispute resolution in the public sector began in the United States, where models of public conflict resolution have emerged that fit the institutional context rather well. However, there is hardly a perfect contextual match, if any, between the United States and other countries in terms of scale, of cultural, political, administrative and legal arrangements, and of processes within which public decision negotiations occur. The "American model" and its attendant simulations have traveled far and wide. Despite the fact that the chapter authors teach in very different public decision contexts, not only have they learned the same principles, but they are also using largely the same instruction materials and simulations. There are some good reasons for this: as we have rediscovered by comparing our experiences, some of the negotiation prescriptions developed in the North American context do travel very well at their most general level. For example, seeking mutually beneficial trade-offs or attending to relationships seem to have no contextual downside. Perhaps that is so partly because some stakeholders' tendencies, such as focus on short-term individual consequences at the expense of long-term collective outcomes, seems to transcend continents. However, to become useful at the practice level, the generally valid prescriptions within the Negotiation 2.0 framework may have to be tuned to context specifics; and some locally-adapted prescriptions may have to be generated.

In the process of identifying which prescriptions are robust, which are in need of adaptation, and what new prescriptions are needed to navigate different contexts, we may discover that some of the latter may also travel well back to the United States. This kind of comparative work may be necessary for an added reason. Globalization of economies and externalities makes necessary and likely the negotiation of international agreements that require mutual understanding of differing decision contexts. Successful international negotiations (e.g., the Law of the Sea) and failed ones (e.g., the Copenhagen negotiations over climate change) suggest that while international agreements are possible, they require attention to precisely the contextual, not just cultural, differences we are highlighting here.

Notes

[1] Negotiation 1.0 and 2.0 (as in the title of this chapter) refer to the different generations of negotiation pedagogy as described in earlier volumes in this series.

[2] For reasons more fully described by Christopher Honeyman, James Coben, and Andrew Lee (see *What Have We Learned*, in this volume), the project's early use of the computer metaphor to describe its critique and revitalization agenda was largely abandoned as the project itself matured.

[3] We believe it is equally important for instructors in other fields to characterize their negotiation contexts and include in their teaching the skills necessary for those specific contexts.

[4] In volume two of the RNT series, the editors and a number of chapter authors used the term "wicked" to describe problems that exhibit some combination of the following features:

- The problem is ill-defined and resists clear definition as a technical issue, because wicked problems are also social, political, and moral in nature. Each proposed definition of the problem implies a particular kind of solution which is loaded with contested values. Consequently, merely defining the problem can incite passionate conflict.
- Solutions to a wicked problem cannot be labeled good or bad; they can only be considered better or worse, good enough or not good enough. Whether a solution is good enough depends on the values and judgment of each of the parties, who will inevitably assess the problem and its potential solutions from their respective positions within the social context of the problem.
- Every wicked problem is unique and novel, because even if the technical elements appear similar from one situation to another, the social, political, and moral features are context-specific.
- A wicked problem contains an interconnected web of sub-problems; every proposed solution to part or the whole of the wicked problem will affect other problems in the web.

See Honeyman and Coben (2010: 440), citing generally Rittel and Webber (1973), Ritchey (2005-2008) and Conklin (2005).

[5] For example, Paula Garb and John Whitely (2001) describe how two warring parties in the Caucasus were able to reach agreements on how to run a hydroelectric facility that spanned the territories under their control, and allocate its benefits. Crucial to this cooperation was the presence of engineers from both sides, who helped refocus the negotiations around the practical matters of running the facility.

[6] For example, a negotiation may have to comply with a "sunshine law" that requires the process to be open to some form of broader public involvement. The U.S. legislation on sunshine laws provides a useful example and can be found at http://sunshinereview.org/index.php/State_Open_Meetings_Laws (last accessed May 2, 2012). Similarly, a mediator may not be able to offer legal advice unless she has qualifications that are recognized under the law for doing so.

[7] At times, the conflict assessment report can conclude that a specific situation is not ripe for tackling, is too polarized, or has a severe power imbalance, so that mediation or consensus building is unsuitable or unlikely to succeed.

[8] Weaker parties can also take on facilitating roles, helping to improve communication and problem-solving while using that position to keep their interests on the agenda.

[9] This example illustrates that while the specifics differ, some public decision situation characteristics are not unique to a location. Thus the same attention to short-range individual interests uncovered by the students in a Japanese prefecture trumps collective long-range interests in a Northeast Ohio watershed, preventing necessary adaptations to predicted effects of climate change. The situation characteristic that travels across the Pacific Ocean in these two examples is the underlying Commons Dilemma structure of the incentives compelling stakeholders in both cases to make choices they may live to regret.

[10] The much-needed Geographic Information Systems (GIS), now standard in most planning agencies and in many other organizations making decisions with spatial consequences, is a good model for this approach of sending change agents into the real world. GIS adoption was slow as agency staffs were reluctant to train for and adopt the new (complicated) technology. Graduates of planning programs equipped with the skills became the change agents, as they increasingly *demanded* to use GIS at work until the practice percolated. By now, not only do most agencies use it, they have also adopted shared base maps allowing them to share necessary data.

References

Conklin, J. 2005. Wicked problems and social complexity. In *Dialogue mapping: Building shared understanding of wicked problems*, edited by J. Conklin. New York: Wiley.

Costantino, C. A. and C. S. Merchant. 1996. *Designing conflict management systems*. San Francisco, CA: Jossey-Bass.

Cutcher-Gershenfeld, J. and M. Watkins. 1999. Toward a theory of representation in negotiation. In *Negotiating on behalf of others: Advice to lawyers, business executives, sports agents, diplomats, politicians, and everybody else*, edited by R. H. Mnookin, L. Susskind, and P. C. Foster. Thousand Oaks, CA: Sage.

De Carlo, L. 2005. Accepting conflict and experiencing creativity: Teaching "concentration" using *La Francilienne* CD-ROM. *Negotiation Journal* 21(1): 85-103.

Druckman, D. 2006. Uses of a marathon exercise. In *The negotiator's fieldbook: The desk reference for the experienced negotiator*, edited by A. K. Schneider and C. Honeyman. Washington, DC: American Bar Association.

Ducsik, W. D. 1986. *Public involvement in energy facility planning: The electric utility experience*. Boulder, CO: Westview Press.

Elliott, M., S. Kaufman, R. Gardner, and G. Burgess. 2002. Teaching conflict assessment and frame analysis through interactive web-based simulations. *International Journal of Conflict Management* 13(4): 320-340.

Fisher, R., W. Ury, and B. Patton. 1991. *Getting to yes: Negotiating agreement without giving in*, 2nd edn. New York: Penguin.

Fuller, B. 2011. Enabling problem-solving between science and politics in water conflicts: Impasses and breakthroughs in the Everglades. *Hydrological Sciences Journal* 56(4): 576-587.

244 EDUCATING NEGOTIATORS FOR A CONNECTED WORLD

Garb, P. and J. M. Whiteley. 2001. A hydroelectric power complex on both sides of a war: Potential weapon or peace incentive? In *Reflections on water: New approaches to transboundary conflicts and cooperation*, edited by J. Blatter and H. Ingram. Cambridge, MA: MIT Press.

Honeyman, C. and J. Coben. 2010. Navigating wickedness: A new frontier in teaching negotiation. In *Venturing beyond the classroom: Volume 2 in the rethinking negotiation teaching series*, edited by C. Honeyman, J. Coben, and G. De Palo. St. Paul, MN: DRI Press.

Kaufman, S. 2011. Complex systems, anticipation, and collaborative planning for resilience. In *Resilient organizations: Social learning for hazard mitigation and adaptation*, edited by B. Goldstein. Boston: MIT Press.

Kim, D-Y. 2007. *The challenges of consensus building in a consolidating democracy: Diesel vehicles and urban air pollution in Korea*. Saarbrücken, DE: VDM Verlag.

Lewicki, R. J. and A. K. Schneider. 2010. Instructors heed the who: Designing negotiation training with the learner in mind. In *Venturing beyond the classroom: Volume 2 in the rethinking negotiation teaching series*, edited by C. Honeyman, J. Coben, and G. De Palo. St. Paul, MN: DRI Press.

Lewin, K. 1947. Frontiers in group dynamics: II. Channels of group life; social planning and action research. *Human Relations* 1(2): 143–153.

Matsuura, M. 2007. *Localizing public dispute resolution in Japan: Lessons from experiments with deliberative policy-making*. Saarbrücken, DE: VDM Verlag.

Miller, G. and R. Dingwall. 2006. When the play's in the wrong theater. In *The negotiator's fieldbook: The desk reference for the experienced negotiator*, edited by A. K. Schneider and C. Honeyman. Washington, DC: American Bar Association.

Mnookin, R. 2010. *Bargaining with the devil: When to negotiate, when to fight*. Chicago, IL: Simon & Schuster.

Ozawa, C. 1991. *Recasting science: Consensus-based procedures in public policy making*. Boulder, CO: Westview Press.

Ritchey, T. 2005-2008. *Wicked problems: Structuring social messes with morphological analysis*. Swedish Morphological Society. Available at http://www.swemorph.com/pdf/wp.pdf (last accessed May 20, 2012).

Rittel, H. W. J., and M. M. Webber. 1973. Dilemmas in a general theory of planning. *Policy Sciences* 4: 155-169.

Schneider, A. K. 2005. *From commitment to implementation: The report of the world commission on dams after five years*. Berkeley: International Rivers Network.

Shell, R. 2000. *Bargaining for advantage: Negotiation strategies for reasonable people*. New York: Penguin.

Shmueli, D., S. Kaufman and C. Ozawa. 2008. Mining negotiation theory for planning insights. *Journal of Planning, Education & Research* 27(3): 359-364.

Susskind, L. 1999. Commentary: The shifting roles of agents in interest-based negotiations. In *Negotiating on behalf of others: Advice to lawyers, business executives, sports agents, diplomats, politicians, and everybody else*, edited by R. H. Mnookin, L. Susskind and P. C. Foster. Thousand Oaks, CA: Sage.

Susskind, L. and J. Cruikshank. 1987. *Breaking the impasse: Consensual approaches to resolving public disputes*. New York: Basic Books.

Susskind, L. and J. Cruikshank. 2006. *Breaking Robert's rules: The new way to run your meeting, build consensus, and get results.* New York: Oxford University Press.

Ury, W. L., J. M. Brett, and S. B. Goldberg. 1988. *Getting disputes resolved.* San Francisco: Jossey-Bass.

Zartman, I.W. 2006. Timing and ripeness. In *The negotiator's fieldbook: The desk reference for the experienced negotiator*, edited by A. K. Schneider and C. Honeyman. Washington, DC: American Bar Association.

❧ 10 ❧

Ethics in Legal Negotiation:
A Cross-Cultural Perspective

Andrea Kupfer Schneider, Ellen Deason, Dawn Chen
*& Zhouxh Xiahong**

Editors' Note: From Chinese and American perspectives, the authors consider a Chinese negotiation class, when presented with an ethical problem or two, as a lens. They examine the implications of the students' decisions for Chinese negotiations, particularly in an environment of law practice. In turn they use these as the basis for an analysis of the larger implications of a rapid and disorienting series of recent changes in Chinese law and legal practice.

Introduction

The *Rethinking Negotiation Teaching* Conference held in May of 2011 in Beijing presented numerous opportunities to expand one's view of negotiation and the issues presented from a variety of international perspectives. One such opportunity was the privilege of watching a negotiation class and observing both the students negotiating and the classroom debrief. The particular negotiation simulation raises issues of disclosure – both whether disclosure is required under the law and whether it is mandated by some set of moral values. The negotiation and the debriefing led to a discussion among conference participants

* **Andrea Kupfer Schneider** is a professor of law at Marquette University Law School in Milwaukee, Wisconsin. Her email address is andrea.schneider@ marquette.edu. **Ellen Deason** is the Joanne Wharton Murphy/Classes of 1965 and 1973 professor of law at The Ohio State University Moritz College of Law in Columbus, Ohio. Her email address is deason.2@osu.edu. **Dawn Chen** is an arbitrator for The China International Economic and Trade Arbitration Commission (CIETAC) and the Beijing Arbitration Commission (BAC) and an adjunct professor at China University of Political Science and Law in Beijing, China. Her email address is dawnchen2010@hotmail.com. **Zhouxh Xiahong** is a professor of law at Jilin University School of Law in Changchun, China. Her email address is zhouxh@jln.edu.cn.

of differences between the United States and China, which proved quite interesting. This essay expands on that conversation. First, we outline in more detail what we observed during the class. Second, we discuss the current situation in China in terms of ethics codes, requirements, and education. Finally, we offer suggestions on teaching cross-cultural negotiation in both the United States and China, given the differences in approach.

An Ethics Class Within a Chinese Negotiation Class

Conference participants observed a negotiation class taught by our colleagues Andrew Wei-Min Lee and Vivian Feng Ying Yu at Peking University. The class is taught in English, and the students who are taking the class are obviously some of the best and brightest – Peking is the one of the best universities in China, and all of the students we met already spoke beautiful English. This was all the more impressive since their English-speaking skills were all classroom-taught and not from travels abroad or endless television watching.

The class negotiated a version of the DONS simulation from Harvard's Program on Negotiation.[1] In this case, lawyers are negotiating a settlement between a woman and the man whom she infected with a deadly disease (think early-day AIDS with no cure). He has quit his job and has given away all of his possessions. The catch is that the man was just tested again and, it turns out, does not actually have the disease. He is in the 0.1 percent of the population that is immune. He tells his lawyer not to tell the other lawyer or the woman, because he wants her to suffer and pay him as much as possible. On the woman's side of the negotiation, it turns out that she has recently inherited a significant amount of money, and does not want this fact shared with the other side. She wants to protect the money to support her young daughter after she herself dies from the disease. Should either of the lawyers reveal their "secret" in the negotiation? (For those of you who are not familiar with the simulation, STOP: What would *you* do?)

The students negotiated – in English – in a courtyard of the university, with four or five conference participants observing each negotiation. They then discussed the negotiation with those observers, as Professor Lee rotated among the groups to get a sampling of the content. After ten to fifteen minutes of discussion, all the groups reconvened in the classroom for a large group debriefing led by Professor Lee.

In the small groups, the visiting observers responded to the way each negotiation developed. They were not given instructions on topics to cover in the debriefings, and some participants were not familiar with the DONS problem. As a result, the content of the discussion probably varied among the groups. In both small groups in which co-authors of this chapter participated, conversation centered on how the students had approached the negotiation, what they were trying to accomplish, and the thought process behind their choices. These negotiations had quickly moved to haggling over very specific monetary terms. The observers explored other possible, mostly interest-based, approaches with the students.

There was some discussion about the information that the lawyers had been instructed not to share, but this topic was not the dominant theme of the small group debriefing. Neither side in the negotiation had disclosed their sensitive information and all of the students said they were comfortable with this decision. They appeared to assume that they had no choice but to follow the client's instructions. The observers raised both utilitarian and strategic questions about what might have been lost by not disclosing, as well as the effects of not disclosing over the long term, when the omissions eventually would become apparent to the other side (the daughter of the dying woman would eventually learn that the boyfriend was healthy, and the lawyers would also likely interact again in other cases). Being ignorant about the professional responsibility framework for lawyers in China, however, the observers in our groups did not discuss the students' decisions to maintain secrecy in the context of ethical rules. The Chinese rules were outside the expertise of the foreign observers, and it would have seemed presumptuous to introduce U.S. or other national rules with which we were familiar.

When we returned to class, it turned out that *none* of the students in any negotiating group had revealed the information. In addition, when all of the information was revealed during the debrief, none of the students seemed perturbed or angry about this situation and how it might have affected their negotiations. Both of these results were rather different from what is often seen in U.S. classrooms when there is "hidden" information. Current U.S. contract law on fraud would void any settlement where a material fact was false – and there was consensus among the observers that the fact of the favorable test result was material.[2] Additionally, under U.S. rules of professional responsibility, a lawyer must correct a misimpression (the health status of the plaintiff) when that is material.[3] (Although the financial information of the defendant is interesting, it is not considered material under U.S. law.[4]) When those of us who have taught DONS or similar cases with secret information in the United States to students who do not reveal the new information (and this clearly does happen in class), we often see a shaming or backlash in the classroom discussion after the negotiation. Students are generally confronted on their lies in terms of the morality of lying about the health condition, as well as suffering strategic and reputational costs when the lie is discovered.[5] Debrief afterwards often focuses on the law, the requirements under the rules of professional responsibility, and reputational costs. Students who have committed the lie often apologize or defend their actions (mistakenly) as required under the rules. Students who are lied to are generally not blasé but rather indignant. It was interesting to the foreign observers that this type of conversation did not occur in the classroom in China.

In addition, neither the students nor the professors in China delved into the conversation of what was required under the law or what a lawyer "should" do – this was rather different from the emphasis on external rules when the same situation gets taught in the United States. Several students emphasized that they would not do anything illegal, leaving foreign observers unsure if the settlement in this case would be fraudulent under Chinese law. Of course, it is rather difficult to draw broad conclusions about what we saw given that the law students were negotiating in a second (or third) language, in front of observers, and that the debrief was conducted in public. The students and their professors could well have been circumspect in their criticism of their peers.

Another possibility is that the questions raised in the debriefing reflected a Confucian approach to ethics that focuses on an individual's internalization of social norms rather than an external rule set (Yu Dan 2006). Students were asked, "What did we learn about being a lawyer?", "What did we learn about who we are now?" and "What did we learn about what kind of person we would like to be?" The last two questions in particular frame the ethical issues from the "inside out," with a starting point of personal ethics, rather than the "outside in" of abiding by external standards.[6] These questions did spark a discussion that seemed similar to aspects of a classroom debrief of this topic in the United States. Many of the students discussed how being a lawyer was different in some way from their conception of themselves as a person – that you have responsibilities to your client, those duties might not agree with your personal morality, and so you need to separate them. This theme is similar to the ongoing debate in academic journals about separating your professional identity from your "regular" identity.[7] Students argued in class that your duty is to protect your client, and that may include lying. It was interesting, however, that one of the students did worry about his reputation among lawyers in Beijing (a city of twenty million!). This definitely brings home the point that professors often make in U.S. classes in

much smaller cities about the importance of building a good reputation in the legal market (Tinsley, Cambria, and Schneider 2006). If
law students even in Beijing worry about their poor reputation for
trustworthiness getting around, we should recognize that mere population size is not sufficient to shield lawyers from their poor reputations and the consequences that come from that.

Lawyers' Ethics and Legal Education in China

Given this class as a backdrop, the next section discusses the framework for legal ethics in China and how it is taught. As China's legal system has been evolving in the last two decades, it is clear that
the ethics rules are also evolving. Both our experience and the current state of the laws and rules outlined below are snapshots along a
changing pathway.

Norms and Lawyers' Codes of Conduct

In China, the framework for lawyers' ethics is prescribed in Article
3 of the Law of the People's Republic of China on Lawyers ("PRCL")
which requires that "in practicing law, a lawyer must observe the
Constitution and laws and adhere to the professional ethics and practicing disciplines of lawyers." (Law of the PRC 2007).[8] More detailed
rules are provided in the Code of Conduct for Lawyers (Code 2004).
The Code sets forth guidelines that govern the practice of law, standards for judging whether a lawyer's acts correspond with these professional requirements and the basis for imposing punishment on
lawyers or law firms that violate the regulations. It contains 190 articles, of which seventeen are specifically related to lawyers' ethics.
Chapter II of the Code, entitled "Professional Ethics of Lawyers," provides basic rules and duties applicable to lawyers. The requirements
include obligations for lawyers to be loyal to the constitution and law,
to be honest and faithful, to be diligent and devoted to their duties, to
protect the interests of the clients, to safeguard the dignity of law, and
to maintain fairness and justice in society according to the law and
rules of confidentiality. Regarding the confidentiality obligation to the
client, both the PRCL and the Code have similar provisions. Article 38
of the PRCL states

> A lawyer shall keep confidential the secrets of the State and
> commercial and secrets of the parties concerned that he or
> she comes to know during his or her legal practice activities
> and shall not divulge the private affairs of the parties con-
> cerned except for the criminal facts and information prepared
> or conducted by the clients or other people which is harmful

to state security, public security or other person's physical or property safety.

Any breach of the confidentiality obligation to the client, as in "divulging commercial secrets or private affairs of a party concerned," may subject the lawyer to a suspension of the law license for three to six months and/or a monetary fine according to the Article 48 of PRCL. Article 9 of the Code also requires a lawyer to keep confidential state secrets, clients' business secrets and personal privacy. Article 59 of the PRCL maintains this confidentiality obligation for former clients as well.

As in other jurisdictions around the world, there are also exceptions to the rules governing confidentiality that sometimes permit the refusal of services or revelation of the confidential information. For example, Article 32 of the PRCL states,

> [a]fter accepting authorization, a lawyer shall not, without good reason, refuse to defend or to represent a client. However, if the matter authorized violates law or the client uses the service provided by the lawyer to engage in illegal activities or the client intentionally conceals the material facts, the lawyer shall have the right to refuse to defend or to represent the client.

In addition, Article 56 of the Code permits lawyers to reveal confidential information if keeping it confidential will result in injury and other criminal conduct, or if the information is harmful to state interests. Also, Article 58 of the Code permits a lawyer to disclose a client's relevant information to protect the lawyer's rights if the lawyer is innocently involved in any client's criminal conduct during the representation process. Similarly, Article 71 of the Code requires lawyers to suggest to clients alternative courses of action, or refuse to proceed if the clients want to engage the lawyer to do something that is prohibited by the law or against the Code. Moreover, Article 19 of the Code requires lawyers not to conduct, or assist clients to conduct, any illegal or fraudulent activities, and Article 17 of the Code states, "The lawyer should not only consider law, but also consider in a proper manner regarding morality, economic, society, politics and other elements relevant to the clients when they provide legal services to clients." If lawyers are engaged in providing false evidence, concealing important facts or intimidating or inducing another with promise of gain to provide false evidence or conceal important facts, they will be subject to civil and criminal liability. In all, although lawyers need to comply with the duty of confidentiality when they provide legal service to their clients, lawyers may not facilitate illegal and fraudulent activities; activities that harm the state and public security; or any activities that could harm other person's physical and property safety.

According to Article 46(4) of the Law on Lawyers, the ACLA and local lawyers' associations shall organize lawyers' training and education on professional ethics and practice, and conduct assessments of lawyers. In practice, the Training Section and the Commission on Professional Education of the ACLA and local lawyers' associations organize professional training both regularly and as needed. Formal training courses and legal seminars focused on different legal issues are organized by the ACLA or local lawyers' associations and are delivered by senior, experienced lawyers or by invited governmental officials who are working on legislation.

In addition to the law governing professional ethics for lawyers, China has laws that state the ethical obligations and regulate the behavior of judges, public prosecutors, notaries, and arbitrators. There are also separate, extensive codes of conduct for each of these law-related professions.[9] Although there is some variation among the codes of conduct and legal ethics rules for the different law-related professions, there are some rules in common. For example, giving or receiving bribes is strictly prohibited for lawyers, judges, and ADR neutrals alike.

Finally, new laws on ethics are now also part of the tests for admission to the bar. Since 2002, individuals must pass the National Judicial Examination before they can provide legal services in China (Meiners and Chen 2007). Professional ethics are part of the required subject matter tested on the examination. It is a closed-book, written exam that consists of four sections: comprehensive knowledge; the criminal and administrative legal system; the civil and commercial legal system; and case analysis. Each section is weighted equally, and lawyers' ethics accounts for less than one-tenth of the points allotted to the first section. Comparing this with the exam points allocated to other legal subjects for the bar examination, the exam points allocated to ethics questions obviously weigh much less. Thus, we would suggest adding more weight for the ethics questions in the bar examination in the future, as to some extent this signals to new lawyers the degree of importance of the professional ethics standards that they need to comply with in their future legal career.

In China, besides ethics questions on the bar examination, new lawyers are also required to take a one-month intensive legal training program designed to ensure quality of service. This includes training courses on legal ethics as well as writing and other legal subjects. The new lawyer is also required to serve one year as an intern-lawyer in a Chinese law firm before he or she can become a practicing lawyer. During this period, the new lawyer cannot handle legal cases or provide any legal services except with the supervision of a qualified practicing attorney. After the internship period, there is a continuing legal education requirement. Every practicing lawyer is required to take a certain number of hours of training courses each year and pass an annual check to maintain her or his status as a lawyer. Failure to complete the legal training courses may impact on further renewal of lawyer's license. Any breach of the PRC lawyer's code or of the code of conduct for lawyers may also result in suspending or losing the lawyer license and/or undertaking any civil or criminal liability.

In addition to the guidance for lawyers in the law and codes described above, China also has a rich tradition of looking to cultural norms and tradition to find moral principles and guidance (Chew 2005). The concept of positive law in the form of statutes and governmental codes, termed *fa*, coexists with a strong traditional reliance on rules of proper conduct based on social and cultural norms, termed *li*. Wejen Chang (2000) describes a centuries-old debate in China between "Legalists," who emphasize predictable order and maintain that the government should rely on the dictates of *fa*, and "Confucians," who argue that the highest, most authoritative guide for behavior is the more flexible *li*, which allows rulers to exercise their discretion in the interests of the community. Confucius taught that observance of *li* would make resort to *fa* unnecessary. While upholding *li*, Confucius denigrated the role of law (*fa*) and legal process. He said, "I can hear a court case as well as anyone. But we need to make a world in which there is no reason for a court case." Confucius believed "that law can convict and execute people, but it cannot teach humanity, kindness, benevolence and compassion" (Rin 1997).

Chinese tradition and culture emphasizes social harmony and a stable social order. The difference, for example, between how mediation has worked in China and in the United States demonstrates these different goals. Mediation in the West has often focused on settlement based on satisfying individual interests, while mediation in China has focused on restoring harmony (Phillips 2009). While the modern view in China is that a robust legal system will definitely help achieve that goal, law in the sense of codes is not regarded as omnipotent, even in the face of societal changes that have accompanied rapid economic development. No matter how robust and mature the legal system is, many do not see it as a guarantee of a safe, stable life and work environment. The extensive promulgation of legislation in many areas may even have contributed to misimpressions in the West about the actual extent of legal change that has occurred (Feinerman

2000: 304–305). Given the discretion of governmental officials consistent with the tradition of *li*, there is a degree of uncertainty about interpretation and enforcement, and there exists, in general, a "discrepancy between what a literal reading of the laws might indicate and the effective meaning of the law" (Chew 2005: 62). And although the legal system is changing in China, the role of personal relationships in a system with a Confucian emphasis on governance by ethics over governance by rule means that personal relationships can be important in how the law is applied (Rivers 2010).

Ethics Education in Chinese Law Schools

It is hard to draw a map of ethics education in Chinese law schools because of the difficulty of collecting information from over 600 law schools and law departments and the lack of nationwide uniform standards for curriculum design for elective courses.[10] Therefore, this discussion is somewhat ad hoc, and is based on the authors' experiences with individual law schools and discussions with law professors. It considers three aspects of legal ethics education: how the course fits into the curriculum; the scope of the course and who teaches it; and available textbooks.

There is a great deal of variation among Chinese universities in the teaching of legal ethics. Some universities do not teach the subject; some devote a portion of another legal course to the topic of ethics; and some offer an independent course devoted entirely to legal ethics. The second pattern is perhaps most prevalent in China.

Even among the law schools that offer an independent legal ethics course, there is no unified practice. These schools include the China University of Political Science and Law, Beijing Normal University, Jilin University School of Law, and the Renmin University School of Law.[11] For example, the Jilin University School of Law offers a thirty-two hour course (two credits) that is required for the more than 300 undergraduates each year, but it does not offer a comparable course for graduate students. In contrast, the Renmin University of China Law School not only offers a thirty-six hour course (two credits) that is required for undergraduates, but it also has a separate elective course for the Juris Master program graduate students. These courses do not focus exclusively on the topic of lawyers' ethics, but incorporate the subject into a course that covers legal professional ethics more broadly. These courses, with names such as "Legal Ethics" or "Legal Professional Ethics," cover the ethical rules applicable to judges, prosecutors, notaries, and arbitrators as well as those designed for practicing lawyers.

There is also variation regarding who teaches legal ethics courses. At China University of Political Science and Law, the practice is to either designate a full-time law professor to teach the course or to invite external legal practitioners to teach together with law school professors. At Beijing Normal University, the semester-long legal ethics courses are taught by invited lawyers, judges, or legal governmental officials. The school believes these legal professionals will bring more practical legal experience and, through the analysis of real cases, law students will gain a better understanding of the importance of learning and observing the legal ethics rules.

There are a number of textbooks edited by Chinese law faculty available for teaching legal ethics courses (see, e.g., Zhang Shihuan 1988; Cao Hong Da 1991; Li Jianhua and Cao Gang 2002; Wang Jinxi 2002; Benson 2008; Liu Zhenghao 2010). These textbooks present the basic principles and norms of legal ethics and the interpretation of these norms. They also provide Chinese and foreign cases and supplementary readings for the students to discuss. In addition, some material on Western legal ethics is available in translation (see O'Dair 2007; Luban 2010).

Implications for Teaching Legal Ethics [12]

The Challenge for Chinese Law Schools in Lawyers' Ethics Education

Although Chinese law schools have established prototypes of a course in lawyers' ethics, they still face challenges to clarify the objectives of the course and to improve its quality and effectiveness.

As professional legal education in China is still at an initial stage, the objectives and functions of teaching legal ethics are not clear. Due to the rapid economic and social transformation over the past few decades, China's legal profession and legal education have undergone dramatic changes. Three decades ago, Chinese lawyers were identified by statute as "state legal workers" (see Provisional Regulation of the People's Republic of China on Lawyers, promulgated in 1980).[13] That emphasis on serving the state changed in the Law of the People's Republic of China on Lawyers, promulgated in 1996, which identified lawyers as "practitioners who provide legal service for society." More recently, the emphasis has changed again, in the Law of the People's Republic of China on Lawyers promulgated in 2007, to identify lawyers as "practitioners who provide legal service for a client" (Huang 2010). If one stops to unpack their implications, these changes are radical.

At the same time, Chinese legal education has also gone through four stages of development: the full restoration and rapid development period (1978-1987); standardization period (1988–97); large-scale expansion period (1998–2002); and the adjustment period (2003–present) (Ji 2010). To date, the Chinese legal profession and legal education have moved forward on a path of specialization and professionalization. As part of that trend, teaching legal professional ethics has come to be considered as important in legal education as legal knowledge and skills (Xu 2007; Huo 2007). But what is the relationship between legal ethics and the legal profession? Can educating lawyers about legal ethics rely solely on completing a course? How, and to what extent, can the teaching of legal ethics contribute to enhance the ethical thinking, self-education, and capacity for self-development of China's lawyers (Qi 2002; Zhang 2010)? Chinese law schools need to find answers to these questions if they want to achieve the goal of training the country's legal talent with a belief in the rule of law and a commitment to being loyal to law and justice.

Another challenge comes from the fact that the current quality and effectiveness of the typical course in legal ethics offered by Chinese law schools is far from ideal. When the course is an optional elective, only a small portion of students select the course, and law school graduates do not have strong professional ethics training. To solve this problem, we believe the current teaching format has to be changed at least in two aspects. One is that the courses should be designed to teach the *method and process* of resolving ethical problems, rather than instilling ethical norms. Second, and relatedly, the lecture-style teaching method should be replaced by a problem-style teaching method (Hamilton and Munson 2011a). To do this, teachers need to transform themselves from being the sole speaker in class into a role as questioner and moderator of classroom discussion. It will be important to train teachers who show promise in these skills, as well as for Chinese law schools to build up high-quality teaching teams to engage in the education and research of legal ethics.

Whether legal ethics courses are taught by law professors or external legal professionals, it is important that they combine theory and knowledge of the rules with real legal practice. This will enable law students to understand the necessity of learning the legal ethics rules and following them in their upcoming legal career. By introducing and analyzing real cases regarding the consequence of breaching legal ethics, students will not only learn what they should or should not do, they will also understand that a breach of legal ethics rules may endanger or ruin their reputation, or subject them to civil or criminal legal liability.

Another important note for those teaching Chinese lawyers who will then do business elsewhere is to make sure that Chinese lawyers understand the different ethics codes in the foreign jurisdictions. As we know, there can be significant reputational ramifications to deception even if there are no legal or other direct ethical consequences for the client or lawyer. While some Chinese lawyers may not worry about U.S. rules that do not apply to them, others might. And the effect of a poor reputation would be even more unfortunate if the Chinese lawyer did not know what was expected, and incurred reputational costs without ever considering them.

At a minimum, we hope more Chinese law schools will incorporate legal ethics courses into their curriculum. Following legal ethics rules represents, to some extent, the maturity of a country's legal system, and enhances the quality of the legal service provided by legal professionals.

Teaching Challenges in the United States

In the United States, law schools have longer experience with courses in legal ethics than those in China.[14] Mandated after the Watergate scandal, ethics classes are required for all graduates of U.S. law schools (Pearce 1998). Almost all states also require a separate ethics exam, the Multistate Professional Responsibility Exam (MPRE), to be admitted to the bar. And versions of the Model Rules of Professional Responsibility (previously the Model Code and the Canon of Professional Ethics) date from 1908. That does not mean that there is no room for improvement in the teaching of the subject, for example, by also incorporating the topic into the fabric of substantive courses. Similarly, despite the fact that ethics rules are both taught and applied across the board, the dilemma as presented at the beginning of this article (the DONS problem) confounds a significant number of U.S. lawyers. Art Hinshaw and Jess Alberts (2009), studying lawyers' behavior, used the DONS problem as the hypothetical, when lawyers were asked to hide the fact that the client is now healthy. They found that only one-third of lawyers studied fully reject the client's desire to hide this material information, even though, in doing so, lawyers are assisting their client in committing fraud. We know that U.S. teachers must also remain vigilant in explaining the current ethics rules and law – and in understanding the psychological pull that creates ethical dilemmas for lawyers.[15]

This section, however, will concentrate on the challenges of legal ethics in the setting of an international practice. It is clear that as the practice of law continues to expand internationally, all nationalities need to learn about the assumptions of practice, as well as laws and codes of conduct in other countries.[16] With the growth of transnational and international law practices, U.S. law schools have introduced international perspectives through new courses, study abroad programs, exposure to foreign Masters degree students, and some integration into assigned readings and discussion in traditional courses (Daly 1998; Terry 2005). Mary Daly (1998: 1249) argued that the professional responsibility course needs to incorporate the subject of international legal practice in order to prepare students to be the "first generation of global lawyers." This argument can be extended to other courses, such as negotiation, which typically cover selected aspects of professional responsibility rules.

There are many differences among national lawyer codes of conduct, in terms of both their overall approach and their specific content. Daly (1999) contrasted the law-like enforceable nature of U.S. codes of conduct with the more general norms experienced by lawyers trained in other systems. Moreover, specific differences in the content of codes can pose thorny conflicts-of-law issues for international law firms with offices in many jurisdictions. Which professional standards should apply to a cross-border transaction involving lawyers from many countries, when there is no obvious home or host jurisdiction (Vagts 2000)? And are lawyers required to comply with the host ethical code as well as, or instead of, their home standards (Lonbay 2005)? In the area of negotiations, one can cite the contrast between the requirement of good faith in contractual negotiations, under the codes of many civil law countries, and the *caveat emptor* standard of bargaining under common law (Rubin 1995; Etherington and Lee 2007).

Other differences are rooted in the lawyer's duty to the client, which varies even among Western countries. The U.S. legal culture is regarded as more client-centered than the culture in Europe, where lawyers have duties that are more independent of the client (Leubsdorf 1999; Moore 2005). For example, clients may not be able to waive their attorney's conflicts of interest or professional secrecy rules (Moore 2005). In China, meanwhile, the framework of a lawyer's duty to his or her client is developing and changing rapidly, as lawyers have over just three decades moved from being defined by statute as "state legal workers" to being defined as "practitioners who provide legal service for a client" (Huang 2010), a more client-based conception of their duties.

More specifically for teaching negotiation to U.S. students, how can teachers convey that differences in the legal environment are intertwined with cultural factors? A review of cross-cultural negotiation studies by Cheryl Rivers and Anne Louise Lytle (2007) found significant differences in the extent to which business negotiators from different countries used various ethically ambiguous negotiation tactics (EANTs) such as misrepresentation, false promises, and inappropriate information gathering. For lawyer negotiators, legal ethical codes may be more salient than for business people, but, as Laurence Etherington and Robert Lee (2007) point out, those national professional conduct rules themselves reflect shared cultural beliefs about appropriate lawyer behavior that differ from country to country and culture to culture.[17]

In this context, how does one teach about different understandings of lying without creating crippling stereotypes or unhelpful generalizations?[18] Culture can become a huge roadblock in negotiation as the two sides may have completely different beliefs for ethical obligations, especially when stereotypes exist (Nolan-Haley and Gmurzynska 2009). Additionally, when a party uses EANTs that the other side views as wrong and unethical, it will create distrust and anger between the parties (Rivers and Lytle 2007). Nolan-Haley and Gmurynska (2009) conclude that an appropriate teaching goal is to help students become more aware of and sensitive to the fact that there are differences in cultural value patterns. They suggest discussing the examples of EANTs described in Rivers and Lytle (2007) and asking students to reflect on their own assumptions and behavioral expectations for particular groups. They also suggest a classroom inquiry based on differences in legal systems. In addition to a general awareness of differences in ethical legal traditions, it is important for a lawyer to understand the rules of wherever he or she might be practicing law as well as the evolving customary behavior – all of which are changing rapidly in China.

Similarly, students should have an introduction to the cognitive psychological factors that lead lawyers of all nationalities into ethically challenging waters. For example, bounded ethicality (in which we do not use our ethical lens unless we already view a given decision as an "ethical" decision) often leads lawyers to act in ways that are inconsistent with the ethics they have expressed.[19] Similarly, lawyers make forecasting errors, in which they fail to recognize how the actual pressure of a case can cause ethical issues. In other words, lawyers, like others, predict that they will act ethically when faced with a dilemma in the abstract. If, however, that dilemma actually occurs, a certain percentage of people studied do not follow their overoptimistic assumptions about how they will behave (Diekmann, Tenbrunsel, and Galinsky. 2003). Finally, many unethical actions result from "slippery slopes," where an early ambiguous decision is used to justify later unethical actions. A better understanding of how unethical decisions can be unleashed by seemingly ethical lawyers will help all law students when dealing with these issues.

Conclusion

We again want to note how grateful we were for this opportunity to watch negotiations unfold and be permitted to use these students as our basis for reflections on ethics and cross-cultural implications. The dilemma of confidential information, loyalty to a client, and the requirement to reveal information remains a challenging discussion in the United States. To see the same dilemma presented in China gave us the opportunity to perceive this issue through the evolving norms in China. In an increasingly global professional practice, such information about varying laws, culture, ethics, and expectations is crucial.

In the United States, stories about honesty abound as "the" model for good behavior. We are raised with the apocryphal folktale of our first President, George Washington, stating that "I cannot tell a lie," and refer to President Abraham Lincoln as "Honest Abe." The role models in China are different, and evolving. The reemergence of Confucius, with the focus on *junzi*, a person of great integrity, might result in similar goals for lawyers (Yu Dan 2006). Yet at present, these cultural assumptions are not aligned. Lawyers in both cultures need to know this and understand this as they work in each culture. And, as the law, government, and role of lawyers continues to change in China, we know that we will need to revisit these conclusions.

Notes

[1] The case was adapted from *DONS Negotiation*, available from the Program on Negotiation. Available at http://www.pon.harvard.edu/shop/dons-negotiation/ (last accessed June 15, 2012).

[2] In the United States, there is, nonetheless, a substantial part of the legal population that remains unclear on the definition of a material fact. In a study by Art Hinshaw and Jess Alberts (2011) based on the DONS problem, only 19% of the lawyers surveyed agreed to a similar request by the now healthy plaintiff *not* to disclose his situation to the other side. But another 19% were not sure what they would do (Hinshaw and Alberts 2011: 29).

[3] Rule 4.1 of the Model Rules of Professional Conduct provides:
Rule 4.1 Truthfulness In Statements To Others
In the course of representing a client a lawyer shall not knowingly:
(a) make a false statement of material fact or law to a third person; or
(b) fail to disclose a material fact to a third person when disclosure is necessary to avoid assisting a criminal or fraudulent act by a client, unless disclosure is prohibited by Rule 1.6.

[4] If the financial information were, for example, the basis of the deal, then this information is material. See Restatement (Second) of Contracts, Sections 161, 164, as well as Comment 2 to Rule 4.1. Since here the financial informa-

tion is not the basis upon which the parties are making the contract, it is not material.

[5] For example, reputation is extremely important in negotiation when uncertainty exists about the strategy the other party might use, or the level of trust. If no such indication is given, one might ask herself, what is his or her reputation? Are they a hard bargainer? Or are they relationship-based and negotiate for mutual gain? Therefore, the outcome in many negotiations will completely depend on the perceived reputations of the negotiators, and if negative, this will be at the expense of their clients (Tinsley, Cambria, and Schneider 2006. See also Glick and Croson 2001).

[6] We thank Jayne Docherty for this insight.

[7] For example, Patrick J. Schiltz (1999) maintains that most unethical behavior does not start from making a huge unethical decision but rather from the day-to-day mundane decisions in which your ethics are eroded little by little. He argues for the habit of acting ethically in all of your actions. In the business context, Anne Tenbrunsel writes that when business people view a decision as a "business" decision versus an "ethical" decision, there are similar mistakes. In other words, all day to day decisions need to be made through an ethical lens (Tenbrunsel and Messick 2004).

[8] The Supreme People's Court of the People's Republic of China, *Law of the People's Republic of China on Lawyers*, May 22, 2002, available at http://en.chinacourt.org/public/detail.php?id=100 (last accessed June 15, 2012).

[9] For example, the China International Economic and Trade Arbitration Commission (CIETAC) code of conduct for arbitrators consists of fifteen articles and the Beijing Arbitration Commission (BAC) Ethical Standards for Arbitrators (http://www.bjac.org.cn/en/Arbitration/Standards.html) consists of fourteen articles. The Code of Conduct for judges contains ninety-six articles and there is a separate set of legal ethics rules for judges that contain thirty articles. The public prosecutor's ethics rules contain forty-eight articles.

[10] There is a standard curriculum design applied nationwide for required courses offered in Chinese law schools. In 1998, the Chinese Ministry of Education established fourteen core courses (required courses) for the legal education of undergraduates. These courses are jurisprudence, Chinese legal history, constitutional law, criminal law, criminal procedure law, civil law, civil procedure law, administrative law and procedure, economic law, commercial law, intellectual property law, international public law, international economic law, and international private law. Environmental resources law and labor and social security law were later added as required courses.

[11] As an example of Renmin's commitment to teaching legal ethics, Prof. Liu Jihua spoke on "Ideas, Aims and Missions of China's Legal Education," "Description, Forecast and Views of China's Legal Ethics Education" and "Education Methods on the Cultivation of International Legal Expert" respectively. Available at http://www.law.ruc.edu.cn/commu/ShowArticle.asp?ArticleID=19375 (last accessed June 15, 2012).

[12] Given the variety of expertise, the suggestions on how to change the Chinese legal ethics teaching come from Professors Chen and Xiahong while the suggestions on how to change the U.S. legal ethics teaching come from Professors Schneider and Deason.

[13] See generally http://www.chinalawdeskbook.com/pdf/CLD%20Ch3.pdf (page 73+) (last accessed September 7, 2012), referring to the Provisional Regulations of the People's Republic of China on Lawyers (adopted August 26, 1980 by the 15th Sess. of the Standing Committee of the 5th National People's Congress), art. 1.

[14] China is not unique in this comparison. Laurel Terry (2000) reports that in many counties legal ethics education is not even available as an elective in law school curricula. Instead, student/lawyers are assumed to learn these principles as part of the practical training period that is required before one can become a practicing lawyer.

[15] For more articles on improving effectiveness of teaching ethics in legal education, see Browne, Williamson,and Barkacs (2006); Hamilton and Monson (2011b); and Donner (2010).

[16] For further reading on global perspectives and initiatives (including European Union directives, the General Agreement on Trade in Services, and developments in multi-disciplinary and multi-jurisdictional practices) that have the potential to affect domestic professional responsibility policies, see Terry (2005; 2007).

[17] It may be important to distinguish between differences in the framework established for negotiation by national legal cultures (and rules) and cultural influences on how individuals from different cultures operate in those legal settings. Interestingly, in the Chinese legal environment, Cheryl Rivers (2010) found that business negotiators from *both* China and Australia indicated that they would not always adhere to Chinese law. Her exploratory study suggests that negotiators' predictions about enforcement of the law and their sense of the significance of the breach were more important factors for both sets of negotiators than their national cultural background.

[18] For further reading on understanding the differences in ethics as it relates to lying, see Lachman (2007) and Schiltz (1999).

[19] For more on "bounded ethicality," see Bazerman (2011).

References

Bazerman, M.H. 2011. Bounded ethicality in negotiations. *Negotiation and Conflict Management Research* 4(1): 8–11.

Benson, L. (ed). 2008. *Legal professional ethics.* Beijing: Beijing University Press.

Browne, M. N., C. L. Williamson, and L. L. Barkacs. 2006. The purported rigidity of an attorney's personality: Can legal ethics be acquired? *Journal of the Legal Profession* 30: 55-78.

Cao, Hong Da (ed). 1991. *Judicial Ethics Tutorial.* Taiyuan, China: Shanxi Education Press.

Chang, Wejen. 2000. Foreward. In *The limits of the rule of law in China,* edited by K. Turner, J. Feinerman, and R. Guy. Seattle: University of Washington Press.

Chew, P. 2005. The rule of law: China's skepticism and the rule of people. *Ohio State Journal on Dispute Resolution* 20(1): 43-67.

Code of Conduct for Lawyers ("Code") (for trial implementation, promulgated March 20, 2004) enacted by the All China Lawyers Association (ACLA). Available at http://www.chinalawandpractice.com/Article/1692834/Channel/9934/The-All-China-Lawyers-Association-Lawyers-Code-of-Practice-Trial-Implementation.html (last accessed June 15, 2012).

Daly, M. C. 1998. The ethical implications of the globalization of the legal profession: A challenge to the teaching of professional responsibility in the twenty-first century. *Fordham International Law Journal* 21(4): 1239-1295.

Daly, M. C. 1999. The dichotomy between standards and rules: A new way of understanding the differences in perceptions of lawyer codes of conduct by U.S. and foreign lawyers. *Vanderbilt Journal of Transnational Law* 32(4): 1117-1162.

Diekmann, K., A. E. Tenbrunsel, and A. D. Galinsky. 2003. From self-prediction to self-defeat: Behavioral forecasting, self-fulfilling prophecies, and the effect of competitive expectations. *Journal of Personality and Social Psychology* 85(4):672-683.

Donner, T. A. 2010. Negotiating across borders: Ethical constraints, attorney's practice guide to negotiations. Eagan, MN: Thomson Reuters West.

Etherington, L. and R. Lee. 2007. Ethical codes and cultural context: Ensuring legal ethics in the global law firm. *Indiana Journal of Global Legal Studies* 14(1): 95-118.

Feinerman, J. V. 2000. The rule of law imposed from the outside: China's foreign-oriented legal regime since 1978. In *The limits of the rule of law in China*, edited by K. Turner, J. Feinerman, and R. Guy. Seattle: University of Washington Press.

Glick, S. and R. Croson. 2001. Reputations in negotiation. In *Wharton on Making Decisions,* edited by S. J. Hoch, H. C. Kunreuther, and R. E. Gunther. Hoboken, NJ: Wiley.

Hamilton, N. W. and V. Monson. 2011a. Answering the skeptics on fostering ethical professional formation (professionalism). *The Professional Lawyer* 20(4): 3-7.

Hamilton, N. W. and V. Monson. 2011b. The positive empirical relationship of professionalism to effectiveness in the practice of law. *The Georgetown Journal of Legal Ethics* 24(1): 137-185.

Hinshaw, A. and J. K. Alberts. 2011. Doing the right thing: An empirical study of attorney negotiation ethics. *Harvard Negotiation Law Review* 16: 95-162.

Huang, Zhenzhong. 2010. On the change of nature and their position in the transition period of new China's lawyers. *Law Review* (Wuhan) 162(4): 52-58.

Huo, Xiandan. 2007. Reflection on China's legal education. *Beijing: China University of Politics and Law Press* 69.

Ji, Xiangde. 2010. The difficulties and prospects of the current legal education in China. *Journal of China University of Political Science* 18(4): 50-58.

Lachman, A. J. 2007. Are they just bad apples? Ethical behavior in organizational setting: An introduction. *Professional Lawyer* 33: 33-40.

Law of the People's Republic of China on Lawyers (first promulgated May 15, 1996, revised in 2001 and 2007). Available at http://en.chinacourt.org/public/detail.php?id=100 (last accessed June 15, 2012).

Leubsdorf, J. 1999. The independence of the bar in France: Learning from comparative legal ethics. In *Lawyers' practice and ideals: A comparative view*, edited by J. J. Barceló III and R. C. Cramton The Hague: Kluwer Law International.

Li, Jianhua and Cao Gang (eds). 2002. *Legal ethics*. Changsha: Central South University Press.

Liu, Zhenghao (ed). 2010. *Legal ethics*. Beijing: Beijing University Press.

Lonbay, J. 2005. Legal ethics and professional responsibility in a global context. *Washington University Global Studies Law Review* 4(3): 609-616.

Luban, D. 2010. *Lawyers and justice: An ethical study*. Trans. D. Rui. Beijing: China University of Politics and Law Press.

Meiners, D. and J. Chen. 2007. Professionalization in the Chinese legal system: Current education and certification of Chinese lawyers. *The Bar Examiner* 76(2): 29-40.

Moore, N. J. 2005. Regulating law firm conflicts in the 21st century: Implication of the globalization of legal services and the growth of the "mega firm." *Georgetown Journal of Legal Ethics* 18(2): 521-550.

Nolan-Haley, J. and E. Gmurzynska. 2008. Culture – The body/soul connector in negotiation ethics. In *Rethinking negotiation teaching: Innovations for context and culture*, edited by C. Honeyman, J. Coben, and G. De Palo. St. Paul, MN: DRI Press.

O'Dair, R. 2007. *Legal ethics: Text and materials*. Trans. Zhu Liyu andYuan Gang, Beijing: Remin University of China Press.

Pearce, R. G. 1998. Teaching ethics seriously: Legal ethics as the most important subject in law school. *Loyola University of Chicago Law Journal* 29: 719-739.

Phillips, F. P. 2008. Commercial mediation in China: Challenge of shifting paradigms. In *Contemporary issues in international arbitration and mediation: The Fordham papers,* edited by A. W. Rovine. Leiden: Martinus Nijhoff.

Qi, Yanping. 2002. On the legal ethics education on modern legal education. *Science of Law* (Xian) 121(5): 12-21.

Rin, Xen. 1997. *Tradition of law and law of tradition: Law, state, and social control in China*. Westport, CT: Greenwood Press.

Rivers, C. 2010. Negotiation ethics across cultures: An examination of the influence of law and codes of ethics. Presented at *23rd Annual Conference of the International Association for Conflict Management*, Boston.

Rivers, C. and A. L. Lytle. 2007. Lying, cheating foreigners!! Negotiation ethics across cultures. *International Negotiation* 12(1): 1-28.

Rubin, M. H. 1995. The ethics of negotiation: Are there any? *Louisiana Law Review* 56: 447-476.

Schiltz, P. 1999. On being a happy, healthy, and ethical member of an unhappy, unhealthy, and unethical profession. *Vanderbilt Law Review* 52: 871-951.

Tinsley, C. H., J. Cambria, and A. K. Schneider. 2006. Reputations in negotiation. In *The negotiator's fieldbook: The desk reference for the experienced negotiator*, edited by A. K. Schneider and C. Honeyman. Washington, DC: American Bar Association.

Tenbrunsel, A. E. and D. M. Messick. 2004. Ethical fading: The role of self-deception in unethical behavior. *Social Justice Research* 17: 223-236.

Terry, L. S. 2000. A survey of legal ethics education in law schools. In *Ethics in academia*, edited by S. K. Majumdar, H. S. Pitkow, L. P. Bird and E. W. Miller. York, PA: The Pennsylvania Academy of Science.

Terry, L. S. 2005. U.S. legal ethics: The coming of age of global and comparative perspectives. *Washington University Global Studies Law Review* 4(3): 463-533.

Terry, L. S. 2007. A "how to" guide for incorporating global and comparative perspectives into the required professional responsibility course. *St. Louis University Law Journal* 51(4): 1135-1159.

Vagts, D. F. 2000. Professional responsibility in transborder practice: Conflict and resolution. *Georgetown Journal of Legal Ethics* 13: 677-698.

Wang, Jinxi (ed). 2002. *Introduction to lawyers' professional rules of conduct*. Beijing: National School of Administration Press.

Xu, Xianming. 2007. The responsibility of legal education. *China Reform News* (Beijing), June 21.

Yu, Dan. 2006. *Confucius from the heart: Ancient wisdom for today's world*. London: Pan Books

Zhang, Shihuan (ed). 1988. *Judicial ethics*. Shanghai: Shanghai People's Publishing House.

Zhang, Zhiming. 2010. Legal professional moral education in china: Description, prediction and opinions. Available at http://www.hngf.gov.cn/theory (last accessed June 15, 2012).

෴ 11 ෴

Redefining Beauty: Negotiating Consumption and Conservation of Natural Environments

*Charles A. Lawry, Sanda Kaufman & Anita D. Bhappu**

Editors' Note: Many people who are learning cross-cultural negotiation are studying the subject for utilitarian reasons, because they expect to negotiate commercial, industrial, or governmental issues across cultures. They may not immediately perceive the relevance of aesthetics. But to a significant extent, any of these kinds of negotiations is likely to have an environmental component, even when the presenting issues in the negotiation do not appear to be primarily "environmental" in content. Thus it becomes germane to a surprisingly large range of people that perceptions of what is appropriate environmentally have a consumption-versus-conservation element that is, at some fundamental level, about differing cultural perceptions of what is useful – and what is beautiful. The authors analyze some of the implications, including the perception that better cross-cultural training and wider travel is helping many people to appreciate others' views of beauty. That leads to a degree of aesthetic and social "convergence" that will be needed in future, for very practical purposes.

Introduction

How to reach international environmental agreements – for example, to reduce industrial pollution and CO_2 emissions – is a broad and complicated question, of interest to both negotiation and environmental

* **Charles A. Lawry** is a doctoral student and a research associate for the consumers, environment and sustainability initiative at the Norton School of Family & Consumer Sciences, University of Arizona. His email address is calawry@email.arizona.edu. **Sanda Kaufman** is professor of planning, public policy and administration at the Levin College of Urban Affairs, Cleveland State University. Her email address is s.kaufman@csuohio.edu. **Anita D. Bhappu** is PetSmart associate professor and co-director of the consumers, environment and sustainability initiative at the Norton School of Family & Consumer Sciences, University of Arizona. Her email address is abhappu@email.arizona.edu.

scholars. While global environmental issues and their consequences deserve research and policy attention, international negotiations over such concerted action should be informed by an understanding of the cultural differences that can influence the negotiation process and its outcomes. One such difference concerns how people from across cultures define and value nature, in terms of both its aesthetic beauty and the economic and health benefits that accrue to them from the existence of natural ecosystems.

Perceptions of natural beauty vary considerably across cultures, drawing both from people's understanding of natural phenomena and from the spiritual values that they espouse as a result of their respective histories and experiences. Consequently, there is no shared metric for natural beauty that can be easily factored into negotiated treaties. Any mutual understanding that we might forge in international environmental agreements has to come from an awareness and appreciation of the cross-cultural definitions of natural beauty, as well as some insight into how individuals in different societies reconcile their consumption of natural environments with efforts to conserve these ecosystems. Such knowledge can shed light on the attitudinal component of environmental policies and regulations that is rooted in culture, and may require special attention during negotiations, because it can contribute to the intractability of international conflicts.

Teaching students how to approach environmental agreements across borders also presents challenges in the classroom, given current negotiation pedagogy. As instructors, we do not just contend with transferring existing negotiation wisdom. Rather, we have to make do with students' current lack of understanding about international environmental negotiations, as well as with the more general lack of effective tools to develop in students an awareness and appreciation of values that are different from their own. In this sense, reality and the classroom share the same difficulty when it comes to instilling in negotiators an understanding of different cultures. We are either looking into our own culture from within (as an ingroup member with the attending biases) or exploring another culture from without (using outgroup mental models such as our own values hierarchy), either of which is bound to lead us astray. Therefore, in the classroom we run the risk of offering and reinforcing biased interpretations, in more or less apparent ways.[1]

It is rather difficult to illustrate effectively the profound and subtle international differences that can affect the process and outcomes of negotiations in a culturally bound classroom. In this chapter, therefore, we explore definitions of natural beauty that are reflected in approaches to conservation/consumption of natural ecosystems in the

United States, China and Japan, and which undoubtedly influence international environmental agreements involving these nations.[2] In doing so, we propose that this chapter can be used as a pedagogical tool for conveying to students not only how cultures can differ in conceptualizing and valuing nature but also that such differences find expression in physical environments. As such, this chapter can make these differences accessible for negotiators to observe and appreciate, thereby helping to conquer the challenge of surfacing cultural differences in a classroom without requiring extensive ethnographic studies for which neither instructors nor students may be equipped.

The current practice for sensitizing students to cross-cultural values is to use role-plays in which students act as negotiators from different cultures, in necessarily simplified situations.[3] We explore here the possibility of accomplishing the same goal by accessing students' own experiences[4] and available information about different cultural perspectives on the environment, in a way that conserves the physical and cultural complexity inherent in such a comparative study. To this end, we will strive in this chapter to convey (without essentializing) mainstream East Asian and American worldviews of natural beauty, and to identify some cross-cultural linkages between Chinese, Japanese and American values that should be integrated into the pedagogy and practice of international environmental negotiations. We begin by reviewing definitions of natural beauty in China, Japan and the United States, followed by a discussion of how these worldviews are relevant to negotiations. We conclude by outlining implications for negotiation pedagogy and practice.

Definitions of Natural Beauty

As researchers and even as travelers, we have noticed how China, Japan and the United States evolved different, country-specific balances between environmental conservation and societal consumerism. The untamed national parks in the United States exemplify the prevailing American conceptualization of natural beauty. In contrast, in China and Japan the beauty of nature is embodied in very carefully designed and scrupulously tended gardens and city parks that Americans might regard as "artificial" and not representative of nature, even if they find them aesthetically pleasing. What might be driving such apparent differences in physical design?

Several researchers who compared Chinese and Japanese gardens and city parks to the national park system in the United States have concluded that fundamentally different worldviews have shaped the planning, design and use of these public spaces, where people admire localized forms of natural beauty (Callicott and Ames 1989; Bruun

and Kalland 1995; Asquith and Kalland 1997; Saito 2002). Whereas
traditional Chinese and Japanese worldviews construe the boundaries between people and nature as fuzzy and deserving of attention,
American perspectives have historically differentiated clearly between
areas for human activities and nature.[5] As will be discussed in the following sections, Chinese, Japanese and American attitudes towards
consumerism and conservation are rooted in these different yet historical worldviews about the relationship between people and nature.
To examine the antecedents of this seemingly inconsequential difference in physical design, we now review briefly some of the philosophies that underscore the traditional worldviews of natural beauty in
China, Japan and the United States respectively.

China

The traditional Chinese attitude toward natural beauty has been characterized as *organismic*, meaning that it is rooted in the perception
of interdependence between humans and nature. Robert Weller and
Peter Bol (1998) conjectured that this point of view is reflected in, and
even may stem from, the Chinese philosophy of Cosmic Resonance
Theory and in the practice of Feng-shui. Both reify the organismic
worldview of natural beauty that frames people and nature as intertwined into a holistic entity.

Cosmic Resonance Theory, the intellectual foundation for Taoism
and Neo-Confucianism in China, posits that an atomistic force (Qi)
connects all people, events and objects (Weller and Bol 1998). Qi, according to Cosmic Resonance Theory, animates humans, animals and
elements of nature such as trees, mountains, rocks and water. Tu Wei-
Ming (1989: 116) noted in his study of Chinese views of nature that
the ancient meaning of Qi specifically invoked the psychophysiologi-
cal properties of blood and breath. Over time, that meaning has been
gradually semanticized to signify "matter energy." Chinese scholars
have henceforth conceptualized Qi not only as incorporating people
and nature together, but also as the hallmark of a universalist (rather
than anthropocentric) worldview. To wit, "[t]o see nature as an external object out there is to create an artificial barrier which obstructs
our true vision and undermines our human capacity to experience
nature from within" (Tu 1989). Thus the concept of Qi effectively dis-
solves a barrier – considered artificial – and frames humans and nature as permeable, overlapping entities.

Feng-shui, an ancient art of placement also known as *geomancy*,
is based on a perspective of natural beauty similar to that of Cosmic
Resonance Theory. In his discussion of the connection between Feng-
shui and nature in China, Ole Bruun (1995) summarized the central

tenet of Feng-shui as follows: a verdant socioecological setting leads to prosperity, while a destitute socioecological setting leads to suffering and demise.[6] Consequently, rural and urban dwellers wishing to become successful and prosperous should pursue the goal of bringing the universe and nature into their physical environments through the practice of Feng-shui (Bruun 1995). As such, Chinese people sometimes seek the advice of geomancers or Feng-shui artists for the design of gardens, homes, office buildings and gravesites. Geomancers dedicate their attention to the shape of the landscape and flow of water in order to capture and balance the flow of Qi (Bruun 1995). Thus the art of Feng-shui is believed to regulate the interconnection of humans and nature, which led Bruun (1995: 185) to deem Feng-shui a "borderline science" that operates at the boundary of society and nature.

In his monograph on Chinese *scholar gardens*, R. Stewart Johnston (1991) added that Chinese gardens also reflect the organismic worldview of people's interaction with nature. He noticed that to escape urbanity from time to time, pre-modern scholar-officials privately enjoyed scenic vistas afforded by the miniaturized elements of urban gardens that surrounded their places of study, such as the Confucius Temple in Beijing. Rather than protecting nature from urban influences, these gardens drew nature into city life through cultivated landscapes imbued with symbolism. Garden designers strategically arranged rocks to symbolize nearby mountain peaks and added small murmuring streams to symbolize rivers. They also incorporated curvilinear elements that embodied Feng-shui, such as curving streams, twisted branches or dragons, in order to maximize the flow of Qi (Johnston 1991). In concert with the organismic worldview, it does not seem that Chinese intellectuals perceived these traditional gardens as distinct, but rather as simultaneously a part of nature and of the human experience.

Chinese garden design is clearly rooted in the Chinese experience with and understanding of the vast natural environment, and in philosophical accounts and spiritual values that have evolved over the centuries of China's history. Although Western-like concepts of urban development and public space have swept across China of late, the traditional gardens continue to fulfill the Chinese worldview of natural beauty. Gardens thrive in conjunction with the pulsating scenes of technological progress and consumerism in China (Weller and Bol 1998). These technological and consumer societal domains of everyday life merge with the spiritual and philosophical experiences of Chinese gardens, which ontologically codify humans and nature into an organismic unit.

Japan

Japanese worldviews of natural beauty bear some resemblance to Chinese worldviews, with some very notable differences. Although Japanese traditions also construe people and nature as an organismic unit, their relationship tends to exist within a "liminal zone" where idealized landscape imagery is appreciated from a distance rather than through immersion (Asquith and Kalland 1997). According to Yuriko Saito (2002), a preference for blurred boundaries and edges is constitutive of Japanese aesthetic tastes. The liminality is characteristic of traditional Shinto and Buddhist beliefs. Buddhism stresses the impermanence of things and the totality of being. Kami – the sentient beings of the Shinto religion – are considered by the Japanese as neither human nor spirit. They have the freedom to reside in natural elements, celestial bodies or even people. In this view, natural phenomena become the offspring of kami, reaffirming their liminal state between humans and nature (Asquith and Kalland 1997).

Admiration for the impermanence of nature is most readily apparent in Japanese architectural and landscape designs. Traditional architectural spaces in Japan flow from one room into the next, bringing the outside into the inside and vice versa. Old and contemporary vernacular architecture alike accomplish this through use of light, low structures made of natural materials, especially wood despite the fact that it is a scarce resource in Japan. Light partitions typically divide rooms and further contribute to the sense of blurred boundaries. The contrasts present in architectural spaces illustrate the traditional Japanese practice of blurring continua, with opposing realities and coexisting spaces (Saito 2002). In the Japanese view, the urban world is not perceived as encroaching upon nature, nor is nature perceived as necessarily purifying the urban world. The same idealized form seen within a garden may be equally appreciated within art, literature, fashion, toys or technology.

Japanese gardens, similarly, blur the boundaries between culture and nature. Joy Hendry (1997) described Japanese gardens as mediating between culture and nature by conceptually residing inside, but physically existing outside. Upon entering a traditional Japanese garden, a viewer is immersed in an idealized version of nature stemming from the liminality of being both inside and outside, as well as the transformation of wild nature into a perfect form (Asquith and Kalland 1997). Whereas this transformation in Chinese scholar-gardens primarily occurred through the manicuring of the gardens in accordance with local customs and beliefs, Japanese gardens transfer distant landscapes into locally experienced natural (miniaturized) carefully positioned elements (e.g., rocks, trees and water) that allow

observers to interact safely with wild nature through perfect, controlled garden scenery (Hendry 1997).

In contemporary Japan, urban gardens, villages and parks continue to function as miniaturized safe-havens. Hendry (1997) contended
that gardens in Japan mediate between the presence of (wild) foreigners and (tame) local traditions. The traditional Japanese worldview of
natural beauty as reflected in garden design reveals to an extent how
the urban Japanese reconcile nature with modern day consumerism
and industrialization. By framing nature as composed of desirable
and idealized elements, Japanese gardens help viewers see through
the dirt and grit of city life and its less-than-aesthetic components
– power lines, garbage or highways (Asquith and Kalland 1997). For
example, Japanese worldviews of natural beauty permit people to
take in the ambiguous boundaries between the Tokyo Bay, the city
of Tokyo, and the distant Mt. Fuji looming in the background, without perceiving them as separate entities. According to Asquith and
Kalland (1997: 15),

> contextualization allows for multiple concepts of nature to co-
> exist: the wild and threatening nature which sometimes plays
> havoc with people and landscape; or the other nature in its
> most cultivated form, a garden, a dwarfed tree (bonsai), or
> a soft drink in a vending machine. It is in the latter idealized
> form that nature is most appreciated by the Japanese.

As in the Chinese case, the physical environment (here, insular rather
than seemingly limitless) has shaped Japanese garden design that
also draws from spiritual values. Japanese and Chinese worldviews
of natural beauty – one liminal and the other organismic – share a
unique fondness for idealizing landscapes. The gardens rooted in
these views are both carefully constructed models of nature, greatly
valued by the public not least due to their scarcity and to a traditional
lack of easy access to real natural landscapes. Borrowing from Claude
Levi-Strauss' structuralist framework, Asquith and Kalland (1997)
described Japanese worldviews of natural beauty as wrestling with
nature continua anchored in three dichotomies: cooked–raw, wrapped–
unwrapped and tame–wild. Both the Japanese and Chinese garden
practices (manicured in different ways) are the result of worldviews
that gravitate toward the cooked and tame ends of the Levi-Strauss
continua, driven by the East Asian cosmologies of Shinto, Buddhism,
Feng-shui, Taoism, and Neo-Confucianism respectively.

United States

In contrast to Chinese and Japanese perspectives, American world-views of natural beauty tend toward the raw and wild ends of the continua described by Asquith and Kalland (1997). Thus instead of using public works to build gardens as monuments, the United States instituted wilderness preserves and national parks where nature can be safeguarded, publicly accessed and "consumed" in its pristine, un-tamed state. National park systems, now prevalent throughout the world, may well be an American invention (Nash 1970; Machlis and Field 2000; Saito 2002). There is little evidence to suggest that any government-supported national park systems existed anywhere else prior to the establishment of Yellowstone National Park in Wyoming in 1872. According to Roderick Nash (1970), Yellowstone was the world's first major wilderness preserve created with the public inter-est in mind.

The historical path to the present can contribute to our under-standing of the outcomes we see today, both in terms of views of na-ture and in how they are reflected in gardens or parks. At the outset, American colonists were determined to cultivate the soil in an effort to "civilize" the wilderness. However, as urbanization spread westward from the initial colonies, people began to seek a different relationship with nature (Saito 2002) and even came to fear the disappearance of natural landscapes. Euro-American settlers came from relatively highly urbanized settings and from a tradition that had accumulated a considerable philosophical distance from nature. Perhaps as Nash (1970) put it best "[c]ities, not log cabins, produce Sierra Clubbers." In other words, the American worldview of natural beauty evolved from a longing for what had been lost in time as urbanization cre-ated a boundary between people and nature. In contrast, Japanese and Chinese cultures had shaped their views of natural beauty during their early (rural) histories (Saito 2002) when contact with nature was more immediate, and they managed to preserve the continuity of this outlook to this day.

In her discussion of how American worldviews of natural beau-ty shifted from taming to preservation, Saito (2002) argues that the strategies for choosing and designating "pristine" sites as national parks often included criteria such as the natural history of the area and its spatial-temporal immensity (e.g., Niagara Falls). This ap-proach is quite different from the traditional Chinese and Japanese concepts of natural beauty, which call for people to admire the wil-derness at a distance through idealized (artificial) garden and park landscapes, often constructed in the midst of urban areas.

Rather than regarding society as part of nature (as reconstructed in Japanese and Chinese gardens), the American conceptualization of natural beauty led to preserved natural scenic landscapes and national parks, to conserve natural features at a distance from everyday life. American urban dwellers take in natural beauty in its own (natural) context. In parks, visitors tend to interact with nature as guests of the natural world, rather than seeing themselves as part of it. The American national park system resembles an environmental caretaker model, where the need to set aside land for conservation often entails the notion of stewardship for the public interest, including future generations.

As a result of this outlook, Americans tend to consider that consumerism and materiality infringe upon nature. Instead, in the dominant Judeo-Christian tradition,[7] nature is seen as a divine gift that came with strings attached – a caretaker duty that implies the setting of protective boundaries even when they imply giving up some economic value in the process.[8] By comparison, Japanese and Chinese worldviews merge consumerism, society and nature. The Chinese and Japanese display an ambivalent relationship with (reconstructed) nature, which is often challenging for Westerners to understand (Asquith and Kalland 1997). In turn, Chinese and Japanese people may find perplexing the American view of natural beauty as separate, and in its wild state.

In summary, traditional Chinese and Japanese worldviews of natural beauty reflect a preference for merging nature with their consumer society, as exemplified by the East Asian traditions of manicured urban gardens and parks. Mainstream American attitudes, on the other hand, tend to place consumerism and society in opposition to nature, as reflected in their vast national park system, which is protected from human encroachment. In light of these cross-cultural differences, we now consider the implications of Chinese, Japanese and American worldviews of natural beauty for negotiation pedagogy and practice, with specific reference to the context of international environmental agreements.

Implications for Negotiation Pedagogy and Practice
This chapter aims to contribute to one of the goals of the Rethinking Negotiation Teaching project, namely to innovate in negotiation teaching by developing tools to convey the complexity of international negotiations. The urgent need to develop students' cross-cultural understanding can be attributed in part to globalization and to the fact that some global resources – nature is an example – are shared, limited and threatened unless we successfully negotiate collective agree-

ments to safeguard them across borders. But most instructors and students do not have direct experience with international negotiations, let alone environmental agreements. However, global issues are increasingly seeping into national politics, so ultimately each country must choose to address them, whether unilaterally or jointly.

One example of a global issue that affects everyone is climate change. Despite wide recognition of the problem, there is no international (or intra-national, at least in the United States; see Honeyman et al., *The "Deliberation Engine,"* in this volume) consensus on how it should be addressed. In fact, there is much reluctance to devote resources to either prevent or mitigate climate change effects. Negotiations of global climate change treaties have so far repeatedly failed, or ended in rather vague plans for continuing the efforts, with no binding agreements. The topic of natural beauty and its valuation in different cultures is one way to introduce students to several of the obstacles present in negotiating global climate change treaties. It provides a nuanced, non-normative pedagogical tool to develop useful analytical skills in students. Chief among them is the ability to probe cultural elements that lead to certain negotiation stances and to devise proposals that take them into account, thereby increasing the likelihood of agreement and action..

At a first level, the actual topic of garden design and the underlying attitudes toward natural beauty could constitute an assignment of discovery: students might be asked to investigate and speculate on antecedents of observed garden design features (based on readings and images) with a class discussion that could bring out the differences and reveal the underlying variation in worldviews. At a second level, when possible, students might be asked to engage in a similar exercise by drawing on their own travel experiences. The latter task could be focused on other designs such as urban open spaces or markets that are prevalent across cultures and exemplify different worldviews. This exercise becomes full-fledged adventure learning if visiting (to another region or country) can be carried out as part of a class assignment. At a third level, our chapter can serve as a model for building an awareness and appreciation for other phenomena/activities that are carried out differently across cultures. The effectiveness of any such exercise in helping students become sensitive to cultural differences and in acquiring tools for understanding specific cultures resides in the debriefing of their experiences.[9]

All of the above pedagogical strategies, however, should be contextualized and informed by the changing cultural landscape, so as not to affirm simplistic cultural stereotypes. Moreover, having an understanding of the historical context that could have influenced definitions of natural beauty and approaches to conservation/consumption of natural ecosystems in the United States, China and Japan should enhance students' ability to approach environmental agreements across borders effectively. Therefore, we now provide some of this context.

The Changing Cultural Landscape

People around the world live surrounded by our natural environments, even if in urban areas this is no longer readily apparent. Apart from cultural differences, we are biologically identical up to very small, insignificant, mostly appearance-related variations (Pinker 2002). It is, therefore, interesting to attempt to tease out the considerable differences in the very basic and ubiquitous relationship we have with our natural surroundings, which we might have expected to vary less than in actuality. What might account for these cultural differences? The temptation is great to ascribe observed garden styles – a reflection of people's attitude toward nature – solely to the spiritual values held by people in various countries, and even to find virtue in some and fault in others from the perspective of our own environmental values.[10] However, we should resist this temptation and turn it into a learning opportunity.

Drawing on our knowledge of relevant cognitive biases (for example, Birke and Fox 1999; Korobkin and Guthrie 2006; Birke 2010), we should distinguish between what is likely present in the makeup of various cultural outlooks and our (often mistaken) attributions. We are apt to learn when analyzing cultural differences as much from our findings as from our analytic process, which should highlight the many biases that we are at risk of activating in forming our judgments during negotiations.

For example, to understand cultural differences in the perception and valuation of nature, we might also want to consider historical differences that may have led to people's conceptualization of their relationship to nature. China and Japan are among the oldest civilizations. Old civilizations evolved slowly. What we construe as fast-paced modernity is but a speck on the timeline of human evolution. The same is true for perspectives on the natural environment, over which people had little dominion at the outset, but which gradually came to be "tamed" as new technologies allowed. The various philosophies and spiritual values in which the Chinese and Japanese anchor their relationships to nature may have developed ex-post to reflect and rationalize, rather than necessarily lead to, these relationships.

The diminutive yet very organized Japanese gardens, where plants do not always occupy a central place, may reflect, for example, a sense of triumph of an insular people over an inclement nature where earthquakes and typhoons are commonplace experiences that can violently and quickly destroy built structures. Perhaps the work-intensive sand arrangements in some Japanese gardens, constructed painstakingly only to be raked away in a flash and seemingly without regret, tell the story of short-lived structures that fall prey to natural forces and, therefore. should not be overly worshipped. The size and sparseness of these gardens may reflect the high value set on scarce productive land.

Another contributor to control and precision exhibited in Japanese gardens may be the political system, which for the better part of the country's history has been autocratic. Emperors made things happen and showcased them. They sought to leave legacies of their passing, taking advantage of available manual labor to construct intricate structures surrounded by designed nature. To this day, tourists might notice with surprise Japanese gardeners using delicate tools to clip the wayward blade of grass on a lawn where most of us would hardly notice it. The fluid boundaries between the natural and the built environments may be a graceful result of the necessity to pack much in small spaces, as well as the need to build light and sparse structures to reduce the damage to them and their replacement cost in the event of frequent earthquakes and storms. Shaped by these natural and political contexts, people's perspective on nature and its beauty might well evolve toward liminality. At the very least the latter accommodates its context well even while seemingly derived from philosophical and religious tenets.

By comparison, Chinese gardens tend to be larger, possibly because of the vastly greater space availability as well as the scale of the Chinese natural landscape elements that they represent. However, similarly to Japanese gardens, Chinese gardens are also stylistically reflective of control, possibly for the dual reasons of the historic slow evolution of control tools, as well as a predominantly autocratic political system. There too, emperors and philosophers left lavish legacies with help from plentiful labor. The Chinese organismic perspective also accommodates well the natural and political context.

Thus, it is not surprising to find that along the centuries the Chinese and Japanese gardens alike received justification and backing in unifying philosophies that helped people make sense of their circumstances. Why and to whom does it matter whether the philosophical underpinnings of their perceptions about natural beauty led or followed? This issue is important pedagogically because it highlights that the natural conditions and the historical evolution of cultures are universally key to understanding observed customs and belief systems. However, this link is not deterministic; similar political conditions can yield different outlooks in natural and cultural contexts that vary, as is the case with neighboring China and Japan.

Tool availability and the development of technology are related to people's relationship to nature (seeing oneself as part of nature vs. dominating the environment for one's needs). This is supported by the observation that before the arrival of Europeans on American shores, Native Americans – whose control over natural phenomena were relatively limited when compared to their Western contemporaries – had a relationship with their nature that was closer to the traditional Japanese and Chinese worldviews than to current American attitudes. Although today we tend to account for the historic Native American relationship with nature in spiritual terms (which might be true today but not necessarily in the past) and hold these attitudes as normative models to be emulated for sustainability, we lack counterfactual evidence of how the attitudes of Native Americans might have evolved had technology afforded them more control over their surroundings. In fact, some of the examples[11] offered by Jared Diamond (2005) suggest that when humans had tools to dominate their surroundings, people around the globe developed views of nature closer to the modern American perspective, and often used these tools to destroy their natural surroundings, which in turn led to their own demise.

That autocratic political systems could account in part for the emergence of controlling gardening styles is supported by the fact that European kingdoms (e.g., France, England, and Germany) in their heyday also produced very artificial "natural" environments around their palaces, for reasons quite similar to those of the Chinese and Japanese upper classes. The United States is relatively young by comparison to Japan and China, and even to Native American cultures, although arguably Western European values predominated in early America even though they developed much later in history than in China and Japan. These old European (early American) perspectives, however, were modified by the new physical and social contexts of the United States, which were very different from Europe both in terms of scale and content.

At the outset of American colonization, nature was an entity to be conquered for survival. Later, with the industrial revolution, physical conditions in urban areas were deplorable whereas natural environments were preserved because they were more difficult to reach, which is when nature became seen as an ideal in the American worldview. This change in attitudes contributed to the innovative creation of national parks and the protection of unique landscapes.

Nowadays, American views of nature are quite diverse, rather than monolithic. Judith Layzer (2010) proposed two useful concepts to anchor the two ends of the American contemporary range of views of nature. At one end, we find *deep ecologists* who do not see humans as having to be privileged in any way but rather as being on equal footing with other living things that form ecosystems. In other words, they view themselves and others as part of nature. Deep ecologists perceive population and economic growth as grave threats to ecosystems. They do not consider the value to people of various ecosystem components to be an important consideration in conservation decisions, and would rather curtail human activities than harm natural ecosystem elements (Layzer 2010). At the other end of this continuum of American views of nature, *cornucopians* value natural elements only insofar as they have some utility (aesthetic, economic, recreational) for humans. In other words, they have a consumer's attitude toward nature. They privilege economic growth and trust that eventually a technological fix will come along to help us overcome any challenges that stem from overuse of limited natural resources (Layzer 2010). The perceptions of the value of nature, people's place with respect to it, and the role of technology in producing solutions to problems generated either by limited natural resources or by their deterioration form a useful set of dimensions for characterizing American contemporary views of nature and locating them on the continuum between deep ecologists and cornucopians.

In addition to cultural differences rooted in the histories, technological and political contexts of different places around the world, we should add scale as a factor possibly accounting for part of the observed attitude differences toward nature. The countries we chose for analysis in this chapter serve well to illustrate the scale argument. China and the United States are the third and fourth largest in the world (at roughly 3.7 million square miles each, compared to Japan, in 62nd place with .15 million square miles). In terms of population, China is in first place (1.4 billion, 2010 China census), the United States is in third place (312 million as of September 6, 2011, U.S. Census) and Japan is in tenth place (at 128 million as of June 1, 2011, Official Japan Statistics Bureau). Thus, the United States has only eighty-four people per square mile, compared to China's 360 people and Japan's 876 people per square mile. Experiencing nature under these very different circumstances cannot but affect people's worldviews.

It should come as no surprise that the smallest gardens with the most artificial (controlled and minutely managed) appearance are found in the smallest, most densely populated and most natural resource-deprived of the three countries – Japan (which is sixty-six percent urbanized, with much of the rest of the land, and even some urban land, devoted to rice production.) Nor is it surprising that the idea of vast natural conservation areas should emerge in the United States, which has relatively large tracts of uninhabited land (judging by the fact that in 2008 it was eighty-two percent urbanized, meaning that the average density belies the concentration of population on a fraction of the available land). China's vast population is only fifty percent urbanized, with a considerable amount of accessible land being occupied by villages devoted to food production. Therefore, although its vast territory still harbors some natural areas, China may be less able (physically and economically) than the United States to engage in nature conservation, should it be inclined to do so.

Conclusion

Over the past century, societies have opened more to one another than in the past, and traveling among continents became relatively easier and more frequent. Economic globalization and communication technologies further reduced physical and cultural distances among countries. As a result, Chinese, Japanese, and American worldviews of natural beauty have intermingled and converged to some extent. For instance, the High Line Park in New York City is reminiscent of Japanese and Chinese gardens. The (in places) frosted glass-floored park, which is elevated above more than a mile of streets, affords subtle views of city landmarks while visitors meander through manicured gardens. The High Line appears to erase traditional boundaries between humans and nature. Mid-nineties American consumers and architects drew inspiration from Japanese design. During the 1990s, middle-class Americans became fascinated with the practice of Feng-shui in their homes. In turn, during the twentieth century China and Japan have created a few national parks of their own that are Western in spirit, in the sense that they are dedicated to protecting the wilderness for public consumption through tourism.

At the very least, these emergent developments support the notion that consumers, architects and urban planners have become particularly open to different worldviews over the years. They also offer hope that as more and more people encounter and experience other cultures, their awareness and appreciation of diverse cross-cultural values will increase. Our comparison of prevailing worldviews of nature, as well as their antecedents, in China, Japan, and the United States has revealed several similarities and differences that undoubtedly influence international environmental negotiations. Notably, no one perspective on nature – its beauty or its value – has generated more sustainable or responsible ecological protections, despite rhetoric to that effect.

Notes

[1] The tendency to be unaware of our own lack of any genuine understanding of other cultures except through the prism of our own has been called "cognitive egocentrism." It is defined as "the projection of one's own mentality or 'way of seeing the world' onto others" (Elkind as cited in Landes 2007: 846). It entails attributing to members of other cultures our own values, interests and modes of thinking as if they were universal, despite much research and experiential evidence that many are not. The perils for negotiation are self-evident. For example, we may fail at following some of our most cherished general prescriptions – such as finding out the others' interests and mutually beneficial tradeoffs – because they hinge on our ability (severely diminished in multi-cultural contexts) to decipher interests and values and how they might be satisfied in cultures other than our own.

[2] We selected these three exemplar countries/cultures because of their geographic and cultural distances from each other, and because some of their physical and history similarities and differences allow us to explore various hypotheses.

[3] Nadja Alexander and Michelle LeBaron (2009) offer a robust critique of using role-plays for this purpose, in particular, the pitfalls of asking students to take on a cultural identity other than their own.

[4] Our proposed approach to teaching about cultural differences by using students' direct experience with one physical element – gardens – and encouraging them to discover the cultural reasons leading to very different designs is a member of the family of adventure learning devices described in other chapters of this volume.

[5] A current example is the ongoing protracted conflict unfolding in Boulder, Colorado, over deep ecologists' attempt to close off to hikers many of the local nature trails to protect plant and animal habitats they claim would be harmed by the mere presence of humans on designated paths.

[6] This is reminiscent of Western planning theories at the turn of the twentieth century, rooted in belief in a similarly strong connection between people and their (urban) environment. Accordingly, physically fixing up neighborhoods was expected to remedy the social ills brought about by deep poverty. In turn, this perspective, by the mid-twentieth century, led to the urban renewal movement, which however failed to bring about the expected results. Expectations may have been either too high, or outright unfounded. While links between physical and social environments may be present, the direction of causality is not clear and therefore acting on it is fraught with perils.

[7] While this tradition has been interpreted to mean that people were given dominion over nature and freedom to exploit it, alternative interpretations have framed it as commanding the caretaker role. For example, the Old Testament commands humane treatment of living things and a sabbatical (seventh) year of rest for land used in agriculture.

[8] Environmental regulations limiting the kinds of activities permitted in national parks (even when they might bring profit, as through the exploitation of natural resources, or enjoyment, through recreational activities) reflect the American caretaker stance toward natural beauty.

⁹ For more information on the role of debriefing, see Deason et al., *Debriefing the Debrief* and Deason et al., *Debriefing Adventure Learning* in this volume.

¹⁰ Besides causing us to attribute to others our own values, our cognitive egocentrism also leads us to judge the past from the perspective of our current values and circumstances, which are often very different from those of years past even within the same culture.

¹¹ A good example is Rapanui – Easter Island – whose population perished after having destroyed the last trees in the quest for building ever more monumental statues, which was an awe-provoking technological feat (Diamond 2005).

References

Alexander, N. and M. LeBaron. 2009. Death of the role-play. In *Rethinking negotiation teaching: Innovations for context and culture*, edited by C. Honeyman, J. Coben, and G. De Palo. St. Paul: DRI Press.

Asquith, P. J. and A. Kalland. 1997. Japanese perceptions of nature: Ideals and illusions. In *Japanese images of nature: Cultural perspectives*, edited by P. J. Asquith and A. Kalland. London: Curzon Press.

Birke, R. 2010. Neuroscience and settlement: An examination of scientific innovations and practical applications. *Ohio State Journal on Dispute Resolution* 25(2): 477-529.

Birke, R. and C. R. Fox. 1999. Psychological principles in negotiating civil settlements. *Harvard Negotiation Law Review* 4(1): 1-57.

Bruun, O. 1995. Feng-shui and the Chinese perception of nature. In *Asian perceptions of nature: A critical approach*, edited by O. Bruun and A. Kalland. London: Curzon Press.

Bruun, O. and A. Kalland. 1995. *Asian perceptions of nature: A critical approach*. London: Curzon Press.

Callicott, B. and R. Ames. 1989. *Nature in Asian traditions of thought: Essays in environmental philosophy*. Albany: State University of New York Press.

Diamond, J. 2005. *Collapse: How societies choose to fail or succeed*. New York: Penguin Group.

Elkind, D. 1967. Egocentrism in adolescence. *Child Development* 38(4): 1025-1034.

Hendry, J. 1997. Nature tamed: gardens as a microcosm of Japan's view of the world. In *Japanese images of nature: Cultural perspectives*, edited by P. J. Asquith and A. Kalland. London: Curzon Press.

Johnston, R. S. 1991. *Scholar gardens of China: A study and analysis of the spatial design of the Chinese private garden*. Cambridge: Cambridge University Press.

Korobkin, R. and C. Guthrie. 2006. Heuristics and biases at the bargaining table. In *The negotiator's fieldbook: The desk reference for the experienced negotiator*, edited by A. K. Schneider and C. Honeyman. Washington, DC: American Bar Association.

Landes, R. 2007. Edward Said and the culture of honour and shame: Orientalism and our misperceptions of the Arab-Israeli conflict. *Israel Affairs* 13(4): 844-858.

Layzer, J. A. 2010. *The environmental case: Translating values into policy.* Washington, DC: CQ Press.

Machlis, G. and D. Field. 2000. *National parks and rural development: Practice and policy in the United States.* Washington, DC: Island Press.

Nash, R. 1970. *The call of the wild: 1900-1916.* New York: George Braziller.

Pinker, S. 2002. *The blank slate: The modern denial of human nature.* New York: Penguin Books.

Saito, Y. 2002. Scenic national landscapes: Common themes in Japan and the United States. *Essays in Philosophy* 3(1): 1-23.

Tu, W. M. 1989. The continuity of being: Chinese vision of nature In *Nature in Asian traditions of thought: Essays in environmental philosophy*, edited by B. Callicott and R. Ames. Albany: State University of New York Press.

Weller, R. P. and P. Bol. 1998. From heaven-and-earth to nature: Chinese concepts of the environment and their influence on policy implementation. In *Energizing China: Reconciling environmental protection and economic growth*, edited by M. B. McElroy, C. P. Nielsen, and P. Lydon. Cambridge: Harvard University Press.

ᘓ 12 ᘔ

Following the Golden Rule and Finding Gold: Generosity and Success in Negotiation

*Lela P. Love and Sukhsimranjit Singh**

Editors' Note: *This chapter picks up where* The Psychology of Giving and Its Effect on Negotiation *(Chamoun and Hazlett 2009),* Finding Common Ground in the Soil of Culture *(Bernard 2009), and* Re-Orienting the Trainer to Navigate – Not Negotiate – Islamic Cultural Values *(Bernard 2010) left off earlier in the RNT series. The authors argue that principles of generosity are strongly supported by principles common to all the world's major religions, and that it follows that precepts that are widely shared (in theory) might yet be taught to be actually followed in negotiation practice. This, they contend, would have major effects not only on the general level of cooperation vs. competition, but on the specific, material as well as spiritual, well-being of the negotiators as individuals. There is a paradox, though: the spiritual benefit inures to you only if you* don't *strategize to achieve it.*

> "Wise souls don't hoard; the more they do for others the more they have, the more they give the richer they are."
> (Lao Tzu)

Introduction
Our friend, who is a landlord, told us a curious story. He rented an apartment in a lovely old Victorian house to a couple, who were very

* **Lela P. Love** is the director of the Kukin Program for Conflict Resolution and the Cardozo Mediation Clinic at Benjamin N. Cardozo School of Law in New York. Her email is love@yu.edu. **Sukhsimranjit Singh** is a lecturer of law, associate director of the center for conflict resolution, and director of the LL.M. program at Willamette University College of Law in Willamette, Oregon. His email address is singhs@willamette.edu.

happy with the arrangement. Happy, that is, until they discovered that a cat of the previous tenant had urinated for a period of time in an upstairs closet. The discovery led to uncovering a drenched carpet that needed to be replaced, a floor that was permeated with the odor of cat urine and affected floor moldings. It gets worse. When the carpet was pulled up in the closet it was clear that it couldn't be replaced without replacing the carpet for the entire room. The landlord had to devote several weekend days to address the situation, as well as many thousands of dollars (he worked in another city during the week). He became increasingly irritated that the tenants made no week-time efforts to move the situation forward (e.g., applying coats of urine extractor and later floor sealer that required periods of time between applications), feeling that they could have been more proactive during the week when he was away. When the rent check arrived, the landlord reported that he held the envelope in his hands and thought, "If they deducted something from their rent, I will be annoyed and disappointed." However, when he opened the envelope and found that the full rent was paid, he immediately returned one half of the rent to the tenants. Their generosity in not asserting an arguable claim begot his, creating an infection of generosity. The tenants gained a reduced rent and a top-of-the line new carpet – one much better than the old carpet. The tenants stayed patient and appreciative as repairs dragged on, and ultimately the landlord had an upgraded apartment and happy tenants.

One can only imagine the downward spiral that might have occurred if the tenants had made a grab for reduced rent.

This story suggests that one of the consequences of generosity may be that it creates generosity in others (or, conversely: grabbiness generates grabbiness) and, in the end, generosity may benefit all in terms of both material and emotional well-being, leading, as in this case, to cooperation and mutual benefit. The chapter examines generosity, a precept endorsed by major religions, as a good negotiation practice.

We recognize that most scholarly articles base their claims on quantitative or qualitative research whose methodology supports reliability. Certainly, such foundations are wise, given the potential for irrational and erroneous conclusions that behavioral economics has uncovered (Belsky and Gilovich 2009.) Yet not all subjects lend themselves equally well to such treatment; rigorous methodology is not the only source of human wisdom. Generosity, in particular, is a phenomenon people have been considering deeply for a very long time. Thus, undeterred by our admitted lack of science, our claims in this chapter will be based on the teachings of major religions, as well as our own life experiences.

Herb Cohen (1982) opened his best-selling book *You Can Negotiate Anything* with an inscription to his father, which read:

> *In memory of my father, Morris Cohen, whose negotiating strategy was always to give much more than he received. His life spoke an eloquence of its own.*

In contemplating this tribute to Morris Cohen, we were struck by the generosity of the father's approach to negotiation that, to us, seemed more enlightened (and potentially more profitable) than the son's, which included many competitive and "tricky" strategies. Consequently, we ask: Is generosity a good negotiation strategy? The thesis that generosity is a good negotiation strategy is counterintuitive: when we think of negotiation we think of the enterprise as being about getting something we want or need – not about generously giving away things of value. So, how could generosity possibly be a successful approach?

Experience tells us it feels better to be generous than to be defensively competitive, especially when the generosity is reciprocated, and often even when it is not. In addition, and more to the point of this chapter, as in the landlord-tenant story, we have noticed that the people to whom we are generous tend to give a lot back. Habib Chamoun and Randy Hazlett (2009: 152) note in their historical review of lessons to be learned from the ancient and long-successful Phoenician trading culture that, "[g]iving generates great feelings, positive energy and powerful emotions on the other side of the table that can include gratitude and reciprocity, leading the other party to be more open and flexible in future negotiations with the giver." This suggests that generosity actually "pays." In the segments that follow we will explore how generosity "pays" in multiple ways: in the increase of actual or material wealth, the increase in the perception of being wealthy, and the increase of spiritual well-being. As we consider how generosity pays, we will think about it in a broad context: that is, from bazaars to boardrooms, to dealings with family and with strangers.

Generosity Defined

In the six short segments that follow, we will very briefly explore what major religions have to say about the desirability of generosity. "Generosity" as used here refers to giving that includes, and goes beyond, money. Generosity is about sharing what you have, be it energy, food, good humor, time, listening, a smile, an embrace – or money. As such, it is the "greatest expression of one's gratitude to others" (Chamoun and Hazlett 2009: 152). True generosity is marked by an open mind and heart. Generosity includes elements such as kindness, patience and compassion (Dalai Lama 1997). It includes presence: a complete undivided attention, to our children, to our friends, to our families and to our colleagues (Thich Nhat Hanh 1973). Others have called it the joy of giving time, talent, treasure and touch (Blanchard and Cathy 2002; Chamoun and Hazlett 2009).

We look at generosity through the lens of six religions and find commonalities in all. Karen Armstrong (2010: 3-4), a scholar of comparative religion, broadens this commonality by noting:

> *All* faiths insist that compassion is the test of true spirituality and that it brings us into relation with the transcendence we call God, Brahman, Nirvana, or Dao. *Each has formulated its own version of what is sometimes called the Golden Rule,* "Do not treat others as you would not like them to treat you," or in its positive form, "Always treat others as you would wish to be treated yourself" (emphasis added).

The Golden Rule is, in essence, urging generosity – not a calculated quid pro quo, but the giving to others as one would like to receive; or, as discussed later in this chapter, giving to others without expectation of reciprocity.

The widely endorsed wisdom emanating from religious traditions may play a critical role both in negotiation, as well as spiritual advancement. As Jeffrey Seul (2006: 331) offers, "[r]eligion may very well be the primary lens through which one sees oneself and the rest of the world." Religious meaning systems, as Seul notes, define the broadest possible range of relationships – to self, others, the universe and God (2006: 324; see also Seul 1999). Consequently, religion, for many, shapes both identity and relationships with others, influencing the course of negotiations, as well as other human affairs. Ignoring religious precepts may involve peril: peril to our soul and, perhaps, to our pocketbook. Indeed, as Phyllis Bernard suggested in Volume I of the RNT teaching series, "A next generation negotiator seeks to include faith-based values without forcing agreement on religion itself" (2009: 39). Toward that end, we next, in alphabetical order, examine the precepts on generosity from six major religions.

In the Bahá'í Faith
One of the youngest religions, the Bahá'í Faith addresses generosity under the concept of the relationship between good and evil in man. Abdul'l-Baha describes it as follows:

[I]f a man is greedy to acquire science and knowledge, or to become compassionate, generous, and just, it is most praiseworthy. If he exercises his anger and wrath against the bloodthirsty tyrants who are like ferocious beasts, it is very praiseworthy, but if he does not use these qualities in a right way, they are blameworthy (Hatcher and Martin 1994: 110).

So, being greedy to be generous is praiseworthy. But being generous to gain personal advantage is not. In Baha'i teachings, Shoghi Effendi Rabbani, the first and only Guardian of the Baha'i Faith, strongly condemns anything suggestive of psychological manipulation. Talking about giving, Shoghi Effendi, in a 1942 letter to the National Spiritual Assembly of the Baha'is of the United States, said, "We must be like the fountain or spring that is continually emptying itself of all that it has and is continually being refilled from an invisible source. To be continually giving out for good of our fellows undeterred by the fear of poverty and reliant on the unfailing bounty of the Source of all wealth and all good: this is the secret of right living."[1] It follows that an insincere display of generosity – as a negotiation ploy like hiding your bottom line or playing good cop/bad cop – would be a mistake.

In Buddhism

As a variant to the Golden Rule, Buddhists urge: *Hurt not others in ways that you yourself would find hurtful* (Udana-Varga 5,1).

In Buddhism, generosity (or *dana*) is of one of the Ten Perfections that lead to Buddhahood. Giving leads to happiness as well as to material wealth. Conversely, the lack of generosity leads to unhappiness and poverty. Thus, the more one gives without seeking anything in return, the wealthier one will be (Stone 2008). This point is exemplified by a recent talk in New York City by a Buddhist lecturer at the Kadampa Buddhist Mediation Center, advertised as revealing the secret of wealth. The speaker, Kadam Morten, a well-respected local Buddhist teacher, promised to let the audience in on how to acquire worldly well-being. It turned out his secret was generosity. He explained that the mind of generosity is an intention, a wish, to give. The person with such a wish already experiences what he or she has as wealth. Conversely, a billionaire with a miserly, hoarding attitude towards his or her money is experiencing it as poverty. His point was that actual money or goods may be unrelated to the experience of wealth in a meaningful way. A generous poor person can feel wealthy in giving away half of their only loaf of bread.

Additionally, the Buddhist idea of karma posits that all of our actions – good and bad, generous and selfish – plant seeds that blossom and will return to us. So, there is a practical element to a spiritual practice. If you do something good to others, as noted above – something generous – some day, in this life, or another life, that good deed will flower and your "good karma" will return with blessings for you. The same is true for bad karma. This idea of karma suggests that it is worthwhile to be generous because it will come back, like a boomerang, with blessings or with curses – a form of active cosmic justice.

So, generosity leads to the experience of feeling wealthy. And it leads to good karma being in store. In other words, generosity will pay.

In Christianity

The New Testament of the Bible advises following the Golden Rule. *So in everything, do to others what you would have them do to you, for this sums up the Law and the Prophets* (Matthew 7:12).

Why this advice? A general social and psychological principle of reciprocity suggests that what we do for others will come back to us (see Cialdini 2006). Sometimes it comes back amplified. The Biblical commandment, however, is notably NOT: Do unto others *so that* they will give unto you. There is no calculated quid pro quo in the admonition. In the Bible, the Golden Rule is meant to be heeded in human intercourse for spiritual, rather than monetary, wealth. Nonetheless, we believe a link between spiritual and material advantage makes doing the generous deed prudent on multiple levels.

In Hinduism

According to the Hindu vision of karma, there are necessary and sufficient conditions that account for the successes and misfortunes in the life of every living being. The individual reaps only what he sows, no more, no less. Every act is both the result of forces set in operation by previous acts and the cause of the future actions (Organ 1974).

For a Hindu, one's attitude towards a possession has equal or higher significance than the mere possession itself. An attitude of a generous mind brings happiness. Like Christianity and Sikhism, the Hindu religious text *Isa Upanishad* says that true enjoyment and peace lie in detachment from wealth.

Another famous Hindu text, the Bhagavad Gita, speaks of three types of giving: "A gift that is given without any expectation of appreciation or reward is beneficial to both giver and recipient. A gift that is given reluctantly and with the expectation of some advantage is harmful to both giver and recipient. A gift that is given without any regard for the feelings of the recipient and at the wrong time, so causing embarrassment to the recipient, is again harmful to both giver and recipient" (Bhagavad Gita 17.20-22).

In addition, in Hinduism, any giving that is motivated by selfish considerations loses its value from the spiritual point of view, and generosity (*dana*) includes physical, intellectual and spiritual service (Sugirtharajah 2001).

In Islam

Islam provides extensive guidelines for its adherents pertinent to generosity. The Qur'an, in verses 2:272, reads, *Whatever they expend, it reverts to yourselves and Those who...spend...from what He has provided for them hope for a business that will never slacken* (35: 29). The Qur'an also outlines the benefits of generosity. Such benefits are others' affection, respect, popular support, and freedom from any rage (Tabataba'I 2000: 183).

In Islamic teachings, generosity provides for cooperation – the basis of human society. Under Islam, generous hospitality is treated as a desired value, even in business negotiations. In Middle Eastern culture, hospitality is more than mere courtesy; "it is an expression of sacred obligations dating to times that some believe even predated Islam" (Bernard 2010). In Islam, like other religions, generosity is not just limited to money; as one Islamic scholar puts it: "one must not suppose that the holy faith of Islam asks our beneficence only through sacrifice of wealth" (Mohammad 2000: 184).

Among other benefits, Islamic teachings emphasize, long-term relationships are established through generosity.

In Judaism[2]

The Torah's commandment "Love thy neighbor as thyself" (Leviticus 19:19) is a reflection of the Golden Rule. Indeed, the mandate, *mizvah*, of performing acts of loving-kindness, *gemilut hasadim*, is one of the highest priorities in the Jewish tradition. Imitating God's ways, *imitatio Dei*, is at the highest level of religious practice, and, since the Jewish faith views God as a performer of acts of kindness, doing such acts is a form of imitating God's ways. This concept forms one of the pillars of Jewish ethics (Harvey 2009). The Torah commands acts of generosity towards both an enemy and a brother: "If thou meet thine enemy's ox or his ass going astray, thou shalt surely bring it back to him again" (Ex. 23,4); "Thou shalt not see thy brother's ox or his sheep go astray, and hide thyself from them, thou shalt in any case bring them unto they brother" (Deut. 22, 1-3). This commandment requires unilateral acts of generosity.

Judaism's take on generosity is also reflected in the principle of *tzedakah*, or the obligation of charitable giving. For adherents, *tzedakah* is a weighty responsibility that should be discharged with great care and thought (Dosick 1995). In the words of Rabbi Yitzchok Adlerstein, "The Torah regards us as custodians of money for the poor. We can take chances with our own funds, but not those that belong to others" (Adlerstein 1999: 59). The quality of our *tzedakah* is more important than its quantity. Being in accord with this imperative for charity and generosity is a requisite of spiritual well-being.

In Sikhism

A major teaching of Sikhism, a relatively young (15th Century) religion, includes *Kirt Karna* (earning honest livelihood), *Naam Japna* (meditation) and *Vand Ke Chakna* (sharing with generosity). A thread that connects all three values of Sikhism is generosity or *"dya"* (as said in Punjabi). A Sikh's daily prayer *Japji Sahib* promotes the importance of generosity by saying "without generosity there is no religion" (Randhawa 1970: 63).

A common practice among Sikh Gurudwaras (Sikh Temples) is the service of *langar* (a free community kitchen), which serves food to others – sometimes to hundreds and thousands –
every day. The concept of *langar* started from the first Sikh Guru, Guru Nanak, and the tradition is to spread equality among all (by making attendees sit on the same ground and by sharing a meal together; by treating class, caste, religion, and gender with indifference) and to distill the importance of *sewa*. *Sewa*, loosely translated to English, means service – though a deeper translation symbolizes generosity from *tann* (body), *mann* (soul) and *dhann* (time and money).

Generosity from *tann, mann and dhann* signifies something important for negotiators. Like all major spiritual traditions, Sikhism teaches its adherents to share with heart, mind and other resources. It also teaches against having big expectations. A calm and fulfilled mind, as per Sikhism, does not expect or seek reciprocity. Such a mind should foster trust in business or personal relationships through right intentions and equanimity.

Generosity in Practice: An Example from Istanbul

In Turkey, ignoring all the advice in this chapter, Lela tried her wings as a competitive bargainer in the Eastern bazaars. She was operating, however, on what proved to be an erroneous assumption that the negotiation exercise was comprised primarily of positional and competitive bargaining. Offer low, make few and small concessions, and – after a long time – pretend to walk out and (when that does not work) accept the lowest offer. Or, try to split the difference. But these tactics did not work. Despite being well-schooled in the "negotiation dance" and the ingredients of competitive bargaining, the use of extreme positions achieved indifferent responses. What was missing?

A particular incident in an Istanbul bazaar illuminated how generosity comes into play in supposedly "competitive" bargaining. Lela tells the following story:

I had only thirty minutes to stay in the bazaar, as my ship was leaving port, and I felt quite pressured about time. I was tired of trying to bargain for everything – nor was it particularly fun. My last item to procure was a small charm to ward off the Evil Eye for my daughter's charm bracelet. I went into a shop and the merchant asked $20 for a charm that was the correct size, promising at the same time to get it properly attached to the bracelet I carried. I said "Done!" thinking I would make the merchant happy and knowing that the charm was probably worth a quarter of that. No whittling away at the offer, simply a resounding "OK." The deal was sealed but the merchant was sour. It was not a fair price, and I had done something wrong by accepting it. So, to try to make amends, I looked at him and said, "I am in a great hurry. If you can get this charm soldered onto my charm bracelet in fifteen minutes (he had to take it to a shopkeeper some distance away), then I will happily pay you $20. If it takes you sixteen minutes, though, I'll only pay you $15. If it takes you eighteen minutes, I'll only pay you $10. If it takes you twenty minutes, you'll give me the charm for free AND promise to have my bracelet back – whether or not the charm is soldered onto it, as I will be anxious about missing my ship. Deal?" The merchant was ecstatic and accepted the deal. A stop watch came out. His fastest son was put into action. His friends gathered to monitor the race against time. In the meantime we discussed politics and gold charms. Fifteen minutes later (the bracelet with attached charm came back in under ten minutes) the merchant was giving me his card, wanting to see me again in Istanbul or in America, and also giving me other trinkets to supplement the gold charm. Everyone had had a good time.

Bazaar (or any) bargaining is about both a transaction and a social interaction – and a generosity of spirit that ultimately will result in a fair price. Play with your bargaining counterpart, have a good time, accept his offer of tea and talk, and you both will find an acceptable exchange. What you give is your time, energy and good humor. Yes, there is a "negotiation dance" around extreme positions and denigrating and aggrandizing remarks about the wares at issue. But eliminate the generosity of spirit and the deal will not prosper.

The Importance of Sincerity
Generosity must be perceived as such by the receiver. If the receiver perceives a gesture as an attempt to buy them off, if they sense a trick

or a manipulative move, an otherwise generous gesture can have the opposite of the intended consequence. For example, take the following scenario:

> Imagine you arranged over the internet to rent an apartment in Berlin to attend a two week course at Humboldt University. You also arranged to share the apartment with a colleague from Italy who is also taking the course. The apartment cost 450 euros for two weeks, as it is a thirty-minute bus ride from the Mitte (the center of town) and Humboldt.
>
> When you arrived in Berlin, the apartment was fine, but your roommate never appeared. She was, however, at the program on Monday morning, and she told you that her plans changed when her boyfriend decided to come with her to Berlin. She tried to call you but never got an answer. She left a voicemail message for you, but you did not get it because you don't check voicemail. She simply forgot to send an email or a text, which is how you always communicate.
>
> It seems that everyone in the program has housing, though you haven't asked about other Humboldt students, as you don't want an absolute stranger for a roommate.
>
> You would like her to pay you 225 euros, her share of the apartment cost. She says she cannot afford that, but is willing to pay seventy-five euros. You don't want to have bad feelings with another student, but you don't know if you can find someone acceptable to take her place. You do enjoy having more space to yourself, but you're paying more than you planned. Would you accept the seventy-five euros?

We asked one of two versions of this question to fifty-seven students in a negotiation and mediation course at Humboldt University in Berlin in the summer of 2011 (see Appendix). The question immediately above was posed to the first group of students. Approximately sixty-eight percent of this group of students accepted the offer of seventy-five euros to resolve the situation – or nineteen out of twenty-eight.

Another group was given a questionnaire with the same language as above, except that one additional paragraph was included at the end of the hypothetical. It said:

> You [the offeree] went to coffee with her to discuss this and she generously offered to pay the bill for coffee and pastry, which you appreciated and accepted. You also felt good that she was concerned that the situation was difficult for you. You did not accept her proposal for seventy-five euros at the

time. You told her you would think about it. Do you accept her offer?

Offerees who were treated to coffee tended to decline the offer: only eleven accepted the offer and eighteen declined, an acceptance rate of thirty-eight percent. We did not ask for an explanation, but we suspect that the generosity was not generous enough – or, perhaps, was insulting under the circumstances, or perceived as manipulative. Or, perhaps, giving the offeree time to think about the offer might have meant that the phenomenon of loss aversion does not influence the immediate response, as it might for the first group.

The numbers tested are too small to say anything conclusive, except perhaps that generosity, like apology, is not simple. Drawing the analogy with apology further and comparing the research on apology (see, e.g., Brown and Robbennolt 2006), one might venture that it may be essential that the generosity be perceived as sincere and as in keeping with the overall situation. Here, where the offeror "owed" 225 euro, the coffee and pastry might have seemed paltry.

We also understand that generosity may be experienced and be received differently depending on the culture of the people involved. In some cultures, for example, acts of generosity are the norm. In Middle Eastern cultures, for example, negotiations often begin with generous hospitality, which is "not merely secular but also sacred" (Bernard 2010). However, the discussion of generosity and culture are beyond the scope of our present chapter.

The Right Thing for the Wrong Reason

What if you became persuaded by this essay, but misread it, and regularly engaged in acts of generosity as a negotiation ploy to get a better deal for yourself? Would such calculated generosity work in the same way that true generosity might? The experiment above is one cautionary example.

We suspect that anything disingenuous can be ferreted out for what it is, and ultimately will not work. Real generosity lies not in asking for anything in return, and further, not offering something in expectation of a *quid pro quo*. It is the experience of being on the receiving end of real generosity that triggers generosity in return.

On the other hand, various religious traditions counsel doing good deeds *even if* the doer's heart is not in the right place. The correct state of mind may then follow from the good acts, and, in any case, the good karma created will someday rebound to bless the good actor.

The Risk of Exploitation

In the Prisoner's Dilemma game, it is now well known that the best strategy over time is *Tit-for-Tat*. Following that strategy, a negotiator is cooperative (generous) to begin with – but when their counterpart is competitive (greedy) the negotiator reciprocates in kind. After this exchange the negotiator once again signals cooperation. The most effective negotiator is willing to suffer some losses (as compared to the negotiator who exclusively claims value) in order to change the overall game to cooperation (Axelrod 1984). One way of looking at this is that there is a price for being generous, when generosity is exploited.

Generosity responded to by relentless greed will ultimately be withdrawn, however, as in the *Tit-for-Tat* strategy. In the world of negotiation, it would be unwise to give away the store. Nonetheless, the initial display of a generous intent should, on average, have better consequences.

In *Howards End*, E. M. Forster (2000) described an incident in which a character leaves his umbrella in a theater, and it is taken by another. After the incident, the character regrets that he did not jealously guard his property. Forster, through another character, comments that some losses will be incurred by adopting a more trusting attitude towards human nature, but that if your trust is betrayed it is "rent to the ideal." Where generosity is taken advantage of, at least the generosity was not exercised in expectation of reciprocity, and it can be seen as "rent to the ideal."

Conclusion

Consider this real-life story. A U.S. company ("shipping company") contracted to build and operate an offshore vessel which would process and store oil produced by an oil field in the Middle East. This was the largest vessel of its kind in the world and was specially designed for use at a particular oil terminal. The vessel left the shipyard where it was being constructed a few days late, and the terminal owner abrogated the contract "because of" the late delivery (as it was entitled to do under the contract) – and then renegotiated the contract with the shipping company to a much lower daily rate. In other words, the terminal owner perceived the game as one of "hardball": because the vessel was specially built for the particular terminal and could not be used elsewhere in the world, the terminal took advantage of the late delivery to obtain a much better deal from the shipping company.

About sixteen months later, the terminal wanted some special equipment installed on the offshore vessel, as now legally required by the local environmental authorities. The terminal offered to pay the full cost of the installation, and also to pay the shipping company an additional daily amount to compensate for the cost of operating the new equipment. While the shipping company believed the cost of operating the new equipment would be no more than a few hundred dollars per day, sensing that it had the terminal over a barrel, and in an effort to try to recoup some of the losses caused by the cancellation of the original contract, it requested an increase in the daily rate for the vessel in the amount of $15,000 per day.

The terminal viewed this as extortion. They found another way to comply with the environmental requirement, without paying the shipping company a single additional dollar.

A year later, the shipping company and the terminal met to discuss extending the contract. Each needed the other – the offshore vessel was essential for the success of the terminal, and the shipping company had no other opportunity for the vessel. Yet they could not close on certain key issues: the terminal recalled having been held up by the shipping company and vowed never to let it happen again, even though they were the original "hardball player" in the deal. In other words, the shipping company's effort to extort $15,000 per day for something that was at best worth a few hundred dollars per day created a level of distrust which undermined the bargaining. At the same time, the shipping company never forgot that the terminal cancelled the original contract even though the vessel was only a few days late.

Is it fanciful to imagine what might have happened had the terminal been forgiving with respect to the relatively minor delay at the shipyard, or had the shipping company offered to operate the new equipment at no charge? We think not (and see Rose 2006 for practical support, in another industry where "hardball players" are not uncommon). Generosity here would have taken its inverse form, of not being opportunistic when an opportunity presents itself. We think the big contract, so crucial to both companies, would likely have been concluded without unnecessary transaction costs and delays. Instead, these very real companies are now mired in impasse over every small issue.

Why was generosity neglected by these negotiators? Beyond religious teachings, we believe generosity should be seen as a basic human value relevant in commercial, and other, dealings. As Robert Ashby, a well-known British humanist, said, "Our evolved history and moral sensibility have given us shared human values and the ability to empathize with others" (Ashby 2001: 59). Many of us are generous in our daily lives with our colleagues, family and friends. When we negotiate, should we lose this attitude of magnanimity, and raise our defenses? What pays off better – short term and long term? Ask the shipping company and the terminal owner.

So, what do you "know" about negotiation that you do not find in the books? Does a warm smile help lead to a good deal? Does "breaking bread together" help? By all means, study up on best alternatives to a negotiated agreement (BATNAs), zones of possible agreement (ZOPAs), and positions and interests. But do not neglect what you know in your heart and what you learn from religion. You might get the best deals, in the long run, if you are generous – and generous about not being too "strategic," too.

Notes

We would like to thank Professors Jim Coben and Ellen Waldman for their helpful feedback on the draft and Kukin Program Fellow Glen Parker for his thoughtful input.
[1] Cited in *Baha'i Funds and Contributions*, p. 16 (Also available at http://bahai-library.com/compilation_funds_contributions).
[2] The authors thank Rabbi Adam Berner for his many insights.

References

Abdu'l-Baha. 1981. *Some answered questions.* Whitefish, MT: Kessinger Publishing.

Adlerstein, Y. 1999. Let the giver beware. *Jewish Action* Winter 5760: 59.

Armstrong, K. 2010. *Twelve steps to a compassionate Life.* New York: Knopf.

Ashby, R. 2001. Charitable giving without religion. Alliance(6)1. Available at http://www.alliancemagazine.org/en/content/march-2001 (last accessed November 28, 2012).

Axelrod, R. 1984. *The evolution of cooperation.* Cambridge: Basic Books.

Belsky, G. and T. Gilovich 2009. *Why smart people make big money mistakes.* New York: Simon Schuster.

Bernard, P. 2009. Finding common ground in the soil of culture. In *Rethinking negotiation teaching: Innovations for context and culture*, edited by C. Honeyman, J. Coben, and G. De Palo. St. Paul, MN: DRI Press.

Bernard, P. 2010. Re-orienting the trainer to navigate – not negotiate – Islamic cultural values. In *Venturing beyond the classroom: Volume 2 in the rethinking negotiation teaching series*, edited by C. Honeyman, J. Coben, and G. De Palo. St. Paul, MN: DRI Press.

Blanchard, K and S. Truett Cathy. 2002. *The Generosity factor.* Grand Rapids, MI: Zondervan.

Brown, J. G. and J. K. Robbennolt. Apology in negotiation. In *The negotiator's fieldbook: The desk reference for the experienced negotiator*, edited by A. K. Schneider and C. Honeyman. Washington, DC: American Bar Association.

Chamoun, H. and R. Hazlett. 2009. The psychology of giving and its effect on negotiation. In *Rethinking negotiation teaching: Innovations for context and culture*, edited by C. Honeyman, J. Coben, and G. De Palo. St. Paul, MN: DRI Press.

Cialdini, R. 2006. *Influence: The psychology of persuasion*. New York: Harper Paperbacks.

Cohen, H. 1982. *You can negotiate anything*. New York: Bantam Books.

Cole, O. 2010. *Understanding Sikhism*. Edinburgh: Dunedin Academic Press.

Dalai Lama. 1997. *Healing anger – The power of patience from a Buddhist perspective*. New York: Snow Lion Publications.

Dosick, W. 1995. *Living Judaism: The complete guide to Jewish belief, tradition and practice*. New York: Harper Collins Paperback.

Forster, E. M. 2000. *Howards End*. New York: Penguin Books.

Harvey, W. Z. 2009. Grace or loving kindness. In *Contemporary Jewish religious thought*, edited by A.A. Cohen and P. Mendes-Flohr. London: The Free Press

Hatcher, W. and J. Martin. 1994. *The Baha'i Faith – The emerging global Religion*. Wilmette, IL: Baha'i Publications.

Lao Tzu (Translated by Ching T.) 1997. *A book about the way and the power of the way*. Boston, MA: Shambhala Publications.

Mohammad, A-H. 2000. *The Qur'an: An introduction*. London: Routledge.

Nhat Hanh, T. 1975. *The miracle of mindfulness: An introduction to the practice of meditation*. Boston: Beacon Press.

Organ, T. 1974. *Hinduism-historical development*. New York: Barron's Educational Series.

Randhawa, G. S. 1970. *Guru Nanak's Japuji*. Amritsar: Guru Nanak Dev University Press.

Rose, D. 2006. Ulysses and business negotiation. In *The negotiator's fieldbook: The desk reference for the experienced negotiator*, edited by A. K. Schneider and C. Honeyman. Washington, DC: American Bar Association.

Seul, J. R. 1999. Ours is the way of God: Religion, identity, and intergroup conflict. *Journal of Peace and Religion* 36(5): 553-569

Seul, J. R. 2006. Religion and conflict. In *The negotiator's fieldbook: The desk reference for the experienced negotiator*, edited by A. K. Schneider and C. Honeyman. Washington, DC: American Bar Association.

Stone, B. 2008. A list of Buddhist lists: The ten perfections. Available at http://bstonedesigns.com/buddhist_lists/ten_perfections.html (last accessed November 28, 2012).

Sugirtharajah, S. 2001. Traditions of giving in Hinduism. Alliance (6)3: 17-21.Available at http://www.alliancemagazine.org/members/pdfs/full/VOL_06_NO_3.pdf (last accessed November 28, 2012).

Tabataba'I, M. and A. Tabatabai. 2000. *Islamic teachings-an overview*. New York: Mostazafan Foundation of New York.

Appendix

Imagine that the following has happened to you here in Berlin:
You arranged over the internet to rent an apartment in Berlin for the two weeks you are here. You also arranged to share the apartment with a colleague from Italy who is also taking the course at Humboldt University. The apartment cost 450 euros for two weeks, as it is a thirty-minute bus ride from the Mitte (the center of town) and Humboldt.

When you arrived in Berlin, the apartment was fine, but your roommate never appeared. She was, however, at the program on Monday morning, and she told you that her plans changed when her boyfriend decided to come with her to Berlin. She tried to call you but never got an answer. She left a voicemail message for you, but you did not get it because you don't check voicemail. She simply forgot to send an email or a text, which is how you always communicate. It seems that everyone in the program has housing, though you haven't asked about other Humboldt students, as you don't want an absolute stranger for a roommate.

You would like her to pay you 225 euros, her share of the apartment cost. She says she cannot afford that, but is willing to pay seventy-five euros. You don't want to have bad feelings with another student, but you don't know if you can find someone acceptable to take her place. You do enjoy having more space to yourself, but you're paying more than you planned.

You went to coffee with her to discuss this and she generously offered to pay the bill for coffee and pastry, which you appreciated and accepted. You also felt good that she was concerned that the situation was difficult for you. You did not accept her proposal for seventy-five euros at the time. You told her you would think about it. Do you accept her offer? **Check one:**

_____ yes   _____ no

The second questionnaire was identical to the one above except that it did not have the highlighted paragraph.

ଓଃ 13 ଞ

Debriefing the Debrief

Ellen E. Deason, Yael Efron, Ranse Howell, Sanda Kaufman, Joel Lee & Sharon Press[*]

Editors' Note: An afterthought; a rushed invitation for general comments; some PowerPoint slides flashed at the end of an exercise; a pre-prepared reading list of "take away lessons" . . . . do these sound familiar? The authors argue that all too often, good intentions for thorough debriefing of negotiation exercises degenerate into something disappointing, or even pointless. They contend that debriefing is too critical an element in overall learning to be defensibly treated this way. In a thorough analysis that should also be read in conjunction with the same authors' treatment of debriefing adventure learning specifically (chapter 14 in this volume), they first outline a choice of goals; then analyze the characteristics of good debriefing work, and discuss some general approaches; and then outline predictable challenges and some tactics for handling them. As is appropriate for the project's increasing focus on the differences between student groups (see Lewicki and Schneider, Instructors Heed the Who, chapter 3 in Venturing Beyond the Classroom), the authors end by discussing how debriefing might be tailored for specific audiences.

[*] **Ellen Deason** is the Joanne Wharton Murphy/Classes of 1965 and 1973 Professor of Law at The Ohio State University Moritz College of Law in Columbus, Ohio. Her email address is deason.2@osu.edu. **Yael Efron** is a lecturer of law and head of academic administration at Zefat Academic College School of Law in Zefat, Israel. Her email address is yaele@Zefat.ac.il. **Ranse Howell** is a senior training consultant and mediator at the Centre for Effective Dispute Resolution (CEDR), London, UK. His email address is rhowell@cedr.com. **Sanda Kaufman** is a professor at the Maxine Goodman Levin College of Urban Affairs and director of the Master of Arts program in environmental studies at Cleveland State University, Cleveland, Ohio. Her email address is s.kaufman@csuohio.edu. **Joel Lee** is an associate professor at the Faculty of Law, National University of Singapore. His email address is joellee@nus.edu.sg. **Sharon Press** is an associate professor of law and director of the Dispute Resolution Institute at Hamline University School of Law in St. Paul, Minnesota. Her email address is spress01@hamline.edu.

Introduction

Debriefing is not limited to teaching negotiation, or even to teaching. It is used in such diverse settings as medical and nursing education, business, counseling, and military operations.[1] In the education context, the debrief is a post-experience analytic process that is an indispensable element in the journey of experiential learning. Done well, debriefing provides an opportunity for participants to reflect on their progress, and enables them to carry away lessons that enhance their knowledge and skills. The debrief provides the crucial "so what" to the teaching exercise.

Debriefing is complicated and demanding, yet it has not received as much attention in the literature as design and implementation of simulations (Lederman 1992). Unfortunately, debriefs of negotiation activities are not always done well, and there is little guidance for structuring and conducting a successful debrief. Too often, a debrief degenerates into "an afterthought or a rushed invitation for general comments" (Alexander and LeBaron 2009: 194). We have also observed trainers conduct debriefs by flashing up PowerPoint slides at the end of exercises and reading lists of "take away lessons." Without effective debriefing, negotiation exercises fall short of achieving their optimal learning potential.

This chapter seeks to stimulate thinking on designing and conducting debriefings in teaching negotiation. It draws on the authors' experiences teaching negotiation in a variety of contexts and with a variety of participants. Some of us teach students in a classroom setting. Others conduct training workshops. Many do both. We teach students in law, urban planning, conflict resolution, and more. We train individuals from a wide range of professions, such as business persons, government officials, and lawyers. We teach in the United States, Europe, the Middle East, Asia, Africa, Central America, and Australia, often to groups with mixed national backgrounds. We concur on many points, but occasionally differ in our approaches.

We believe that a good debrief is essential to teaching negotiation well. It should make the experiences of the learning activity come alive. It should connect those experiences to the content of the course and assist participants in putting theory into practice and constructing their own lessons. It should make the process feel personal and real, and increase the likelihood that the students will remember and use their new learning. It should help students develop the habit of reflecting on their practice. The effectiveness of a simulation role-play or other experiential learning activity depends to a great extent on the effectiveness of the debriefing.

This chapter primarily considers debriefing simulated negotiations in the form of role-play exercises, which are the most common method of teaching negotiation (Movius 2008; Alexander and LeBaron 2009; Ebner and Kovach 2010). For a consideration of the special issues involved in debriefing adventure learning experiences, see our companion chapter (Deason et al., *Debriefing Adventure Learning*) in this volume. This chapter applies generally to both teaching and training, and we use the terms "teach," "train," and "facilitate" interchangeably except where the context indicates distinct meanings. Similarly, until the final section when we discuss the differences between executive-style workshops and the academic setting, we do not distinguish between "participants" and "students" or "classes" and "workshops" unless we make an explicit contrast.

The chapter begins with a discussion of the goals of conducting a debrief and of the importance of debriefing for the learning process. We then outline the characteristics of good debriefing and describe general approaches to debriefing. Next, we explore the challenges entailed in debriefing and make some suggestions about ways to address them, including a section with ideas for designing debriefing structures. We then outline a series of functional steps for debriefing negotiations. Finally, we close the chapter with a section on tailoring debriefing for specific audiences.

Goals of Debriefing

A negotiation exercise is an unaccompanied immersion: students are asked to jump into the situation and handle it on their own. By necessity, instructors deliver their contribution outside this experience, i.e., before and after it. Before the exercise, this input may come through lectures, discussion of readings, the planning of the exercise, and preparatory briefing or instructions. After the exercise, the instructor's input comes through debriefing. This is the point at which a carefully constructed discussion with clear analytic lessons is crucial to the teaching of negotiation skills (Susskind and Coburn 2000).

A primary purpose for debriefing is to develop and reinforce the learning goals for the exercise. Thus, a good debrief begins in the planning stages for the exercise, with very carefully thought out and articulated learning goals for the activity (even if those goals may not be articulated in advance to the students). Then, the plan for the debriefing should be aligned closely with the goals for the exercise. The debriefing should also reinforce the function of the exercise in the broader context of the course or workshop, which as Lynn Cohn and her colleagues (2009) stressed in the training context, should be designed based on a careful assessment of the overall goals. It is essential to create a close linkage between that foundation of general goals, the content and skills conveyed to the participants, the specific purpose(s) of the exercise, and the debrief.

While using analogical reasoning and observational learning in combination with simulations shows promise for improving knowledge transfer about negotiation (Nadler, Thompson, and Van Boven 2003; Movius 2008), currently the typical educational tool used with simulations is principle-based learning. Often an instructor designs an exercise to give students a chance to apply negotiation principles by using a factual setting that encourages students to practice concepts presented through reading, lectures, or discussion. In this context, the crucial role of debriefing is to tie the specific applications in the exercise back to the broader concepts and to solidify those lessons. The debrief should elicit reactions and observations from the participants about the application in the exercise and, embedded within the discussion, review the concepts and explore how they could be applied in other situations. In some cases, it may also be possible to use the debrief to assist the participants to transfer lessons from the class to their real-world contexts by helping them anticipate what they will do in the future.

Instructors may also plan a negotiation experience to generate new realizations and change practices or approaches. Without an effective debrief, however, this experience might have little pedagogical benefit. It can leave untouched the baggage of habits, cultural legends about negotiation, and poorly-understood basic concepts such as "win-lose" or "win-win." It can even confirm for some the false conclusion that they are master negotiators who always get the best of their opponents. The debrief is the step that processes the experience, challenges students' assumptions, and fosters new approaches in the future.

Other goals may be less directly tied to course content. In the educational setting, negotiation exercises and their debriefing can play a role in students' general professional development. For example, if law students have not yet taken a clinic or had work experience that has exposed them to representing a client, practicing negotiation skills may bring them closer to a sense of being a lawyer than the doctrinal content of many of their other courses. The debrief is an important part of this process. If it is conducted as a conversation among professionals, honoring and acknowledging the knowledge and experience each individual brings to the learning enterprise, it can help students develop a professional identity (Rudolph, Simon, Raemer, and Eppich 2008). Furthermore, presenting the debrief as a model for ongoing self-assessment encourages students to develop as reflective practitioners (Schön 1983) engaged in continual learning.

Contributions of Debriefing to Learning

Learning is understood as a process in which the learner internalizes concepts and principles, leading to new thought patterns and changed actions (Kolb 1984). During the debriefing of a negotiation simulation, this internalization takes place through reflection and feedback. Reflection has been defined as the collection of "intellectual and affective activities in which individuals engage to explore their experiences in order to lead to new understandings and appreciations" (Boud, Keogh, and Walker 1985). Although the definition is phrased in terms of an individual activity, in debriefing reflection occurs at a group level as well. This can help students make sense of their experience not only by exploring their own observations but also by gaining insights from the reactions of their peers.

The importance of reflection for effective debriefing is supported by the theoretical work of several scholars who emphasize the role of reflection in moving a person from an unexamined experience to new understandings for future actions. John Dewey (1933) pioneered the idea of reflective thinking as education, seeing the process as not only an intellectual activity, but also an emotional one. Donald Schön (1983) maintained that professionals face complex situations that cannot be resolved by technical tools alone, and proposed an approach to professional learning facilitated by reflection. He coined the term "reflective practice" to describe the discipline of examining the values, assumptions, and knowledge-base that drive one's professional practice.[2] Kurt Lewin's (1951) cyclical model of adult learning alternates between a concrete experience and analysis of that experience. In the cycle articulated by David Kolb (1984), after an experience in which learners gather information, their reflections on that experience lead them to formulate new generalizations and abstract concepts, which they then test in new situations. This process of alternating exploration, action, and reflection is central to adult learning (Brookfield 1986).

Debriefing is also an opportunity for feedback to participants not only from the teacher(s), but also from their fellow participants or an observer. Effective feedback is one of the main elements in the "learning curve" concept introduced by Newell and Rosenbloom (1981). A review of the literature on simulations in medical education concluded that feedback is the most important feature of this form of medical education (Issenberg et al. 2005). Feedback can also promote the acquisition of negotiation skills (Patton 2000).[3] Thompson (1998) highlights studies demonstrating the importance of feedback to building negotiation skills and concludes that "effective negotiation requires practice and feedback" (Thompson 1998: 8). It is considered especially important in learning behavioral negotiation skills, as distinguished from learning negotiation theory and concepts (Williams, Farmer, and Manwaring 2008).[4]

Characterizing the Effective Debrief

In suggesting ways to improve negotiation role-plays, Nadja Alexander and Michelle LeBaron (2009: 194) stress the importance of debriefing them "specifically and completely." We have identified the following as important additional characteristics. An effective debrief:

- Focuses on the process of interaction. Dialogue among the participants and between the facilitator and participants allows essential articulation of insights.
- Draws on the experience of the participants by eliciting reactions and encouraging reflection on the activity.
- Explicitly connects the exercise, which has been tailored for a specific purpose, to the course material. The facilitator needs to be able to weave participants' comments into this structure.
- Offers additional information from negotiation theory and experimental and field research. This helps tie the experience to reasons behind behaviors, interaction patterns, effectiveness of strategies, and quality of outcomes.
- Models behaviors that reinforce past lessons or preview future ones. This makes the debrief a link in the chain of activities in a course or workshop.
- Lasts long enough to be comprehensive and to underscore the importance of the activity.

In a nutshell, a good debrief is the opposite of a recipe. Its distinguishing mark is that it gives students the tools to analyze specific situations and make choices informed by an understanding of why certain techniques might work or how they might be adapted to work. A good debrief empowers students with the knowledge they need to react in the negotiation moment, however different it might be from past experiences.

General Approaches to Debriefing

The specifics of conducting a debriefing vary depending on the teaching context (whether an academic course or professional training), the professional and cultural context, the participants' background, and the time allotted. There are commonalities, however, and we discuss here two general approaches with contrasting pedagogical underpinnings.

We call the first approach *deductive,* in that debriefing starts with a presentation to the students of the lessons to be gleaned from the exercise. Then the participants are invited to share their experiences and the facilitator uses their responses to illustrate those learning points or to generate discussion around exceptions to the learning points. The second approach is a more *inductive* process. The facilitator first elicits reactions and responses to the experience and then uses them to build up to the lessons. In this approach, the experiences are the raw materials from which students construct their personal learning. Metaphorically, this second approach is akin to weaving a tapestry from threads contributed by the students. The image on the tapestry, and the point of the discussion, will not be clear until the facilitator pulls the strands together and the lessons emerge.

Both approaches have advantages and disadvantages. The deductive approach is easier and faster to conduct. Because instructors identify the lessons at the outset, they can facilitate a relatively brief and targeted discussion. This is comparatively straightforward because the initial road map of the lessons provides structure for the discussion and makes it easy for the students to recognize the "take away" points. On the negative side, even though this approach has the participatory element of asking students about their experiences, presenting the conclusions first has a prescriptive effect. It turns students into confirming responders rather than initiators, and might as such inhibit student reflection.

The second, inductive, approach offers the advantage of encouraging participants to construct their own knowledge. However, these debriefs usually take longer. The facilitator has to build the lessons from the responses, and it takes time to elicit sufficient comments to concretize the lessons. These debriefs can also be more challenging, especially for instructors with limited experience in debriefing, because the lessons must be constructed in real time. With the participants not privy to the road map of the lessons, the facilitator has to keep track of responses and manage the discussion to develop the intended points. The "open-endedness" of this conversation can also be somewhat unsettling for the participants. But it makes them less likely to jump to premature closure, which leaves them more open to discovering and learning lessons that are personally meaningful but go beyond the instructor's plan.

The consensus among the authors of this chapter favors the second, more elicitive approach. We believe that a debrief is more likely to create learning that students will actually retain if their own reflections lead to the conclusions. This is apparent when a student announces in a debrief – often with great enthusiasm – a realization she made on the basis of the exercise. Even when a point has previously been made in a reading assignment and again in prior class discussion a student may not absorb it until she discovers it herself, as she becomes aware of her experience.

Many of the chapter's authors, however, modify the purely inductive approach by using questions to organize the debrief. This gives the process more structure, although it also makes it less open-ended. In this variation, the debrief is a highly interactive process, in which the facilitator asks questions of the group to guide their learning and uses the responses to continue and develop the discussion. The goal is to draw on what the participants actually experienced and tie their comments to what the facilitator planned (or hoped) would be discovered in the exercise. Instructors can retain many of the benefits of the purely inductive approach by asking open-ended questions (such as "what worked well?" or "what was hard for you?") along with more focused questions, and by using planned discussion points and questions only as starting points. We prefer to conduct the debrief in free form, taking cues from what participants say and bringing out examples of student behaviors we observed during the exercise.

When using an inductive approach, it is useful to conclude with a summary that incorporates what the students have shared as well as any important additional points that were not articulated. Instructors may present this summary on a previously prepared slide, flip chart or a handout, so that the "take away" points are clear. It can be similar to the information that students would get at the start of a deductive debrief. The summary makes up for any gaps in the discussion and ensures that the debrief links the experience to its objectives and places it in the larger context of the course or training.

Challenges to Successful Debriefing and Suggested Remedies

The requirements of an effective debrief pose significant pedagogical challenges for trainers. In this section, we outline some of the issues – psychological and social, facilitative, and logistical – that teachers often face, and we explore approaches and techniques to help address them.

Psychological and Social Challenges

Participants face psychological challenges during debriefs. Self-reflection can be uncomfortably revealing of shortcomings, and there is also a natural reluctance to receive criticism.[5] Resistance to change is a common theme in education, as reflected in numerous studies (Patton 2000). Trainers face the challenge of fostering an atmosphere of safety that enables participants to seek feedback and to strive for improvement.

Criticism also creates social challenges through threats to the role of individuals in a group (Patton 2000). One factor is that dissecting a participant's behaviors may have an effect on the individual's standing in the group. Another is that exercises with an opportunity to double-cross a negotiating partner can provoke sympathies and antipathies with lasting effects in the classroom (see Welsh 2012). A debrief needs to defuse threats to the self-worth and reputation of participants in order to preserve an environment conducive for learning.

To create a safe environment for everyone to express their views, the facilitator must model openness and tolerance. An effective way to do this is to listen with respectful curiosity and the goal of understanding, and then to utilize responses to further the discussion. This shows the value of each person's contribution, provides space for the participants to explore and digest their experiences, and demonstrates that the discussion is a safe place to discuss concerns. Consider overtly encouraging a spirit of experimentation during exercises, which can moderate reactions to role-play dynamics and threats to reputation. The goal is to foster a sense of community that encourages the growth of all.[6]

Facilitation Challenges

No matter how experienced the teacher, facilitating a debrief involves challenges in terms of participant dynamics and managing contributions. Many of these challenges are common in facilitating any discussion, but they may be more pronounced during debriefs where students are being asked to dissect their performance and to describe personal reactions and feelings. Perhaps the best general facilitation advice parallels what we teach our students about negotiation: combine thorough preparation with flexibility in the moment. A debrief will rarely turn out the way one has planned it. But if one can keep in mind the goals of the debrief and be flexible in utilizing responses, learning objectives can be met.

Preparation means identifying the objectives of the exercise, and planning lines of questioning and summary points in advance so that the instructor is ready to use the debrief to further those objectives. It is also vital to know the details of the fact pattern for the exercise in order to follow nuances in the discussion, and to the extent possible, it is very helpful to observe the students doing the exercise. Jotting down examples of student interactions prepares the facilitator to enrich the debrief; students cannot always be counted on to volunteer their experience, but will usually respond to prompts. More generally, preparation also means being comfortable with the subject matter. Ideally, the teacher should be familiar not only with what she intends to cover, but also with related material that speaks to the experience the students are likely to have.

These forms of preparation are also helpful in alleviating a trainer's anxiety; an inductive debriefing style can be intimidating. There is no pre-planned content to deliver – just an open forum. This can be uncomfortable for some because it feels as if the conversation can go anywhere (or nowhere). On occasion, they may even hold rather heated discussions – a sign of engagement, but with the risk that the instructor will lose control. Facilitators need to strike a balance between allowing adequate space for the discussion and steering it back to the purpose of the exercise. Thorough preparation and clarity about those purposes assists greatly with this ambitious goal.

Flexibility is necessary to adapt to the unanticipated directions participants may introduce into the conversation. Planning the goals of the exercise and the debrief, as opposed to the minutiae of specific questions, supports flexibility by preparing the instructor to relate unexpected comments to the larger picture. Curiosity and concentration are also practices that support flexibility in debriefing. (See Efron and Ebner 2010 for suggestions on cultivating curiosity and openness in preparation for leading a training.) During the discussion, stay in the moment with the students. Listening carefully to their experiences is essential in order to be able to make meaningful connections in an agile debrief.

In terms of more specific facilitation challenges, there are a number of common difficulties to be expected during debriefing conversations. We suggest some skills instructors can cultivate to address them.

"The sound of silence"
Sometimes, it is difficult to get responses from the room with a general invitation. People have a variety of reasons for reticence: they may not want to be first, or to risk sounding stupid, or they may not understand. Silence can also be an expression of the psychological or social factors discussed above, or it can reflect something as simple as postprandial or late evening timing. Some reframing and encouragement may be necessary to elicit responses. A specific person might be invited to respond to start the conversation. This, and the facilitator's reaction to the response, will hopefully lead to more fruitful discussion. If, however, after several open questions and prompts there is still silence, it may be necessary to fall back on using a pre-written set of learning points on a slide or a flip chart, which can help guide the discussion and prompt responses from even the most difficult group.

"The Dominant Party"
Occasionally someone in the room dominates the discussion or pronounces views in a definitive way. This may dissuade others in the

room from speaking, reducing the variety of views and preventing a full discussion. Furthermore, silent participants may be less likely to process the experience in personal terms, and they lose the benefit they would gain from articulating their insights. The most constructive approach is to encourage the involvement of the rest of the room without alienating the dominant party or marginalizing his view. Instructors can do this by asking for other views. If necessary, the facilitator might have to single out a couple of specific people for their responses. In extreme circumstances, the facilitator may need to speak to the "dominator" individually.

"Missing the point"

At times a participant offers an observation that is either irrelevant, off-point, or simply wrong. A related challenge is when a group is stuck on discussing specific outcomes or other topics that do not have general applicability. As in the case of the dominant party, the challenge is to address the problem without alienating that person or group or discouraging participation. It is therefore better not to ignore this type of response. It may be possible to use the response to open a discussion by linking it to something that is relevant. Done this way, the participant making the initial response will both learn and feel included. Alternatively, the teacher can acknowledge the response as one possible way of seeing things, but then elicit different views from others who might challenge it. This gives the person who offered the initial response an opportunity to rethink it in light of what other participants have to say, which may be more palatable than a counter from the facilitator.

"Runaway emotions"

After some role-plays, especially prisoner's-dilemma-type exercises or simulations designed to raise ethical issues, some participants may feel wronged or upset about having been double-crossed. Even without an element of deception, there is likely to be an emotional component to students' sense of their performance in the role-play. While emotions can be an important aspect of the learning process, helping students manage them is necessary to keep the debrief on track. Allowing some venting at the beginning of the debrief may pre-empt this difficulty. Some of us also suggest that reassuring participants that emotions are a human mechanism for dealing with issues that matter, and praising those who take the learning experience so seriously, can help replace hostility with pride. An analogy to a real-life negotiation process can also be helpful to deal with emotional overflow. Asking students how emotions might affect the negotiation process and other participants in real-life negotiations is one way to refocus the discussion on broader themes.

"The mosaic"

Anyone who has taught knows that the more heterogeneous a group is – in terms of initial skills, interests, experience, and educational background – the more difficult it is to teach the class at the appropriate level and to manage the variety of contributions. This, however, is a challenge that can be turned into a valuable asset. Diversity in the classroom microcosm can be treated explicitly as mirroring the diversity of perspectives that participants will encounter in their professional negotiations. Thus, differences among students can illustrate key negotiation points related to the effects of differences in perceptions, substantive knowledge, life experiences, and culture. Instructors may want to use every opportunity to draw attention to these differences and explore how they affect negotiation processes and outcomes, reminding students that agreements are often made possible by differences in preferences rather than similarities.

Logistical Challenges

Time constraints

Insufficient time for adequate debriefing is one of the most common challenges faced by negotiation teachers. Trainers struggle with how to distribute time among conveying theoretical elements, experiential exercises, and their debriefing. Inadequate time for a debriefing session undermines its effectiveness and, given its importance, limits the learning experience. It is especially difficult for the teacher to stay elicitive and fully foster self-discovery when time is short. When there is insufficient time, the debrief tends to become more of a presentation than an interactive discussion. And, even if the process is interactive, everyone may not have a chance to speak. In short, inadequate time for a debrief risks compromising important goals of the process.

One rule of thumb in the educational context is to allocate, as a starting point, twenty-five percent of the total exercise time to debriefing (Hertel and Mills 2002). This may need to increase with a large group, a group unfamiliar with debriefing, or a complex activity. In contrast, others advocate longer timeframes. Steinwachs (1992) runs debriefs for at least as long as the experiential part of the exercise. In nursing education, where simulations are widely used, some advocate allotting three times the length of the experiential portion to debriefing (Arafeh, Hansen, and Nichols 2010). In actual practice, however, nursing educators tend to allocate from ten to fifty percent of the total exercise time to reflection and debriefing (Brackenreg 2004). For

negotiation simulations, some of the co-authors of this chapter esti-
mate that debriefing can fulfill most of its potential if approximately
twenty-five percent of the exercise time is dedicated to the debriefing
session. In any event, variation in the duration of debriefing should be
related to the complexity of the exercise and the learning objectives.

Whatever the length of time planned for debriefing, it is important
to keep the exercise on schedule. Cutting off negotiation in the middle
can be difficult for students who feel that they could reach agreement
with just a little more time. But the debriefing will have to absorb
the time overrun. In deciding when to stop an exercise, it may help
to consider how much additional learning, if any, students would get
from continuing it. There may be a point of diminishing educational
returns after which students will benefit much more from debriefing
than from continuing the exercise. Although students typically seek
the satisfaction of completing an agreement, the educational goals of
an exercise may not require this, and some lessons may be stronger if
not all students reach one.

The timing for the debriefing session

When is the optimal time to conduct debriefing – immediately after
a negotiation exercise, or later, once the experience has sunk in? The
nursing literature on simulations advocates debriefing immediately
in order to productively focus the emotions that will naturally arise
when students begin to analyze their performance following a simulation (Arafeh, Hansen, and Nichols 2010). Pedagogically, immediate
feedback makes it easier to connect behaviors to outcomes and, therefore, to the need for changed behavior. In addition, students remain
engaged and they remember details. However, logistically, there is the
problem that negotiating groups will inevitably complete the activity at different times. An immediate debrief may keep some students
idling while others continue their negotiation. Moreover, there simply
may not be time to conduct a full debriefing process, especially within
the constraints of a class period.

In order to adapt to timing constraints, it may be advantageous
to postpone the debrief until the following session, particularly with
a complicated simulation exercise (high stakes, multi-party, multi-
issue) that may require an entire class period to negotiate. With this
approach, students should be asked to take a few minutes to jot down
their impressions, either in free form or with some guidelines, to help
them recall their experiences in the later discussion. Alternatively,
some negotiations can take place outside class. This may call for using
some of the alternative designs for debriefing that we discuss below.

In addition to logistic considerations, there are some pedagogical
advantages to separating the role-play and the debrief. It takes time to

ponder one's actions, their consequences, and their desirability. Some distance between the experience and the discussion can help students cool off and bring perspective to their analysis. Debriefing effectively must balance both needs – to process the experience directly and immediately, and to allow sufficient time for reflection. Admittedly, semester-long classes offer more options than workshops.

Number of participants

Although there is some indication that many negotiation classes are taught in groups of under thirty students (Patton 2000; Williams and Geis 2000), larger classes are not uncommon. Trainers sometimes work in teams of two or three, and may have more influence over the size of a workshop, but usually they too lack the luxury of matching the number of participants to the number of training staff. Thus in both settings there are often more working groups of students engaged in role-plays than teaching staff. As a result, instructors cannot observe each negotiation entirely, which limits their ability to provide feedback. Furthermore, with large numbers of negotiation groups, there are more experiences to discuss, and this makes whole-group debriefing sessions more complex. Especially when combined with time limitations, an unwieldy number of students imposes significant constraints on full participation during a debrief.

One response to size is to break the class into smaller groups led by adjunct instructors for simulation exercises and debriefs. Other solutions involve varying the design of the debriefing structure, as discussed in the following section.[7]

Designing a Debriefing Structure

Some of the challenges of debriefing can be best addressed by considering alternative methods for debriefing and selecting a structure suited to the specific exercise. In a typical negotiation class, several groups negotiate the same role-play exercise simultaneously and the entire class reconvenes at the end of the role-play for an in-class debriefing session. An advantage of this format is that all students can benefit from the varied experiences of the small negotiating groups. However sole reliance on this approach has many of the disadvantages, discussed above, that are associated with immediate debriefing in a large group. Rather than automatically adopting this structure, an instructor should consider varying it with other approaches.

Many of the authors of this chapter have experimented with debriefing methods designed to respond to some of the logistical – and other – challenges that trainers face. Self-assessment or other written reaction is one approach that expands the scope of reflection.

Discussion in small groups is an additional, productive way to complement traditional whole-group discussion. We also discuss the benefits of whole-group discussions and ways to adapt them to large groups.

Personal Assessment

One way to overcome the reluctance participants have to share their shortcomings, fears, and concerns with others, while simultaneously encouraging participants to examine their assumptions and performance, is to use a self-assessment instrument.

Yael Efron and Noam Ebner have developed personal assessment sheets to guide reflection at each debriefing point in the exercise: before it begins, half-way through (if applicable), and at the end. The sheets are not handed in to the teacher nor shared with anyone, but participants are encouraged to keep them for future reference. This promotes candid reflection over time, and provides a perspective on skill improvement throughout the course. A sample set of questions for a simulation exercise emphasizing negotiation skill-building is included in Appendix A. The questions can be tailored to fit other goals as appropriate for the training session.

A related, less guided, approach is to ask the students to spend a few minutes after the exercise recording their immediate reactions and observations. This helps engage all students in the subsequent discussion. It can also enable that discussion to occur or to continue during the following class period if the time left at the end of the negotiation is not long enough to do justice to a full debrief.

Small-group Discussions

Most of the chapter authors rely, to varying degrees, on small-group discussions among those who participated in the same role-play group. This allows participants to share confidential role information and to provide personal feedback to each other. The small group may be more comfortable for discussion than the plenary format, allowing some students to be more forthcoming. These discussions also help smooth the timing problem created when some groups finish negotiating earlier than others. Substantively, the discussions can highlight different perspectives on the group's shared experience and prime participants to offer their viewpoints in the large-group discussion. There, the small groups' experiences can be used as examples to demonstrate common themes or diverse approaches.

A logistical challenge for small group debriefs is having too few trainers to lead the discussions. While groups can hold discussions without a facilitator, this may not be ideal. One solution is to assign a student to act as a "coach" in each group. The coach acts as an observer during the role-play and leads a discussion in the small group after the exercise. The coach is equipped with a set of specific questions to bear in mind while observing the exercise and to use as the basis for the discussion.[8] Additionally, the coach is tasked with preventing the small-group discussion from becoming a simple, play-by-play rehash of the negotiation or – even worse – a continuation of the negotiation itself. Teachers can rotate the observer role among participants over the course of the training, as this role can aid in solidifying learning.

Whole-class Discussions

Personal assessment and small-group discussions cannot, however, fully substitute for traditional whole-group debriefing. A whole-class discussion guided by a facilitator is preferable for creating a learning opportunity that draws on others' experiences and insights. Drawing attention to the commonalities and the differences in participants' courses of action in the negotiation has the beneficial effect of easing participants' concern about acknowledging their mistakes, and it encourages them to explore different tools and techniques in further experiences.

Plenary discussions help create a shared language and experience based on the role-plays which carry on throughout the continuation of the course or training. For example, the phrase "There is always a round nine," was used in a debrief of a prisoner's dilemma-type role-play in which the students were surprised by a ninth round when they thought the exercise was over. The phrase came to signify the importance of keeping the future in mind when considering relationship building and was later used whenever relationship building actions were discussed in debriefing other exercises.

It may be necessary, however, to modify the traditional large group format to respond to logistical issues. With a group so large that discussion is unwieldy, Steinwachs (1992) suggests using a fishbowl debriefing technique. She puts ten to twenty students in an inner circle to participate directly in the conversation; the rest of the group observes from an outer circle, but can rotate in and become an active participant by standing behind someone's chair. An alternative we have used is to limit the interaction within the whole group to reports from the smaller groups. Or, when observers are used, they can report during the plenary session.

Additional Vehicles for Debriefing

Reflective journals or papers can also be used to supplement traditional in-class debriefing. Like self-assessment sheets, journals used at the beginning of the debriefing process help students reflect in preparation for group discussions. A post-discussion journal assignment extends the analytical learning process by requiring each student to organize his or her thoughts and debrief on an individual basis, and gives a quiet student an avenue to articulate his reactions (Petranek, Corey, and Black 1992). Charles Petranek (2000) argues that students learn much more when oral debriefing is followed with written debriefing. The drawbacks, however, are the time commitments for students to prepare the reflections and for faculty to evaluate the papers and provide feedback. For more on using reflective journaling, see McAdoo (2012).

Reviewing a video in a small group is another way to conduct a debriefing, and is particularly suited to providing feedback on student performance. Williams and colleagues (2008) developed a method using webcams to record students practicing negotiation micro-skills, which they combine with reflective journal entries that are informed by watching the recording. For more examples of such methods, including suggestions for making them less labor- and time-intensive for teachers, see Matz and Ebner (2010), Ebner and Kovach (2010), and Manwaring and Kovach (2012).

Functional Stages of Debriefing

Whatever debriefing methods the instructor selects, the course of the debrief should be carefully planned to bring out the points of the exercise, but at the same time should foster a natural discussion with and among the participants. Barbara Steinwachs (1992) divides the debriefing process into three phases: description, analogy/analysis, and application.[9] We suggest structuring these phases using the following steps, which are a variation of stages proposed by the American Society for Training and Development[10] and are based on a composite of the facilitation and elicitation approaches used by the authors of this chapter. As observed by Steinwachs (1992), participants are often reluctant to move out of the earlier descriptive phases. Allocating time for each stage can help ensure that the discussion reaches the steps for analysis and future application.

Step 1: Encourage Venting and Expression of Emotion

A significant challenge in starting a debrief is separating participants from the story line of the simulation. Participants find it difficult to detach from the role they have been playing and to adopt a learning stance towards themselves and their experience (Ebner and Efron 2005). Participants often want to relive the story or account for their various moves – to work out their anger or frustration, or communicate their sense of accomplishment. Trainers want to shift the focus instead to the dynamics, the tools used, and the skills practiced. This requires students to transition from their roles in the simulation back into seeing themselves as participants in a learning exercise. This identity prompts a more analytical mode that allows them to generalize and draw conclusions from their experience.

Dealing with emotions can help with the transition. After the participants have had an opportunity to vent, stress that the role is over, the negotiation is done, and that they should let things go rather than carry the negotiation into the debriefing session. In addition, discussing emotions explicitly at the start of the debrief can not only help prevent "runaway emotions" from later hijacking the debrief, but it can also harness emotional energy and constructively redirect it toward learning. Emotions have effects on interactions during the role-play that need to be explored (Nelken, Schneider, and Mahuad 2010), and discussing participants' feelings is a way to intensify and personalize the analysis of the experience for participants (Brackenreg 2004; Fanning and Gaba 2007). New understandings that change behaviors need to be realized on an emotional, as well as a cognitive, level (Patera and Gamm 2010).

Step 2: Define Debriefing Goals and Set a Mutually Respectful Tone [11]

State clearly what you hope they will gain from this experience in terms of the goals of the exercise. Announcing the goals of the debrief helps students locate their experience in the broader perspectives of the course, and also gives the trainer objective grounds for bringing the discussion back on point if it wanders too far afield. During the first debrief of a training, the instructor may find it helpful to tell students that it is an opportunity to transform their simulation experience into practical lessons.

This is also the time to set an appropriate tone for the debrief by demonstrating respect for the participants and their experiences. This is particularly necessary when students' experiences and conclusions differ from the ideas that the instructor wants to convey. Above all, the debrief should be a conversation. This invites interaction and fosters collective possibilities for learning that exceed what any individual could achieve on their own (Baker, Jensen, and Kolb 1997).

Step 3: Explore the Experience

Some of the authors of this chapter typically begin their debriefs by asking how many of the groups reached agreement, eliciting the main points of the agreements (or, if one was not reached, where the negotiations left off), and recording these results on the board or a flip-chart. The danger in doing this is that it can send a signal that the end result of the negotiation matters more than the process, and reinforce some students' tendencies to judge their performance based on a comparison to results from other groups. If this step is skipped, however, students often need to describe what happened in their group, and the conversation keeps circling back to that topic. Like the process of surfacing emotions, reporting results can allow participants still engrossed in the exercise to transition to an analysis. In addition, the agreements are often instructive. For example, they may show a great variety of possible outcomes and demonstrate students' creativity in generating options.

Other co-authors prefer to begin with a question related to the theme of the exercise. Starting with a good, clear, open question invites responses that can open up many avenues of discussion. This question should ask for subjective experience rather than an objective response. That way, everyone has a valid response to contribute and the debrief models openness to different perspectives. For example, to begin a discussion of how negotiation outcomes can be evaluated, the opening question might probe whether students feel their negotiation was successful. Then one can segue into why participants felt it was a success (or not) and use those responses to develop possible criteria for measuring success. In a debrief aiming to illustrate a number of points, the instructor should have a good first question for each point. Sequencing the topics is also important so that each one opens up the discussion of the next.

Step 4: Focus on Training Goals and Develop Learning

The heart of debriefing is a discussion with the students about their experience, highlighting aspects that illustrate specific negotiation theory points and best practices, and emphasizing key lessons that might apply to other situations. To that end, the discussion needs to link the experience to the learning objectives of the exercise. The difficulty of creating this link should not be underestimated. When there is a lack of clarity about the goals, this invites an unfocused discussion, reducing the effectiveness of the debriefing. Often when students are confused it may be because trainers are confused.

Facilitators who have clearly articulated their goals to themselves can use students' responses to advance the discussion in a number of ways. Clarifying questions are one way to use a response to expand on useful points and create more material from which to concretize lessons. Douglas Stone (2000) counsels that good follow-up questions arise from the learning points appropriate for the session, and can help dissect how participants are connecting their experiences to their conclusions. One can also use responses to illustrate desired behavior, reinforce past lessons, or foreshadow future lessons. The more an instructor is able to put every role-play experience into perspective and bring out repeatedly some of the key lessons – such as preparation, best alternative to a negotiated agreement (BATNA), and mutually beneficial tradeoffs – the more likely it becomes that students will understand and retain what we teach.

Step 5: Look to the Future

After the negotiation experience has been processed and connected to theory and process points, the debrief can help prepare students to transfer their new knowledge to other settings (with an appropriate admonition that context matters and negotiations will differ). To promote this transfer, one technique is to question students about what they would do differently if negotiating in a related, but different situation. A series of "What if . . .?" questions can bring out contingencies to prompt rethinking of strategies. One of us elicits from each student a "nugget of wisdom" – an observation about behaviors, expectations met (or not), the negotiation process, or an outcome – that might inform future negotiations. This part of the debrief is specifically directed toward promoting reflective practice habits.

Step 6: Pull the Threads Together

At the end of the debrief, it is important to pull together the threads of the discussion. If the discussion has been rich, this concluding summary will have more meaning for the students than if the instructor had simply provided a take-home message. Pulling the threads together can be as straightforward as using a flip chart to summarize the discussion in terms of each of the lessons. A prepared slide can be a starting point if it is supplemented with suggestions from participants. It is helpful to allow participants to consult these points throughout the course or training. Consider posting any prepared debriefing materials (such as your planned questions) and the results of each group's negotiation on the web or, more simply, post any flip chart pages on the wall for future reference.

Step 7: Celebrate Success

Several of this chapter's authors believe that it is helpful pedagogically to close a debrief by acknowledging the success of the participants. Especially in the concentrated day-long format of a workshop, it is not unusual for the group to be worn out by the end of the debrief, and anxious to end the session. This can diminish the participants' ability to absorb information. Moreover, fatigue seems to promote pessimism, so stressing points for improvement might translate in a tired participant's mind into a feeling of being "no-good." For this reason it is important to "[c]elebrate success and encourage optimism. Remind participants that if the use of particular skills, techniques, and tools enabled them to achieve changes in [the simulation exercise], they can help them do the same in reality" (Ebner and Efron 2005: 392).[12]

One way to acknowledge success is to end a debrief with a festive ceremony of signing the agreements the parties reached. Another possibility, particularly appropriate at the end of short courses, is to award certificates and take pictures of the group. To reinforce particular behaviors, the trainers might announce notable accomplishments or mark specific advances with a round of applause. Or, the identification of achievements can come from the group in a "take-away" session in which each participant shares one key learning point or identifies what he or she is most proud of from the day. Throw in a bowl of candy from which each participant can take some sweets prior to his or her announcement and it's a celebration.

Tailoring the Debrief for Specific Audiences

In this final section, we analyze adjustments for debriefing based on who is participating in the training. (On the importance of tailoring overall training design to participants, see Lewicki and Schneider 2010.) Some of the challenges of debriefing are different in an executive workshop format than for university education. Within an educational setting, the discipline can make a difference. And adjustments need to be made, in both workshops and the classroom, for the participants' language and culture.

University Education vs. Executive Workshops

While this chapter's prescriptions are intended generally to apply to both academic teaching and executive training, there are some notable differences in conducting debriefs between these two settings. The need for assessment, experience of the participants, their relationships, and the time structure are factors influencing debriefing decisions that often differ between the two contexts. As a result, a debrief (even of the same exercise) will likely be different in both content and style.

In an academic setting, the instructor is responsible for assessing whether students have mastered the material, and for grading that mastery. (See Ebner, Efron and Kovach 2012.) Grading permits the academic instructor to fashion certain incentives that are not available in the workshop context. For example, making participation in classroom discussion a component of the grade can help encourage participation in the debrief. But the eventual need to grade can also influence the content and emphasis of debriefs. In contrast, in an executive-style negotiation training, the participants are primarily responsible for their own learning, and debriefing does not need to be shaped with an eventual assessment in mind.

In an academic setting, the instructor may occasionally need to be directive to ensure that the important points of the lessons have been covered and to connect the exercise to basic concepts. Some of the authors feel that, in contrast, executive-style trainings offer more leeway to take cues from the participants and allow them to glean the lessons that are most relevant to them. On the other hand, other authors find that they are more likely to use the deductive approach in an executive workshop than in the classroom. Busy people may want a quick "take away" and may not have the patience to be led to formulating insights.

Participants in academic courses and executive trainings are likely to have very different real-life experience. While a debrief should always connect in meaningful ways to the participants' past negotiation experiences and allow them to learn from one another, there is often more depth of experience to work with in a training. Executive trainers work with adults who often have an extensive work history; they may even have more hands-on negotiation exposure than the trainers themselves. In contrast, students may have no experience of some of the situations in the role-plays. These different knowledge bases necessarily affect the starting point and content of a debrief, and influence the richness of the learning environment. In workshops, the greater depth of experience also creates a potential for the debrief to provide opportunities for reflection, perspective taking, and exchange of ideas, rather than serving primarily as a vehicle to convey basic negotiation concepts.

Experience can also pose challenges and reduce receptiveness to new ideas. In trainings, participants' perceptions of their experience level, even when that does not correspond to actual skills, shape their expectations about how they should be taught. They may also expect more hands-on activities (depending on their cultural background) and be more comfortable expressing discontent if the training content does not meet their expectations.

In addition, executive training participants may work in the same agency or company and know each other well. Students may, or may not, know each other from prior classes, but they are unlikely to have shared work experience. The extent of a shared background and participants' comfort level in dealing with each other can lead to different dynamics among participants. Receiving criticism from, or in front of, peers is always sensitive, but particularly so during in-house trainings. When individuals will continue to work together after the training, there is a strong need to save face with one's colleagues – particularly if employees are in the same training program as their supervisors. This is an especially important factor when the training relates to a core skill that might be a measure of one's value to the organization, as with in-house negotiation training for lawyers, managers or sales professionals.

Another difference between debriefing in academic courses and executive trainings is the length and structure of the contact time. In a semester-long course, instructors have time to develop a deeper familiarity with student participants than is possible with the brief exposure in a workshop. One consequence is that executive debriefs often require the trainer to be a quick study and be particularly flexible. Participants' needs may be harder to predict and the debrief is more likely to deviate from preplanned goals. Trainers must be able to follow participants' interests closely and adapt the debrief accordingly.

The compactness of a workshop may be an advantage in that participants are focused on nothing else and completely immersed in the subject. But there are limits to what can be absorbed in one sitting, and fatigue can limit the effectiveness of a workshop debrief. Compared to the compressed format of a workshop, the duration of an academic course gives classroom facilitators greater leeway in selecting what to cover in any particular debrief. If a topic is appropriate for a later negotiation, the teacher has an option to postpone discussion if time is short. The academic course format also allows other techniques for dealing with inadequate time, such as asking students to record their thoughts for discussion during the next class. These time management techniques are not available to trainers. In theory they may have less need for them, with a longer block of workshop time that is not constrained by the duration of a class meeting. But in reality there is never enough time, and the structural options for responding to this challenge are more limited in the workshop setting.

Perhaps the most important consequence of the concentrated learning in a workshop is that participants do not have a debriefing opportunity for guided reflection over time. There is no opportunity to gradually develop realizations that build on their earlier work. One way to counteract this disadvantage of the workshop setting is to schedule follow-up sessions to encourage further reflection and check on progress in applying the workshop lessons. Another approach is to build an online support group and use it for communication between workshop/course sessions, or even post-workshop, with several added benefits in terms of relational and group dynamics (see Bhappu et al. 2009).

Academic Discipline or Participant Background

While many of the authors teach law students, Kaufman teaches public and urban affairs students. Because most of them seek careers in the public sector, she aims to equip students with the skills needed to become effective and reflective negotiation *parties* in the context of multi-party public decision-making. This context for the course shapes debriefings regardless of the specific objectives of the exercise. Each debrief is directed not only at the particular goal of the role-play, but also toward helping students connect to the big picture of negotiating in the context of public decisions. (For a discussion of teaching negotiation for public decisions, see Matsuura et al., *Beyond "Negotiation 2.0"*, in this volume.) For example, with a prisoner's dilemma-type exercise, the debrief sorts out the dynamics the students have experienced and develops examples of real situations that present similar incentives. What differs – and is driven by the specific audience – is that the debrief also covers strategies for mitigating the effects of such incentives in public decisions, as well as possibilities for structural change.

Compared to business or law students, public affairs students often tend to be relatively less competitive in classroom role-plays. Their orientation toward public service combines with normative messages in other courses to enhance their desire to compromise, which they often confuse with cooperation. To help them become effective negotiators on behalf of their future constituencies and to impart the habit of reflective practice, Kaufman emphasizes this issue in debriefs throughout the course. She makes a special effort to help students differentiate between compromise and cooperation, and to convey that cooperation is a strategic choice they should adopt only when they expect a better outcome than with other strategies.

Law students might conduct the same role-plays, and debriefs might similarly emphasize inter- and intra-group dynamics, different ways to approach a negotiation situation, making a strategic choice as to which approach to take, and encouraging reflection. But the focus on specific lessons in debriefing likely differs. Some law students tend toward a competitive and adversarial approach. In addition, they may have difficulty seeing things from the perspective of others. During debriefings, there is frequently an "aha!" moment when students realize that there are ways of achieving one's goals (or those of one's clients) apart from competition. Law students' worldview is therefore "complexified" by the negotiation exercise and the debrief.

Since law students will often represent clients, it is important to design exercises and focus debriefing to bring out issues of authority, internal and external negotiations, and principal-agent tensions. Acting as an agent is not unique to law students; representation of constituencies is a topic that needs a lot of attention with public policy students. But in the legal context, especially with regard to settlement negotiations, it is particularly appropriate to emphasize principal-agent tensions and the ethical and professional responsibility questions that may arise. In addition, other topics, such as evaluating litigation prospects as a party's BATNA, are more uniquely relevant to legal settlement negotiations and may require not only emphasis in debriefings, but also specially tailored exercises.

Native Language and Culture

Language can have a significant effect on participation in the debriefing process in either an academic or workshop setting. In a class conducted in English with non-native speakers, as is common with international groups, the facilitator may need to adjust some debriefing techniques. Simple steps can be taken to aid comprehension. For example, it may help participants if they can read some of the key questions for the debrief on the instruction sheet for the exercise or on a PowerPoint slide, rather than only hearing them. Joseph Stulberg and his colleagues (2009) offer a number of suggestions for minimizing communication barriers in conducting negotiation workshops for global professional groups, many of which are relevant to debriefing (see also Abramson 2009).

Trainers faced with language differences should be prepared to adjust their expectations regarding student response time. As an example, a group of lawyers from North Finland participating in a workshop offered in English by one of the co-authors took a very long time to respond to questions, because they needed time to think and process. What can seem like an eternity of silence to a facilitator is but a moment to students dealing with a language that is foreign to them. Longer response times may translate into the need to allocate a longer time for debriefing, or to limit the scope of the debrief and carefully select key questions.

We have observed that participants in a workshop conducted in what is, for them, a foreign language may also need extra encouragement to participate. This may be due not only to hesitancy with the language, but also to a learning style preference influenced by background and culture, such as an educational experience dominated by lectures (see Kovach 2009). Such students may be uncomfortable with role-playing itself, which may carry over into discomfort with the debrief. Some students may not be comfortable with speaking up in a classroom at all. Other individuals may not be accustomed to the heavy use of questions in debriefing. They may instead expect the facilitator to act as an expert and impart instruction, rather than eliciting lessons from students. Awareness of differences in educational approaches and expectations in different cultural settings, and explicit acknowledgement of this awareness, can help relieve some of the tension.

Other cultural factors, including organizational or professional culture, may also influence the discussion dynamic. For example, with a group of officials from Nigeria, the importance of power and status in the group caused participants to feel ill at ease offering their opinions before the most senior person had spoken, and when they did speak they did not express disagreement with him. Whatever the cultural or language reasons for lack of participation, with a less active group the trainer will have to "lead from the front," while still encouraging dialogue (even if there are spells of uncomfortable silence).

Conclusion

We close with the observation that most of the little advice available on debriefing is, like our own, based primarily on experience. Given the importance of debriefing to experiential learning, the negotiation field could benefit from research on what makes the process effective, and from the development of tools to assess debriefs. In addition, most negotiation teachers learn how to lead a debrief by remembering their own teachers' practices, and through the experience of doing debriefs. We suggest that negotiation teachers develop the reflective habit of applying debriefing principles to analyze their own debriefs. After debriefing a negotiation exercise, instructors should reflect systematically by asking what happened, how it felt, what challenges they encountered, what worked well, what might account for their experience, and what they could do differently the next time. It might be helpful to enlist a colleague to observe a debrief and then participate in debriefing *that* experience.

Notes

We thank John Lande for his thoughtful comments on a draft of this chapter and Rebecca Kells for research assistance.

[1] See Lederman (1992) for descriptions of the use of debriefing in military contexts and with psychological studies involving deception of subjects, where it serves different functions than in the educational setting.

[2] Schön (1983) differentiated between the reflection that occurs during practice, "reflection-in-action," and the reflection that occurs in critically thinking back about practice, "reflection-on-action," which is the type of reflection

in a debriefing. A third form of reflection, "reflection-for-action," integrates the outcomes of the first two into reflection to guide future behavior.

[3] Patton (2000) cites research conducted by Professor Israel Unterman of San Diego State University comparing agreements that were achieved at the end of negotiation sessions conducted by students, who received concrete and specific feedback in negotiation training, with agreements reached by businessmen whose negotiation skills were acquired through experience alone. The students, who received practice and feedback, reached better results than the businessmen.

[4] Gerald Williams and colleagues (2008) advocate the use of deliberative practice, a method that relies heavily on feedback, for teaching negotiation skills. Participants practice: 1) a well-defined task; that is 2) challenging but achievable; they receive 3) immediate feedback on their performances and outcomes; 4) they correct their errors; and 5) they repeat the tasks until performance becomes routine (Ericsson 1996: 20-21).

[5] It is not uncommon for some students to react to criticism by explaining what they really meant to communicate, or blaming the others' behaviors and showing themselves to be "right," rather than reflecting on what could be learned from the experience for the future.

[6] Some commentators emphasize this process goal over content goals. Baker, Jensen, and Kolb (1997: 8-9) believe that the work of the facilitator should be "shaped by the intention to create a hospitable, receptive place to hold a conversation, rather than by the intention to make certain things happen." The values that underlie this approach include:

> a profound respect for each participant in the conversation, including the assumption of the wisdom each has to offer; the inclusiveness of voices, meaning that even those who have traditionally been excluded must not only be present but be heard; an assumption that reflective listening is at least as important in the conversation as active speaking: the fundamental importance of allowing silence to provide space for reflection and deep listening; a readiness that is essential for learning; and an openness to surprise and the unanticipated must be welcomed.
>
> (Baker, Jensen, and Kolb 1997: 9)

[7] Physical space can be another logistical issue. If there is any flexibility, thought should be given to finding an appropriate location. Ideally each group should have its own space for the negotiation, so that the shared space where the debrief will be conducted is available for returning participants who have completed their activity (or their small group discussion). The debriefing space should allow everyone to hear and see each other easily, as well as to see any flip charts or PowerPoint slides that are used to collect observations or debriefing points.

[8] The questions can address specific skills discussed earlier in class (e.g., "Look for and note any active listening elements exhibited by the parties," or "Observe and note the parties' choices for use of questions in this negotiation"). They can address theories students have learned or concepts that the teacher wishes to highlight (e.g., "What was the apparent choice of negotiation strategy employed by each party?" or "How did the relationship between the parties change over the course of the negotiation?"). In some of the courses where this technique is used the coach prepares a written report on the discussion that contributes to his or her grade.

⁹ For other formulations of debriefing phases, see Lederman (1992), Rudolph and colleagues (2008), and Zigmont and colleagues (2011).

¹⁰ Writing for the American Society for Training and Development (ASTD), Sivasailam Thiagarajan (1996: 526-527) suggests a debriefing structure consisting of a series of questions in the following sequence: 1) inquire about participants' feelings; 2) explore what happened in the exercise to aid recall and "discover similarities, differences, and patterns"; 3) ask what participants learned, to encourage them "to come up with generalizations and to test them"; 4) prompt participants to consider how their simulation experience relates to the real world; 5) pose "what if?" questions to encourage participants to apply the experience in new contexts; and 6) conclude with "what next?" to "encourage action planning based on insights from the activity." Alternative frameworks for structuring questions have been suggested by Gaw (1979), Thiagarajan (1992), and van Ments (1999).

¹¹ If the trainer is using personal assessment as part of the debrief, and if time permits, this might be an appropriate point to suggest some personal reflection. Allow five to ten minutes for participants to fill out their personal assessment sheets. This quiet, reflective, and personal activity not only enhances self-awareness, but also helps prepare for discussion in the subsequent steps.

¹² Other co-authors take a more cautious approach to celebrations, especially to the promise of a carry-over to real negotiations. Simulations are never quite like reality, and Kaufman maintains that trainers owe students a frequent reminder of this point. Truth in advertising means that teachers should not oversell a promise that what worked in the classroom setting will work in the same way in a real situation.

References

Abramson, H. 2009. Outward bound to other cultures: Seven guidelines. In *Rethinking negotiation teaching: Innovations for context and culture*, edited by C. Honeyman, J. Coben, and G. De Palo. St. Paul, MN: DRI Press.

Alexander, N. and M. LeBaron. 2009. Death of the role-play. In *Rethinking negotiation teaching: Innovations for context and culture*, edited by C. Honeyman, J. Coben, and G. De Palo. St. Paul, MN: DRI Press.

Arafeh, J., S. Hansen, and A. Nichols. 2010. Debriefing in simulated-based learning: Facilitating a reflective discussion. *The Journal of Perinatal and Neonatal Nursing* 24(4): 302-09.

Baker, A. C., P. J. Jensen, and D. A. Kolb. 1997. In conversation: Transforming experience into learning. *Simulation and Gaming* 28(1): 6-12.

Bhappu, A., N. Ebner, S. Kaufman, and N. Welsh. 2009. Online communication technology and relational development. In *Rethinking negotiation teaching: Innovations for context and culture*, edited by C. Honeyman, J. Coben, and G. De Palo. St. Paul, MN: DRI Press.

Boud, D., R. Keogh, and D. Walker. 1985. *Reflection: Turning experience into learning*. London: Kegan Page.

Brackenreg, J. 2004. Issues in reflection and debriefing: How nurse educators structure experiential activities. *Nurse Education in Practice* 4(4): 264-70.

Brookfield, S. D. 1986. *Understanding and facilitating adult learning: A comprehensive analysis of principles and effective practices*. San Francisco: Jossey-Bass.

Cohn, L., R. Howell, K. Kovach, A. Lee and H. de Backer. 2009. We came, we trained, but did it matter? In *Rethinking negotiation teaching: Innovations for context and culture*, edited by C. Honeyman, J. Coben, and G. De Palo. St. Paul, MN: DRI Press.

Dewey, J. 1933. *How we think: A restatement of the relation of reflective thinking to the educative process.* Lexington, KY: D.C. Heath.

Ebner, N. and Y. Efron. 2005. Using tomorrow's headlines for today's training: Creating pseudo-reality in conflict resolution simulation games. *Negotiation Journal* 21(3): 377-394.

Ebner, N. and K. K. Kovach. 2010. Simulation 2.0: The resurrection. In *Venturing beyond the classroom: Volume 2 in the rethinking teaching series*, edited by C. Honeyman, J. Coben, and G. De Palo. St. Paul, MN: DRI Press.

Ebner, N., Y. Efron, and K. K. Kovach. 2012. Evaluating our evaluation: Rethinking student assessment in negotiation courses. In *Assessing our students, assessing ourselves: Volume 3 in the rethinking negotiation teaching series*, edited by N. Ebner, J. Coben, and C. Honeyman. St. Paul, MN: DRI Press.

Efron, Y. and N. Ebner. 2010. Get ripped and cut before training: Adventure preparation for the negotiation trainer. In *Venturing beyond the classroom: Volume 2 in the rethinking negotiation teaching series*, edited by C. Honeyman, J. Coben, and G. De Palo. St. Paul, MN: DRI Press.

Ericsson, K. A. 1996. The acquisition of expert performance: An introduction to some of the issues. In *The road to excellence: The acquisition of expert performance in the arts and sciences, sports and games*, edited by K. A. Ericsson. Mahwah, NJ: Lawrence Erlbaum Associates.

Fanning, R. M. and D. M. Gaba. 2007. The role of debriefing in simulation-based learning. *Simulation in Healthcare* 2(2): 115-125.

Gaw, B. A. 1979. Processing questions: An aid to completing the learning cycle. In *The 1979 annual handbook for group facilitators*, edited by J. E. Jones and J. W. Pfeiffer. San Diego, CA: University Associates.

Hertel, J. P. and B. J. Mills. 2002. *Using simulation to promote learning in higher education: An introduction.* Sterling, VA: Stylus Publishing.

Issenberg, S. B., W. C. McGaghie, E. R. Petrusa, D. L. Gordon, and R. J. Scalese. 2005. Features and uses of high-fidelity medical simulations that lead to effective learning: A BEME systematic review. *Medical Teacher* 27(1): 10-28.

Kolb, D. A. 1984. *Experiential learning: Experience as the source of learning and development.* Englewood Cliffs, NJ: Prentice-Hall.

Kovach, K. K. 2009. Culture, cognition and learning processes. In *Rethinking negotiation teaching: Innovations for context and culture*, edited by C. Honeyman, J. Coben, and G. De Palo. St. Paul, MN: DRI Press.

Lederman, L. C. 1992. Debriefing: Toward a systematic assessment of theory and practice. *Simulation and Gaming* 23(2):145-160.

Lewicki, R. J. and A. K. Schneider. 2010. Instructors heed the who: Designing negotiation training with the learner in mind. In *Venturing beyond the classroom: Volume 2 in the rethinking negotiation teaching series*, edited by C. Honeyman, J. Coben, and G. De Palo. St. Paul, MN: DRI Press.

Lewin, K. 1951. *Field theory in social sciences*. New York: Harper & Row.

Manwaring, M. and K. K. Kovach. 2012. Using recordings. In *Assessing our students, assessing ourselves: Volume 3 in the rethinking negotiation teaching series*, edited by N. Ebner, J. Coben, and C. Honeyman. St. Paul, MN: DRI Press.

Matz, D. and N. Ebner. 2010. Using role-play in online negotiation teaching. In *Venturing beyond the classroom: Volume 2 in the rethinking negotiation teaching series*, edited by C. Honeyman, J. Coben, and G. De Palo. St. Paul, MN: DRI Press.

McAdoo, B. 2012. Reflective journaling assignments. In *Assessing our students, assessing ourselves: Volume 3 in the rethinking negotiation teaching series*, edited by N. Ebner, J. Coben, and C. Honeyman. St. Paul, MN: DRI Press.

Movius, H. 2008. The effectiveness of negotiation training. *Negotiation Journal* 24(4): 509-531.

Nadler, J., L. Thompson, and L. Van Boven. 2003. Learning negotiation skills: Four models of knowledge creation and transfer. *Management Science* 49(4): 529-540.

Nelken, M., A. K. Schneider, and J. Mahuad. 2010. If I'd wanted to teach about feelings I wouldn't have become a law professor. In *Venturing beyond the classroom: Volume 2 in the rethinking negotiation teaching series*, edited by C. Honeyman, J. Coben, and G. De Palo. St. Paul, MN: DRI Press.

Newell, A. and P. S. Rosenbloom. 1981. Mechanisms of skill acquisition and the law of practice. In *Cognitive skills and their acquisition*, edited by J. R. Anderson. Hillsdale, NJ: Erlbaum Inc. Publishers.

Patera, M. and U. Gamm. 2010. Emotions – a blind spot in negotiation training? In *Venturing beyond the classroom: Volume 2 in the rethinking negotiation teaching series*, edited by C. Honeyman, J. Coben, and G. De Palo. St. Paul, MN: DRI Press.

Patton, B. M. 2000. On teaching negotiation. In *Teaching negotiation: Ideas and innovations*, edited by M. Wheeler. Cambridge, MA: PON Books.

Petranek, C. F. 2000. Written debriefing: The next vital step in learning with simulations. *Simulation and Gaming* 31(1): 108-118.

Petranek, C. F., S. Corey, and R. Black. 1992. Three levels of learning in simulations: Participating, debriefing, and journal writing. *Simulation and Gaming* 23(2): 174-185.

Rudolph, J. W., R. Simon, D. B. Raemer, and W. J. Eppich. 2008. Debriefing as formative assessment: Closing performance gaps in medical education. *Academic Emergency Medicine* 15(11): 1010-1016.

Schön, D. A. 1983. *The reflective practitioner: How professionals think in action*. New York: Basic Books.

Steinwachs, B. 1992. How to facilitate a debriefing. *Simulation and Gaming* 23(2):186-195.

Stone, D. 2000. Thoughts on facilitating discussion about negotiation. In *Teaching negotiation: Ideas and innovations*, edited by M. Wheeler. Cambridge, MA: PON Books.

Stulberg, J. B., M. P. Canedo Arrillaga, and D. Potockova. 2009. Minimizing communication barriers. In: *Rethinking negotiation teaching: Innovations for context and culture*, edited by C. Honeyman, J. Coben, and G. De Palo. St. Paul, MN: DRI Press.

Susskind, L. E. and J. Coburn. 2000. Using simulations to teach negotiation: Pedagogical theory and practice. In *Teaching negotiation: Ideas and innovations*, edited by M. Wheeler. Cambridge, MA: PON Books.

Thiagarajan, S. 1992. Using games for debriefing. *Simulation and Gaming* 23(2): 161-173.

Thiagarajan, S. 1996. Instructional games, simulations, and role-plays. In *The ASTD training and development handbook: A guide to human resource development*, 4th edn., edited by R.L. Craig. New York: McGraw-Hill.

Thompson, L. 1998. *The mind and heart of the negotiator*. Upper Saddle River, NJ: Prentice Hall.

van Ments, M. 1999. *The effective use of role-play: Practical techniques for improving learning*, 2nd edn. London: Kogan Page.

Welsh, N. 2012. Making reputation salient: The reputation index. In *Assessing our students, assessing ourselves: Volume 3 in the rethinking negotiation teaching series*, edited by N. Ebner, J. Coben, and C. Honeyman. St. Paul, MN: DRI Press.

Williams, G. R., L. C. Farmer, and M. Manwaring. 2008. New technology meets an old teaching challenge: Using digital video recordings, annotation software, and deliberate practice techniques to improve student negotiation skills. *Negotiation Journal* 24(1): 71-87.

Williams, G. R. and J. M. Geis. 2000. Negotiation skills training in the law school curriculum. In *Teaching negotiation: Ideas and innovations*, edited by M. Wheeler. Cambridge, MA: PON Books.

Zigmont, J. J., L. J. Kappus, and S. N. Sudikoff. 2011. The 3D model of debriefing: Defusing, discovering, and deepening. *Seminars in Perinatology* 35(2): 52-58.

Appendix A

Personal Assessment Sheet
Professionalism demands constant learning and improvement.
Reflect on these questions – they will help take you to the next level.

Before Game Begins:
When negotiating, I feel my strongest quality or ability lies in using the following skills:

The skills I would like to improve or enhance are:

At Simulation Mid-point:
Describe a point in the negotiation where your strongest quality or ability was best demonstrated. How did the use of this specific element advance the negotiation?

Describe a point of difficulty in the negotiation. What skill or tool might you have used (focus on yourself, rather than on others!) to advance the negotiation?

What skill/tool would you like to develop or practice during the rest of the negotiation?

After Simulation Conclusion:
Describe a point in the negotiation where your strongest quality or ability was best demonstrated. How did the use of this specific tool advance the negotiation?

Describe a point of difficulty in the negotiation. What skill or tool might you have used (focus on yourself, rather than on others!) to advance the negotiation?

What is the most significant insight you found during this exercise, regarding the practice of negotiation? How will I be using it in your future negotiations?

०३ 14 ०

Debriefing Adventure Learning

Ellen E. Deason, Yael Efron, Ranse Howell,
*Sanda Kaufman, Joel Lee & Sharon Press**

Editors' Note: This chapter (which should be read in conjunction with the same authors' Debriefing the Debrief, chapter 13 in this volume) addresses the special conditions which attach to efforts to debrief adventure learning. The same real-world authenticity that is the most attractive feature of adventure learning, they point out, introduces predictable problems – beginning but not ending with the mundane failure of negotiating groups to return to class at the same time, when the debrief has been scheduled. But it gets worse than that, in ways the authors cheerfully outline. The authors follow with a number of suggestions, which collectively should help students get the most out of the exercise – and help the teacher sleep better the night before the exercise.

Introduction
Negotiation adventure learning is a type of experiential learning that takes teaching negotiation out of the academic or executive training

* **Ellen Deason** is the Joanne Wharton Murphy/Classes of 1965 and 1973 Professor of Law at The Ohio State University Moritz College of Law in Columbus, Ohio. Her email address is deason.2@osu.edu. **Yael Efron** is a lecturer of law and head of academic administration at Zefat Academic College School of Law in Zefat, Israel. Her email address is yaele@Zefat.ac.il. **Ranse Howell** is a senior project manager and mediator at the Centre for Effective Dispute Resolution (CEDR), London, UK. His email address is rhowell@cedr.com. **Sanda Kaufman** is a professor at the Maxine Goodman Levin College of Urban Affairs and director of the Master of Arts program in environmental studies at Cleveland State University, Cleveland, Ohio. Her email address is s.kaufman@csuohio.edu. **Joel Lee** is an associate professor at the Faculty of Law, National University of Singapore. His email address is joellee@nus.edu.sg. **Sharon Press** is an associate professor of law and director of the Dispute Resolution Institute at Hamline University School of Law in St. Paul, Minnesota. Her email address is spress01@ hamline.edu.

classroom and into real environments.[1] The Rethinking Negotiation Teaching project has experimented with adventure learning (Coben, Honeyman, and Press 2010), and stimulated scholarship on both its use as a negotiation teaching tool and reactions to that use (Cohn and Ebner 2010, Kamp 2010, Larson 2010, Manwaring, McAdoo, and Cheldelin 2010, Panga and Grecia-de Vera 2010, Press and Honeyman 2010). Student assessment in the context of adventure learning is discussed by Sharon Press and colleagues in Volume 3 in this series (2012). This chapter examines debriefing adventure negotiation exercises.

Negotiation Adventure Learning

Adventure learning in negotiation is inspired by "adventure education," which can be characterized as providing a learning opportunity that is experiential, authentic and real, is set outside the traditional classroom, has an element of real or perceived risk, and often relies on collaboration (Manwaring, McAdoo, and Cheldelin 2010). In negotiation teaching, it has been developed as a complement to role-play exercises. The prescribed scenarios, preselected facts, and designated interests of role-play exercises provide the advantage of a common framework for the simulated negotiation and allow instructors to design exercises to convey particular lessons. In contrast, adventure learning emphasizes real negotiations with "authenticity as a priority" (Coben, Honeyman, and Press 2010: 110). It typically involves sending teams into the community with missions that will stimulate negotiations, both amongst the group members and with others. Alternatively, instructors can find negotiation authenticity when students try to apply concepts learned in class to actually buying a car or dealing with a colleague at work. In addition to authenticity, adventure exercises provide an element of the unexpected that adds excitement to a course or training and creates opportunities for unanticipated lessons that flow from students' experiences.

Manwaring, McAdoo, and Cheldelin (2010: 122) describe two different philosophies for adventure learning, which lead to different types of adventure learning assignments, namely "orientation" and "disorientation."

> In the orientation approach, participants are given direct, explicit instructions about what they should do and why. . . . In the disorientation approach . . . students are *not* explicitly told the nature and purposes of the activity in advance. Instead, they may be given incomplete, oblique, or misleading instructions, or no instructions at all.

At the Istanbul and Beijing conferences held as part of the Rethinking Negotiation Teaching project, small groups participated in negotiation adventure exercises that used both approaches. In Istanbul, the assignment with orientation took place in the Grand Bazaar or Spice Market. Groups were instructed to negotiate a purchase of food for the entire conference to share, negotiate for something else the group decided to buy, observe these and other negotiations, and interview sellers about their strategies. The disorientation assignment was designed to stimulate intra-group negotiations; groups selected and took photos that best represented various themes, such as the crossroads of the sacred and the secular, and the most dangerous thing observed during a walk through the city (Coben, Honeyman, and Press 2010). In Beijing, participants joined Chinese law students from a negotiation class to purchase and eat lunch, followed by a walk around the Peking University campus to find and photograph certain landmarks. Participants were also asked to reflect on negotiations that they encountered during their weekend in Beijing (Ebner, Coben, and Honeyman 2012; Honeyman, Coben, and Lee, *What Have We Learned*, in this volume).

One can easily see the importance of the debrief in the context of *disorientation* adventure learning, where some students may not understand or appreciate what they have learned until they participate in a debrief that highlights important elements of negotiation. However, the debrief for adventure learning activities *with orientation* is equally important if participants are to learn as much as possible from their experiences. Reports from both trainers and students suggest that debriefing, and careful planning for debriefing, is especially important with all adventure learning activities (Panga and Grecia-de Vera 2010; Press and Honeyman 2010). As with any debrief, this planning should enable the teacher to connect the content of the debrief to the goals of the exercise. It also should take account of the distinctive challenges of negotiation adventure learning.

General Principles of Debriefing

In *Debriefing the Debrief* (Deason et al., in this volume), the authors set ambitious goals for the function of debriefing in traditional role-plays.

> It should make the experiences of the learning activity come alive. It should connect those experiences to the content of the course and assist participants in putting theory into practice and constructing their own lessons. It should make the process feel personal and real, and increase the likelihood that the students will remember and use their new learning. It

should help students develop the habit of reflecting on their practice.

All of these goals are equally applicable to debriefing in the setting of adventure learning. Similarly, many of the principles that apply to debriefing a simulation role-play are also relevant to adventure learning. We emphasize that an effective debrief exhibits the following characteristics, which we reproduce here for convenience:

- Focuses on the process of interaction. Dialogue among the participants, and between the facilitator and participants, allows essential articulation of insights.
- Draws on the experience of the participants by eliciting reactions and encouraging reflection on the activity.
- Explicitly connects the exercise, which has been tailored for a specific purpose, to the course material. The facilitator needs to be able to weave participants' comments into this structure.
- Offers additional information from negotiation theory and experimental and field research. This helps tie the experience to reasons behind behaviors, interaction patterns, effectiveness of strategies, and quality of outcomes.
- Models behaviors that reinforce past lessons or preview future ones. This makes the debrief a link in the chain of activities in a course or workshop.
- Lasts long enough to be comprehensive and to underscore the importance of the activity.

Special Considerations in Debriefing Negotiation Adventure Learning

In addition to these general principles, there are special considerations when debriefing an adventure learning negotiation exercise. This section explores their implications. We consider the nature of negotiation adventure learning goals, the sheer number of experiences and their complexity, special logistical challenges, possible resistance from participants, and ethical and cultural dimensions of adventure learning exercises.

First, the objectives of an adventure learning exercise, while related to negotiation theory and skills, may be more general and tied less directly to elucidating specific pre-planned points than in a typical role-play. For example, the goal may be any one (or more) of the following: to have students interact together "outside their comfort zones"; to experience a negotiation in which they had a real stake in the outcome (not "just" a simulation); and/or to put "theory into practice." In addition, the goals may not be articulated specifically to the participants or even easily recognizable from the context, as in the case of an "oblique" or "disorienting" exercise designed to stimulate internal team negotiation and implicit learning (Coben, Honeyman, and Press 2010; Manwaring, McAdoo, and Cheldelin 2010; Press and Honeyman 2010).

The nature of the objectives in negotiation adventure learning, especially with a disorienting approach, puts a greater burden on the debriefing process to develop the learning points, because participants are less likely to be able to formulate the points on their own. Therefore, it is important that the instructor anticipate some clear and manageable lessons that will likely be raised by the negotiation adventure exercise. The facilitator needs to avoid the temptation of squeezing all the learning that can be gained from the richness of reality into a single debrief. Yet the facilitator also needs to be open to incorporating unanticipated lessons that may even draw on concepts or theories that have not yet been discussed in class. Clarity about goals and flexibility about specific lessons are necessary to effectively shape the debriefing discussion as it develops. A clear summary of take-home lessons at the end of the debrief is particularly important given the more "amorphous" nature of the adventure learning experience.

Second, participants' adventure learning experiences tend to be more varied and far less predictable than in a traditional role-play. The same is true when students report on actual negotiations in their lives, which can be instructive even though all the students did not share the experience. The potential lessons from these experiences are, in turn, likely to be richer and reflect the complexity of real situations, which is so difficult to capture in role-plays. As a result, facilitators and participants alike may be surprised by unplanned insights.

This variety of experiences and potential insights suggest the wisdom of using an inductive approach to debriefing negotiation adventure learning. As described in *Debriefing the Debrief* (in this volume), an inductive approach builds lessons from participants' responses, and encourages them to construct their own knowledge as opposed to starting with a set of pre-identified lessons. This requires the trainer to be comfortable with uncertainty and skilled at drawing out lessons from examples.

Adventure negotiation assignments that lend themselves to student presentations, such as a photography exercise (see Coben, Honeyman, and Press 2010), combine the strengths of the inductive approach with a degree of structure in the debriefing. The presentation format gives groups leeway to distill and organize their own learning points through the process of preparing for their presentations. Then the instructor can use the presentations as raw material for a whole class discussion aimed at articulating lessons.

Along with the complexity and variety of adventure experiences, the instructor cannot observe the details of what went on, and thus, far more than in a typical role-play, must rely on student self-reports. But participants filter both their perception of the experience, and what they report, by such factors as their knowledge, frames (Donohue, Rogan, and Kaufman 2011), and level of familiarity with the situation. This means instructors are likely to hear only what *students* frame as important, and that may be mediated by what they think will make them look good. This informational challenge suggests modifying a purely inductive discussion with prepared questions, both to help shape what students regard as important and to stimulate reflection.

Third, there are also distinct logistical challenges to debriefing negotiation adventure learning. Debriefing with the whole group immediately after the experience is often impractical because small groups typically finish their exercises at different times and may be spread out over an entire city if an exercise sends them far afield (Coben, Honeyman, and Press 2010). Yet because of the diversity of experiences in adventure learning, there is much to be learned from a discussion that includes all the groups and thus draws on all the experiences. We offer some suggestions below for ways to combine whole group interactions, small group discussions, and other vehicles for debriefing. With a complex debriefing structure, and especially when parts of the debrief will occur after a time lag, it is helpful to equip students with some tools for storing observations. These could include techniques such as "stop, reflect, record" moments during the experience, assigning one person in each group the role of observer/reporter, preparing a group report at the end of the experience, or journaling.

In addition, allocating sufficient time is a crucial logistical consideration for debriefing negotiation adventure learning. While adequate time for debriefing is always at a premium, even more time may be needed than with a role-play. The inductive approach to debriefing that we recommend for adventure learning is time consuming, and the debrief needs to process the wide variety of experience to be expected with adventure learning. One technique that relieves some of this time pressure is to allocate at least part of the debriefing time to simultaneous small group discussions, which permit wide participation in a limited time period. Journaling used in conjunction with a later large-group discussion is another possibility; the instructor can focus on selected topics in the discussion while reassuring students that their full reflections will be read.[2]

Fourth, there may be resistance to the whole adventure learning agenda among some participants. Adventure learning exercises run a higher risk than role-plays of being perceived by some participants as "pointless." Participants in the adventure learning activities at the Rethinking Negotiation Teaching conference held in Istanbul in 2010 reported problems with lack of motivation and an inability to connect the activity to clear learning objectives, which undermined some of the small group dynamics following the oblique exercise (see e.g., Panga and Grecia-de Vera 2010). One of this chapter's authors observed a similar reaction when using an adventure learning photography assignment with executive groups in trainings focused on enhancing their negotiation skills. The exercise was not what they were expecting and they initially found it strange, unfamiliar, and uncomfortable.

In the executive training example, a clearly focused debrief was essential to help participants understand the usefulness and applicability of the exercise. When participants have doubts about adventure learning, the debrief needs to show how the activity relates to actual negotiation practice. In addition, as we urge in the context of role-plays, debriefs should help students process the emotional content of exercises (Nelken, Schneider, and Mahuad 2010), which may mean probing the causes of resistance.

Fifth, with some exercises, negotiation adventure learning may raise ethical or cultural issues that would not come up in a traditional role-play, and that will need debriefing along with the negotiation lessons. If, for example, students are asked to negotiate something for free, the debriefing should ask students to consider the consequences for the real individuals in the interaction.[3] When the exercise entails interacting with persons from a different culture, it may be appropriate for the debrief to touch on the perils of cognitive egocentrism – the commonly shared tendency to interpret an experience through the lens of our own culture. This can lead participants to mistakenly attribute to others the same values and priorities as their own, and to interpret interactions in terms of what they would mean in their own culture. Often, it will be appropriate for a debrief in this setting to discuss the possible effects of our cultural frames on participants' interpretation of their experience.

Structures for Debriefing Negotiation Adventure Learning

As techniques for debriefing adventure learning develop, one promising approach that responds to many of these challenges is to structure multiple layers of debriefing, using individual reporting and small group processes as well as whole-group discussion. In addition to the need for a nuanced reflection to sort out one's own experience, there is much to learn from the different experiences of other groups. In order to give everyone a chance to participate and to develop all these perspectives, debriefing may need to be accomplished in stages, spread over time.

In the experiments with adventure learning at the Beijing conference (see Ebner, Coben, and Honeyman 2012; Honeyman, Coben, and Lee, *What Have We Learned*, in this volume), and at the earlier conference in Istanbul (see Coben, Honeyman, and Press 2010), small groups debriefed the experience prior to a whole-group interaction. In Beijing, participants were also asked to fill out individual reporting sheets. Multiple forms of debriefing can also be used and adapted in other teaching settings. In executive trainings, one of the authors uses small group discussions prior to a full group debrief to fill the gap while waiting for the other groups to complete their exercises. In Sandra Cheldelin's graduate level course, students submitted reflection papers on their experience and debriefed both within their adventure learning groups and as a whole class (Manwaring, McAdoo, and Cheldelin 2010).

It is too soon to suggest an ideal structure, and indeed the best format for debriefing may vary with the type of adventure assignment. In Istanbul, the small group debriefing seemed to work better for the exercise that was clearly oriented toward negotiation than for the oblique exercise. For the former, participants were remixed so the groups reflected a variety of experiences, and each group was led by a facilitator. For the latter, participants stayed in the same group and did not have a facilitator. But the perceived success of the debriefing may have had more to do with the nature of the adventure – oriented or disoriented – than with the structure of the group.

In Beijing, the assignment encouraged some debriefing within the participant group at the end of the exercise. The following day, small groups for debriefing were formed based on who was seated at a particular table. The students who had participated in the exercise were not present; the debriefing groups did not correspond to the groups that had participated in the activity; and there were no assigned facilitators. Due to the size of the overall group and time constraints, the large group debriefing was limited to short reports consisting of one point from each small group. Reactions among participants to this debriefing varied; satisfaction was perhaps linked to the quality of the discussion in the small group, where most of the discussion took place.

The wisdom of using multiple levels of debriefing has been borne out in Cheldelin's classroom. She reported that very few of the students' reflection papers discussed the oblique negotiation activity (based on a photography assignment). She suggested that they were sufficiently "disoriented" that they did not *recognize* the negotiations that occurred, either when they happened or in their reflections. But later, when the groups presented their photographs to the class as a whole, their presentations focused on their intra-group negotiations. Thus by that stage of the debriefing process, because of either the multiple opportunities for reflection or the leavening effect of time, they had become aware of these negotiations, and focused productively on them in retrospect (Manwaring, McAdoo, and Cheldelin 2010).

Conclusion

Given the growing enthusiasm for adventure learning and the corresponding increase in its use, it is critical that instructors consider how to debrief the adventure learning experience appropriately and effectively. Facilitators must pay attention to all of the considerations involved in conducting debriefs of more traditional role-play simulations and in-class group activities, which are relevant as well for adventure negotiation debriefing. In addition, instructors must prepare for the challenges unique to adventure learning. As negotiation teachers continue to develop adventure learning exercises, they also need to experiment with modes of debriefing. We urge them to devote as much thought and energy to planning the debrief as they do to planning the exercise itself.

Notes

[1] We intend our comments to apply to debriefing negotiation adventure learning in both academic settings and executive training programs. The terms "teacher," "trainer," "instructor," and "facilitator" are used interchangeably.
[2] Another strategy for dealing with time limits is to use a more deductive approach: explain up front what the exercise was supposed to illustrate and then put the burden on the participants to select for discussion the observations that they think are most related to the goals of the adventure. There is a risk that the students may not be the best judges of relevance, but without such self-screening there is a risk that the group will try to discuss too many different experiences and will miss key lessons.
[3] For instance, should the person be told that the students are engaged in a learning exercise? When? Should they be compensated in any way for their pains? Are there limits to what students may ask of others in their quest to learn about negotiation?

References

Coben, J., C. Honeyman, and S. Press. 2010. Straight off the deep end in adventure learning. In *Venturing beyond the classroom: Volume 2 in the rethinking negotiation teaching series*, edited by C. Honeyman, J. Coben, and G. De Palo. St. Paul, MN: DRI Press.

Cohn, L. P. and N. Ebner. 2010. Bringing negotiation teaching to life: From the classroom to the campus to the community. In *Venturing beyond the classroom: Volume 2 in the rethinking negotiation teaching series*, edited by C. Honeyman, J. Coben, and G. De Palo. St. Paul, MN: DRI Press.

Donohue, W., R. Rogan, and S. Kaufman (eds). 2011. *Framing matters: Perspectives on negotiation research and practice in communications*. New York: Peter Lang.

Ebner, N., J. Coben, and C. Honeyman. 2012. Introduction: Assessment as mirror. In *Assessing our students, assessing ourselves: Volume 3 in the rethinking negotiation teaching series*, edited by N. Ebner, J. Coben, and C. Honeyman. St. Paul, MN: DRI Press.

Kamp, A. 2010. Is what's good for the gander good for the goose? A "semi-student" perspective. In *Venturing beyond the classroom: Volume 2 in the rethinking negotiation teaching series*, edited by C. Honeyman, J. Coben, and G. De Palo. St. Paul, MN: DRI Press.

Larson, D. 2010. Adventure learning: Not everyone gets to play. In *Venturing beyond the classroom: Volume 2 in the rethinking negotiation teaching series*, edited by C. Honeyman, J. Coben, and G. De Palo. St. Paul, MN: DRI Press.

Manwaring, M., B. McAdoo, and S. Cheldelin. 2010. Orientation and disorientation: Two approaches to designing "authentic" negotiation learning activities. In *Venturing beyond the classroom: Volume 2 in the rethinking negotiation teaching series*, edited by C. Honeyman, J. Coben, and G. De Palo. St. Paul, MN: DRI Press.

Nelken, M., A. K. Schneider, and J. Mahuad. 2010. If I'd wanted to teach about feelings I wouldn't have become a law professor. In *Venturing beyond the classroom: Volume 2 in the rethinking negotiation teaching series*, edited by C. Honeyman, J. Coben, and G. De Palo. St. Paul, MN: DRI Press.

Panga, S. S., Jr. and G. B. Grecia-de Vera. 2010. A look at a negotiation 2.0 classroom: Using adventure learning modules to supplement negotiation simulations. In *Venturing beyond the classroom: Volume 2 in the rethinking negotiation teaching series*, edited by C. Honeyman, J. Coben, and G. De Palo. St. Paul, MN: DRI Press.

Press, S., N. Ebner, and L. P. Cohn. 2012. Assessing the adventure. In *Assessing our students, assessing ourselves: Volume 3 in the rethinking negotiation teaching series*, edited by N. Ebner, J. Coben, and C. Honeyman. St. Paul, MN: DRI Press.

Press, S. and C. Honeyman. 2010. A second dive into adventure learning. In *Venturing beyond the classroom: Volume 2 in the rethinking negotiation teaching series*, edited by C. Honeyman, J. Coben, and G. De Palo. St. Paul, MN: DRI Press.

ༀ 15 ༂

Bringing the Street to the Classroom and the Student to the Street: Guided Forays into Street-wise Negotiations

Habib Chamoun-Nicolas, Boyd Fuller, David Benitez &
*Randy Hazlett**

Editors' Note: Many writings in this series have argued for greater authenticity in training and teaching, including getting students out of the classroom. No greater authenticity in negotiation teaching settings is likely to be found than in the authors' experiments with teaching students who are actually at work negotiating, while they really are at work. The authors argue that two key attributes of authenticity are served by this technique: repeated engagement, as distinct from isolated role-plays, and expanded stakes, where the student stands to gain or lose in an immediate career sense. Not only is the training, at least in part, actually performed at work, but the students are observed closely by people who are associated with management. The authors report on early experiments in a multinational business setting (in Mexico and the United States), and a public policy setting in Singapore.

* **Habib Chamoun-Nicolas** is an honorary professor at the Catholic University of Santiago Guayaquil-Ecuador and an adjunct professor and member of the executive board at the Cameron School of Business at the University of St. Thomas in Houston, Texas. His email address is hchamoun@keynegotiations.com. **Boyd Fuller** is an assistant professor in the Lee Kuan Yew School of Public Policy, National University of Singapore. His email address is boyd.fuller@nus.edu.sg. **David Benitez** is CEO of Intelligent Mexican Marketing (IMM). His email address is david.benitez@inteli-mex.com. **Randy Hazlett** is president of Potential Research Solutions and Christian Artist's Workshop in Dallas, Texas. His email address is rdhazlett@sbcglobal.net.

Introduction

Extending negotiation experiences, such as role-plays and real, ongoing negotiations or projects, beyond the purview of one class or course can improve learning outcomes. In this chapter, we discuss several experiments in which students have been taken out of the classroom to engage in or be coached through intensive negotiation experiences. These experiences extend teaching beyond the classroom through *repetitive engagement,* with the same experience across multiple classes and, in some cases, through *expanded stakes,* by evaluating students' performance in the negotiations and, in some cases, by engaging students while they take part in real life negotiations.

In the next section, we discuss the typical role-play, and critiques of it that have emerged during the Rethinking Negotiation Teaching project. Then we introduce our pedagogical experiments and how they encourage the extension of the learning cycle.

Role-plays for Teaching Negotiation

Alternative dispute resolution (ADR) is a practice, as well as a literature. Teaching about ADR requires preparing students so that they can practice their skills immediately after the course, as well as giving them ideas and frameworks to enable long term reflection on and improvement of those skills. As such, negotiation pedagogy has made extensive use of experiential methods for student learning, including negotiation role-plays.

To understand how our experiments moved beyond the typical role-play, it is first important to understand the place of role-plays in the learning cycle. There are two common approaches to learning using experiential tools. The first, more deductive approach is to introduce certain concepts and practices to students, ask them to practice those elements during the negotiation role-play or other experiential method, and then reflect upon what they have learned from that experience. The second, more inductive approach starts with the experience, and lets the students identify which aspects of the lessons (puzzles, mishaps, and successes) they want to reflect upon. The aspects they choose to reflect upon may have been covered by the class' concepts and frameworks, or may go beyond them.

Both learning approaches can be placed on the same learning cycle of planning-action-observation-reflection-planning (Kolb 1984), shown in Figure 1.

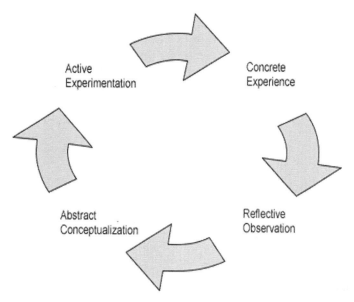

Figure 1: Kolb's Cycle of Experiential Learning

When a negotiation role-play is used within one class, the instructors typically aim to have the students leave the class with a few take-home lessons that will increase their understanding and that they will be able to practice in later role-plays or, even better, real-life negotiations. The benefits of this interaction between analysis and doing are well established. Research indicates that hands-on learning adds to student retention and satisfaction in the learning process (Roblyer 2006). However, as others in the Rethinking Negotiation Teaching project have noted, the effectiveness of using role-plays is limited.

Moving Beyond the Typical Role-play

Nadja Alexander and Michelle LeBaron (2009) challenged the efficacy of such role-plays in the first volume of the Rethinking Negotiation Teaching series, arguing that students sometimes do not find such role-plays compelling or applicable to their daily lives, and that students can often either under- or over-act their roles, further making the negotiation experience unrealistic. These authors do not call for the end of role-plays *per se* (though their title implies so), but instead argue that role-plays need to be supplemented with other experiential pedagogical methods, such as adventure learning (in which students engage in real-life negotiations or other kinds of interactions) and micro-exercises that focus on one particular negotiation activity, e.g., active listening.[1] Overall, many authors in the Rethinking Negotiation Teaching series have echoed this call for more realistic negotiation experiences for students to engage in, including those that go beyond the classroom and class time (see Nelken, McAdoo, and Manwaring 2009; Coben, Honeyman, and Press 2010; Manwaring, McAdoo, and Cheldelin 2010; Panga and Grecia-de Vera 2010). This chapter looks at the authors' pedagogical experiments using both more realistic simulations and real life negotiation experiences in their courses.

First, since typical role-play exercises are conducted within one class, the students have to engage in a new role-play for the next class. Even if that new role-play allows them to practice the same skills and concepts as covered in the previous role-play, the student will still spend at least part of the class time getting warmed up to the role, the other players, and other dimensions of the role-play scenario. Furthermore, any lecture or readings will typically introduce new concepts and skills. The end result is that we tend to leave it up to students' initiative and cognition to continue the learning about the skill or theory touched upon in the simulation. The lack of real stakes and real student engagement mentioned above is the second limitation that our experiments seek to overcome.

The pedagogical experiments we describe here fit with the spirit of more realistic negotiation experiences beyond the classroom and class time, but they are different from the experiments described in the earlier two volumes produced by the Rethinking Negotiation Teaching project. Some are efforts to make negotiation simulations more real and effective by extending the time of their implementation across multiple classes and allowing for reflection on them in each class. Others place students in real-life negotiation scenarios that are close to what they might do in their professional jobs. More specifically, they are experiments distinguished from traditional role-plays by two characteristics: repetitive engagement and expanded stakes.

Repetitive Engagement

The first characteristic that distinguishes these pedagogical experiments is related to *repetitive engagement*. The online simulations and real-life negotiations described here last beyond the duration of one class. All of the techniques described here extend the negotiation experience over multiple class sessions, with each session providing an opportunity for feedback, reflection, and re-strategizing for the continuing negotiations. Repetitive engagement allows multiple iterations of the learning cycle as students plan, act, observe, reflect, and re-plan. We also hope that using the same scenario or real-life negotiation experience for multiple learning cycles reduces the time spent on other activities commonly found in simulations – e.g., the need to "get in character," to learn and adapt to a new scenario, to learn and adapt to new negotiating partners.

When simulations are extended, instructors can help the students go through multiple iterations of the learning cycle in each related class. Students can try to achieve the same goal multiple times, iteratively improving their understanding and application of the concepts without having to start over again in a new context and role that have to be deciphered and internalized. In fact, even if the students or instructors choose to focus on new challenges and ideas as the negotiation progresses, there are still benefits, because the students can focus on strategies and observations rather than expending effort in warming up to a new scenario or role.

Expanded Stakes

The second distinguishing characteristic of the experiments is *expanded stakes*. This applies more to the experiments in coaching that will be described below. The stakes in these negotiations are real and personal. The students may be negotiating as part of their job, or doing a class project that involves real clients and real outcomes. In this sense, the pressures to perform, the interpersonal dynamics, and the many other complexities are closer to, or actually are, what they will experience when they leave the classroom. In addition, classroom teaching can be enhanced by high level, interactive "street-wise" experiences with coaching (Barreto 2009; Sosa 2012).

Before we proceed to analyze our experiments, it is important to state a few common assumptions and starting points that the authors share. First, we all teach the seven elements framework (Fisher, Ury, and Patton 1991)[2] in our classrooms as one way of analyzing and preparing for negotiations. Second, we believe that there is much to learn from reflective engagement with an ongoing negotiation experience (see Druckman 2006). Third, our students come from a variety of cultures, languages, professions, and settings, that influence their expectations, interpretive frameworks, and other ways of making sense of the world (see Goh et al., *As We See It*, in this volume). We acknowledge and encourage students to identify potential differences, while still providing the "seven elements" and other frameworks as a starting point for discussions. Then, we deal with differences as they arise, in class discussion, one-on-one sessions with students, and other media of reflection and analysis.

In the next section, we describe how we used role-plays that extended beyond one class session. The two subsequent sections describe pedagogical experiments in which the instructors follow and coach students who are engaging in real-life negotiation practice. The first of these experiments revolves around a class project in which the students work together to identify a topic, convene stakeholders, and facilitate a dialogue with outside stakeholders. In the second of these experiments, the instructor shadows and coaches one or more students as they engage in their professional negotiations. In the last section we provide a summary of what we have learned from conducting these experiments and from comparing our experiences, and conclude by proposing improved experiments for the reader and ourselves.

Using Extended Role-Plays

Extended role-plays (i.e., beyond one class and learning cycle) were designed for students to continue engaging the concepts learned in class, to continue following up with the concepts to ensure applications, and to reflect upon experiences in subsequent classes. Here the authors present the use of online negotiations as a tool to allow students to learn and apply concepts asynchronously and synchronously. This section describes the experiment in more detail.

Using an Online Simulation to Teach Negotiations at Business Schools

A way of teaching negotiation at the Cameron School of Business at the University of St. Thomas which we have found very useful was to engage students in actual negotiations, rather than exclusively role-plays, using an online simulation program developed by the University of Maryland's ICONS project.[3] We have used several ICONS simulations, such as Nigeria Oil; Borders, Environment, and Trade of the Americas; and European Union. We will describe how we used these and invite other professors to use similar platforms that help connect the students more into a real case simulation.

The Borders, Environment, and Trade in the Americas simulation is a multi-party, multi-issue negotiation that can extend the MBA student's business exercise experiences. We wanted the students to be exposed to a more realistic case simulation in which they can act as diplomats of specific countries, do research, and understand domestic issues, positions, strategic needs, and strengths and weaknesses. Also, we wanted the students to develop a coalition-forming strategy to gain negotiation power. Students had an opportunity to think and strategize regional multilateral agreements and bilateral agreements, depending on needs, issues, and positions.

Also very important was the students' mixed-mode communication experience while negotiating. This simulation was designed to be used as an outside-of-the-classroom negotiation. Students could feel and experience the difference between negotiating online, sending messages, delivering and receiving emails, and conducting online chats as opposed to traditional face-to-face meetings. Multi-mode communicating is more representative of an actual negotiation.

How ICONS connects with the course

Our course was an International Trade and Negotiation MBA special topic summer course at the University of St. Thomas. Learning from both the most famous negotiators in history, the Phoenicians, and the modern ICONS Project simulation, we used a syllabus that covered the following topics:

- International trade and negotiations
- Basic principles of negotiation
- Single-issue two-party distributive negotiation to collaborative negotiation
- Single-issue multi-party cases to multiple-issue multi-party negotiations
- Internal vs. external negotiations
- Culture and negotiations
- Commercial vs. diplomatic negotiations
- Negotiate like a Phoenician (Taking a look at history to see what the best historical negotiators did and how the student can apply it in today's environment) (Chamoun and Hazlett 2007)
- Deal methodology and the use of "tradeables" (Chamoun and Linzoain 2004)

The ICONS simulation was in addition to in-class material, and was conducted online outside of class. At every classroom meeting, we dedicated ten minutes to discuss the ICONS simulation and what the students needed to do in each session.

Simulation timing

The MBA course was a six-week summer course. We met every Monday and Wednesday evening. In the first two weeks, students performed research on their specific assigned country, completed the country worksheet, filed their position paper, and developed their strategy.

Students were asked to send at least three messages per week and three questions per week to other countries for the first three weeks. In the second week, when we noticed some students had failed to answer inquiries from other countries, we set as a rule of the simulation that everyone not answering an inquiry from others would be penalized in the game. Subsequently, everyone started communicating more frequently.

By the third and fourth week of class, we specified that students needed to exercise conferencing features in ICONS to schedule online discussions and formulate proposals. We initiated a rule that a country needed to submit at least one proposal by the fourth week of class, and that others needed to respond. In the fourth week of class, we set a rule that students needed to do conferencing at least once a day. Scheduling conferencing was the most difficult task. The MBA students are professionals with very busy schedules, so setting specific times for country combinations was quite difficult.

We left the conferences open in the fifth week, checked the messaging between countries, and determined which countries wanted to have private conferencing. Finally, we set country conference combinations based on the students' messaging aspirations and expectations. After conferencing, the students had an opportunity to vote for proposals and write their final assignment reaction paper.

In the sixth week, we opened all the conversations on the simulation, so that the students could go back and read the messaging of the different countries and reflect on what really happened in the negotiation. They analyzed coalition formation and how this helped or hindered the negotiation strategy.

Teacher and student roles

Our role as teachers was to observe and give directions via e-mail outside of the simulation. We wanted the students to discover and learn as much as they could on their own after being given instructions in the classroom but before doing the simulation outside of the classroom. We examined simulation messaging daily, noting proposal postings and requests for conferencing. We sent email reminders as needed to promote messaging, proposals, and conferencing, depending on course stage.

We provided ICONS materials to the students to guide their progress, such as the country worksheet, the position paper, proposal and strategy guidelines, and then the reaction paper. We helped them with debriefing questions to prepare for the reaction paper, which we found was very helpful in meeting student expectations.

We facilitated the next steps in the simulation without getting directly involved in them. We found the process more important than the actual subject they were negotiating. We instructed students to look at actual newspapers to find out how the true negotiations progressed among the countries they have represented: Venezuela, United States, Mexico, Colombia, Peru, Honduras, Ecuador, Chile, Argentina, etc. We tried to guide the students with the simulation to be as realistic as possible by looking at real online newspapers, as well as information that the ICONS Project had provided through many resourceful avenues.

Learning objectives and assessment

The learning objectives were:

- To think critically
- To learn to do team work
- To persuade and communicate effectively
- To learn the complexity of negotiating online
- To conduct regional (multilateral) and bilateral agreements
- To learn the negotiation process by doing
- To use tactics of negotiation effectively
- To analyze the effect of diplomatic negotiations on their own business
- To understand the effect and stability of coalitions and their power in negotiation.

The students, in our view, reached these goals. Students conducted face-to-face exercises in the classroom and reflected upon the lessons learned in the simulation. Students communicated and negotiated more collaboratively by the end of the course.

Student feedback

A couple of the student comments, which we think are typical, may help provide a sense of their reaction concerning the class and simulation. According to the students' survey responses at the end of the course:

> The ICONS Project Simulation and class material helped us think deeper and differently about the various negotiation strategies and the ways in which negotiation can take place.

> [T]he most exciting part of the course is the International Negotiation ICONS Simulation exercise which allows students to experience and play an active role in the negotiation process on an international scope. This by far is the most useful part of the course, because it combines every element and principle of negotiation taught and allows the student to apply all of them extensively in a real-life context. The online Negotiation course was a challenging and extremely enjoyable experience which taught us very valuable lessons that we will use for the rest of our lives in situations both professional and personal.

We have used the ICONS Project Simulation three additional times: once using the Nigeria Oil simulation with students from Mexico, Guatemala and the United States simultaneously, a second time using a European Union Negotiation simulation with U.S. students, and last with the Borders, Environment, and Trade in the Americas simulation with European students.

The bottom line in teaching students negotiation in a real-life context, we think, is that if you as a teacher can link learning to doing, you will be more effective. This differs from negotiation teaching using only role-plays, because it expedites the application of concepts in the real world. The instructor becomes a coach, facilitating and supplementing learning in and out of the classroom, and creating situations where students can explore different modes of learning synchronously and asynchronously.

Recommendations
For teachers preparing to participate in an ICONS simulation for the first time, we recommend[4] the following:

- Give the students a two-week period to research their country. Have them deliver a country worksheet, position paper, strategy, and proposal by the third week. Encourage students to set forth at least one multilateral proposal and one bilateral.
- Preclude email messages between students outside of the simulation.
- Encourage students to log into the simulation frequently to check for messages.
- Allocate classroom time to set the conferences while everyone is present.

The instructor needs to monitor information flow, and periodically encourage students to be more active, as well as remind students of the time window for voting on proposals and the deadline to deliver the reaction paper.

Bringing the Class to the Street and the Street to the Class

In this section, we describe two experiments we have conducted in which our students engage in real-life negotiation activities and the instructors provide guidance and coaching. The first of these experiments revolves around a class project: convene a dialogue on a topic of some controversy that is also related to a governance issue. The second of these experiments situates the instructor as both a shadow and coach while students engage in their professional negotiations.

For both experiments, one of the key pedagogical tools we employed was coaching. Coaching is a process in which one person (the coach) supports another (the "coachee") in the latter's effort to improve a certain personal or professional goal (Kauffman and Bachkirova 2008). In our case, the instructors are the coach and our students the coachees. The coaching processes described here revolve around the students' experiences in real-life negotiations. The instructors meet the students multiple times during the course of the teaching period to help the students identify skills they need to improve or goals they want to achieve; develop approaches to try; and then debrief with those students in the next meeting to help them revise their strategy as the negotiations proceed. More detail on the coaching that each author used will be provided below.

Experiment One: Convening Policy Dialogues in Singapore

At the Lee Kuan Yew School of Public Policy, National University of Singapore, the course "Advanced Negotiation: Convening Policy Dialogues" requires that students convene a dialogue on some policy topic by the end of the semester. This course is "advanced" in that a) it follows a basic negotiation course in which the seven elements and other core negotiation concepts are taught and b) it extends the concepts to intra-group negotiations, as well as convening multi-stakeholder policy dialogues.

This course has two real-life negotiations in which students engage. First, the students are required to convene a dialogue on a policy issue that a) they choose as a group; b) involves stakeholders; and c) is an issue around which there is at least some disagreement among stakeholders. As examples, previous classes have convened dialogues around Singapore's immigration policy, the faculty's pedagogical policies, the preservation and display of maritime artifacts, and Singapore's potential use of nuclear and grid management technologies to meet its long-term energy needs.

Second, the students need to negotiate internally as they choose a topic, choose what activities they will do to make the dialogue happen, assign tasks, and otherwise go through the process of convening a dialogue, facilitating the meeting, and making a report on it. These negotiations are different from the situations that they encounter in the basic negotiation course because: a) the outcome of the negotiation has very real impacts, not only on their grade, but also potentially on their self-confidence, reputation, and curriculum vitae; and b) the negotiations occur within a group that sees itself as a team. In fact, much of the class reflection time is spent on helping students realize how they tend to assume that they all have similar interests when they are in the same group: when they discover disagreement, they tend to argue instead of negotiate. Those with the same interests only require clarification of the facts; those with different interests, like in any other negotiation, need to identify and meet needs through trades, collaborations, compromises, etc. With regard to this chapter, the rest of this section focuses on: a) the impact that using a real negotiation experience has on student learning, and b) the use of coaching as a tool for reflection and learning in this course.

Learning Objectives

There are two broad sets of learning objectives for this course. The first set of learning objectives revolves around the convening and facilitation of policy dialogues. For example, the instructor will encourage the student groups to start assessing the stakeholders, their interests, possible agendas, the context, and other factors that will allow them to determine whether to hold a dialogue, who needs to be invited, what the dialogue will try to achieve, and what process the participants will follow. Student groups will also learn about the need to go out and meet prospective participants and other interested parties, not only to assess their interests and willingness to participate, but also to build participant trust in the process and work through the agenda with their input until it is legitimate.

The second set of learning objectives revolves around the application of the basic negotiation concepts in real practice. As the students think about how to design the dialogue, for instance, they can use the "Seven Element Framework" and other tools. This class, however, is also about using the tools in intra-group processes. In most negotiation role-plays, the setting is inter-organizational, a setting which provides at least some permission for disagreement and possible non-cooperation should it be impossible to reach a suitable deal. The class group does feel that it has the luxury of non-cooperation, but there tends also to be a strong norm of cooperation. The latter often becomes strong enough that many students find it difficult to remember that they as individuals might have different interests – despite the instructor's constant reminders.

Coaching

For the course, students need to meet with the instructor three times during the semester: the first time after approximately three weeks have passed, the second about four to five weeks later, and the last either just before or after the dialogue.[5] In class, the instructor provides both on-the-spot observations of emerging dynamics and some perspective on crucial moments in the students' deliberations and after-meeting reflective discussions.

Each group coaching session lasts forty-five to sixty minutes. The first session starts with the professor asking the students to quickly identify their strengths as a negotiator. Next, the instructor asks the students to identify a few particular negotiation (including here facilitation as well as convening) skills that the students feel that they could improve. Once that is done, the students are asked to identify one of those skills as something they will work on during the next three to four weeks. This work can occur in class as well as outside, in other negotiation situations that students might find themselves in, though most students choose in-class situations. For the identified skill, the student then spends the rest of the coaching session choosing one or two ways that they will practice that skill in the upcoming weeks. For example, if a student decides that they want to work on building relationships with people they find difficult, they might identify a person and develop a set of activities that they will undertake for approaching them.

The second coaching session follows much the same procedure, though it starts differently. In the first part of the interview, the instructor will ask the student to explain how their experiment went and what they learned from it. After that, the student will be asked to identify what skill they would like to work on over the next three to four weeks, and a strategy will be developed. The third coaching session is similar to the second one, with an additional few minutes spent on wrapping up the coaching relationship. The last two coaching sessions are also used to assess students' abilities to learn in the field by analyzing negotiation situations and then devising the adjustments to their negotiation strategy (see Fuller 2012).

In-negotiation Interventions

Besides providing ongoing coaching, the instructor for this course observed most meetings of the group. These observations had two purposes. First, a portion of the students' assessment was based on their performance in applying negotiation skills during the meetings. Second, the instructor would stop the meeting once or twice to point out good, surprising, and ineffective negotiation moments and behaviors as they became apparent. During these ten minute interruptions, the instructor briefly described what he saw and asked the students to analyze its causes, and what they could do about it as individuals and as a group.

In practice, it was always a struggle to choose which moments were important and interesting enough to merit an interruption. Most meetings had more than enough such moments; knowing which ones to choose was crucial. Sometimes an intervention was more of an interruption than a useful teaching moment, because the group lost momentum. Similarly, there was a careful balance between making a point and allowing *students* to come to that point themselves. The latter often requires more time, and while it may produce more learning, it also hinders their ability to conduct the meeting fruitfully. It also risks increasing their frustration and sense of failure, and in turn reducing their motivation for the course.

The instructor must also keep a careful eye on the balance between students learning from their struggles and keeping a sense that the project is doable and worthwhile . Almost all students will willingly recognize that they learn most from the struggles they encounter; yet each class also encounters moments where it begins to lose hope. Over the years, the instructor has spent more time highlighting their progress, working to keep them motivated, while simultaneously allowing them to fall into fairly predictable challenges. For example, at the beginning of the semester, the instructor will strongly encourage the students to choose a person or committee that keeps an eye on the overall process and its targets and deadlines. Inevitably, the groups so far have either not chosen that person or sub-group or, in the one case where they did choose two individuals, the appointed students gradually forgot to maintain that role. While this instructor encourages the students from time to time to go back to this perspective, he does not force the issue.

Lessons learned

Following are the lessons that the instructor has learned teaching this course. These lessons draw from in-depth discussions that the instructor has had with many students during and after the course and from the feedback given during the university's official student assessment of the course. The main lessons are:

- **Students find the coaching very useful**. In general, students have found the coaching sessions to be very useful for developing their skills. All students surveyed to date have counted the coaching as a useful tool for identifying skill and understanding gaps and working to improve them.
- **Students learn most from their struggles.** In each class, the instructor and students have observed that the group learns much from the struggles it undergoes. Students have mixed feelings about this. They generally acknowledge that most of the lessons could not have been learned unless they went through the difficult patches. At the same time, they sometimes feel quite frustrated – and a few may remain so for the remainder of the course. So far, the main negative impact of this is on the teaching evaluations, where, for one out of the four years this approach has been taught, the teaching evaluation was lower than usual.
- **The instructor must carefully and constantly evaluate the benefits and risks of interventions, both in the classroom and in coaching sessions.** As mentioned earlier,

the instructor observes the students in most of their meetings and engages them in the analysis of particular moments and outcomes. This provides insights and prompts students to be more reflective about their negotiation strengths and weaknesses. At the same time, temptations to resist are letting these moments go on too long and speaking too much. Students often look to the instructor to provide observations and ideas about what they ought to do. Such an approach, however, is both: a) something provided during the classroom time; and b) counterproductive to the purpose of the coaching session, which is to develop not only their negotiation skill but also their ability to reflect, learn, and re-strategize as reflective negotiators in the future. Therefore, the instructor must make sure to constantly give the reflective and strategizing role back to the students.

- **Students' failure to implement the strategies from previous coaching sessions is an opportunity for learning.** Reflective exercises like coaching can do well even if students do not do what they plan. When students do what they plan, the outcomes of their actions can be discussed, and the effectiveness of their planned strategy assessed. When, on the other hand, they do *not* do what they had planned, the instructor can encourage the student to identify why they did not conduct the experiment. From this, the student would have a better idea of the barriers they face in improving and implementing their negotiation skills. The new strategy they develop would, with luck, take these into account, or even address them exclusively as a separate and necessary step before seeking to improve the skill they first identified as important.

Experiment Two: Coaching Students in Street Negotiations

Some of the authors designed a course for a real client, known as Barcel USA, with an overarching client objective to position Mexican salty snacks in the United States. The students were employees of the firm, and the instructors had the challenge to co-design a training program with Barcel executives that would not only help the participants to focus on concepts and skills of negotiations, but also make sure participants *implemented* what they learned, and aligned it with company strategies. Coaching was a crucial element in this course.

For this course, our coaching is what we call "negotiation shadowing plus." This methodology, essentially coaching students who are engaged in real-life negotiations, expands experiential learning beyond the traditional role-plays, simulations and case studies. The instructor sees students engaged in ongoing, real-life negotiations, and coaches them as they seek to improve their performance. This is a results-oriented methodology that not only helps the students achieve their self-development objectives, but also the objectives of the negotiation in which they are engaged. There are four phases of the methodology: a) introspection; b) self vs. corporation awareness (the identification of self-development objectives through reflection with company objectives); c) conflict and negotiation core concept studies (e.g. Negotiation 101); and d) onsite implementation of learning and feedback.

Real-life negotiations

After the first training and negotiation teaching session at Barcel USA with traditional role-play and case studies, we realized we needed to change the teaching approach. Our approach was not leading us to the immediate results we expected, especially in terms of alignment with the company objectives. Therefore, we refocused the training based on participants' real-life negotiations.

Participants learned from their own real, ongoing cases. In other words, based on participants' concrete experience, the instructor shadowed or coached the negotiation concepts examined in class. Following the experiment, we resumed classroom sessions to reflect upon what we observed and what we learned. Subsequently, we were able to teach advanced negotiation concepts which helped conceptualize what students actually experienced. We encouraged participants to experiment based on our concepts and experiences as the learning-through-application cycle as described by Kolb (1984) continued.

For the specific course described here, Barcel USA's objective was to position several products made in Mexico in large supermarkets in the United States. At least partly as a result of this "shadowing plus" training, we believe, not only did the distribution company position several products at strategic store locations all over the United States, but it also positioned one product as one of the bestselling salty snacks in the United States. The company's annual revenues increased by forty percent and sales exceeded $100 million. The experiment was repeated in another distribution company, Intelligent Mexican Marketing (IMM). IMM is a company that is growing extremely fast and has experienced fifty percent annual growth for four years in a row.

Setting and tracking learning objectives

We believe this systematic approach to teaching negotiation works only if we align the teaching objectives with specific company objectives and parallel the teaching concepts with real case applications. If the participants need to obtain specific objectives for their job scope and activities, then the course is designed around those objectives. For example, suppose the company distributes salty snacks and candy in the United States in two different channels: independent supermarkets and chain stores. After basic instruction, negotiation course instructors designed a plan to visit stores representing both channels, with the task of applying what students learned and getting focused results.

The authors developed an assessment tool to measure student effectiveness on a Likert scale from one to five in five different areas. The areas of evaluation during a client visit were:

a) **Empathy**. Did the participant develop empathy on the client visit? Did he ask questions? Did he understand the other side? Is the relationship developing?

b) **Avoiding internal objections and responding to external objections.** Internal objections are self-generated barriers, such as a lack of confidence, while external objections are barriers the client gives, such as "it is too expensive" or "I don't need it." (Participants were asked beforehand to prepare a list of the most common objections and the most likely responses.)

c) **Understanding other needs and interests**. Did the participants ask questions to understand the interests of the other side?

d) **Satisfying the needs of the other.** Is he actually getting the problems solved? Were options generated?

e) **Closing.** Is he actually closing the deal? Were the negotiation objectives covered for both sides? Did our student apply principles learned to close the deal? How effective was his understanding of the concepts and their application?

Before designing this observation-based tool, authors Chamoun and Hazlett created a participant self-evaluation questionnaire that was used as both pre-test and post-test to measure course effectiveness. This tool used a scale of 1-5 in all of the questions (1 meaning they do not apply (or lack skill in applying) a particular negotiation concept and 5 meaning they use and are skillful in application). Analyzing more than 500 response sets, participants' self-scores increased on average from 3.34 to 3.90, a modest measure of course effectiveness, albeit simply a self-assessment. An observation-based tool chronicling student performance during actual negotiations before and after instruction was expected to provide a better gauge of coaching effectiveness and student learning. Using one workshop that included applying principles "on the street" as an example, class mean scores across all five categories rose from 1.59 to 3.41 as pre and post-course evaluations. We assert that the observation-based rating is more representative of the initial state than self-evaluation scores, and the difference logged in application-based assessment is a stronger indicator of change. The ability to close positively all prepared real negotiations improved from a typical rating of "not closing, or being afraid to ask" to "has the courage to ask." The actual indicator of success, on a scale from 1 to 5 (1 being unsuccessful, 5 being "very successful") changed similarly: the average participant's ability to close deals increased from 1 to 4 after they "went to the street."

Lessons learned

This chapter is really about the *progression* of negotiation teaching, from classroom instruction with role-plays toward coaching students through real job negotiations, which we call street-wise negotiation. Here are some observations within both Barcel USA and Intelligent Mexican Marketing (IMM). We believe they have applied to all associates involved in the course.

a) The first negotiation in which they succeed is the internal one with oneself – their own case. They understand how things could be accomplished if they are properly negotiated.
b) They understand that they don't sell, they negotiate.
c) They lose their fear to ask for things. Suddenly, nothing in the organization is non-negotiable.
d) Training as part of a workgroup encourages individuals to pursue similar goals; it creates a new standard of accomplishment and unifies group wants.
e) Diversity in the training group enriches the experience. Sometimes the positive inertia engages the non-believers. It encourages change toward a new mindset.
f) They transform their approach to work from "unprepared" meetings to a fully prepared sales force. They seek their objectives with a new level of intensity.
g) People understand the relevance of "closing the circle." Not only do they prepare in advance, but they also close all initiatives they start.
h) The relationship between theory and practice is key.

Fernando Guadarrama, one of our many Barcel USA students (and a former Regional Sales Manager) commented on the process,

> I have witnessed how effective coaching is to bring negotiation skills instruction to the field. We decided to approach a client that we had lost and that we had not been able to recover after many failed attempts on our part. The client had a

very high sales potential but until then had refused to accept our products back into her business and did not even want to speak with us again. My sales team's negotiation behavior was such that they were afraid to ask questions. It was also difficult for them to listen, and at times they didn't have the courage to walk away. After reflecting on this in class and strategizing with my sales team a plan of action to change this behavior, we went to visit this client. I am convinced that because Dr. Chamoun-Nicolas and I were present, my sales representatives felt not only motivated, but also probably obligated to experiment (with) the negotiation methodology that they had just learned. I noticed my sales representatives changed behavior by following Dr. Chamoun's advice on-site. They learned how to ask questions, to listen, and to take breaks when necessary. Once the source of the negotiation problem was identified, my sales representatives were able to offer the client exactly what she needed, and in return we got her business back. My sales representatives, at a reflection session after this experiment, expressed that they felt empowered by this learning experience and that they would certainly continue using the negotiation strategies in the future.

Future work
We believe there are benefits to both self-assessment and observational-based rating tools. A single, unified, validated tool that includes self–and third–party evaluation can assist the student as well as the coach in evaluating the learning experience.

Conclusion
Whether or not the reader is prepared to accept our assertions, which we concede are not yet provable, we believe that our experiences show at a minimum that it is possible to introduce concepts in the classroom, and then place students in role-plays or real negotiations in which they have to apply and reflect upon those ideas. It is also possible to put students in negotiation experiences, and then ask them what they found most interesting, difficult, or surprising, and to use those discussions in turn to elicit teaching points. We have found both ways to work.

In our experience, "going to the street" first, with appropriate prior planning, captures the attention of the participants more. Students tell us that they only realize how difficult it is to practice their skill and improve their outcomes when engaged in a long, multi-session, and higher-stakes negotiation.

Some are surprised by the quick turnaround of results that can occur when they deliberately experiment with new techniques midway through the negotiation, and after some reflection and even coaching. This motivates the students to pay closer attention to the case studies used later in the classroom.

Such turnarounds can take longer when the negotiation is multiparty and occur among people who see themselves as a team, which is what occurs within the public policy course. Students in these courses often struggle to get a handle on the process and make the group work effectively. Successes that happen along the way are balanced by new challenges, as students struggle with the complexities of negotiating within a team and convening a real dialogue. Some form groups that meet after or before class sessions to debrief their experiences and strategize how to improve their outcomes. Almost all students grudgingly admit that this repeated encounter with small successes and constant struggles is valuable as a learning experience. The successful completion of the dialogue is also a powerful motivator and a significant accomplishment.

The two characteristics that distinguish the pedagogical experiments described here from traditional role-plays are repetitive engagement and expanded stakes. Having the students go through *multiple learning cycles* during one negotiation seemed useful, whether or not the later cycles considered the same skills, behavior, or moments as the first one. Students focus more on what they are doing and what is happening, rather than trying to catch up to the constantly changing negotiation role-plays and other scenarios. When they focus on the same skill for multiple learning cycles, they begin to understand that skill or concept in a deeper way, moving beyond each concept (which generally sounds simple enough on its own) to the real challenges and mishaps that occur when we try to apply it in real-life situations.

Expanding the stakes has also proved very useful for our courses. Students treat these negotiations, whether extended role-plays or real-life interactions, more seriously. The degree of their emotional and personal involvement is noticeably heightened, and the sense of satisfaction and accomplishment when completing the real-life negotiations is clear.

When we align the negotiation teaching objectives with the participants' concrete experiences, this seems to yield the right environment to anchor the participants' interest to learn, to help participants see the value of learning since it would immediately help them resolve a real case, and to create a virtuous cycle of learning. Knowing the specific interests of participants is essential (see Lewicki and Schneider 2010). That interest, for MBA students, could be extra course credit, a better grade, or more effective resolution of their own cases. Whatever the interest may be, the instructor needs to develop a teaching methodology that considers the participants' interest and which will help not only keep him or her on track, but also motivate to learn.

The authors intend more experiments in the future with a similar experimental design basis, to address course participants' real needs. In other words, if we are going to follow Kolb's cycle of experiential learning effectively, we need first to find the right environment to create concrete experiences as stepping-stones. Second, we must design more sophisticated tools to help students follow the learning cycle effectively and link concrete experience with negotiation theory, and ongoing experience with ongoing reflection. Third, we need to find ways for students to engage more effectively with each other in making sense of, and trying to improve the outcomes of, their negotiations. Fourth, the instructors must have a follow-up and coaching plan to apply actively what is learned from step two, and to feed the results back into the concrete experience environment (see Figure 1). Finally, in order to make all this happen, we need to expand the scope of role-plays to multiple consecutive training classes or courses, and expand the stakes for the students beyond those typical in classroom work.

Notes

[1] For additional constructive advice on effective use of role-play, see Ebner and Kovach (2010).

[2] For a description of the seven elements (relationship, communication, interests, options, standards, alternatives and commitments), see Patton (2005).

[3] As part of the Center for International Development and Conflict Management at the University of Maryland, College Park, the ICONS Project offers complex simulations that can be conducted either face-to-face or through its customized web-based communication system, ICONSnet. For brief descriptions of available simulations, see http://www.icons.umd.edu/training/simulations (last accessed April 25, 2012).

[4] We also envision ICONS Project simulations as an avenue for furthering research, by analyzing the different negotiations with different students from different countries.

[5] The timing varies in each course because students are in charge of setting the schedule for their activities. Some try to get the dialogue done earlier, others (more commonly) do this near the end of available time.

References

Alexander, N. and M. LeBaron. 2009. Death of the role-play. In *Rethinking negotiation teaching: Innovations for context and culture*, edited by C. Honeyman, J. Coben, and G. De Palo. St. Paul, MN: DRI Press.

Barreto, L. 2009. *The role of ontological coaching on assuring quality: An approach for the professional competencies of the employees.* Master Thesis, UAT, Mexico.

Chamoun, H. and P. Linzoain. 2004. *Deal-guidelines for a flawless negotiation.* Houston, TX: KeyNegotiations.

Chamoun, H. and R. Hazlett. 2007. *Negotiate like a Phoenician.* Houston, TX: KeyNegotiations.

Coben, J., C. Honeyman, and S. Press. 2010. Straight off the deep end in adventure learning. In *Venturing beyond the classroom: Volume 2 in the rethinking negotiation teaching series*, edited by C. Honeyman, J. Coben, and G. De Palo. St. Paul, MN: DRI Press.

Druckman, D. 2006. Uses of a marathon exercise. In *The negotiator's fieldbook: The desk reference for the experienced negotiator*, edited by A. K. Schneider and C. Honeyman. Washington, DC: American Bar Association.

Ebner, N. and K. K. Kovach. 2010. Simulation 2.0: The resurrection. In *Venturing beyond the classroom: Volume 2 in the rethinking negotiation teaching series*, edited by C. Honeyman, J. Coben, and G. De Palo. St. Paul, MN: DRI Press.

Fisher, R., W. Ury, and B. Patton 1991. *Getting to yes: Negotiating agreement without giving in*, 2nd edn. New York: Penguin.

Fuller, B. 2012. Interviews as an assessment tool. In *Assessing our students, assessing ourselves: Volume 3 in the rethinking negotiation teaching series*, edited by N. Ebner, J. Coben, and C. Honeyman. St. Paul, MN: DRI Press.

Kauffman, C. and T. Bachkirova. 2008. Spinning order from chaos: How do we know what to study in coaching research and use it for self-reflective practice? *Coaching: An International Journal of Theory, Research & Practice* 1(1): 1-7.

Kolb, D. A. 1984. *Experiential learning experience as a source of learning and development.* Upper Saddle River, NJ: Prentice Hall.

Lewicki, R. J. and A. K. Schneider. 2010. Instructors heed the who: Designing negotiation training with the learner in mind. In *Venturing beyond the classroom: Volume 2 in the rethinking negotiation teaching series*, edited by C. Honeyman, J. Coben, and G. De Palo. St. Paul, MN: DRI Press.

Manwaring, M., B. McAdoo, and S. Cheldelin. 2010. Orientation and disorientation: Two approaches to designing "authentic" negotiation learning activities. In *Venturing beyond the classroom: Volume 2 in the rethinking negotiation teaching series*, edited by C. Honeyman, J. Coben, and G. De Palo. St. Paul, MN: DRI Press.

Nelken, M., B. McAdoo, and M. Manwaring. 2009. Negotiating learning environments. In *Rethinking negotiation teaching: Innovations for context and culture*, edited by C. Honeyman, J. Coben, and G. De Palo. St. Paul, MN: DRI Press.

Panga, S. and G. B. Grecia-de Vera. 2010. A look at a negotiation 2.0 classroom: Using adventure learning modules to supplement negotiation simulations. In *Venturing beyond the classroom: Volume 2 in the rethinking negotiation teaching series*, edited by C. Honeyman, J. Coben, and G. De Palo. St. Paul, MN: DRI Press.

Patton, B. 2005. Negotiation. In *Handbook of dispute resolution*, edited by M. L. Moffitt and R. C. Bordone. San Francisco: Jossey-Bass.

Roblyer, M. D. 2006. *Integrating educational technology into teaching*, 4th edn. Upper Saddle River, NJ: Prentice Hall.

Sosa, C. 2012. *Propuesta para un nuevo orden educativo, Formativo y de capacitación profesional y laboral.* Buenos Aires, Argentina.

🕸 16 🕸

Negotiation and Professional Boxing

Habib Chamoun-Nicolas, Randy D. Hazlett, Russell Mora,
Gilberto Mendoza & Michael L. Welsh*

Editors' Note: In this groundbreaking piece, a group of authors with unimpeachable expertise in one of the least likely environments ever considered for negotiation analyze what is actually going on in the professional boxing ring. Their surprising conclusions take the facile claim of our field that "everybody negotiates" to a whole new level. Not only does this chapter serve as a kind of extreme-case demonstration of why students should consider learning negotiation to be central to any occupation they may take up in future; it might well serve as inspiration for some new studies in other fields in which negotiation may previously have been thought irrelevant.

Introduction

Referee Judge Mills Lane, a former marine and decorated fighter in his day, was blindsided. Mills, a late substitution due to an objection from the Tyson camp, issued an early blanket warning to keep punches up. According to our own analysis of the fight video (Boxingsociety. com 1997), defending heavyweight champion Evander Holyfield gained an early advantage with a characteristic forward lunging style. Following a punch, Holyfield would lock up with the smaller Mike Tyson, shoulder-to-shoulder, applying force throughout. Holyfield finished the round clearly in the lead. At the 2:28 mark in the second, a

* **Habib Chamoun-Nicolas** is an honorary professor at Catholic University of Santiago Gua yaquil-Ecuador and an adjunct professor and member of the executive board at the Cameron School of Business at University of St. Thomas in Houston, Texas. His email address is hchamoun@keynegotiations.com. **Randy Hazlett** is president of Potential Research Solutions and Christian Artist's Workshop in Dallas, Texas. His email address is rdhazlett@sbcglobal.net. **Russell Mora** is a Las Vegas boxing referee. His email address is russellmora@cox.net **Gilberto Mendoza** is the vice-president of the WBA (World Boxing Association). His email address is gjmendoza@wbanews.com. **Michael L. Welsh** is the auditor of the WBA. His email address is admin@michaellwelsh.com.

leaning Holyfield popped Tyson's right brow with his head, causing an immediate issue of blood. Tyson appealed to Referee Lane, who called a timeout at 2:20. He separated the fighters and verbally confirmed that the cut resulted from a head butt rather than a legal blow. As the blood trickled unexamined and unchecked, Referee Lane called for immediate resumption to action. At the 1:39 mark, Tyson looked for Referee Lane for help as the head-forward, pushing style persisted. The referee called time at 0:36 after an obvious Holyfield shove that sent Tyson bouncing against the ropes. Judge Lane addressed Holyfield saying, "You know better than that!" The next tie-up took nearly twenty seconds for Lane to pry apart the fighters, as repeated instructions to "let him go" went unheeded.

During the break, the cut doctor spent the entire time working around the eye of Mike Tyson. After the bell for round three, Lane immediately called time and sent Tyson back to his corner for his mouthpiece. As action resumed, Tyson exploded with a flurry of targeted blows, prompting Holyfield to toss Tyson back to recover distance. Tyson immediately returned to the offensive, forcing Holyfield to backpedal for the first time. Tyson seized control of the ring. It took Lane nearly fifteen seconds to break a clinch and migrate from wrestling back to boxing. At 1:13, Holyfield delivered a blow, unseen by Lane, yet cited by the announcers as below the belt. After a series of crushing blows on Holyfield, Tyson missed with a left hook only to find himself in the familiar head-to-head clinch position. Tyson rotated his head at the 0:40 mark. Holyfield leapt back in a reactive circular motion to reveal a chunk of his ear now missing. Referee Judge Mills Lane called time at 0:35. Tyson followed the retreating Holyfield and heaved him into the ropes. Lane propelled himself between fighters to regain control of the timeout period.

After blood was rinsed from the ear, Referee Lane examined Holyfield without verbal exchange. A minute into the timeout, Lane found the boxing commissioner ringside and summoned him forward. Lane explained, "He is disqualified. He bit his ear. He is out. He is disqualified. He bit his ear. I can see the bite marks." When the commissioner questioned the disqualification ruling as appropriate, Judge Lane conferred with the doctor saying, "He bit his ear. Can he go on?" The Doctor replied a simple, "Yes." Lane immediately concluded the proper consequence was a two-point deduction. After nearly a two and a half minute delay, the round continued. Tyson resumed the role of aggressor, but after fifteen seconds, he found himself in proximity of Holyfield's opposite ear and bit down. The infraction went undetected until after the bell, at which point Referee Judge Mills Lane disqualified Tyson.

Through this vignette, we gain insight not only into the dynamics of a heavyweight fight, but also into the intricacies of conflict management as conducted by a professional boxing referee. Conscripted to enforce the rules for the integrity of the sport, to ensure the safety of the opponents, to score the fight in partial determination of the proper outcome, and to manage the flow of the competition for value to the fans and promoters, the professional boxing referee must be adept at making split-second conflict management decisions, with the ability to adapt to the dynamics of a fight and the situational needs of the moment. He must balance the needs: to be the ultimate authority on allowable behavior; not to dictate tactics, but to react to combatants' actions; to influence conformance in future behavior of people who come with premeditated goals to inflict physical pain and harm.

We see in the Holyfield-Tyson match Judge Mills (who, for a time, was a county court judge in real life) in the role of a boxing referee. At times, we see him making decisive judgments, negotiating with opponents, allowing questionable tactics, issuing warnings, conferring with officials, executing penalties, breaking the action to gather facts, reprimanding participants jointly and separately, and ultimately pronouncing the victor. We see the need for the impartial conflict manager to balance his roles as gatekeeper of the rules and arbiter of relationships in this contracted sporting event. To do so effectively, the professional boxing referee must exhibit not one conflict management style, but the situationally-appropriate style to influence the desired result. This is possible if the dominant style balances rules and relationships, such that the referee can increase or decrease either as appropriate, and temporarily adopt one of the more traditional styles in conflict management.

While "win-win" strategies are often valued in negotiation, in sports, and in particular, professional boxing, it would appear to the casual observer that certain conflict resolution styles might be absent, with combatants strategically pursuing a win-lose result. The boxing literature, also, has little to say on negotiation strategies as tools for conflict resolution, outside of contracts and fees. Still, both behind-the-scenes negotiations and persuasive tactics in the boxing ring itself between opponents, managers, promoters, and officials are rich in possibilities for analysis. The results of a little investigation suggest that previous conceptions of how "everybody negotiates" have, if anything, under-recognized the spectrum of conflict resolution styles active in professional boxing, and by implication, perhaps in other highly contentious environments.

In an effort to analyze what is going on in boxing from a negotiation perspective, we will make some adaptations to the well-known

Thomas-Kilmann instrument. While the Thomas-Kilmann tool has proven useful in analysis of negotiation styles for decades, we suggest some modifications and alternative imagery, to portray classifications pertinent to the sport of professional boxing. We therefore take the liberty of supplanting traditional conflict management style labels of competing, collaborating, compromising, avoiding, and accommodating with *Fight Like a Spartan, Facilitate Like a Phoenician, Judge Like Solomon, Avoid Like a Politician,* and *Delegate Like a Diplomat,* respectively. In most cases, the new classification scheme simply adds clarity; however, the compromising and accommodating styles, seldom encountered in combative sports, and in particular by professional boxing referees, are replaced with more meaningful counterparts representing similar partitioning between cooperation and assertiveness. Anecdotal examples are pulled from boxing history to illustrate the complexity of the sport and how the adapted negotiation style tool can be used to classify social behaviors between participants. The intent of the tool is to assist boxers, referees, promoters, and managers in decision-making by recognition of styles and ramifications in this adrenaline-pumping sport of split-second judgments. This specific article focuses upon conflict management styles exhibited by the "third man" in the ring – the professional boxing referee. In a learning environment, the style descriptions and examples would be supplemented with video evidence, documenting behaviors across multiple learning modes for maximum teaching effectiveness.

Classifying Negotiation Styles

Robert Blake and Jane Mouton (1964) introduced a simple five-category scheme for classifying negotiation style, yielding the primary interaction styles: competing, collaborating, compromising, avoiding, and accommodating. From here forward, we make the distinction between negotiation and conflict management style for reasons that will become apparent. The refined assessment tool by Kenneth Thomas and Ralph Kilmann (1974) has been used extensively to identify primary modes of interaction in individuals regarding tendencies toward cooperation and assertiveness. The ability to identify style, and tactics characteristic of a specific style, can aid in developing appropriate strategies to get to closing. Indeed, self-evaluation to identify one's own dominant style also holds value in both guiding successful negotiations and identifying skills for possible development. Conflict management styles can be dynamic, with multiple styles exhibited according to shifting needs. Thus, it is important to be familiar with techniques and methods that are flexible enough to avoid an impasse. Identification of styles is one such tool to guide the successful negotiator.

Win-win scenarios are generally not the ideal for either party in war and sports. Sporting events, such as the Olympics, have often superseded the political landscape, offering national pride to the winner, along with boasting rights that may not be possible on the battlefield. With much literature aimed at integrative negotiations, we step back to examine negotiations in sports. In particular, we evaluate negotiations and conflict management styles in a sport more akin to war than most – professional boxing. Through case studies and vignettes, we get an often behind-the-scenes look at the complex world of boxing decision-making. While professional boxers enter the ring with the intent to dominate their opponent by inflicting pain, they do so under contractual obligation to abide by a set of rules. Most rules in boxing are centered around the avoidance of unfair advantage. Thus, for example, we have weight ranges and prohibitions against illegal blows. We have preset time lengths and subdivision into rounds. Combatants agree to be assessed on a point system by predetermined judges, provided fighters are able to successfully complete the appointed maximum duration. The successful referee enforces the rules of engagement without drawing undue attention to himself. In some of the most successful bouts, the referee is the "invisible third man" in the ring.

Adapting the Classification of Conflict Management Styles for the Boxing Context

In sports, and professional boxing in particular, it is not readily apparent that parties cooperate with one another to any recognizable degree. Many would rather see only two of the traditional style designations as appropriate: competing and avoiding. As fighters are both vying for a win and working to incapacitate their opponent or his ability, nearly everyone in boxing would categorize a fight as maximum assertiveness without cooperation. Fighters, however, do cooperate to a significant degree to ensure a fair outcome, with significant value for themselves, their business partners, and the fans that ultimately finance the sport. In addition, they cooperate by agreeing to abide by the rules of boxing. They cooperate by agreeing to abide by the instructions of the referee, who serves as both observer and judge.

The referee is present for close-hand inspection of tactics, exercise of penalties, protection of participants, and adjudication. The skilled referee is constantly moving to get the best point of observation, and is ready to intervene in an instant, while avoiding interference. The referee is working with both participants, allowing them to spar within the agreed set of rules, but quick to act on either's behalf should there be a violation or safety concern. The referee must command the respect of fighters often double his size, and thrust into situations where emotion often overrides intellect as participants move in and out of positions of dominance. In the balance of this chapter, we focus on conflict management styles from the perspective of the professional boxing referee. But first, we adapt the traditional terminology of Thomas and Kilmann, to make it more recognizable within the context of a combative adjudicated sport (see Figure 1).

Competing – Fight Like A Spartan

The Spartans were ancient Greece's most formidable warriors, with a "win at any cost" attitude, solidified with viable, time-proven battle strategies and an unswerving sense of honor. Boxers will rapidly associate with this style, and exhibit it most often in pre-fight rhetoric and assertion of fight control in the ring. It will be most often conferred on the aggressor and is most visible between boxers content to go "toe-to-toe." The referee also must use this style, however, to command the respect of the fighters in order to maintain control of a bout. Overuse of this style by a referee, however, is not appreciated by fans, who want the fighters to control the outcome. The best referees will judiciously exercise their competitive style, choosing to exhibit enough authority to ensure safety and fairness without being the center of attention.

Collaborating – Facilitate Like A Phoenician

The style high in cooperation and assertiveness we re-label as *Facilitate Like a Phoenician*. The Phoenicians were an ancient Mediterranean people known for their negotiation skills (Chamoun and Hazlett 2008). In a prolonged period of regional conquest, the Phoenicians made themselves more valuable as business partners to the political and military powers in play than as a subjugated people. Thus, we associate conflict management styles that involve a high degree of cooperation and concern for effectiveness with these highly skilled negotiators of the past.

Boxers will not see themselves as collaborating in the ring, beyond the agreement to abide by the rules; however, this style is often exhibited unknowingly. For example, few fights will continue long without one fighter assuming the role of aggressor. Fans get unruly with sparse interaction, ultimately leading to one fighter assuming an alternate style. In fights where mutual respect has been substantiated, combatants may actually work together to conserve energy. The counterpunch is a reactive strategy that depends on actions of the other. Each fighter creates windows of opportunity for themselves and the other. As for the referee, he is an impartial judge; yet he is ready to assist either combatant when unfair advantage has been levied through either an infraction of the rules or physical incapacitation. While physical domination is a fighter's goal, illegal blows include those when a fighter is unable to defend himself. Boxers and their corner representation make appeals throughout a match. The degree to which this information is processed into decision making is up to the referee. While this may on the surface resemble arbitration rather than negotiation, the professional boxing referee operating with this style is open to input from participants and is actively engaged with the fighters. The referee in this style could also be interpreted as negotiating with himself for the benefit of the fighters and the sport. The good referee works with both fighters, while not showing favoritism beyond the enforcement of fight protocol.

Compromising – Judge Like Solomon

This style is perhaps the one most in need of alternate imagery from the original language of Thomas and Kilmann. Compromising means making concessions to the other in order to gain ground on those terms most important to you. Sportsmen do not typically envision compromise as a useful style. However, if we examine the motivating forces (the axes in the style chart), we find a related style, also a balance between cooperation and assertiveness. This style can easily move into any of the other styles with small shifts in motivation. We choose to rename this style *Judge Like Solomon* to capture the keen sense of fairness exhibited by Solomon, as recorded in Hebrew scripture: in particular, the incident of the two women approaching Solomon with but one child, both claiming to be the mother. Exercising great wisdom, he called for the child to be cut in half (ostensibly a compromise), giving an equal portion to each woman. The woman yielding her claim, in order to save the child, was awarded the baby, as having shown herself to be the true mother. What appeared at first to be an extremely bad compromise was thus revealed instead to be judiciousness of a high order. We believe there is wisdom in the fact that the two *could* be confused.

While combatants may not claim to operate in the arena of compromise, the appropriate strategy strikes a balance between offense and defense, aggression and caution. The skilled fighter can operate with such a balance, reserving opportunity to both seize advantage and protect against disadvantage. Sometimes the best "cooperative" strategy is simply to wait, to prolong the window of opportunity. Meanwhile, the professional boxing referee seeks to use this conflict management strategy for preference, working with the combatants, but ever ready to interject himself between fighters as the authority

figure in the ring. We envision this style, therefore, not as one of compromise in its classic sense, but rather as one of judicious and decisive
balance.

Avoiding – Avoid Like a Politician

We can easily identify the avoidance tactic with politicians who place
reputation and votes over positions and policies. The avoiding strategy
is often portrayed in boxing as both an offensive and defensive tool.
Against a slower opponent, a boxer may choose to maintain advantage through constant motion. Avoiding can also be used to great advantage if there is a marked difference in reach. While the jab seldom
results in a knockout, it scores points nevertheless. Avoidance could
likewise be a tactic to counter an obvious advantage in power. A boxer knowing he cannot effectively trade blows toe-to-toe can exercise
avoidance. From a conflict management style, *Avoid Like a Politician* is
low on both the cooperation and assertiveness scales. That does not
make it an ineffective strategy in boxing, as exhibited by the younger
Ali in his extensive use of motion, captured in his mantra "float like
a butterfly, sting like a bee"; however, it is not a desirable dominant
conflict management strategy for a boxing referee. Such a referee fails
to control a fight, endangering the lives of the combatants. Under
some circumstances, a referee can avoid micromanagement of a fight
without giving undue advantage; but a referee exercising avoidance
too much will be seen as disengaged or ill-equipped for the position,
especially at the professional level.

Accommodating – Delegate Like a Diplomat

The accommodating style is quick to please, surrendering leadership
or control; but while this type of behavior is exhibited in sports, it
is seldom seen in boxing referees. Thus, we have labeled this conflict management style as *Delegate Like a Diplomat*. A diplomat goes to
great lengths not to offend and always errs on the side of relationship.
This style is seldom effectively used by boxers, though there is historical precedent in Ali's *rope-a-dope* strategy deployed against a younger,
stronger, but less durable Foreman. The tactic coined as *rope-a-dope*
by Ali refers to an invitation to the opponent to take uncountered
punches while he assumes a low-energy, highly protective stance using the ringside ropes as shock absorbers. Using his arms and gloves
as protective equipment to avoid debilitating damage, he planned to
tire the opponent with extended invitations to *take their best shot*. Once
his opponent's energy was spent, Ali became the aggressor.

    In general, to surrender (temporarily) to the opponent is almost
always a defensive strategy by a hurt fighter trying to protect himself

just long enough to regain his faculties. A referee using the delegating strategy of conflict management may purposefully bend the rules to protect a fighter or counter an advantage.

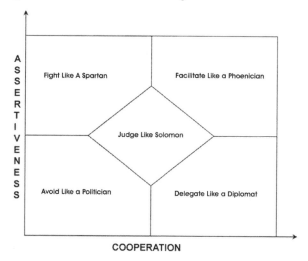

Figure 1. Proposed Thomas-Kilman conflict management styles reinterpreted for application in combative adjudicated sports.

A referee using this strategy can easily be viewed as one showing favoritism in the ring. Another form of delegation concerns scoring, knowing there are other judges scoring the fight. The referee could get so involved with other aspects of officiating as to lose track of his responsibility to score the fight properly. In this case, he is not delegating to the combatants, but rather to the other professional judges, who however lack the referee's ability to manipulate his frame of reference for optimal viewing angle. The professional boxing referee ought to have the most reliable assessment of scoring blows. Another example of delegating by the referee would be indirectly addressing conflict to preserve relationship or, as in the case of Holyfield-Tyson, seeking higher authority, as in a boxing commissioner or doctor.

Table 1 categorizes how each of these five conflict management styles would offer a different response to the delivery of a low blow by one fighter against another.

CONFLICT MANAGEMENT STYLE	ACTION
Fight Like a Spartan	Stop the action and penalize the guilty fighter
Facilitate Like a Phoenician	Stop the action and verbally warn both fight
Judge Like Solomon	Stop the action, issue a warning, and assess the ability of the violated party to continue
Avoid Like a Politician	Let the fight continue as long as both fighters are physically able
Delegate Like a Diplomat	Stop the action and warn each corner

Table 1. Illustrative potential actions in response to an illegal punch.

In the *Fight Like a Spartan* style, the referee would immediately exercise a penalty based upon his observation and interpretation of the facts. In the *Facilitate Like a Phoenician* style, the referee would acknowledge the observation and recite the rules to both parties equally, to preserve relationships. In the *Judge Like Solomon* mode, the referee would stop the action and exhibit concern for both the rules and the fighters, especially the one who was placed at a disadvantage. In the *Avoid Like a Politician* style, the referee would apply the adage, no harm, no foul. As *Delegate Like a Diplomat*, the referee might fail to address the combatants directly, preserving relationships and choosing rather to allow the coaches in each corner to police the actions of their principals. These are all actions that can and do take place in boxing in response to the identical in-ring infraction.

Historical Precedents for Dominant Conflict Management Styles

While we have identified the preferred dominant style for conflict management for a professional boxing referee as *Judge Like Solomon*, all styles have found their place in history in prominent matches. For illustrative purposes, we will describe a few here. We note that dominant referee style can change with combatants, as well as changing with time and experience.

Case 1. Jersey Joe Walcott vs Ezzard Charles, June 5, 1952

This was the fourth meeting between heavyweights Jersey Joe Walcott and Ezzard Charles. Charles had won the first two fights. In their third meeting, Jersey Joe Walcott defeated Charles to take the title with what many analysts still list as one of the greatest knockouts in boxing history. This fight made history on many fronts. It was the first sporting event to be broadcast on national television. It also represented the first heavyweight championship bout to be refereed by a black man, Zach Clayton. The fight went the distance with Walcott getting a unanimous, yet controversial decision. Clayton was heavily criticized for his role as referee. The August, 1952 issue of *The Ring* magazine ran the cover story, "Who Really Won That Fight? Joe or Ezzard?"[1] *Jet* ran an Inside Sports column by A. S. "Doc" Young containing a blistering rebuff of the referee.

> Obtruding all over the place, obstructing action as well as view, he [Clayton] unashamedly displayed his innate longing for the spotlight, a burning desire to be the star. . . He advised Charles against imaginary low blows, but allowed Walcott a punch to Ezz' thigh. Ignoring in-fighting as part of the game, he roughly separated boxers as soon as they touched bodies. He allowed Walcott to hit on the break. And, presuming himself to be a doctor, he went to Charles' corner and wiped a medicant from his eye. (Young 1952: 51)

Life magazine (1952) likewise reported, "According to a majority of the sportswriters at ringside, Charles easily outpointed Walcott, even though Joe was aided no end by Referee Zack Clayton, who kept nagging Charles about imaginary low blows while seeming to encourage the champion."[2]

While sports reporting (not to mention refereeing) can certainly be biased, we want to focus on the conflict management style(s) visible in these descriptions. Perhaps Clayton's behavior was affected by his unique place in history, or his knowledge of the national television broadcast. The contention that Clayton drew attention to himself over his role illustrates high assertiveness with low cooperation–which we would describe as a *Fight Like a Spartan* style. Thus, he competed with the fighters, controlling actions during and between rounds, and by some accounts overtly showing bias.

Case 2. Muhammad Ali vs George Foreman, October 30, 1974

George Foreman continued his march as decorated Olympic champion into the professional arena, and gained the heavyweight title by defeating Joe Frazier, setting up a fight between Foreman and Ali. Ali executed his "rope-a-dope" strategy, allowing Foreman to openly punch him while using the ropes to partially support his frame. Referee Zach Clayton allowed extensive use of holding on the part of Ali. When Foreman tired, Ali took the offensive. Foreman was floored in the eighth round. While Foreman quickly rose to his feet, appearing to beat the count, Clayton called the match at the 2:58 mark in the round. Though perhaps the count of announcer Bob Sheridan and Referee Clayton were out of synch, the broadcaster had only reached eight. Clayton did not appear to evaluate Foreman when he got up. Clayton ended the fight rather than allow the match to proceed to the next round. While the decision remarkably did not draw much controversy, it is illustrative of a shift in conflict management style over the younger Clayton (see Case 1). The failure to intervene and strictly enforce rules demonstrates the *Avoid Like a Politician* style. Few believe that a longer match would have yielded a different result, potentially explaining the absence of a formal protest. Using his prerogative as referee, Clayton decided Foreman should not continue. The decisive action to end the fight exemplifies the Judge Like Solomon style.

Case 3. Andre Berto vs Freddy Hernandez, November 28, 2010

Freddy Hernandez was 29-1 going into the fight with welterweight champion Andre Berto. About a minute into the fight, Freddy Hernandez went down hard. Referee Russell Mora immediately intervened and sent Berto to a neutral corner. Hernandez struggled to his feet and spit out his mouthpiece. The boxer staggered toward Referee Mora who was evaluating the body motion and eyes of the challenger from close range. At the count of eight with a wobbly Freddy Hernandez on his feet, Mora called the fight.

While paying fans hate such brevity in boxing, and fighters find such early exits embarrassing, Referee Mora clearly portrayed the *Judge Like Solomon* conflict management style. Steve Carp, of the Las Vegas Review-Journal, wrote, "A left jab followed by a left hook followed by a big right hand dropped Hernandez, and after he wobbled upon getting to his feet, he was clearly in no condition to continue . . ." (Carp 2010). Mora asserted not only the right but the need to decide for himself that he was seeing a fighter no longer able to defend himself. While the ruling drew controversy, the style depicted is unambiguous.

Case 4. Robert Guerrero vs. Michael Katsidis, April 9, 2011

As center ring instructions are given, Katsidis yells to Guerrero, "What are you looking at?" The initial round was the beginning of a great chess match. In the second round, Guerrero has a glove touch the canvas after an exchange, but Referee Russell Mora ruled this a trip, and took no action. The commentators, Jim Lampley and Max Kellerman, repeatedly insisted that the referee missed a knockdown. The commentators continued to replay the so-called missed knockdown, but they were unable to see that both fighters' feet were entangled. While boxers score with knockdowns, slips and trips are not rewarded. However, the referee missed a glove wipe. Anytime a fighter's glove touches the canvas for any reason the referee must wipe his gloves. By the end of the seventh round, Guerrero took an obvious lead. In the eighth, Katsidis hit Guerrero with an apparently intentional low blow.

When a boxer commits an intentional foul and has gained an unfair advantage, the referee may deduct a point for the intentional foul, as Mora did. Unfortunately, Katsidis continued his low blow attack, causing the referee to deduct yet another point. The second point deduction was more complicated, and was not understood by the commentators. An illegal low blow is not only one on the cup of a fighter, but also any punch below the navel or the hips. In the ninth round, Guerrero returns the favor and hits Katsidis with a low blow. The referee deducted a point from Guerrero, with the mindset that a strict enforcement of low blows was necessary to maintain a clean and fair fight. The strict enforcement cleaned up the fight. With no more infractions, Kitsidis and Guerrero continued to fight hard until the final bell and a unanimous decision for Guerrero.

Whether accidental or out of frustration, low blows constitute a rules infraction by combatants and a break in the cooperative agreement. Recognizing this as such, and knowing the danger to fighters by blows that are deemed illegal, the referee had to regain control with decisive action. With cooperation at a low point, maximum assertiveness was required. The actions of Referee Mora shifted to *Fight Like a Spartan*, evoking maximum allowable penalties for each infraction without further warning. Exercising penalties brought the fighters into "cooperation" – i.e., the resumption of a fair fight.

Case 5. Yuri Foreman vs. Miguel Angel Cotto, June 5, 2010

Yuri Foreman faced Miguel Angel Cotto in his first defense of the World Boxing Association world light middleweight title, on the first boxing card in the new Yankee Stadium. In the seventh round, Foreman slipped when his braced knee buckled. As the fight resumed, Foreman heavily favored his knee. The injury compromised Foreman's mobility, allowing Cotto to connect repeatedly. After a few more falls, Foreman's trainer threw a towel into the ring midway through the eighth. At that traditional symbol of surrender, the ring was flooded by members of both corners as well as event officials. However, sensing no imminent danger, Referee Arthur Mercante Jr. conferred with Foreman, inquiring if he wanted to continue. Receiving an answer in the affirmative, Mercante cleared the ring, and the fight resumed. Foreman crumbled again early in the ninth, but this time it followed a solid left hook.

The referee promptly halted the fight. Defending his decisionmaking, according to ESPN boxing writer Dan Rafael (2010), Mercante responded in a post-fight interview, "The towel came in the heat of the battle. They had a good exchange going. I felt it wasn't necessary to stop it. I didn't know where it [the towel] came from. There was no need to stop the fight. They were in the middle of a great fight. That's what the fans came to see. I felt I did the right thing to let it continue."

Faced with an unexpected symbol of surrender, Referee Mercante exercised both a high degree of cooperation and assertiveness. Following identification of the trainer as the source, he chose to disregard the opinion of the corner and consult the boxer himself to discern if the fighter could continue. Calling the fight because of a trainer's action would have delegated his authority. Contrary to popular belief leading to the saying *throwing in the towel*, this action does not, according to the rules of boxing, trump the referee's authority to end a match. Asserting his professional opinion and authority, he did what few would have done after everyone, including the fighters, had turned the ring into a post-fight ritual. Taking the opportunity to substantiate his assessment with additional information directly from the fighter, Referee Mercante exhibited the *Facilitate Like a Phoenician* conflict management style. Mercante elevated the option of the fighter to continue over the opinion of his trainer. When his opinion was later swayed in deference to the injured fighter's well-being, he ended the match.

Case 6. Muhammad Ali vs. Joe Frazier, October 1, 1975

In a fight marketed as the "Thrilla in Manila," Ali defended the heavyweight title in this third matchup with Joe Frazier. Contrary to his early-career "constant motion" strategy and his "outlast him" strategy that secured the title from George Foreman, Ali was convinced that he could trade blows with Frazier. The early rounds went to Ali, but Frazier showed he still could muster respect at the highest level, taking the middle rounds. By the end of the fourteenth round, Referee Carlos Padilla, Jr. had to direct Frazier to his corner due to eyesight deterioration. Ali said later of his retreat to his corner (Kram 1975), "It was the closest thing to death that I could feel." Frazier's trainer, Eddie Futch, refused to let Frazier continue into the final round.

The choice of Referee Carlos Padilla, Jr. to officiate the fight had been a controversial one primarily due to his small stature (Samaco 2009). At 160 pounds, some challenged his ability to command respect, and thus control the fight between heavyweights, especially of this caliber. Padilla warned Ali against holding and was repeatedly seen pulling Ali's arm down whenever it wrapped around Frazier's nape. Padilla exercised good balance between cooperation and assertiveness, representing the *Judge Like Solomon* conflict management style.

Conclusion

The reinterpretation of conflict management styles for combative sports, and professional boxing in particular, leads to specialized imagery that better fits the substance of what we argue is largely a disguised negotiation. In particular, the compromising style is replaced with a more meaningful interpretation, for competitive sports, of the balance between cooperation and assertiveness. Classification of styles aids in self-awareness, along with better management of interactions with others displaying tendencies identifiable using this schema. Conflict management styles can be dynamic, but dominant styles can emerge as primary. Sports examples help solidify terms and concepts for audiences who are not familiar or comfortable with negotiation theory or traditional classroom learning experiences. Roles that are typically projected to display only one or two styles, due to the win-lose nature of the game, turn out on examination actually to cover a wide gamut of possible styles. Perhaps the terminology as applied here to the professional boxing referee could be extended to other participants and other sports, revealing still more venues in which negotiation is pervasive if generally unrecognized.

Notes

[1] See http://boxrec.com/media/index.php/Ring_Magazine:_August_1952 (last accessed May 17, 2012).
[2] "Walcott staves off a challenger." *Life*, 16 June 1952, 33.

References

Blake, R. R. and J. S. Mouton. 1964. *The managerial grid*. Houston: Gulf Publishing.
BoxingSociety.com. 1997. Mike Tyson vs Evander Holyfield (Fight 2) (June 28), available at http://boxingsociety.com/allboxing/full_fights/mike-tyson-vs-evander-holyfield-fight-2.html (last accessed May 16, 2012).
Carp, S. 2010. Berto keeps welterweight title with quick KO of Hernandez. *Las Vegas Review-Journal* (November 18). Available at http://www.lvrj.com/sports/berto-keeps-welterweight-title-with-quick-ko-of-hernandez-110930999.html (last accessed May 16, 2012).
Chamoun-Nicolas, H. and R. D. Hazlett. 2008. *Negotiate like a Phoenician*. Kingwood, TX: KeyNegotiations.
Kram, M. 1975. Lawdy lawdy he's great. *Sports Illustrated* (October 13) 43(15): 20-27.

Rafael, D. 2010. Cotto overcomes Foreman, bizarre night. *ESPN.com* (June 9), available at http://sports.espn.go.com/sports/boxing/columns/story?columnist=rafael_dan&id=5256515 (last accessed May 16, 2012).

Samaco, M. L. 2009. Carlos Padilla, Jr. – The greatest Filipino international referee. *PhilBoxing.com* (April 12), available at http://philboxing.com/news/column-1146-23385.html (last accessed May 16, 2012).

Thomas, K. W. and R. H. Kilmann. 1974. *The Thomas-Kilmann conflict mode instrument.* Tuxedo Park, NY: Xicom, Inc.

Young, A. S. 1952. Inside sports. *Jet,* 19 June, 51.

☙ 17 ❧

Adapting to the Adaptive:
How Can We Teach Negotiation
for Wicked Problems?

Jayne Seminare Docherty & Leonard Lira*

Editors' Note: This chapter picks up where the "wicked problems team" left off in Venturing Beyond the Classroom: *with the need to formulate effective teaching strategies for an exceptionally important area of inquiry, in which our understanding is, as yet, far short of perfection. Docherty and Lira are examples of professionals whose students cannot wait for anything close to perfection: both in peacebuilding and in the military, a professional must work with the understanding that is available. It is significant that in their very different environments, Docherty and Lira have been learning from each other, adapting ideas from the military into peacebuilding and vice versa, in order to formulate teaching programs that can work even within the single perspective of either discipline. Their experiments are groundbreaking, and of importance to many other professional fields.*

Introduction
In prior writings in this series (Chrustie et al. 2010; Honeyman and Coben 2010; Docherty 2010; Lira 2010), we and our colleagues in the "wicked problems team" explored the nature of wicked or adaptive

* **Jayne Seminare Docherty** is a professor at the Center for Justice and Peacebuilding at Eastern Mennonite University in Harrisonburg, Virginia. Her first book *Learning Lessons from Waco* was an analysis of the Federal Bureau of Investigation's attempt at hostage negotiation with the Branch Davidian sect, and her subsequent work has frequently involved the intersection and relationships between uniformed forces and civil society, ethnic minorities, and religious groups. Her email address is jayne.docherty@gmail.com. **Leonard Lira** is a Lieutenant Colonel in the U.S. Army and an assistant professor in the Department of Joint, Interagency, and Multinational Operations of the Command and General Staff College at Fort Leavenworth, Kansas. His email address is leonard.lira@us.army.mil.

problems and the challenges of using negotiation to deal with such problems. We drew the concepts from two different sources, which use different terms, as part of our attempts to understand our experiences working in complex conflict situations. We will use wicked and adaptive interchangeably. We will also discuss an important recent book by Peter Coleman and his colleagues (2011; see also *Playing the Percentages in Wicked Problems*, chapter 20 in this volume), which uses concepts from chaos and complexity theory to explain intractable conflicts better; these we consider to be one form of a wicked or adaptive problem.

Because the subject matter may be unfamiliar to the reader, we will begin with a degree of recapitulation of the team's 2010 writings. Readers already familiar with this material may wish to skip to page 387. For the purposes of this chapter, the term "wicked" describes problems that exhibit some combination of the following features:

- The problem is ill-defined and resists clear definition as a technical issue, because wicked problems are also social, political, and moral in nature. Each proposed definition of the problem implies a particular kind of solution, and one that is loaded with contested values. Consequently, merely defining the problem can incite passionate conflict.
- Solutions to a wicked problem cannot be labeled good or bad; they can only be considered better or worse, good enough or not good enough. Whether a solution is good enough depends on the values and judgment of each of the parties, who will inevitably assess the problem and its potential solutions from their respective positions within the social context of the problem.
- Every wicked problem is unique and novel, because even if the technical elements appear similar from one situation to another, the social, political, and moral features are context-specific.
- A wicked problem contains an interconnected web of sub-problems; every proposed solution to part or the whole of the wicked problem will affect other problems in the web.

(See generally Rittel and Webber 1973; Ritchey 2005-2008; and Conklin 2005.) This stands in sharp contrast to the nature of problems that the planning profession has labeled "tame." As summarized by Tom Ritchey (2005-2008: 1), a tame problem:

- Has a relatively well-defined and stable problem statement.
- Has a definite stopping point, i.e., we know when a solution is reached.
- Has a solution that can be objectively evaluated as being right or wrong.

- Belongs to a class of similar problems that can be solved in a similar manner.
- Has solutions that can be tried and abandoned.

The concept of an adaptive problem as contrasted with a technical problem is taken from the work of Robert Kegan and Lisa Laskow Lahey (2009). As Kegan and Lahey (2009: 31) have learned through extensive practice, "meeting adaptive challenges requires first an adaptive *formulation* of the problem (i.e., we need to see exactly how the challenge comes up against the current limits of our own mental complexity), and, second, an adaptive *solution* (i.e., we ourselves need to adapt in some way)." Technical problems, while they may be very complicated, do not require that we grapple with naming a new problem clearly and make changes in *ourselves* in order to deal with them.

This is a significant observation, and therefore worth expanding upon. It is a misunderstanding of wicked problems to think they can be tamed by getting the parties to recognize and accept objective information. To illustrate, some of our colleagues asked whether construction contracts for a massive project such as the Big Dig in Boston would constitute a wicked or adaptive problem. They argued that the Big Dig was ill-structured and wicked but became quite tame as the parties learned the requirements for solving the problems they were facing. In response, we offer that if the parties simply needed to gather more information or improve the way they shared information to solve their problem, then it was a difficult technical problem, rather than "wicked." Technical problems can be very complicated; but their complexity is typically diminished through gathering more or better information, or improving shared access to information.

Some problems are both technically complex and wicked: reducing the emissions of greenhouse gases is an example. The development of the necessary technology is complex. But the creation of socio-political, legal and economic systems that will support the development and deployment of such new technologies is definitely a wicked problem, some would say it is a "super wicked" (Levin et al. 2007; Lazarus 2009)[1] In fact, it is an example of the kinds of large-scale systems change problems that we argue require a different understanding of negotiation.

Perhaps negotiation as currently taught and practiced rests on an unconsciously held mental model of conflict as a technical problem. This would help to explain why adaptive or wicked problems have been so little discussed in the arena of negotiation and teaching negotiation, even though parts of the field of conflict resolution have been deeply preoccupied with wicked problems in the form of intractable conflicts.[2]

According to Douglas Noll (2001), an attorney writing on mediate. com, adaptive problems do not fit into the framework of mediation, and we think his claims can also be applied to negotiation. In his words:

> If people recognize the problem and can repeat a well-worked solution, then normal mediation processes are efficient. For example, lawyers who have experience negotiating the settlement of automobile accidents are engaging in technical work. The mediator simply acts as an honest broker to facilitate the distributive negotiation. *There is no adaptive problem because no views, values, behaviors, or assumptions need to be changed.*
>
> In situations that call for adaptive work, however, the parties must *learn their way forward.* This is the work of peace-making, not generic mediation. Even when a peacemaker has some clear ideas about what needs to be done, implementing change often requires serious and substantial adjustments in people's lives. (Emphasis added)

We read Noll's list of sample adaptive problems – "adaptive problems typically involve partnership disputes, turf wars within large organizations, family business conflicts, employment conflicts (harassment and discrimination), marital dissolutions and other relationship or identity conflicts" – as further validation of our claim that such problems are not limited to the unstable and violent contexts where we work. (See the stories by Howard Gadlin and Jamil Mahuad, in particular, in this team's prior effort, Chrustie et al. 2010.)

We presume Noll is talking about problem-focused mediation rather than transformative mediation (Bush and Folger 1994); at least his example of mediating accident claims seems to be framed in a problem-focused manner. Readers who advocate for transformative mediation have likely already balked at Noll's observations. We urge them not to disengage from our argument on this basis. While we see transformative mediation as one effort to include personal and relational change in the mediation process, in our view it misses the mark for grappling with complex wicked problems. Transformative mediation focuses on personal and relational transformation without discussing how such transformations actually alter the problem at hand.[3]

In a similar vein, we pondered whether Noll's idea of "learning their way forward" applied only to alterations in the parties' subjective views and attitudes rather than alterations in their understanding of objective variables. We concluded that this is not actually a helpful question, for the same reason that Bush and Folger's transformative mediation model misses the mark. *The concept of a wicked problem rests on a view of the world that claims there is no neat and clear distinction between so-called objective variables and our so-called subjective understanding of them.* Or, to put it differently, wicked problems coalesce around our socially negotiated collective answers to five worldviewing – yes worldviewing a verb, not worldview a noun – questions:

- What is real?
- How is what we consider real organized?
- What is valuable (not valuable) about what we deem real?
- What constitutes authentic knowledge?
- What should we do? (Docherty 2001: 52)

In that respect, wicked or adaptive problems are deeply structured by the *meaning-making processes* that the parties employ to organize the world and respond to it in ways they deem effective and proper.

Our Context: Our Work

In our work, the wicked problems we deal with are also called intractable conflicts. Until the publication of Coleman's (2011) book *The Five Percent: Finding Solutions to Seemingly Impossible Conflicts*, most researchers focused on finding the root source or essence of intractable conflicts. By Coleman's count, the literature identifies fifty-seven (!) root causes of intractable conflicts. Coleman and his colleagues took an adaptive approach to intractable conflicts when they shifted the focus from finding *the* cause to seeing intractable conflicts as a system.

> As soon as one looks more deeply into the collection of fifty-seven factors, which are each *the* source of intractability, it becomes clear that there is something even *more basic* that intractable conflicts seem to share. These essences, all fifty-seven of them, are often connected to one another in a very particular way. They tend to be linked in such a way that they *support and reinforce* one another. In other words, they function like a system: one complicated, well-oiled system. That is their essence (Coleman 2011: 35).

Once this idea is written down, it is difficult not to say, "Well, of course! Intractable conflicts are systems and they require a systems approach! Perhaps our episodic- or encounter-focused mediation and negotiation practices can't deal with the whole system!"

But it took Coleman and his colleagues at the International Project on Conflict and Complexity fifteen years of conducting *research* and gathering *evidence* in order to develop a robust new view of the intractable conflict problem. In this work, they were assisted by peacebuilding *practitioners* who have been tackling conflicts as complex systems – without the benefit of an adequately negotiated language for talking about conflict systems – for at least thirty years. And their new explanation, their adaptive way of looking at intractable conflicts[4], will probably flourish because it will be used by peacebuilding practitioners and by *educators* in peacebuilding programs, such as the one at Eastern Mennonite University's Center for Justice and Peacebuilding, where Jayne divides her time between teaching and practice.

It is worth noting that Coleman's book was developed, in his own words, by "a motley crew: an unlikely mix of social psychologists, an anthropologist, an astrophysicist, complexity scientists, conflict specialists, and peacemakers" (Coleman 2011: xi). In other words, to even *conceive* of a new way of thinking about the problems presented by intractable conflicts, the world of academia had to break with some of its own established practices, including the propensity to work in disciplinary silos, the attitude that true knowledge comes from pure research which should then be used to inform practice, and a tendency to force faculty members to choose between "pure" and "applied" research. Wicked or adaptive problems do indeed require that we *change ourselves* – as practitioners, researchers, educators, and students – if we want to address them effectively.

The next evident problem to be addressed is how those who have developed ways of working with such problems through trial-and-error practice and those who have conducted research that helps explain such problems can effectively teach others to employ various skills, including negotiation, when they encounter wicked or adaptive problems. Perhaps just as important, how do we teach them about the *limitations* of negotiation, and about ways to effectively integrate negotiation activities with other processes when dealing with such problems? Here, we return our attention to the primary focus of the Rethinking Negotiation Teaching project.

Our audience, we presume, will include both practitioners and teachers. In our view, teachers who want to address these problems need first to immerse themselves in the practice of working with them. Fortunately, these sorts of problems are not that uncommon. While Coleman's group is focused primarily on the five percent of conflicts that have become sustained and violent, and while both Gadlin and Mahuad (Chrustie et al. 2010) have engaged in what might be called rather elevated levels of practice, Noll (2001), correctly in our view, points out that the same dynamics are applicable in conflicts very close to home and easily accessible to many practitioners and teachers.

Practitioners, in our experience, improve their practice when they attempt to teach others what they have figured out in practice.

Bridging this practice/teaching divide is probably as important for re-thinking negotiation teaching as was bridging all of the academic/practice divides in order to more accurately describe and explain the dynamics that create Coleman's five-percent problems, or what we have been calling wicked or adaptive problems. Therefore, this chapter and the next two will tack back and forth between discussions of negotiation practice and of the practice of teaching negotiation.

We (the authors) also comprise a motley and unlikely, albeit small, crew.[5] Leonard is a U.S. Army officer approaching negotiation from the field of military arts and science.[6] Jayne is a professor in a peacebuilding program.[7] In addition to teaching negotiation, we both have field experience using negotiation to address complex problems in situations that are unstable. Leonard served two tours in Iraq, including a tour where his primary focus was providing security and reconstruction for Taji, a district in the northern part of the Baghdad province. His unit's two main tasks were to train the Iraqi security forces (police and army) and to assist the local government in "standing up" and operating. Jayne works in Lebanon, Thailand, and Myanmar (Burma), where she teaches and coaches local parties working incrementally and nonviolently to move their societies toward more just, sustainable, and inclusive patterns of social, political, and economic governance.

We have both learned about the limitations of what is typically taught in a negotiation class or training when the context is unstable, the problems are ill defined, the legitimacy of the negotiators is unclear, and the parties have entered Coleman's "landscapes with very strong and coherent attractors for destructive interactions and weaker, less coherent, latent attractors for more constructive types of interactions" (2011: 85). In earlier papers (Docherty 2010; Lira 2010) we used the concept of wicked problems that originated in the field of design and planning (Rittell and Webber 1973) and more recently entered the arena of military sciences (Greenwood and Hammes 2009) as a framework for exploring the disconnect between what we were taught about negotiation and the realities we faced on the ground. We also used the concept of adaptive problems (Kegan and Lahey 2009), which we appreciated because it emphasizes the need for self-reflection and a willingness to change oneself in order to deal with the problem at hand. Our colleague, Calvin Chrustie, who has long experience as a crisis negotiator with the Royal Canadian Mounted Police and as a U.N. peacekeeper, agreed with our ideas about the nature of the problems we were confronting. And Gadlin and Mahuad, who work in less chaotic and less potentially violent settings, agreed with us that wicked problems are more common than is typically acknowledged in the teaching of negotiation (Chrustie et al. 2010). At the conference in Beijing, other project participants, largely those teaching in the field of public policy, supported this view.[8]

Now we are working in our respective domains on ways to teach others how to use negotiation in situations similar to the ones we encountered. Jayne actually has two sets of students – university students in a graduate program, and leaders in Lebanon, Thailand, and Myanmar (Burma). Leonard's students are primarily U.S. nationals, with a few international students from allied countries in the mix, while Jayne's students at the university come from around the world and, of course, her students in other countries are from cultures other than Jayne's home culture.

Most of Leonard's students are mid-career military officers from the United States and allied countries, but his classes also include students from other federal government agencies, such as the departments of State, Justice, Agriculture, and Labor. Jayne's university students range from entry-level to mid-career members of a variety of different professions, including development, education, policing, post-conflict reconstruction and recovery, community organizing, politics, and government. In the field, her "students" are a mix of high-ranking decision-makers and lower-ranking individuals who will be working as staff for political and military leaders of armed groups and newly elected officials in transitional governments.

Leonard's students will most likely be working in situations where they are using negotiation while *also* conducting or authorizing the use of kinetic operations.[9] Some of Jayne's university students will work in the same arenas where Leonard's students operate, but without the capacity to apply – and often with a deep skepticism about the value of – kinetic operations.[10] Some will work in situations where the presence of forces willing and able to use policing force in support of security and stability for the general populace – rather than in support of warlords or powerful groups working on their own behalf – would be a welcome change from the prevailing chaos. Other students will never see direct violence; instead, they will be working to alter conditions of structural violence[11] that leave entire communities in the grip of poverty and truncated life opportunities. These students are dealing directly with deep-rooted, intractable conflicts and with the consequences of structural violence in their own communities and countries.

In spite of these differences, the contexts in which our students work are similar. In those settings, governance systems[12] are typically absent, non-functional, or considered illegitimate by significant parties. Alternatively, there may be competing governance systems vying for legitimacy.[13] Violence – overt or structural – or the threat of violence is a given. The patterns of interaction among the parties are dominated by what Coleman calls negative attractors "made up of many elements from feelings and beliefs to group rules for conflict to national holidays and institutions. These elements are tightly linked through reinforcing feedback loops that intensify and spread the negativity and pull of the conflict over time. Additionally, they possess a set of loops that provides inhibiting feedback, which discourages or prohibits de-escalation or other changes in more constructive directions" (2011: 85). The problems to be addressed usually meet most or all of the criteria for being deemed wicked or adaptive, and many are part of Coleman's five percent (the most intractable conflicts).

In addition to facing similar problems, we are now using the same framework *to design* our courses. Leonard introduced Jayne to David Kolb's "Experiential Learning Model" (ELM), which is widely used at the Army Command and Staff College (see Appendix below for a detailed explanation of ELM).

Jayne was already using participatory teaching processes that elicit the experience and knowledge of the students, but she started using the Kolb model to improve the design of all of her courses and workshops. At this point, Jayne has used ELM and insights about negotiating wicked problems to improve her workshops and the training materials developed in those workshops. At the university, she has used ELM to modify courses that include small elements of negotiation teaching, and she recently designed and taught a course (Narrative Negotiation) that focuses on negotiating wicked or adaptive problems. Her course is described in *Teaching Three-Dimensional Negotiation*, chapter 19 of this volume.

Leonard uses the ELM, somewhat modified from Kolb's theory, in all of the courses he teaches (see Appendix). In his electives, he tries to expand this model to establish a "reflective practicum" method. This method requires his students to work their way through complex problems by conducting sub-group exploration of as many variables of the problem as they can, consolidated group synthesis of those variables, and then group evaluation of the variables from their selected wicked problem, to develop a course of action to engage the problem. Leonard's reflective teaching method will be detailed in *Making it up as You Go*, chapter 18 of this volume.

Based on these experiences, we considered writing a prescriptive paper about how to teach negotiation for wicked problems; it was, in other words, tempting to put up another "product" to compare with the training and education programs we wanted to critique. However, doing so would run counter to one of the biggest lessons from our field experience: *context matters!*

If context matters in the field, then it also matters in the classroom where we are preparing negotiators for the field. It matters who our students are, and it matters where they will be working in the future. This is not just a plea for the development of more complex and field-relevant exercises or cases. Wicked, or adaptive, problems require the development of negotiators with high levels of self-awareness and a willingness to engage in self-change in order to deal with the problem. Negotiators for wicked problems also need to develop a significant capacity for critical and creative thinking about how to support positive changes in the socio-political-economic context within which they are operating.

For these reasons, we think readers will benefit more if we show *the process by which we developed our courses*, as well as the description of the courses. This will reveal where we have similar and divergent ideas about the theories behind negotiating wicked or adaptive problems. It will also help others, who are preparing negotiators for different contexts, to think about how they would design context-appropriate courses and trainings.

In this chapter, we lay out our shared thinking about the ways that negotiating in the context of wicked problems differs from negotiating problems that are more common. Or rather, to be consistent with our own paradigm, we lay out our *current version* of our *socially negotiated understanding* of the ways that negotiating in the context of wicked problems differs from negotiating more common problems. Then we identify suggested goals of negotiation teaching when preparing students to deal with wicked problems. We also explain the ELM method of teaching and some general guidelines for using it to design negotiation courses or training. Finally, we challenge the idea that negotiators can be prepared to deal with wicked problems using only classroom or training room activities. In our view, there is a need for further field-based reflective practicum activities in order to prepare highly skilled negotiators capable of dealing with wicked problems. In the next two chapters (*Making it up as You Go* and *Teaching Three-Dimensional Negotiation*) we respectively describe in greater detail the courses we have developed or are developing to teach our respective students.

A New Framework for Thinking About Negotiation for Wicked Problems

In conflict situations, wicked problems frequently but not always take the form of long-term, intractable conflicts that are typically a multi-dimensional mix of issues *only some of which can be addressed through the transactional negotiation processes currently emphasized in courses and short trainings* (Avruch 2006). As Robert Ricigliano (2006: 56) observes:

> ... it is not that the existing negotiation canon is invalid, but that needs and values cannot, for the most part, be satisfied at the transactional level alone. Rather, values and need-based conflicts are often addressed through the interplay over *time* of progress at the *transactional* level (e.g., specific negotiated outcomes) with changes that occur at the *contextual* level...
>
> Conflicts that involve issues of identity, fundamental values, and/or basic human needs require consideration of two critical contextual elements: structures and social relations between groups in society. Structures refer to the systems and institutions in society that are designed to meet people's basic human needs for identity, security, vitality, and community. These systems and institutions include governance, security, rule of law/human rights, social services (education, healthcare), environmental/natural resources, and media and civil society. Social relations refers to the state of relations between groups in the society, be they based on ethnicity, race, religion, class, clan, etc. It refers to the levels of trust between groups, the lever of inter-group tensions, inter-group perceptions, and the various dynamic interactions between groups (e.g., victim-oppressor, relative deprivation, etc.). *Often the deeper roots of protracted conflicts are in the contextual dimension* (emphasis added).

We would agree with Ricigliano, but we would add that it is a mistake to use the concept of "negotiation" to refer only to transactional (or direct dispute-settlement) activities. We believe that the mental model that dominates negotiation teaching makes it difficult to consider wicked or adaptive problems precisely because the term negotiation is reserved solely for transactional negotiation. It is more helpful to understand transactional negotiations as problem-focused processes that are, themselves, a consequence of *social negotiations*. Parties enter into transactional negotiation through a process of negotiating the following: What is (and is not) a problem suitable for transactional negotiation (Docherty 2001); how to define (or frame) the problem to be negotiated (Caton Campbell and Docherty 2006); the site (dispute domain) in which to negotiate (Miller and Dingwall 2006); which parties have a right to enter into the negotiation process, and how the participants should conduct themselves (what scripts they may or may not use) during negotiation (Stolte, Fine, and Cook 2001). In stable settings, these things may have long since been more-or-less settled, so that the social negotiation is not on most people's minds. In our settings, they are very much "live" issues.

Before proceeding further, we should explain the conceptual foundations of our multi-dimensional model of negotiation. We are reflective practitioners at heart. Our primary concern is effective practice. Consequently, we start with a multi-faceted problem derived from the field. How can negotiation as we currently understand and teach it be used to:

- Help communities and societies deal with problems of violence and instability,
- Help communities and societies move from oppressive systems of governance to more inclusive systems of governance, and
- Help negotiators deal with wicked or adaptive problems more generally?

We have already seen that parties can only deal with wicked or adaptive problems if they change: a) their mental maps of the problem; and b) their understanding of what their future will be like as a result of making the first change. This might be something as relatively non-threatening as altering ideas about construction to accommodate a planetary reality of permafrost. But it might be something as threatening to identity, values, and privilege as altering ideas about their roles, status, and future living arrangements with other individuals or groups.

We (the authors) have been most involved in conflict situations where whole groups of people must engage in processes of social transformation in order to deal with their shared problems. In other words, multiple groups need to shift their collective consciousness so that their reality is refined by consensus (for a quick overview, see http://en.wikipedia.org/wiki/Social_transformation.) Or to put it another way, in the situations where we are working, human communities need to grapple with their usually unspoken and unexamined answers to the five worldviewing questions listed above.

The answers to those questions are found not in formal treatises or doctrines, or at least not only in such documents; they are found primarily in the *lived* answers to questions such as:

- How should men and women interact?
- How should elders and youth relate to one another?
- How should material resources be allocated among diverse communities?
- What is the proper way to "tell the story of our people"?
- What constitutes the good life?

- What kind of evidence is considered valid and reliable when we make truth claims?
- Who gets to participate in collective decision-making and how is collective decision-making done properly?

Even though some aspects of some of these questions (and thousands of other questions like them) can be crafted into problems amenable to transactional negotiation, there is no way to convene a bargaining process to answer these types of questions directly. The answers are lived into, through a variety of processes of communication that we are calling *social negotiations*.

To make sense of our practical questions and our concept of social negotiation, we need to lodge them in a paradigm that fits the questions, a way of understanding the world in which a concept of social negotiation even makes sense. Following Gareth Morgan (1980) and our own experience in practice, we assume multiple paradigms can and do exist simultaneously within disciplines of study and practice. From a top level (alternate realities) perspective, we are clearly operating from a paradigm that focuses on the ways that people individually and in groups *construct* their world, including their personal lives, their shared lives, and their societies. There are many schools

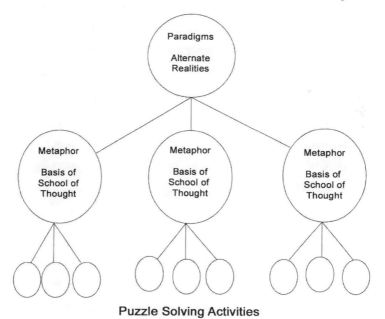

Puzzle Solving Activities

Based on Specific Tools and Texts

Figure 1. Paradigms, metaphors, and puzzle solving: three concepts for understanding the nature and organization of social science (Morgan 1980: 606)

of thought in psychology (see, e.g., Burr 1995; Parker 1998; Gergen 2009) and sociology (see, e.g., Goffman 1959: Berger and Luckman 1966; Giddens 1979) that fall under this broad paradigm. Theory and research in this paradigm focus on the same problem: How do humans, in society, create their worlds and themselves? It is no accident that our teaching methodology is grounded in the social constructivist learning theories of Lev Vygotsky (1978: 1986) and the transformative pedagogy of Paolo Freire (2009).

Social constructionists have their internal (intra-paradigm) squabbles about whether the real focus should be on small group interaction, or on the interactions between individuals or primary groups and larger social structures. We would say: *Both are important; we want to know how micro (individual) level, meso (group) level, and macro (social) level changes can be coordinated to have peace writ large (Anderson and Olson 2003) effects.* Social constructionists argue about whether individuals are constrained or empowered by the structures in which they interact. From our experience, we would say: *Both, and the really interesting question is how people use their opportunities to alter the pattern of constraints and empowerment for themselves and others.* Social constructionists debate whether the engine of change is primarily human agency or environmental forces. We would say: *Some of each, and the interesting question for a practitioner is whether we put our energy toward empowering the agents or shaping the environment to promote the desired changes.*

It should be obvious by now that we are pragmatists. As such, we prefer to start our conversation at the middle level of metaphor rather than the top level of paradigm. According to Morgan (1998), who proposed seven metaphors for organizations, *"all* organization and management theory and practice is based on images, or metaphors, that lead us to understand situations in powerful yet *partial* ways" (1998: 358). Morgan identifies the following metaphors for organizations: machine, organism, brain, culture, political system, psychic prison, process, and system of domination. Similar metaphors are found in sociological research and in other forms of practice including our own fields of the military arts and peacebuilding. Each metaphor is interesting and *partially* accurate, but more important; each metaphor is *useful* in its own way (See Gadlin, Schneider, and Honeyman 2006). Morgan argues that an effective leader learns to use multiple metaphors "to 'read' and understand what is happening in an organization" (Morgan 1998: 251). We would make the same claim for anyone working with conflict and with parties in a conflict.

When facing a wicked problem or an intractable conflict we find it most helpful to use the metaphor of society as an emergent system.[14] The word emergent is going to show up a lot in these chapters.

Sometimes we use it to describe an unfolding and unpredictable process of change. But when we say society is an emergent system, we are using technical language from the study of chaos and complexity theory, sometimes known as the study of self-organizing, adaptive systems. We are applying that technical language to society in a metaphorical manner to illuminate aspects of society that need attention in order to deal with an adaptive problem.

The basic building blocks of a self-organizing, adaptive system are agents, schema, and simple rules. Agents in an emergent system can be anything, as long as they are able to follow simple rules and make "choices" based on information coming from their environment. Some examples of agents in emergent systems are: insects, slime mold, birds, fish, or human beings (individually or in groups).[15] Simple rules guide the choices of the agents and "schema are mental templates that define how reality is interpreted and what are appropriate response[s] for . . . given stimuli" (Dooley 1996: 3) – in other words, which rules to apply in this case. Birds in flocks or fish in schools might have the following rules: stay close together, but not too close, move toward food, and flee from predators. The resulting emergent systems are flocks of birds or schools of fish that swoop through the sky or the water as if they have a shared mind.

The big difference between insects, slime mold, fish or birds and human beings, is the fact that "man is the symbol-using (symbol-making, symbol-misusing) animal" (Burke 1966: 16). Burke goes on to say man [sic] is the "inventor of the negative (or moralized by the negative), separated from his natural condition by instruments of his own making, goaded by the spirit of hierarchy (or moved by the sense of order), and rotten with perfection" (1966: 16). In other words, human emergent systems differ from the emergent systems of fish, birds and slime mold because human beings are capable of making value-based choices – and engaging in values-based disagreements – about what is good or right.

The central point we are making here is this: Human beings are active, creative participants who construct their social world, not passive, conforming objects of socialization. Individually and in groups, they have the ability to accept, challenge, and/or renegotiate the rules and roles that are sustained by cultural norms, organizations, and institutions. In emergent terms, they can *renegotiate* the schema or mental templates *and* the rules by which they operate *and* the purpose or goal of the larger system. This renegotiation can be a messy process, but it is often so gradual as to escape notice. During both positive periods of rapid change (e.g., moving from war to peace) and negative periods of such change (e.g., dealing with the consequences of a massive natural disaster), however, the problem of social negotiation rises to our attention.

In this way, our metaphor of society as an emergent system plus our observations of what happens to those emergent systems during times of turmoil leads us to a multi-dimensional understanding of negotiation that we posit is a more accurate description of the breadth and depth of negotiation as a lived social reality. *Social negotiation* is used, consciously or not, continuously to constitute and sustain or modify the *context,* including dispute domains and the rules and roles that guide participants in a transactional negotiation.[16] *Dispute domain negotiation* is used to frame specific problems and locate them in a particular socio-cultural setting where they can be negotiated using (culturally shaped) *transactional negotiation* processes.

Figure 2 reminds us to consider all three interlocking types of negotiation. Problems become wicked, in part, because the three types of negotiation become disconnected from each other. This happens when the views, values, behaviors or assumptions about when, where and how to negotiate specific problems are no longer supported by a negotiated social order that enjoys adequate legitimacy, or when shared assumptions about what is negotiable or who is allowed to negotiate fall apart. Problems also arise when the results in one negotiation create negative feedback that entrenches rather than resolves conflict in another domain. The results of transactional negotiations sustain or modify the results of social negotiation, including the legitimacy (or lack thereof) of dispute domains. Social negotiations can create new dispute domains, delegitimize existing dispute domains and even overthrow or negate prior agreements achieved through transactional negotiation. Carefully selected transactional negotia-

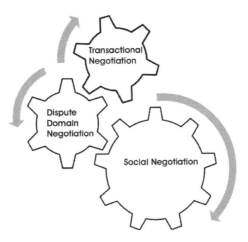

Figure 2: Interconnected Types of Negotiation

tions can be used to alter the socially negotiated order in positive directions, but carelessly or malevolently chosen transactional negotiations can throw societies into turmoil.

Most negotiation courses or training focus in detail on transactional negotiation, perhaps focus marginally on dispute domain negotiation, and typically focus not at all on social negotiation. This limited focus *may* work just fine for some types of conflicts. Nevertheless, as we suggested above, many more cases than commonly thought may require simultaneous attention to the three types of negotiation. Certainly, the kinds of problems we (Leonard and Jayne) have dealt with in the field demanded a multi-dimensional approach to negotiation, and we are now trying to figure out how to teach others to take this approach. Following Ricigliano, we do not question the validity of the current canon of negotiation topics and practices, but we do question their *adequacy* for dealing with wicked problems.

One of the first things negotiators need to learn when dealing with wicked or adaptive problems is that the overall problem cannot and will not be altered *only* or perhaps even *primarily* through transactional negotiations. In the words of Ambassador John McDonald,

> [t]here is no such thing as an 'intractable' conflict. To obtain positive results, the following are necessary ingredients at the government and citizen levels: building trust, demonstrating goodwill, deploying mutual peacebuilding skills, and having profound dedication to creating peace (2006:721).

As a pioneer with Louise Diamond of multi-track diplomacy (1996), Ambassador McDonald was one of the first to recognize that peace comes to a conflicted society not primarily from top-level peace negotiations, but from sustained multi-dimensional engagement of the entire society. Our concept of social negotiation builds on this multi-track tradition with an added emergent systems orientation to social structures and relationships, as constantly under negotiation through myriad formal and informal interactions. Social negotiations *may* improve relationships so that people can engage in dispute domain negotiations to identify or create legitimate arenas for dealing with the problems that have been identified by the *people* as most important for altering their social systems and relationships in directions *they* deem positive. Engaging *consciously* in this process is a good description of peacebuilding.

Ambassador McDonald adds that obtaining funds for this kind of work is the most difficult element. We would add, however, that coordinating other activities with transactional negotiations is another significant problem. *Insofar as we inadvertently teach negotiators to ignore*

the relationship between transactional negotiation and social and dispute do-
main negotiations, our students and we (teachers of negotiation) may be part of
the problem and not part of the solution in cases of complex conflict.

Here is a short list of some of the problems that we have seen
when transactional negotiation is used inappropriately in relation to
adaptive or wicked problems.

- The problem to be negotiated is poorly chosen; it is of interest only to a small group of parties or it is imposed by outside
  actors.
- The framing of the problem is not inclusive; any agreement
  reached will benefit some parties and harm others, thereby
  further exacerbating underlying social, political, or economic
  imbalances.
- The dispute domain being used is considered illegitimate by
  some parties or by their constituents; any agreement emerging from that domain will be considered illegitimate.
- The negotiators are disconnected from the people; everyone
  at the table is part of an elite segment of society with its own
  interests in maintaining a problematic status quo ante.

In short, transactional negotiations done poorly can make the overall
problem far worse than it was before the negotiations. Other activities must be used prior to, in tandem with, and subsequent to negotiations *if the transactional negotiations are going to have a positive effect on*
the larger problem (Docherty 2005: 2010). Negotiators do not need to
be experts in all of the "tools" that are used to transform complex
conflicts, but they do need to know that other tools exist; they need
to be willing to learn *in situ* which tools are needed prior to, during,
and after transactional negotiations; and they need to learn how to
coordinate their activities with those of others working on the conflict
(Brown et al. 2004).

Adaptive problems, by definition, require that the parties change
themselves in order to deal with the problem. Because we are talking about complex social conflicts, the changing of self is, therefore,
necessarily *group change,* not just personal changes by key players. This
makes the relationship between at-the-table and behind-the-table
negotiations more complicated than is usually understood. Jayne's
experience with armed resistance/liberation groups indicates that the
"set of loops that provides inhibiting feedback, which discourages or
prohibits de-escalation or other changes in more constructive directions" (Coleman 2011: 85) operate at the group level as well as the
individual level. These loops are operationalized through organizational norms, procedures, and codes of silence that lock members into
a "groupthink" that is impervious to available information that would

question established views, ideas, or policies. The high in-group bonding forged through years or even decades of struggle makes it difficult for individuals to challenge the established group norms, rules, and conflict strategies. Structural factors such as an inability to leave the territory controlled by the group and risk factors such as an inability to protect family members from possible reprisals from others in their own movement or organization perpetuate the larger conflict by obstructing reality-based thinking and creativity.[17] Jayne has not worked directly with the government side of the conflict, but she has heard from colleagues working with those parties that the same dynamics are at play.

We are talking here about complex negotiations embedded inside complex negotiations, as each party adjusts its own sense of identity, purpose, goals, and (frequently) internal power dynamics and organizational structures. Within each party, there is usually an internal struggle between moderates, who want to negotiate, and hardliners who prefer competitive (even combative) strategies (see Honeyman 2006). In this context, a successful transactional negotiation about a carefully chosen smaller issue *can* be part of a confidence-building process that helps the moderates in all of the parties build constituencies strong enough to support bigger negotiations and resilient enough to endure the setbacks that are an inevitable part of dealing with a complex problem. In this situation, negotiators must become adept at analyzing the structural, cultural, and relational dimensions of the behind-the-table negotiations of all of the parties (see Caton Campbell and Docherty (2006) for a sample case, and Docherty and Caton Campbell (2006) for the behind-the-table negotiation issues related to that case).

Our proposed multi-dimensional framework for understanding negotiation necessarily links to a dynamic understanding of culture that goes well beyond the do's and don'ts list that all too often gets used in negotiation trainings. We agree with Kevin Avruch (2004: 393) that trying

> to learn about another culture from lists of traits and customs is akin to trying to learn English by memorizing the OED: all vocabulary, no grammar. This method is particularly ill suited if what one is trying to master in another culture is a dynamic process to begin with – a process such as negotiation.

We would take the culture problem a step further. There are no culturally neutral individuals who enter into another culture; negotiation is *always* a cultural encounter, and one's own culture is always a part of the equation. (See, e.g., Goh, et al., *As We See It* and Stulberg,

Kwon, and McCormick, *How Different is "Different,"* chapters 5 and 6 in this volume.) Connecting the problem of culture to the necessity for self-change as part of dealing with adaptive problems, we have concluded that negotiators need to become symmetrical anthropologists (Docherty 2004) capable of observing culture (their own and others') in action. This implies that we must teach negotiation in a manner that involves students in self-reflection, and not just the mastery of skills.

Rethinking Negotiation Teaching Objectives and Methods

Once we know what students need to learn, we can articulate the learning outcomes/objectives/ goals (Gagne et al. 2004) for a course, for a workshop, or for a curriculum. We will say more in the next chapters about whether it is possible to use single courses or workshops to prepare negotiators for wicked or adaptive problems.

When teaching adult students, the goals need to be concrete, practical, and applicable to real problems recognized by the students. Broadly speaking, our goal is to educate negotiators capable of dealing with the kinds of problems we and others have encountered in the field. When we make that broad goal more concrete, we identify the following learning outcomes:

- Students will be able to transfer core negotiation skills (many of them taught in current negotiation courses or trainings) to new, complex, and evolving situations.
- Students will be able to think critically and creatively about the role and limitations of transactional negotiation as a tool for dealing with wicked problems.
  - They will be able to identify and prioritize transactional negotiable problems that will help alter the wicked or adaptive problem in positive directions.
  - They will be able to recognize elements of the problem that require other interventions that support a social renegotiation of relationships and structures.
  - They will be able to coordinate transactional *and* social negotiation activities.
  - They will be able to identify available dispute domains, articulate the strengths and weaknesses of each domain option, and make coherent choices about when, where, and how to negotiate specific issues that drive the larger conflict.

- Students will be able to manage the ongoing information gathering and analysis processes necessary to negotiate effectively in a changing context.
- Students will be able to manage the negotiation process while it is in progress, and they will be prepared to *alter* the negotiation process as necessary given changes in the broader context.

The first objective on the list above is a problem for all negotiation teachers, whether they are focused on wicked problems or not. According to Michael E. Roloff, Linda L. Putnam, and Lefki Anastasiou (2003: 823) few programs actually assess whether training increases participants' knowledge or their ability to apply that knowledge to new situations. By transfer, we mean that a negotiator is able to take a concept or skill and apply the underlying principles of that concept or skill to an entirely new situation. The new situation may be related to the situation used in the classroom or training – in other words, it may be in the same general domain of practice – or it may be a situation quite different from the one used in teaching. To be classified as new it must be distinctive enough to test the ability of the negotiator to do two things. First, she must recognize patterns of difference and similarity, in order to make judgments about the applicability of the knowledge gained in the classroom to this situation. Then she must make adjustments in the application of the knowledge and skills to suit the new situation.

The ability to transfer negotiation knowledge to new situations is predicated on the critical and creative cognitive skills of the negotiator. Roger Fisher, William Ury, and Bruce Patton make this clear in their third step for *Getting to Yes* methodology. They indicate that negotiators need to "invent" options (Fisher, Ury, and Patton 1991: 56–80). However, they warn that the creative thinking required for this is stymied by "judging prematurely, searching for a single answer, assuming that the negotiators' pie is fixed in supply, and leaving to the opponent the solution of his or her problems" (1991: 57). They offer four prescriptions to invent creative options: "separate the act of inventing options from the act of judging them; broaden the options on the table rather than look for a single answer; search for mutual gains; and invent ways of making their decisions easy" (1991: 60). Their prescription indicates that critical and creative thinking applied to negotiators' skills is necessary to assess each new situation and develop the best creative course of action; therefore, it needs to be developed in the student and should be a desired outcome of any course on negotiation.

We have already discussed above why students need to be able to coordinate negotiation with other activities when dealing with a wicked problem. If one accepts the concept of wicked problems and the uniqueness of each situation as well as the argument that every action we take in relation to the problem alters the situation, then it is clear that negotiators need to master skills for continuous information gathering, assessment and adaptation of their negotiation strategy. (See Calvin Chrustie's analysis, in *Playing the Percentages in Wicked Problems*, in this volume, of the Bosnian conflict of the 1990s.) Negotiators require the ability to formulate and adapt a negotiation strategy based on changes to the context of the situation in which they are using their skills. Given that the contexts in which negotiators practice their skills are imbued with human variables, causing an unpredictable reaction for every action taken, the negotiator needs to possess the ability to assess and modify negotiation strategies developed at the beginning of her intervention.

While the development of both transferable knowledge and conceptual problem solving abilities is necessary for successful negotiators, adaptive problems demand much more. Not only must a negotiator possess certain domain knowledge of negotiation skill application, and the ability to conceptualize solutions based on that domain knowledge, but she should also be able to manage the implementation of those solutions. She must develop the ability to apply judgment to negotiation situations that require decisions on the selection of a reasonable course of action. The inability to do so could lead to failed negotiations where all other variables would indicate that it should succeed (Neale and Bazerman 1985: 49).

Given these learning outcomes, we are designing courses that combine experiential and reflective methodologies. Most negotiation courses focus on the acquisition of skills rather than reflection on one's own assumptions about negotiation. In other words, in our educational and practitioner experience, we have either received experiential (skills focused) or reflective training or education, but rarely both together. We think this gap needs to be closed to prepare negotiators to deal with wicked or adaptive problems.

In researching how to do this efficiently and effectively, we did not find much help in the educational research literature or negotiation's academic literature. Consequently, we offer in the next two chapters examples of methods, both experiential and reflective, that we have adopted in teaching several courses where negotiation skills were being conveyed. Both of us believe that negotiation skills are central enough to our practice that they should be incorporated into other courses, and not taught only in specialized negotiation courses.

So some of the techniques we describe have been incorporated into other courses, while some are taught in a full negotiation course.

Rethinking Negotiation Teaching through Experiential Learning Methods

As a way of organizing the development of experiential teaching methods, we have both used an experiential method employed by the U.S. Army Command and General Staff College (CGSC). This method is adapted from David Kolb's "Experiential Learning Model" (ELM) composed of five steps:

- Concrete experience;
- Publish and process;
- Generate new information;
- Develop; and
- Apply.

Kolb developed the ELM based on the work of the Russian cognitive theorist L.S. Vygotsky, who theorized, "learning from experience is the process whereby human development occurs" (Kolb 1983: xi). According to Kolb, learning is best stimulated by creating a "dialectic tension and conflict between the immediate concrete experience" and contemplation of the analytical theory that addresses the phenomena that the participating student is experiencing (1983: 9). To Kolb, this conflict between experience and theory was the "central dynamic in the process of experiential learning" (1983: 9–10).

The faculty and staff development division at the CGSC teach the faculty to employ Kolb's ELM in their entire curriculum (U.S. Department of the Army 2008). As can be seen in the Appendix, the way in which CGSC operationalizes the model takes into account all possible learning styles, by having the lesson or course flow in a pattern that uses an approach from each of the learning modes.

Kolb identified essentially four different modes of learning, which exhibit four distinct abilities of students: concrete experience abilities, reflective observation abilities, abstract conceptualization abilities, and active experimentation abilities (1983: 30). The concrete experience ability is an orientation toward being involved in experiences and dealing with immediate human situations in a personal way. The operative skill in this ability is to feel, versus think; thus, it influences the affective domain of human knowledge. The reflective observation ability orients on understanding the meaning of ideas and situations through observation and describing them without bias. The emphasis is on observation of how events are occurring in the observed environment and developing an intuitive understanding, versus figuring out what is the exact action required to make events occur. The abstract conceptualization capability orients on using logic, ideas, and concepts to think through the issues, versus the use of feelings. This ability emphasizes theory building over intuitive understanding. The active experimentation ability orients on actively influencing the environment through practical application, to see what occurs, instead of passively reflecting on what is observable in order to gain an understanding (1983: 68–69).

It is important to note that while Kolb identifies these four learning modes as distinct, they do not necessarily exhibit themselves distinctly in individuals. In fact, individual students can exhibit a combination of each of these abilities in varying amounts. Kolb attempts to map this by utilizing a learning style inventory, developed to categorize how much of each learning mode an individual may exhibit (at the time of the inventory.) The inventory is presented as a multiple-choice instrument which, when graded, will list how much each of the capabilities listed above are exhibited in an individual. Depending on how this maps out for each individual, their basic learning style is identified and labeled. For example, if the individual student exhibits the preponderance of capabilities that are characterized as abstract conceptualization and active experimentation, Kolb labels their learning style as convergent. Convergent learners seek practical application of theory to experience in order to solve problems. They reason deductively and prefer technical tasks to interpersonal tasks, thus demonstrating control in the expression of their emotions.

If the individual student exhibits a preponderance of capabilities of concrete experience and reflective observation, Kolb labels this learning style as diverging. This learning style is the polar opposite of the converger. A divergent learner will intuitively notice relationship patterns. Divergers will look for multiple alternatives to understanding issues and solving problems by viewing concrete experiences through many perspectives. They tend to be imaginative and emotion-oriented.

If the student exhibits a preponderance of capabilities associated with concrete experience and active experimentation, then Kolb labels that individual learning style as an accommodating learning style. This style is characterized as learning best by doing things, adaptable to change, and impatient with waiting to intuitively solve a problem. Accommodators will learn by trial and error.

In polar opposite to this learning style is the student who demonstrates a preponderance of capabilities associated with abstract conceptualization and reflective observation. Kolb labels the student with those types of capabilities as an assimilator. Assimilators are comfortable with building theoretical models to understand issues and problems. They will reason inductively and are less concerned with humans or their emotions, and more focused on abstract ideas (see Figure 3 below).

Based on the identification of these learning styles, Kolb adopted his experiential learning model. Kolb based his learning model on two continua that form a quadrant out of combining the polar opposites, in the learning modes that create the learning styles:

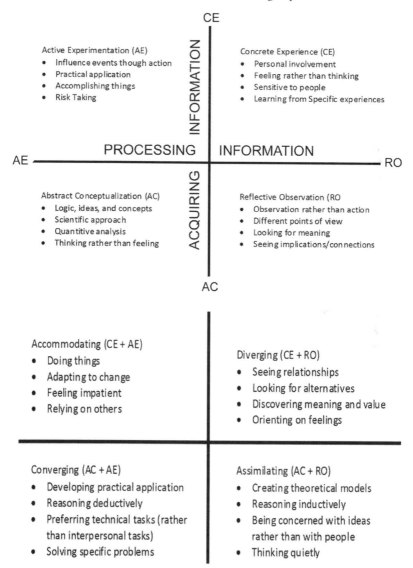

Figure 3: Kolb's Experiential Learning Model.

Crucially, ELM *reverses the order of many negotiation courses*. Rather than providing input on a theory or idea (for example claiming value and creating value) and then putting the students into a role-play, game or simulated activity to practice applying the concept, we start with experience. The experience used in the classroom needs to be designed with enough complexity to engage the students, and it needs to be recognizable as an "authentic" field-based problem. This argues against the development of generic role-plays or games for teaching negotiation, and it argues for the development of rich, complex activities that are suited for particular groups of students. In chapters 18 and 19, we will describe in greater detail some strategies for creating powerful experiential activities for a variety of students without having to create the activities anew for each group.

There is no right or wrong answer during the experiential phase of ELM. The focus is on shared discovery. Cultivating an attitude of wonder and discovery during the experiential phase – what John Paul Lederach, Reina Neufeldt, and Hal Culbertson (2007) refer to as "re-mystifying practice" – is critically important. It sets up the basis for double-loop learning (Argyris and Schön 1978) or reflecting on our theories-in-use, which Chris Argyris and Donald Schön also call our "strategies for getting what we want." Wonder and discovery allow the students to uncover their own attitudes, assumptions, beliefs and patterns of behavior – some of which they will need to "unlearn" in order to become better negotiators of wicked problems. (See Scott Peppet and Michael Moffitt (2006) for more on learning and unlearning in negotiation pedagogy.) Unlearning is a significant feature of reflective learning and professional development; we will have more to say about this in chapters 18 and 19.

Reflective learning continues during the "publish and process" phase when students and teachers step back from the experience and unpack what happened. Who did what in what order? Why did they do that? What does that mean for the way we are thinking about the problem at hand? What worked well? What did not work well? Where did we see disagreements about how to proceed? What do these disagreements reveal about assumptions and attitudes? How did our combined assumptions and attitudes promote or prevent successfully defining a negotiable problem, and locating a dispute domain in which we could negotiate?

Only after the students have experienced a challenging problem and discovered what they can from that problem does the instructor step in with new information. She adds ideas, theories and research that might shed new light on what just transpired during the experiential and publish/process phases. In this way, students are able to connect a concrete, lived experience to the new ideas.[18]

Reversing the input of new ideas and experiential learning process is supported by the new brain research and the cognitive sciences. It is a concrete expression in the classroom of a paradigm shift that has led a growing number of researchers to

> the conviction that the proper units of knowledge are primarily *concrete,* embodied, incorporated, lived; that knowledge is about situatedness; and that the uniqueness of knowledge, its historicity and context, is not a 'noise' concealing an abstract configuration in its true essence. The concrete is not a step toward something else: it is both where we are and how we get to where we will be (Varela 1999: 7).

Looking ahead to the students' anticipated real-world situations, the group (students and instructor) contemplates what it would look like to apply the new learning in situ. Together they are able to anticipate and plan for the transfer of learning to real-world settings. We recommend that students have at least two and preferably three or more opportunities to work with complex cases. In each experience, they will adapt and apply what they have already learned to a new case and *reflect on the process* by which they achieved (or did not achieve) a transfer of learning from one experience to another. These subsequent classroom experiences are opportunities for the instructor to observe whether and how students are applying what they are learning. After that, the instructor can give each student detailed, direct feedback about where she needs to focus her personal development as a negotiator. Students can also give *each other* feedback, which cultivates attitudes and practices needed to work effectively on the teams that are a necessary feature of addressing wicked problems.

Conclusion

We have two primary conclusions, based on our experience as practitioners and educators. First, students of negotiation need to learn about the relationship between transactional negotiation and social and dispute domain negotiations. Failing to appreciate that relationship in cases of complex conflict may contribute to the social problems they intend to help solve. Second, using an experiential- and reflective- based method of teaching negotiation students about this relationship has been one way we as educators have tried to do this.

We both believe that the ELM approach to classroom teaching will yield negotiators who are better prepared to deal with wicked or adaptive problems. However, we do not think this is enough to achieve that goal. As a matter of principle as well as efficacy, we believe it is misleading to say that participants can learn what they need to know to negotiate wicked problems in a single class or workshop. (See Crampton and Tsur, *Negotiation Stands Alone*, in this volume, as to some possible career implications of the sheer amount of learning involved. Note also that Tsur's key examples are of highly experienced military officers.) This does not mean that we are arguing that negotiators require a lot of formal education in order to deal with wicked problems. Jayne has used these teaching techniques successfully in workshops with participants without significant formal education.[19] But getting participants to actually transfer what they have learned in the safety of a workshop to their far more tumultuous and risk-laden lives requires continued coaching and support. Nor do we anticipate students taking a single semester-long or intensive course on negotiating adaptive problems to successfully apply their new knowledge to real cases. We believe courses or workshops need to be followed up with real-world practice accompanied by coaching or mentoring and/ or opportunities to apprentice with more experienced negotiators. This will also be addressed in more detail in chapter 19 (and again, in Crampton and Tsur, *Negotiation Stands Alone*).

Notes

[1] Generally speaking, we see complex engineering and technical problems as wicked when they also involve adjusting deeply held beliefs and/or entrenched patterns of human behavior, and their social, political, and legal institutions. It is probably more helpful to think about technical problems and wicked problems as occupying a continuum, with some grey area in between where a problem might be "sort of" wicked.

[2] For an earlier effort to unpack unspoken mental models that influence the way we approach negotiation, see Jayne's chapter "The Unstated Models in our Minds" in *The Negotiator's Fieldbook* (Schneider and Honeyman 2006).

[3] Narrative mediation (Winslade and Monk 2000; Winslade and Monk 2008), on the other hand, focuses on both personal change and the way that changing our story about a situation opens up new options for living more constructively into a transformed future. We see promise in this approach; Jayne is developing her course based on narrative practices and it will be called Narrative Negotiation.

[4] It is not just these problems that are adaptive; the solutions also require a complex and adaptive set of structures. See also Calvin Chrustie's focus on development of suitable structures, in *Playing the Percentages in Wicked Problems*, in this volume.

[5] Our "crew" is actually larger than the two authors of this particular chapter. At various times and for different purposes it has included Calvin Chrustie, Chris Honeyman, Howard Gadlin, Jamil Mahuad, David Matz, and Rachel Parish.

[6] Military Arts and Science, as an academic field, could be considered a subset of Political Science or Public Administration as it is taught in the professional military education institutes that are accredited to confer a Master of Military Arts and Sciences academic degree. The U.S. Military's expanded roles in counterinsurgency, peace, and humanitarian operations have caused

the military to question some of its fundamental principles and traditional thinking about its purpose. This has led to a re-examination of professional education methodologies and concepts, to incorporate theories and concepts from other fields such as political science, economics, and anthropology.

[7] The study of peacebuilding may be seen as an outgrowth of the field of conflict analysis and resolution. The concept of peacebuilding and its practices and scope are not well established. See Henning Haugerudbraaten (1998) for an overview of the debates about peacebuilding – what it entails, who does it, and how it is accomplished. Jayne's university program and practice are organized around the following definition:

> Peacebuilding is the set of initiatives by diverse actors in government and civil society to address the root causes of violence and protect civilians before, during, and after violent conflict. Peacebuilders use communication, negotiation, and mediation instead of belligerence and violence to resolve conflicts. . . The ultimate objective of peacebuilding is to reduce and eliminate the frequency and severity of violent conflict. See http://en.wikipedia.org/wiki/Peacebuilding.

While there is a growing role for peacebuilding professionals, peacebuilding activities are usually undertaken in conjunction with other professions such as development, education, the pursuit of justice through formal and informal means, trauma healing, leadership training, organizational development and governance reform.

[8] Sanda Kaufman, in particular, noted that so-called wicked problems (though she did not like that term) are the norm rather than the exception in design and public policy arenas. We agree. However, the fields of public policy and applied peacebuilding have yielded a mix of approaches to these problems, some more useful than others. We particularly appreciate the work of John Forester (1999, 2009), John Paul Lederach (1997), Stephen Daniels and Gregg Walker (2001), Peter Adler and others (2000; 2002). They do not try to impose linear, problem-solving processes on conflicts that are inherently non-linear and emergent. Unfortunately, their practices have not yet penetrated most negotiation classrooms.

[9] "Kinetic operations involve application of force to achieve a direct effect, such as artillery, infantry, aviation, and armored offensive and defensive operations. Non-kinetic operations are those operations that seek to influence a target audience through electronic or print media, computer network operations, electronic warfare, or the targeted administration of humanitarian assistance. It is important to note that many operations do not fall neatly into one category or another. For example, a security patrol may have the power to apply force (a kinetic operation), but over time, if its consistently professional conduct earns it the respect of the local populace, its presence can become a non-kinetic effect – if not a complete operation in itself" (Richter 2009:104). The military profession makes the claim "Among all professions, our calling, the Profession of Arms, is unique because of the lethality of our weapons and our operations."

[10] The growing challenge of civilian peacebuilders working alongside military units in locations of instability has led to increased dialogue about civil-military cooperation. See Robbert Gabrielse (2007) for a discussion of the problems related to coordinating development, diplomacy and defense agencies in the same challenging context. When we add non-governmental organizations (NGOs) to the mix, the problem is even more complicated (Franke, 2006; Gourlay, 2000). This logically leads us to speculate about the need for

cross-training between our students. For now, however, we are each focusing on what it takes to teach our own students how to negotiate wicked or adaptive problems.

[11] The concept of structural violence is commonly ascribed to Johan Galtung (1969). For our purposes the description and explanation of structural violence developed by James Gilligan (1996) is a good summary of the problem. Structural violence is evidenced by "the increased rates of death and disability suffered by those who occupy the bottom rungs of society, as contrasted with the relatively lower death rates experienced by those who are above them." These excess deaths are non-natural; they are a consequence of the stress, shame, discrimination, and denigration that results from lower status.

[12] Governance describes the process of decision-making and the process by which decisions are implemented (or not implemented). The term governance can apply to any group decision-making process and the systems for ensuring implementation of collective decisions. Thus, we can talk about governance in corporations, international organizations (e.g., United Nations, International Monetary Fund, World Bank), national or local political systems, organizations (including civil society organizations and non-governmental organizations or NGOs), faith-based organizations, or traditional societies (e.g., clan-based or tribal systems).

[13] In many parts of the world, people live under multiple governance systems – post-colonial systems, tribal or clan systems, and religious systems – and disputes over the legitimacy of these systems is a constant source of uncertainty and conflict. This is not, however, only a problem in post-colonial societies. Similar disruptions to governance systems can take place in modern bureaucratic settings, for example after a corporate merger. See Docherty (2005) and the work of Walton, Cutcher-Gershenfeld, and McKersie (1994; 1995).

[14] Notice that we value the concept of society as an emergent system because it is useful, not because it is "true" in some ultimate sense. There are other ways of looking at society that are equally accurate and equally interesting and revealing. The real test for a practitioner wanting to deal with a situation is whether a way of thinking about the problem yields insights that can guide action, and whether those actions achieve outcomes deemed to be positive. And as soon as we talk about positive outcomes, we point to the fact that all forms of social practice, including negotiation, are loaded with ethical assumptions. Elsewhere, Jayne has argued that "every negotiation encounter involves social ethics (general societal principles of right and wrong) and not just procedural ethics (typically incorporated into professional codes of conduct)" (Docherty 2010: 499).

[15] See the video on emergence located at http://www.youtube.com/watch?v=gdQgoNitl1g&feature=related (last accessed December 12, 2012).

[16] Individuals or groups with lower social status may be allowed at the table, perhaps even required to be at the table by a rule such as UN 1325, which requires women's participation in negotiations to end armed conflicts. Or they may be prohibited from participating in negotiations on their own behalf. Furthermore, once in the negotiation how they may speak, what they may say, when they may talk, and the personal consequences as a result of their negotiation behaviors are all shaped by socially negotiated norms. See for example Tinsley, Cheldelin, Schneider and Amanatullah (2009) or Bowles and Babcock (2008) regarding the social and economic consequences for women as compared with men when negotiating for compensation in the workplace.

[17] The bad news is that groups and societies locked in these conflicts create fractal patterns that start to permeate all parts of the society. (See Gadlin, Matz, and Chrustie, *Playing the Percentages in Wicked Problems*, chapter 20 in this volume.) Domination and control mechanisms or zero-sum conflict patterns operating at the largest social level are repeated in schools, religious communities, businesses, families, and so on. The good news is that fractal patterns can be disrupted at any level and disruptions in the pattern can cascade over into other areas. This is why Coleman (2011) focuses on "local actionables" (137) and argues we need to "aim to alter patterns, not outcomes" (95). The art of peacebuilding is largely in selecting the domains that are ripe for changing patterns of thinking and acting and knitting those domains together to maximize the spillover effects of change.

[18] Laurence de Carlo (2005) has developed a similar teaching process that indicates that the input of new information, ideas and research need not be strictly sequential. Using a CD, he makes ideas, research, and theories about negotiation available to students during an extended (multi-week) learning process. The students decide whether, what and how much of the material to use. During debrief sessions, the materials are discussed, and students often alter their use of the material in subsequent weeks. In our view, this creates a meta-level learning experience where students are learning to be reflective, creative practitioners capable of sorting through a lot of information "in the moment" – which is what they will need to do in real negotiations. Jayne has done something similar in strategic peacebuilding classes, but the materials she gives students tend to be tools such as manuals for planning interventions rather than summaries of pure research. In workshops with participants working in second languages or participants with minimal formal education, this strategy would need to be significantly modified.

[19] We do not like the mental model of education implied by the word training. Jayne prefers the idea of a workshop, which implies that the participants and the instructors all bring critical information into the process where they engage in shared learning and discovery. Indeed, much of Jayne's thinking presented here and in prior papers on negotiating wicked problems was learned in collaboration with workshop participants in Lebanon, Thailand, and Myanmar. Similarly, Leonard prefers to use the term "practicum" as used by Donald Schön in his 1995 book *Educating the Reflective Practitioner*. Much of Leonard's thinking, similar to Jayne's, is based on experience gained in collaboration with his elective seminar students utilizing a "practicum" or "workshop."

References

Adler, P. S. 2002. Science, politics, and problem solving: Principles and practices for the resolution of environmental disputes in the midst of advancing technology, uncertain or changing science, and volatile public perceptions. *Penn State Environmental Law Review* 10(2): 323-344.

Adler, P. S., R. C. Barrett, M. C. Bean, J. E. Birkhoff, C. P. Ozawa, and E. B. Rudin. 2000. *Managing scientific and technical information in environmental cases: Principles and practices for mediators and facilitators.* Washington, DC: Resolve, Inc., U.S. Institute for Environmental Conflict Resolution, and Western Justice Center Foundation.

Anderson, M. and L. Olson. 2003. Confronting war: Critical lessons for peace practitioners. Cambridge, MA: The Collaborative for Development Action, Inc.

Argyris, C. and D. A. Schön. 1978. *Theory in practice: Increasing professional effectiveness.* San Francisco, CA: Jossey-Bass.

Avruch, Kevin. 2004. Culture as context, culture as communication: Considerations for humanitarian negotiators. *Harvard Negotiation Law Review* 9: 391-407.

Avruch, K. 2006. The poverty of buyer and seller. In *The negotiator's fieldbook: The desk reference for the experienced negotiator,* edited by A. K. Schneider and C. Honeyman. Washington, DC: American Bar Association.

Berger, P. L. and T. Luckman. 1966. *The social construction of reality: A treatise in the sociology of knowledge.* New York: Anchor Books.

Bowles, H. R. and L. Babcock. 2011. *Relational accounts: A strategy for women negotiating for higher compensation.* Available at research.hks.harvard.edu/publications/getFile.aspx?Id=322 (last accessed March 3, 2013).

Brown, J. G., M. Caton Campbell, J. S. Docherty, and N. A. Welsh. 2004. Negotation as one among many tools. *Marquette Law Review* 87(4): 853-860.

Burke, K. 1966. *Language as symbolic action.* Los Angeles, CA: University of California Press.

Burr, V. 1995. *An introduction to social constructionism.* New York: Taylor & Francis Group.

Bush, R. A. B. and J. P. Folger. 1994. *The promise of mediation: responding to conflict through empowerment and recognition.* San Francisco, CA: Jossey-Bass.

Caton Campbell, M. and J. S. Docherty. 2006. What's in a frame? In *The negotiator's fieldbook: The desk reference for the experienced negotiator,* edited by A. K. Schneider and C. Honeyman. Washington, DC: American Bar Association.

Chrustie, C., J. S. Docherty, L. Lira, J. Mahuad, H. Gadlin, and C. Honeyman. 2010. Negotiating wicked problems: Five stories. In *Venturing beyond the classroom: Volume 2 in the rethinking negotiation teaching series,* edited by C. Honeyman, J. Coben, and G. De Palo.. St. Paul, MN: DRI Press.

Coleman, P. T. 2011. *The five percent: Finding solutions to seemingly impossible conflicts.* New York: Public Affairs.

Conklin, J. 2005. Wicked problems and social complexity. In *Dialogue mapping: Building shared understanding of wicked problems,* edited by J. Conklin. New York: Wiley.

Cutcher-Gershenfeld, J. E., R. B. McKersie, and R. E. Walton. 1995. *Pathways to change: Case studies of strategic negotiations.* Kalamazoo, MI: W.E. Upjohn Institute for Employment Research.

Daniels, S. E. and G. B. Walker. 2001. *Working through environmental conflict: The collaborative learning approach.* Wesport, CT: Praeger Publishers.

De Carlo, L. 2005. Accepting conflict and experiencing creativity: Teaching "concertation" using *La Francilienne* CD-ROM. *Negotiation Journal* 21(1):85-103.

Diamond, L. and J. McDonald. 1996. *Multi-track diplomacy: A Systems approach to peace,* 3rd edn. West Hartford, CT: Kumarian Press.

Docherty, J. S. 2001. *Learning lessons from Waco: When the parties bring their gods to the negotiation table*. Syracuse, NY: Syracuse University Press.

Docherty, J. S. 2004. Culture and negotiation: Symmetrical anthropology for negotiators. *Marquette Law Review* 87(4): 711-722.

Docherty, J. S. 2005. *The little book of strategic negotiation: Negotiating during turbulent times*. Intercourse, PA: Good Books, Inc.

Docherty, J. S. 2006. The unstated models in our minds. In *The negotiator's fieldbook: The desk reference for the experienced negotiator*, edited by A. K. Schneider and C. Honeyman.Washington, DC: American Bar Association.

Docherty, J. S. 2010. "Adaptive" negotiation: Practice and teaching. In *Venturing beyond the classroom: Volume 2 in the rethinking negotiation teaching series*, edited by C. Honeyman, J. Coben, and G. De Palo. St. Paul, MN: DRI Press.

Docherty, J. S. and M. Caton Campbell. 2006. Consequences of principal and agent. In *The negotiator's fieldbook: The desk reference for the experienced negotiator*, edited by A. K. Schneider and C. Honeyman. Washington, DC: American Bar Association.

Dooley, K. 1996. Complex adaptive systems: A nominal definition. *The Chaos Network* 8(1): 2-3.

Fisher, R., W. Ury, and B. Patton. 1991. *Getting to yes: Negotiating agreement without giving in*, 2nd edn. New York: Penguin.

Forester, J. 1999. *The deliberative practitioner: Encouraging participatory planning processes*. Cambridge, MA: MIT Press.

Forester, J. 2009. *Dealing with differences: Dramas of mediating public disputes*. New York: Oxford University Press.

Franke, V. 2006. The peacebuilding dilemma: Civil-military cooperation in stability operations. *International Journal of Peace Studies* 11(2): 5-25.

Freire, P. 2009. *Pedagogy of the oppressed*, 30th anniversary edn. New York: Continuum.

Gabrielse, R. 2007. A 3D approach to security and development. *Consortium Quarterly Journal* (VI)2: 64-74.

Gadlin, H., A. K. Schneider, and C. Honeyman. 2006. The road to hell is paved with metaphors. In *The negotiator's fieldbook: The desk reference for the experienced negotiator*, edited by A. K. Schneider and C. Honeyman. Washington, DC: American Bar Association.

Gagne, R. M., W. W. Wager, K. Golas, and J. M. Keller. 2004. *Principles of instructional design*, 5th edn. New York: Wadsworth Publishing.

Galtung, J. 1969. Violence, peace, and peace research. *Journal of Peace Research* 6(3): 167-191.

Gergen, K. J. 2009. *An invitation to social construction*. Newberry Park: Sage.

Giddens, A. 1979. *Central problems in social theory: Action, structure, and contradiction in social analysis*. London: Macmillan.

Gilligan, J. 1996. *Violence: Reflections on a national epidemic*. New York: Vintage Books.

Goffman, E. 1959. *The presentation of self in everyday life*. New York: Doubleday.

Gourlay, C. 2000. Partners apart: Managing civil-military cooperation in humanitarian interventions. *Disarmament Forum*. Available at http://www.unidir.org/pdf/articles/pdf-art131.pdf (last accessed December 12, 2012).

Greenwood, T. C. and T. X. Hammes. 2009. War planning for wicked problems. *Armed Forces Journal*. Available at http://www.armedforcesjournal. com/2009/12/4252237/ (last accessed December 12, 2012).

Haugerudbraaten, H. 1998. Peacebuilding: Six dimensions and two concepts. *African Security Review* 7(6): 17-26.

Honeyman, C. 2006. Using ambiguity. In *The negotiator's fieldbook: The desk reference for the experienced negotiator*, edited by A. K. Schneider and C. Honeyman. Washington, DC: American Bar Association.

Honeyman, C. and J. Coben. 2010. Navigating wickedness: A new frontier in teaching negotiation. In *Venturing beyond the classroom: Volume 2 in the rethinking negotiation teaching series*, edited by C. Honeyman, J. Coben, and G. De Palo. St. Paul, MN: DRI Press.

Kegan, R. and L. L. Lahey. 2009. *Immunity to change: How to overcome it and unlock potential in yourself and your organization*. Boston, MA: Harvard Business School Press.

Kolb, David A. 1983. *Experiential learning: Experience as the source of learning and development*. Upper Saddle River, NJ: Prentice Hall, Inc.

Lazarus, R. 2009. Super wicked problems and climate change: Restraining the present to liberate the future. *Cornell Law Review* 94: 1153-1233.

Lederach, J. P. 1997. *Building peace: Sustainable reconciliation in divided societies*. Washington, DC: United States Institute of Peace.

Lederach, J. P., R. Neufeldt, and H. Culbertson. 2007. Reflective peacebuilding: A planning, monitoring, and learning toolkit. Available at http://www.eldis.org/assets/Docs/43157.html (last accessed December 12, 2012).

Levin, P. K., B. Cashore, S. Bernstein, and G. Auld. 2007. *Playing it forward: Path dependency, progressive incrementalism, and the "super wicked" problem of global climate change*. Paper presented at the International Studies Association Convention, Chicago, IL. February 28-March 3.

Lira, L. 2010. Design: The U.S. Army's approach to negotiating wicked problems. In *Venturing beyond the classroom: Volume 2 in the rethinking negotiation teaching series*, edited by C. Honeyman, J. Coben, and G. De Palo. St. Paul, MN: DRI Press.

Masterman, M. 1970. The nature of a paradigm. In *Criticism and the growth of knowledge*, edited I. Kakatos and A. Musgrave. Cambridge, UK: Cambridge University Press.

McDonald, J. W. 2006. A new future for Kashmir? In *The negotiator's fieldbook: The desk reference for the experienced negotiator*, edited by A. K. Schneider and C. Honeyman. Washington, DC: American Bar Association.

Miller, G. and R. Dingwall. 2006. When the play's in the wrong theater. In *The negotiator's fieldbook: The desk reference for the experienced negotiator*, edited by A. K. Schneider and C. Honeyman. Washington, DC: American Bar Association.

Morgan, G. 1979. Response to Mintzberg. *Administrative Science Quarterly* 24: 137-139.

Morgan, G. 1980. Paradigms, metaphors and puzzle solving in organization theory. *Administrative Science Quarterly* 25(4): 605-622.

Morgan, G. 1998. *Images of organization: The executive edition*. San Francisco, CA: Berrett-Koehler Publishers, Inc.

Neale, M. A. and M. H. Bazerman. 1985. The effects of framing and negotiator over confidence on bargainer behavior. *Academy of Management Journal* 28: 34-49.

Noll, D. 2001. The role of the peacemaker: Adaptive versus technical work. Available at http://www.mediate.com/articles/noll3.cfm (last accessed December 12, 2012).

Parker, I. 1998. *Social constructionism, discourse and realism.* Newberry Park: Sage.

Peppet, S. R. and M. L. Moffitt. 2006. Learning how to learn to negotiate. In *The negotiator's fieldbook: The desk reference for the experienced negotiator*, edited by A. K. Schneider and C. Honeyman. Washington, DC: American Bar Association.

Richter, W. E. 2009. The future of information operations. *Military Review* 89(1): 103-113.

Ricigliano, R. 2006. A three-dimensional analysis of negotiation. In *The negotiator's fieldbook: The desk reference for the experienced negotiator*, edited by A. K. Schneider and C. Honeyman. Washington, DC: American Bar Association.

Ritchey, T. (2005-2008). *Wicked problems: Structuring social messes with morphological analysis.* Swedish Morphological Society. Available at http://www.swemorph.com/ (last accessed December 12, 2012).

Rittell, H. W. J. and M. M. Webber. 1973. Dilemmas in a general theory of planning. *Policy Sciences* 4: 155-169.

Roloff, M. E., L. L. Putnam, and L. Anastasiou. 2003 Negotiation skills. In *Handbook of communication and social interaction skill*, edited by J. Greene and B. Burleson. Mahwah, NJ: Lawrence Erlbaum.

Stolte, J. F., G. A. Fine, and K. S. Cook. 2001. Sociological miniaturism: Seeing the big through the small in social psychology. *Annual Review of Sociology* 27: 387-413.

Tinsley, C. H., S. I. Cheldelin, A. K. Schneider, and E. T. Amanatullah. 2009. Women at the bargaining table: Pitfalls and prospects. *Negotiation Journal*, 25(2): 233-248.

U.S. Department of the Army. 2008. *CGSC "Experiential Learning Model" Job Aid.* Faculty and Staff Development Division, Command and General Staff College.

Varela, F. J. 1999. *Ethical know-how: Action, wisdom and cognition.* Stanford, CA: Stanford University Press.

Vygotsky, L. S. 1978. *Mind in society*, 14th edn. Cambridge, MA: Harvard University Press.

Walton, R. E., J. E. Cutcher-Gershenfeld, and R. B. McKersie. 1994. *Strategic negotiations: A theory of change in labor-management relations.* Cambridge, MA: Harvard Business School Press.

Winslade, J. and G. D. Monk. 2000. *Narrative mediation: A new approach in conflict resolution.* San Francisco, CA: Jossey-Bass.

Winslade, J. and G. D. Monk. 2008. *Practicing narrative mediation: Loosening the grip of conflict.* San Francisco, CA: Jossey-Bass.

Appendix

CGSC ELM Model Based on Kolb

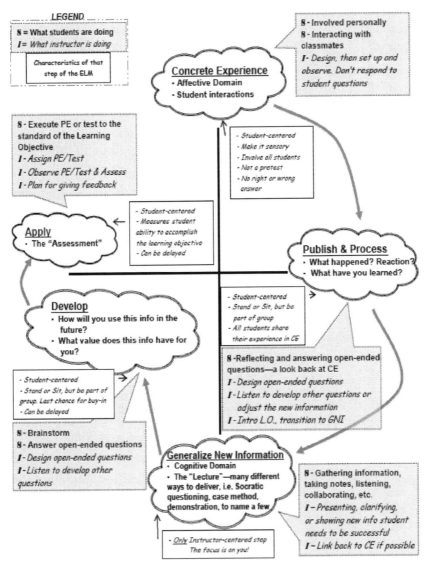

The Experiential Learning Model (ELM) Job Aid, Faculty and Staff Development Division, U.S. Army Command and General Staff College. Ft. Leavenworth, Kansas

❧ 18 ❧

Making it up as You Go: Educating Military and Theater Practitioners in "Design"

Leonard L. Lira & Rachel Parish*

Editors' Note: Following directly from the preceding chapter, Lira and Parish lay out a potential example of a training course for "wicked problems," finding unexpected parallels in two completely different professional environments: the theater and the military. The authors demonstrate how an elective "Design" course in the U.S. Army Command and General Staff College parallels the development of theater professionals. This matches the insights of Jayne Docherty, a professor of peacebuilding, in the previous chapter and the one which follows.

Introduction

Negotiation is a practice of "social creation." It is a *creative* practice because the goal of negotiators is to change the current social condition described in a conflict by creating, or facilitating the creation of, a new *social condition*, wherein the parties to that conflict can come to a negotiated solution. The creation of that solution thus advances the interest of the parties, the negotiators, and society (see Blanchot et al., *Education of Non-Students*, in this volume). Negotiation, therefore, as Herbert Simon (1996) once indicated about engineering, medicine, business, architecture, and painting, is concerned not with the necessary (what is), but with the contingent (what can be), and thus how to create, or design, that condition. Since there is a critical and cre-

* **Leonard L. Lira** is a Lieutenant Colonel in the U.S. Army and an assistant professor in the Department of Joint, Interagency, and Multinational Operations of the Command and General Staff College at Fort Leavenworth, Kansas. His email address is leonard.lira@us.army.mil. **Rachel Parish** is Artistic Director of Firehouse Creative Productions, a London-based theater company that specializes in collaborative theater. Her email address is rachel@firehousecreativeproductions.com.

ative reasoning requirement to do this in negotiation, the field may benefit from the same type of "design" thinking that other creative practices such as architecture, art, music, dance, etc., utilize in their professional education courses. If the field of negotiation were to adopt "design thinking" as a part of its curricula, it would also be following the lead of other practitioner fields outside the arts that have already revamped their programs for "executives, educators, doctors, and lawyers" (Korn and Emma 2012: B1).

The premise of this chapter is that to educate and train students in negotiation, perhaps we can apply pedagogical methods similar to those that other creative practices use to educate and train *their* practitioners. While this chapter does not outline a specific course in negotiation, it does use one such course to illustrate the possibilities, and to propose a generalizable method of instruction in design thinking that curriculum developers could tailor for negotiation. To demonstrate the utility of "design-thinking based" pedagogy, this chapter provides examples from the disparate fields of theatrical and military arts. From these examples, we can explore parallels that may demonstrate, for developers and teachers of negotiation curricula, a creative educational approach that is probably well-suited to practitioners who will have to deal with "wicked problems" as discussed in the preceding chapter.

Design Thinking and Negotiation

Mathematics and systems science literature from the middle of the twentieth century introduced early concepts of "Design" in the specialized term-of-art sense defined below. Eventually it began to influence other disciplines, principally architecture (Spillers 1974: 5), but also social sciences (Simon 1996), and the problem-solving processes, policy-making, and planning curricula of disparate fields such as business administration, public management, city and regional planning, education, engineering, industrial design, communication design, policy sciences, and social work (Olsen 1982: 5).

Design's definition, as modified from the above literature and used in this chapter, is that it is a goal-directed problem-solving activity which incorporates collaborative and participatory methods that involve critical and creative reasoning (Olsen 1982). At first look, conventional wisdom may find it counterintuitive that negotiation and design activities are related. However, Richard Buchanan (1992) articulates four domains of design. These domains are helpful in differentiating between subcategories of the above definition and isolating points where the creative processes of design and negotiation converge.

The first domain Buchanan describes is commonly associated with graphic design, in which designers use symbolic and visual communication. The second, meanwhile, is in the creation of "material objects" such as the design of "clothing, domestic objects, tools, instruments, machinery, and vehicles" (Buchanan 1992: 9). Both of these domains may appear remote from our field's concerns. Some may see the creative process as intuitive in these areas, whereas not everyone will see the requirement for so intuitive a creative process in a negotiation context .

However, in Buchanan's third and fourth design domains the requirement for a more explicit creative process in design, and how that process relates to the negotiation process, becomes more apparent. According to Buchanan, the third area is "the design of activities and organized services, which include the traditional management concern for logistics, combining physical resources, instrumentalities, and human beings in efficient ways and schedules to reach specified objectives" (Buchanan 1992: 9). The fourth area is the "design of complex systems or environments for living, working, playing, and learning" (Buchanan 1992: 10).

These last two areas are associated with managers, planners, lawyers, architects, engineers, and other practitioners who provide social services or deal with human problems as part of their practice. In other words, they are consistently devising creative and negotiated social solutions (see Docherty and Lira, *Adapting to the Adaptive*, in this volume). Thought of in this manner, one can easily associate the activities of negotiation that these practitioners use with the activities of design that they apply to create solutions to problems in their own professions. The thinking that goes into both types of activities is "design thinking" and consists of "places of invention . . . where one discovers the dimensions of design thinking by a reconsideration of problems and solutions" (Buchanan 1992: 11).

More readily, negotiation practitioners who deal with organizational conflict already widely use the term "dispute systems design," and the literature of that specialty generally acknowledges that one form or another of negotiation will be a primary, if not *the* primary, detail activity within the systems design frame (Ury, Brett, and Goldberg 1988). So at one level a relationship between negotiation and some form of "design" is already common knowledge among at least a subset of negotiation professionals. However, it is more debatable whether the full range of potentially useful concepts of "design" as developed by other professions and in other contexts has yet been examined, let alone thoroughly adapted, for possible use in dispute systems design.

Negotiation as a Creative Practice

As discussed by Jayne Docherty and Leonard in the preceding chapter, negotiation experts clearly recognize negotiation as a creative practice. In this, the parallels to at least some forms of *art* are becoming more obvious and worth further exploration. The role of the artist as a social critic, of course, has long been widely understood. But the concept of the artist as an "operating" figure, a leader – inherent in the concept of Design above – is now growing. Therefore, a discussion of art as a discipline raises the possibility of useful sidelights on efforts to incorporate Design thinking into negotiation, whether in the military or other professions, from experience in the very different domain of art. We will explain further in the discussion below.

A summary of a growing body of research, in particular the British "Artist-as-Leader" research project, puts it this way:

> Artists lead through their practice. One quality of experiencing art is that artists enable us to see the world differently. Our focus is on the ways in which this provides leadership. This is what we mean by leading through practice. Currently, artists are increasingly choosing, or being called upon, to work more directly within social, cultural, economic, and political processes. This is a trajectory that has a complex history in which art is increasingly active in the formulation of cultural processes (Douglas and Fremantle 2009).

Seen within this context, art increasingly takes *people* to be its main material, and often defies traditional categorization into form. However, art practices that share the same basic material as negotiation (people), and particularly those practices that involve:

a) an emphasis on spoken or written forms of communication and

b) working directly with groups of people who will co-create the design

stand to be most relevant to this discussion. The form most obviously fitting these criteria is theater, particularly collaborative theater.

For reasons described elsewhere in this volume (see Blanchot et al., *Education of Non-Students*), Rachel's London-based theater company effectively puts her in the role of an artist-leader. She describes what is for practical purposes a Design problem:

> *As, in effect, an "artist-leader" myself, I listen a lot and let what I hear guide my actions. When I heard contemporaries working in new theater in London say consistently, "there is a lack of creative space," I was curious to figure out what this meant. It turned out that this*

"space" meant a space: 1) to really think laterally; and 2) to connect meaningfully at the start of a creative process with other collaborators. Writers were lonely, actors felt like they were tools, designers felt they were brought in far too late in the creative process to have a meaningful impact. So, I set up a Big Idea workshop.

The Big Idea workshop is a week-long exploration of something that we're wrestling with in contemporary life; belief, time and power are the three ideas we've tackled through this platform so far. Once a year, I gather together groups of artists interested in pushing their boundaries and engaging with collaborative theater making. Over this week we throw open wide the questions about this theme. We debate, have presentations, write, devise, and create. I work as the instigator, creating the platform for the creativity of others to flourish and find form. After the week's workshop, interdisciplinary teams form around ideas generated in the workshop. I work with these teams to develop, draft, dramaturg, and find producing outlets for their products.

This work sits squarely within the context of artistic practice explored in Anne Douglas and Chris Fremantle's description of the Artist-as-Leader research project, cited above. It is also led by a design-thinking approach similar to the fourth variety outlined above, "design of complex systems or environments for living, working, playing and learning." Artists such as Suzanne Lacy, Helen Mayer Harrison and Newton Harrison, Barbara Steveni and John Latham are among those whose work as "artist-leaders" has been the subject of a comprehensive research study relevant to this discussion. As part of this research, Douglas, a professor at Gray's School of Art, identifies that such artists

> think about the long term implications of their actions where most other areas of production or service are expedient, solving the problem on hand and in the immediate context. They are capable of working across hierarchies and social groupings, enabling individuals to transcend barriers of discipline, belief and specialism (Douglas and Fremantle 2009: 7).

The work carried out by many artists working in this area speaks to a shared dedication, much like the overlap Leonard describes of his shared work with Docherty: *a mutual interest in a common theme to design solutions to social problems; the conception and creation of a future condition, artificially created by human interaction.*

Activities in this area of practice are often about the *way* of working rather than a catalogue of a series of products. This does not mean the quality of the outputs need suffer, and indeed it is often the existence of the end goal that can provide common ground and guidance in difficult times. To emphasize this point, Douglas states

> *many artists and other related roles would place the emphasis in terms of creativity and quality in the process as well as its end result, considering its conceptualization and articulation and even its power to create change"* (2009: 13).

Similarly, many writers on negotiation, mediation and dispute systems design have valued the normative effects of these processes on the parties' ability to work constructively and creatively in the future as highly as, or even more highly than, the immediate prospects for settlement (see, in particular, Bush and Folger 2005). There is overlap of other kinds, too, between the arts and negotiation (see, e.g., LeBaron and Honeyman 2006, Honeyman and Parish 2013). This area of arts practice and the recent research around it provide a rich background of complementary findings that could be of interest to strategists of Design and related teaching in the military as well as in other professions.

Reconsidering a Foundational Text

Roger Fisher, William Ury, and Bruce Patton indicate the need for a creative process in negotiation in their third step of the *Getting to Yes* methodology. Recall that the third step requires negotiators to "invent" options (Fisher, Ury, and Patton 1991: 56–80). They articulate their prescription to create negotiation options in their circle chart, which depicts a process to determine what is wrong and then to devise actions that negotiators might take to solve what is wrong by shuffling back and forth between real world practicalities and theoretical propositions (1991: 68). It is a simple four-step process:

1) identify the problem;
2) analyze the problem;
3) develop general approaches; and
4) develop specific actions to solve the problem.

It is also a concept that undergirds much of contemporary negotiation instruction. In practice, however, this instruction tends to occur not in the circular pattern designed by Fisher, Ury, and Patton, but rather in a linear step-by-step process.

In this sense, the field of negotiation may have followed the same pattern of development as the design field, in that it implemented variations of linear models that essentially held two distinct phases: problem definition/analysis and problem solution/synthesis (Buchanan 1992: 15). We would offer three observations about the application of Fisher, Ury, and Patton's approach to inventing negotiation options in general negotiation pedagogy, observations which have previously been made in other contexts by earlier critics of design thinking. First, the creative process of developing solutions generally does not follow a simple linear process. (For a demonstration of how failure to understand this can undermine a peacekeeping process, see the Bosnia discussion by Calvin Chrustie in *Playing the Percentages*, in this volume.) Fisher, Ury, and Patton imply this by fashioning their four-step process into a circular pattern, rather than a linear pattern. This demonstrates a *shuffling back and forth between* the theoretical and practical applications of problem analysis and solution creation. But not all their followers have really understood this element.

Second, the negotiation problems that are pervasive in wicked problems in particular – as encountered by practitioners of other professions who may not be negotiation experts per se but nonetheless use negotiation to achieve their goals – are not easily rendered into linear analysis and synthesis. And third, the Fisher, Ury, and Patton four-step process, in and of itself, offers a means of *practice,* not education. That is to say, it is prescriptive enough to articulate the practice of creating negotiation solutions, but not descriptive enough to generalize to a larger curriculum of negotiation study.

Thus, the majority of negotiation curricula apply Fisher, Ury, and Patton's steps for inventing negotiation options under the assumption that there are definitive conditions or limits to negotiation problems. In contrast, we contend, like Buchanan's assessment of Horst Rittell and Melvin Webber's wicked problems, that most social negotiations of human problems are in fact indeterminate, meaning that they have no "definitive conditions or limits" (1992: 15). Therefore, the development of negotiation solutions to these human problems may be best served through the application of the same design thinking that other types of creative practitioners use when dealing with wicked problems, as in Rachel's example above. It is in this sense that we assert that the activities of negotiation are in a fundamental way "design" activity.

Negotiation as Design Activity

Similarly to the design field, the negotiation field is *integrative.* In this instance, we are not using the term in reference to the dichotomy between integrative and distributive tactics within a negotiation; we mean that all negotiation, even when it is heavily distributive, *must* draw from multiple sources of expertise and ideas (e.g., a factory official negotiating price and delivery dates with a supplier is likely to talk internally with people from sales, marketing, production, engineering and so on.) According to Buchanan, in the broadest terms, the design field's diverse practitioners, professions, and academic disciplines are drawn together in the activities of design because "they share a mutual interest in a common theme: the conception and planning of the artificial" (1992: 14). By artificial, Buchanan means any condition created which is not natural, or found naturally, but human-made, such as graphic art, a new toaster, an urban plan – or the creation of a negotiated settlement. As in other professions that employ design, a wide variety of practitioners from very diverse fields of practice use negotiation out of necessity, to create new social situations in which they or their practices must live and operate.

Two ready examples are the authors of the preceding chapter. As disparate practitioners, Docherty and Leonard are drawn towards the field of negotiation because they share a mutual interest in a similar common theme, to design solutions to social problems: the conception and creation of a future human condition, artificially created by human interaction. In this manner, the creative processes of both design and negotiation intertwine in liberal arts and social sciences.

Another example, superficially far removed from the military but in our opinion highly relevant, again comes from Rachel's work in theater. Below she outlines a typical design setting and activity that occurs during improvised group auditions.

In a room in an old office building, a group of actors who do not know each other meet for the first time in an audition situation. They are each there to show themselves to be the best person for a particular role or roles. They are grouped in with several people, some of whom are their competitors and some of whom are applying for unrelated jobs. They are presented with a task: Together, as a group, create the first scene of the play – in twenty minutes. They have come to the audition having read the whole play, but they are not to use the scene itself in the task. What they have instead is a few guidelines: The scene has three movements, which I outline for them to follow (the protagonist is revealed, there is a battle, the antagonist is revealed and the protagonist suffers). I also give them a list of fifteen "ingredients" to include in the scene (including a moment of silence, a moment of pure fear, the demonstration of "supervillain" powers, flying, a choreographed dance, a song sung, an explosion, etc.). They then must improvise a solution – a scene to perform to the people who are considering hiring them. No leader is set in this task and there is no prescribed starting point, not even a prescribed performance space. They must work it out between themselves with the clock ticking and in a high stakes situation. Once the instructions are given, the improvisation has begun.

In this recent audition process, I worked with twelve groups of performers with this very task. Each group has a completely differ-

ent approach to devising a solution and arriving at a performance. Several points emerge that make for a successful process and product. You can't be afraid to fail. Without a starting point, you have to just begin – a simple movement of a chair can spark in someone else a new idea/solution to another part of the project. Everyone must take part, but there is no set pattern of participation. The project is shared and joint responsibility must be taken: complete commitment to the project is required. A lot of what is created will be useless. Yet these experiments always provide some moment of brilliance that can be extracted from the solution in the improvisation and used in a considered and crafted staging of a scene. These moments that are created through improvisation would not have happened outside of a collaborative and networked process.

In addition to this improvised section of the audition, there is a one-to-one section in which the performer has a chat with the director, and in which the performer reads sections of the script:

The main purpose of the auditions is to establish the tone of the process clearly and to start a conversation with your future collaborators. An audition of this sort conveys a lot of information to the performer; in addition to the techniques we will use, they also learn that they will have a lot of responsibility to collaborate, that they will have to expend a lot of physical energy, that they will take a lot of risks, that they will always be listened to, etc. What a director looks for is a set of people who will be best suited to work together on the process that lies ahead. There are always specific criteria that come into play, according to the particularities of the process that lies ahead, and there is very little intuition that comes into play in putting a team together.[1]

Below, we will discuss a military equivalent.

Design Education and Negotiation
Buchanan foresaw the expansion of design thinking into both the liberal arts and social sciences. His quote below states as much:

As the field of design matures in the coming years, we will begin to teach design as a liberal art of contemporary culture. In other words, we will include within our programs individuals who come to study design but with no intention of entering into professional design practice. They will study design as a preparation for many other types of careers, in the same way that students today study literature or natural science or history or social science (Buchanan 1998: 66).

From this starting point, it is easy to see how the utilization of design thinking and education in many professions and practices has grown to include negotiation.

The political scientist Herbert Simon attempted to develop a general "teachable doctrine about the design process" for professions in his book, *The Sciences of the Artificial* (1996: 113). Simon's description of design relates closely to "Design" as known by other professionals. For example, even though he recognized design's origins in the engineering profession, he emphatically states:

> Engineers are not the only professional designers. Everyone designs who devises courses of action aimed at changing existing situations into preferred ones. The intellectual activity that produces material artifacts is no different fundamentally from the one that prescribes remedies for a sick patient or the one that devises a new sales plan for a company or a social welfare policy for a state. Design, so construed, is the core of all professional training; it is the principal mark that distinguishes the professions from the sciences (1996: 111).

To Simon, design theory focuses on how professionals should think social constructs ought to be created, thus searching for a "satisficing" design instead of an "optimized" design.

Donald Schön, meanwhile, has sought to establish "processes which practitioners bring to situations of uncertainty, instability, uniqueness, and value conflict" (1983: 49). He addressed how to teach this new theory of knowledge to design thinkers of all professions by contending that "professional education should be redesigned to combine the teaching of applied science with coaching in the artistry of reflection-in-action" (Schön 1990: xii). Specifically, he recommends that professional education follow the "deviant traditions of education for practice as studios of art and design, conservatories of music and dance, athletics coaching, and apprenticeship in the crafts, all of which emphasize coaching and learning by doing" (1990: xiii).

Schön (1983) labels this educational methodology the "reflective practicum." He describes the process of this reflective seminar as one in which teachers coach students into conducting "reflection-in-action." Schön defines reflection-in-action as the ability of professionals to think about what they are doing while they are doing it. For Schön, the way to teach how to manage the areas of professional practice that are not easily determined, i.e., operating in complex adaptive (i.e., in this series' terms, wicked problem) settings, such as social negotiation in human conflict settings, is through the ability to reflect as you work through the problem and apply previous experience to new situations. Schön describes the practicum as:

> (A practicum is) a setting designed for the task of learning a practice. In a context that approximates a practice world, students learn by doing, although their doing usually falls short of real world work. They learn by undertaking projects that simulate and simplify practice; or they take on real-world projects under close supervision. The practicum is a virtual world, relatively free of the pressures, distractions, and risks of the real one, to which, nevertheless, it refers. It stands in the intermediate space between the practice world, the "lay world of ordinary life, and the esoteric world of the academy . . . The work of the practicum is accomplished through some combination of the student's learning by doing, her interactions with coaches and fellow students, and a more diffuse process of "background learning (1983: 37-38).

Some professional educational institutions are following Schön's prescription. In fact, business schools today are looking at how to modify their educational methodologies to incorporate this different approach. In a 2005 special report in Bloomberg BusinessWeek, Louis Lavelle and Jennifer Merritt ventured that "business schools have been trying to inject design thinking into their curriculum for well over a decade, with mixed success" (2005: para. 6). In *Negotiation Stands Alone* (chapter 26 in this volume), Alexandra Crampton and Michael Tsur take this further, discussing Tsur's conclusions from years of practice and teaching of crisis negotiators in terms of a necessary body of experience that far exceeds what can be achieved in normal "school" environments, even those that include a practicum. It is not irrelevant that Tsur argues that some of the most promising "new" professional negotiators in his proposed advanced professional structure are likely to be experienced military officers.

Design Education for Military Practitioners

As a profession, the military is lately coming to incorporate design thinking and design education into its professional military education curriculum. For example, the Army's Command and General Staff College (CGSC) devotes six hours to Design in its core curriculum, and an additional twenty-four hours to Design as an elective course (Lira and Culkin 2011). This must be evaluated in the context of a great number of specialty subjects competing for very limited student time, such that even the six hours represent a notable shift in priorities. The six hours are devoted to explaining design thinking and how the Army incorporates design into planning doctrine. However, the twenty-four hour elective course (see Appendix for a detailed course outline) actually applies an example of Schön's practicum. Throughout this course, instructors attempt to follow David Kolb's experiential learning model (discussed in Docherty and Lira, *Adapting to the Adaptive*, the preceding chapter in this volume), melded with Schön's reflective practicum process. The twenty-four hours of the course are therefore broken into three segments, consisting of a deconstructive module, a constructive module, and a reflective module. (The hours applied to each module, again, are based on the tight scheduling constraints at CGSC. For all intents and purposes, a course developed elsewhere along the three modules – deconstructive, constructive, and reflective – can shape the number of hours according the time constraints that apply to the particular teaching environment.)

In the deconstructive module, the course breaks down the process of design, explaining the theory and praxis behind it. Instructors introduce Design as a term-of-art concept, and the rationale for design thinking is discussed with the students. Although the first module describes the concept of design as non-linear, it has the students sequentially analyzing the parts of the concept, so that they gain an in-depth knowledge of the concept's components. This module follows the experiential learning model (ELM) detailed in the preceding chapter in this volume (Docherty and Lira, *Adapting to the Adaptive*).

In the constructive module, the course teaches the students about design according to Schön's recommended model, i.e., by having them practice it. The instructors divide the students into design teams, and set them upon what Rittell and Webber (1973) would call a "wicked problem." The students therefore learn the principles of design by *applying them in a case study*, centered on complex human-based problems that they wish to change artificially through some sort of problem-solving intervention. One example that students have used is the violence induced by drug wars along the Mexican-American border. The students conduct the design activities to develop the design concept that articulates their understanding of the problem and its solution in the form of a graphic and narrative depiction. They then brief their design concept before a critique board, which judges the students on their creative as well as critical reasoning. This experience forces students to articulate very complex issues, problems, and potential solutions clearly and concisely. Since the entire exercise is fundamentally an intra-group negotiation under other terminology, in the language of the Rethinking Negotiation Teaching (RNT) project the exercise also constitutes a form of "adventure learning" of the "oblique" type, in which a team must negotiate internally in order to accomplish a set goal (see volume 2 in the RNT series, chapters 7-10, Honeyman, Coben, and De Palo 2010).

Finally, in the reflective module, instructors expose the students to the learning methodology, and facilitate their reflection of their learning, through a seminar-type discussion and an online reflective forum, where students consider various aspects of applying and learning design fundamentals. In the online forum, the students answer open-ended questions that motivate them to wrestle with the complexities of the problem and to reexamine their decisions and the solutions they selected. Through the application of the deconstructive, constructive, and reflective modules, the design elective attempts to integrate the best of both experiential and reflective learning. The benefit of this is that through experiential learning, students gain new knowledge for the long term. Through reflective learning, students can transfer that new knowledge to settings never before experienced by the learner – thus (the instructors hope) helping them to become more adaptive and effective in changing environments.

The Course Outline

The instructors applied the ELM and a reflective-practicum-style teaching methodology in designing this course. The overall objective was for instructors to facilitate learning by harnessing the students' personal experiences, critical and creative thinking skills, and focused application of new concepts in a "reflection-in-action" method.

There are five fundamental steps in the ELM:[2]

1) Concrete Experience (CE) – The instructor presents an activity or text that evokes individual responses from the students. Students can then actively connect personal experience to the subject matter.

2) Publish & Process (P&P) – The instructor attempts to link the concrete experience to the lesson learning objective. Students understand better that their discussions are part of a larger context, connected to the curriculum.

3) Generalizing New Information (GNI) – The instructor presents new information to the students based upon readings and other pre-assigned work.

4) Develop – Students reflect on how this new information will affect their lives professionally and personally.

5) Apply – Students conduct an exercise – e.g., write a paper, orally present a report, or coordinate an activity – which employs the general concepts introduced during the lesson. The instructor assesses their performance in accordance with established standards defined in the curriculum.

A detailed class-by-class overview (twelve two-hour lessons) is reproduced in the Appendix. The instructors organized each lesson (represented by shaded blocks) according to specific steps in the ELM. For instance, lessons one and two introduced the concept and rationale for design; this served as the Concrete Experience & Introduction. Lessons three and four addressed the "What/How design?" and correlated with the Publish & Process and Generalize New Information steps. The first four lessons approached the material in a deconstructive manner – i.e., they sequentially analyzed the methodology of the doctrinal concept. During lessons five through eleven, students personally learned the principles of Design ("Develop") by applying them in a case study centered on the complex border issues with Mexico. In the final lesson, students presented their initial design concepts to an audience of Command and General Staff instructors who had not participated in their planning. This experience forced the student teams to articulate very complex issues, problems, and potential solutions clearly and concisely. In addition to the staff-training benefits, the students could reflect on their experiences during a question-answer period afterwards. Furthermore, students considered various aspects of applying and learning design fundamentals in online discussion boards.

An allotment of reflection time assumed that students brought intellectual preconceptions about design to the course. Many students wanted to know more about design in order to validate or disprove their self-developed hypotheses. Some of their concerns centered on how design (broadly termed as "conceptual planning" in Army Field Manual 5-0) links into predominantly detailed planning processes such as the Military Decision Making Process (MDMP).[3] Others wondered about the expected products and how Design is being disseminated and developed throughout the joint military and interagency professions. The instructors found that asking open-ended questions about these topics effectively enabled motivated students to wrestle with these issues in class and thereby better understand the nature of design as it applied to their experience and practice. It was the instructors' impression, based on this feedback, that *not* addressing these topics in class or via the virtual discussion board would likely have become a barrier to further learning. (For more on this theme, see Deason et al., *Debriefing the Debrief*, in this volume.)

Design as Negotiation Pedagogy
After the course, both instructors and students responded to a post-course survey. The survey suggests multiple lessons learned (Lira and Culkin 2011), all very likely applicable to course designers and instructors of negotiation elsewhere.

Lessons Learned (Joint Perspectives)

Both instructors and students reported the desire of the students to practice design in an exercise that dealt with a relevant "real world" issue, as opposed to a real world location incorporated into a fictitious scenario, or an exercise with both a fictitious location and scenario. The students reported that when the exercise contained any fictitious aspects, they would not as readily see the exercise's relevance to what the students perceived as their world. To respond to their appetite in this regard, the instructors focused on an exercise selected from a current crisis widely reported in the media, i.e., the narcotics gang war along the U.S. and Mexico border.

Lessons Learned (Student Perspectives)

One of the biggest issues reported by students was that they wished they had previous examples, or "schoolhouse solutions," to use as a framework for developing their solutions. But the instructors were concerned that the students might become "fixated" on those design solution examples, which after all were created for problems in other contexts, and lose the opportunity to practice developing creative solutions for the problems they were currently confronting. The instructors based this concern on the potential problem of fixation as documented by Nigel Cross (2005) and Greg Lawson (1980). Cross cites a study by D. G. Jansson and S. M. Smith, who studied senior students' and experienced professional mechanical engineers' solution responses to design problems. They compared groups from both sets, with one group charged to design a solution to their problem with no examples given, and the other group provided with examples of previous design solutions. Their comparison found that the latter group appeared to be "fixated" by the example designs, producing solutions containing many more features from a single option (the example design) than did the solutions produced by the groups not shown any examples. The not-so-obvious problem with this is that in complex settings that may vary greatly depending on the context, solution sets that work in one setting may not work in another setting. According to Cross, providing specific examples may therefore act against the development of creativity in the development of solutions to complex problems.

We will discuss a theater equivalent below.

Lessons Learned (Instructor Perspectives)

Another lesson that the course authors learned was that students reported better understanding if prompted with open-ended questions during the reflective module. Students reported in post-course evaluations that they felt this enabled them to internalize the learning objectives of the course better. Combined with experiencing the problem at first hand, students reported that this also elicited a better understanding of how they made their decisions and whether those decisions were conducive to solving the problem presented.

The instructors also reported learning in the process of delivering their course that they needed to apply the lessons of the course without preaching a *method or procedure*. In the course of solving the problem, each design team developed its own style, dynamics, and general group understanding of the problem. Each group articulated the problem, along with a broad operational approach to solve it, differently from the other groups. The instructors surmised that the dynamics of organizational decision-making required such an "instant organization" to take on and exhibit the traits and thinking patterns of the organizations' inhabitants, i.e., the team members themselves. This would be no different from any negotiation team's composition and personality. (And indeed, it is quite similar to Rachel's experience with different audition groups.) Therefore, during the elective the instructors allowed the diverse characteristics of each group to develop naturally. Task organization, such as adopting or assigning leader, recorder, or researcher roles, evolved on their own. Additionally, each group internally decided and developed the manner in which the group would brief the problem statement and solution. Instructors reported that this appeared to allow greater group buy-in. Furthermore, it enhanced the group's ability to express to outsiders the type of problem they encountered in the exercise and how to deal with it. (For more on the value of allowing students to design parts of a course themselves, see Nelken, McAdoo, and Manwaring 2009.)

Finally, another issue instructors reported dealing with was deciding how to evaluate the learning of the students, and grading their design products. How does an instructor evaluate critical and creative thinking, let alone teach it in design or negotiation? Schön (1990) offers two methods for design evaluation: the "instructor method" (desk criticism, in Schön's terminology), or the critique board (Design jury) method. The instructor method only requires the student to present to the instructor and then receive an evaluation. The problem with this method, according to Schön (1990), is that the student may tend to emulate the instructor's creative and critical style (a form of fixation), while the instructor, seeing what he/she perceives to be correct – because it is what he/she would have done – does not provide an accurate assessment.[4]

The critique board method, meanwhile, requires the student to present the design product to a board of evaluators, who are experienced in his/her design field (for the military student, that field is the Military Decision Making Process). The problem with *this* method is that if the student does not have time to develop the design products to the point where they can be fairly exhibited to outsiders, and instead only the internal participants understand them, the external evaluators may be observing a product for which they have no context and little understanding of how it was developed.

Lawson and several other Design scholars have documented this description of a working Design product – used for internal understanding – and a presentation design for such a product. If the course is too short, affording the students time only to develop a rough design product, the individual teacher evaluation is best. If, on the other hand, there is ample time for the students to develop a presentation-level product, then the instructors follow Schön's recommendation to conduct a critique board. In the end, in the sample CGSC course, the instructors felt that the process of creativity and critical thinking was a more important outcome of the course than the products developed. Here too there is a useful parallel to collaborative theater, in this instance to the thinking behind Rachel's "Big Idea Workshop" discussed above. A great many other considerations, many of which are just as relevant to assessment of students in this environment as in others, will be found in *Assessing Our Students, Assessing Ourselves* (Ebner, Coben, and Honeyman 2012), volume 3 in the RNT series.

On reading Leonard's first draft of this chapter, Rachel was particularly drawn to the above point on the potential problem of fixation: "*the instructors reported concern that the students would become fixated on those design solution examples, created for problems in other contexts, and lose the ability to develop creative solutions for the problems they were currently confronting.*" Douglas discusses a distinction made by anthropologists Elizabeth Hallam and Tim Ingold (2007), on the nature of creativity within policy discourse. The distinction they draw is between innovation and improvisation, with innovation being product focused and looking towards the past, and improvisation being process focused and forward looking. They go on to characterize improvisation in terms of four key qualities: being generative, relational, temporal, and the way people work in daily life as well as in reflective creative practice. Creating a culture of improvisation in designing a process is a key to sidestepping the pitfall of fixation.

Again Rachel offers a connecting example:

Recently I was commissioned by the Ideas for Creative Explorations Research Institute at the University of Georgia to develop a piece of performance about food. My approach, as described in the Informal Education chapter of this book, is one designed to engage a broad spec-

trum of people in each of the stages of creative practice. The goal is to make a good show. It is equally to involve an array of individuals within a community to contribute to a conversation through creativity. I ran workshops with artists exploring the relationship to food, which operated very much like the "big idea" workshops. Colleagues and I also met with individuals, to listen to their ideas, feelings, and memories of food.

These meetings were partly arranged and partly happenstance, facilitated by stopping individuals in the street or in their place of business, or arranging meetings with them if they worked in an industry related to food. We listened, but did not have an agenda, and this made all the difference. The stories, information and investment people made into the project were very strong. Individuals talked, wrote, and contributed to the project very openly and repeatedly.

Because we were not there to judge, but rather to understand, people wanted to give more, and they admitted to feeling free to contribute more honestly than otherwise. In this kind of approach, new ideas flourish, surprising connections can be made, and the problem of fixation is sidestepped. This is done by designing situations, creating conditions of discourse and collaboration, and making room for improvisations and space for shared creativity.

We believe that experiences such as this, generated in the theatrical community, may well prove valuable both for practitioners from stereotypically hierarchical professions, such as military officers who are attempting to get their minds around Design, and for peacemakers presented with much the same problem in their very different professional community (see Docherty and Chrustie, *Teaching Three-Dimensional Negotiation,* in this volume).

To sum up, Design, like negotiation, is not a linear activity. Nor is it an activity that follows a purely analytical train of thought. On the contrary, it is creative, recursive and non-linear. Therefore, the methodology to teach it should match its application by practitioners – broadly, in the same way that Rachel's audition process modeled the way the company would work once the actors and other professionals were selected. Since the military method of practice is in other ways, of course, very different from the collaborative theater method, in the CGSC's conditions a *deconstructive* module of instruction is necessary to break down the concept's components. Having successfully completed this, instructors should immerse students in a *constructive* module, in which they learn by doing. Then the course should give time to the students to be *reflective*, while they are still doing their activity, so they can better internalize what they are learning.

Conclusion

This chapter contends that both design thinking and negotiation are activities of social creation. Like design education, negotiation education could benefit from the integration of experiential and reflective learning methodologies – at least some of which have been highly developed in other fields, such as theater. This suggests that a welcoming attitude toward unconventional sources might allow methods to be adapted economically and without a sustained campaign to reinvent the wheel.

As examples, the vignettes Rachel provides represent education activities just as much as does the elective course example provided by Leonard. Rachel's examples may contain less formal structuring, but, like Leonard's examples, they take place within a pool of practitioners. The only differences she would make between application of these principles with students in formal educational settings and with individuals working professionally in the field come in evaluation practices.

One lesson that Rachel's work in theater has reinforced in this chapter is that we teach largely through our actions, rather than through our directives. This is where Design is clearly important, and requires the educator to have a healthy engagement with reflective thinking about her own work before she can outline a curriculum *and* while she delivers it. A learning practice with a design that displays a balance of structure and flexibility will communicate the importance of these skills to the learner. The design itself can impart to the student skills that are necessary to do the job required of them in the future. Instructors guide their student practitioners in bringing a flexible approach to creative problem solving if they demonstrate this through the form and content of their (the educator's) practice. As Leonard's approach outlines, this can equally be done in the highly formal settings of military education as it is through Rachel's work in theater.

The description of the "design elective" above demonstrates that both reflective practice and ELM learning methodologies can be integrated in a course that contains deconstructive, constructive, and reflective modules. This combination allows students to analyze the concepts studied, practice the concepts, and reflect while practicing the concepts. By combining experiential and reflective learning in this manner, students can gain new knowledge for the long term, and internalize that knowledge enough to be able to transfer it to new problems never before experienced. This helps them become more adaptive and effective in rapidly changing negotiation environments – which, as Howard Gadlin, David Matz and Calvin Chrustie (*Playing the Percentages in Wicked Problems,* in this volume) and Chrustie et al. (2010) demonstrate, are increasingly being recognized as characterizing not only the 21st century military and peacemaking professions, but also many other professional environments that are not so obviously implicated. Modeling the Design education curriculum within a negotiation curriculum may provide negotiators, as Nigel Cross (2005) would say, with a "designerly way of knowing" how to identify and solve complex [negotiation] problems.

Notes

[1] The reader may find similarities here to Calvin Chrustie's discussion of the design and formation of a crisis negotiation team, in Bosnia and elsewhere, and the difficulties some members have had in comprehending and adapting to the equivalent demands for creativity, flexibility and systems thinking. See *Playing the Percentages in Wicked Problems,* chapter 20 in this volume.
[2] CGSC, Faculty Development Program, Fort Leavenworth, Kansas. See also Kolb 1984; Conner 1997-2007.
[3] The military decision making process is an iterative planning methodology used by the Army to understand the situation and mission, develop a course of action, and produce an operation plan or order.
[4] In a world which often valorizes the related concept of apprenticeship, it is worth noting that this concern is not just "academic." It was one of the core criticisms of then-current training practice in a field closely related to negotiation, which starting in the 1980s led to a comprehensive effort to rethink skills, training and selection of mediators. See Honeyman 1988, Honeyman et. al 1995 and the numerous intermediate publications cited therein. And, for an updated "take," see the annotated bibliography of the International Mediation Institute (http://imimediation.org/assessing-mediators-an-annotated-bibliography, last accessed Nov. 16, 2012).

References

Buchanan, R. 1992. Wicked problems in design thinking. *Design Issues* 8(2): 5–21.
Buchanan, R. 1998. Education and professional practice in design. *Design Issues* 14(2): 63–66.
Bush, R. B. and J. Folger. 2005. The promise of mediation: The transformative approach to conflict, rev. edn. San Francisco: Jossey-Bass.
Chrustie, C., J. S. Docherty, L. Lira, J. Mahuad, H. Gadlin, and C. Honeyman. 2010. Negotiating wicked problems: Five stories. In *Venturing beyond the classroom: Volume 2 in the rethinking negotiation teaching series,* edited by C. Honeyman, J. Coben, and G. De Palo. St. Paul, MN: DRI Press.
Conner, M. L. 1997-2007. Learning from experience: Overview of experiential learning. *AgelessLearner.com.* Available at http://agelesslearner.com/intros/experiential.html (last accessed Nov. 16, 2012).
Cross, Nigel. 2005. *Designerly ways of knowing,* 1st edn,. London: Springer.

Douglas, D. A., and C. Fremantle. 2009. *The artist as leader: Research report.* Aberdeen: Robert Gordon University.

Fisher, R., W. Ury, and B. Patton. 1991. *Getting to yes: Negotiating agreement without giving in,* 2nd edn. New York: Penguin

Hallam, E. and T. Ingold (eds). 2007. Creativity and cultural improvisation. New York: Berg.

Honeyman, C. 1988. Five elements of mediation. *Negotiation Journal* 4(2): 149-158.

Honeyman, C. et al. as Test Design Project. 1995. *Performance-based assessment: A methodology, for use in selecting, training and evaluating mediators.* Washington, DC: National Institute for Dispute Resolution. Available at www. convenor.com/madison/method.pdf (last accessed Nov. 16, 2012).

Honeyman, C., J. Coben, and G. De Palo (eds). 2010. *Venturing beyond the classroom: Volume 2 in the rethinking negotiation teaching series.* St. Paul, MN: DRI Press.

Honeyman, C. and R. Parish. 2013 (forthcoming). Movement in three acts. *In Making movement matter: Conflict, dance and neuroscience* (working title), edited by M. LeBaron, C. MacLeod, and A. Acland. Chicago: American Bar Association.

International Mediation Institute. 2012. *Assessing mediators: an annotated bibliography.* Available at http://imimediation.org/assessing-mediators-an-annotated-bibliography (last accessed Nov. 16, 2012).

Kolb, D.A. 1984. *Experiential learning: Experience as the source of learning and development.* Englewood Cliffs, NJ: Prentice Hall.

Korn, M. and R. Emma. 2012. Forget b-school, d-school is hot: "Design Thinking" concept gains traction as more programs offer the problem-solving Courses. *Wall Street Journal,* June 7, U.S. edition, sec. Marketplace.

Lavelle, L. and J. Merritt. 2005. Tomorrow's b-school? It might be a d-school. *BusinessWeek: Online Magazine,* August 1. Available at http://www.businessweek.com/magazine/content/05_31/b3945418.htm (last accessed Nov. 16, 2012).

Lawson, B. 1980. *How designers think: The design process demystified,* 4th edn. Boston: Architectural Press.

Lira, L. and D. T. Culkin. 2011. Teaching design: Challenges and opportunities in national security curriculum. Paper presented at the 69th Midwest Political Science Conference, Chicago, IL. Available at http://www.mpsanet.org/Conference/ConferencePapers/tabid/681/q/Lira/year/2011/Default.aspx (last accessed Nov. 16, 2012).

Nelken, M., B. McAdoo, and Manwaring, M. 2009. Negotiating learning environments. In *Rethinking negotiation teaching: Innovations for context and culture,* edited by C. Honeyman, J. Coben, and G. De Palo. St. Paul, MN: DRI Press

Olsen, S. A. 1982. *Construction management and engineering.* New York, NY: John Wiley & Sons.

Rittel, H. W. J. and M. M. Webber. 1973. Dilemmas in a general theory of planning. *Policy Sciences* 4: 155–169.

Schön, D. A. 1983. *The reflective practitioner: How professionals think in action,* 1st edn. New York: Basic Books.

Schön, D. A. 1990. *Educating the reflective practitioner: Toward a new design for teaching and learning in the professions,* 1st edn. San Francisco: Jossey-Bass.

Simon, H. A. 1996. *The sciences of the artificial,* 3rd edn. Cambridge, MA: MIT Press.

Spillers, W. R. 1974. *Basic questions of design theory.* Amsterdam: North-Holland Pub. Co.

Ury, W., J. A. Brett, and S. Goldberg. 1988. *Getting disputes resolved: Designing systems to cut the costs of conflict.* San Francisco: Jossey-Bass.

Appendix

A559 Course Overview: twelve meetings, two hours each

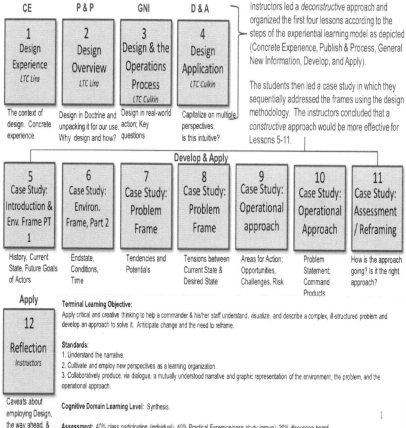

ೞ 19 ಬಿ

Teaching Three-Dimensional Negotiation to Graduate Students

Jayne Seminare Docherty, with Calvin Chrustie*

Editors' Note: *In a conscious parallel to the preceding chapter, Docherty describes an initial experiment, developed largely from Chrustie's practical experience, with teaching "wicked problems" to graduate students in peacebuilding at a Mennonite university. The collaboration between a professor of peacemaking on the one hand, and a highly experienced police officer and peacekeeper on the other, is as significant to the development of our field as the flow of information, experiments and ideas back and forth between the peacebuilding professional environment and the Command and General Staff College of the U.S. Army, discussed in chapter 17 in this volume, and further amplified in this chapter.*

Introduction
In a previous chapter (*Adapting to the Adaptive*, in this volume) Jayne Docherty and Leonard Lira elaborated on the concept of three-dimensional negotiation, which they argue is more appropriate than inter-

* **Jayne Seminare Docherty** is a professor at the Center for Justice and Peacebuilding at Eastern Mennonite University in Harrisonburg, Virginia. Her first book *Learning Lessons from Waco* was an analysis of the Federal Bureau of Investigation's attempt at hostage negotiation with the Branch Davidian sect, and her subsequent work has frequently involved the intersection and relationships between uniformed forces and civil society, ethnic minorities, and religious groups. Her email address is jayne.docherty@gmail.com. **Calvin Chrustie** is an inspector within the Royal Canadian Mounted Police and has held various negotiation and conflict management positions, including former team leader of the Conflict Negotiation Team, team leader of a Hostage Negotiation Team, and member of a Canadian international response group to overseas kidnaps. He also has extensive practice in a multitude of conflict situations domestically and abroad, including with the United Nations and other agencies in the Middle East, the Balkans, and Africa. His email address is calchrustie@hotmail.com.

est-based negotiation when addressing complex protracted conflicts. The assumptions behind three-dimensional negotiation are summarized as follows: *Transactional negotiations*, which are the problem-focused processes emphasized in standard negotiation courses, are actually a consequence of *social negotiation*. Furthermore, parties enter into transactional negotiation through a process of negotiating the following: What is (and is not) a problem suitable for transactional negotiation (Docherty 2001); how to define (or frame) the problem to be negotiated (Caton Campbell and Docherty 2006); the site in which to negotiate (Miller and Dingwall 2006); which parties have a right to enter into the negotiation process, and how the participants should conduct themselves (what scripts they may or may not use) during negotiation (Stolte, Fine, and Cook 2001).The result is a more complex, but more realistic and complete, understanding that all negotiations involve *social negotiation* and *dispute domain negotiation* in addition to the more commonly studied and taught *transactional negotiation.* The fact that in many everyday settings most of these elements of social negotiation are "settled" before the transaction begins (or before the onset of the particular dispute) obscures, but does not change, this relationship.

Three-dimensional negotiation as an approach to conflict emerged as a consequence of ongoing conversations and prior writing collaboration. In the past three years Jayne and Leonard have also been trying to figure out how to *teach* three-dimensional negotiation. Leonard integrated design thinking into teaching negotiation at the Army's Command and General Staff College (CGSC) (see Lira and Parish, *Making it up as You Go,* in this volume). Jayne used improvisational theater techniques and an emergent scenario based on a real case introduced by Calvin Chrustie to teach professional peacebuilders at the Center for Justice and Peacebuilding at Eastern Mennonite University about three dimensional negotiation, as described in this chapter.

For those readers not familiar with either the military arts and sciences[1] or professional peacebuilding[2] it might seem unusual that Leonard and Jayne were wrestling with similar problems related to teaching negotiation to professionals. But closer consideration of the realities facing our students reveals that they are often working side-by-side in situations where:

- Governance systems[3] are unclear because they are absent, non-functional, or considered illegitimate by significant parties or because there are competing governance systems vying for legitimacy.[4]
- Violence – overt or structural – or the threat of violence is a given.

- Negative attractors "made up of many elements . . . [that] are tightly linked through reinforcing feedback loops that intensify and spread the negativity and pull of the conflict over time" dominate the patterns of interaction among the parties. "Additionally, they possess a set of loops that provides inhibiting feedback, which discourages or prohibits de-escalation or other changes in more constructive directions" (Coleman 2011: 85).

In other words, our students are working with intractable conflicts that meet most or all of the criteria for being deemed wicked problems.[5] Consequently, they are compelled to focus on all three dimensions of negotiation if they want to succeed in reducing violence and altering the socio-political, cultural, and economic contexts that gave rise to the violence in the first place.

Starting Assumptions about Teaching Negotiation

Leonard started with the premise that all negotiation "is a *creative* practice because the goal of negotiators is to change the current social condition described in a conflict by creating, or facilitating the creation of, a new *social condition,* wherein the parties to that conflict can come to a negotiated solution" (Lira and Parish, *Making it up as You Go,* in this volume). Therefore, he reasoned, negotiation requires design thinking. Jayne too started with the premise that negotiation is creative, as well as with an understanding of process design that was influenced by dispute systems design (Ury, Brett, and Goldberg 1988; Costatino and Merchant 1995), the growing emphasis on design, monitoring and evaluation (or learning) in peacebuilding practice (Lederach, Neufeldt, and Culbertson 2007), and three years of field experience teaching negotiation to parties attempting to transform violent conflicts in Myanmar. She also drew on her prior experimentation with incorporating theater techniques into other courses.

From these similar starting points, Leonard and Jayne concluded that if they were serious about teaching three-dimensional negotiation, they would need to shift their mental model of teaching. Typical negotiation courses or trainings focus on helping students acquire skills, but the underlying and unexamined epistemological assumptions remain squarely in a paradigm of "banking education" (Freire 2009: Ch. 2), which assumes students are blank slates upon which the instructor needs to inscribe new knowledge. The student needs to be taught how to see and work with interests and not just positions, taught how to create as well as claim value, taught how to identify win-win options, how to go to the balcony . . . and the list goes on. In terms of skills, the student needs to be taught how to embody and instantiate practices of communication, reasoning, and problem solving that are useful in negotiation.

Yet students, in this paradigm, are not being invited into a "liberatory" education that raises critical consciousness, unlocks creativity, and empowers them to re-narrate their worlds. They are instead being asked to imbibe new ideas and adopt new practices that so-called experts agree are accurate and useful. Nor are students being asked to adapt and modify new ideas and practices to their own realities, which they and not the teacher know best.

When you start with the assumption that teaching negotiation is about transferring knowledge and developing skills, it makes sense to employ short, focused games, activities and thought exercises around carefully crafted cases. The cases are designed to "reveal" the previously invisible realities of negotiable problems – in other words, they are designed to bring the student into the teacher's narrative about the world. The related activities are designed to give the students opportunities to practice skills that make sense in the world the teacher has revealed.

If, however, we accept the argument that all transactional negotiations are interconnected with social negotiation and dispute domain negotiation,[6] then our students arrive in our classes as experienced negotiators. At a minimum, they are participants in the continuous process of social negotiation, even if they are not conscious of that reality. As adults, they are almost certain to have participated in some form of dispute domain negotiation, even if they did so without conscious attention to the process. And they are familiar with forms of transactional negotiation that make sense within the world they and their communities have socially negotiated, which may or may not be a world shared by the instructor. While all cultures appear to have developed methods of transactional negotiation, we should not assume that their communities have arrived at the same form of transactional negotiation that gave rise to what is taught in standard negotiation courses or trainings. That particular form of transactional negotiation was developed in a particular milieu (Western business settings) by a particular group of individuals (mostly well-to-do white men) for particular purposes (Docherty 2010: 489, also Greenhalgh and Lewicki 2003: 26).

Leonard and Jayne both assumed their students already knew something about negotiation. Therefore, they incorporated critical engagement with the students' existing knowledge into their courses, and they emphasized reflective practice as an essential part of a negotiator's toolkit. In short, they designed their courses to include opportunities for students (and professors) to "unlearn" as well as learn new things about negotiation. (See Docherty and Lira, *Adapting to the Adaptive* in this volume for a full discussion of the pedagogical principles behind Leonard's and Jayne's courses.)

Negotiation as a Game (Finite or Infinite?)

The use of a game metaphor for describing negotiation is so pervasive that it has disappeared into the background for many of us. But what kind of game is negotiation? Well, that may depend on whether we are talking about social negotiation or transactional negotiation. According to James P. Carse, "There are at least two kinds of games. One could be called finite, the other infinite. A finite game is played for the purpose of winning, an infinite game for the purpose of continuing the play" (1986: 3) and bringing as many persons as possible into the play.

Social negotiation is an infinite game; it does not have a clear start and stop time, the rules can be changed, some players can enter or exit the game, the players can "play with" the boundaries of play, and there are no outside referees to enforce rules and regulate play. Transactional negotiation, on the other hand, is more often described in terms reserved for finite games. Even when the game of transactional negotiation is played cooperatively, we still talk about who did better and who did worse in the process; we rank the participants in terms of the outcome. (In formal classes, this is sometimes done explicitly, for purposes of student assessment [Coben 2012].) The game is played for a particular purpose in a bounded period of time. Even if some negotiators sustain ongoing relationships, each round of play (each negotiation encounter) can be viewed and evaluated separately.

"Finite games can be played within an infinite game, but an infinite game cannot be played within a finite game. Infinite players regard their wins and losses in whatever finite games they play as but moments in continuing play" (Carse 1986: 8). Jayne would go further in connecting these two forms of negotiation games. In negotiation, the outcomes of transactional negotiations (finite games) feed back into social negotiations (infinite games) in ways that alter the infinite game. And the infinite game of social negotiation exposes issues and problems that are amenable to transactional negotiation. Participants in the infinite game of social negotiation can agree to step into the finite game of transactional negotiation, or they can use other methods for dealing with problems and conflicts.

If this game metaphor is helpful for explaining the interconnected processes of social and transactional negotiation, then we can think about the task of teaching negotiation to others as an example of teaching others how to play a game. But what kind of game are we trying to teach? Are we teaching students to play the infinite game or the finite game? Are we adequately teaching them how the finite and infinite games intersect and interact?

Many activities used in typical negotiation pedagogy are quite clearly finite games. Participants are given a situation, a role, a set of rules, some pointers regarding what constitutes skillful play, and criteria for evaluating the outcomes of their play. The instructor starts the game and ends the game and evaluates the results of the play. Who did better or worse in the play? Who achieved better or worse outcomes? Some teaching games are even scored numerically. When organized this way, even the most complex cases become artificially simplified in the minds of the game players.

What gets left out of play when we teach negotiation this way? Pretty much everything needed to deal effectively with protracted social conflicts[7] (Azar 1990), because those problems absolutely require "players" who are skilled at social negotiation, transactional negotiation *and* the connections among those different games.

The rest of this chapter will be Jayne's description of the course; hence a switch to the first person singular. This is not intended to minimize Calvin's contribution to the course, which was formative, as described below.

Using an Emergent Scenario to Teach Negotiation

To overcome the limitations of existing approaches to teaching negotiation, I developed a course where the students and I created an emergent scenario using improvisational theater techniques and game design activities. (See Lira and Parish, *Making it up as You Go*, in this volume, for more on the use of theater in our field.) The course was taught over three weekends, with the class sessions running from 8:30 a.m. until 5:30 p.m. on Friday and Saturday. Each weekend was dedicated to one dimension of negotiation: social negotiation (January 20 and 21), dispute domain negotiation (February 10 and 11), and transactional negotiation (February 24 and 25). Students were also expected to meet and work between sessions, and they did so with great enthusiasm.

Fourteen students were enrolled in the course. It would have been more effective to have about twenty students, but the group was large enough to run the course. As is typical with the classes in my department's master's program, the group was older, more experienced and more internationally diverse than in many classrooms.[8]

I handed out flip cameras or similar devices and asked students to record their between-class meetings and private negotiations. In the classroom, we used cameras to capture small group and plenary sessions, with the small group sessions being convened in pre-designated stage areas. I have hours of video yet to be fully analyzed, but there are some interesting clips that illustrate the depth of conversations that arose out of having students develop full characters rather than assume roles. During the semester, students watched some of their own videos, and found this enlightening and helpful for developing their characters and thinking about the issues. The following description of the class and reflections on why it worked and how it could be improved are necessarily incomplete, since they do not fully reflect the experiences and views of all the participants. However, the students will have a voice in this chapter via quotations from some of their journals.

Identifying a Case

Emergent scenario is not another name for simulation. Simulations are typically finite games, even when they are complicated. An emergent scenario goes beyond even the most daring and creative ideas developed by Noam Ebner and Kimberlee Kovach (2010) in response to an earlier declaration by Nadja Alexander and Michelle LeBaron (2009) that role plays are far insufficient for the needs they are generally used to address. Even Daniel Druckman's marathon exercise (2006) is more structured and scripted than an emergent scenario, as is the Laurence de Carlo CD-ROM simulation of environmental conflict resolution in France (2005).

An emergent scenario starts with a dramatic event and an invitation to the participants to build a world within which that dramatic event has meaning.

The world, and therefore the negotiable problem or problems that arise from that world, is co-created by the participants, acting in characters that they animate in ways similar to an actor giving life to a character. This stands in marked contrast to the assigned roles in simulations, which emphasize the goals of the parties and thereby privilege a rational-actor model of the person. In many simulations relationships, emotions, cultural norms, and values are all implicitly or explicitly treated as problems that get in the way of rational negotiation. In truth, however, those messy facets of our lives are central to who we are, what we desire, and how we interact with others, including how we interact with others in negotiation. In protracted social conflicts the conflict is deeply embedded in cultural norms and relationships; it is woven into the emotional responses of the parties and it creates its own logic (i.e., its own rationality).

In an emergent scenario, as in real life, the "world" emerges from the interactions of participants who are bundles of relationships, roles, emotions, and values as well as goals that are amenable to bargaining, trading and problem solving. In short, the world created in the classroom is *negotiated into reality* through the interactions of the participants who bring their whole selves into the process. The created world, like the real world, is unpredictable. The problems to be negotiated are identified and framed by the participants. I anticipate that every time I teach an emergent scenario, even with the same prompt, the case that develops will be different, because the class members will create a different version of the world; the one thing the worlds will have in common is that the dramatic event the class starts with will make sense within every world that is created.

In our course, we started with *Luna: Spirit of the Whale,* a made-for-television film about a real-life conflict in British Columbia in 2001-2002. In addition to the dramatic film, we had documentary film materials and some behind-the-scenes information from Calvin Chrustie, a Royal Canadian Mounted Police officer who had led the RCMP team working on the case. Calvin is also a co-author of a prior chapter in this series about negotiating wicked problems (Chrustie et al. 2010). In a real sense, therefore, Calvin, as a practitioner, originated key components and materials used for the course.

The drama started when a juvenile orca whale became separated from his pod and showed up near Gold River, British Columbia. The whale was known by three different names. Scientists referred to him as L98, which is the number he was assigned as part of his pod. The public, after a naming contest sponsored by a newspaper, called him Luna. The local First Nations community (the Mowachaht/ Muchalaht) called him Tsux'iit (tsu' – keet), which was the tribal name of their late chief Ambrose Maquinna, because they believed the spirit of their chief – in keeping with their traditional beliefs – had migrated to the whale.[9]

The class immediately had to grapple with social negotiation when they tried to understand the beliefs of the Mowachaht/Muchalaht as compared with the way *reporters* described their beliefs. Reporters used the term "reincarnated" to describe the Mowachaht/Muchalaht claims about Tsux'iit. Many members of the dominant culture had trouble accepting this claim, because their understanding of reincarnation did not fit with the fact that the orca was already alive when the Chief died. Members of the public and some government officials concluded that the Mowachaht/Muchalaht advocates were making this claim to advance their cause, not because they really believed the orca was Chief Maquinna. The actual Mowachaht/Muchalaht belief is more about the chief's spirit "migrating into" rather than being "born into" an orca or a wolf.

Exploring the Context of the Luna Case

The directors of the film give Luna/Tsux'iit status as a character in the world of Gold River; he is not treated as a part of nature to be controlled or managed by human beings even though some members of the community would opt to treat him that way. In making this narrative choice, they capture the underlying worldviewing conflict (Docherty 2001) between the First Nations band and the Euro-Canadian community in a manner that gives us a window onto the protracted social conflict in British Columbia (B.C.).

So, what is the background of the protracted social conflict?

British Columbia is unusual within Canada because most of the First Nations groups in B.C. never signed treaties with the colonial power (Great Britain) or with the subsequent Federal and Provincial governments. Many students in my class did not know that the relationship between First Nations groups and the Crown (i.e., the British colonial power) was shaped by the *Royal Proclamation of 1763*, which decreed that First Nations should not be disturbed in their use and enjoyment of the land. The proclamation also provided that only the Crown could purchase land from First Nations groups, and could only do that through treaty making. In this manner, the *Royal Proclamation* set the framework for negotiating with First Nations based on co-operation instead of conquest.

This is not to say that there were no elements of conquest and domination between the Federal and Provincial governments of Canada and the native peoples. In fact, there were many instances of abuse and domination, including efforts to eradicate native cultures by placing students in residential schools where they were forced to speak English and forbidden to speak their own languages; economic and educational discrimination; the placement of First Nations children in foster care, and many other policies and practices that attempted to destroy native cultures through assimilation.

One of the most far-reaching policies of repression was the 1927 *Indian Act*, which made it a criminal offense for a First Nation to hire an attorney for the purpose of pursuing a land claim settlement.[10] Not surprisingly, there were no historical treaties signed subsequent to that date. This freezing of the treaty process had particularly negative effects on the western provinces, including B.C., where most First Nations groups had not negotiated treaties prior to 1927. Not having treaties in place has had long-term negative effects on everyone living in the province

The economy of B.C. is based largely on resource extraction (fishing, mining, and timber), and the unresolved land claims eventually paralyzed the economy. The issues are well summarized on a website intended to help teachers explain the problems arising from a lack of treaties in the province.

> Uncertainty about the existence and location of Aboriginal rights create uncertainty with respect to ownership, use and management of land and resources. That uncertainty has led to disruptions and delays to economic activity in B.C. It has also discouraged investment.

> The consequences of not concluding treaties are lost economic activity as well as escalating court costs and continued uncertainty. Key benefits of negotiated settlements are economic and legal certainty as well as harmonized arrangements between the different levels of government.

> A 2009 Pricewaterhouse [sic] Cooper study, commissioned by the B.C. Treaty Commission, showed that the sooner treaties are settled the bigger the benefits for First Nations and all British Columbians. Those benefits include investment, jobs and economic development (http://www.aadnc-aandc.gc.ca/eng/1100100016299/1100100 016300).

The process for correcting these problems began in 1992, when "Canada, British Columbia, and the First Nations Summit, representing the First Nations . . . created the British Columbia treaty process. This process is aimed at building a relationship with B.C. First Nations based on respect and trust that will result in treaties, thus settling the uncertainty associated with unresolved land claims in B.C." (Auditor General 2006: vii). Twenty years later the Treaty Process is still not complete.

By 2006, it was clear to the Auditor General's Office that the treaty process was stalled for a number of reasons. It was expensive and time consuming for all three parties (First Nations and provincial and federal government). The process often raises more questions than it answers. And the gap between the positions of the parties is large and difficult to bridge (Auditor General 2006: 10). Furthermore, the legal, political and economic conditions have changed in the past ten years in ways that negatively impact the Treaty Process (p. 11).

From a peacebuilding perspective, the Treaty Process has not made progress because it was flawed in its design. The Treaty Process is essentially a high level political negotiation to regularize relations between First Nations peoples and the Provincial and Federal government of Canada. In that respect the treaty negotiations (taken collectively) are similar to a peace process to move a country from war-to-peace after an internal conflict, but it has not been conceived that way. Because the relations between the First Nations groups and the governments have not been overtly violent, the parties are also involved in other more immediate negotiations about resources and economic development, *which were not considered in the design of the Treaty Process*. So the various negotiation processes run alongside one another and tangle things up. Every dispute over a resource impacts the treaty negotiations and every treaty negotiation impacts the way parties approach conflicts over resources. When resource based conflicts get loaded onto a political negotiation that should be serving as a process for building legitimate governance structures and relationships, the short-term issues of economics distort the political conversations.

In the face of stalled Treaty Negotiations the government and First Nations appeared, in 2006, to be creating "an emerging policy" under the title "the New Relationship." The goal was to create "an opportunity for all First Nations, whether inside or outside the treaty process, to work with the province to make decisions about the use of land and resources" in order to "strengthen relationships between the three parties" (p. 11). However, in the absence of clarity about the linkage between the government's New Relationship and treaty policies, the First Nations groups were playing a "wait and see" game.

Even when Luna/Tsux'iit/L98 arrived in Gold River in 2001, treaty negotiations appeared to be stalled, and some First Nations groups were looking for other means to settle specific resource claims so that they could get on with development and meeting the basic needs of their peoples. Yet these larger governance conflicts were hanging over every encounter between First Nations groups, the government and other stakeholder groups in the province. In other words, the whale, whatever name we use for him, definitely entered into a social, political, economic, and cultural setting of a wicked problem or a protracted social conflict.

The different attitudes about Luna/Tsux'iit/L98 are understandable only in the context of these background conflicts. Some commercial fishermen saw Luna as a nuisance, once he moved into "their" harbor, both because he was eating "their" fish and because he was playing with and damaging their boats and equipment. Local business leaders were inclined to see him as an economic boon because he generated tourist traffic. Some, but not all, in the Mowachaht/Muchalaht community saw him as their late chief and, therefore, a free, independent creature with the right to make his own decisions about where he would live. Some First Nations leaders thought that

Tsux'iit/Luna might even be used as a rallying point around which to mobilize an uprising or confrontation with the dominant community and/or the government officials. The employees of the Department of Fisheries and Oceans (DFO) – the federal agency responsible for regulating fishing and protecting wildlife – had different views about Luna/L98. Some DFO employees saw him primarily as a potential danger to boats and humans, while others were more concerned about his welfare and the health of his pod. Some of the DFO personnel were also concerned about the cultural rights of the First Nations community. Media and the general public saw him as a cute creature with a sad story. Whale scientists saw L98 as "lost" and in need of return to his pod for his own health and the long-term viability of the whale population. The Royal Canadian Mounted Police (RCMP) were concerned about keeping order. Off camera and never discussed in the film, they were keeping an eye on the situation for any signs that some individuals might decide this was an opportunity to use violence in their cause.

Given only minimal comment in the film was the issue of the impact of aquaculture in Northwest Canada generally and B.C. specifically. Large corporations had been developing "fish farms" where they raise farmed Atlantic salmon off the coast. Fish farms were less likely than other resource extraction operations to be shut down in court, because the coastal waters were not subject to competing ownership claims in the same way that land-based resources were contested. The practice of aquaculture has expanded significantly since the incident with Luna and today the fish farms, many owned by large Norwegian companies, have proliferated along the coast. While they provide employment opportunities, they are also controversial for environmental reasons.

Around the time that Luna/Tsux'iit/L98 showed up, the controversy over farmed salmon was starting to heat up. Environmental scientists and activists were alleging that sea lice from the farmed salmon were responsible for the dramatic and sudden collapse of several major salmon runs in B.C., a catastrophe that was negatively affecting the First Nations and Euro-Canadian communities. In the film, there is a brief mention that Luna/Tsux'iit had damaged a fish farm, and the late chief, Ambrose Maquinna, had been working on issues related to stopping or regulating fish farming in the area. This was not the primary focus of the film, but for those who identified the whale as Tsux'iit, any damage he did to fish farms could be interpreted as continued comment from Chief Maquiina and a motivation to increase resistance to aquaculture operations in the area.

Establishing the Context for Our Emergent Scenario

In many simulation-based classes, the professor would take a case such as the one described above and decide which issues should go to negotiation, which parties should participate, and how the negotiations should be organized. This information would be *given to* the students, who would also be *assigned* roles and negotiating goals. Much of the real-life consequences of a protracted social conflict and much of the messiness and stubbornness of a wicked problem would thus be sanitized from the classroom experience. An emergent scenario is set up differently, through a process of building a world and developing multi-dimensional characters.

In situations of protracted social conflict, there are multiple, interconnected issues, not all of which are suitable for negotiation. For example, negotiation does not address past historical harms and community traumas. Those drivers of conflict need to be addressed through other interventions, including activities such as truth-telling and reconciliation processes, community dialogues, and public commemoration of difficult historical events. When peacebuilders approach real wicked problems, they have to coordinate multiple interventions and identify those issues that might usefully be negotiated as part of the effort to transform the overall conflict. An emergent scenario, unlike a simulation, replicates this reality. Therefore it is never clear, at the beginning of an emergent scenario, which issues will be negotiated and which issues will be managed in other ways or left unaddressed.

After watching the dramatic film and the documentary video, the class members and I discussed the issues described above. We started by clarifying the immediate dramatic conflict of Luna/Tsux'iit/L98; we applied conflict analysis techniques that all of the students learn in their first course in the degree program. In addition to discovering the problems with stalled treaty negotiations, we learned that the conflicts over aquaculture had grown more heated since 2002. Eventually, someone said something like, "I wonder what would happen if Luna showed up now?" We all thought that was a really interesting question, so we decided that our emergent scenario would be set today, rather than in 2001-2002 when Luna/Tsux'iit/L98 actually appeared.

Based on that foundational decision, we divided the task of building the world for our conflict scenario into two parts: creating the local community and enriching our understanding of the context.

Creating a Realistic Community

During the remainder of the first class session – approximately a day-and-a-half – we focused on building the local community in which Luna 2 would appear. The students created and introduced their characters. They were asked to introduce themselves as real people, not just as persons with an opinion about Luna 2. To accomplish this they developed personal biographies using theater techniques to build characters.

Uta Hagen (1973) recommends preparing for stage roles by doing weeks or months of research into the daily life of a character. She also argues for focusing on the subjective aspects of the character's life. If you are preparing to play Nina in *The Sea Gull* . . .

> You must look for, and identify with, and make use of not only your (Nina's) clothing and underclothing, the details of your room (washbowls with pitcher and soap and heavy linen towels, the kind of bed and bedding, curtains, scrubbed flooring, icons, prayer habits) but also with what you read, what's forbidden or allowed. How do you write? By candlelight, kerosene, gaslight? If you write a note to Konstantin, on what kind of paper, with what kind of pen and ink, etc.? Then explore your specific task of getting ready for an outing (Hagen 1973: 137).

I did not ask the students to go quite this far in developing their characters, but I did emphasize Hagen's advice to focus on the subjective level and build emotional connection with the character.

The result was the development of a community of complex characters rather than a classroom of "flat" representatives of positions. One student reflected on the difference between playing a role and developing characters in our emergent scenario this way:

> I have gone through much training that involved role-plays, and have become more and more concerned about the efficacy of and the impact of the role-plays. Too often the role that is played emphasizes one or two problematic features that make it easy to love or hate that role. This flat description and personification of someone does not assist skill development . . . . [I]t perpetuates stereotypes and provides comic relief to often tense training situations (#6).

As with many participants, #6 chose a character that would challenge him to think outside his ordinary frame. He opted to be an elected official, and he did a lot of work getting inside the thought process and life reality of political leaders. As a consequence he developed a much greater appreciation for the pressures on political leaders when they confront complex social conflicts, particularly those that blend scientific or technical issues with the social, political and economic challenges of supporting healthy development.

One of the Canadian students (#11) was both excited to have a Canadian case chosen for the course and offended by some of the ways others were portraying Canadians. Once she got past her reaction, however, she recognized the opportunity to identify and reflect on her own unconsciously held assumptions. She took on the role of a Canadian government official from the DFO. She wrote, after watching the film,

> I felt my tendency to demonize or simplify those with whom I don't agree, and desired to face that by putting myself in the shoes of the "Government" worker who is only trying to keep his job . . . . It was a nuanced experience that prompted me to reflect on my identity, my narratives, and how I can begin to shift my own stories to be able to integrate with the stories of others (#11).

If you are wondering how students develop realistic characters, part of the answer is that they draw on their own lives in the same way that a professional actor draws on her own life when animating a character. Even if an actor spends weeks or months researching the life of Nina in *The Sea Gull*, becoming intimately familiar with Nina's daily life right down to the underwear she wears and the books she is or is not allowed to read, ultimately the emotional dimensions of the character come in part from the inner life of the actor. Uta Hagen will not play Nina the same way Susan Sarandon plays Nina.

After the first class session, some students were still having difficulty getting into their own character and engaging with the other characters in the scenario. This was probably difficult, in part, because the students knew each other well from other classes. For example, one student wrote:

> . . . everyone in the class had [their] own worldview toward negotiation on issues and we each took our own characters. It was very interesting, but [at] the same time, it was too confusing for me. Every time I met the other character, I need to understand not just one person's worldview but two (real world person and character). Such like the movie "Inception" I need to dive twice into other people's worldview (#7).

He suggested that he and others might need more assistance getting into character.

The assistance came from a fellow student, who developed a very detailed process of creating a genealogy for her character. We used that process at the beginning of the second session to help everyone round out his or her character. Later, this same student developed a second character when she realized that her character (Kit) *could not* attend a particular meeting, but her character's son (Sean) would be front and center at that meeting. For the remainder of the course, she used a simple costume prop – a baseball cap – to indicate who was showing up for a conversation. Cap forward was Kit; cap backward was Sean. The rest of the community quickly grasped the differences between Kit and Sean. It was fascinating to watch others interact quite differently with Sean and with Kit even though they knew they were talking to their classmate. From a pedagogical perspective, it was useful to cultivate and rely on a few students who were really able to develop complete and well-rounded characters. They modeled the process and others were able to follow their example.

Another challenge for some students occurred when our Japanese student presented herself as speaking for Luna. Her character claimed a background in process work that enabled her to channel the orca's feelings. This, as much as anything, illustrates the difference between a role-play and an emergent scenario. This kind of person would never be scripted into a traditional negotiation role-play, even though such persons are often present in the local community. If a role-play did include this character, she would probably be played with irony, more of a caricature than a real character. In our class, this character was well rounded and utterly sincere.

This is not to say she was immediately welcomed into the student-created "world of Gold River." Many members of the emergent community thought she was a crackpot. And some of the First Nations community members were offended by what they perceived as disrespect for their beliefs by some "New Age, hippie outsider." On the other hand, I reminded the students that every complex conflict draws into the engagement someone with views outside the norms of the community. Eventually, everyone opted to deal with her character respectfully, and in one case she played a bridge between competing worldviews in a way that no one else could have played it. With her there, there was little chance that Luna's needs or wishes would be forgotten. She even challenged the aboriginal community regarding their proposed plans to help "manage" Luna.

In the first weekend session, the community members got to know one another through a series of dyadic and small group encounters in character. Only after the students had a sense of the persons in their emergent community did we identify sub-groups in the community that might be the basis for what professional conflict interveners call parties to the conflict. Because the students had developed complex characters, they were aware from the beginning that each sub-group had internal tensions and conflicts based on identity, historical conflicts and worldview differences.

Enriching Our Understanding of the Context and Conflict

I assumed primary responsibility for developing more details about the surrounding social, political and economic context for the emergent scenario. Because this was the first time we were using this scenario and I was occupied during the class sessions with facilitating the character development process, this had to wait until after the first weekend. Between the first and second weekends students also did a lot of research and forwarded relevant documents for my consideration. In the future, I will launch the course with background materials already organized. But I am sure that more research will be needed, because no two emergent scenarios are exactly the same, and things change!

Our research on current conditions in B.C. revealed that conflicts over fish farms have gotten much worse in the past ten years, and the treaty negotiations are still stalled. But all is not frozen in place because of lack of progress on the treaty negotiation. Quite interesting from a conflict management perspective were the First Nations communities that had decided to make agreements with the government outside of the treaty process in order to meet the needs of each respective community.

As the designated "game master," I made some decisions about the scenario, as we would resume it in the next class meeting. I decided to change First Nations groups because the Mowachaht/Muchalaht community has been significantly altered as a result of their encounter with Tsux'iit. I also did not want the students trying to replicate the community from the film, and I wanted them to explore the way a similar conflict would evolve if it involved a First Nations community that had made different choices about how to handle the protracted social conflicts in B.C. I opted to use the Heiltsuk people as our First Nations group, because they have not met in treaty negotiations with the government since 2003, but they have reached interesting agreements about co-managing a conservancy district and other ways of creating economic development and economic stability in their area (see http://www.gov.bc.ca/arr/firstnation/heiltsuk/default.html).

I relocated the Heiltsuk people geographically to the same area where Luna had appeared ten years ago so that the students would not need to grapple with a geographic change on top of the other changes we were making. I moved the issue of the fish farms and fishing resources to the fore because those conflicts have, in fact, escalated in the province. If another whale appeared today under similar circumstances, it is reasonable to assume that the drama of the whale would highlight the conflicts about aquaculture.

I kept the profile of Heiltsuk tribe intact and referred students to their extensive web site (located at http://www.firstnations.eu/fisheries/heiltsuk.htm) for more information. I rather arbitrarily (not to mention unkindly) scripted the demise of their chief, Bob Anderson, who has an extensive public record of opinions including videos available on the web. This meant that while he was deceased in our emergent scenario, we had access to his public persona, which made him a very real character in our world, particularly since one of the tribal members developed her character as his widow.

Based on this research, I presented the following conflict summary to the class via email.

- Luna Two (L2) showed up in Heiltsuk waters shortly after the chief died;
- L2 is drawing public attention;
- L2 has damaged two fish farms – the owners want the whale removed, because they are liable for damage done to native fish populations when their fish escape *and* they lose money on the fish themselves;
- DFO and the government in general are being pressured by all groups to "do the right thing" re: L2 *and* re: fish farming, but what is the "right thing"?

I also gave everyone a list of the cast of the characters from the class and an extensive list of video resources and print materials to absorb. The materials included information about efforts to address the conflicts over fish farming, including a long-delayed report from the *Cohen Commission*, which was investigating the environmental impact of fish farming.[11] This gave them an opportunity to grapple with the role of science in complex environmental conflicts, and I gave them readings related to this issue (Adler et al. 2000; Adler 2002).

The video materials were particularly useful for revealing the world of the ongoing conflicts in B.C. For example, one video documentary follows mayors from B.C. communities on a trip to Norway, where they learn about aquaculture (http://vimeo.com/12042048). All of the mayors are Euro-Canadian and they all express hopes that this kind of development can revitalize the B.C. economy. The film includes interviews with environmental opponents to expanded fish farming; again, all of these individuals interviewed are Euro-Canadian. No one in the video mentions the unresolved treaty issues as one reason that the economy of B.C. is in trouble, and no one refers to the needs or rights of the First Nations groups. In other videos, only First Nations issues are addressed and no one mentions the larger economic decline that impacts everyone (http://www.youtube.com/watch?v=Ojey_ GYsbi0; http://www.youtube.com/watch?v=4j01Aj-40ug). As often happens in protracted social conflicts, the parties appear to live in different realities, even though they probably interact on a daily basis.

In addition to developing their characters and immersing themselves in the materials, various subgroups were asked to convene meetings prior to the next class session. For example, the First Nations characters were asked to convene a Tribal Council meeting and representatives from DFO, the elected officials, and the fish farm managers were asked to attend a meeting about aquaculture development in the province where they would have informal conversations. Some participants opted to have casual meetings in character between sessions – the types of chance encounters that happen in real life at the grocery store or the post office.

While continuing their social negotiations, the students were also preparing for our session, which would focus on identifying venues and processes for managing various conflicts including identifying some issues that are amenable to formal negotiation.

Negotiating What to Negotiate and How to Negotiate It

The second class session was dedicated entirely to the very messy process of deciding which issues can be handled through negotiation and which issues need to be handled some other way, or perhaps even put on hold until later. The students read materials on the concept of legal pluralism, which is a situation that arises when multiple systems of governance or multiple systems for addressing conflicts compete for legitimacy. Legal pluralism is very common, but rarely discussed in negotiation classes. In protracted social conflicts, legal pluralism is always a problem. The Luna scenario forces students to grapple with this issue, as is illustrated by this journal entry written by the student playing the widow of the Chief.

> The overarching challenge associated with discerning the difference between Band, Provincial and Federal authority over land and water use exemplifies the way that legal pluralism impacts this case. While I thought we had a legal agreement with the Province of British Columbia related to our authority over the land, water and wild life, I later found that it would not be valid until ratified by the Canadian Federal Government. Together, these overlapping governmental bodies, including local, provincial and Federal legal systems, rep-

resent multiple pathways to pursue legal action on behalf of
the interests of the Band. However, if not correctly navigated,
the Band could expend scarce financial resources pursuing
various options within the network of interlocking legal systems, only to find that one successful treaty is negated by another legal loophole. Choosing the right arena/domain for the
dispute at hand is crucial for the Band at this juncture. (#3)

Discovering this problem in character, where her emotional self and
identity were present, was far more powerful than reading about it in
a paper.

Another dimension of identifying a dispute domain for negotiation in a protracted conflict involves improving relationships through
dialogue as well as making process decisions through shared deliberation. This is perhaps the most difficult part of teaching three-dimensional negotiation. In real life, the processes for setting up a complex
negotiation take months or even years. Putting this process on fast-
forward in an emergent scenario is tricky.

We set the room up to have different meeting spaces, making
them as private as possible. (Hint: For emergent scenario teaching
you need a lot of space, and options for breakout rooms.) Each group
met to discuss the issues as they understood them and to decide what
problems they considered suitable for negotiation, what problems
they wanted to handle in another way, and what kind of negotiation
process they would like to try using. For several hours they met in
their groups, and sent emissaries to other groups, and convened small
meetings to negotiate process.

Some individuals had created boundary-spanning characters –
for example, the Heiltsuk man who also owned a commercial fishing license and was also a member of the Pacific Trollers Association,
which meant he was friends with the predominantly Euro-Canadian
commercial fishermen. He spent time running between meetings and
informally carrying messages and information. But he also experienced some suspicion from his different peer groups. Others had created personal bonds that complicated their relationship as parties to
a conflict. For example, Kit (a professional fisher) was a widow and
high school classmate of the Chief's widow, Leila. They had shared
some time together outside of class when Kit visited Leila after the
Chief's funeral. The class learned the value and the limitations and
complexities created by boundary spanners and personal relationships that transcend the conflict.

After several hours of working on the issue, and feeling more
rather than less confused about how to design a dispute domain that
would support negotiation, we stepped out of characters and con-

vened back into a class setting. It was here that we learned how helpful it could be to step into and out of the emergent scenario for the purpose of teaching and learning. (For more on a related theme, see Deason et al., *Debriefing the Debrief* and *Debriefing Adventure Learning*, in this volume.) We continued this process for the remainder of the course, and we learned that it was important to signal clearly when we were making those transitions. It helped to develop some embodied practices (see Alexander and LeBaron, *Embodied Negotiation*, in this volume) to mark the transition point: "shaking off" our character or putting our character back on.

As students-teachers and as a teacher-student (see Freire 2000) of peacebuilding and not as characters, we developed a large conflict map for our case, and we then reviewed process design options and principles of good process design. We grappled with questions such as: How do you sort out issues that might be negotiable from those that can't be negotiated? How do you identify issues that *if* they were negotiated might transform the more protracted social conflict? How do you negotiate buy-in for a negotiation process? Who can and who cannot serve as a convening agent for negotiations?

These were without question the richest process design discussions I have ever had with students, because even though they were out of character, they were emotionally attached to the situation, not just working on an intellectual puzzle. This proved to be a very enlightening exercise. It made me realize that when we teach process design, we do not force students to view the design from deep within a stakeholder identity, and that is a problem that needs to be corrected. As a side note: this emergent scenario taught empathy skills far more effectively than any training activities.

After our design discussion, the students went back into their characters and groups to consider process options. Their discussions were different now, because they could all see how something that looked good on paper might not look so good to some of the stakeholders. They could also see how rational, linear process design privileges the viewpoints of some stakeholders over others, and why some parties might think of transactional negotiation as a game rigged against them.

The students concluded that no process would be designed if we left it all to the parties. So they decided to hire a facilitator. That led to a negotiation over who would hire the facilitator and how she would be paid. Again, a common issue in process design had a lot more resonance for the participants. This also made me realize that students were getting a lot of experience with "at the table" or transactional negotiation simply through the process of designing a dispute domain. In the future, I think this opportunity for practicing transactional negotiation could be highlighted and improved.

The parties agreed that a facilitator hired by the Suzuki Foundation (http://www.davidsuzuki.org/) would be acceptable, and I was hired to serve as the facilitator. Together, we agreed that rather than having the facilitator conduct private interviews and prepare a report on the issues that might be negotiable, she would facilitate a public listening process. Again, we did a mini-negotiation over the process design for the listening sessions. This allowed us to discuss issues of fairness and efficiency as well as issues of transparency and confidentiality. And then we conducted the listening process.

In this way we created a "fast forward" version of dialogue and deliberation processes that might take months or years in a real case, rather than just skipping over that messy part of the whole process. For the students, this closed the gap between dialogue, deliberation and decision-making (see for example Nixon 2012; Saunders 1996). And in our teaching/learning roles, we had rich discussions about why this is an issue in our field, what happens when citizens engage in dialogues but the dialogues don't inform the top level negotiations, and what kinds of options others have developed for connecting dialogue with decision-making.

Transactional Negotiation

The third weekend was scheduled for transactional negotiation, which requires the creation of a focused agenda of issues that are suitable for negotiation. The participants had identified the co-management agreement between the Heiltsuk tribe and the Provincial government as an area where some progress achieved through negotiation would help to transform the larger conflicts. Acting as "game space designers" we agreed that "Dr. Jane Foster" (me, again) from Eastern Mennonite University would facilitate the negotiation process, and that she would be paid out of a *Co-Management Implementation Fund (CMIF)* that was created using contributions from:

- DFO,
- The Heiltsuk Economic Development Corporation (HEDC) (http://www.coastfunds.ca/read-our-stories),
- The BC Salmon Farmers Association (http://www.salmon-farmers.org/),
- A special fund created by the Provincial government (sponsored by Minister Lake), and
- The Pacific Trollers Association (http://www.island.net/~pta/).

The government ruled that CMIF could not accept donations or support from corporations. Two parties to the conflict, Mr. Tuna (an aquaculture executive) and Denis (a local owner of a fish farm)[12] negotiated to make contributions to the B.C. Salmon Farmers Association to support CMIF. This was permitted by the government and deemed acceptable by the other parties.

The participants also agreed that negotiations would focus around three goals:

1) Address some specific issues related to the safety of Luna and keeping Luna from damaging property or creating a danger to others.

2) Help the participants set up a system for co-management of ocean related resources (ocean fish, fish farms, and salmon runs affected by ocean conditions).

3) Build the foundations for a sustainable Co-Management Program.

Within these boundaries, I developed the type of planning forms and technical information more commonly used in negotiation simulations. Each party received information about their near-term, mid-term and long-term (3 years out) goals and interests for the issues of: a) Luna 2; b) Co-Management Program; c) Fisheries/Ocean Issues; and d) Other Issues. Each party had other issues that were not technically on the agenda, but that they might try to move onto the agenda. This, too, is realistic. They also received information on the monetary and material resources they had on hand. They were free to expand on and refine their goals and interests and they could prioritize the issues as they wished, but they were required to work within the resources as outlined on their handouts.

We also noted at the outset that in order to convene these negotiations the parties had to have made *frame concessions*, including:

▪ The government and Euro-Canadian communities are agreeing to work inside a frame that says "Luna 2 is tied to the Heiltsuk people."

▪ The Heiltsuk people have agreed to accept that Luna 2 needs to be "managed" as part of the larger ecosystem.

Again, the students could really feel how difficult those concessions were for the various parties. They understood that reframing the situation in order to get to the table was a very complicated and difficult process of negotiation in its own right, because reframing can involve identity threats.

The groups prepared separately for the negotiation sessions, and then they sent representatives to the negotiation table, which was convened in a fishbowl so everyone could watch. Because they sent representatives to the table, not all characters had a role at the table. This meant that many students were observers of the negotiation, and they did not have a chance to be at the table practicing the skills of transactional negotiation. I was concerned they would feel cheated, but they were completely attentive to the process, took extensive notes, and in the debriefing process they made very astute observations about how their classmates had negotiated.

Among the students enrolled in our class, many do not aspire to being at the table as parties to a complex conflict. They are embarked on career paths that will involve designing, supporting and facilitating negotiation processes, i.e., helping others to negotiate more effectively. I think this is why they were happy to observe.

When I teach the class again, however, I will add a fourth weekend. With the help of a teaching assistant, I will review the videos captured on the flip cameras to identify interesting "micro-negotiation" encounters. These will form the basis for practicing negotiation at the table in the fourth weekend. Everyone will get some practice with transactional negotiation and the class will be able to review the development of the scenario and contemplate "what could have been" if they had made other choices.

How Did the Class Work, Overall?

The course was organized using the ELM model (see Docherty and Lira, *Adapting to the Adaptive*, in this volume), which organizes learning in this order: concrete experience, "publish and process" (reflect on what you did), generalize new information, develop and anticipate how you will use it, and then apply the knowledge. In the extended scenario, I discovered it was important to do the full ELM circuit repeatedly, in bite-size chunks. We all needed to stop the scenario periodically to review what we were learning. It was in these moments that I delivered mini-lectures or we engaged the readings they had done prior to class. I can tell from their journals that the materials they read stuck with them, because they could understand them in reference to an immediate life experience.

From my perspective, the emergent scenario process is a much more realistic way to teach negotiation. It forces students to grapple with *social ethics* and *social responsibility* to parties not at the negotiation table in a manner that rarely, if ever, happens in the standard negotiation classroom (Docherty 2010: 498-501).

The emergent scenario has enough of the uncertainty and complexity of real cases without overwhelming the students. The key is finding a balance between scripting and leaving things open for creativity. Several students commented on the importance of this balance and the way we managed it. What intrigued me, however, was the way some of them connected finding the "sweet spot" of balance between scripting and creativity to the process of recognizing the power of worldviews as drivers of conflict.

> The concept of three level negotiations in which worldviews of participants are acknowledged as important determinators [sic] of behavior and decision making is something that I haven't encountered thus far, even though negotiations are a field that I have researched before . . . I believe that the emergent scenario was the crucial part for understanding negotiations from a different perspective. Even though we had a general context and description of actors, the possibility to develop our characters enabled us to create our own worldviews within the scenario. In this way we are able to see how the worldviews inform the behaviors and the decision making as a part of a negotiation process (#2)

Overall, the emergent scenario process seemed to promote a lot of self-reflection about the students' own worldviews and their past experiences with conflict:

> I am not sure whether it is possible to separate the people from the problem entirely since we tend to automatically tangle issues with our backgrounds, memories, egos and positions. While I was surprised by my initial judgment in regards to the Canadian government's position, whom I unintentionally accused of being rude and unsympathetic to the tribes, I realized later that my accusation had much to do with my background. I channeled my anger about Afghanistan, where soldiers from the U.S. and the European countries are engaged in a prolonged war . . . (#9)

As in other classes where I have used dramatic films to set up activities, the *Luna* film evoked a variety of responses – shaped by culture and emotional reactions – from students. This type of response rarely happens if I start a class with a written case study. For example:

> The person from the [DFO] head office arrived in Gold River with a clear plan in mind. . . He had little regard for the position of the new chief in the community and this was clearly evident when he walked into the office and joined the conversation that his field officer was having with the chief. As a person from a culture different from North America, I found the attitude of the person from the head office disrespectful. However, I also thought it was important for the band to fol-

low the rules of the land because I am from India, a country
where people selectively follow rules based on their status in
society, the amount of money they have, or their political connections . . . But what were the rules in the scenario in the
film, and did I have the insight to interpret them correctly?
. . . [when we watched the documentary about First Nations
relations with the government]. . . Suddenly, I was not sure
whether I knew what was right or wrong because my orientation suddenly changed. The people from the First Nation had
been treated so unfairly! . . . I felt indignant. . . (#5)

Because the students in our program are primarily mid-career professionals, they also reflect on past experiences and anticipate applying
knowledge to future practice. We ask them to do this quite often, but
I usually find their reflections very cognitive and not deeply reflective. What I discovered in their journals was that the emergent and
uncertain aspects of our case invited more nuanced and much deeper
and more complex comparisons to past practices. In fact, some of the
students adopted characters that harkened back to their own past experiences with cases of complex conflict. Their journals included particularly rich insights at multiple levels – self-awareness about past
choices and behaviors, insight into the actions of others from past
cases, and "AHA! moments" about their earlier case. In future, I will
flag the opportunity to try on a role for the purpose of reflection on
past experience as well as for the purpose of the negotiation class
itself.

I was also struck by how effective this teaching process was for
helping students think about transferring what they were learning to
other situations. They did not all learn exactly the same thing, and I
would not expect them to, given how many backgrounds were represented in the class. But each student identified lessons that seemed
useful for him or her, including many deeply personal reflective lessons about personal behavioral tendencies or biases. Given how well
we come to know our students, I was fascinated with how well each
student focused on a personal lesson I thought they needed to consider in order to become more reflective practitioners.

More than half of the class talked in detail about what they
learned and how they were using it (or would use it in future) *in
relation to very concrete problems*. The journals followed a logical pattern
that looked like this: "I used to do x and y. In the emergent scenario,
I tried _____ and I watched my colleagues do _____, now when I
go back to my work, I am going to do a and b, because _____." This
was not some vague parroting of concepts and ideas. They were really
envisioning specific changes in behavior.

Conclusion

Following my students down the reflective path, I will end with some things I learned and things I will do differently.

First, while the process of teaching with an emergent scenario is nerve-wracking when you are not sure it will work, it does work. I will enter into it with confidence. I will trust the process and trust the students. They get really hooked on this and more fully enter into being teachers-students than they do in other courses.

Second, this takes a lot of time. Preparing between classes, answering questions and inquiries from the parties in the conflict (i.e., the students who take this work really seriously and really get into their roles), making the best use of the video materials that are produced so that students can reflect on their own performance in something closer to real time... all of this requires person power. But at least in our program, I think I have some solutions. We have students learning to use technology as part of their preparation for peacebuilding work; this is part of our arts and peacebuilding focus. I plan to offer some of them an opportunity to practice their technical skills by helping with the course. We also teach a facilitation course, and we have students wanting more facilitation experience. I am considering enlisting them for the times in the course where groups want facilitation. Perhaps we will even create a "jobs board" where would-be facilitators can post their qualifications and the negotiation class or even one or two groups from the class can select and "hire" an outside facilitator. Or, my biggest radical vision. . . organize a *whole semester* around an emergent scenario, with some students participating to learn negotiation, some students participating to learn process design, and others participating to learn facilitation skills. (Certain aspects of the course described by Fox and Press in *Venturing Home*, in this volume, might be seen as something of a prototype for this idea.)

Finally (for now), going back to the beginning setup of the class, I will modify the character preparation process. I plan to ask students to prepare a genealogy (using the technique developed by the student) and a genogram as part of developing their character. A genogram is a pictorial display of a person's family relationships. It is more than a family tree, because a genogram uses symbols that help the person completing it identify repetitive patterns of behavior. Each student in the master's program is asked to develop a genogram for the purpose of identifying family conflict patterns as an assignment in the conflict analysis course. This assignment is part of the CJP commitment to developing reflective practitioners who are self-aware and willing to embrace personal as well as social transformation. The students could easily do a genogram for their characters.

I will also ask each participant to identify those parts of his or her character's life that are not public, but are nevertheless important for understanding the character's response to conflict. Finally, I plan to invite other students not enrolled in the course to serve as interviewers, in order to help each participant refine and develop her character. This will actually give other students an opportunity to practice interviewing skills.

Notes

[1] Military Arts and Science, as an academic field, could be considered a subset of Political Science or Public Administration as it is taught in the professional military education institutes that are accredited to confer a Master of Military Arts and Sciences academic degree. The U.S. Military's expanded roles in counterinsurgency, peace, and humanitarian operations have caused the military to question some of its fundamental principles and traditional thinking about its purpose. This has led to a re-examination of professional education methodologies and concepts, to incorporate theories and concepts from other fields such as political science, economics, and anthropology.

[2] The study of peacebuilding may be seen as an outgrowth of the field of conflict analysis and resolution. The concept of peacebuilding and its practices and scope are not well established. See Henning Haugerudbraaten (1998) for an overview of the debates about peacebuilding – what it entails, who does it, and how it is accomplished. Generally speaking, however, the focus of peacebuilding is on identifying and altering the root causes of violent conflict.

[3] Governance describes the process of decision-making and the processes by which decisions are implemented (or not implemented). The term governance can apply to any group decision-making process and the systems for ensuring implementation of collective decisions. Thus, we can talk about governance in corporations, international organizations (e.g., United Nations, International Monetary Fund, World Bank), national or local political systems, organizations (including civil society organizations and non-governmental organizations or NGOs), faith-based organizations, or traditional societies (e.g., clan-based or tribal systems).

[4] In many parts of the world, people live under multiple governance systems – post-colonial systems, tribal or clan systems, and religious systems – and disputes over the legitimacy of these systems are a constant source of uncertainty and conflict. This is not, however, a problem only in post-colonial societies. Similar disruptions to governance systems can take place in modern bureaucratic settings, for example after a corporate merger. See Docherty (2005) and the work of Walton, Cutcher-Gershenfeld, and McKersie (1994; 1995).

[5] Our conversations gained traction when we discovered the concept of wicked problems, which originated in the field of planning but was being applied to the challenges facing the military in Iraq and Afghanistan. "Wicked problems are ill-defined, ambiguous and associated with strong moral, political and professional issues. Since they are strongly stakeholder dependent, there is often little consensus about what the problem is, let alone how to resolve it. Furthermore, wicked problems won't keep still: they are sets of complex, interacting issues evolving in a dynamic social context. Often, new forms of

wicked problems emerge *as a result* of trying to understand and solve one of them" (http://www.swemorph.com/wp.html). We and other colleagues wrote a series of papers about negotiating wicked problems, and finally (!), we are writing about *teaching* negotiation for wicked problems. See Chrustie et al 2010; Docherty 2010; Honeyman and Coben 2010; Lira 2010.

[6] For a more detailed discussion, see Docherty and Lira, *Adapting to the Adaptive*, in this volume (noting that "*[s]ocial negotiation* is used, consciously or not, continuously to constitute and sustain or modify the *context*, including dispute domains and the rules and roles that guide participants in a transactional negotiation. *Dispute domain negotiation* is used to frame specific problems and locate them in a particular socio-cultural setting where they can be negotiated using (culturally shaped) *transactional negotiation* processes").

[7] "In brief, protracted social conflicts occur when communities are deprived of satisfaction of their basic needs on the basis of the communal identity. However, the deprivation is the result of a complex causal chain involving the role of the state and the pattern of international linkages. Furthermore, initial conditions (colonial legacy, domestic historical setting, and the multicommunal nature of the society) play important roles in shaping the genesis of protracted social conflict" (Azar 1990: 12).

[8] The class was made up of: One Afghan NGO leader (female), a Chilean attorney (male), a Macedonian social activist (male), a Korean journalist and a Korean NGO leader (both male), a Canadian teacher (female), a Canadian school counselor (male), three U.S. citizens (one female university faculty member, one female pastor, one male policy advocate), one Nigerian pastor (male), one Syrian social activist (male), one Indian businessman (male), and a Japanese law professor/social activist (female). The age of the participants ranged from late 20s to almost 60, with an average age in the 30s.

[9] SPOILER ALERT: Luna/Tsux'iit/L98 actually has a biography on Wikipedia that documents his birth in a whale pod, disappearance and presumed death, his reappearance off the coast of BC, and his eventual death in an accident involving a tugboat http://en.wikipedia.org/wiki/Luna_%28killer_whale%29.

[10] *Fact Sheet: British Columbia Treaty Negotiations.* Aboriginal Affairs and Northern Development Canada. Available at http://www.aadnc-aandc.gc.ca/eng/1100100016299/1100100016300 (last accessed March 3, 2013).

[11] The Cohen Commission was established in November 2009 by Prime Minister Stephen Harper as a "Commission of inquiry into the decline of sockeye salmon in the Fraser River." Its report was scheduled for delivery October, 2010, but was delayed until October 29, 2012. See generally www.cohencommission.ca (last accessed March 3, 2013).

[12] This was an interesting place where I used my discretion as game space designer to create a realistic (but perhaps not completely real) set of relationships. Student #5 (a male entrepreneur) created a character that "owned" fish farms in Gold River, while student #7 introduced himself as Mr. Tuna, the new country director for a Norwegian transnational fisheries company. I have no idea if this is how the fish farms actually operate, but I moved the business model used by poultry growers and large poultry corporations (which I happened to be familiar with) to fish farming in B.C. I gave Mr. Tuna and Denis (the two characters) a business model and showed them how that model created opportunities and risks for both of them and how it relied on their own negotiations that are embedded in the wider context.

References

Adler, P. S. 2002. Science, politics, and problem solving: Principles and practices for the resolution of environmental disputes in the midst of advancing technology, uncertain or changing science, and volatile public perceptions. *Penn State Environmental Law Review* 10(2): 323-344.

Adler, P. S., R. C. Barrett, M. C. Bean, J. E. Birkhoff, C. P. Ozawa, and E. B. Rudin. 2000. *Managing scientific and technical information in environmental cases: Principles and practices for mediators and facilitators.* Washington, DC: Resolve, Inc., U.S. Institute for Environmental Conflict Resolution, and Western Justice Center Foundation.

Alexander, N. and M. LeBaron. 2009. Death of the role-play. In *Rethinking negotiation teaching: Innovations for context and culture*, edited by C. Honeyman, J. Coben, and G. De Palo. St. Paul, MN: DRI Press.

Azar, E. 1990. *The management of protracted social conflict: Theory and cases.* Aldershot, UK: Dartmouth Pub. Co.

Carse, J. 1986. *Finite and infinite games.* New York: Simon and Schuster, Inc.

Caton Campbell, M. and J. S. Docherty. 2006. What's in a frame? In *The negotiator's fieldbook: The desk reference for the experienced negotiator*, edited by A. K. Schneider and C. Honeyman. Washington, DC: American Bar Association.

Chrustie, C., J. S. Docherty, L. Lira, J. Mahuad, H. Gadlin, and C. Honeyman. 2010. Negotiating wicked problems: Five stories. In *Venturing beyond the classroom: Volume 2 in the rethinking negotiation teaching series*, edited by C. Honeyman, J. Coben, and G. De Palo. St. Paul: DRI Press.

Coben, J. 2012. Empowerment and recognition: Students grade each other's negotiation outcomes. In *Assessing our students, assessing ourselves: Volume 3 in the rethinking negotiation teaching series*, edited by N. Ebner, J. Coben, and C. Honeyman. St. Paul, MN: DRI Press.

Coleman, P. T. 2011. *The five percent: Finding solutions to seemingly impossible conflicts.* New York: Public Affairs.

Costatino, C.A. and C. S. Merchant. 1995. *Designing conflict management systems: A guide to creating productive and healthy organizations.* San Francisco, CA: Jossey-Bass.

Cutcher-Gershenfeld, J. E., R. B. McKersie, and R. E. Walton. 1995. *Pathways to change: Case studies of strategic negotiations.* Kalamazoo, MI: W. E. Upjohn Institute for Employment Research.

De Carlo, L. 2005. Accepting conflict and experiencing creativity: Teaching "concertation" using *La Francilienne* CD-ROM. *Negotiation Journal* 21(1): 85-103.

Docherty, J. S. 2001. *Learning lessons from Waco: When the parties bring their gods to the negotiation table.* Syracuse, NY: Syracuse University Press.

Docherty, J. S. 2005. *The little book of strategic negotiation: Negotiating during turbulent times.* Intercourse, PA: Good Books, Inc.

Docherty, J. S. 2010. "Adaptive" negotiation: Practice and teaching. In *Venturing beyond the classroom: Volume 2 in the rethinking negotiation teaching series*, edited by C. Honeyman, J. Coben, and G. De Palo. St. Paul, MN: DRI Press.

Docherty, J. S. and M. Caton Campbell. 2006. Consequences of principal and agent. In *The negotiator's fieldbook: The desk reference for the experienced negotiator*, edited by A. K. Schneider and C. Honeyman. Washington, DC: American Bar Association.

Druckman, D. 2006. Uses of a marathon exercise. In *The negotiator's fieldbook: The desk reference for the experienced negotiator*, edited by A. K. Schneider and C. Honeyman.Washington, DC: American Bar Association.

Ebner, N. and K. K. Kovach. 2010. Simulation 2.0: The resurrection. In *Venturing beyond the classroom: Volume 2 in the rethinking negotiation teaching series*, edited by C. Honeyman, J. Coben, and G. De Palo. St. Paul, MN: DRI Press.

Freire, P. 2000. *Pedagogy of the oppressed,* 30th anniversary edn. New York: Continuum.

Greenhalgh, L. and R. J. Lewicki. 2003. New directions in teaching negotiations: From Walton and McKersie to the new millennium. In *Negotiations and change: From the workplace to society*, edited by T. A. Kochan and D. B. Lipsky. Ithaca: ILR Press.

Hagen, U. 1973. *Respect for acting*. Hoboken, NJ: John Wiley and Sons.

Haugerudbraaten, H. 1998. Peacebuilding: Six dimensions and two concepts. *African Security Review* 7(6): 17-26.

Honeyman, C. and J. Coben. 2010. Navigating wickedness: A new frontier in teaching negotiation. In *Venturing beyond the classroom: Volume 2 in the rethinking negotiation teaching series*, edited by C. Honeyman, J. Coben, and G. De Palo. St. Paul, MN: DRI Press.

Lederach, J. P., R. Neufeldt, and H. Culbertson. 2007. Reflective peacebuilding: A planning, monitoring, and learning toolkit. Available at http://www.eldis.org/assets/Docs/43157.html (last accessed December 17, 2012).

Lira, L. 2010. Design: The U.S. Army's approach to negotiating wicked problems. In *Venturing beyond the classroom: Volume 2 in the rethinking negotiation teaching series*, edited by C. Honeyman, J. Coben, and G. De Palo. St. Paul, MN: DRI Press.

Miller, G. and R. Dingwall. 2006. When the play's in the wrong theater. In *The negotiator's fieldbook: The desk reference for the experienced negotiator*, edited by A. K. Schneider and C. Honeyman. Washington, DC: American Bar Association.

Nixon, P. 2012. *Dialogue gap: Why communication isn't enough and what we can do about it, fast*. Singapore: John Wiley and Sons Singapore.

Office of the Auditor General of British Columbia. 2006. *Treaty negotiations in British Columbia: An assessment of the effectiveness of British Columbia's management and administrative process*. Victoria, British Columbia. Available at: www.fns.bc.ca/pdf/BCAGTreatyNeg_Report3.pdf (last accessed December 17, 2012).

Ricigliano, R. 2006. A three-dimensional analysis of negotiation. In *The negotiator's fieldbook: The desk reference for the experienced negotiator*, edited by A. K. Schneider and C. Honeyman.. Washington, DC: American Bar Association.

Saunders, H. 1996. Prenegotiation and circum-negotiation: Arenas of the peace process. In Managing global chaos, edited by C. Crocker, F. Hampson, and P. Aall. Washington, DC: United States Institute of Peace.

Stolte, J. F., G. A. Fine, and K. S. Cook. 2001. Sociological miniaturism: Seeing the big through the small in Social Psychology. *Annual Review of Sociology* 27: 387-413.

Ury, W. L., J. M. Brett, and S. B. Goldberg. 1988. *Getting disputes resolved: Designing systems to cut the costs of conflict.* San Francisco, CA: Jossey-Bass.

Walton, R. E., J. E. Cutcher-Gershenfeld, and R. B. McKersie. 1994. *Strategic negotiations: A theory of change in labor-management relations.* Cambridge, MA: Harvard Business School Press.

෫ 20 ෬

Playing the Percentages in Wicked Problems: On the Relationship between Broccoli, Peace-keeping, and Peter Coleman's *The Five Percent*

*Howard Gadlin, David Matz, & Calvin Chrustie**

Editors' Note: *In the initial joint effort of the Rethinking Negotiation Teaching Project's "Wicked Problems" team (Chrustie et al. 2010), the authors began with the more dramatic, international and violent settings, and worked from there to demonstrate how these problems also operate within less violent environments, such as city politics and the internal doings of a large organization. Here, in an effort to assess for teaching purposes a major new work in the field* (The Five Percent, *by Peter Coleman), the authors begin in the opposite order, and scale up their discussion from the most modest of beginnings – a vegetable – to conclude with analysis of one of the most contentious and unstable disputing environments: peacekeeping.*

* **Howard Gadlin** has been ombudsman, and director of the Center for Cooperative Resolution, at the National Institutes of Health since 1999. Previously he served as ombudsman for the University of California – Los Angeles (UCLA), the Los Angeles County Museum of Art, and the University of Massachusetts, Amherst. His email address is gadlinh@od.nih.gov. **David Matz** is a professor in the Graduate Programs in Dispute Resolution at the University of Massachusetts/ Boston in Boston, Massachusetts, and principal at The Mediation Group in Brookline, Massachusetts. His email address is davidematz@gmail.com. **Calvin Chrustie** is an Inspector within the Royal Canadian Mounted Police and has held various negotiation and conflict management positions, including former team leader of the Conflict Negotiation Team, team leader of a Hostage Negotiation Team, and member of a Canadian international response group to overseas kidnaps. He also has extensive practice in a multitude of conflict situations domestically and abroad, including with the United Nations and other agencies in the Middle East, the Balkans, and Africa. His email address is calchrustie@hotmail. com.

Introduction

One could hardly choose a more modest, common-or-literally-garden variety starting point than a vegetable. But one type of vegetable is, as it happens, a peculiarly good place to start a discussion of wicked problems: broccoli.

Consider the humble broccoli from the point of view of structure, and it begins to serve as a metaphor for organization. Each floret is almost a miniature copy of the whole plant: look at a single floret and you know what the larger plant looks like. This feature – self-similarity – is part of what defines a fractal, an object in which the same type of structure appears on all scales. (The famous Mandelbrot set, below, is another view of a fractal: each node is a replica of the larger whole.)

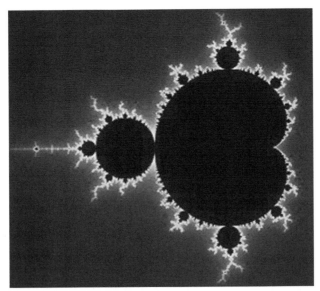

Fractals have turned out to be a useful concept for people who study organizations, because they help describe "one of the identifying

characteristics of a complex adaptive system. The same patterns of behavior or relationship appear in multiple places and times across the organization" (Olson and Eoyang 2001: 109). As a metaphor[1] fractals alert us, when working in complex organizations, to expect similarities in different parts and levels of the organization: similar patterns of communication, similar tensions and anxieties, similar relationships within and across the organizational units and hierarchy. However, recognizing those similarities is not the same as really *understanding* them, or appreciating how they are connected to an organization's problems; and it certainly does not tell us how to address them.

Fractals are one of the more interesting features of *complex adaptive systems*, which have been described and analyzed in an area of inquiry called complexity theory. Without delving into all the fine points of complexity theory, we can point to two other features of problems and conflicts within complex adaptive systems that make them especially interesting for people interested in conflict and negotiation: 1) They sometimes produce problems and conflicts that are seemingly intractable; and 2) These conflicts often seem to be self-perpetuating. These are the sorts of problems that are at the center of Peter Coleman's *The Five Per Cent* (2011). While Coleman's book concentrates on intractable conflicts (the five percent of conflicts that are not amenable to understanding and resolution through the application of conflict resolution and negotiation principles that are successful with most conflicts), his analysis actually has quite profound implications for the study of all complex problems.

Problems within complex adaptive systems are especially fascinating because they challenge our assumption that all conflicts can be resolved, as well as our belief that a path to resolution will be possible if we know all there is to know about a conflict and how it got to be as it is. These problems, referred to by some as wicked problems, resist both understanding and resolution. (Note: not all wicked problems are "intractable," even though they share many of the same features.) In a wonderfully insightful book, Dietrich Dorner (1996: 37-42) identifies four features of complex systems that help us understand why problems within them often seem intractable. First is *interrelatedness* – the existence of many interrelated parts. Any action that affects one part of the system will also affect many other parts of the system, both directly and indirectly. Second is *intransparency* – one cannot discern every important factor affecting a system, at least not in advance of attempting to intervene in that system. Third, *internal dynamics* – the interrelated factors develop and proceed independent of external control. To begin to understand a complex problem we have to observe its development over time. Finally, *incomplete/incorrect understanding* – complex systems cannot be fully understood, and we cannot know in advance of attempting to intervene how the variables are related to one another and how they influence one another.

Usually when people speak of wicked problems they are referring to large and complex multi-party situations that seem almost impossible to resolve. Certainly, some of the most intriguing and challenging conflicts facing those who would be dispute resolvers are of that sort. Such conflicts seem to have a life of their own, almost independent of the ostensible parties to the conflict. These are conflicts with a history; they are embedded in social systems and structures, and cannot be addressed by resolving individual instances. (See our team's Five Stories chapter in volume 2 in this series, Chrustie et al. 2010.)

And with this, we can now to turn to *The Five Percent*. One of the virtues of Coleman's book is that he provides an incredibly rich, broad, and intricate framework within which we can begin to think critically about the task of handling a wicked problem, without falling into despair about the enormity of the challenge.

What's 5% Worth? *David Matz*

Though he never uses the term, Peter Coleman in his book *The Five Percent* takes the *idea* of wicked problems seriously. (In this chapter, for consistency with this team's other writings, I will use the term wicked problems, even in quotations, where Coleman says "the 5%.") He argues not primarily for a different set of techniques, but rather for a different way of thinking, a way of thinking that grows precisely from the way in which wicked problems differ from ordinary ones. This dovetails rather well with the analysis of other members of this team: see Docherty and Lira, *Adapting to the Adaptive*, and Lira and Parish, *Making it up as You Go*, in this volume. But because Coleman is first out of the gate with a complete book, not to mention an important one, his book deserves to be the primary subject of this chapter.[2]

Coleman is committed to an accurate description of how these wicked problems work, but he seems to be even more committed to sympathy with our limits as humans – as individuals and as collectivities – and the ways in which these problems are wicked because *we* are limited. Perhaps the deepest question in his book is: how can one fight cynicism, how can one stimulate energizing hope in the face of our limits, in the face of the mismatch between the difficulty of the problems and the failings of human beings, in the face of our dismal historical record with such wicked problems? (World War I is one of his favorite examples.) Much of our conflict resolution literature reaches for hope by using slogans, elevator speeches, and four-point steps that fit on the back of a professional card. Like any activist-scholar, Coleman too is selling an approach; but he refuses to sacrifice his respect for the complexity of the issues to make his sale.

Coleman's model describes what goes on in the head of a party to a conflict, and it starts with this idea: "human beings are driven toward consistency and coherence in their perception, feeling, thinking, behavior and social relationships. This is natural and functional" (Coleman 2011: 68). Coherence in its more extreme form makes clear and comfortable who the good guys and the bad guys are, and it provides "a stable platform for action. These are not trivial things, especially for disputants engaged in exhaustingly difficult conflicts." Coherence, however, can also become dysfunctional. It encourages a party to blot out new or challenging data or options or feelings. Coherence is the enemy of complexity. Coherence is comfortable and seductive; the more intense the conflict, the more attractive the coherence, the more difficult it is to be open to complexity. But the path to the resolution of conflicts lies in complexity. Coleman cites a number of research studies to support the twin ideas that openness to complexity enhances openness to resolution, and that integrating new views and feelings (i.e., embracing complexity) are crucial steps in moving toward resolution.

Coleman draws on a number of ideas from complexity science. He pictures wicked problems, for example, as a dynamic flow of loops in which many parts of a conflict influence many other parts, and in which A can influence B and B can, via C for example, influence A. No one part can be said to cause any single outcome. Linear, cause-and-effect thinking is thus minimized. And as Coleman's charts and pictures illustrate, a wicked problem has a huge number of such loops. The influence-loop approach focuses attention primarily on relationships among the many interacting pieces of the conflict. The book provides steps for creating such a conflict map and several examples of analyses (Coleman 2011: 124), and also describes "visualizing software" developed by Coleman that acts as an aid in describing and analyzing the conflict.

Describing a conflict by using loops and as many dynamics and points of influence as one can devise seems useful to identifying the points at which a party or an intervener can apply pressure. The conflict map also creates intellectual space,[3] and a tool for being as accurate and comprehensive as possible in the descriptive stage. Such a mode of analysis for a wicked problem, embodying and describing complexity, will blur or even obliterate the good guy-bad guy distinctions. It will also, by giving one a sense of overview of everything that is going on, provide a sense of mastery and confidence. Such confidence is essential, according to Coleman's model, to lure an individual away from the depths and dangers of coherence. Coleman also provides an inventory of ways to work with the loops to "dismantle negative attractors."

> With concept mapping the goal is not necessarily to get it right. The goal at this stage is to get it different: to try to reintroduce a sense of nuance and complexity into the stakeholders; understanding of the conflict. The goal is to try to open up the system: to provide opportunities to explore and develop multiple perspectives, emotions, ideas, narratives, and identities and foster an increased sense of emotional and behavioral flexibility. To rediscover a sense of possibility (2011: 133).

(The experimental, "try something" overtones of this matches our own team's preliminary conclusions, in chapters 24-27 of volume 2 in this series. This theme is further developed in our colleagues' depictions of their current teaching approaches, in chapters 17-19 and 21 in this volume.)

A further attraction of the book is that Coleman has gathered much research and organized it around his model, giving the findings a resonance they might not have standing alone. One insight reported is that "disputants in an ongoing relationship need somewhere between three and a half to five positive experiences for every negative one, to keep the negative encounters from becoming harmful" (Coleman 2011: 98.) This idea gives the conflict map a welcome hint at quantification and shape.

Some of the ideas Coleman adopts are intriguing, though also puzzling. He defines a wicked problem as occurring when the influence patterns pushing toward coherence become "self organizing. This means they will continue to grow and spread, no matter what anyone tries to do to stop them. They become virtually impervious to outside influence. . . . When this occurs, conflicts cross a threshold into intractability." (p. 85.) What does this mean? All conflicts are to some extent out of the control of any individual, because the other party almost always holds some form of veto. Does Coleman mean that a conflict becomes intractable (i.e., a wicked problem) when a party loses control of itself? If so, what is the value of Coleman's book to a party? Is there some notion here about degrees of control?

The model does present some deep difficulties, difficulties inherent in wicked problems. The model describes the workings of a person's mind, and it gives an intervener with the goal of changing that mind a theory from which to work, i.e., opening it to greater complexity. But what does it do for the party? It is a strength of the theory that it illustrates the powerful incentives for a party to cling ever tighter to coherence and, as the conflict wears on or grows in intensity, to reject complexity. But how does a party get the willpower to overcome this pull? Coleman acknowledges this difficulty when he says that

> the press for certainty and coherence is a basic tendency in life greatly intensified by conflict, especially [wicked problem] conflict. And it often contributes to our total misreading of events. This tendency of course is *nearly impossible* to be mindful of when we are caught up in a [wicked problem] (2011: 99).

Moreover, while the model does seem more useful for an intervener who, through interviews of many players, has access to the complexities illustrated in the charts and loops, does a party, even one who wants such complexity, have access to the necessary information? Perhaps the implied point is that only an intervener can help a party think through the problem.

For someone who has worked with people in the thrall of a wicked problem, this book provides a completely plausible, intuitively attractive, description of what is going on in their heads. The insistence on spelling out the flows of influence – toward coherence, toward complexity – are compelling. What the theory leaves out, however, is any way of assessing which influences are more important than others. Which are worth the effort they will take? Which might take priority in time? Coleman does give it a try (2011: 139) when he identifies foci like "local actionables" (i.e., do what you can do), support things that already work toward complexity, and (most interestingly) identify "individuals who . . . embody the different conflicting identities and tensions inherent to the conflict" (2011: 141).

Elsewhere in the book Coleman says that making priority judgments is the party's job – i.e., the theory will not help out much. In a book emphasizing complexity, the relative absence of clues about how to navigate among so many choices is a major inadequacy. This is another way of saying, as Coleman does, that too much complexity is as problematic as too much coherence, though for different reasons. But the book is therefore less strong on helping an intervener cope with the prescribed increase in complexity. Coleman worries that all of our usual lenses for seeing complexity filter out too much or the wrong things. But by failing to provide an alternative lens, and a rationale for why it is better, he leaves the option of no lens. Staring a while at any of his charts will be quite adequate to induce a longing for *some* lens.

I would propose that in sorting out such priorities, the impact of conflict must give a special role to the uses of coercion, and the implications for control of self and control of others: the more wicked the

problem, the higher the perceived costs of "losing," the more significant the impact of coercion. Our field is allergic to the uses of power,
and often ignores it or defines it out of the problem.[4] Coleman's model
does not identify power as a special concern, but it does leave room
for such concerns. I would suggest that the appropriate place for its
consideration is in the prioritizing of ways to influence complexity.

The model makes room for, but I think substantially underesti-
mates, the fact that almost all individuals in wicked problem situations are in organizations that exist to some extent with the purpose
of *re-enforcing an individual's commitment to coherence*. To change the individual, one must change the organization – exactly as Howard Gadlin
describes below. About this, the book is silent. As it also is about the
yet larger question: if the wicked problem is large enough to engage
significant parts of the society, how does this model lend itself to a
process of social change? The tools we have for making social change
are essentially those of conventional politics plus Saul Alinsky. We use
leadership, political parties, pressure groups, demonstrations, coalitions, and public decision-making. Would Coleman's theory work in
the political realm? Though this critique may be asking no more than
that he write another book, I would like to express some skepticism
about whether the nature of politics is consistent with the enhance-
ment of complexity. (For more on a related theme, see Honeyman et
al., *The "Deliberation Engine,"* in this volume.)

Scaling up the Fractal to Organizational Level: *Howard Gadlin*

For people who work in organizations, problems and disputes of the
kind we address here provide both a challenge and an opportunity. A
challenge because they divert attention away from the mission of the
organization; an opportunity because they can offer a window into
the dynamics of the organization, provided one does not get totally
absorbed in the idiosyncratic qualities of each particular dispute or
problem.

Usually when we think of "individual" problems or conflicts we
also think in terms of the psychological characteristics of the particular individuals involved in the problem situation, and we focus on
those characteristics and the nature of the relationship or interaction
between the individuals involved. In some instances we also take into
account the impact of the specific problem and others in the organization; but generally, the problem is seen as a reflection of the qualities
of the people involved. Yet we can also view individual problems or
disputes as *reflections of organizational dynamics*, symptoms as it were of
the structure and dynamics of the organization. To do this, we have to

direct our attention *away* from the compelling qualities of the parties to a dispute and the drama of the issues in conflict, and attend instead to aspects of the situation that are not immediately visible.

Typically, problems that are thought of as "individual" disputes, such as an allegation of power abuse by a supervisor or a conflict between two co-workers in a laboratory, are seen primarily as something to be resolved. There is work to be done and the conflict is a distraction. But often, these sorts of disputes reveal the impact of features of the organization to which managers and employees pay little attention, even when faced with problems, like these, that are seen as interfering with attending to the main purpose of the organization.

Let me illustrate by describing my work. I am an ombudsman, and as such I have two major areas of responsibility. The first involves helping individuals who come for assistance to address and resolve their concerns, problems or conflicts. The second involves identifying systemic problems within the organization – policies, practices, and procedures that regularly elicit or exacerbate tensions, conflicts and/ or dysfunction – and bringing those problems to the attention of the appropriate organizational leaders, and then pressing them to attend to those problems.

If one attends to individual cases with an eye toward identifying and understanding the contribution of systemic factors, the task of "resolving" the matter is broadened, and even redefined. There is a distinction between settling a dispute and resolving conflict. Settling a dispute is generally a matter of helping the parties involved come to an agreement, or reach an understanding that satisfies their individual concerns. Resolving a conflict, I would argue, almost always involves addressing systemic factors that underlie, elicit, and sustain individual disputes. Settle a dispute without resolving underlying conflicts and a new dispute will pop up in its place. If we are not to be limited to dispute settlement, we need to address individual disputes with an eye toward understanding them in the context within which they emerge and exist.

One way to move toward such intervention is by asking an expanded set of questions about the dispute, questions that go beyond identifying individual motives, interests and positions and that are designed to uncover the ways in which the dispute is embedded in and reflects the organizational context within which it occurs. Here is such a set of questions, grouped around five aspects of a dispute that will have to be understood if the underlying conditions of the dispute are to be addressed. The questions in **boldface** are designed to point to systemic factors.

1) Problem
   - What are the issues to be addressed?
   - What are the conflicts to be resolved?
   - What are the time constraints on the situation?
   - **Is there a policy or procedure contributing to this problem?**
   - **What systemic organizational issues does the problem illustrate?**
   - **What features of the organization are fueling or sustaining this conflict?**
   - **What does it mean that this conflict has arisen? Might this conflict be representative of similar/related issues elsewhere in the organization?**

2) People
   - Who are the key parties to the problem?
   - What are the perspectives of the disputants?
   - **Do the parties or perspectives "represent" the concerns of others who are like them within the organization?**
   - **Who has a stake in keeping things as they are?**

3) Power
   - How is power distributed among the disputants?
   - What power do the individual disputants have?
   - What does each disputant have to gain or lose?
   - Who most needs the conflict resolved?
   - **How will addressing/resolving this conflict affect the power structure of the organization?**
   - **Is there an organizational history to this situation?**
   - **What are the politics of the situation?**

4) Positions/Interests
   - What is each disputant's opening position?
   - What interests and concerns are informing their positions?
   - **What organizational interests are reflected in these interests?**
   - **What organizational problems are reflected in these interests?**
   - **How is the reward or incentive structure of the organization related to this conflict?**

5) Process
   - What intervention possibilities exist?
   - Which interventions are best suited to the concerns of the disputants?

- **Does this situation call for systemic intervention?**
- **Which intervention will best lay the groundwork for systemic intervention?**
- **What sorts of systemic intervention would be most appropriate?**

It will be immediately evident to the reader, when she encounters Calvin Chrustie's analysis below, that so long a list of questions is a good illustration of his argument for a conscious "intelligence capability." This is implicated even in the ostensibly "manageable" environment of a single organization and a single presenting issue. In more complex and unstable environments, a full-blown intelligence team is highly desirable – yet even in the more conflictually modest circumstances I describe here, the press of time, the unwillingness of many participants to delve into sensitive areas, and conventional assumptions as to the role of a mediator can easily militate against pursuing such questions to the point of getting useful answers. I recognize that I am fortunate in having an organizational mandate to press for such answers; not every conflict professional presented with similar problems has similar organizational support. But perhaps attention given to the subject, such as in the current stream of writings, will eventually help to form the intellectual basis for a broader claim on the necessary organizational resources (not to mention the necessary organizational grit).

Identifying the relevant policies, practices, distributions of power and reward structures within an organization helps us appreciate the context within which individual problems and disputes take form. But these elements do not, by themselves, allow us to fully grasp the dynamics of interconnections among the disputing people or departments within the organization. Nor do they help us to appreciate the role played by that dispute or problem in maintaining and reproducing the organizational dynamic. As we approach an individual problem with an eye toward possible intervention, we must keep in mind that

1) Every person and organizational unit (department, division, etc.) is part of a larger system;
2) All are reacting to and contributing to tensions, problems and conflicts in the system;
3) Where in the organization the problem develops depends on where and how they are interconnected to the others in the system;
4) Problems or conflicts that develop are often an exaggeration or complication of some feature or process in the system that contributes to the stability and continuity of the system;

5) Problems or conflicts that develop are often the "solution" to problems or conflicts that have not been recognized or identified as such.

Let me illustrate with a brief case history. Two professional level employees, each the head of a branch in the same division and each with highly specialized technical knowledge, were referred by their supervisor to my office, with the request that I work with them to help resolve what appeared to be intense personal conflicts and animosity. Their two branches had to work very closely together, and each branch was dependent on some of the output of the other branch in order to be able to do their work properly. The ongoing conflicts between the two branch chiefs were affecting the work quality and output of both branches. The administrator who referred them was especially anxious about their dispute, and wary of trying to help address it, because of the identity differences between the disputing parties. One was a Muslim man, the other a Jewish woman. It was clear that the administrator believed/feared that it was these differences that fueled their conflict and that, in some way, their apparent animosity was about those differences.

When I met with them, the tension and mutual dislike was immediately apparent, although at no point during the time I worked with them did either of them give any direct indication that religion or gender was, for them, a salient factor. But from the beginning, my questions of them focused as much on the systemic issues, as illustrated in the five elements of conflict above, as it did on the details of their individual dispute. However, in addition to inquiring about the history and organizational context (policies, practices, etc.) of their conflict and observing their interpersonal interactions, I spent a considerable amount of time asking about the specific details of their conflicts: what *exactly* did they fight about, when did such fights arise, how did others react when they fought, who benefited the most/least, and who suffered the most/least when they fought? One aim of many of these questions was to help reveal

1) If there were (unrecognized) positive organizational *purposes* being served by the dispute and tensions between the two; or

2) If there were (unrecognized) organizational *failings* that were being compensated for by the dispute and tensions between the two.

One consequence of the intervention was that it enabled them to reframe their understanding of what the fights were about. At the beginning each had raised sharp criticisms of the other's work and managerial style, and also of the other's role in the division. He focused on what he felt was the personal nature of her criticisms, privately and publicly, of him and his work and the work of his staff. He saw her as undermining the ability of the branch chiefs to function as a team, and felt the need to support others whom she also criticized. She focused on what she felt was a lack of rigorous standards on his part, and attributed deficiencies in some of the division's products to failings of his team. However, as we examined their conflicts in the broader organizational context they began to attend to features of the division that had never been discussed before.

One of the most striking was that there was no process and no opportunity for the branch chiefs to gather and critically examine and improve the work being done in their division, the processes employed for allocating tasks, and the methods of communication and collaboration between branches. In addition, the branch chiefs were not receiving critical feedback from the division director, either on a project-by-project basis or in the annual performance evaluation reviews that were (on paper, at least) required. As these observations accumulated, the disputants began to see their disputes as filling an organizational void. Any work group and every employee needs to be able to assess their own performance and to receive feedback from others about their performance. As we analyzed the situation, they began to see that their dispute was a symptom of an organizational problem that had not previously been either identified or addressed. They agreed that they would go together and speak about this with the division director (the very person who had referred them). They also came to see – with some assistance from me – that they each had responded differently to the same organizational failing – the lack of crucial team reflection and feedback: she, by assuming the role of critic and he, by assuming the role of maintainer of group cohesiveness. They agreed, again with some guidance from me, that if and when the division did correct the underlying problem, *she* would refrain from taking the lead in offering critical remarks, and *he* would attempt to offer criticisms as well as support at branch chief meetings.

This agreement and reframing did not mean that their animosity was gone and a collegial relationship established. The combination of past history and strong personal differences made a positive relationship unlikely. But the reframing reduced the burden that their personal relationship had to carry. No longer did it have to serve as the vehicle for an organizational failing; it was reduced to a manageable personal tension and dislike that did not threaten the effectiveness of the larger work group.

Notice that in the example above, while we see the impact of features of the larger organization in what is first presented to us as "a dispute between two coworkers" our steps toward resolution have to proceed on two levels – the dispute between the individuals, and the *system* within which their conflict arose. However, one of the complexities of organizations is that "successful" interventions at the level of the individual can sometimes be at odds with "successful" intervention at the systems level. This is especially likely if organizational polices are designed so that they address systemic problems as if they were individual issues.

Think of the example of racial discrimination. While it is generally acknowledged that racial discrimination is a systemic feature and should be against the law, racial discrimination is primarily addressed through the processes by which a given individual who believes they have been discriminated against may bring formal charges (within organizations) or lawsuits. Essentially, these charges have to be supported by proof of prejudicial thinking or motivation on the part of the person charged. But recent research demonstrates that, although some direct prejudice-based discrimination still exists, increasingly important factors are the much subtler social processes and patterns of exclusion that are not grounded in overt racial prejudice (Sturm 2001). If this is true, then it is quite likely that the very processes by which job discrimination complaints are pursued *exacerbate* the tensions between those who feel discriminated against and those who believe discrimination is a thing of the past. The EEOC reports that roughly one percent of allegations of racial discrimination are upheld in court. In my experience, most of the minorities interpret this finding as further indication of racial discrimination and of the existence of a system that is stacked against them. At the same time, most non-minorities interpret these results as an indication that allegations of racial discrimination are generally without foundation and that racial discrimination is no longer a problem. The subtler elements of a continuing problem go unremarked on both sides, and therefore the central issue remains largely unaddressed.

A similar problem exists within organizations that have dispute resolution processes designed to address complaints of racial discrimination through mediation. An individual allegation of discrimination might be negotiated so that a particular dispute could be "settled"; but that certainly does not mean that the broader issue of racial discrimination has been resolved. Indeed, typically the person bringing the complaint of discrimination is convinced that he or she has been treated that way because of his or her race. The person charged believes with equal vehemence that that is not the case. It is rare that a mediated agreement includes any sort of recognition that discrimination took place. So each of the parties leaves the dispute that has been ostensibly "settled" without an answer to the fundamental question that led to the complaint – "was this person discriminated against?" – and, I would assert, without a fundamental change in their basic belief about whether or not racial discrimination is a factor. Even if we grant that the mediation process has enhanced the parties' understanding of each other and the reasons for their conflict, we would not fool ourselves into believing that we or they understood the broader issue, or that we knew how to resolve it.

The point here is not to denigrate mediation programs that attempt to address complaints of discrimination, or the well-intentioned people who design and implement such programs. What is useful about the dilemma of these programs for our purposes here is that they illustrate on a thoroughly mundane, everyday level the nature of wicked problems, and the complexity of the effort to attempt to solve major social problems – especially those that are anchored in long-standing social conflicts.

We will conclude this chapter with a discussion of what the emerging analysis of wicked problems seems to offer for one of the largest-scale disputing environments, i.e., peacekeeping.

The Fractal Blows Up: *Calvin Chrustie*
One of the practical uses of fractals has turned out to be in digital photography: fractals are the mathematical basis of software that now allows an image to be enlarged enormously, without the usual extreme loss of focus and sharpness.[5] Perhaps there is a workable analogy here, as we turn our attention to a part of our team's experience that is particularly close to Coleman's central interest (intractable conflict) – i.e., peacekeeping. Peacekeeping, as I use the term, is broader than some may think: it includes managing the more complex community conflicts and disputes, such as those over natural resources, as well as managing international violent conflicts, i.e., wars.

Both David Matz and Howard Gadlin in this chapter have provided valuable insight and analysis of Coleman's writings. Similarly to David, I have found Coleman's book insightful and helpful in its comprehensive understanding of how one should think when relating to wicked problems. Coleman's detailed analysis of the multifaceted elements at play is impressive. I would like to relate this discussion to my past two decades' experience as a practitioner in a range of conflicts, including interpersonal and workplace conflicts, community conflicts, and more complex environments all the way up to peacekeeping. In doing so, I must acknowledge the limitations of a first effort to codify twenty years of experience. At this time I can offer only a preliminary sketch of this difficult area, and I hope that the reader will be prepared for a good helping of errors and omissions.

I offer these thoughts in public at this stage in hopes that others will broaden, deepen and help me clarify them.

Our chapter's opening discussion about broccoli really is a good place to start thinking about wicked problems; the self-similarity that defines a fractal resonates with me as a helpful metaphor for understanding the ways the structure of complicated problems replicate themselves. This leads me to look at the structure of a wicked problem as needing a matching *process* structure, one specifically designed to deal with that specific problem.

In this next portion, I hope to expand on some conceptual frameworks that I have found useful when working within 5% conflicts. While the complexity of these disputes will often escape the best efforts of practitioners, including those who consider applying some of these concepts to be discussed, I have found these conceptual tools (or models or frameworks, depending on how you look at them) useful in enhancing if not the resolution, at least the mitigation of these conflicts. While there is an exhaustive list of practical considerations that *could* be applied, including many of those written about by other well known practitioners such as the United States Institute for Peace Peacemaker's Toolkit (see http://www.usip.org/publications/peacemaker-s-toolkit), it is my intention to focus here on one model that I have found instrumental in managing and mitigating wicked problems: the Structure→Strategy→Process→Outcome model. However, before explicating this valuable model, I offer some thoughts on the necessity of sophisticated conflict intelligence capability and the dangers of oversimplication, particularly the danger of focusing too narrowly on theory rather than pragmatic response.

Conflict Intelligence Capability

According to Larry Woocher,writing in a special report on conflict assessment and intelligence analysis for the United States Institute of Peace, "[o]ne of the axioms of international conflict management and peacebuilding is the importance of developing a deep understanding of a situation before acting" (2011: 2). Accurate conflict analysis is indeed critical. But the conflict management's field focus on analysis has come at a high price – inattentiveness to creating and maintaining organizational *structures*, accompanied by robust processes that allow for "intelligence" to be maintained throughout all phases of engagement, not just during an initial analysis/assessment phase. This includes direction to the intelligence teams, collection of information, processing the information, analysis of the information and timely sharing and distribution of the information.

Risks of Oversimplification: What Should a Practitioner Actually Do?

I concur with Coleman as to the likelihood of oversimplification of wicked problems. My personal experience suggests that so-called "experts" often use skills and tactics and processes, sometimes as a mediator or negotiator, or facilitator, or with a small group of negotiators, mediators or facilitators, without looking at the broader needs dictated by the complexity of the issues or problems. Also consistent with David Matz's review, I think Coleman's effort at describing the thinking required to engage in resolving complex/wicked problems, while partly defined in the book, leaves a certain degree of ambiguity as to what a practitioner is actually supposed to *do*. So while his analysis of the problems is excellent, Coleman's treatment of practical action is missing something. He talks about the dangers of oversimplification, and also the importance of not over-complicating matters. His treatment, however, is that of a theoretician: it is insightful and complex, but at the expense of pragmatism – at least, from the point of view of someone who must actually handle these cases.

Below, I will use one such case setting I worked in – the Bosnian war – to illustrate this. But first, I will use Howard Gadlin's fractal approach to describe what I see as a pragmatic response to an actual conflict that is also to be addressed using Coleman's larger theory. I believe my take on this is quite consistent with our earlier description of broccoli.

Let us start with the smallest unit operating in such a conflict, the individual negotiator. I would begin by highlighting the importance of *humility* as a basic characteristic in the negotiator or other professional handling a wicked problem. This includes understanding that I, the negotiator, am not a particularly central figure, just a piece of a larger mechanism for dealing with the conflict. I look at the conflict as a theater, and I conceive of my own role not as actor, director or star, but more as a stage manager, facilitating the production and outcomes of the theater experience. I focus on building the sets, guiding the actors; I have enough distance from the actors to provide some objectivity and allow for strategic decision-making, and with the benefit of perspective (consistent with the teachings of Sun Tzu), to allow for engagement and identifying opportunities that are consistent with the philosophy of aikido. I use intelligence and information to assess when to engage, and when not to engage and instead to "go with the flow of the river." The structure I favor allows for strategic oversight, not the continuous engagement that often distorts and crowds the perception of the actors. This, I hope, mitigates the risk identified by Coleman as getting caught in the web of coherence, complexity and emotional traps.

Structure→ Strategy→ Process→Outcome

Avedis Donabedian, in pioneering analyses of health care, has written about *structure* (how the system of care is configured and descriptions of its components) and *process* (how care is delivered) as influencing *outcomes* (including mortality, functional status, quality of life, and patient satisfaction) (Peters et al. 2009: 6-7; see generally Donabedian 2002, Donabedian 2005, and closer to our field, Miller and Dingwall 2006).

When I first saw this particular triumvirate of concepts, it rang true to me for purposes of analyzing my own experience in conflict management. I have since tried to use it consciously. Along with this I have relied on some concepts derived from organizational behavior theory. These include the ostensibly straightforward, but often mis-applied importance of consciously using structures and processes to enhance efficiency and effectiveness. This parallels some of the writings in the last decade or two in the field of conflict management systems by Roger Fisher and William Ury (1991), and then William Ury, Jeanne Brett, and Steven Goldberg (1988). The concepts I have been trying to apply are also closely related to those that Leonard Lira, Jayne Docherty and our other colleagues in this team have been writing in this series. The common factor, again, is the necessity to create a structure within which an *appropriate* process can be created to obtain the necessary outcomes. These structures obviously need to take into consideration the fractal nature of conflict earlier highlighted.

Yet contrary to all of these conclusions, in practice we often focus on tactics and processes – or we focus on theory without reference to practice, as highlighted by Coleman in his book. One of the biggest gaps between useful theory and effective practice is the importance of structure, and professionals' common failure to focus on that.

An example, of course, is essential, if the reader is to understand what I am talking about. Unfortunately, my recent and current examples, including First Nations issues in Canada and elsewhere, handling major protests over G8 meetings, peacekeeping problems, and issues in the Horn of Africa (where I have worked with kidnapping issues) raise continuing security concerns, because some of the structural and process elements, not to mention the outcomes, would refer to classified information. Accordingly, I will use a more historical example, from my earlier experience in Bosnia. My personal point of reference is the peacekeeping field, a context that I recognize most people (especially most civilians) are simply unfamiliar with. The complexity of negotiating in a war context is unique. Civilians typically think of negotiation and war primarily in terms of high-level diplomatic negotiators trying to end the war. Thus, for example, they might be familiar with the press coverage of the Dayton negotiations resulting in the signing of a general framework agreement for peace in Bosnia and Herzegovina in 1995; but they never see or likely think much about the daily negotiations that we were doing on the ground. At the time, this example, like my other experiences there, did *not* use the structure/strategy/process/outcome model, because I was then unaware of it. I believe better outcomes would have resulted, at least in part, if that model had been employed.

It might also help to reflect here that the military recognizes a distinction between three levels of engagement in a conflict: strategic, (long term plans/objectives), operational (short to medium-term objectives/activities, including the coordination and synchronization of tactical activities and processes), and tactical (the day-to-day engagement and management of linear processes). Military doctrine focuses most on the critical decisions at the middle, operational level. I have learned from this that our responses need to be commensurately focused there. Thus, effective thinking is not primarily about the group of ten tanks on the battlefield in the Middle East moving toward a border. That is "tactical," those ten tanks. The coordination with *other* tanks, with the air force, with an intelligence operation dispersing misinformation among the enemy, all the moving parts that together are greater than the sum of those parts; that is the operational level, and that is what we must primarily concern ourselves with as peacekeepers, just as the military does in its domain.

In chapter 25 of volume 2 in this series (see Chrustie et al. 2010: 456-458), I described the nature of my work in Bosnia as a wicked problem:

> . . . The warring parties themselves were ambiguous in their commitment to resolving the exchange issues during the course of the conflict. Many warring military and paramilitary groups continued to capture, kidnap and withhold the casualities of war because the prisoners and even the deceased were seen as valuable commodities at the various negotiation tables within the larger context of the conflict. In some instances, the warring parties would collect human beings and even the remains of casualties in order to build their own power vis-à-vis other negotiations. They used the fate of the human beings (alive or dead) under their control to advance their interests in negotiations over freedom of movement, ceasefires, claims to territory and other issues.
>
> Even though some leaders of the warring factions were clearly violating the Geneva Convention, others among the leaders exhibited independent thinking similar to that shown

by [United Nations Protection Force] (UNPROFOR) personnel who tried to assist with the exchange negotiations. These
leaders were genuinely seeking the international community's support and assistance in the mediation and resolution
of the exchange issues. But the net result of the pressures
against negotiating issues of exchange was the creation of a
fragile and tenuous negotiation process that was subject to
numerous negative influences.

The issues were not easy to resolve or even to frame effectively for negotiation. For example, the parties, including
individual negotiators directly involved in the process, were
torn between their long-term and short-term interests. POWs
and hostages, if released and turned over, were potential witnesses to war crimes and other human rights violations. Even
the deceased could provide evidence of mass murders and
genocide. And the allegations were likely to be leveled at some
of the key military and civilian leaders, including some individuals associated with the exchange process. Achieving the
release of one's own people was a political coup, but releasing
the people held by one's own group had the potential to create
other problems, including an escalation of tensions and further violence when the evidence carried by the released individuals (alive or dead) came to light. Whether the resolution
of a POW, kidnap or body exchange was defined as the "end
game" or as a "means to an end," serving other negotiation
objectives was also fluid. Most often, it was difficult to ascer-
tain what the interests of the parties really were, due to the
complex web of influencing factors that were ever-changing
and unpredictable.

Generally speaking, negotiators are taught that a certain
level of transparency and information sharing is one key to
the negotiation process. But the exchange negotiations were
complicated by the high levels of risk associated with sharing
information. It is difficult to negotiate effectively when, as
happened to Calvin, even telling Side A whom he was meeting with on Side B resulted in Side A mounting a large special
forces operation to capture friends and family of the negotiator for Side B. This was a dramatic situation, but overall it
was not unusual to have a negotiation process lead to other
kidnappings or loss of life, as each party tried to use coercion
and threats to alter the decision-making of the other party.

The behaviors described above are difficult to comprehend if they are not set in the context of history. Many of

the parties involved as either hostages or family to the hostages, and even many of the negotiators, were survivors or first generation children of individuals who had survived the concentration and POW camps of World War II, including the extermination camp of Jasenovac. And if they were not affected by historical traumas, many of the negotiators had witnessed recent violence and experienced deep personal loss, including the murder of relatives, as a consequence of the ongoing war. The relatively fresh memories of death camps, torture, and brutality and the immediate experience of violence gave rise to intense feelings of fear and hatred amongst the parties. For example, a senior Serb civilian was kidnapped in a small village near Rajic. The brother of the elderly Serbian male kidnapped, his only living relative, sought Calvin's assistance in securing his brother's release. Both the hostage and his brother were in their late sixties.

Months of negotiation ensued, during which the brother of the hostage shared with Calvin that both he and the hostage were orphans from a local WWII concentration camp. When the camp was liberated in 1945 by the Allies, a Yugoslavian couple adopted them, because the boys had lost their family in the concentration camp. Half a century later in 1993, one of them *again* found himself in a detention camp. The tools of active listening and expression of empathy seemed wholly inadequate for working with such traumatized individuals. And the task of negotiating a resolution or series of resolutions capable of bringing the POW and kidnap crisis to an end seemed well out of reach of individuals equipped only with the toolkit of negotiation skills provided in typical "Negotiation 1.0" courses and trainings.

Furthermore, a victim image frequently invoked by language used in discussions of negotiation teaching (e.g., in the paragraph above, deep personal loss/trauma/fear) can be inadequate or mis-leading to describe some of the people one must negotiate with, who may be better described in terms of "players." For example, Calvin recalls attempting to secure the release of a certain high-ranking Croatian military officer who was kidnapped in 1992. A meeting was set up with a senior Serbian military intelligence officer to secure a response from the Bosnian Serbs as to their willingness to release the Croatian general, then being held in a detention center. The meeting was with one of the aides to the infamous top Bosnian Serb General Ratko Mladic – to this day, wanted for war crimes in the Hague, but uncaptured.[6] The Serbian Colonel started by asking, "Who was the first victim in World War II?" Calvin responded, "I don't know." The Colonel looked across the table and asked "Who was the first victim in the Korean War?" Again, Calvin responded, "I don't know."

The Colonel continued on with several more wars over several more decades, with the same response. He then sat up, and with a serious and respectful tone, through the interpreter, stated, "The first victim in all these wars is the same, the *truth*." A thirty-minute discussion ensued, which Calvin quickly realized would be unproductive. What emerged (i.e., the message that General Mladic, via his aide, effectively delivered that day) was characteristic of Calvin's experience not only in the former Yugoslavia but in other conflict zones, including Iraq, Israel and East Africa: there is often layer upon layer of lies and misinformation, to protect the truth for a multitude of strategic reasons. The implication for conflict practitioners is that in these conflict-ridden environments, the ability to analyze the issues, the interests, the positions and most important, the truth is often difficult, if not impossible.

While the escalation and unresolved issues related to POW exchanges, kidnappings and other related issues occurred within the context of the larger conflict, history reveals that they were an important factor in *fueling* the conflict. In Coleman's language, these factors contributed to a negative "basin of attraction." Indeed in other conflicts, even where the actual substantive conflict has been mitigated to a significant degree, these kinds of "attractors" have often continued for years thereafter, and may even fuel the resumption of conflict. In World War II, Vietnam and other wars the POW issues, for example, continued long after the main conflict was over.

The example above took place, in my view, in the *absence of any organized analysis* of how such issues affected the former Yugoslavia. My on-the-ground perception was that a year and a half into the war, any activities conducted by the UN in this regard were haphazard and driven by the goodwill of individuals, versus part of the formal mission and strategy of the UN. In my dealings with the heads of the Exchange Commissions for two of the three warring parties, Dragin Bulajic (president of the Bosnian Serb Exchange Commission) and his counterpart, Ivan Grujic (president of the Croatian Exchange Commission), both officials repeatedly shared their frustrations with me concerning the lack of engagement, focus or support on the part of the UN. Its engagement in a more thorough manner in mitigating these critical conflictual issues would certainly have helped on a direct level. I believe it would also have helped lessen the tensions on a larger level. Both these senior representatives of the warring parties, certainly, acknowledged and identified the importance of resolving these issues *in the context of the larger conflict* in bringing peace to their respective countries.

Yet instead of focusing on these issues, the typical analysis of the conflict – consistent with Coleman's thesis – was focused on reporting on the *symptoms* of the conflict (particularly in the form of Daily Situational Reports, which included the number of mortar impacts, the number of troop movements, paramilitary operations, weapons smuggling and any other "significant" events). In other words, the reporting was focused on the most tactical activities, while there was very little analysis of their relationship and the relationship of other factors to the underlying conflict, and specifically to those factors that, if they did not initially give rise to the conflict, certainly perpetuated it – such as, in my view, the kidnap, POW and body exchange issues. This focus is consistent with what an individual policeman charged with restoring immediate order might do; but it has little to do with addressing the root causes and drivers of the conflict. In that respect, the UN approach was haphazard, linear, and often, purely reactive in its response to an incident (e.g., a request from local authorities to engage in an exchange), versus any kind of systematic approach.

In contrast, a systematic approach would have demanded a consistent analysis of the issues, with a resulting relevant strategy, followed by a structure and various processes to match. (I will expand on these critical elements below.) The normal response, by contrast, was that a local military or government official would ask for something, and the UN would respond – but with no strategy underlying the action, and no appreciation of the relative significance or insignificance of any given issue. This fits with Coleman's discussion of responding to symptoms, not causes. In most cases, as Coleman would predict, people responded to complexity by avoiding it, because it was overwhelming.

The structure→strategy→process→outcome model, however, provides a way to think about how to affect these "attractors" in a constructive way. It is my own modification of the more typical structure→process→outcome model – though as a practitioner, I am well aware that theorists may have developed something similar or even further articulated, but in which I am not schooled. The following diagram represents the model, and is simple enough, on its surface:

Structure→strategy→process→outcome.

While such a diagram might imply that the *sequence* is s-s-p-o and then stops, however, this is not actually intended as linear, but as recursive, for all the reasons outlined by Lira and Parish, in *Making it up as You Go*, in this volume. Ongoing analysis and the fluid nature of the conflict dictate what the actual next step will be.

Structure, including the necessity for conflict intelligence applications

On the ground in Bosnia, the command structure was linear (in fact, geographically based), an approach that devalued ongoing intelligence capability and undermined the ability to respond effectively to a constantly changing, and often, chaotic environment.

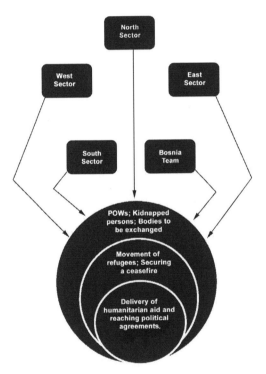

Figure 1: The Bosnia Command Structure. (For graphic simplicity, the arrows (representing each sector's efforts) are not shown as reaching all three "subject" circles described in the text below, but of course they did in practice.)

Individual sectors lacked any concrete internal team structure. Moreover, to my knowledge, there was little or no strategic communication consideration in the peacekeeping effort in Bosnia. What was occurring and being reported in the field was at the operational and/or tactical level, including the negotiations relative to three very distinct sets of problems, each involving ever increasing numbers of people and complexity: 1) individual POWs, kidnapped or missing persons, and bodies to be exchanged; 2) movement of refugees, ensuring freedom of movement and securing a ceasefire; and 3) delivery of humanitarian aid and reaching political agreements.

In Figures 2 and 3, I offer what I believe to be a much more effective structural approach. Here, the structure is organized fractally, with each sector having its own robust conflict intelligence and analysis capability and conflict team structure.

First, as detailed in Figure 2, each sector would have an internal conflict team structure that would promote/encourage communications both intra- and inter-sector. External support groups such as

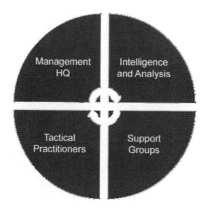

Figure 2: Proposed Conflict Team Structure Within Each Sector

cultural advisors, strategic alliance groups, and third-party intervenors would have a specific report and control point (represented here by an individual quadrant), as would tactical practitioner team members such as negotiators, mediators, and facilitators.

In Figure 3 (see next page), the angled arrows represent each sector's recursive intelligence collection and analysis, designed to focus at the strategic level of communications. As even this first attempt also shows, a structure that could credibly be used in managing a wicked problem is itself likely to be somewhat complex and multifaceted. But that complexity allows for a host of strengths, not just the predictable drawbacks of complexity. The strengths include a particularly critical element: ongoing and "predictive" intelligence analysis (as opposed to the above-described status reports of symptoms of the conflict). Conflict by its very nature demands prediction; yet wicked problems make prediction difficult, without a robust structure that includes the essential elements for conflict analysis, such as collection of information/ research, processing that information, analysis, and

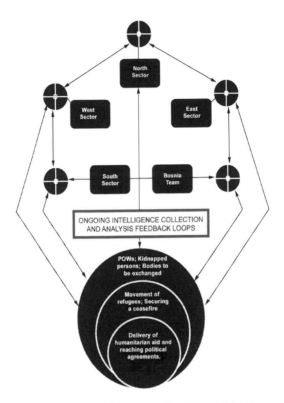

Figure 3: A Revised Bosnia Command Structure. See Figure 2 for the content of each small circle. (For graphic simplicity, the arrows (representing each sector's efforts) are not shown as reaching all three "subject" circles described in the text above, but of course they would in practice.)

distribution/sharing. Rarely in all the conflicts I have participated in have these considerations actually been incorporated in the approach to the conflict.

Instead, I have witnessed two typical responses to conflict. The first is that of a negotiator or mediator heightening his own personal awareness, taking the time to analyze the conflict more comprehensively, but without having a structure, team, mechanism or processes in place to conduct this with the necessary skills and tools to do it properly. The second response I have observed has been in the form of theoretically robust structures in conflict zones, known as fusion or Intel centers, but whose scope is often limited to the military and tactical elements of the conflict. What is important to winning on the battlefield, e.g., avoiding casualties and identifying the next immediate threat, does not necessarily help to develop a strategy of peaceful resolution, or to mitigate the threat through a multifaceted approach including the use of negotiators, mediators, community development, psy-ops and political and economic initiatives.

To be effective at approaching a wicked problem, then, will require a correspondingly complex and multidimensional approach. This has undoubted costs. But until leaders involved in conflict are willing to open themselves up to such new and more elaborate approaches, the old ways of business will lead those involved in managing wicked conflicts to the usual outcome of frustration and failure.

Equally important, such a structure allows for *resilience*. Most wicked problems, as Coleman describes, are frustrating, long-term and exhausting. Building structures like this allows for negotiators, mediators and other conflict managers to be replaced as necessary – or simply to take the time to be reflective. This too sustains forward movement, making it less dependent on a given individual.[7] A structure that can last as long as the wicked problem also deals with the reverse issue – the likelihood that many so-called experts will leave almost as fast as they arrived. With that kind of turnover goes a loss of knowledge, relationships, trust and insight. Creating a structure allows sustaining and building upon the forward movement of any one individual's conflict mitigation and management. Mediators, negotiators and peacemakers thus need to consider a more robust systems approach to conflict, versus the traditional linear approach utilizing one or a group of mediators/negotiators.

Strategy

The second strength that a structure like the one diagrammed in Figure 3 allows for is strategy. The benefits of strategy in *military* operations have been well known since the days of Sun Tzu (see 1910/2012 translation), and account for a huge proportion of military history. To develop strategy, analysis is required – which is built into this structure. However, the structure must allow for the ability to develop, plan, and constantly modify the strategy. This means it must have the personnel and resources to focus on tomorrow's activities, not merely today's crisis. Once the strategy is developed, it needs a mechanism within the structure to command and control the activities, to ensure consistent focus on the mission, to manage any conflicting activities, to ensure that all the moving parts of the structure and the team are in sync, and most important, to ensure that the operation maintains the "speed, flow and direction" of the conflict mitigation or management activity.

There may be times to pause the activities, to avoid fueling the conflict; there may be times to shift the direction quickly, to exploit new peace opportunities; there may be times when new barriers appear, which perhaps would benefit from some outside perspective and experience. This includes the insight and awareness to avoid the destructive political, cultural and psychological "landmine" issues inherent in all wicked problems. In addition to "built-in outside experts," however, such a structure also proactively identifies, and formerly builds and maintains, critical strategic alliances.

Identifying, developing and sustaining relationships with strategic allies is time- and resource-dependent. Creating a structure focused on this potentially aids in having the right people proactively engaged at the right times to allow for effective forward momentum in overcoming the inevitable obstacles, resistance, barriers and spoilers. This should result in an improved ability to outmaneuver the spoilers of peace; greater wisdom to know when to pause in order to avoid stepping into highly volatile issues; and better insight into the when, where, who and what of latent opportunities for collaboration. Building structures in advance through planning allows for the full power of a strategic approach, as compared to a reactive one.

Once a suitable structure is in place, a strategy is developed based on the ongoing analysis. This will identify various *processes* or *channels* of engagement. For me, defining these better will have to be a "next phase" in my approach to thinking about wicked problems. I can at least, however, outline the processes that I think would be implicated in the Bosnian structure, shown in Figure 4 on the next page.

I can also note which elements were, in my view, missing in practice. For simplicity, I will discuss these as text elements keyed to the several elements of the Figure 4 diagram. I freely admit that this diagram is imperfect in many ways. Because diagrams and flow charts have been known to be excerpted and to then take on a life of their own, I should emphasize that it is offered here merely as the best I can manage at the present stage of thinking through these issues, not as anything rigorous, and certainly nowhere near anything "definitive." Yet even this first attempt to codify a suitable structure would, I think, have improved greatly on what my colleagues and I had available in Bosnia. Had I understood these matters better then, I would have used it.

Process
With the structure outlined in Figure 3, the HQ conflict management team could have assumed responsibility in developing a strategic communications strategy, and with the support of other subject matter experts, could have leveraged the activities in the field in relationship to POW negotiations, and gleaned broader community and political support for their resolution. In such a communication stream, the messaging should be consistent and in support

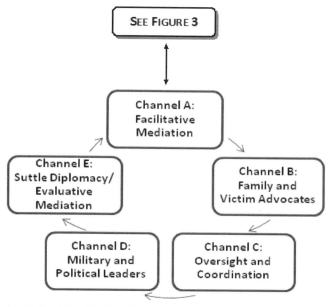

Figure 4: Relationship of Revised Bosnia Command Structure to Outside Channels

of the other channels. The target audience here is the larger community – associates of those engaged directly in negotiation/mediation processes, and persons of influence *outside* such channels.

This concept includes political leaders, persons of influence within the warring factions, potential spoilers of peace, and the community at large. This channel must be in sync with the other channels, but it has many options, and according to the "sync needs" of the moment can use communication means such as television, literature, town hall meetings/public forums, radio, Internet, and/or blogs to carry the message. In Coleman's description of "the 5%," I would suggest, the majority of such conflicts are multiparty disputes. Relying solely on communication with those directly engaged has typically resulted in failure. Thus a strategic channel for communication targeting the larger audience is critical.

Often, key players and persons of influence are not engaged in the actual negotiation/mediation processes – thus the need for a broader communication strategy, to ensure that efforts are made to address the potential role of those outside the formal resolution processes. Often there is misinformation being generated and shared amongst the warring factions, including intentional propaganda as well as simple miscommunication. Efforts must be made to enhance the accuracy of the information from all sides, and to nullify efforts to undermine the negotiation/mediation processes.

In the former Yugoslavia there has been literature confirming the use of "psy ops" (functionally, strategic communication under another name, though the phrase "psy ops" often has pejorative connotations that derive from being sneaky, which peacekeepers must avoid). Nevertheless, I suggest, there was a lack of an overall communication *strategy*. In my view, this was largely due to the lack of a formal structure within the UN tasked with resolving these issues. Building a conflict team structure such as outlined in Figure 3 would allow for working with psy ops groups, other strategic communication resources, and next, those who are described below in Figure 4 as "channels." Inherent in this proposal is a change in the usage of the word "channel." This is deliberate.

Channel A is directed at the designated government representatives who are directly responsible through their positions for assisting in the resolution of the conflict – or in some cases, in the escalation of the conflict. Traditionally, negotiators, mediators and peacemakers have consistently focused their structures and processes (i.e., all of their resources) in engaging with these players. Yet my experience is that most of the engagement has been performed without any formal structure; the interactions have been informal, or semi-formal at best.

In Bosnia, quite often if not consistently, the lead organization for mediation in these processes was the International Committee of the Red Cross (ICRC). Where possible, the UN did embed an observer into the facilitative mediation process led by ICRC. For instance, in the former Yugoslavia, in some cases the UN Military Liaison Officers assumed that role; in other cases, UN police or UN civil affairs officers assumed that role. Unfortunately, because there was no formal structure, such third-party support in addition to the ICRC was minimal, leaving the warring parties to their own means to resolve complex issues. If the ICRC was unable through its typically confidential, facilitative process to reach an agreement, the outcome was loss of life, torture, and the escalation of tensions. At the very least, a structure within the UN with observers who were *consistently* embedded into the facilitative mediation processes, with some central coordination and oversight, would have allowed the UN to glean valuable insights into the causal factors of the tensions, identifying opportunities for potential resolution and trust building. (I note Coleman's discussion that it takes between three and a half and five positive experiences for every negative one to build trust. The reader can easily imagine what the ratio was in Bosnia.) Clearly, this by itself would not have been enough. But even such mere "presence" of the international community would have enhanced, to some degree, the willingness of the warring parties to act in good faith.

Channel B: This channel is essentially focused at engaging family, friends and associates of missing persons, a "victim liaison" role. This may include conducting prison visits, providing "proof of life" for the negotiations if required, and ensuring that the families and their associates mobilize (where possible) community and political support to resolve the POW/missing persons/body exchanges.

Quite often, the players from the warring factions may resort to utilizing the victims for other political or military gains; the well-being and safe return of POWs or missing persons, or the respectful return of casualties, becomes a tool or weapon in the war. Equally often, the warring parties may avoid engaging or maintaining transparent dialogue with the families, if they opt to use the victims' situation for ulterior motives. A process such as channel B provides the UN negotiators/mediators with an opportunity to engage with these families, and leverage them for securing political and community support in resolving the volatile issues. This may include the family providing negotiators/mediators with additional opportunities to engage with community and political leaders, in an effort to advance the processes in channel A. To accomplish this effectively, a structure that allows for constant relationship-building and communication with the families is critical. In the former Yugoslavia, however, structure and resources were absent in this family liaison role, and the negotiators engaged in channel A processes were required to assume this role as well. This placed additional responsibilities on those tasked with managing very complicated processes associated with channel A, and as a result, negatively affected the "speed, flow and direction" of *those* negotiations. Having a specific mechanism in place – i.e., several officers with a standing assignment as liaison to the families – would thus have bolstered channel A in addition to its direct functions. Here again, the absence of formal structure limited the effectiveness of the processes involved.

Channel C: This is the oversight and coordination prong, to reduce conflicts among other processes, to leverage opportunities, to apply pressure when barriers arise, and to infuse all of the other processes with real-time analysis and intelligence. This prong represents the part of the structure where strategy evolves into operations, and it is intended to provide constant looping of assessments and feedback between the many processes. This prong also provides support and guidance to the field operatives concerning nuances of culture, history, politics and current events which they have no time to track directly and which may significantly impact their respective processes.

Channel D: This is designed to proactively build relationships with key military and political leaders who can assist in the mitigation and/ or resolution of the POW, missing persons and body exchange issues.

As stated previously, channel A is the primary such channel; but as noted above, the facilitative mediation process led by ICRC constantly ran into barriers, resistance and challenges that could not be resolved or even addressed by those "at the table." It is entirely consistent with Coleman's analysis that additional structures and processes would have to be put into place to create strategic alliances, to amplify the mediators' power and influence.

This is especially applicable if the process needs to shift more towards something resembling "evaluative" mediation, such as a shuttle diplomacy-and-negotiation process in which the peacekeepers themselves engage more assertively. Failure to provide for this element is a significant predictor of the typical stalemate expected by Coleman's analysis. In situations such as the Bosnian conflict, that includes loss of life and escalation of tensions. On the ground in that conflict, I assumed this role myself, in addition to managing other processes; a more structured approach, with others tasked specifically with this role, would have been far more effective.

Channel E: In addition to mediation processes facilitated by such agencies as the ICRC, consideration should be given to a parallel "evaluative" mediation, which would include bouts of shuttle diplomacy.

Outcome

This process, as I conceive it, would be a UN-supported process that would perform the functions the ICRC is ill-equipped to do, such as moving the parties through difficult barriers. It would allow the ICRC to remain neutral in its facilitative definition, as its charter requires, without sacrificing the good that a more intensive/robust approach can sometimes bring. This could have helped to keep the overall mediation efforts from repeatedly stalling out. I have witnessed the ability in other cases to run both evaluative and facilitative processes in tandem, by independent (but cooperative) mediators.

This, admittedly, requires a high degree of continuing analysis, risk management and communication with the parties, to ensure that one process does not compromise the other process, but instead enhances it. The corresponding structure would consist of various UN mediators/negotiators and intelligence personnel, forming an integrated team (military, civilian, and police), specifically tasked with these negotiations/mediations. In my view, those attached to the F prong would not only work behind the scenes between warring parties on sticking points that were frustrating the ICRC mediation, but would seek resources to "create value" (when one side needs something new put on the table to justify to its own constituency its logical next move), identify innovative solutions for joint gains, proactively identify impending barriers, and organize an "all hands on deck" approach when that is what it will take to resolve the impending problems in advance. In terms that have been used to describe labor mediators, this kind of role has been called a "dealmaker," in comparison to the ICRC's "orchestrator" role (Kolb 1983). In Bosnia, due to the sensitivity of channel A and the reputational and trust issues that concerned ICRC, many such initiatives and sidebar negotiations took place between the warring parties and myself, when such sticking points were encountered. Again, however, a formal structure with proper resources would have helped.

The structure outlined here is far from perfect. My purpose in offering it is simply to highlight the importance of *structure* to support *processes* which will in turn result in more effective *outcomes* in wicked problems. Today's practitioners, especially over the last decade, have increased their focus in both theory and practice on self-awareness and self-reflection (see, e.g., Fox and Press, *Venturing Home*, and Goh et al., *As We See It*, in this volume). There is an unequivocal need for practitioners dealing with wicked problems, however, to add to this a greater awareness of how to build structures to assist and support their process work.

The structures themselves will require complexity, as Figures 2-4 suggest. At the same time, they must be designed to be fluid, flexible and capable of responding to dynamic events within the conflicts. Typically, the warring factions themselves create a structure (e.g., in the former Yugoslavia, the Exchange Commissions) to address such issues as POWs etc., as they obviously know these issues will become volatile and perpetuating factors. Yet in Bosnia the UN failed to consider a structure of its own designed to address what was obviously a key issue in a "5%" conflict, choosing instead to rely on the simplicity of design of a "UN military, UN police and UN civil affairs" structure. While there are likely a host of reasons for the existing structures of the UN in peacekeeping operations, experience suggests that the UN could have done better in view of the complexity of the conflict. Nor did the UN build subsidiary structures within the larger structure to address the key and perpetuating issues associated with POWs. In summary, and in my experience in other conflicts, structure is one of the last things that practitioners consider.

The reasons for this are themselves complex, and may relate to a combination of ego, inexperience, and exhaustion. In 1993, while still an extremely inexperienced practitioner of conflict management, I recall being summoned to UN HQ by senior officials during the Bosnian negotiations. I was brought before the UN Commissioner of UNCIVPOL, Commissioner Michael O'Reilly, who was kind enough to praise my work in this area. He then asked if there was anything the UN could do to assist and support my efforts. He asked that I keep him advised, and said he and other leaders would ensure that I secured the support to continue on with these critical negotiations. With the benefit of hindsight and the impetus of this writing, and as a student of dispute resolution since my experience in the former Yugoslavia, I have recently reflected on my then response.

My response, I regret to say, was typical of those I have since observed with many practitioners: an egocentric response seeking support to continue on with my efforts, to continue to be allowed to participate in these high risk and politically sensitive negotiations. Had I had the benefit of more experience, or had I honed my self-reflective skills (which occurred only later, as a result of studying such thinkers as Daniel Bowling and Michelle LeBaron) I would have put more thought and less emotion into my response.

What was really required, to sustain the work I and others had started, and to mitigate the loss of life and the torture that was occurring on a daily basis, was to focus on designing an effective *structure*, such as the one depicted in the previous pages. If we are to improve our abilities in managing, mitigating and resolving the "5%" conflicts, we must enhance our awareness not just of the self, but equally, of the techniques and needs for building structures to amplify the effectiveness of our processes. In other words, we must learn to treat as a matter of routine, and to execute, the pattern **Structure→strategy→ process→outcome.** In addition, we must in the future prepare those venturing forth to such assignments to ensure that our mediation and negotiation processes truly consider the strategic, operational and tactical levels of conflict engagement to be distinct, with the tactical day-to-day engagement and management of linear processes coming only after strategic and operational decisions.

Conclusion

The past twenty years' development of our field has, at least, made it easier to perceive some of the deficiencies in our practices; and that is, perhaps, a start toward being able to train and deploy professionals who are readier to deal with the complexities. As one of the key complexities, it bears repeating that the processes outlined above are not linear, let alone fixed. They are instead constantly modified based on analysis, feedback, assessments and opportunities, successes – and failures. All of these processes must operate in line with the strategic objectives and the overall strategy, and these too shift over time.

In that respect in particular it feels wrong to label this section of our chapter a "conclusion"; the very concept is too misleading, in view of the work-in-progress reality as I perceive it. Perhaps it is appropriate, however, to refer to a way station, and a milestone. At best, my colleagues and I in this chapter have arrived at a way station, perhaps representing a definable bit of progress along a path that is certainly going to remain both confusing and arduous, and that is probably unfinishable in any of our lifetimes. To the extent that this analysis may be useful to others, however, it owes a good deal to Peter Coleman's book. That, indeed, is a milestone.

Notes

[1] For more on the value of metaphors in negotiation, and indeed the inevitability of thinking in them, see Gadlin, Schneider, and Honeyman 2006.

[2] It should be noted that Coleman's book is not about "negotiation" as such. Its relevance in negotiation is that it provides a way of describing a *context* for negotiation. Yet it is on all fours with the thrust of this team's conclusions to date; see particularly Docherty and Lira, *Adapting to the Adaptive*, in this volume. And it may go further, by giving a negotiator working within this context a clearer sense of the alternatives available to self and other. What it says more profoundly is that negotiation can be made more effective by using Coleman's larger intellectual construct. This is no small accomplishment, and no small contribution to the larger agenda of the negotiation field.

[3] Note the parallel discussion by Rachel Parish of "creative space," in *Making it up as You Go*, in this volume.

[4] Not always, however. See, e.g., Korobkin 2006, Bernard 2006, and Honeyman 2004.

[5] One reviewer of the eponymous software product Genuine Fractals claimed to be routinely making 40″ x 60″ prints from a 15 megapixel file, and sometimes prints up to ten by thirteen feet, with success. This is a very high degree of enlargement. Genuine Fractals 6 Review, by Jon Canfield, available at http://www.photographyblog.com/reviews_genuine_fractals_6.php (last accessed January 23, 2013).

[6] In May 2011, approximately a year after this excerpt was first published, Mladic was found, arrested and extradicted to the Hague, where he is currently on trial for war crimes, crimes against humanity, and genocide. See generally http://en.wikipedia.org/wiki/Ratko_Mladi%C4%87 (last accessed January 13, 2013).

[7] Here I speak as a practitioner who was once called unexpectedly from Vancouver into a government department's weekend meeting in Ottawa – and then dispatched directly to the Horn of Africa, without even the opportunity to go home and pack. I was gone almost a year, partly because there was no structure for "spelling" me once I had become familiar with the conflict. The number of times an experienced practitioner faced with this kind of deployment has begged off, or resigned, or demanded transfer while the work was still under way and with no suitable replacement in sight, is difficult to know; but I suspect it is high. The neutral agencies find it all too easy to blame the resulting failures on the parties.

References

Bernard, P. 2006. Power, powerlessness and process. In *The negotiator's fieldbook: The desk reference for the experienced negotiator*, edited by A. K. Schneider and C. Honeyman. . Washington, DC: American Bar Association.

Chrustie, C., J. S. Docherty, L. Lira, J. Mahuad, H. Gadlin, and C. Honeyman. 2010. Negotiating wicked problems: Five stories. In *Venturing beyond the classroom: Volume 2 in the rethinking negotiation teaching series*, edited by C. Honeyman, J. Coben, and G. De Palo. St. Paul, MN: DRI Press.

Coleman, P. 2011. *The five percent: Finding solutions to seemingly impossible conflicts*. New York: Public Affairs.

Donabedian, A. 2002. An introduction to quality assurance in health care. Oxford: Oxford University Press.

Donabedian, A. 2005. Evaluating the quality of medical care. T*he Millbank Quarterly* 83(4): 691-729.

Dorner, D. 1996. *The logic of failure*. New York: Basic Books.

Fisher, R., W. L. Ury, and B. Patton. 1991. *Getting to yes: Negotiating agreement without giving in*, 2nd edn. New York: Penguin.

Gadlin, H., A. K. Schneider, and C. Honeyman. 2006. The road to hell is paved with metaphors. In *The negotiator's fieldbook: The desk reference for the experienced negotiator*, edited by A. K. Schneider and C. Honeyman. Washington, DC: American Bar Association.

Honeyman, C. 2004. The physics of power. *Marquette Law Review* 87(4): 872-874.

Kolb, D. M. 1983. *The mediators*. Boston, MA: MIT Press.

Korobkin, R. 2006. On bargaining power. In *The negotiator's fieldbook: The desk reference for the experienced negotiator*, edited by A. K. Schneider and C. Honeyman. Washington, DC: American Bar Association.

Miller, G. and R. Dingwall. 2006. When the play's in the wrong theater. In *The negotiator's fieldbook: The desk reference for the experienced negotiator*, edited by A. K. Schneider and C. Honeyman. Washington, DC: American Bar Association.

Olson, E. E. and G. H. Eoyang. 2001. *Facilitating organization change*. San Francisco: Jossey-Bass/Pfeiffer.

Peters, K. E., B. C. Mueller, N. E. Stoller, and S. Gupta. 2009. Structure-process-outcome quality measures. In *Encylopedia of health services research*, edited by R. M. Mullner. Thousand Oaks, CA: Sage Publications

Sturm, S. 2001. Second generation employment discrimination: A structural approach. *Columbia Law Review* 101: 458-568.

Sun Tzu (translation 2012, 1910). *The art of war.* Available at http://suntzu-said.com/ (last accessed January 23, 2013).

Ury, W. L., J. Brett, and S. Goldberg. 1988. *Getting disputes resolved: Designing systems to cut the costs of conflict*. San Francisco: Jossey-Bass.

Woocher, L. 2011. *Conflict assessment and intelligence analysis: Commonality, convergence, and complementarity*. Washington, DC: United States Institute of Peace. Available at http://www.usip.org/publications/conflict-assessment-and-intelligence-analysis (last accessed January 23, 2013).

C3 21 ຂ

Teaching Wickedness to Students:
Planning and Public Policy, Business, and Law

Sanda Kaufman, Roy Lewicki & James Coben*

Editors' Note: Many readers of this book, and this series, may start out thinking that of all the problems and all the issues and all the techniques they need to engage with as teachers of negotiation, at least they can leave "wicked problems" to specialists in international, environmental, race relations and other "intractable" conflict. Howard Gadlin's analysis in chapter 20 of the role of wicked problems inside any large organization should be enough to give pause to that complacency. This chapter's three authors normally encounter students who are more "typical," recent-graduate-level, and classroom-oriented than the midcareer military professionals discussed by Leonard Lira and Rachel Parish in chapter 18, or the often middle-aged, returning students in the graduate program in peacebuilding described by Jayne Docherty in chapter 19. The authors candidly assess barriers and offer up a series of practical recommendations for teaching "wicked problems" in planning and public policy, business, and law programs.

Introduction
Should we even try to teach about "wicked problems" in planning school, business school, or law school negotiation courses? Can we

* **Sanda Kaufman** is a professor of planning, public policy and administration at Cleveland State University's Levin College of Urban Affairs. Her research spans negotiation, intervention, framing and intractability in public conflicts, participation in public decisions, decision analysis, risk communication, and program evaluation. Her email address is s.kaufman@csuohio.edu. **Roy J. Lewicki** is the Irving Abramowitz memorial professor emeritus in the Max M. Fisher College of Business at The Ohio State University. His email address is lewicki_1@fisher.osu.edu. **James Coben** is a professor of law and senior fellow in the Dispute Resolution Institute at Hamline University School of Law, and co-director of the Rethinking Negotiation Teaching project. His email address is jcoben@hamline.edu.

hope to do so with any effectiveness? Keeping in mind a key wicked-problems principle – that context matters – we assess below the potential value, and the prospects, of a serious attempt to incorporate wicked problems teaching in three distinct teaching domains.

We begin with Sanda Kaufman because planning and public policy often involves wicked problems. From her perspective, this is not new material. If you examine planning and public policy challenges long enough and with enough depth, she argues, you realize that they are all complex (and often wicked); and planners and policy makers know it. That said, Sanda goes on to describe how planners and policy types still fall into typical traps (zeroing in on the technical problem at hand to the exclusion of the rest; isolating problems in ways that limit tradeoffs; etc.). The teaching recommendation: teach ways of thinking, rather than teaching solutions; teach humility; demand "thick" stakeholder analysis; and recognize that not everyone can do this (some skills cannot be taught).

Roy Lewicki then succinctly describes why business school negotiation training has systematically ignored the skills critical for solving wicked problems. He explores three root causes: 1) an intellectual heritage based on a bilateral negotiation perspective; 2) a controlling economic paradigm that favors outcome maximization, from a partisan point of view, over issues/perspectives (many non-economic) that are often more characteristic of wicked problems; and 3) research paradigms, influenced by economics and psychology, which tend to isolate contextual factors and oversimplify complex problems. Roy then describes how these forces shape the business school negotiation teaching agenda, and concludes with recommendations for change, including a call for better exchange between negotiation teachers across disciplines, as well as between effective practitioners and teachers.

James Coben closes by focusing on a much narrower question: what exactly will he *do* differently in his two-credit (1400 classroom minutes[1]) law school negotiation course, the next time he teaches it? Noting that the traditional negotiation "canon" (see Lande et al., *Principles for Designing Negotiation Instruction*, in this volume) is necessary to provide the transactional tools necessary to handle many typical lawyering assignments, Jim goes on to posit that lawyers have an ethical obligation to assist their clients to critically examine dispute definition (and be open to the possibility that the "presenting" binary dispute is, in fact, a symptom of a systemic conflict that will necessitate different negotiating tools and tactics, to address it with any success.) He follows with a modest proposal: four "small" shifts in his teaching agenda that should help prepare students to effectively take on this ethical obligation.

Planning and Public Policy (Sanda Kaufman)

What is Wickedness (in public decision making)?

We used to say that (policy, planning and environmental) public disputes are symptoms of an underlying conflict. Resolving them does
not mean we have resolved the conflict, which can only be managed
(a spin of Horst Rittel and Melvin Webber (1973), who were speaking
of social problems). Conflicts that drag on for years, and flare up in
various disputes that subside and reappear repeatedly, are indicative
of the presence of wicked problems.

Context matters, indeed. What and how to teach about how to
handle wicked problems in a negotiation situation may vary, in accordance with the specific roots, manifestations and consequences of
"*wickedness*" and the means at the parties' disposal. We see this variation reflected in the chapters that address wicked problems in this
volume. In the realms of public decisions – planning, public policy,
administration and management – "wicked" problems stem from situations with characteristics overlapping neatly with the hallmarks of
"complexity,"[2] including:

- Highly interdependent social systems that often interact with
  the natural environment: for example, the building of the U.S.
  highway network in the 20th century – beneficial to the economy and to people's lives at a time when fossil fuel energy appeared plentiful – has also led to urban sprawl around many
  cities. Not only has urban sprawl fragmented and impaired
  natural habitats, it has also contributed to central cities' decline, and no longer appears economically or environmentally
  sustainable. Interdependence effects are aggravated by the
  threshold nature of change in some systems. In social-ecological systems, changes do not necessarily occur gradually in
  proportion to inputs, but rather in stepwise fashion, when certain input thresholds are reached. These systems tend to have
  a fractal nature (similar levels of complexity at all scales), and
  exhibit unpredictability, and "openness" – the lack of precise
  boundaries for either problem definition or solutions. We see
  many of these characteristics at work in global climate change
  processes and effects, so it is less than surprising that there is
  no agreement on either the problems climate change poses or
  on effective solutions.

- Slow feedback from decisions: consequences tend to exceed
  the decision makers' life spans. This trait infuses heightened
  uncertainty in momentous decisions that are costly now, with
  (imperfectly known) consequences for many over the long

haul, when those who made the decisions will not incur their effects. This is coupled with diminished learning: wrong models of reality that drive today's decisions fail to be invalidated because by the time sufficient evidence accumulates, it can no longer be traced back to its causes. Accountability is also lacking over such long time periods, inducing more overconfidence and risk-taking in decision makers than would be the case if feedback occurred swiftly. Those who built the highway systems did not foresee rising fossil fuel prices, the consequences of lead pollution or acid rain, or the contribution of emissions to climate change. They cannot in any practical way be held accountable for decisions from which they benefited that turned out to have broad negative consequences. In turn, current decision makers will not have to account for their mistakes. Although we have numerous examples of past decisions that had unpredicted consequences and turned out unwise in the long run, in general today's decision makers do not seem to have understood that they are just as unable to predict the future accurately as their predecessors.

Planning and other public decisions shape the physical space, which has memory. Spatial effects of decisions endure and are cumulative. Since we cannot start over when we realize the error of our past ways or understand better some cause-effect linkages, we have to build on what already exists. Previous decisions with spatial consequences have restricted our options for the future, and our current decisions continue to narrow the set of future alternatives. For example, although we now find suburbs problematic for a host of reasons (inefficient use of land and of public resources, fragmentation of natural habitats, social isolation, etc.) we cannot recreate metropolitan space according to our current understanding and circumstances. Nor can we accede to some deep ecologists' demands to restore land to its pre-colonization state. This inability to backtrack and start over has been called path dependence, and has a parallel in negotiations. It means that some outcomes that were possible in a system at the outset (or acceptable to negotiators at the beginning of a dispute) become infeasible (or unacceptable to negotiators) in time, as various decisions are gradually implemented in the system and leave their mark (or as negotiators move from one proposal to another). In addition, in both social-ecological systems decisions and in negotiations, intervening implementation issues, defaults on interim agreements, and commons incentives alter the situations sufficiently in time to render some initially desirable solutions infeasible or unacceptable.

People make individual and joint choices at various scales that affect the physical and social environments. Their thinking is afflicted by cognitive difficulty with large amounts of information; limited knowledge about how socioeconomic and natural systems work and interact; a tendency to focus on one cause and one effect at a time; confusion between correlation and causality; mental models that do not correspond well to reality; impatience; and other difficulties that impair understanding, predictions, the generation of solutions that match the complexity of the targeted systems, and learning from past mistakes (Dörner 1994).

Wickedness – in the guise of surprising, unintended decision consequences that are sometimes irreversible by the time they are detected, and that accrue to others than those who reaped the short-term benefits – emerges at the intersection of highly complex situations with people's difficulty in dealing with them, and with institutional arrangements that partition the space of decisions (e.g., Bazerman and Watkins 2004). In the example of the U.S. highway system, the current generation lacks the resources for altering the resulting interlinked spatial configurations – which amply benefited some in past generations – to reduce reliance on automobiles and promote less polluting and less carbon-intensive transportation means. Moreover, attempts to implement system-wide change to adapt to new circumstances give rise to protracted conflicts. In the context of interdependent social-ecological systems, change often means perceived and real winners and losers.

Some of the current disputes around wicked problems at scales ranging from local to global include: to frack or not to frack; calls to dismantle the O'Shaughnessy Dam (built in 1913) that forms the Hetch-Hetchy Reservoir in the Yosemite National Park; and preventing or mitigating effects of global climate change. Negotiations over the design of national policies such as health care or reforming tax and immigration laws or intervening in intra- and international wars (e.g., Syria, Mali, Asia's Pacific Rim) also have some of the attributes of wicked problems, due to the scale of both the problems and consequences to very large numbers of different people.

These examples suggest that because globally interacting systems are involved, wicked problems can emerge at very different spatial scales, and may have consequences exceeding the geographic location of their source. We also get the sense that not all wicked problems are equally severe. However, if we attempted to generate "wickedness criteria" we would be confronted not only with serious measurement challenges, but also with conflicts stemming from value differences. We might have to weigh contemporary suffering and loss of life against the (predicted) quality of life of future generations; environmental damage versus damage to human systems; or the geographic distribution of sacrifices today for a promised collective future (though one neither necessarily evenly distributed nor certain to be better.) Thus one aspect of the wickedness of planning and policy problems resides in implied value choices we may be reluctant to formulate, let alone implement. This is one of the drivers of the intractable quality of conflicts surrounding wicked problems.

Note that complexity, wickedness and intractability intersect. Wickedness and complexity share several characteristics. So do wicked problems and intractable conflicts. However, not all complex problems are wicked; also, intractable conflicts are not necessarily rooted in wicked problems. For example, value conflicts are difficult but not wicked, as seen in longstanding conflicts surrounding abortion, gun control, gay rights, some international disputes and some lengthy planning disputes. Some wicked problems share with intractable conflicts a duration that exceeds even the longest of human life-spans. In fact, we deem conflicts to be intractable when they seem to have no end in [our] sight. Nevertheless, history is replete with conflicts that ended after decades, and even centuries, during which they surely appeared intractable to their contemporaries. Time plays a (largely unpredictable) role in wicked problems too, in the delay between decisions and results, often in areas other than where they were enacted.

To summarize, planning and public policy wicked problems involve many parties, unfold over long time periods with low feedback, tend to entail consideration of few decision factors relative to the scale of the problem, and hinge critically on correct mental models of reality (because causal links are difficult to verify and effects are difficult to attribute to causes, due to the time lags between action and consequence). Nothing stands still in systems that have numerous quasi-independently moving parts and lack precisely definable boundaries, so it is difficult to accumulate experience or to predict consequences which are at times irreversible.

Where Does Negotiation Come Into Wicked Planning and Policy Decisions?

Wicked problems cut across physical, political and organizational boundaries. They occur in contexts in which resources are limited, where some irreconcilable interests, risk preferences and values are in play, and where numerous needs compete for attention. Wicked problems require decisions that entail politically and morally difficult tradeoffs between present and future, local and other scales, various issues and various interest groups. For the individuals directly involved, conflicts between self-interest and the broader (organizational or public) interests are also always present.

Within democratic societies, public decisions that attend to wicked problems require negotiations among stakeholders, including both those having specific decision mandates and others able to claim a place at the decision table. The negotiation processes that yield implementable public decisions are often resource- and technical information-intensive, lengthy, complicated, and context-specific, involving numerous parties with varying levels of skill, experience, creativity, responsibility and commitment.

Teaching Negotiations in a "Wicked" Context

In light of the nature of planning and public policy decisions and their likelihood of encountering or even giving rise to wicked problems and to serious conflicts, what should we teach students (or planning and public policy professionals) and how? The answers may vary in terms of actual content and means, but we might at least explore some objectives and prescriptions.

I propose that we should strive to help students become effective stakeholders, able to participate in negotiated decision processes and to represent their own and their constituencies' interests. This means equipping students with approaches and tools, rather than specific fixes, in recognition of both the uniqueness of each decision context and the shared characteristics of complex situations as well as sources of wickedness and intractability.

Some prescriptions: We should model in the classroom ways of thinking and interacting with others that can surface, and help avoid, wicked traps. We should show that we expect problems to be difficult to unpack and understand, solutions to be difficult to devise and implement, results to surprise us, and the future to be difficult to predict. We should strive for specificity, and discourage discussions in terms of generalities that obscure responsibilities and resource limits, or that contain implicit value judgments. We should surface our cognitive shortcomings. Whenever possible, we should explore scenarios of alternative courses of action and their consequences, rather than considering one solution. We should show respect for the real stakeholders of situations discussed in class, and assume them to be rational even when they do not conform to our own notions of rationality. We should avoid Manichaean attitudes, apply healthy doses of doubt to information especially when it *conforms* to our own worldviews, and surface frames and differences between factual knowledge and our own and others' beliefs. We should model humility – the sense that we may not understand as much as we think we do (hubris is particularly dangerous in a wicked context) – and admit that the best answer to many negotiation questions is "it depends."

This is a tall order, much easier said than done, especially within a single negotiation course. Perhaps learning how to become a skillful public decision maker should not be relegated to negotiation courses. Rather, some of the necessary skills, such as recognizing the hallmarks of wicked problems and preparing for negotiation through thorough systems and stakeholder analyses, can be included in several other courses and in projects in the same way as it would be necessary in practice. After all, we do not bring up ethics only in an ethics course, or data analysis only in a quantitative methods course. Ideally, as the primary vehicle for making public decisions, negotiation should come up whenever such decisions are discussed. Perhaps we might engage our colleagues in efforts to identify where and how they could include negotiation insights and skills in their courses on other topics. Nevertheless, we are still left with the task of teaching within a short time span about negotiation practices that unfold over long time periods, in multiple venues, in continuously changing circumstances, and with high stakes that are often outside students' experience, and therefore more difficult to understand.

Arguably, teaching public decision negotiation while contending with wicked problems requires addressing complexity-related topics, which is not necessary when teaching negotiation in other contexts. We may need to devote time to developing "thick" stakeholder analyses, as well as understanding the role of context, scale, and institutional structures that shape the decision making processes. One key skill is recognition of the incentives implicit in specific contexts, such as the commons dilemma incentives (Hardin 1968) that tend to contribute to intractability in public disputes. For example, commons incentives account at least in part for repeatedly failed international negotiations over global climate change.

Another set of skills that tends to be specific to public decision negotiations and is particularly difficult to convey in a classroom setting is negotiation process design. It too runs against time limits, the need for practice and the fact that this activity lies outside most students' experience. Perhaps one of the best vehicles for conveying some of these negotiation skills is apprenticeship with seasoned negotiators or mediators (for a deeper discussion, see Matsuura et al., *Beyond "Negotiation 2.0,"* in this volume), rather than classroom work.

In the process of teaching negotiations we need to encourage multiple understandings of wicked problems, and expose students to others' ways of thinking. (It is nigh impossible to negotiate with others whose thinking we dismiss as illegitimate, irrational or ill-motivated because it is different from our thinking.)[3] We need to instill a healthy skepticism of one-cause, one-fix solutions. We also need to insist on rich explorations of decision consequences across systems, and of the meaning of non-decisions (or no-agreements): failing to make a decision is a decision too. It may seem to be an expeditious way of avoiding some negative consequences, but it amounts to deciding to live with a (stable or deteriorating) status quo. We may also need to convey the real possibility that wicked problems may linger beyond our lifetime, and that we do not have a "fix" for every problem we can describe.

Finally, we the teachers and trainers may have to recognize that perhaps some skills cannot be taught (and we ourselves may not have mastered them either). Negotiating public decisions requires personal talent, a high degree of empathy, charisma, leadership, patience, and the ability to share credit for successes and shoulder the blame for failures. We may want to select our "decision heroes" and study their qualities. We should honestly convey to students that not everyone is cut out to be a negotiator in the context of wicked problems.[4]

Business (Roy Lewicki)

Why Business School Training in Negotiation Skills Has Ignored the Skills Critical for Solving Today's Wicked Problems

Negotiation training in business schools has fundamentally ignored a negotiated approach to wicked problems.[5] What are the origins and causes of this orientation (or misorientation)? The reasons can be traced to three basic causes, all of which are rooted deep in the intellectual heritage and evolution of "business negotiation" theory and teaching practice.

The intellectual roots of business negotiation

First, the intellectual heritage for the study of negotiation in business has been the bilateral negotiation model: that is, individual on individual, or group on group. The primary applications were the earliest and most visible sources: labor relations and industrial purchasing. The dominant influence was the growth of more formalized labor relations through the late 1800s and early 1900s. The historical roots of this heritage lie in the evolution of the Railway Labor Act. The initial roots of the Act, in turn, were in the late 1800s, and were designed to introduce mandatory government arbitration into crippling commercial labor strikes. The Act led to a stream of additional legislation through the late 1800s and early 1900s; the early initiatives were designed to regulate abusive labor practices, but over the long term, evolved into formalizing the "modern" collective bargaining process. Thus, the earliest roots of writing on business negotiation can be traced to observing negotiation dynamics as they occurred in the collective bargaining process, a bilateral process primarily conducted by union and management. But this process was always conducted in the shadow of the federal government, which occasionally intervened to both "rectify" abusive practices and terminate strikes that were against the national interest, as well as to provide intermediaries (arbitrators and mediators) who could intervene to break shorter term deadlocks.

A second intellectual root was drawn from the purchasing profession, where buyer and seller squared off over price and quantity. While purchasing was largely seen as a "clerical activity" for much of the early 1900s, the demand for scarce raw materials and the post-war boom required the purchasing function to evolve into a more sophisticated transaction process. Today, the purchasing field has evolved into a highly sophisticated process of managing purchasing, logistics and supply chain management (Wisner, Tan, and Leong 2011). A third intellectual root was occasionally drawn from international diplomacy, but that tradition did not strongly influence theory and development until years later.

The practical problems associated with effectively "managing" labor negotiations or the purchasing function engaged academics with strong social science backgrounds in economics and psychology/sociology. These conversations evolved into what has been called the industrial relations and organizational behavior approaches (c.f. Kochan and Verma 1983; Walton, McKersie, and Cutcher-Gershenfeld 2000 for summaries of this evolution). In the negotiation area the most dominant transitional theory building can be traced back to Richard Walton and Robert McKersie (1965). Working with some of the early industrial relations sources and the then-contemporary analytical tools of social psychology and sociology, these authors "reframed" the more technical issue-based dynamics of these complex negotiations into four major "subprocesses": Distributive bargaining; integrative bargaining; attitudinal structuring and intraorganizational bargaining. Remarkably, these subprocesses – particularly the first two – tend to dominate the pedagogical approaches still in use. Theoretical grounding for the current approaches can also be found in the work of Jeffrey Rubin and Bert Brown (1975), Dean Pruitt (1981) and Howard Raiffa (1982), who significantly elaborated upon the tools and techniques of integrative or "principled" negotiation.

This intellectual tradition has tended to "bound" what is taught/studied in negotiation in a number of interesting but often unrecognized ways (obviously, none of these are absolutes, but they strongly influenced the evolution of theory and research in the field):

a) An ongoing assumption that negotiation is mostly a bilateral dynamic – labor vs. management, buyer vs. seller.

b) An ongoing assumption that most "important" negotiations are distributive – i.e., they are fundamentally about competitive processes, although there has been creeping enlightenment about the importance of integrative, "win-win" processes. Almost all students who come to learn about negotiation in our classrooms bring the presumption that they are there to enhance their distributive deal-making skills.

c) An ongoing assumption that "business negotiation" was largely to serve the interests of managers, both as advocates for themselves and as advocates for the "owners" (shareholders) whom they represent as agents. Hence, most of the prescriptive writing to managers about "how to negotiate" has been both asymmetric and prescriptive – i.e., how to behave as an "effective" negotiator in a bilateral negotiation, either when representing one's own interests or when acting as an agent for others' interests in a bilateral context (Kochan and Verma 1983).

d) Even going back as far as labor relations in the 1920s-30s and the creation of the Railway Labor Act, the prescribed "intermediary" roles of mediators and arbitrators was "outsourced" to other professions, like law, public policy and diplomacy. Third-partyship (of almost any form – e.g., Ury 2000) – and the associated bridge-building skills – is still a hugely neglected topic in business schools, and when taught, generally only addresses how managers can use facilitation skills in the resolution of interpersonal disputes or in facilitating teamwork dynamics. Thus even though Walton and McKersie talked about other "sub-processes" in labor relations, such as intraorganizational bargaining and attitudinal restructuring, these threads have generally been ignored in negotiation training or relegated to other parts of a curriculum. The consequence is that business education in negotiation favors the advocacy perspective, as opposed to an orientation designed to bring parties together across complex problem boundaries, and the associated skills of doing so.

An active dialectic

Second, as noted earlier, most management education in today's business schools is an active dialectic between two major intellectual traditions: economics and psychology. Economists attempt to prescribe how business (and business persons) should operate based on principles of economic rationality, while psychologists study how and why humans don't always behave consistently with economic rationality, and prescribe what to do about those deviations. Thus, even in the descriptive and prescriptive approaches to negotiation behavior, the economic paradigm is never very far away, implying that the primary emphasis for defining negotiation goals should be by measuring "outcome maximization" in economic terms and from a partisan perspective. Completely left out of many of these discussions are the sociological, ethical, legal and/or political perspectives on these issues – dimensions of a problem that often make it "wicked" – and/or these perspectives are marginalized in factor of "solutions" based on clear economic rationalities such as profit maximization or shareholder value.

The influence of economics, mathematical modeling and game theory

Third, research paradigms for *studying* negotiation in the organizational behavior and applied economics tradition have been heavily influenced by the research traditions of the same two fields: economics, with a heavy focus on mathematical modeling, game theory and optimization, and experimental psychology, with its heavy focus on laboratory-based simulations, hypothesis-driven deductive approaches to research, and selection of only one or two variables at a time for examination. Both of these research approaches tend to eliminate or isolate the "contextual" factors that overwhelm complex negotiations and enhance wicked problems, hence oversimplifying the complex reality of wicked problem negotiations and problem solving processes. Within the business school traditions, ethnographic or case studies of complex situations have been continually undervalued as "less serious" and "less rigorous" research. "Cases" tend to be seen as teaching vehicles, not as complex research analyses, which further marginalizes the complex situational and time-line dynamics that make some problems "wicked."

Finally, because business school education is also dominated by the frameworks of traditional economics, the general presumption has been that there are "markets" of buyers and sellers and that in the event one cannot strike a deal with seller X in market A, one almost always has alternative choices of other sellers in other markets, and/or that conditions in market A may change so that alterations in price or terms may become attractive to seller X. Almost no attention has been actively given to worlds in which there are no alternative sellers and/ or where altering the "terms of sale" is not a viable possibility – also a characteristic of a wicked problem.[6]

Pedagogical Implications

So, what have been the pedagogical implications of these three forces for the teaching of negotiation in schools of business and management?

First, business education is almost always limited to a dialectic between the economic and the psychological. Almost no attention is given to the legal, political, ethical or the sociological – either in the discipline's analytical tools or in valuing these perspectives on business problems. My guess is that these conceptual bases run through the training in (some) other professional schools; but not business.

Second, most of the "core" teaching scenarios/teaching methods have focused on interpersonal dynamics, behavior in the context of game theoretic (simple) economic models, and distributive/integrative processes. These topics will comprise the first fifty-seventy percent of the content of any university-based seven- or ten-week negotiation course.

Third, the complex, "wicked" problems which pervade our broader society are given only marginal treatment in the business school, and usually in nonrequired "elective" courses such as business and society, environmental management, urban planning, economic development and healthcare management. Moreover, the learning methods in these classes tend to be through case method or guest speaker, in which the greater emphasis is dominantly placed on problem diagnosis, while greatly insufficient treatment is given to inventing and implementing complex solutions and evaluating their practicality or implementability. In short, the more "wicked" the problem, the less likely we are to be using proactive, action-learning methods to access it and experiment with solutions. In many cases, we do not even teach the tools of complex problem analysis, as advocated by Dörner – cognitive biases, etc. (see generally Matsuura et al., *Beyond "Negotiation 2.0"*, in this volume).

Finally, and surprisingly, there remains an active, ongoing gap between "knowing" and "doing" in the management professions (Pfeffer and Sutton 2000). This gap has been pointed out by many, both in terms of many areas where there is valid research knowledge that is not being adequately implemented, and in terms of situations where prescriptive action is being given which ignores a credible base of established research findings. A paper by Sanda Kaufman,

Christopher Honeyman and Andrea Kupfer Schneider – *Why Don't They Listen to Us?* (2007) – has shown how this dynamic persists in the training and implementation of negotiation skills as well.

It would be wise to end with some prescriptive implications. Here are three:

a) There needs to be improved interchange between the effective practitioners and the dominant shapers of the field's pedagogy, to introduce creative new ways to teach about the parameters of wicked problems and some tools for moving forward their resolution. Training in negotiation and dispute resolution should focus on the complex dynamics of wicked problems. Creation of a handful of useful classroom simulations/cases/scenarios focused around the parameters of these disputes (c.f. Lande et al., *Principles for Designing Negotiation Instruction*, in this volume), as well as structured processes for "debriefing" and extending these scenarios, would enable more active instruction in this area.

b) Attention should be given to creating "biographical profiles" and "case studies" of skilled professionals who are skilled handlers and solvers of wicked problems. This would help foster new training and development initiatives.

c) Finally, there needs to be improved interchange between negotiation teachers across disciplines as to the "missing pieces", both in conceptual models and/or in pedagogical tools for training negotiators and intermediaries.

In short, we need cleaner theory, but also enhanced ways to train practitioners in the complex dynamics of highly complex disputes. It is time for business faculty who teach negotiation – in collaboration with colleagues from related disciplines – to move beyond an emphasis on the simple buyer-seller market transactions, and move toward models and teaching approaches that engage the more challenging, socially complex, "wicked" problems that face society (*including* business as a key stakeholder). Much of this can be accomplished through "advanced" elective courses in negotiation, but can also be enhanced by developing instructional packages of materials (cases, role-plays, videos, teaching notes) that would further enable this instructional initiative.

Law (James Coben)

> *"Small moves, Ellie. Small moves."*
> *(Carl Sagan, screenplay for* Contact*)*

The Wicked Problem Challenge

When Christopher Honeyman, Giuseppe De Palo and I first conceived the Rethinking Negotiation Teaching (RNT) project, none of us anticipated the series of chapters addressing wicked problems. Yet here we are.

These collected writings challenge me as a law school negotiation teacher to examine the "unconsciously held mental model of conflict as a technical problem" and acknowledge that some problems "cannot and will not be altered only or perhaps even primarily through transactional negotiation" (Docherty and Lira, *Adapting the Adaptive*, in this volume). Furthermore, the writings make it easy to see that my current negotiation teaching focuses on "linear movement through identifiable steps and stages (which of course has never been *entirely* the case)," that "can be analyzed largely in terms of 'technical' change – with the negotiator or intervener applying an external set of tools to solve a problem" (Chrustie et al. 2010: 451). This approach works well enough for "tame" problems that are amenable to solutions that are deemed "technical" (Docherty 2010: 481-482).

Wicked problems, in contrast, "require 'adaptive' responses that require negotiators or intervenors to modify their own views and behaviors, rather than merely applying tools to a problem outside themselves" (Chrustie et al. 2010: 451, citing Kegan and Lahey 2009). Focus only on the presenting problem, argues Jayne Docherty (2010: 484), and you run "the risk of doing great harm and making the problem even worse." Instead, argues Docherty, you "*must* negotiate problems related to the social order, which manifest in their conflict over defining the problem and in their conflict over judgment frames for assessing the legitimacy of their negotiation process, as well as the merits of proposed solutions" (2010: 484).

Wise practice in such a context involves a far broader (indeed, intimidating) set of activities than in the normal negotiation toolkit I provide my law students. It means adding such things as "conflict assessment; convening the parties and their representatives; learning together about each other, the evolving context, and options for resolution; negotiation; and monitoring implementation of the agreement, followed by possible renegotiation" (Docherty 2010: 484, citing Forester 1985).

Challenging indeed. Yet lawyers, perhaps better than some, might "appreciate" (in more ways than one) how dispute settlement often carries with it a host of "whack-a-mole" problems for clients – what Howard Gadlin (*Playing the Percentages*, in this volume) much more eloquently summarizes as follows:

> Settling a dispute is generally a matter of helping the parties involved come to an agreement, or reach an understanding that satisfies their individual concerns. Resolving a conflict, I would argue, almost always involves addressing systemic factors that underlie, elicit, and sustain individual disputes. Settle a dispute without resolving underlying conflicts and a new dispute will pop up in its place. If we are not to be limited to dispute settlement, we need to address individual disputes with an eye toward understanding them in the context within which they emerge and exist.

Structural Limitations

How, if at all, can I include this new information, taking into account the full treasure trove of topics not in the standard canon of negotiation? (For a complete but succinct list of syllabus-expanding possibilities, see Lande et al., *Principles for Designing Negotiation Instruction*, in this volume.)

My answer is guided in part by three observations about law negotiation education: First, the vast majority of my students get only a single shot at a negotiation course: two academic credits out of the eighty-eight required to graduate, a grand total of 1400 classroom minutes. (For insights into what becomes possible when given something like triple that amount of time, see Fox and Press, *Venturing Home*, in this volume.) Second, I am training future lawyers to be agents; lawyers who have a duty of loyalty to their clients and cannot ethically[7] "force them" to view their conflict (which they often frame as a "dispute" with a particular individual party, rather than as a conflict within a much more complex and multi-party universe) through a complexity/wicked problem lens. Third, I believe like John Lande (2012), that I have a primary duty to prepare students for the negotiations that they are most likely to encounter in their day-to-day post-graduate practice.

The Lawyer as Counselor

There is room within these structural limitations to at least consider the proposition that wicked problem "thinking" is relevant to a very broad range of "everyday" problems, and certainly not just intractable conflict. This includes situations lawyers regularly encounter, notwithstanding most clients' tendency to present their conflict as a binary dispute with a single "opponent."

Moreover, I believe there is a case to be made that a lawyer/agent negotiator has an ethical duty to explore with clients the potential systemic (inevitably complex, sometimes wicked) implications of whatever "dispute" a client presents. The American Bar Association's Rule of Professional Conduct 2.1 states that

> [i]n representing a client, a lawyer shall exercise independent professional judgment and render candid advice. In rendering advice, a lawyer may refer not only to law but to other considerations such as moral, economic, social and political factors, that may be relevant to the client's situation.

The published comment to the rule adds, with respect to "Scope of Advice," that

> [a]dvice couched in narrow legal terms may be of little value to a client, especially where practical considerations, such as cost or effects on other people, are predominant. Purely technical legal advice, therefore, can sometimes be inadequate. It is proper for a lawyer to refer to relevant moral and ethical considerations in giving advice. Although a lawyer is not a moral advisor as such, moral and ethical considerations impinge upon most legal questions and may decisively influence how the law will be applied.

I believe that the modern ADR movement within U.S. law schools is partly a battle joined over how aggressively to interpret and operationalize this rule obligation and comment. Some thirty years ago, Carrie Menkel-Meadow fired the first salvo with her seminal work *Toward Another View of Negotiation: The Structure of Problem-Solving*, in which she asserted that:

> Although litigants typically ask for relief in the form of damages, this relief is actually a proxy for more basic needs or objectives. By attempting to uncover those underlying needs, the problem-solving model presents opportunities for discovering greater numbers of and better quality solutions. It offers the possibility of meeting a greater variety of needs both directly and by trading off different needs, rather than forcing a zero-sum battle over a single item (1984: 795).

This was radical stuff at the time, with Menkel-Meadow suggesting that lawyers go well beyond legal issues (their "familiar" turf) to consider a wide range of client interests, including the impact of solutions on client relationships, social needs of the parties, personal feelings, psychological consequences of negotiated success or failure, and ethics concerns (1984: 802). Her recommendations included the then startling idea that "the lawyer ranks the client's preferences in terms of what is important to the client rather than what the lawyer assumes about the 'typical' client" (1984: 804).[8]

In 1995, Paul Brest weighed in with the commonsense notion that "lawyers in everyday practice are called upon to help clients arrange their future affairs in dynamically changing situations where the facts, as well as the law, are anything but determinate" (1995: 7). How dynamic a world were these lawyer problem-solver pioneers envisioning? Certainly not as dynamic as the one the wicked problem writers describe for us today. Yet even in 1995, there was acknowledgment that "most real-world problems do not conform to the neat boundaries that define and divide different disciplines" (Brest 1995: 8).

Move forward seven years to Jackie Nolan Haley's masterful article *Lawyers, Non-Lawyers And Mediation: Rethinking The Professional Monopoly From A Problem-Solving Perspective*, in which she drew the direct parallel between the theory and practice of problem-solving as an approach to lawyering and developments in the ADR and mediation movements more generally (2002: 246). In that classic work, Nolan-Haley summarized "[t]he essential attribute of a problem-solving orientation is a focus on parties' underlying needs and interests rather than on their articulated positions" and documented that a "rapidly growing literature admonishes lawyers to shed adversarial clothing, think outside the litigation box, embrace creativity, create value, and move into the twenty-first century as problem-solvers rather than as gladiators" (2002: 246).

These scholarship efforts helped to transform how law teachers, and particularly ADR professors, conceptualized the work of lawyers – and with a nod to the controlling ethical rule, the role of lawyer "as counselor." But they also helped frame a narrative struggle that continues to this day – as one classic counseling text frames it: traditionalists vs. problem-solvers.[9] Thus, for example, just last year my Hamline colleagues (and RNT contributors) Sharon Press and Bobbi McAdoo felt compelled to make the case for problem-solving being made part of the "core" law school curriculum, out of the concern that "marginalizing" problem-solving activities into "siloed" upper-level elective courses contributes to the perception that ADR is soft, when compared to what "real lawyers" do (McAdoo, Press, and Griffin 2012: 40-41).

In other words, in the law schools, we are still waging the fight to make "legitimate" the problem-solving model of lawyering and negotiation that Menkel-Meadow advocated for thirty years ago. So when thinking about wickedness in the law school context, it pays to remember that the law profession (and legal education) is still one grappling with even the most modest of conflict definition expansions, albeit one that I would argue the ethical rules invite us to engage in.

A Modest Proposal

Keeping this larger battle in mind, I am "going small" with my response, believing that a wicked problem focus grounded in the lawyer's ethical obligation to be an effective "counselor" gives me a way of reaching students with a message that conforms with their own expectations of applicable professional and educational norms (see Lande et al., *Principles for Designing Negotiation Instruction*, in this volume).

Accordingly, the next time I teach a two-credit negotiation law course, I will add the following learning objective to my existing list:

- Students will be able to think critically about the role and limitations of transactional negotiation as a tool for dealing with systemic conflict, including complex and wicked problems.

(For a much more robust set of possible wicked problem learning objectives, including the one mine is based on, see Docherty and Lira, *Adapting to the Adaptive*, in this volume.)

My "Small Moves" Recommendations

To operationalize my wicked problems learning objective, I will do four specific things. The first two are relatively "easy" in terms of time and implementation; the third and fourth are more demanding – for the students and the teacher.

1) Expressly examine the assumptions and limitations of technical transaction negotiation

The week one reading assignment will include a set of excerpts from the wicked problem chapters of the RNT project. As the course progresses and we study the distributive and problem-solving models detailed in the course textbook,[10] I will routinely ask students to articulate the assumptions built into the models we are studying, specifically inviting a wicked problems perspective. One prompt that I believe will be especially effective with law students is regularly to ask a question inspired by Howard Gadlin (*Playing the Percentages*, in this volume): "If we are not to be limited to dispute settlement, how might we address individual disputes with an eye toward understanding them in the context within which they emerge and exist?"

2) Expand the list of planning questions to be used in every negotiation

Like most law teachers, I provide a negotiation planning form for my students. I will continue to do so. However, I will give them an additional assignment: How would they propose to modify the planning form to take account of systemic conflict, complexity, and even wicked problems? After students generate their own responses, I will distribute Howard Gadlin's list of questions[11] from *Playing the Percentages*, in this volume, which offers his own take on how to "tease out" systemic factors underlying conflict.

3) Use at least one "complex" simulation

As Jayne Docherty and Calvin Chrustie (*Teaching Three-Dimensional Negotiation*, in this volume) so eloquently frame it:

> Many activities used in negotiation pedagogy are quite clearly finite games. Participants are given a situation, a role, a set of rules, some pointers regarding what constitutes skillful play, and criteria for evaluating the outcomes of their play. The instructor starts the game and ends the game and evaluates the results of the play. Who did better or worse in the play? Who achieved better or worse outcomes? Some teaching games are even scored numerically. When organized this way, even the most complex cases become artificially simplified in the minds of the game players.
>
> What gets left out of play when we teach negotiation this way? Pretty much everything needed to deal effectively with protracted social conflicts (Azar 1990), because those problems absolutely require "players" who are skilled at social negotiation, transactional negotiation *and* the connections among those different games.

Docherty and Chrustie are far from alone in describing the foibles of simplified simulations (see generally Druckman 2006 and Alexander and LeBaron 2009). "To really 'get' the parties' and lawyers' perspectives," argues Lande (2012: 127), "students need to have more extensive interactions than are possible by simply "parachuting" into a single-stage simulation."

The problem, of course, is the "paucity of rich, reality-like simulations" (Matsuura et al., Beyond "Negotiation 2.0", in this volume). As Roy already advocated above, we need to create more. Fox and Press (*Venturing Home*, in this volume) describe their own ambitious effort – a series of interactions between an American high technology start-up and a Chinese technology manufacturing company (both based on actual publicly listed companies) "where students could research the real organizations and related issues as the course progressed." In Fox and Press's simulation, the students are assigned to their company throughout the course, over time "developing their own corporate culture and making decisions based on an increasingly rich and complex identity and history of decisions." Lande (2012: 128-136) provides a host of insights regarding his own creation and use of multi-stage negotiation simulations in law school classrooms. Sanda Kaufman (Matsuura et al., *Beyond "Negotiation 2.0"*, in this volume) describes two public policy domain simulations – *Francilienne* (De Carlo 2005) and *Silver County* (Elliott et al. 2002) that offer models for immersing students in rich pools of factual information (e.g., media interviews, websites, agency documents, interviews with multiple stakeholders).

Too intimidated to create your own simulation? Then you might consider Daniel Druckman's *Uses of a Marathon Exercise* (2006), detailing how to use case-studies to explore complexity. And for you risk-takers? Jayne Docherty (*Teaching Three-Dimensional Negotiation*, in this volume) offers up a detailed description of her use of "emergent scenarios" (a large-scale class exercise that starts with a "real" event and "an invitation to the participants to build a world within which that dramatic event has meaning"). As Docherty explains, "[t]he world, and therefore the negotiable problem or problems that arise from that world, is co-created by the participants, acting in characters that they animate in ways similar to an actor giving life to a character."

4) Include at least one adventure learning exercise

Chapters 7-14 of volume 2 of the RNT series fully explore the challenges and benefits of adventure learning, what Melissa Manwaring, Bobbi McAdoo and Sandra Cheldelin (2010: 127) summarized as involving "'direct, active, and engaging learning experiences that involve the whole person and have real consequences,' and that bring learners 'out of their comfort zone . . . no matter where the location and how physically risky or active the mode of learning may be'" (citing Prouty, Panicucci, and Collinson 2007: 4). Such learning offers, among many other things, "multiple forms of authenticity," the opportunity for participants "to be highly intentional about how they approach the negotiation aspects of the activity," and "an opportunity for students to collaborate in a meaningful way and build relationships" (Manwaring, McAdoo, and Cheldelin 2010: 139).

To this list, I would add one more major benefit: the potential that "real life" will surface complexity far better than any planned or scripted simulation. Indeed, some negotiation activities conducted by students in the "real world" may even move beyond the boundaries of the emergent scenario approach endorsed by Jayne Docherty above. Just by way of a quick example, in the 2011 and 2012 iterations of Hamline's Practice, Professionalism, and Problem-Solving course, a required first year class (see generally McAdoo, Press, and Griffin 2012), we asked students to form groups of three to four people and go off campus to participate in an external negotiation of their choosing. Most of my own students in the fall of 2011 took on relatively straightforward transactional assignments (e.g., negotiating purchases at a pawn shop; procuring discounts for class members at a local coffeehouse; reserving the best table and happy hour extras at the corner bar, including in one case getting agreement from the DJ to allow them all to dance the Macarena – no doubt inspired by my prior mention of Roy Lewicki's delightful assignment to "go out and collect "no's"). The post-exercise graded journals and classroom discussion were entertaining and occasionally enlightening, touching on a wide variety of emotional and cognitive reactions to the experiences.

But one group in particular stood out. They chose to engage in a neighborhood land use issue – the desire of a small group of community members to build a dog park. What the students initially thought was a "routine" planning matter quickly emerged as a far more complex and long-festering conflict about neighborhood gentrification and class and race dynamics. In the students' words, "they got much more than they bargained for." Of course, the real learning was mine: I had not given them a vocabulary to describe what they were experiencing, not to mention my failure to provide any concrete tools to actually engage constructively in helping to frame and work on the community's challenges. Hopefully, the students participating in the next iteration of my two-credit negotiation course will fare slightly better, having benefited from my four "small moves."

Conclusion

We began this chapter by posing two questions: Should we even try to teach about "wicked problems" in planning school, business school, or law school negotiation courses? Can we hope to do so with any effectiveness? Our answers: Yes and yes. But much work remains to be done.

Over twenty-five years ago, the National Institute for Dispute Resolution underwrote the development of complex negotiation scenarios for use in business and law schools; several of those scenarios are still viable today. Several years following that, the Hewlett Foundation undertook a massive initiative of funding dispute resolution centers on university campuses, and several of those centers (Harvard and Northwestern, in particular) developed the rich portfolio of simulation materials that dominate today's training market.

To make real progress in teaching "wickedness" to students, it would seem to us that it is time for a "third wave" of pedagogical development, staffed by interdisciplinary teams, that would stimulate new classroom experiments in teaching and the concomitant theory development necessary to move us forward.

Notes

[1] It is worth noting, in light of other writing in this volume concerning the "truncated" nature of typical executive teaching, that this is actually less class time than the common 40-hour training course is able to provide. That implies that any assumption by regular faculty of the superiority of their teaching environment warrants a closer look. (For more on a related theme, see the *Epilogue* to this volume.)

[2] While wickedness often is seen in complex situations, complex problems are not all wicked. A complex system is one "with numerous components and interconnections, interactions or interdependence that are difficult to describe, understand, predict, manage, design, and/or change" (Magee and de Weck 2004: 2). Complex systems exhibit several defining characteristics, including feedback, strongly interdependent variables, extreme sensitivity to initial conditions, fractal geometry, self-organized criticality, multiple metastable states, and a non-Gaussian distribution of outputs (Kastens et al. 2009; for detailed information on these characteristics, see the *Introduction to Complex Systems* page at http://serc.carleton.edu/NAGTWorkshops/complex-systems/introduction.html [last accessed March 1, 2013]). Simple interactions between numerous agents give rise to complex situations and emergent behaviors; order intertwined with chaos. Still, not all of these systems contain the other *elements* of a wicked problem.

[3] An example is political impasse over almost any national policy decision in the past several years: politicians have become unable to negotiate over party lines as they impugn each other's motives and ways of thinking.

[4] In a related vein, see Crampton and Tsur, *Negotiation Stands Alone*, in this volume.

[5] A wicked problem "rests on a view of the world that claims there is no neat and clear distinction between so-called objective variables and our so-called understanding of them" (Docherty and Lira, *Adapting to the Adaptive*, in this volume).

[6] For more on this theme, see Avruch 2006.

[7] As summarized by Stefan Krieger and Richard Neumann in *Essential Lawyering Skills*, one of the most popular lawyering skills texts: "Regardless of whether the relationship is traditional or participatory, the law of agency, professional responsibility, malpractice, and constitutional criminal procedure provide that certain decisions are reserved to the client and may not be made by the lawyer. The law of agency matters because the client is a principal

whose agent is the lawyer. If the lawyer makes decisions reserved to the client, the lawyer can be disciplined under the rules of professional responsibility, or held liable in malpractice, or both" (2011: 25). See, however, Korobkin and Guthrie 2006.

[8] Three decades later it is hard to remember that this actually needed to be expressly said.

[9] "Contrast the client-centered conception of problems with a more traditional view. Under the traditional conception, lawyers view client problems primarily in terms of existing doctrinal categories such as contracts, torts, or securities. Information is important principally to the extent the data affects the doctrinal pigeonhole into which the lawyer places the problem. Moreover, in the traditional view, lawyers primarily seek the best 'legal' solutions to problems without fully exploring how those solutions meet clients' nonlegal as well as legal concerns" (Binder, Bergman, and Price 1991: 17).

[10] I use Russell Korobkin's *Negotiation Theory and Strategy*, 2nd edition (2009).

[11] "Here is such a set of questions, grouped around five aspects of a dispute that will have to be understood if the underlying conditions of the dispute are to be addressed. The questions in **boldface** are designed to point to systemic factors.

1) Problem
   - What are the issues to be addressed?
   - What are the conflicts to be resolved?
   - What are the time constraints on the situation?
   - **Is there a policy or procedure contributing to this problem?**
   - **What systemic organizational issues does the problem illustrate?**
   - **What features of the organization are fueling or sustaining this conflict?**
   - **What does it mean that this conflict has arisen? Might this conflict be representative of similar/related issues elsewhere in the organization?**

2) People
   - Who are the key parties to the problem?
   - What are the perspectives of the disputants?
   - **Do the parties or perspectives "represent" the concerns of others who are like them within the organization?**
   - **Who has a stake in keeping things as they are?**

3) Power
   - How is power distributed among the disputants?
   - What power do the individual disputants have?
   - What does each disputant have to gain or lose?
   - Who most needs the conflict resolved?
   - How will addressing/resolving this conflict affect the power structure of the organization?
   - Is there an organizational history to this situation?
   - What are the politics of the situation?

4) Positions/Interests
   - What is each disputant's opening position?
   - What interests and concerns are informing their positions?
   - **What organizational interests are reflected in these interests?**

- **What organizational problems are reflected in these interests?**
- **How is the reward or incentive structure of the organization related to this conflict?**

5) Process
- What intervention possibilities exist?
- Which interventions are best suited to the concerns of the disputants?
- **Does this situation call for systemic intervention?**
- **Which intervention will best lay the groundwork for systemic intervention?**
- **What sorts of systemic intervention would be most appropriate?**

See Gadlin, Matz, and Chrustie, *Playing the Percentages*, in this volume.

References

Alexander, N. and M. LeBaron. 2009. Death of role-play. In *Rethinking negotiation teaching: Innovations for context and culture*, edited by C. Honeyman, J. Coben, and G. De Palo. St. Paul, MN: DRI Press.

Avruch, K. 2006. The poverty of buyer and seller. In *The negotiator's fieldbook: The desk reference for the experienced negotiator*, edited by A. K. Schneider and C. Honeyman. Washington, DC: American Bar Association.

Azar, E. 1990. *The management of protracted social conflict: Theory and cases.* Aldershot, UK: Dartmouth Pub. Co.

Bazerman, M. and M. Watkins. 2004. *Predictable surprises: The disasters you should have seen coming, and how to prevent them.* Cambridge, MA: Harvard Business School Press.

Binder, D. A., P. Bergman, and S. C. Price. 1991. *Lawyers as counselors: A client-centered approach.* St. Paul, MN: West.

Brest, P. 1995. The responsibility of law schools: Educating lawyers as counselors and problem solvers. *Law and Contemporary Problems* 58: 5-17.

Chrustie, C., J. S. Docherty, L. Lira, J. Mahuad, H. Gadlin, and C. Honeyman. 2010. Negotiating wicked problems: Five stories. In *Venturing beyond the classroom: Volume 2 in the rethinking negotiation teaching series*, edited by C. Honeyman, J. Coben, and G. De Palo. St. Paul, MN: DRI Press.

De Carlo, L. 2005. Accepting conflict and experiencing creativity: Teaching "concentration" using *La Francilienne* CD-ROM. *Negotiation Journal* 21(1): 85-103.

Docherty, J. S. 2010. "Adaptive" negotiation: Practice and teaching. In *Venturing beyond the classroom: Volume 2 in the rethinking negotiation teaching series*, edited by C. Honeyman, J. Coben, and G. De Palo. St. Paul, MN: DRI Press.

Dörner, D. 1989. *The logic of failure: Recognizing and avoiding error in complex situations.* New York: Metropolitan Books.

Druckman, D. 2006. Uses of a marathon exercise. In *The negotiator's fieldbook: The desk reference for the experienced negotiator*, edited by A. K. Schneider and C. Honeyman. Washington, DC: American Bar Association.

Elliott, M., S. Kaufman, R. Gardner, and G. Burgess. 2002. Teaching conflict assessment and frame analysis through interactive web-based simulations. *International Journal of Conflict Management* 13(4): 320-340.

Forester, J. 1985. *Critical theory, public policy, and planning practice.* Cambridge, MA: MIT Press.

Hardin, G. 1968. The tragedy of the commons. *Science* 63(3859): 1243–1248.

Kastens, K. A., C. A. Manduca, C. Cervato, R. Frodeman, C. Goodwin, L. S. Liben, D. W. Mogk, T. C. Spangler, N. A. Stillings, and S. Titus. 2009. How geoscientists think and learn. *Eos* 90(31): 265-266.

Kaufman, S., C. Honeyman, and A. K. Schneider. 2007. Why don't they listen to us? The marginalization of negotiation wisdom. In *Négociation et tranformations du monde,* edited by C. Dupont. Paris: Editions Publibook.

Kegan, R. and L. L. Lahey. 2009. *Immunity to change: How to overcome it and unlock potential in yourself and your organization.* Boston: Harvard Business School Press.

Kochan, T. and A. Verma. 1983. Negotiations in organizations: Blending industrial relations and organizational behavior approaches. In *Negotiating in organizations,* edited by M. H. Bazerman and R. J. Lewicki. Beverly Hills, CA: Sage Publications.

Korobkin, R. 2009. *Negotiation theory and strategy,* 2nd edn. New York: Aspen

Korobkin, R. and Guthrie, C. 2006. Miswanting. In *The negotiator's fieldbook: The desk reference for the experienced negotiator,* edited by A. K. Schneider and C. Honeyman. Washington, DC: American Bar Association.

Krieger, S. H. and R. K. Neumann, Jr. 2011. *Essential lawyering skills: Interviewing, counseling, negotiation, and persuasive fact analysis,* 4th edn. New York: Aspen.

Lande, J. 2012. Teaching students to negotiate like a lawyer. *Washington University Journal of Law and Policy* 39(1): 109-144.

Magee, C. L. and O. L. de Weck. 2004. Complex system classification. *Fourteenth Annual International Symposium of the International Council On Systems Engineering (INCOSE).* Available at http://hdl.handle.net/1721.1/6753 (last accessed March 1, 2013).

Manwaring, M., B. McAdoo, and S. Cheldelin. 2010. Orientation and disorientation: Two approaches to designing "authentic" negotiation learning activities. In *Venturing beyond the classroom: Volume 2 in the rethinking negotiation teaching series,* edited by C. Honeyman, J. Coben, and G. De Palo. St. Paul, MN: DRI Press.

McAdoo, B., S. Press, and C. Griffin. 2012. It's time to get it right: Problem-solving in the first-year curriculum. *Washington University Journal of Law & Policy* 39: 39-108.

Menkel-Meadow, C. 1984. Toward another view of negotiation: The structure of problem-solving. *UCLA Law Review* 31: 754-842.

Menkel-Meadow, C. 1999. Taking problem-solving pedagogy seriously: A response to the Attorney General. *Journal of Legal Education.* 49: 14-21.

Nolan-Haley, J. M. 2002. Lawyers, non-lawyers and mediation: Rethinking the professional monopoly from a problem-solving perspective. *Harvard Negotiation Law Review* 7: 235-299.

Pfeffer, J. and R. Sutton. 2000. *The knowing-doing gap*. Boston, MA: Harvard Business School Press.

Prouty, D., J. Panicucci, and R. Collinson. 2007. *Adventure education: Theory and applications*. Champaign, IL: Human Kinetics.

Pruitt, D. 1981. *Negotiation behavior*. New York: Academic Press.

Raiffa, H. 1982. *The art and science of negotiation*. Cambridge, MA: Belknap Press.

Rittel, H. W. J. and M. M. Webber. 1973. Dilemmas in a general theory of planning. *Policy Sciences* 4: 155-169.

Rubin, J. and B. Brown. 1975. *The social psychology of bargaining and negotiation*. New York: Academic Press.

Ury, W. L. 2000. *The third side: Why we fight and how we can stop*. New York: Penguin.

Walton, R. E. and R. B. McKersie. 1965. *A behavioral theory of labor negotiations: An analysis of a social interaction system*. New York: McGrawHill.

Walton, R. E., R. B. McKersie, and J. Cutcher-Gershenfeld. 2000. *Strategic negotiations: A theory of change in labor management relations*. New York: Cornell University Press.

Wisner, J. D., K. C. Tan, and G. K. Leong. 2011. *Principles of supply chain management: A balanced approach*. New York: Cengage.

❧ 22 ❧

Embodied Conflict Resolution: Resurrecting Roleplay-Based Curricula Through Dance

*Nadja Alexander & Michelle LeBaron**

Editors' Note: Moving on from the same authors' seminal 2009 critique of the overuse of role-plays in negotiation teaching, Death of the Role-Play (chapter 13 in Rethinking Negotiation Teaching), Alexander and LeBaron have taken the rapidly increasing enthusiasm for experiential learning in a new direction: multiple intelligences. Their particular interest is in a use of experiential learning that focuses on kinesthetic intelligence, employing actual physical movement, particularly dance, to unlock creativity in other mental domains, as well as to encourage authentic participation by people whose skills are not primarily verbal or mathematical. Those who may be inclined to be skeptical should note that this work is receiving increased attention among people whose dominant skills are definitely verbal: this chapter serves as a brief introduction to a project whose longer work is to be published soon by the American Bar Association.

"I would believe only in a God that knows how to Dance." Friedrich Nietzsche

Introduction
M: *Who would have thought that many conflict resolution trainers have second thoughts about the use of role-plays?*
N: *I guess we are not alone!*

* **Nadja Alexander** is a professor and director of the International Institute for Conflict Engagement and Resolution (IICER) at Hong Kong Shue Yan University. Her email address is nadjaalexander@me.com. **Michelle LeBaron** is a professor of law and director of the Program on Dispute Resolution at the University of British Columbia in Vancouver, Canada. Her email address is lebaron@law.ubc.ca.

M: *No, some trainers have voiced concern about the standardization of the whole role-playing scene!*

N: *No pre-work . . .*

M: *Which means that participants are unprepared . . .*

N: *And may reject the entire experience, or at least not take it on board as something to integrate into their own practice . . .*

M: *How can they really experience conflict without being led safely to a context in which they can access and connect their own experience to that of another?*

N: *It's like throwing people into the deep end . . .*

M: *Yes, and some can't swim!*

N: *You mean they . . .?*

M: *Quite possibly, but the instructor might never know, especially if there is limited debriefing and post-work for role-plays.*

N: *Gosh . . . so if not everyone can swim, what's something they can do?*

M: *They can breathe.*

N: *And if they can breathe, they can move.*

M: *And if they can move, they can . . .*

N: *Dance!*

M: *Precisely!*

After writing a piece entitled *Death of Role-play* (Alexander and LeBaron 2009) we received many responses from conflict resolution trainers, mediators and other readers. As mediators, we had watched with mounting dismay a tendency toward "roteness" in conflict resolution pedagogy, in particular in practice areas involving multiple repeat mediations based on the same technical subject-matter, e.g., landlord-tenancy disputes or bank-customer disputes. We worried that this tendency was reinforced by "canned" role-plays. As conflict resolution trainers, we wondered about the effectiveness of this approach to foster mindful, responsive and emotionally skilled practice. Consequently, we critically examined the widespread use of multiple standardized role-plays in mediation and negotiation training, to awaken fresh interest in why we do what we do as conflict resolution trainers and, through our critique, to provoke responses and conversation. By publishing *Death of Role-play*, we hoped to stimulate increased creativity, reflexivity and methodological diversity in conflict resolution and mediation training.

Death of Role-play appeared to hit a nerve. Readers, like us, did not desire to abolish role-plays altogether. In fact, many continued to rely heavily on standardised role-plays, while acknowledging questions about the ways they and others were using these ready-made resources. As will be explained in more detail in the next section, our concerns with this ubiquitous teaching method included its inflexibility; too-frequent appeal to dramatic excesses of participants; limited adaptability across cultures; and dubious generalizability to actual conflict interventions.

In this chapter, we elaborate on a set of alternatives to standardized role-plays that are more dynamic and embodied, and therefore more likely to yield proficiency in practice. Borrowing from fine arts, neuroscience and intercultural communication among other interdisciplinary fields, we explain why dance and movement are useful and even essential components of conflict resolution education (Honeyman and Parish 2012). From our own and others' experiences in the field we examine why practitioners and parties can benefit from the gifts of mirror neurons, somatic empathy and other recently-elaborated insights, if they only step away from their tables and – yes, we mean it – dance! Shall we?

Who Said What About Role-Plays and Why?

In *Death of Role-play* (Alexander and LeBaron 2009) we critiqued the use of role-play in negotiation training, from a number of perspectives. We questioned its cultural appropriateness as a methodology, illustrating how participants from some ethno-cultural groups are uncomfortable with pretending to impersonate others. Drawing upon relational-identity theory (Shapiro 2006), which highlights the variability of human behavior according to context and roles, we examined the utility and resonance of prescribed, standardized scripts with which participants may have limited experience or connection. Our discussion also probed pre- and post-work, exploring the adequacy of preparation and advance briefing when role-plays are used. Finally, we questioned whether the dramatic adventure of playing a role actually results in durable and reproducible new behaviors in post-course interventions (Lewicki 2000; Movius 2004; Druckman and Ebner 2008; Van Hassalt, Romano, and Vecchi 2008).

In the 2009 chapter, we suggested that continuing the current over-reliance on culturally-encapsulated, standardized scenarios and character roles could prove to be the death of the popular pedagogical vehicle known as the role-play. Christopher Honeyman and James Coben (2010: 2) picked up on this theme when, drawing upon feedback from an international group of negotiation teachers, they wrote that

> . . . negotiation teachers:
> 1) over-rely on "canned" material of little relevance to students; and
> 2) share an unsubstantiated belief that role-plays are the one best way to teach.

Here, we re-engage with this topic, exploring it in the light of embodied pedagogy. Can we find ways to vary training methodologies that are culturally sensitive, foster creativity, and meaningfully develop third-party capacities for our globalizing world? Can essential elements of embodied practice be identified that apply across training methodologies and cultural contexts? How can we take a giant leap forward and move beyond role-play-based training to multi-sensory, experiential, and culturally fluent training activities that may include – but by no means be limited to – role-playing?

Since the publication of *Death of Role-play* in 2009, significant international attention has been directed to innovative ways of enhancing and complementing role-play methodologies with diverse experiential learning approaches. For example, the second (Istanbul, 2009) international conference on Rethinking Negotiation Teaching was shaped around a series of adventure learning activities with a focus on authenticity, real life engagement, creativity, and the role and value of emotional experiences (Honeyman and Coben 2010: 2-3).

In this chapter, we place the spotlight on experiential learning of a different type. We explore possibilities of using dance and movement-based activities to supplement, complement, inspire and potentially transform experiential education, and take it to a new level of teaching and learning potential. This includes both "somatic" and "kinesthetic" dimensions of such activities – in other words, attention to and experience of the body "from the 'inside out,'" as well as of the body in motion, through the complex interplay of sensation, emotion, and cognition (Hervey 2007). From our experiences as educators and interveners in diverse contexts, from law firms, corporations and universities to conflicted communities from first and third world regions, we have observed the vitality and usefulness of embodied methodologies. Not only are they vital because role-play methods have been over-used, creating a need for more balance and diversity in pedagogical methods, but also because the complex issues and identities at stake in today's conflicts call for multiple modalities of intervention. Training must help third parties develop the capacities to work effectively not only in cognitive realms, but also in emotional, physical, imaginative, intuitive and spiritual dimensions.

Our experience has taught us firsthand the importance of a multi-modal approach. Working with women, youth and chiefs from remote villages in the fragile and transitional economies of the Pacific and Africa has opened our eyes to the traditional transformative power of dance in many non-Western cultures. In indigenous settings around the world, people have long used dance, movement, music making, storytelling, mime, theatre and ritual to surface and address conflict.

In such contexts, kinesthetic elements are understood as integral to resolving conflict, making decisions and effecting change.

Shifting our attention to modern industrialized societies, we note the mushrooming trend of health and mindfulness retreats that focus variously on achieving balance and perspective through mental relaxation and nurturing the body. There is also a significant increase in the popularity of ancient pilgrim trails – taking a period of days, weeks or even months apart from fast-paced lives to walk in rhythms that gradually re-connect physical, natural and spiritual aspects of being (Nolan 2010). These and other developments indicate an increasing collective questioning of the widespread focus on rationally-oriented production and linear achievement in modern Western society.

The artificial and still deeply entrenched separation of mind and body; logos and ethos; and brains and brawn is a legacy of the eighteenth century Age of Enlightenment, also referred to as the Age of Reason. In order to preserve the purity and perceived superiority of intellectual reason, cognitive intelligence was separated from the arts, skills and other intelligences associated with physicality, creativity, imagination and emotionality. As a result, the Western intellectual tradition yielded pedagogy in universities and professional training contexts that privilege rational functioning, often to the exclusion of other senses and intelligences. Such approaches can be described as "disembodied" because they block access to, and reject, ways of being and knowing that explicitly engage the body. This intellectual privileging has continued despite recent acknowledgement of the importance of kinesthetic approaches to learning (Grinder and Bandler 1976; Coffield et al. 2004; BenZion 2010a; 2010b).

The Western philosopher Friedrich Nietzsche recognized the inadequacy of this approach when he turned his back on the academic circles and institutions of the nineteenth century. Nietzsche recognized what neuroscientists are now confirming, namely that the Cartesian assumption of mind-body splits is unfounded, and sound thinking and decision-making involve the synergy of multiple intelligences (Damasio 1994; 1999; Barsalou et al. 2003; Niedenthal et al. 2005: 186; Koch 2006). In other words, knowledge in the sense of "know-why" is inextricably linked to "know-how" and is optimally situated in bodily experience and somatic memory. Today, fields as diverse as neuroscience (see, e.g., Niedenthal et al. 2005; Barsalou et al. 2003), political science (see, e.g., Young 1980; Heyes 2007; Butler 1993), education (see, e.g., Coffield et al. 2004; BenZion 2010), dance therapy (see, e.g.,Berroll 2006; Bloom 2006; Hervey 2007), and philosophy (see, e.g., Givler 1924) have begun to explore and attest to the significance of aesthetics, emotional intelligence, and somatics to all areas of human activity.

If conflict resolution education is to be effective, then we must ask ourselves how concepts and skills integral to resolving conflict can be learnt and taught in ways that (re-) connect them with physical dimensions of emotion, intuition and imagination. Given that cognition and emotion are braided processes that cannot be separated from the body as an instrument of knowing, training methods that target or isolate the intellect can no longer be seen as defensible. It is time that conflict resolution caught up with these developments, reflecting them in its pedagogy. In the next section, we examine why dance and movement are particularly potent tools for training repertoires.

Just as unexplored terrain can seem dangerous to the untraveled mind, so body-based work can feel risky and threatening to people whose attention has been focused from the neck up. Yet working in a universe that tries to match competing rationalities of conflict parties without accessing the richness of physical resources is a bit like passing on a feast in favor of a bowl of watery gruel: it is far less enjoyable and truly unnecessary when abundance is available.

Dance, The Moving Imagination

Dance teachers are fond of saying, "if you can walk, you can dance." We would go one step further and suggest that if you can breathe, you can move, and if you can move, so too, you can dance. Dance is, after all, our moving imagination. It is the kinesthetic manifestation of expression, or as modern dance pioneer Martha Graham famously exclaimed, "Dance is the hidden language of the soul."

Of course, Martha Graham and her contemporaries were working at a time when an essential "true" and stable core identity was taken as a given. Modern dance was meant to give this core "authentic expression." In the protean world of the twenty-first century, complex dynamics of identity and meaning-making are understood to animate conflict. As Robert Lifton (1999) has written, solving contemporary conflicts calls for suppleness, creativity and resilience. Those who would intervene in contemporary conflicts are therefore less focused on the imprecise idea of working with stable core personalities and more concerned to help parties find ways through labyrinths of contested meanings and identity-shaped narratives (Foster 1997, 1998; Desmond 2001).

Dance and movement help with these challenges because they assist parties to bypass conscious stories of conflict, while summoning creativity as they:

- articulate and recognize deeply-rooted feelings and needs;
- embrace new ways of knowing through heightened mind-body (somatic) sensations, connections and awareness;

- develop increased awareness of inner geographies where habitual responses to conflict reside, thus increasing repertoires of possible conflict behaviors; and
- experiment physically with new ways of being for the future.

In the conflict resolution field, we are witnessing increasing interest in, and applications of, embodied knowledge. Consider the application of meditation principles focused on breath and self-awareness in the practice of mindfulness mediation (Riskin 2002). Breathing is the most vital activity for the human body. It massages our organs, carries oxygen to all parts of body and feeds the brain. By slowing down and controlling breath, we expand and deepen our capacity to focus on different levels of dialogue, problem-solving and understanding.

During the third Rethinking Negotiation Teaching conference (Beijing, 2011) Vivian Feng Ying Yu demonstrated her use of the ancient Chinese art form of calligraphy to bring slowness and centeredness into her life and her conflict-related work. The process of engaging in calligraphy summons meditation, beauty and creativity in the practitioner, and is said to engender a higher state of creative mind. What if negotiation trainers and practitioners tried calligraphy as a core practice both in preparation for intervention and as a training activity? Forget your haste to memorize the top twenty brainstorming techniques! Instead, find a quiet corner and "lose yourself" in the deep concentration and sense of flow and inner calm that comes with practicing calligraphy, meditation, yoga or tai chi. Practicing calligraphy can become a way of life bringing a calm confidence and creative state to inform everything the calligrapher does, including negotiation.

At the Beijing conference, Andrew Wei-Min Lee and Vivian Feng Ying Yu also introduced the Chinese ritual of the tea ceremony, to facilitate a decelerated pace and corresponding somatic attention to breath, body and being. Tea ceremonies assist those participating in them to connect with one another through the meta-language of embodied silence; they generate an unspoken dialogue that communicates a meta-message of connection, respect and interdependence. As we participated in both calligraphy and the tea ceremony, we noticed increased calm and concentration, and became intrigued about the applicability of these body-based practices to our work.

While these practices involve slowing down, they do not necessarily undermine efficiency. Many negotiation trainers will have heard of the maxim "You have to go slow to go fast." Perhaps these meditative practices are a vehicle for doing just that! Slowness in the tea ceremony or calligraphy does not involve sloth, laziness or other negative attributes associated with its vernacular usage. Rather slowness refers to what musicians call the *tempo giusto,* the pace that is "just right," that maximizes our ability to access the combined wisdom of our bodies and our minds (Honoré 2004). In negotiation contexts, slowness can be nurtured through a wide variety of practices. It may involve doing visualization and breathing exercises, or using Reiki or therapeutic touch to calm nerves before or in challenging negotiation contexts. It may involve preparing and serving tea to those involved in a negotiation. Slowness can foster a calm and centered approach even in the midst of an aggressive environment, adding to people's confidence, and enhancing abilities to think clearly and make smart decisions in pressured situations.

In another example of embodied work, constellation methodology (Hellinger 2007; Sparrer and Onn 2007) challenges participants to create physical and emotional maps of conflict that yield insights and possibilities outside the reach of conscious cognitive processes. By inviting people to "stand in" for parties in conflict, a synthetic pattern is unfolded that may mimic the actual conflict dynamics, yielding insights for parties or third parties. The use of constellations and other related work offers participants creative opportunities to develop a deep somatic understanding of underlying issues and relationships from a systemic perspective. Likewise, conflict resolution workshops which integrate elements of meditation and physical self-awareness encourage participants to access their inner dancers as they examine ways they move in personal relationships and how they respond to conflict (Sparrer and Onn 2007).

In yet another illustration, Augusto Boal's *Theatre of the Oppressed* (1974/2000) – directly influenced by Paulo Freire's *Pedagogy of the Oppressed* (1970/2000) – has been used worldwide to engage disadvantaged communities in processes of reflection, innovation, decision-making and collaborative law-making (legislative theatre). Participatory theatre has been used by inmates, trade unionists and hospital workers; by peasants and workers, students and teachers, artists, social workers, psychotherapists, and non-profit organizations. It has empowered people with marginalized voices and supported the development of innovative solutions to conflict precisely because it uses the embodied and symbolic language of theatre rather than conventional approaches. Theatre of the Oppressed and Diamond's Theatre for Living are powerful vehicles for articulating often-excluded, undervalued, or ineffable realities of those in conflict, and generating creative practical solutions (Diamond 2007).[1]

Whether simple attention to breath or more elaborate body-based methods are used, many negotiators and negotiation educators will find aspects of their work reflected in the above discussion. Few of them, however, would think of using dance as resource. Dance and movement have long enjoyed legitimacy as transformative vehicles in therapeutic circles. The application of dance therapy principles to help people deal with the aftermath of violent conflict is one area where the mind-body connection is nurtured and the ruptured threads in those areas may be healed. Therapeutic use of creative movement has yielded profound effects in accessing and processing traumatic memories and strong emotions, stored in the body – making these precious aspects of conflict conscious, less charged, and more accessible (Rothschild 2000; Koch 2006; Homann 2010; Berroll 2006; Winters 2008).

For some, this discussion may seem to take us far from the everyday understanding of the term "dance" and have little connection with recognized forms of dance such as the fox trot, hip-hop, jazz or classical ballet. Let us take a look at a standard dictionary definition. The New American Dictionary defines dance as:

1) a series of movements that match the speed and rhythm of a piece of music; and

2) a particular sequence of steps and movements constituting a particular form of dancing.

The first definition is much narrower than our understanding of dance. We are not aiming to train participants to move in ways that match pace and rhythm to a particular piece of music. In fact, movements that clash with a given rhythm or defy a prescribed tempo can be just as communicative in revealing undercurrents and group dynamics.

The latter definition is broader, referring to a patterned sequence of movements as dancing. But when do emerging forms get recognized as dance? Hip-hop, for example, was not always a recognized form of dance. It grew from expression and commentary on everyday life, yet today is a recognized dance form with a huge following. In recent years, hip-hop has become an accessible catalyst for conflict transformation in marginalized youth culture from south central Los Angeles to South Africa. Various other forms of contemporary dance continue to push the envelope and challenge the boundaries of what is recognized as dance, and what is not.

Still, many people harbor the illusion that they do not dance, at least not outside specific occasions. By defining dance, these standard explanations have effectively confined dance, creating a sense that dance is a thing that artists do, not something we all do in our everyday lives. A look at colloquial language tells another story (Gadlin, Schneider, and Honeyman 2006). "I'm afraid I stepped on her toes," we say, or "How can we shift the painful dance between us?"

In conflict, references to dance are frequent. Seeking to identify issues, we urge others to "stop dancing around the topic." When offered an outcome, we may "waltz around the offer," playing for time and seeking to look at the proposal from different angles. In the German language, the phrase "to dance at several weddings" (*auf mehreren Hochzeiten tanzen*) provides an equivalent to the English, "to have your cake and eat it too" – words often uttered in situations involving some level of tension or conflict. Similarly, "to dance on someone's nose" (*jemandem auf der Nase rumtanzen*) means to "walk all over someone." Muhammad Ali uses dance as a metaphor for boxing when he says, "The fight is won or lost far away from witnesses – behind the lines, in the gym, and out there on the road, long before I dance under those lights" (Cevallos 2010: 15). Then there is the ubiquitous "negotiation dance" referring to the sequence of strategies and "moves" negotiators make as they work towards agreement. Mark Young and Erik Shlie (2011), for example, explore the metaphors of the dance of positions, the dance of empathy and the dance of concessions. Once we begin to notice dance as a powerful metaphor that is well-integrated in our everyday communications, conflicts and resolutions, we realize its potency as a way of understanding situations and offering mobility in stuck places.

In this chapter, we embrace dance and – more broadly – movement, as forms of embodied expression not limited to a recognized sequence of movements. Dance is and should be available to anyone who wants to explore it, regardless of rhythmic and coordination ability. Dance extends to all forms of movement whether visible to the human eye or not. Dancing on the inside, beneath your skin, or in your mind's eye can be every bit as expressive, exhilarating and exhausting as a vigorous jive. Indeed, it is possible to be very calm on the outside and feel vibrant on the inside, or to move vigorously on the outside from a deep, calm center. Thinking of dance this way, it becomes inclusive, accessible and much less threatening to many people who might not feel confident "dancing" in a public space.

We would go so far as to contend that you cannot *not* dance. What happens if you see a day of your life as a dance? You become aware of your movements: their rhythms, textures and nuances as they express inner states, as they affect others, and as they influence the relational fields around you. Imagine you are on a crowded subway during morning rush hour. How does your body shift, slide, pause and adaptively dance around the physicality of others? How do you breathe and situate your kinesthetic awareness in the space? What attitudes are communicated by your dance? What do the textures of your movements say? Do you experience the crowded subway as oppressive and invasive as you press yourself against a wall and close your eyes, feigning sleep? Or does your presence comfortably fill the space in and around your relational field? The "frame" of dance brings a clear focus on nuances of spatial, place-related influences we navigate every day. Was your day spent at a computer working on a long document? How did your posture shift over time? What were the physical sensations you experienced during that day: heavy/light; tense/relaxed; alert/sleepy; engaged/detached? How did the walk to the refrigerator whisper relief to your muscles, coaxing your circulation to restoration? When your cat brushed against your leg, did you hug back? When your partner called to check on dinner plans, did your state change? These are the kinds of questions that arise from "thinking dance."

If you still feel resistant to the notion of dance as a staple of conflict resolution training, please join with us in jettisoning images of negotiators switching business suits for tutus. Consider times when you have experienced a breakthrough in a problem or received a sudden insight. Often, movement is a catalyst, whether in the form of a walk in the park or mopping the floor. Neurobiologically, we will see that there are good reasons for this. In addition, conceptualizing relations between people in conflict as a dance takes away from binary zero/sum, simplistic notions that pervade much colloquial conflict language. Dancing, as anyone who has tried ballroom dance with a partner can attest, is complex and requires attunement to the others' intentions and the environment, and sympathetic responses to surprises. Let us explore more of the fruitfulness of these ideas as we examine the links between dance and kinesthetic communication.

Dance and Kinesthetic Communication

The immense volume of literature around the notion of kinesthetic or body language and nonverbal communication points to the power of kinesthetic communication. A new book, *Making Movement Matter: Conflict, Dance and Neuroscience*, connects dance and kinaesthetic communication to conflict transformation and negotiation (LeBaron, MacLeod, and Acland 2012). Too much literature, however, has focused on translating the language of the body into words, rather than encouraging the exploration of communication at a kinesthetic level through breath, body awareness and movement in relation to others (Riskin 2002; Freshman 2010; Riskin 2010).

Expressive arts therapy, in particular dance therapy, has been at the forefront of experimentation with "dance language" grounded in physical experience. In intercultural or post-conflict settings from Iraq to Haiti to Bolivia, from Sub-Saharan Africa to Israel to Peru, expressive arts modalities have been applied for decades to address conflict-related trauma. This work has consistently revealed the capacity of expressive, embodied practices to shape and re-shape identities, understandings, and relations. By engaging the creative and imaginative capacity of individuals in addressing situations of conflict or trauma, these methods have been potent in generating change in both mental and material domains (Levine and Levine 2011).

One of the concrete reasons that embodied communication proves effective in conflict and post-conflict settings is that it can quickly and deeply foster inter-group trust, receptivity, and flexibility when encountering the unfamiliar. This is captured succinctly in the comments of one student from a tango dance class.

> Learning to be a good Argentine Tango follower is about surrender. So in Saturday's "Followers' Workshop" we practiced exercises in trust (yes, gently tipping to the side or backwards or frontwards with our eyes closed, trusting that someone would break the fall), feeling our partner's weight change and again, with eyes closed, being in tune with and following our partners' movement around the floor. I had to slow down, let go of everything else on my mind, and be totally present in the moment. . . . Leave a desire for control at the door. And take the lesson home.[2]

As you read this comment, consider the parallels to negotiation skills. How often do we encourage students to trust the process and surrender to it without worrying about the outcome? And what about the skills of mindfulness and being in the present? Sound familiar?

In another example, Diane Levin's *Dog's Tale* (2011) highlights the power of kinesthetic and emotional wisdom in a mediation setting and reminds us of the limitations of our rationality. The story, from one of her mediation sessions, is set out below.

> A husband and wife came to me, seeking help with their divorce. In addition to the real and personal property they had acquired during many years of marriage, they had also run a business together for many years, so untangling their lives was complicated, with many difficult decisions to face.
>
> Just hours before their meeting with me, the wife called to ask if they could bring their dog with them. "He's very sweet and well-behaved," she said, "and I think we'd both feel better if he were there with us." An animal lover myself, I had no objections and encouraged her to bring the dog along. The husband and wife soon arrived, followed by an enormous

dog, one of the biggest I'd ever seen. After they introduced themselves and their dog to me, their dog drank deeply from the water bowl I'd provided for him and curled up in the corner of my conference room with his head on his paws. He didn't close his eyes but remained watchful, looking from one of his humans to the next.

The mediation began. The one issue not in contention was what they wished to do in planning for their dog following the divorce. They were working in consultation with their vet and an animal behavior expert to come up with a visitation schedule and residence plan that would meet their dog's best interests. With that issue set aside, we began identifying and working our way through the other issues to be addressed. Not surprisingly, the discussion became emotional. First, the wife raised her voice, pressing her case against the husband's proposal. The dog suddenly stood up from his corner, strode to the wife's side, sat down beside her and leaned against her, resting his head in her lap. She stroked the dog's head, and her voice assumed its normal tone. After a few minutes, the dog returned to his corner. Soon it was the husband's turn to become agitated, and as the volume of his voice began to rise, the dog once more stood up, came to his side, leaned against him, and rested his head in the husband's lap.

And so it went. Sensitive issues were raised, one spouse or the other became upset, and time and again, there the dog would be, leaning against the person who needed his comfort most in that moment, the great furry head resting upon a knee. The moment would pass, clarity would come, the anger would evaporate, the discussion would progress, and back the dog would go to his corner.

We took up a particularly difficult issue next. As the conversation continued, both husband and wife became increasingly agitated. I could see that the mediation was approaching that make-it-or-break-it moment. This was where it all falls apart, or it all comes together.

For a brief second or two I gathered my thoughts, thinking how best to frame what needed to be said to shift the discussion into "make it" territory away from "break it." As I was about to speak, I felt something warm and heavy lean against me. I looked down, and there was the dog, his head resting in my lap this time, looking up at me with his dark brown eyes. Evidently this time I was the one who needed support, at least in the judgment of this wise dog.

The husband and wife both stopped in mid-sentence, their voices falling silent. In amazement, they gaped at the dog with his head in my lap. Then, tension broken, they each smiled, shaking their heads. In an instant, the moment had changed. They were laughing now. "How about if we . . .," said one. "Great idea," said the other, "how about if we also . . ."

A few minutes later, they were standing up and hugging each other, the most difficult issues addressed to their mutual satisfaction. Their dog bounded about the room, his tail wagging.

Kinesthetic communication and body language are considered to be an expression of bodily-kinesthetic intelligence, which Howard Gardner (1993) has identified as one of the different types of intelligences that humans possess. In the next section we consider these multiple intelligences and their links with dance.

Dance and Multiple Intelligences

In the 1980s, Howard Gardner wrote about the concept of multiple intelligences, among them the linguistic, logical, musical, bodily-kinesthetic, spatial-visual, interpersonal, intrapersonal, naturalist, spiritual, and existential (Gardner 1993). Such work effectively demonstrated that conventional conflict approaches – so often linear, verbal, deliberative, and disembodied – are insufficient to address the diversity of human modes of understanding. When we come to see the self as a multi-faceted perceptual, expressive and relational center, engaging multiple intelligences becomes integral to engaging complex and diverse individuals in conflict settings.[3]

Neuroscience has recently explored how many forms of intelligence – cognition, emotion and attitudes – are embodied. For example, Antonio Damasio (1994), among others, examines the physicality of emotion and shows us that what we come to experience as "emotions" are in fact interpretations of physical sensations. Examples of physiological expressions of feelings recognizable to many of us include goose bumps, blushing, sweaty palms, shortness of breath, butterflies in the stomach and other manifestations of energy in the body. Physical sensation not only informs our perception, but also structures or limits it: the autonomic nervous system which controls our ability to access thoughts, discover new ideas, and change our behavior is shaped by physical contact and rhythm from an early age, and influenced by physical cues in later life (Ledoux 1998; Porges 2004, 2009; Homann 2010: 3). Because all perception is filtered through the body, with its corporeal memory of experiences including trauma, the body shapes and limits our understandings of and responses to the world. Much of this is precognitive; therefore it becomes crucial to directly engage the body to bring perceptions, judgments, and emotions to a conscious level of choice (Merleau-Ponty 1964: 5; Merleau-Ponty 1968: 253; Diprose 2002: 174). Seasoned conflict practitioners know the role that intuition or gut feeling can play in reading situations; increasing body awareness can work to enhance perception of the subtle cues and signals – both internal and external – in which such intuition is grounded.

Just as the body shapes perception, so too can embodied approaches re-shape it. Physical practices have been shown to have significant effects on cognition, learning, mood and motivation. Physical exercise not only promotes development in these areas, but does so relatively quickly (Neeper et al. 1996; Widenfalk, Olsen, and Thoren 1999; Cotman and Engesser-Cesar 2002; Meeusen et al. 2006; Berg 2010). As well, embodied practices that emphasize proprioception (awareness of the body in space) and encourage internal attunement have been shown to have beneficial effects on the neurophysiological regulation systems that foster openness to change and receptivity towards others (Schore 2003). Thus, an accent on physical dimensions and engaging these dimensions through movement can lead directly to conceptual, emotional and behavioral shifts.

In fact, the body has been shown to play a role in mental processes where we least expect it. Research has shown that mental processes once thought disembodied are, in fact, physical phenomena. Almost 100 years ago, researcher and philosopher Robert Chenault Givler (1924), drawing on the neuro- and physical sciences of the time, found that the expression of physical and bodily experiences influence understandings of, and meaning ascribed to ethical notions such as what constitutes right and wrong. This line of inquiry continues today. For example, in her review of research linking body awareness and movement to decision-making, Lenore Hervey (2007) highlights Warren Lamb's system of movement pattern analysis and its application to corporate settings. Essentially, the research confirms that all processes of decision-making have observable kinesthetic elements, both shaping and being shaped by relational factors. In other words, our bodies play an integral part in conflict, communication and choice-making.

Understanding the influence of the body in shaping perception, responses, and relations is a complex task. While there is evidence for certain pan-human expressions and gestures (Ekman and Friesen 1986), it has also been shown that our bodies interpret and code the world around us in culturally specific ways. Anthropologist Judith Hanna (1990) explains that cultural differences are usually reflected in movement and that paying careful attention to the body can therefore reveal pivotal cues to cultural differences, uncovering nuances, textures and relational habits relevant to conflict. At the same time, she warns that phenomenological experiences and expressions also differ from person to person. This is because relationships between body and self are rooted not only in biology but also deeply in social and cultural forms including rituals, rites of passage and festivals. Both collective and individual identities are expressed via movement; it is a language that reveals whole worlds to an attuned observer. It is also a language which, Hanna suggests, may be a more accurate, less filtered and adulterated communication vehicle than spoken language.

Dance also heightens kinesthesia, or awareness of both one's own and others' bodies; in fact, learning about the subtle cues, demands and tendencies of one's own body has been linked to understanding empathy, or how *other* moving bodies might feel (Foster 1982: 13; Noland 2009: 13). Dance therefore provides an essential avenue to more accurately perceiving not only personal states but others' personal and cultural positions.

Recent work in neuroscience has explored empathy as an embodied phenomenon. When people observe or plan actions, motor neurons become activated in the same way as they do when the action is actually being performed (Jeannerod 1994, 1997). As well, neuroscientists have found that the area of the brain associated with pain and affective experiences is activated when witnessing the pain or fear of others (de Gelder et al. 2004; Jackson, Meltzoff, and Decety 2005.) When people watch each other move, their brains are essentially practicing ways of relating to others. The human capacity to imitate, learn, and feel with others is, at base, a kinesthetic experience (Dosamantes-Alperson 1984; Dosamantes-Beaudry 1997; Berroll 2006; Hervey 2007: 98-9; Winters 2008; Berlucchi and Aglioti 2010).

In addition, dance and movement have been shown to stimulate new neural pathways and shift cognitive habits. Understanding the neuromuscular transformations that accompany movement can reveal the inner grammar of cultural and social patterning. In addition, movement releases emotions and latent memories, uncovering new connections between people, and fostering alternative interpretations of personal, cultural and political transactions (Bloom 2006; Noland 2009; Homann 2010). Out of this kinesthetic intelligence, new vantage points and solutions can surface, as parties develop awareness and choices about what was previously unconscious (Homann 2010.) The acknowledgment and incorporation of kinesthetic dimensions into conflict intervention could maximize resources available for transformation of intractable conflict. For example, imagine that a group is struggling with a complex series of issues related to an environmental problem. Watching or participating in a dance or movement experience on ecology, diversity, harmony and balance may deepen conversations and introduce vitality, nuance, and texture to the well-worn tracks of disagreement.

Malvern Lumsden describes the richness of body-based resources this way:

> Our sense of what is real begins with and depends crucially upon our bodies, especially our sensorimotor apparatus, which enables us to perceive, move, and manipulate, and the detailed structures of our brains, which have been shaped by both evolution and experience (Lumsden 2010: 4, citing Lakoff and Johnson 1999: 17).

Neuroscientists have demonstrated something that dancers and others have long known: that all decision-making involves rational *and* emotional processes centered in the body, so we cannot observe, think or respond clearly without our bodies and our feelings. Emoto-cognitive processes cannot be neatly excised from each other, but occur in concert. The body is an essential channel into understanding and engaging these processes. Thus we can engage our kinesthetic and emotional intelligences to help us move through differences with less resistance than if we rely on rational thinking alone to find our way out of negative feelings or into positive thoughts. As negotiation practitioners and teachers incorporate insights from neuroscience and dance theory and practice, we will be better able to assist people with complex problems.

Building Dance and Movement-Related Intelligence

In dealing with challenging conflict situations, we need diverse inner resources and intelligences. Chief among these is somatic, or movement-based intelligence. This way of knowing assists us in drawing on physical cues and resources to:

- Sense and shift group, interpersonal and intrapersonal dynamics;
- Discern physical movements in others that signal internal changes;
- Discern changes in vocal rhythms that may relate to shifts in attitudes, relationships or perspectives;
- Notice via physical cues when processes are safe or unsafe for others; and

- Learn ways of working with strong emotions using breath and movement to promote flexibility rather than rigidity.

Here are some suggestions for cultivating somatic intelligence, along with tips on increasing it:

- Notice your physical responses to stress and conflict, and learn ways to center and calm yourself through using breath, visualization or movement;
- Adopt a physical practice in your life: an activity, or an art form like dance. Keep a journal about what you learn about your body and its ways of signaling as you engage in this practice.

In negotiation contexts you can:

- Incorporate centering techniques when tensions are high – the simple act of breathing deeply or shaking limbs can do wonders in shifting mental and emotional states;
- Pay careful attention to nonverbal cues, devising an internal interpretive map as the process proceeds;
- Respond effectively to spatial, temporal and kinetic dimensions of negotiation; if dialogue reaches an impasse, suggest changing postures or positions in the room; if empathy proves difficult, incorporate subtle forms of physical or conceptual mirroring; if a direct approach is not shifting dynamics, use a creative or embodied method to help parties "step out" of entrenched antagonistic roles;
- Use physical language to give implicit permission to parties to attend to physical needs and cues. For example: "My back needs to stretch. How about taking a few minutes to get our circulation going?"

In preparing for negotiation workshops in multi-party contexts, invite people to consider how they hold themselves, their postures toward others, and their attunement to personal physical signals as a way of increasing somatic awareness and choice. Movement-based practices can assist people to learn ways to tap the body's wisdom so that it is available even in the midst of stressful negotiations.

These strategies for negotiation will be more accessible if they have been practiced in advance. Hervey (2007) describes an activity where she asks training participants to move in relation to values that she calls out to the group. To debrief, participants discuss the process of moving and how they chose ways to move in relation to the values. Hervey observes that values like justice or fidelity evoke diverse responses from participants. As they examine movement choices, participants develop more awareness of the nuances, complexities and diversity of relationships to these values. These insights can support increased effectiveness in negotiation: as people recognize complexity in relation to values, they are more able to discern and respond to complexity in negotiations.

In another example of applied somatic practice, University of British Columbia business law professor Janis Sarra recently convened an interdisciplinary movement-based workshop on fairness.[4] With the assistance of two professional dancers, academicians used movement to examine corporeal aspects of fairness. Participants reported that movement assisted them in examining and deepening their understandings of fairness, deepening their capacities to work with the subtleties of fairness in their theorizing and practice. The possible applications of movement-based strategies to negotiation training are infinite. But it is also useful to ask how these approaches might link to existing methods, including role-plays.

How Do Dance, Movement and Role-plays Relate to One Another?

Now, hang on a minute, some of you may be thinking. We have just discussed at length the notion of dance as embodied expression. Isn't that exactly what role-plays do? Embody learning by inviting movement and experiential applications to a given scenario? So aren't we already "dancing"?

Well, yes and no. Yes, role-plays and a whole range of other activities do engage kinesthetic learning styles more than traditional classroom teaching such as lectures. And it is true that negotiation education has traveled a long way from the hierarchical days of predominantly theory-based, one-way oral communication between professoriate and participants. However, as explained previously, acting out a prescribed role within a limited time frame does not necessarily maximize learning. Deep insights arise more consistently and powerfully from authentic somatic experiences than from synthetic role-plays that operate at arm's length from participants' real lives. In the next section, we consider how the ideas in this chapter can enhance role-plays and other experiential methods in negotiation training.

Preparation

As negotiation teachers, we emphasize the importance of the setting of a process. We explain the importance of establishing a collaborative atmosphere, where parties can feel safe to voice their concerns without retribution and to engage creatively in problem-solving without being pre-judged by others. Safety is a paramount concern in using body-based approaches, particularly because these tend to be outside participants' experiences and comfort zones.

Lumsden (2010) explains the importance of creating a safe space where the rules of the regular learning setting are suspended and students can behave and move freely, differently and authentically. He stresses that the requirement of safety encompasses both physical and emotional elements, as the space should offer participants a link "between the internal and external worlds, facilitating the exploration of new ways of being and emotional expression, and experimenting with new dimensions of existence."

How can this be achieved? Creating an environment which evokes playfulness, creativity, warmth and isolation from the "outside world" is a good start. In the much acclaimed 2010 British historical film drama *The King's Speech*, King George VI works with an Australian speech therapist, Lionel Logue, to overcome his debilitating speech stammer. In one scene, Logue transforms the cold, impersonal but very stately room from which the King will make his speech into a cozy, inviting and very safe space draped with throws, curtains, rugs and cushions from the rooms in which he and King George VI had trained and rehearsed. The warm and familiar environment has an immediate relaxing effect on the King, both mentally and physiologically, and he goes on to make one of his most powerful speeches.

Similarly, it may be useful to make colorful props or art supplies available to participants of negotiation workshops, encouraging a variety of modes of expression. Inviting participants to bring objects of special significance to place in a circle or ritual space in a training room can also invoke a sense of safety and "home."

While we may not have access to cozy rooms or custom-built dance studios, there is much we can do to enhance the somatic possibilities of training spaces. For example, participants can be encouraged to bring soft balls, non-fragile objects, scarves and other props. If you do not have access to a private space, see what can be done to "block out" the outside world, e.g., using old sheets, sofa covers and blankets as curtains. Bring in inflatable furniture – it is light and easy to transport. Consider how to integrate the restroom, kitchen, breakout or hallway spaces into the training space. How can you use creativity to design a comfortable, informal learning space?

In addition to preparing the physical space, think about how you frame the training in announcements and materials sent to participants. Mark Young and Erik Schlie (2011: 202) advocate the use of the dance as a metaphor for negotiation training on the basis that it "challenges such dichotomous constructs as fight versus flight, harmony versus war, and adversaries versus partners." They posit that "creatively accessing a [dance] metaphor [...] can help us understand more of the varied facets of negotiation and approach the field in a

more differentiated way." Using dance as a metaphor to frame negotiation language from the very start is a powerful way to invoke safety
and spaciousness.

Applications

So how might dance intelligence manifest itself in a negotiation
workshop? Here are some ideas you might like to try in your next
workshop or training session. Feel free to vary aspects to suit your
training needs. Be creative!

- Working with peripheral vision: Before students move into
  a role-play, ask them to form a circle and fix their eyes on a
  point on the opposite side of the room. Without moving their
  eyes from their chosen point, ask participants what they can
  see beyond it. For example, can they notice the color and texture of the walls, ceiling or floor? Can they (without moving
  the focus of their eyes) see any surrounding furniture or objects? How many people in the circle can they take into view,
  and what can they notice about them – clothing, hair, color?
  Invite participants to move across the room keeping their eyes
  on a point, navigating around people and objects as they go.
  In this second activity, movement is added to the use of peripheral vision, thereby heightening focus and self-awareness
  while expanding visual horizons. The debriefing that follows
  can address peripheral vision as a physiological skill for negotiators as well as a metaphor for how people experience
  conflict in very narrow ways. Negotiation thus becomes an
  exercise in supporting self and other to expand frames of reference. This exercise may also be a metaphor for the ability to
  identify resources that may not be obvious to those directly
  involved in the conflict.

- Embody excellence in negotiation: Invite participants to find
  a space of their own and to draw an imaginary circle of excellence in front of them into which they will step during the
  activity. Ask them to think of someone they consider to be an
  excellent negotiator and to imagine this person in the room
  with them. Now ask participants to notice as many details
  as they can about the negotiator. For example, how does the
  person hold themselves, move and sit; how do they express
  themselves through facial and bodily gesture; how do their
  eyes move and speak; how do they sound and feel? As participants calibrate these details, they step into their imaginary
  circle of excellence, close their eyes, and emulate and embody
  these characteristics. This can be a very powerful and trans-

forming experience for many, especially those who identify well with their chosen person. This activity is best done immediately prior to a role-play and at a stage in the training when participants have a realistic idea of what excellence in negotiation looks like.

- What's your ginch? "Ginch" is Canadian dancer Margie Gillis' expression for the embodied equivalent of what conflict interveners might call tension, impasse, deadlock or just plain being stuck (Gillis 2013a). We all can identify ginches in our body, so this activity draws upon people's somatic knowledge, inviting analogies between how we address tensions in our bodies and how we address interpersonal tensions. Now for the activity: invite participants to move around the room freely, loosely and comfortably, "dancing" out any discomfort or tension. After some minutes, ask them to identify their biggest, ugliest, most persistent ginch, whether it be a sore neck, nagging knee problem, locked jaw, tight back or other symptom. As they continue to move around the room, suggest to participants that they create space around their ginch and allow it to move and release itself. In other words rather than letting a robust masseur hammer the problem, focus on it and let it breathe, give it the space and time to sort itself out. Gillis sometimes suggests consciously connecting the part of the body in distress with a place in the body where ease is experienced. This can be done by participants individually, or in pairs; either may ease the tension or tightness in a particular area. The applications of this approach to negotiation are obvious; as participants are better able to bring health and well-being to their weak or tense areas, they can surround their emotional and intellectual challenges with a new level of ease and awareness (Gillis 2013b).

- Moving to which music? Select a piece of music with some texture and complexity, perhaps from the "world music" genre. Ask participants to move around the room responding to different aspects of the music, for example the "sad" or "melancholy" themes, the "happy" or "lively" themes, the high or low notes, the percussion, the melody and so on. How does the experience of the music change for participants? Are they "dancing" to the same music each time? How might this translate to their understanding of how different people experience the same conflict?

- Flowing and frozen embodied scenes: Body sculpting activities and other somatic methods of learning can be used in numerous ways to explore negotiation dynamics. Drawing on Hervey's work (2007), participants can work individually or in groups to create a flowing tableau to concepts such as hope, fairness, justice, impasse, resolution, fear, trust and so on. Or they can be invited to create a physical sculpture conveying their experience of a role-play, whether they were a player or an observer. In another variation, they can be asked to create two physical snapshots to communicate the emotional texture of a group before and after a role-play experience. Finally, they can be invited to move in relation to each other in ways that convey their learning about values and ideas like fairness, closure, etc.

- Framing and reframing in the language of dance: As suggested previously, trainers can utilize the metaphor of dance in framing and debriefing activities, and in reframing comments and questions as they arise throughout a training. Using dance language throughout a course – as opposed to just in relation to one specific "dance" activity – helps to normalize the relationship between dance and negotiation and increase participants' comfort and creativity in experimenting and engaging in embodied activities.

- Our experience indicates that integrating these types of activities into training, and interspersing them among role-plays, heightens the level of authentic engagement of participants and improves the overall quality of role-plays and debriefing discussions. Participants who have experienced trainings in which body-based methods were integrated report increased abilities to play roles authentically, and a deeper capacity to share their personal experiences of successful negotiation with others.

Shall We Dance? Reflections and Closing Thoughts

Well, go figure . . . It turns out that dance is not as frightening as I had thought. I started using it as a warm-up in a bi-weekly class on negotiation and conflict resolution and it turned out to be the thing students looked forward to most!

Dance and movement, when used as part of training and framed as patterned physical activities, can help participants shift perspectives and increase physical health at the same time. Though academic cultures are notoriously physically phobic, it makes sense for people with physical bodies to use them! And doing so not only brings people into awareness of where they may be holding tension, it allows them to find ways to release it.

Who knew I could dance? One of the surprising outcomes of using dance and movement in teaching and training contexts is that people who expressed resistance or no affinity were often surprised at the positive impact of both dance and other movement. In one class, participants found ways to talk about mobility which positively affected their relations as a cohort, following movement exercises that included a wheelchair-bound member of their group. Resistance turned to positive anticipation as they moved beyond stereotypes of dance awkwardness and discovered its capacity to transport them into new, more nuanced conversations.

As a mediator and trainer, I am about to start developing my dance intelligence. After all, it's just a step to the left . . .

As conflict interveners and those assisting with negotiations, we ask a lot of disputing clients. We ask them to reveal themselves to us, trust us and expose their vulnerability – while we hide comfortably behind a shield of professionalism. Similarly, as trainers we may find ourselves slipping into the routine of asking participants to role-play while we safely ensconce ourselves behind the veil of "facilitator." Dance intelligence is about using our essential somatic awareness. It helps us access other ways of knowing and being within ourselves, and to recognize them in others. It builds bridges between our inner and outer worlds. As conflict interveners and negotiation trainers, dance intelligence helps us to connect with others and build empathy and trust. It enhances our ability to weave fluently in and among cultures and to reach that deep level of human awareness that the Africans call "Ubuntu."[5] Surely that is what effective negotiation is all about.

Notes

The authors appreciate the research and conceptual assistance of Emily Beausoleil, PhD, candidate at the University of British Columbia, Canada, the research contribution of Honor Lanham, researcher at the Institute for Conflict Engagement and Resolution in Hong Kong, and the editoral assistance of April Chan, law student at Hong Kong Shue Yan University.
[1] See http://www.theatreoftheoppressed.org/en/index.php?nodeID=3 (last accessed April 4, 2012).
[2] See http://myartfullife.wordpress.com/category/dance/ (last accessed April 4, 2012).
[3] For an exploration of multiple intelligences in negotiation, see Alexander and Howieson (2010).
[4] See http://www.explorefairness.pwias.ubc.ca/ (last accessed April 4, 2012).
[5] "Ubuntu" is an African philosophical term which offers an explanation of the essence of what it means to be human and the individual's interconnectedness with others. According to Ubuntu we affirm our humanity when we acknowledge that of others as our humanity is bound up in theirs. See Tutu (1999).

References

Alexander, N. and M. LeBaron. 2009. Death of role-play. In *Rethinking negotiation teaching: Innovations for context and culture*, edited by C. Honeyman, J. Coben, and G. De Palo. St. Paul, MN: DRI Press. Reprinted in *Hamline Journal of Public Law & Policy* 31(2): 459-482 (2010).

Alexander, N. and J. Howieson. 2010. *Negotiation: Strategy style skill*, 2nd edn. Sydney: Lexis Nexis.

Barsalou, L. W., P. M. Niedenthal, A. K. Barbey, and J. A. Ruppert. 2003. Social embodiment. In *The psychology of learning and motivation,* edited by B. Ross. San Diego: Elsevier Inc.

BenZion, G. 2010a. Prevailing the dyslexia barrier: The role of kinesthetic stimuli in the teaching of spelling. In *Neurocognition of dance* , edited by B. Blasing, M. Putke, and T Schack. London: Psychology Press.

BenZion, G. 2010b. Does a change in mathematics instructional strategies lead struggling third grade students to increase their performance on standardized tests? Master's thesis, University of Maryland at College Park.

Berg, K. 2010. Justifying physical education based on neuroscience evidence. *The Journal of Physical Education, Recreation and Dance* 81(3): 24-29.

Berlucchi, G. and S. M. Aglioti. 2010. The body in the brain revisited. *ExperimentalBrain Research* 200: 25–35.

Berroll, C. F. 2006. Neuroscience meets dance/movement therapy: Mirror neurons, the therapeutic process and empathy. *The Arts in Psychotherapy* 33(4): 302-15.

Bloom, K. 2006. *The embodied self: Movement and psychoanalysis.* London: Karnac.

Boal, A. 2000. *Theatre of the oppressed.* Translated by A. Charles and M. O. Leal McBride. London: Pluto.

Butler, J. 1993. *Bodies that matter: On the discursive limits of sex.* London: Routledge.

Cevallos, J. 2010. *Positional hitting: The modern approach to analyzing and training your baseball swing.* Minneapolis, MN: Mill City Press.

Coffield, F., D. Moseley, E. Hall, and K. Ecclestone. 2004. *Learning styles and pedagogy in post-16 learning. A systematic and critical review.* London: Learning and Skills Research Centre.

Cotman, C. and C. Engesser-Cesar. 2002. Exercise enhances and protects brain function. *Exercise and Sport Science Review* 30: 75-79.

Damasio, A. 1994. *Descartes' error: Emotion, reason, and the human brain.* New York: Putnam.

Danasuim A. 1999. *The feeling of what happens: Body and emotion in the making of consciousness.* New York: Harcourt Brace & Company.

de Gelder, B., J. Snyder, D. Greve, G. Gerard, and N. Hadjikhani. 2004. Fear fosters flight: A mechanism for fear contagion when perceiving emotion expressed by a whole body. *Proceedings of the National Academy of Sciences* 101(47): 16701–06.

Desmond, J. C. 2001. Introduction: Making the invisible visible: Staging sexualities through dance. In *Dancing desires: Choreographing sexualities on and off the stage*, edited by J. C. Desmond. Madison, WI: University of Wisconsin Press.

Diamond, D. 2007. *Theatre for living: The art and science of community-based dialogue*. Bloomington, IN: Trafford Publishing.

Diprose, R. 2002. *Corporeal generosity: On giving with Nietzsche, Merleau-Ponty and Levinas*. Albany, NY: State University of New York.

Dosamantes-Alperson, E. 1984. Experiential movement psychotherapy. In *Theoretical approaches in dance/movement therapy*, edited by P. L. Bernstein. Dubuque, IA: Kendall/Hunt.

Dosamantes-Beaudry, I. 1997. Somatic experience in psychoanalysis. *Psychoanalytic Psychology* 14(4): 517–30.

Druckman, D. and N. Ebner. 2008. Onstage or behind the scenes? Relative learning benefits of simulation role-play and design. *Simulation and Gaming* 39(4): 465-497.

Ekman, P. and W. V. Friesen. 1986. A new pan-cultural facial expression of emotion. *Motivation and Emotion* 10(2): 159-168.

Foster, S. L. 1982. *Reading dancing: Gestures towards a semiotics of dance*. PhD Dissertation, University of California, Santa Cruz.

Foster, S. L. 1997. Dancing bodies. In *Meaning in motion: New cultural studies of dance*, edited by J. C. Desmond. Durham, NC: Duke University Press.

Foster, S. L. 1998. Choreographies of gender. *Signs* 24(1): 1-33.

Freshman, C. 2010. Yes, and: Core concerns, internal mindfulness, and external mindfulness for emotional balance, lie detection, and successful negotiation. *Nevada Law Journal* 10(2): 365-392.

Friere, P. 2000. *Pedagogy of the oppressed*. Translated by M. Bergman Ramos. New York: Continuum.

Gadlin, H., A. K. Schneider and C. Honeyman. 2006. The road to hell is paved with metaphors. In *The negotiator's fieldbook: The desk reference for the experienced* negotiator, edited by A. K. Schneider and C. Honeyman. Washington, DC: American Bar Association.

Gardner, H. 1993. *Frames of mind: The theory of multiple intelligences*. New York: Basic Books.

Gillis, M. 2013a (forthcoming). Dance as conflict transformation. In *Making movement matter: Conflict, dance and neuroscience*, edited by M. LeBaron, C. MacLeod, and A. Acland. Chicago: American Bar Association.

Gillis, M. 2013b (forthcoming). Appendix: Experiential exercises mapping dance onto conflict transformation. In *Making movement matter: Conflict, dance and neuroscience*, edited by M. LeBaron, C. MacLeod, and A. Acland. Chicago: American Bar Association.

Givler, R. C. 1924. *Ethics of hercules: A study of man's body as the sole determinant of ethical values*. New York: Alfred A Knopf.

Grinder, J. and R. Bandler. 1976. *The structure of magic II*. Palo Alto, CA: Science and Behaviour Books.

Hanna, J. L. 1990. Anthropological perspectives for dance/movement therapy. *American Journal of Dance Therapy* 12(2): 115-126.

Hellinger, B. 2007. *Das klassische familienstellen.* Die fünf Standardwerke: Die Quelle braucht nicht nach dem Weg zu fragen: Ein Nachlesebuch, Heidelberg, Germany: Carl-Auer Verlag.

Hervey, L. W. 2007. Embodied ethical decision-making. *Amercian Journal of Dance Therapy* 29(2): 91-108.

Heyes, C. J. 2007. *Self-transformations: Foucault, ethics and normalized bodies.* Oxford: Oxford University Press.

Homann, K. B. 2010. Embodied concepts of neurobiology in dance/movement therapy practice. *American Journal of Dance Therapy* 32(2): 80-99.

Honeyman, C. and J. Coben. 2010. Introduction: Half-way to a second generation. In *Venturing beyond the classroom: Volume 2 in the Rethinking negotiation teaching series,* edited by C. Honeyman, J. Coben, and G. De Palo. St. Paul, MN: DRI Press.

Honeyman, C., J. Coben, and G. de Palo (eds). 2010. *Venturing beyond the Classroom: Volume 2* in the *Rethinking Negotiation Teaching Series.* St. Paul, MN: DRI Press.

Honeyman, C. and R. Parish. 2013 (forthcoming). Make a move. In *Making movement matter: Conflict, dance and neuroscience,* edited by M. LeBaron, C. MacLeod, and A. Acland. Chicago: American Bar Association.

Honoré, C. 2004. *In praise of slowness.* New York: Harper Collins.

Jackson, P. L., A. N. Meltzoff, and J. Decety. 2005. How do we perceive the pain of others? A window into the neural processes involved in empathy. *NeuroImage* 24: 771–79.

Jeannerod, M. 1994. The representing brain: Neural correlates of motor intention and imagery. *Behavioral and Brain Sciences* 17(2): 187-245.

Jeannerod, M. 1997. *The cognitive neuroscience of action.* Hoboken, NJ: Wiley-Blackwell.

Koch, S. C. 2006. Interdisciplinary embodiment approaches: Implications for creative arts therapies. In *Advances in dance/movement therapy: Theoretical perspectives and empirical findings,* edited by S. C. Koch and I. Brèauninger. Berlin, Germany: Logos Verlag.

Lakoff, G. and M. Johnson. 1999. *Philosophy in the flesh. The embodied mind and its challenge to Western thought.* New York: Basic Books.

LeBaron, M., C. MacLeod, and A. Acland (eds). 2013 (forthcoming). *Making movement matter: Conflict, dance and neuroscience.* Chicago: American Bar Association.

LeDoux, J. 1998. *The emotional brain: The mysterious underpinnings of emotional life.* New York: Simon & Schuster.

Levin, D. 2011. A dog's tale: A mediation story for the holiday season. *Kluwer Mediation Blog.* Available at www.kluwermediationblog.com (last accessed April 4, 2012).

Levine, E. and S. Levine. 2011. Art in action: Expressive arts therapy and social change. London: Jessica Kingsley

Lewicki, R. J. 2000. Teaching negotiation and dispute resolution in colleges of business: The state of the practice and challenges for the future. In *Teaching negotiation: Ideas and innovations,* edited by M. Wheeler. Cambridge, MA: PON Books.

Lifton, R. J. 1999. *The protean self: Human resilience in an age of fragmentation.* Chicago and London: Chicago University Press.

Lumsden, M. 2010. The moving self in life, art, and community mental health: 12 propositions. *Body, Movement and Dance in Psychotherapy* 5(3): 231-243.

Meeusen, R., P. Watson, H. Hasegawa, B. Roelands, and M. F. Piacentini. 2006. Central fatigue: The serotonin hypothesis and beyond. *Sports Medicine* 36(10): 881-909.

Merkeay-Ponty, M. 1968. *The visible and the invisible.* Translated by A. Lingis. Evanston: Northwestern University Press.

Merleau-Ponty, M. 1964. *Signs.* Translated by R. C. McCleary. Evanston, IL: Northwestern University Press.

Movius, H. 2008. The effectiveness of negotiation training. *Negotiation Journal* 24(4): 509-531.

Neeper, S., J. Gomez-Pinilla, J. Choi, and C. Cotman. 1996. Physical activity increases mRNA for brain derived neurotrophic factor and nerve growth factor in rat brain. *Brain Research* 726(1-2): 49-56.

Niedenthal, P. M., L. W. Barsalou, P. Winkielman, S. Krauth-Gruber, and F. Ric. 2005. Embodiment in attitudes, social perception, and emotion. *Personality and Social Psychology Review* 9(3): 184–211.

Nolan, D. 2010. Spain: A food lover's pilgrimage. *Qantas: The Australian way* available at http://travelinsider.qantas.com.au/spain_a_food_lovers_pilgrimage.htm (last accessed July 12, 2012).

Noland, C. 2009. *Agency and embodiment: Performing gestures/producing culture.* Cambridge, MA and London: Harvard University Press.

Porges, S. W. 2004. Neuroception: A subconscious system for detecting threat and safety. *Zero to Three* 24(5): 9–24.

Porges, S. W. 2009. Reciprocal influences between body and brain in the perception and expression of affect: A polyvagal perspective. In *The healing power of emotion: Affective neuroscience, development, and clinical practice,* edited by D. Fosha, D. Siegel, and M. Solomon. New York: W. W. Norton.

Riskin, L. 2002. Contemplative lawyer: On the potential contributions of mindfulness meditation to law students, lawyers, and their clients. *Harvard Negotiation Law Review* 7: 1-66.

Riskin, L. 2010. Annual Saltman lecture: Further beyond reason: Emotions, the core concerns, and mindfulness in negotiation. *Nevada Law Journal* 10(2): 289-337.

Rothschild, B. 2000. *The body remembers: The psychophysiology of trauma and trauma treatment.* New York: Norton.

Schore, A. N. 2003. *Affect regulation and the repair of the self.* New York: W. W. Norton.

Shapiro, D. L. 2006. Identity: More than meets the 'I'. In *The negotiator's fieldbook: The desk reference for the experienced negotiator,* edited by A. K. Schneider and C. Honeyman. Washington, DC: American Bar Association.

Sparrer, I. and S. Onn. 2007. *Miracle, solution and system: Solution-focused systemic structural constellations for therapy and organisational change.* Cheltenham, UK: Solutions Books.

Tutu, D. 1999. *No future without forgiveness.* New York: Doubleday.

Van Hasselt, V. B., S. J. Romano, and G. M. Vecchi. 2008. Role-playing: Applications in hostage and crisis negotiation skills training. *Behavior Modification* 32(2): 248-263.

Widenfalk, J., L. Olsen, and P. Thoren. 1999. Deprived of habitual running rats downregulate BDNF and TrkB messages in the brain. *Neuroscience Research* 34(3): 125-32.

Winters, A. F. 2008. Emotion, embodiment, and mirror neurons in dance/movement therapy: A connection across disciplines. *American Journal of Dance Therapy* 30(2): 84–105.

Young, I. M. 1980. Throwing like a girl: A phenomenology of feminine body comportment motility and spatiality. *Human Studies* 3(1): 137-56.

Young, M. and E. Schlie. 2011. The rhythm of the deal: Negotiation as a dance. *Negotiation Journal* 27(2): 191-203.

⋘ 23 ⋙

The Influence of Emotion in Negotiations:
A Game Theory Framework

*Habib Chamoun & Randy Hazlett**

Editors' Note: *Perhaps the "other side of the coin" of the preceding chapter, this chapter's authors review what has been learned about long-term relationships from the insights of game theory. They note that game theory's presumption of "rational," interest-maximizing negotiators is a significant limitation, in a world in which is increasingly accepted that we all think from the starting point of our emotions (see Patera and Gamm, Emotions – A Blind Spot in Negotiation Training, chapter 19 in Venturing Beyond the Classroom). Evolutionary game theory, they argue, provides a basis to learn from repeated interactions, which could be adapted by introducing emotional bias into the game theory framework. This would allow game theory to be used in analysis of altruism, empathy, reputation and other phenomena which are becoming more and more important in teaching negotiation. Their analysis also challenges us all to absorb more via a kind of intelligence most negotiators rather desperately avoid exercising: the mathematical.*

Introduction

Meeting the needs of a business partner fosters mutual empathy and creates significant leverage for the present and future deals. It signifies a desire to place relationship over short-term gain. The more significant the need met, the deeper the emotional impact. Game theory provides a powerful platform for analyzing preferred strategies; however, the restriction of game theory to "rational" players leaves

* **Habib Chamoun** is an honorary professor at Catholic University of Santiago Guayaquil-Ecuador and founder of Keynegotiations, LLC. His email address is HChamoun@Keynegotiations.com. **Randy Hazlett** is president of Potential Research Solutions and Christian Artist's Workshop in Dallas, Texas. His email address is RDHazlett@sbcglobal.net.

no direct means to interject emotional influence. Evolutionary game theory gives players opportunity to learn from repeated interactions. While the actions in evolutionary game theory are typically directed by changes in some measure of profit, and thus selfishly motivated, repeated interaction has some semblance to a long-term business relationship. We take advantage of this feature to propose a means for introducing emotional bias into a game theory framework.

Repeated interaction of evolutionary game theory allows parties to assess collaborative tendencies. When the other party consistently acts in a mutually beneficial manner, trust, and therefore mutual empathy, is increased and risk decreased. However, predictability does not connote trust. Zero-sum behavior promotes distrust, magnifying perceived risk in continued interaction. In dealing with human psychology, trust is earned slowly, whereas acts of betrayal promote immediate retraction. Any model of human bias based upon empathy should incorporate such a response function.

In evolutionary game theory, the next move is typically constructed as a function of the prior position and a differential in a value function. We draw an analogy with differential control theory in engineering unit operations. However, we advocate integral control in modeling evolving long-term relationships. Integral control is less reactionary and more stable with respect to fluctuations in behavior, since future choice is a function of the current state and history. Thus, early choices will be sensitive to non-cooperative behavior, but later choices will be guided by cumulative experiences, accommodating the occasional glitch.

We assert that behavior aside from price that promotes mutual empathy acts as a catalyst to accelerate the relationship bonding process. The degree of trust produced in a long-term relationship can be achieved more quickly if there is auxiliary supporting behavior. Thus, we can use evolutionary game theory that incorporates bias in the choice updating scheme as a means to also include elements usually associated with emotions and irrational behavior. With the described modifications to game theory, elements such as gifting outside the deal (Chamoun and Hazlett 2007; 2009) can both accelerate the approach to a Nash equilibrium, if it exists, and shift the equilibrium position.

Game Theory Externals

Rational Behavior

Game theory arose out of a need to reduce subjectivity in decision-making, particularly in social interactions. It borrowed heavily from laws of interacting elements found in the traditional sciences, such as the kinetic theory of gases, with the aim of understanding social relationships. The need to quantify responses couched the practice in economical terms, reducing decisions to those that support or erode individual or social objectives. Roger Myerson (1991: 1) defines game theory as the study of mathematical models of conflict and cooperation between intelligent rational decision-makers, with rationality demonstrated in decision-making driven by the desire to maximize utility. Thus, rational behavior is confirmed by selfish decision-making. It is akin to a Hippocratic oath to do no harm to self. Evaluated directly, altruistic behavior is irrational. This leaves a dilemma, for human behavior is rampant with decision-making for the better good of society or elevating the needs of others over self.

Still, Paul Weirich (2007) reminds us, "There are no dilemmas of rationality." Tom Siegfried (2006: 21) stated, "Game theory does not actually assume that people always behave selfishly or rationally. Game theory tells you what will happen if people do behave selfishly and rationally." Thus, game theory is not the study of human behavior, but merely gives us a mathematical framework that can be useful in comparing alternatives, to make decision-making less subjective.

Emotions and Irrational Behavior

Roy Lewicki and colleagues (2010: 138) state that "perception, cognition and emotion are the basic building blocks of all social encounters, including negotiation, in the sense that our social actions are guided by how we perceive, analyze, and feel about the other party, the situation, and our own interest and positions." Thus, all human interactive behavior is filtered through emotions regardless of whether those emotions remain unexpressed or undemonstrated. The association of emotions with irrational behavior is, therefore, an unfortunate consequence of game theory. Cheyney Ryan (2006: 77), meanwhile, has elaborated on the distinction of philosopher John Rawls between behaving rationally and reasonably. Rational behavior is that consistent with personal goals; reasonable behavior also takes into consideration the impact of personal goals on others. As such, rationality is a capacity, whereas reasonableness is a virtue. One avenue to incorporating emotions is to exploit the definition of irrational behavior as accepting changes in utility that seem unfavorable. This can be accomplished by borrowing the role of temperature from the world of physics. Molecules take seemingly random movements, termed Brownian motion, even under a potential gradient if thermal energy of the molecules is sufficient to overcome local barriers. This principle is captured in simulated annealing, now a standard method in optimization.

Applied initially to local structure problems in the traditional sciences (Kirkpatrick, Gelatt, Jr., and Vecchi 1983), it has found application in social problems, such as neighborhood segregation (Schelling 1971). In simulated annealing, when the environment is "hot," even increases to an objective function are accepted. With time, the environment is allowed to "cool," and choices become increasingly more objective. Like the slow cooling of a glass-like material, the deliberate approach towards equilibrium facilitates a resulting crystalline structure free of stress defects. Analogously, simulated annealing allows jumping out of local minima in favor of a global optimum.

Recognizing rationality as behavior that aligns with choices to increase (maximize) utility, we can introduce temperature in virtually any utility construct in the role of emotions. When we are hot or excited, our choices can run counter to those of an objective decision-maker. When we cool off and are calm, our decisions conform to expectations. To introduce emotions into game theory, we must simply allow for an assessment of emotional state, and recognize a broader spectrum of responses. For application of emotions in repeated games, we must allow the emotional state to be constantly reassessed. Should emotions always run high, there is some probability of choices that are effectively randomized, or at least counter to reason. The challenge to the counterpart is to diffuse strong emotions, restore the benefits of rational thinking, and reduce the risk of counterintuitive choices harmful to one's own utility. Modeling emotions in this fashion is proper when choices are unlinked or less strongly connected to measures of utility. In other words, some emotions "blind us" from using utility as a driver, and as a result, outcomes are more random, or even opposite, than expected. When emotions, such as trust or anger, reinforce or justify specific choices, they should be incorporated directly into the measure of utility.

Emotions and Utility

Emotion can be a powerful motivator or an overwhelming distraction. Eliciting emotion in the other party can likewise compel or repel. For example, Daniel Druckman and Mara Olekalns (2008: 1-11) discuss the role of anger, normally considered a negative response: "Display of anger can be beneficial if used to signal how strongly one feels about an issue, about the fairness of proposed distribution or procedures, or about possible consequences of continuing intransigence." Van Kleef and colleagues (2007) found a positive and significant association between anger and dominating behavior in that an angry negotiator tended to adopt a more competitive stance. Once anger is expressed, it must sometimes be resolved before negotiating issues can resume, if at all (Lewicki, Saunders, and Barry 2010: 299). Prediction of response to identical stimuli is also compounded by social preference. Pro-social people become more cooperative in loss than gain, whereas pro-self people become more cooperative with gain (Carnevale and Keenan 1990; De Dreu and McCusker 1997). Fairness, a driver for all sorts of decisions during negotiations, is also largely a matter of perception, and perceived fairness in procedures as important as fairness in outcomes (Welsh 2006). Unexpressed emotion is perhaps more problematic (Shapiro 2006).

On the other hand, game theory assumes that players can formulate an expression of what they want, and are able to evaluate the consequences of decisions on the basis of impact to their wants, commonly called a utility function. It can be any quantifiable want. In extending game theory to real social contexts, the challenge comes in how to quantify feelings or intermix the rational and irrational into an objective function. Of course, once a new utility function is fully parameterized, all behavior purporting to support increase in utility suddenly satisfies the definition of rational decision-making. This yields us one avenue to incorporate specific emotions or actions linked to certain emotion-driven responses. The sections that follow identify reciprocity, altruism, distributive justice, and mutual empathy as behavior motivators that could possibly be incorporated into an expression of utility.

Reciprocity

Why do a deed perceived to benefit others at a direct cost to our utility? Action in hopes of reciprocation is motivation for a broad spectrum of social behaviors. In discussion of the rule of reciprocity, Robert Cialdini (1993: 17) declared, "we are obligated to the future repayment of favors, gifts, invitations, and the like." Granting unsolicited favors can result in either direct or indirect reciprocity. Direct reciprocity is captured by a tit for tat rule – I scratch your back, you scratch mine. In indirect reciprocity, I scratch your back, someone else will, in turn, scratch mine. Indirect reciprocity in essence relies on actions becoming to some degree public, to complete the circle. According to Deborah Larson (1998: 121), reciprocity, matching of concessions, is difficult to assess without common measures of value. When no such standards exist, norms and customary expectations, such as equity, equality, and need, establish fairness. Equality connotes common reward, whereas equity divides the spoils on the basis of merit. Need, meanwhile, circumvents the concept of parity. Need elevates value. The meeting of needs is a higher form of compensation than the disposition of objects. Reciprocity, of course, need not be in tangible goods.

Reciprocity certainly includes emotions (Keltner and Haidt 1999), either positive or negative. Warm-heartedness expressed by employers produced open-minded employees (Yifeng, Tjosvold, and Peiguan 2008). According to Barry (2007), "Emotionality is not an alternative to cognition at the negotiation table, but rather a complementary force." Good feelings can be pervasive in business and social relationships, yet emotions can also escalate at the expense of reason as the basis for decision-making.

Altruism and mutual empathy

Altruism is defined as helping someone else out at a cost to you with no return benefit. In reality, many altruistic behaviors do result in benefit, but it may come in the form of indirect reciprocity, reputation-building, or simply generation of good feelings for the giver. The giving process fosters mutual empathy, defined as "the experience of being known and accepted deeply by another, being aware of another being aware of you . . . among the most psychologically important human experiences" (O'Hara 1997: 314). Mutual empathy, sometimes referred to as relational empathy, is a strong driver in altruistic behavior. Among the strongest relationship bonds, intergenerational giving and kinship (Wade-Benzoni 2006) are prime motivators for self-sacrifice. However, we also generate relationships through repeated interaction. Relationship changes the dynamics of any interaction or negotiation (Lewicki, Saunders, and Barry 2010). Of course, this can either be positive or negative. In the case of negative relationships, behavior would cease to be altruistic in favor or some form of punishment, even if it costs us.

Distributive justice

Reasoning of the individual leading to decision-making is critical to the understanding of social systems, yet in the absence of sufficient feedback, we only have behavior or behavioral changes as indicators of motivation. According to Daniel Druckman and Cecelia Albin (2009), perceived justice in outcomes increases durability of agreements. The need for equality is commonly expressed in splitting the difference, when a profit window is presented though parity in profit sharing, may not carry identical value to both parties based on effort or need. Agreement on a standard of fairness has a positive impact on negotiations and outcome satisfaction (Lewicki, Saunders, and Barry 2010: 317). Injustice and inequality are thus drivers for change.

Reputation

Networks form group associations that can influence behavior. Social networking brings new clientele based upon independent experience.

According to Martin Nowak and Karl Sigmund (2005: 1291-1298), "Cooperation through indirect reciprocity . . . requires the evolution of reputations and communication of those reputations among the larger group." We are led to believe that name brands are better than generics due to the reputation that follows the product or a spokesperson behind the product. We are also influenced by perceived long-term commitment to a product and pattern much buying behavior on the basis of warranties and brand longevity. Reputation impacts perceived risk.

Repeated Games

Repeated games provide incentives that differ fundamentally from traditional game theory. As such, the study of repeated games launched another branch of study, evolutionary game theory. George Mailath and Larry Samuelson (2006: 9) state, "The common force organizing market transactions is the prospect of future interactions." People simply behave differently with the prospect of future interaction, and indeed, some behaviors are intended to promote such opportunities. In repeated games, however, players may become either more cooperative or more belligerent.

In evolutionary game theory, no single repeated action is guaranteed to maximize utility. In fact, a mixed strategy often maximizes benefit – multiple strategies with defined probabilities of occurrence. The ability to assess the consequences of your actions in formulating a next move strategy depends upon how much you know about the other party's decisions and motivation as well as your own. Also, equilibria in repeated games rely on open-endedness. That is, if players knew in advance the number of rounds, behavior to maximize utility would be affected by the approach toward the end of the relationship (Myerson 1991: 310). Similarly, initial behavior in the absence of trust may be predictably selfish to protect against the unknown, yet there is an incentive to be generous to promote generosity on behalf of others. In essence, early generous behavior can be a catalyst to promote behavior normally reserved for interactions only after a significant history of benevolence (Chamoun and Hazlett 2009).

Risk in Decision-Making

Much psychotherapy deals only with behavior and not the underlying emotions supporting behavior. The goal is to correct behavior. Similarly, physicians treat symptoms rather than causes. Incorporating emotions into behavioral games can also only deal with actions that may result from an undercurrent of emotions. We treat emotions as motivators for an observable action. We do not need to know why if behavior becomes predictable in some fashion. Much decision-making is based upon the degree of fear, ignorance, paranoia, or confidence. We can lump all such factors into the category of making decisions with associated risk. There are tools available to help decision-makers remove subjectivity in assessing risk.

Discounting

Economists use discounting routinely to account for the time value of money. Games also can incorporate discounting, sometimes referred to as patience, in repeated interactions or multiple-round negotiations. In dealing with parties who are not infinitely patient or unequally patient, there is additional risk beyond your assessment of utility that the interaction will terminate in nonagreement. The concept of robustness (Chamoun 2003), the ability to close a deal in few meetings, is closely related due, in part, to cost of continuing negotiations, especially in international markets when considering the cost of travel. Opportunities literally shrink without a deal closing. Roger Myerson (1991: 398) suggests,

> [a] good bargainer should try to create the perception that there is a relatively high probability that bargaining may terminate in disagreement whenever one of his offers is rejected, whereas there is a relatively low probability that bargaining may terminate in disagreement when he rejects someone else's offer.

In other words, make offers firmly, and reject offers politely. Sometimes a suboptimal result is better than no result.

Quantifying Risk

Seldom do business decisions rest on a clear-cut reserve price. Other factors enter the evaluation, some of which are known, while others are intangibles. Even when an outcome can be reduced to a formula, uncertainties exist in the parameter set. Often tools are used to quantify the range of outcomes based upon Monte Carlo computations covering the range of all input parameters. These are all methods to quantify risk in business decision-making. While the expected value may hold particular interest, business decision-makers also rely on estimates of upside and downside potential as percentiles on a cumulative probability curve. Whether these presets are ± one standard deviation, or arbitrarily set at, say ten percent and ninety percent is unimportant. What is significant is that no one value can be treated as representative without additional information, and decision-makers must account for this risk. We assert that pricing games include flexibility in setting reserves. If risk can be further clarified in the course of a negotiation or in a repeated game, better estimates can be produced, allowing players to adjust "risked pricing" on the fly. A portion of such risk involves uncertainties regarding the other party and the perceived tendency toward integrative rather than distributive decision-making.

Similarly, any utility function can be approached as a risked computation. With the ability to allow extraneous probabilities in an expression of utility (Fishburn 1970), direct incorporation of feelings is greatly simplified. Still, "emotions" like trust (technically not a single emotion, but a compound) may perhaps be the easiest to capture, since they are borne out in a pattern of behavior. Trust is gained slowly but easily lost. Many of the classic game theory games, such as The Prisoner's Dilemma, Dove-Hawk, and the Ultimatum game, have trust, or lack of it, at the core of decision-making. Nash showed that in single-play, n-person games, an equilibrium can frequently be achieved where no single player could expect to do any better by unilaterally switching strategies. Evolutionary game theory tells us that patterns of unilateral behavior can maximize utility; however, utility can best be maximized through cooperative behavior and trust in the other party to act in an integrative fashion. Trust is an expression of risk assessment, and is a key to formulating emotional responses into a game theory framework.

Games Incorporating Emotions

Taking Emotional Temperature

The role of temperature masks obvious choices based solely on utility. In simulated annealing, a decision is accepted or rejected based upon the strength of the change in utility measure in contrast with ambient noise. Games, however, usually involve a choice between alternatives with differing consequences, some of which depend on choices of another player. A Nash equilibrium exists if neither player can improve their utility by changing their position with the choice of the other player held constant (Binmore 2007). With binary games, such as Prisoner's Dilemma, this can be easily accommodated by computing a choice based upon relative differences in utility with a decision to accept or reject this choice as a measure of emotional blindness. In a binary choice game, a parameter, θ, can be constructed.

$$\theta = e^{-|U_1 - U_2|/\kappa T(t)} \tag{1}$$

where U_i is the expected utility of strategy i, T is the temperature, possibly a function of time, and κ is an adjustable constant. We can interpret θ as the probability that an energetically unfavorable strategy is adopted. Use of temperature in an Arrhenius expression is not new, but the specific interpretation of θ in binary decision-making is. The product, κT, carries units of energy. If we carry forward this analogy, utility must have the same units. When the utility differential between choices, ΔU, is negligible in contrast to thermal noise, κT, choices are indiscriminant with regard to utility. The basis of choice is controlled by any one of possible emotions, urges, or allegiances. When 4κT =ΔU, we essentially return to rational decision-making, rejecting over ninety-nine percent of decisions resulting in utility degradation. For games with a pure rational strategy, we can compute the emotional energy, κT, using the observed quantity, θ.

$$\kappa T(t) = -\frac{|\Delta U|}{\ln(\theta)} \qquad (2)$$

In games where an equilibrium strategy involves a fixed probability of selection of strategy 1, we can relate the predicted equilibrium probability distribution with the observed one to take the emotional temperature. In repeated games, the emotional temperature can evolve. Historical values can be tracked and projected to aid in future decision-making by a rational counterpart interacting with an emotional player. A prior exercise to assess emotional temperature may be equally fortelling for interactions of subsequent interest.

As in the analogy with chemistry, and in particular with the kinetic theory of gases, such expressions deal with populations. All molecules have dynamically changing energy levels as molecules interact and exchange collision energy. The temperature is not well represented by the energy level of any single molecule at a single point in time. A good assessment of temperature involves taking an average over a large number of samples representing the population, or a large observation time window with a single sample.

Examples

James Andreoni and John Miller (1993: 570-585) reported repeated Prisoner's Dilemma statistics in games designed to test the influence of altruism with the possibility of unknown augmented utility functions that ascribe pleasure from mutual cooperation. Subjects were told that the opportunity to earn a considerable sum existed, as the game was carried out with cash reward. The units of utility were $0.01. Games were played in four modes, but herein, we examine only the first two. Mode one involved computer matching of partners between fourteen subjects for ten rounds of Prisoner's Dilemma with payout functions as shown in Figure 1.

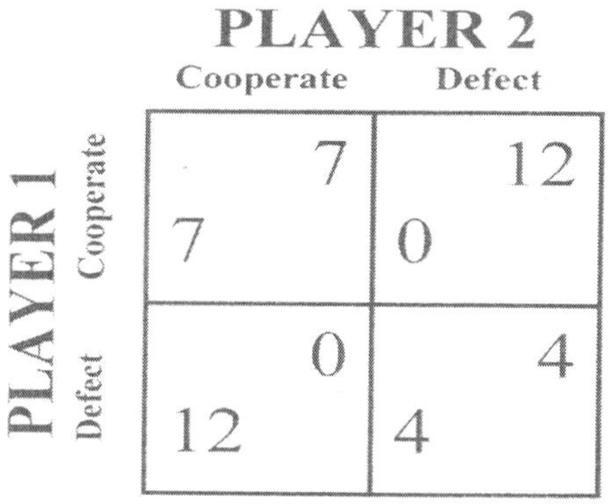

PLAYER 2

		Cooperate	Defect
PLAYER 1	**Cooperate**	7 7	12 0
	Defect	0 12	4 4

Fig. 1 The symmetric Prisoner's Dilemma payoffs as given by Andreoni and Miller(1993)

At the end of each set of ten rounds, partners were rematched for a total of twenty ten-period games. In the second mode, players were randomly paired at each iteration for a total of 200 matchings. To be consistent with the prior game, players were given personal performance summaries every ten rounds of play. The results are reproduced in Figure 2.

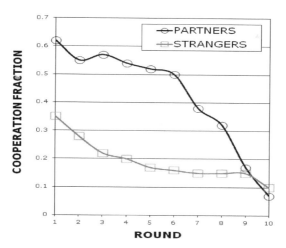

Fig. 2.   Results from repeated play of Prisoners Dilemma with partners for ten rounds each and randomly assigned pairings per iteration. Adapted from Figure 2 of Andreoni and Miller (1993).

Figure 3 shows the average payoffs per round for each mode of play. It should be noted that population averages for both those choosing to cooperate and defect decline as the Nash equilibrium for all to defect is approached.

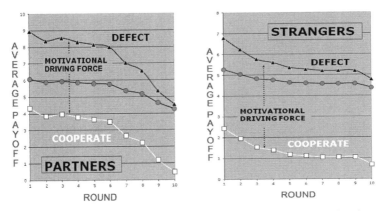

Fig. 3.   Tracking the overall average payout (gray circles) and those who choose to cooperate (white squares) and defect (black triangles) in each round of play: (a) Partners are matched and play ten rounds together; and (b) Players are matched at each iteration, i.e., strangers.

Why would the population succeeding as a whole migrate to lower payoffs for all? First, those who defect are aware of the upside potential of staying with their choice, especially immersed within a population eager to cooperate. Indeed, defectors were rewarded on average much higher than those choosing to cooperate. The risk of joint co-operation for defectors is a loss of five in utility. It is not those who are rewarded for cooperation who are unhappy. Rather, those choosing to cooperate, anticipating a gain in utility of seven but receiving zero reward, can harbor feeling of betrayal and possibly a need for retaliation, a very strong emotion driving change. According to Morton Deutsch (1975: 140), "... there is usually a positive circular relation between the well-being of the individuals in a group (or society) and the well-functioning of that group." Those individuals unhappy with their outcome, though they may be in the minority, drive the group towards stability at the expense of overall population reward. The only way to purge future betrayal is to adopt defection. Still, some may be reluctant to assume the role of traitor trying to capitalize on others, based upon moral principles. There is also a lack of equity in population averages, making fairness also a motivator to defect. However, these players could only sense population statistics as the games progressed. Finally, we see a marked difference in the play of partners, where history plays a role in future dealings, and strangers paired for a one-off game. Most notable is the starting fraction of those choosing to cooperate. Knowing a relationship of ten rounds would proceed, partners were also twice as likely to start play with intention to cooperate. This is the win-win scenario, but it is unstable. The onset of defection eliminates cooperate-cooperate as a sustainable result, as the probability of this outcome pairing decays rapidly.

Still, there is something else happening in the partners mode not evident with strangers. The rate of cooperation decay is mild with partners until it exhibits a precipitous change after crossing the fifty percent threshold. The average payoff for cooperation dramatically drops below the guaranteed payoff for defection. The payoff for indiscriminating players who choose cooperation fifty percent of the time can be computed as 5.75, considerably more than players choosing to cooperate with this frequency were obtaining on average. There may also be an analogy to reaching a percolation threshold in science in which defection has sufficiently "invaded" the interaction, making reward for cooperation a cognitive idealization, like abandoning a sinking ship. Another possible metastable position in repeated games with relationship would be to alternate choices systematically, so each player receives the maximum payout half the time. In this case, such reciprocating players would receive an average payout of 6 – marginally better than for an indiscriminant population and far above the Nash equilibrium payout.

Next, we apply Equation 1 to analyze the initial emotional temperature and its evolution through repeated game play. These results, shown in Figure 4, were normalized with respect to the equilibrium payout.

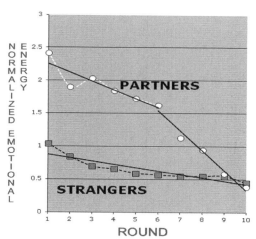

Fig. 4. Extracting a measure of the emotional energy, κT, from repeated Prisoner's Dilemma play for partners (white circles) and strangers (gray squares). Solid lines represent regression in at least squares sense with the slope quantifying a rate of temperature change.

The appropriate activation energy is not that taken from payout difference in Figure 1 for single play, but rather the actual average payouts experienced in the population for the binary choice presented. This difference between average payouts for cooperate and defect is dynamic. While individuals may experience a greater degree of success and disappointment, we concentrate on the population average difference as the risk barrierexperienced in cooperation. The emotional temperature, indicative of making choices using criteria other than provided utility functions, is approximately 2.5 times higher at the onset of game play when a relationship was pending. Even after ten rounds of play, Nash equilibrium is not reached, as some emotional energy persists. Some oscillatory response could be expected in discrete play data, especially for small populations, as players react, gather data, and assess trends. The emotional energy of partners is drained rapidly as rationality prevails following crossing the threshold for indiscriminate players with the associated underwhelming reward. With the distinction provided by Morton Deutsch (1975: 143) between equity and equality as values for the basis of distributive justice, perhaps there was a shift from equality towards equity when social relations entered game play. While this may help explain differences in initial emotional energy between games with partners and strangers, we note the differences in average payouts between those choosing cooperation and defection within each game as potential drivers for distributive justice are remarkably similar, stay fairly constant, and are approximately equal to the difference (four) at the Nash equilibrium.

The same driving force used to compute emotional energy can be recognized as a measure of fairness, though the true range of reward disparity is much larger than this. The other side of the coin of fairness is envy. The population might be assessed as satisfied if only average payout was considered. Only when the population is subdivided, exposing disparities in utility and underlying emotions, can outcomes and population kinetics be reconciled. Key will be taking the concept of emotional temperature as an observable and allowing more creative outcomes by exposing another degree of freedom.

Conclusion

We find it interesting that economics are always performed on forward estimates, but emotions and trust in the other party are predominatly based upon historical information. Game theory can be extended to include parameters related to emotions, thus expanding the definition of rational behavior. It can also be appended to account for emotional blindness, using the concept of emotional energy and temperature. We were able to show how to take the emotional temperature of a player or group based upon a history of action, a parameter which may prove useful in long-term relationships or repeated games. As defined, fairness and fairness history can be used in virtually any game. With more opportunities to portray factors leading real people to real decisions, the landscape for game theory to provide a platform for business and social decision-making becomes usefully enlarged.

Future Work

Similar analysis can be carried out, with variations in payout and rules of engagement, to target different emotions. Such games need to include larger populations for greater statistical significance. It is proposed to go beyond post-game analysis. We plan to propose gaming experiences for use in teaching negotiation concepts that are able to quantify emotions and utilize them in forward modeling, especially games in which trust is the only variable contributing to the measure of risk. Gifting is additionally proposed in the role of a catalyst with the ability to accelerate a relationship. We will explore leveraging existing formulations in chemistry to capture this type of external in social contexts.

Notes

Special thanks to Daniel Druckman, Roy Lewicki, Christopher Honeyman, and James Coben, for all their input, help, and feedback to improve the quality of this chapter.

References

Andreoni, J. and J. H. Miller. 1993. Rational cooperation in the finitely repeated prisoner's dilemma: Experimental evidence. *The Economic Journal* 103(418): 570-585.

Barry, B. 2007. Negotiator affect: The state of the art (and the science). *Group Decision Negotiation* 17(1): 97-105.

Binmore, K. 2007. *Game theory: A very short introduction.* Oxford: Oxford University Press.

Carnevale, P. and P. Keenan. 1990. Decision frame and social motivation in integrative bargaining. Paper presented at the third meeting of the International Association for Conflict Management, Vancouver, Canada.

Chamoun, H. 2003. *Trato hecho: Guía para una negociación sin fallas.* Houston, TX: KeyNegotiations.

Chamoun, H. and R. Hazlett. 2007. *Negotiate like a Phoenician.* Houston, TX: KeyNegotiations.

Chamoun, H. and R. Hazlett. 2009. The psychology of giving and its effect on negotiation. In *Rethinking negotiation teaching: Innovations for context and culture,* edited by C. Honeyman, J. Coben, and G. De Palo. St. Paul, MN: DRI Press.

Cialdini, R. B. 1993. *Influence: The psychology of persuasion.* New York, NY: William Morrow.

De Dreu, C. K. W. and C. McCusker. 1997. Gain-loss frames on cooperation in two person social dilemmas; a transformational analysis. *Journal of Personality and Social Psychology* 72(5): 1093-1106.

Deutsch, M. 1975. Equity, equality, and need: What determines which value will be used as the basis of distributive justice. *Journal of Social Issues* 31(3): 137-149.

Druckman, D. and C. Albin. 2009. Distributive justice and the durabity of peace agreements. Presented at the 22nd Annual International Association of Conflict Management Conference, Kyoto, Japan.

Druckman, D. and M. Olekalns. 2008. Emotions in negotiation. *Group Decision and Negotiation* 17(1): 1-11.

Fishburn, P. C. 1970. *Utility theory for decision-making.* New York, NY: Wiley.

Keltner. D. and J. Haidt. 1999. Social functions of emotions at four levels of analysis. *Cognit Emotion* 13(5): 505-521.

Kirkpatrick, S., C. D. Gelatt Jr., and M. P. Vecchi. 1983. Optimization by simulated annealing. *Science* 220(4598): 671-680.

Larson, D.W. 1998. Exchange and reciprocity in international negotiation. *International Negotiation* 3(1): 121-138.

Lewicki, R. J, D. M. Saunders, and B. Barry. 2010. *Negotiation,* 6th edn. Boston: McGraw Hill Irwin.

Mailath, G. J. and L. Samuelson. 2006. *Repeated games and reputations: Long-run relationships.* New York: Oxford University Press.

Myerson, R. B. 1991. *Game theory: Analysis of conflict.* Cambridge, MA: Harvard University Press.

Nowak, M. A. and K. Sigmund. 2005. Evolution of indirect reciprocity. *Nature* 437: 1291-1298.

O'Hara, M. 1997. Relational empathy: Beyond modernist egocentricism to postmodern holistic contextualism. In *Empathy reconsidered: New directions in psychotherpy,* edited by A. C. Bohart and L. S. Greenberg. Washington, DC: American Psychological Association.

Ryan, C. 2006. Rawls on negotiating justice. In *The negotiator's fieldbook: The desk reference for the experienced negotiator,* edited by A. K. Schneider and C. Honeyman. Washington, DC: American Bar Association.

Schelling, T. 1971. Dynamic models of segregation. *Journal of Mathematical Sociology* 1(2): 143-186.

Shapiro, D. L. 2006. Untapped power: Emotions in negotiation. In *The negotiator's fieldbook: The desk reference for the experienced negotiator,* edited by A. K. Schneider and C. Honeyman. Washington, DC: American Bar Association.

Siegfried, T. 2006. *A beautiful math: John Nash, game theory, and the quest for a code of nature.* Cambridge, MA: Belknap Press.

Van Kleef, G. A., E. van Dijk, W. Steinel, F. Harinck, and I. van Beest. 2007. Anger in social conflict: Cross-situational comparison and suggestions for the future. *Group Decision and Negotiation* 17(1):13-30.

Wade-Benzoni, K. 2006. Giving future generations a voice. In *The negotiator's fieldbook: The desk reference for the experienced negotiator*, edited by A. K. Schneider and C. Honeyman. Washington, DC: American Bar Association.

Weirich, P. 2007. *Equilibrium and rationality: Game theory revised by decision rules.* Cambridge, UK: Cambridge University Press.

Welsh, N. 2006. Perceptions of fairness. In *The negotiator's fieldbook: The desk reference for the experienced negotiator*, edited by A. K. Schneider and C. Honeyman. Washington, DC: American Bar Association.

Yifeng, N.C., D. Tjosvold, and W. Peiguan. 2008. Effects of warm-heartedness and reward distribution on negotiation. *Group Decision Negotiation* 17(1): 79-96.

ᐇ 24 ᐅ

A Game Of Negotiation:
The "Deliberation Engine"

Christopher Honeyman, Peter S. Adler, Colin Rule, Noam Ebner, Roger Strelow, & Chittu Nagarajan*

Editors' Note: *This chapter envisions a negotiation game which can promote learning, as well as fact-finding on any hot-button issue. The authors outline a particular form of online game, in variants separately designed to work with formal education, working professionals, and the general public. The game, as conceived here, is designed to address a mounting problem in negotiations of the largest scale, public issues: an apparently increasing tendency of people and parties to make up their own facts. Global climate change is considered as a test case. A*

* **Christopher Honeyman** is managing partner of Convenor Conflict Management, a consulting firm based in Washington, DC and Madison, Wisconsin. He has directed a 20-year series of major research-and-development projects in conflict management and is co-director of the Rethinking Negotiation Teaching project. His email address is honeyman@convenor.com. **Peter S. Adler** is a public policy consultant and mediator based in Honolulu, Hawaii, following a multiyear term as president of the Keystone Center for Science and Public Policy (Keystone, Colorado and Washington, DC.) His email address is padleraccord@gmail.com. **Colin Rule** is CEO and **Chittu Nagarajan** is Chief Product Officer of Modria.com, an online dispute resolution service provider based in San Jose, California. Colin's email address is crule@modria.com and Chittu's is chittu@modria.com. **Noam Ebner** is an assistant professor at Creighton University School of Law, where he chairs the online master's program in negotiation and dispute resolution. His email address is noamebner@creighton.edu. **Roger Strelow** is a lawyer-mediator in private practice in Fort Myers, Florida. He previously served at various times as assistant administrator of the U.S. Environmental Protection Agency, staff director of the U.S. Council on Environmental Quality in the Executive Office of the President, and as a vice president of General Electric and later of Bechtel Corporation. His email address is rstrelow@comcast.net. The authors would like to thank Todd Bryan, senior associate at the Keystone Center, and marketing consultant Christine Raymond for their advice in the discussions which led to this chapter.

related chapter in this volume, The Education of Non-Students, *assesses the prospects for a related new strategy, using theater, film and games to begin to provide informal negotiation education for the vast majority of the public who will never take any kind of course on negotiation.*

Introduction

There is currently no readily usable online mechanism that enables groups to compare their assumptions while setting aside, for the moment, the positions emanating from these assumptions. Such a system, if it were robust enough, might be able to reveal a great deal about what is really powering a public dispute, showing where the main conflicts of opinion are stemming from.

We believe such a tool could be designed so as to invite what-if experimentation and augment other conflict management techniques. The web-based "deliberation engine" tool we will outline here, by itself, would enable users to explicate a particular problem more fully, and encourage them to explore more options than are currently practicable. Such a device, we think, would also become an informal teaching tool of particular value in an emerging effort to address the public need for more "informal" education in our field (see Blanchot et al., *Education of Non-Students*, in this volume).

Our team may, in fact, go on to develop such a tool ourselves. (Our current design is discussed in this chapter's Appendix.) But recognizing the odds against any one version of any new technological idea actually coming to fruition, we prefer to set forth the concept in detail here, and avoid the risk of playing the "dog in the manger." To put it another way, it is more valuable to us to work toward an increased chance of such an idea being successfully executed by *someone* than to treat it as intellectual property.

This is, in turn, partly because we believe this tool can also become the central and most public element in a larger collaborative toolbox, some parts of which have already been developed. In conjunction with other tools, we think a "deliberation engine" will improve the odds that well-reasoned solutions to public controversies will prevail.

This chapter, in a nutshell, outlines the possibilities of at least one version of an emerging interactive technology tool. The "deliberation engine" is designed to enable multiple users to offer, review, change, or model the different factual assumptions that are brought to bear on a complex or contentious issue.[1] Given the context of this book, we will detail its pedagogical advantages as a tool for teachers to utilize in teaching negotiation and conflict engagement, in addition to its real-problem applications.

Background

We know that different parties use widely varying factual assumptions, especially when they are engaged in an active conflict. By the time an issue is joined in public, these assumptions are often buried under mounds of rhetoric. It is a central tenet of democracy that everyone is entitled to hold and express their own opinion. But for people to believe that they are entitled to their own *facts* is a pernicious and apparently growing trend.

When issues move beyond personal experience, everyone makes tacit assumptions about the "facts"; and it is well demonstrated that "facts" are subject to cognitive bias, especially in contexts laden with emotional controversy (see, e.g., Guthrie and Sally 2006; Shapiro 2006; Korobkin and Guthrie 2006). Compounded by the sheer complexity of the underlying issues in many of today's policy disputes (e.g., in the United States, national health care reform, immigration, Social Security, tax policy, or tort reform, to name a few), this makes it virtually impossible to understand everything that is powering an opposing opinion, even for those significantly interested in, and knowledgeable about, what is going on in a particular area. This inability to see clearly what assumptions another person or group is relying on degrades the ability to conduct civilized and fruitful conversations. And that, in turn, fuels the periodic rise of extreme and unproductive political discourse.

It is human nature to suspect or at least question the motives of anyone who disagrees with you. Over hundreds of years, society has developed tools, for purposes of public debate – the press and formal research are merely the most obvious – that purport to answer the need for reliable facts. Yet in the United States, at least, our most common mechanisms for sifting and winnowing the facts – the press and media generally – have become perceived as increasingly partisan, even as newspaper and TV network budgets for addressing and explaining complex factual situations have shriveled. The rise in viewership of viewpoint-oriented Fox and MSNBC, at the expense of more sober outlets like CNN or PBS, is merely part of a broader trend. Another part of this trend is reflected in the general public becoming more aware that "facts" introduced in controversial debates are often premised on research funded or sponsored by stakeholders, rendering them suspect. Moreover, the same stakeholders who vigorously "spin" facts are often not shy about questioning the impartiality of public institutions historically deemed to be above the fray of partisan purposes, such as the National Academy of Sciences or the Congressional Budget Office.

We believe that, at least in the United States (and perhaps more broadly) it should be possible to improve on this situation significantly, using new technologies and smarter social processes. The formats we envision require relatively economical organizational innovation; many of the key technological elements are available off-the-shelf. We are interested in helping to develop a suite of new mechanisms (some of which are already under way) that will encourage people who believe vastly different things on important topics of concern to understand something of each other's factual assumptions, and to become more inclined to grapple with those differences in a respectful and productive way.[2] We are also eager to engage those in the large but often non-assertive political "center," and to harness their greater proclivity than the more opinionated to seek reasonable compromise resolutions. We will focus here on the central element in the suite: a public, transparency-generating tool that can help turbo-charge dialogue, deliberation and negotiation. We call this tool the "deliberation engine."

Existing Analogues

Several progenitors of the "deliberation engine" exist, and suggest that this should be a do-able enterprise. One category is "fact-checking" systems such as www.factcheck.org and www.snopes.com. These demonstrate both that there is an audience for accuracy and that the business of checking assumptions and representations is neither impossibly laborious nor impractically expensive. The drawback of the existing kinds of tools is that they focus on a single question or sub-issue at a time, and usually on an accusation that someone is stretching the truth or lying outright. This focus leads them to function more like arbiters of truth or "fact police" than as facilitators of good discourse and well-designed problem solving.

A second mechanism consists of repositories of information whose aim is to present both sides of a controversy, without deciding it, in order to provide decision-makers with resources for critical thinking and to provide the general public with the background for making more informed choices. One example of this is www.procon.org.

Detailed background articles in newspapers of record, and the less frequent detailed documentaries on public television, form a third set of important fact-sorting mechanisms. These remain valuable, and can help iron out misconceptions. But they also suffer from increasingly severe time, space and cost constraints. The inability of any one team of writers/producers/editors to easily identify all pertinent sources of information on a particular topic may lead, meanwhile, to accusations of bias. These mechanisms are also passive, one-way communication experiences (with some promising but rare exceptions, such as "balance the budget" tools,[3] or the "choose the best neighborhood" tool discussed below). Most important, they do not allow for Boolean what-if experimentation by interested experts, let alone by "civilian" users or readers.

A fourth mechanism is the "wiki," best known through www. wikipedia.com. This continually growing encyclopedic reference demonstrates that it is possible to allow mass participation, such that persons with limited individual knowledge (but many opinions) can collaborate with relative goodwill to produce a usable article. It is encouraging for our purposes that only a tiny fraction of the topics treated on Wikipedia have generated such heat that a moderator is even necessary (for more on dispute resolution on Wikipedia, see Hoffman and Mehra 2009).

What we suggest draws from all four of these precedents, but would itself be quite different in structure, application and value.

The Deliberation Engine: Components

The deliberation engine as we conceive it consists of several main components. Most obvious is a website, structured to allow one or more users to examine an issue from the perspective of any of the main identified parties to that issue, and also to *modify* that perspective by changing the assumptions behind any element. In some ways, the engine can be seen as a distant relative of the well-known "SimCity" (a city-building simulation video game[4]) and its various progeny, but with real issues and real counterparts. The website is structured so as to make all assumptions and facts easily retrievable, transparent, and visually attractive. SimCity is an excellent demonstration that a manipulable database need not look hideous.

An excellent small-scale example of what we mean by a "deliberation engine" has already been published. For a *New York Magazine* article that asked "What's the best neighborhood in New York?", the magazine retained statistician Nate Silver (of www.fivethirtyeight. com) to assess fifty neighborhoods according to cost and quality of housing, quality of schools, access to transportation, restaurants, entertainment and many more criteria that enter into people's judgments of a desirable place to live. His article (Silver 2010) straightforwardly describes the weighting choices he made, and why.

For our purposes, the most interesting application is not the article itself, nor the topic, but the supplementary website. There, Silver organized what amounts to a deliberation engine of the kind we envision – just on a small scale and for a single, not-very-controversial topic.

Silver invites a user to look at a list of desirable neighborhoods, and then to *modify* the list by inserting the user's own weighting of the criteria. The changing ranking can be seen in real time. We can imagine a young family hunting for a home in "the right neighborhood for us" using this tool. The process could go something like this: the family members engage in discussions. They do not have to agree on all of the variables that seem important, though – no variable is excluded if husband, wife *or* children want it included. This avoids unproductive arguments; if one family member thinks another has offered an absurd criterion, she or he can simply weight it at zero in her ratings. They enter their individual ratings and then weight them.[5] They amalgamate their weightings, discuss them, perhaps agree on a smaller, more focused list, change the variables, add new ones, and then do individual and amalgamated scorings. The resulting information is used to help prioritize possible neighborhoods for their family's search. At a minimum, it is easy to imagine the time stuck in traffic, driving around one ultimately unsuitable neighborhood after another, being reduced; with some real-world families, we suspect that without such help, arguments may become so repeated and acrimonious that everyone gives up, and openly or tacitly agrees to stay in their current tiny apartment.

The New York livable-neighborhood example is at the low end of the complexity scale for the issues we have in mind.[6] Toward the high end are matters such as sustainable energy production, decisions about pandemic vaccination policies, military base closures, or American policies on health care reform. The health care example is emblematic. In the raucous debates with dueling fact-sets and highly divisive polemics, it has been far from clear that the public even agrees on what the topic is. Are we talking about "health *care* reform"? Or is it "health *insurance* reform"? Is it the allocation of scarce health care resources, or is it the reform of public health practices and the promotion of healthier lifestyles? Or, is it the reform of malpractice laws? Or, is it something else again (Medicare costs, abortion, pharmaceutical imports, or some combination of all of the above)?

A step beyond even these is global climate change. Both because of its inherent importance and because its scientific and political complexity provides an excellent challenge to "stress-test" a new suite of tools, we are contemplating building a first set of implementations of the "deliberation engine" around this issue, as described below.

Global climate change has many layers and subsets of issues. To name just three, different parties might find themselves contending over:

1) Whether severe and harmful warming will in fact occur unless there is significant curbing of anthropogenic (human
produced) "greenhouse gases" ("GHG") such as CO2 emissions, as the vast majority of climate scientists and modelers
believe but many other public actors dispute;

2) whether there are enough national security, economic and
other reasons for the United States to mount a major effort
to accelerate replacement of GHG-producing fossil fuels with
alternative, renewable energy sources such as solar and wind,
even if the case for doing so on purely environmental grounds
is subject to reasonable doubt; and

3) whether, if such acceleration is desired, it makes more sense
to increase the cost of fossil fuel generation through a cap-
and-trade or carbon tax scheme, or alternatively, to mount
a "moon shot" type of research-and-development effort, to
reduce the cost of alternative energy through innovation and
efficiency improvements.

All engines have multiple moving parts. In the climate change context, the deliberation engine could encourage focusing on common
questions, where that is desirable and possible. But as we conceive
it, the engine would also be nimble enough to allow different questions to be entered, and/or questions to be put in play with different
parameters. Thus one set of users might take up one fact-intensive set
of questions, such as the reliability of predicted worst-case adverse
effects scenarios. Another might look at the relative efficiencies and
costs of "taxing" fossil fuel generation, or of developing lower-cost
alternative energy systems in order to achieve more rapid replacement
of the former with the latter. Someone else might look at the relative
cost-benefit of cap-and-trade versus a carbon tax. With robust hard-
ware and software (which our particular group has available through
an existing platform, though we are not alone in this), a large variety
of such questions could be accommodated simultaneously. As the effects of asserted answers to one set of questions can be related to the
answers given to another set of questions, a more comprehensive understanding of interrelated issues becomes visible.

The "deliberation engine" on its own would be a powerful tool,
but it is important to note that it can integrate with other tools to
produce an even more effective suite. The development over the last
three decades of public policy facilitation, negotiated rulemaking and
several other strategies is well known, enough so as not to require
discussion here. Another existing related tool is less obvious, however.
In some of our work, we use variants of a specialized collaboration
process called Joint Fact Finding ("JFF"). The procedure requires that

those who are affected by a decision also be involved in framing the research question(s) and identifying, generating, analyzing and interpreting the scientific and technical information that will be used to inform a decision or action. JFF procedures are flexible but have six critical characteristics (see, Adler et al. 2011 and Schultz 2003):

1) They involve multiple stakeholders who may have very different viewpoints;
2) they are collaborative and require people to work together;
3) they are structured, meaning, JFF processes and meetings are not left to chance but are well designed and highly focused dialogues;
4) they are inquiry based and require a robust exploration to understand the problem from all angles;
5) they are interest-based study processes and not forums for arguing political positions; and
6) they are integrative and multidisciplinary. They bring different types of knowledge, information and data to the table.

Nested into a rigorous social process like collaborative JFF, the deliberation engine has enormous problem-solving possibilities. An algorithm that describes how JFF works in the present context might start to look like this:

1) Bring together a group of potential collaborators/opponents.
2) Frame the issues or problems.
3) Develop a list of all possible factual variables that might be pertinent to the issues or problem. Discard none.
4) Clearly separate questions of "fact" from questions of "values," as far as possible; for example "what level of greenhouse gases ("GHG") will trigger each of various severities of warming effects?", versus "what level of climate change seems reasonably tolerable from an overall cost-benefit standpoint?"
5) Identify the fullest possible set of "data" needs that will help inform the fullest possible set of "fact" questions.
6) Populate the fact questions with the fullest possible data sets in ways that allow everyone to see everyone else's suggested or asserted facts.
7) Ensure open enough sources that the methods and assumptions behind any suggested fact can be checked by others with contending views. Where sources and methods are *not* open, data sets are either disqualified or relegated to a secondary or tertiary status.

In such a structure, any time one set of facts is added or challenged, the impacts on other facts are quickly and transparently visible to everyone. JFF actually embodies other important bits and pieces of social process. Yet in current practice, Step 1 alone – bringing people together – can be hard to get a commitment to, not to mention expensive, because the conventional practice of a physical meeting with participants, who are often geographically as well as intellectually distant from each other, requires considerable preparation and coordination. An online equivalent could help parties get beyond a crucial stage when few have yet seen the value of committing to bear such expense. This factor alone could greatly expand the range of issues and of parties that can be drawn into our field's existing processes.

To summarize thus far: our concept is fundamentally a new web-based tool by which anyone can modify a chain of reasoning – but not without admitting their chosen fact base, and with an incentive to support that with credible references or evidence.

The further possibility exists that linking multiple databases may reveal relationships between issues now mostly treated as unrelated; for instance, between expenditures to minimize GHG in order to stem sea-level rises and a possible policy to protect or move at-risk seashore facilities (an issue somewhat similar to the long-running questions about allowing versus banning reconstruction of flood-plain structures harmed or destroyed by past floods.) While that level of integration would not be a first-generation goal, even an early generation could allow for multiple kinds of uses. A "macro" climate change version, for example, would allow people to plug in scenarios for any public policy choice and, in effect, see what is likely to happen. It would allow and even encourage all biased versions of "the facts" to be submitted to transparency and respectful challenge.

But in practice, it is probably more appropriate to begin with a single "pilot" sub-issue within climate change, and build up to the macro level over a series of manageable subtopics. Whether a given topic or sub-topic might have a moderator, a JFF stakeholder group, or even an expert panel to establish the "conventional wisdom" on that sub-topic could be decided by the tool's organizers and users. Even where conventional-wisdom or panel-of-experts opinions exist, though, a user could still modify the resulting premise or number – but the result might show in red, as a revised assumption that others might want to review more closely than most.

Will People Play?

Like any new technology, it is impossible to anticipate all of the uses to which such an engine might be put. With all due humility, therefore, and focusing on our particular work (i.e., the realm of public issues), we currently identify three distinguishable markets for the particular form of this tool we contemplate: educators; professionals directly engaged in public policy (e.g., public policy experts and leaders, facilitators, mediators, and various kinds of partisans); and the general public. At a core level, these potential markets are integrated, but they require different interfaces.

For reasons of efficiency and economy, and because of patterns of professional interests and contacts that might not apply to a different team also interested in this "space," our concept includes testing the tool first with a multinational panel of well-known teachers of negotiation and their students, which we describe as "tier 1" of the structure. The reasons are discussed further below. We think that following initial testing at tier 1, the tool could be quickly adapted and adopted at "tier 2" by professionals directly engaged in public policy. It would also, we think, be used by partisans as well as by more flexible "middle-grounders" who would find they can now more easily and more productively engage in serious debates over new or modified laws, rules, standards, or regulations.[7]

If *partisans*, in particular, can be induced to input data in such a structure, either individually or collectively, and to agree on as much of the baseline data as possible, the prospects would improve further, and two positive consequences would flow at "tier 3" on any given issue (described below as the Public Game.) First, the deliberation engine would acquire widespread credibility and a real depth of information. (Partisans often have handy access to much of the information needed to address any public controversy.) The second consequence from partisan or collaborative participation is financial: It becomes possible to envision financial sustainability based on the now-familiar model of fees payable for customized versions by heavy users.

Ultimately, the most obvious and most widely used format, if our particular model goes forward, will be what we are describing for technical purposes as "tier 3." This is a version with a "lite" interface that is free, open, and accessible to anyone through a website, a portal, or an application for iPads and smartphones, etc. The professional version (tier 2) would be used for heavy applications, and might allow for custom formatting. ("Civilian" users might be able to access a certain number of pages per month, in more standardized format(s), and pay nothing directly, but would support the engine indirectly through advertising. Heavy-duty users would pay subscription fees.) Meanwhile the first version likely to be actually developed (tier 1, for faculty and students) is far from temporary, even though it represents our first foray. As an integral part of the structure, it would continue to provide for low-cost population of the database with new data for any newly mounted topic or issue.

We believe that if and when such a structure is competently offered (whether by us or by others), partisans as well as collaborators
will in fact play, and with gusto. The reasons are not hard to follow:
First, on any issue of perceived importance, no partisan group can
afford to leave any significant playing field of public opinion to its opponents. The moment any one group becomes interested in mounting
its own data on a public database, something of an equivalent is created to a trial in court, in which the worst strategy the opponent can
adopt is to fail to show up at all. Second, those in the middle, who often are not engaged productively in highly polarized debates, should
see a better opportunity for exercising constructive influence within
a consensus-building project, in which posturing is not an advantageous strategy. And third, we are living in a society which already
makes great use of online games, whether they are immersive and
in-depth (e.g., World of Warcraft) or simple and addictive (e.g., Angry
Birds or Farmville).[8] If our design or something similar is implemented well, we think the deliberation engine could become as compelling
as many of the games that currently are consuming hundreds of millions of hours of human attention every year.

Will partisans, in particular, play with good manners? We believe
that Wikipedia is far from unique: there are many and heartening
examples of unmoderated or only lightly moderated conversations in
which public discourse is conducted in a spirit of (relative) mutual respect and a degree of procedural cooperation, even among parties who
are implacably opposed on a policy level. In fact, several of the authors
have earned our living as facilitators and mediators in such settings,
both online and offline. It is routine to us to create such dialogue, often among parties who doubted that it could be done.

At the same time, once such an engine reaches tier 3, we are not
naïve as to the incentives for public policy players to "game" systems,
or ignorant as to the history of such activity with systems much older
than our game. Robust electronic security measures are called for at
that stage. Fortunately, robust security is a feature already developed
for the platform we are working with; and again, we are not the only
potential implementers thus equipped.

Conclusion

In the United States, we live in an age in which public policy is all
but paralyzed by intransigent political conflict. This paralysis is abet-
ted by dysfunctional discussions around complex issues, frequently
disconnected from anything resembling objective facts. Whether or
not we as a group manage to navigate the financial, technical and
other hurdles inevitable in development of an idea into a practical

tool, we would be delighted to see other groups take up the challenge we pose here. Our reasoning is not purely altruistic, either: there are many markets, and even whole industries, which became credible and achieved "scale" only when more than one offering became available.

Notes

[1] There are, of course, complementary ways to view the current state of affairs in public disputes. One of them is a particularly useful sidelight on the exceptionally complex situations we hope the deliberation engine will help to address. In recent years, the concept of an "uncertainty monster" has been gaining traction. Judith Curry and Peter Webster (2011) summarized the emerging concept as follows:

> The "uncertainty monster" is a concept introduced by Van der Sluijs (2005) in an analysis of the different ways that the scientific community responds to uncertainties that are difficult to tame. The "monster" is the confusion and ambiguity associated with knowledge versus ignorance, objectivity versus subjectivity, facts versus values, prediction versus speculation, and science versus policy. The uncertainty monster gives rise to discomfort and fear, particularly with regard to our reactions to things or situations we cannot understand or control, including the presentiment of radical unknown dangers. An adaptation of Van der Sluijs's strategies of coping with the uncertainty monster at the science–policy interface is described below.
>
> - *Monster hiding.* Uncertainty hiding or the "never admit error" strategy can be motivated by a political agenda or because of fear that uncertain science will be judged as poor science by the outside world. Apart from the ethical issues of monster hiding, the monster may be too big to hide and uncertainty hiding enrages the monster.
> - *Monster exorcism.* The uncertainty monster exorcist focuses on reducing the uncertainty through advocating for more research. In the 1990s, a growing sense of the infeasibility of reducing uncertainties in global climate modeling emerged in response to the continued emergence of unforeseen complexities and sources of uncertainties. Van der Sluijs (2005: 88) states that "monster theory predicts that [reducing uncertainty] will prove to be vain in the long run: for each head of the uncertainty monster that science chops off, several new monster heads tend to pop up due to unforeseen complexities," analogous to the Hydra beast of Greek mythology.
> - *Monster simplification.* Monster simplifiers attempt to transform the monster by subjectively quantifying and simplifying the assessment of uncertainty . . . .
> - *Monster detection.* The first type of uncertainty detective is the scientist who challenges existing theses and works to extend knowledge frontiers. The second type is the watchdog auditor, whose main concern is accountability, quality control, and transparency of the science. The third type is the merchant of doubt (Oreskes and Conway 2010), who distorts and magnifies uncertainties as an excuse for inaction for financial or ideological reasons.
> - *Monster assimilation.* Monster assimilation is about learning to live

with the monster and giving uncertainty an explicit place in the contemplation and management of environmental risks. Assessment and communication of uncertainty and ignorance, along with extended peer communities, are essential in monster assimilation. The challenge to monster assimilation is the ever-changing nature of the monster and the birth of new monsters.

[2] It has been estimated that between three and one-half and five positive experiences for every negative one with the other party are required, to get people unmired from a deeply felt dispute. This is a daunting figure, which demands a sustained strategy (Coleman 2011).

[3] A good example would be one hosted by the New York Times, which specifically invited readers to "Make your own plan, then share it online." See http://www.nytimes.com/interactive/2010/11/13/weekinreview/deficits-graphic.html (last accessed September 10, 2012).

[4] A general description of this game and its progeny can be found at http://en.wikipedia.org/wiki/SimCity_(series) (last accessed September 10, 2012).

[5] This method of assigning issues not only value, but also weight, has been used in other negotiation platforms. For example, in iCan Systems' Smartsettle system, parties make offers to one another on multiple issues; however, they also privately rate the degree to which each issue is important to them. This allows the program to seek to optimize each party's outcome, by suggesting offers in which parties might gain relatively more on those issues which are most important to them.

[6] If the underlying structure is made totally available for the user's choice of any issue (one of several possible scenarios), the tool can have *many* possible uses. Three relatively simple examples demonstrate uses at different scales:

- A student and his or her family are trying to decide which of many colleges to consider attending. They could array their specific choices (e.g., Butler, University of Missouri, George Mason, etc.), plug in specific data (location, tuition, transportation costs, music or sports opportunities, etc.), structure and prioritize their criteria, and play with the weightings to refine their hunt for the preferred school for that particular student. Where there are different factual assertions, say the quality of teaching, they are encouraged and helped to find ways to display the differences in quantitative terms, and to evaluate how this relates to the pertinent cost issues.

- An organization working to plan essential cutbacks might use the engine to lay out options, structure criteria, and invite executives in the organization to enter their conflicting assertions about the ripple effects of key decisions. For example, one manager may argue that disintermediation, e.g., trimming whole layers of management, will save core costs by speeding up decision-making. Another might argue that those same actions will actually cascade into additional costs as remaining managers become overworked and make more superficial judgments. The engine will facilitate and encourage these managers to find and set forth data that truly rather than superficially support their respective points of view. The potential quantitative consequences of different cuts can be debated with greater clarity and less office game-playing, leading to sharper understanding of potential impacts.

- The procurement division of a national business, or of a state or federal agency, considering its "green-greener-greenest" purchasing policies for bulk supplies, could set up a customized version of the deliberation engine to compare hundreds of key products from its supply chain. The potential factual assertions can be deliberated with much greater precision, assertions of cost effects can be quantified, and decision choices can be arrayed with increased precision.

These examples are offered for simplicity and variety, not because we will necessarily adopt so open a structure, or necessarily see anything like these three uses as priorities to address. Although new technology applications often have unanticipated but wildly successful applications – indeed, we expect to be surprised by the uses this tool is put to – we are particularly interested in the deliberation engine because of its special relevance to the public policy questions of the day.

[7] Adler notes: In The Keystone Center's current work, diverse projects that could use a deliberation engine right now include managing chemicals of concern; solving the marine debris and ocean plastics problem; reducing greenwashing and the marketplace confusion of hundreds of eco-labels; and developing new interconnected smart grids on the eastern seaboard of the United States. Other issues can arise at any moment, and a deliberation engine that is ready to go with a new implementation twenty-four hours a day could help with the most emergent of public policy issues. On May 8, 2010, for example, shortly after the Gulf of Mexico oil spill, one of the members of Keystone's Board of Trustees wrote: *"We should think about what role Keystone can play in the aftermath of the spill. There will be a debate both about new offshore leases and about needed reforms in regulation and oversight of existing drilling. Like most things, emotion and exaggeration will likely dominate the debate. If ever there is need for science-based dialogue and consensus building, it will be on this. . . ."*

[8] See, e.g., a list of twenty-five "highly addictive" games on Facebook compiled by the design weblog Hongkiat.com, at http://www.hongkiat.com/blog/highly-addictive-facebook-games/(last accessed September 10, 2012).

References

Adler, P. S., T. Bryan, M. Mulica, and J. Shapiro. 2011. *Humble inquiry: the practice of joint fact-finding as a strategy for bringing science, policy and the public together.* Available at http://www.mediate.com/pdf/Joint%20Fact%20Finding.pdf (last accessed September 10, 2012).

Alexander, N. and M. LeBaron. 2009. Death of the role-play. In *Rethinking negotiation teaching: Innovations for context and culture*, edited by C. Honeyman, J. Coben, and G. De Palo. St. Paul, MN: DRI Press.

Coleman, P. 2011. *The five percent: Finding solutions to seemingly impossible conflicts.* New York: Public Affairs.

Curry, J. and P. J. Webster. 2011. *Bulletin of the American Meteorological Society,* Dec. 2011. Available electronically at http://journals.ametsoc.org/doi/pdf/10.1175/2011BAMS3139.1 (last accessed September 10, 2012).

Ebner, N., A. Bhappu, J. G. Brown, K. K. Kovach, and A. K. Schneider. 2009. You've got agreement: Negoti@ting via email. In *Rethinking negotiation teaching: Innovations for context and culture*, edited by C. Honeyman, J. Coben, and G. De Palo. St. Paul, MN: DRI Press.

Guthrie, C. and D. Sally. 2006. Miswanting. In *The negotiator's fieldbook: The desk reference for the experienced negotiator*, edited by A. K. Schneider and C. Honeyman. Washington, DC: American Bar Association.

Hoffman, D. A. and S. K. Mehra. 2009. Wikitruth through Wikiorder. *Emory Law Journal* 59(1): 151-210.

Korobkin, R. and C. Guthrie. 2006. Heuristics and biases at the bargaining table. In *The negotiator's fieldbook: The desk reference for the experienced negotiator*, edited by A. K. Schneider and C. Honeyman. Washington, DC: American Bar Association.

Nelken, M. 2012. Evaluating email negotiations. In *Assessing our students, assessing ourselves*, edited by N. Ebner, J. Coben, and C. Honeyman. St. Paul, MN: DRI Press.

Oreskes, N. and E. M. Conway. 2010. *Merchants of doubt: How a handful of scientists obscured the truth on issues from tobacco smoke to global warming*. New York: Bloomsbury Press.

Schultz, N. 2003. *Joint fact-finding: Adversaries in need of information*. Available at http://www.beyondintractability.org/essay/joint_fact-finding (last accessed September 10, 2012).

Shapiro, D. 2006. Untapped power: Emotions in negotiation. In *The negotiator's fieldbook: The desk reference for the experienced negotiator*, edited by A. K. Schneider and C. Honeyman. Washington, DC: American Bar Association.

Silver, N. 2010. *The most livable neighborhoods in New York: A quantitative index of the 50 most satisfying places to live*. Available at http://nymag.com/realestate/neighborhoods/2010/65374/ (last accessed September 10, 2012).

Van der Sluijs, J. P. 2005. Uncertainty as a monster in the science–policy interface: Four coping strategies. *Water Science Technlogy* 52: 87–92.

Appendix: Our Team's Current Design

We will briefly discuss here how our own conception of a deliberation engine works – in the full knowledge that by doing so, we may be fostering a competitor with a better idea. If that happens, so be it.

Negotiation Teachers and Students as "First Testers"

A number of writings in the first two books in the Rethinking Negotiation Teaching series (beginning with Alexander and LeBaron 2009) critiqued our field's tendency to build scoreable games, as well as role-plays and other teaching devices, around brief, context-free, culturally arbitrary (or distinctly culturally American), and emotionally unrealistic scenarios. Up to now, teachers have typically also found it daunting to try to replicate another aspect of negotiations in real work and public policy environments – the almost inevitable existence of multidisciplinary teams on more than one side. One of our goals has been to create a deliberation engine in such a way that anyone using it will find themselves working with a team of diverse members, as well as negotiating or otherwise relating to a counterpart team that is similarly composed. For any professional in the modern world to imagine that lawyers work only with (or against) other lawyers, that business executives need not take public bodies into account, or that public officials can achieve public goals without the input of business, law and many other kinds of professionals, is naïve in the extreme. We would like to replicate that real-world condition from the outset.

The fact that the Rethinking Negotiation Teaching project, at the time of this writing, can count over 100 leading teachers of negotiation and other professionals among its committed contributors, means that very unusual circumstances now exist, in which multidisciplinary, multinational teams can actually be convened at very low cost for experimental purposes. The fact that our conception uses global climate change as the basis for the early test games lends itself well to convening teams that will include business, law, public policy, planning, natural resources, and peace studies students, all in mixed teams. The fact that three dozen or more countries are represented among the project's contributors reflects the important reality that climate change is indeed a global concern. (Faced with this situation, negotiation exercises that did not transcend national borders would seem poverty-stricken.) The particular versions of such a platform that appeal to us, as well as the issues we propose to address, lend themselves to multinational as well as multidisciplinary teams.

We anticipate that *teachers* will be motivated to engage their students in exercises using the deliberation engine for these reasons, among others:

1) The game's inevitable initial roughness, a characteristic of first-generation computer-based tools everywhere, is counterbalanced by the attraction of being able to tell students, truthfully, that their work is not merely a junior version of "academic" in its most dismissive sense, but an opportunity to take part in a real-world developmental project.

2) Beyond the real-world significance, the game would keep students motivated (see below) and challenged, taking at least a bit of the daily pressure off teachers to provide this motivation and challenge

within the classroom. Similarly, the grading of student performance could be largely programmed in advance, and therefore less labor-intensive than other types of exercises teachers are using.

3) Participation in the game leads to an experience inherently more realistic than some of the previous techniques critiqued in the Rethinking Negotiation Teaching project. The Deliberation Engine, far beyond simply providing a platform for conducting an e-negotiation simulation, supplants existing exercises which are designed to be conducted by email, and provides teachers with new methods for computer-mediated negotiation interactions for purposes of both practice and assessment (see Ebner et al. 2009; Nelken 2012). As a result, by assigning students to participate in the game, teachers stand to improve their own courses, in ways explored in a number of previous project writings that have stressed the need for authenticity.

4) Students engage in a process closely mimicking the reality of the modern business environment: multidisciplinary, multinational teams working together on complex issues. Nothing we do in the classroom as negotiation teachers today comes close to the degree to which these conditions can be modeled through participation in the game.

5) The game does not just provide an excellent learning opportunity, it can also serve as an easy-to-assess evaluation method (see Ebner, Efron, and Kovach 2012).

We expect students' motivation to participate to stem, in turn, primarily from three factors:

1) The novelty of the platform and nature of the interactions incorporated in their assignment would be intriguing.

2) The game presents a real-life opportunity to take a key role in the development of tools for addressing real problems that affect all of humanity.

3) They can be graded on their work, as their participation could be an assessed assignment in their negotiation course.

Tier 2: The Professionals Go to Work

While the initial focus is on teachers and students, which is appropriate in the context of the project which gives rise to this book, in our conception of the suite of tools that is just the beginning. Every major public issue, and many a minor one, seems to generate at least a phase, if not an enduring frustration, of factual incoherence, as between parties who talk past each other without ever grappling with the extreme factual inconsistencies powering their beliefs. Whether public policy or business policy is at issue, mediating organizations have at times created processes specifically for addressing the factual inconsistencies. A notable one is joint fact-finding ("JFF"), described above as used by Keystone.

Tier 2 of the deliberation engine represents, at least in part, an electronic version of JFF. The tier 1 start, compiling from student teams the data and arguments that have been found relatively persuasive or unpersuasive by their negotiating counterparts and their professors (and using the platform's ability to track more and less persuasive arguments and facts *within* a team as well as across teams) provides a team of professionals with a starting place for their own, presumably more sophisticated, inquiry. Since the structure would aggregate not only all information from all iterations of the game on a particular topic, but also the "roll-up" effects and reliability ratings given by observers, students in search of a good grade would have a double incentive to seek out and document *reliable* information to buttress their positions. With enough "runs" at tier 1, in other words, even before the professionals are invited into a particular issue, a significant quantity and variety of data can be amassed, sifted and weighed – at little or no direct labor cost. To a professional, in turn, this "pre-filling, pre-screening" element promises substantial cost savings compared to traditional "hands-on" methods of compiling and evaluating comparable starting data. In turn, the promise of this efficiency makes it possible to charge for use of the platform by professional groups; they will save much more than they will expend.

The time savings alone in mounting a JFF or related exercise, compared to the two years that is typical for the in-person variety of such an exercise, represents an enormous improvement in a professional team's ability to get work done. It also means that it becomes possible for such a team to run the exercise more than once, with different counterparts, to see if the results vary (generating new insights) or are consistent (generating higher confidence.) Either way, the learning expected is substantial, yet much less expensive to generate than by using more traditional approaches.

An additional feature of the technology platform we are working with, and one particularly valuable at tier 2 and tier 3, is the ability to recruit, at very low cost, large numbers of online citizen volunteers, prescreened for typical sources of bias, who are willing to evaluate the propositions set forth by competing parties. Voting with their clicks, they offer a reality check that is also very expensive to match using older approaches. But again, we are not the only group with ready access to large numbers of people online.

The Public Game: Tier 3
Of course, the ultimate purpose of the whole structure as we would create it is not just to serve teachers and students, nor even to serve professionals, but to serve the public. Tier 3 of the structure depends on tier 1 and tier 2 to create and validate data and arguments that can be drawn on and evaluated by the general public, citizen groups, lobbying groups, political parties, business and trade associations – indeed, all of those who participate in our political processes. Unlike the professionals, however, most of those participating at tier 3 do not have an immediate economic incentive to find and sift large quantities of data. Unlike students, they do not get graded, at least not directly. And they are easily overwhelmed by too much information.

In our version, accordingly, tier 3 is designed with an interface significantly different from both the "professional" and the "teacher/student" interfaces. While professionally-staffed business or environmental organizations may opt for a quite sophisticated interface that allows many choices, but also rewards prior practice with the engine, any member of the general public with an interest in a particular issue will be invited to participate too. But such "regular citizens" will not be expected to delve into unreasonable complexity. The interface designed for them would therefore *allow* deep study, but it would not *require* it, and it would be possible to participate meaningfully in a deliberation simply by identifying one's general preferences and political, economic or social stance, and/or one's particular conclusions from the data reviewed, and then joining an "electronic party" (in the negotiation, rather than the political, sense of the term) that has similar beliefs and/or conclusions.

Still, the party's handling of *facts*, as it proceeds to deliberate with parties with very different beliefs, would be subject to the same rigor as the engine applies at tier 1 and tier 2. By clicking on any asserted fact that fails the electronic check for validity, made possible by compiling the most well-accepted facts from tier 1 and tier 2 into the database, any citizen can find out just what about his or her asserted fact had already been rejected – and rejected, part of the time, by people who *started out* making exactly the same arguments he or she is making now. We believe this element is a powerful tool for pushing public debate in the direction of reality-based disputation.

෬ 25 ෨

Negotiation Stands Alone

*Alexandra Crampton & Michael Tsur**

Editors' Note: Yes, the authors concede, "everybody" negotiates: but that's like saying "everybody drives," and then watching aghast when "everybody" climbs into a racing car, or an eighteen-wheeled tractor-trailer. The authors draw from Tsur's experience teaching Israeli hostage negotiators and in other high-pressure environments to argue for an entirely distinct concept of a professional negotiator, one that starts with a rather experienced "student" and builds a sharply different training regimen from there.

Introduction: Getting Past Negotiation 1.0

While this book series began with the shortcomings of "Negotiation 1.0," by way of context as well as contrast this chapter will begin with a brief tribute to the Negotiation 1.0 legacy. First, the popularization of negotiation through books like *Getting to Yes* (Fisher, Ury, and Patton 1991) made negotiation more visible and accessible to millions. The complex contexts and nuances of negotiation were drastically simplified to clear, instrumental tasks and principles that have been widely translated to personal and professional application around the world. Those who have avoided negotiation or resorted to adversarial bargaining now have a method that can be more effective and efficient. The pioneers of the interest-based model also negotiated successfully

* **Alexandra Crampton** is an assistant professor in the department of social and cultural sciences at Marquette University. Her email address is alexandra.crampton@marquette.edu. **Michael Tsur** is founder and director of the Mediation and Conflict Resolution Institute in Jerusalem, and an adjunct professor of negotiation in the law faculty and the business school at Hebrew University of Jerusalem. His email address is tsur-negotiation@012.net.il. This chapter is based on Michael's notes for a longer subsequent writing, based in turn on many years of accumulated practice experience as negotiator, mediator, and trainer in many contexts, including as a member of the Hostage Crisis and Negotiation Unit of the Israeli Defense Forces.

to bring Negotiation 1.0 into professional education, despite criticisms that negotiation cannot be taught.[1] Negotiation has become an accepted specialization within professional practices such as law, business, and public policy. In the process, negotiation acquired a recognized empirical and theoretical literature, fostered through centers of research and practice, academic and professional conferences, and peer-reviewed specialty journals.

Yet this recognition continues to be limited to negotiation at most as a specialization, and more often as a sub-function of other fields, rather than as a profession that might stand alone. Moreover, what professional negotiators practice is usually quite different from the basic and even advanced forms taught in short courses. Professional negotiators are not simply more familiar with navigating the typical terrain of negotiation processes. They become highly skilled at perceiving and understanding nuances of communication and interaction that are hard to evaluate by, or simply overwhelming to, the negotiation novice. In other words, negotiation is a language too difficult for most to speak fluently. And when that terrain seems to dissolve into the high seas of stress, ambiguity, and conflict, a professional negotiator becomes an expert navigator who can guide the principals to safety – or at least a less rocky peace. The necessary intuition and inner qualities of professional negotiators are not universal, and not everyone can become a professional negotiator, even though everyone may benefit from basic negotiation training.

We contend that these "soft skills" and sensibilities cannot be trained didactically, but must be cultivated over time through reflective practice and experience. Several other chapters in this book series hint towards this conclusion. Differences noted between Negotiation 1.0 as "basic" and Negotiation 2.0 as "advanced," for example, offer a start to this conversation. However, taking culture and context as integral rather than additional to negotiation suggests a need to push this idea of advancement further. The result is an argument for a more advanced *concept* of negotiation, a different pool of potential students, and corresponding changes to pedagogy. This then leads to a second argument for establishing negotiation as a stand-alone profession.

In Michael's as yet unpublished work on which this chapter is based, what the negotiation field needs is not a revolution but an evolution: formalizing, structuring, and upgrading negotiation as a stand-alone profession should in no way diminish what went before, and what continues to thrive in many, many venues. The need for evolution is in part due to the complex demands of an increasingly globalized and interconnected world. These demands require professional negotiators to possess both global and local expertise in that there are general areas of expertise (outlined in this chapter) required of all negotiators as well as a need for local adaptation to contexts of culture, region, negotiating parties, and other case specifics. The general role of a professional negotiator is that of a mentor able to stimulate and provide negotiation skills to a growing number of potential end-users within established professions. Business or political leaders, for example, already hire professional negotiators such as crisis negotiators under some circumstances, to help analyze, strategize, and coach them through negotiations when the negotiations are nominally "conducted" by the parties themselves. We propose to build on this for more general usage.

The ideal "students" to mentor for this role have already proven successful in general negotiations within a first or even second career field of practice. They are far from the novice negotiator typified in negotiation pedagogy literature. Early differences between future novice and professional negotiators may even be seen in childhood, when the latter responds automatically to challenges by negotiating options, process, and outcomes with curiosity, respect, and creative thinking.[2] This means that professional negotiation programs would not compete for generic undergraduate or young graduate students. Instead, they should recruit from established professionals, perhaps even those nearing retirement from their original professions. This approach takes advantage of a major demographic trend, which is longevity in the work force. This also incorporates economic trends that both allow and require people to actualize their potential by changing careers. The ideal student of professional negotiation has already become an expert within his or her first career. In the Israeli context, for example, Michael has worked with high-ranking military officers, who typically retire between the ages of forty-five and fifty after years of commanding and managing personnel and operations in a very challenging environment. This work experience makes them potential candidates for negotiation as a second career.

We take up Michael's advanced negotiation concept next, and introduce the skills and sensibilities required for mastery. Space limitations require focusing this discussion down to a brief description of a general course of study of negotiation, such as could be taught globally. (Programs of study better tailored to local specifics, and how to adapt from the general model, will have to be explored in later work.) The introduction offered in this chapter leads to a discussion of the ideal student and program of study to train professional negotiators. Our chapter ends with next steps for formalizing negotiation as a second- or even third-career profession, and a conclusion about innovation and negotiation.

Advancing Negotiation Base Concepts

The first step in developing negotiation as a stand-alone profession is to bring complexity back into base models. The second is to address complexities that were not part of creating Negotiation 1.0, such as distinguishing leadership negotiation and how to negotiate in a crisis or hostage situation.[3] This section begins with the first task and then moves into the second.

Section One: Getting Past Negotiation 1.0

Participants in the Rethinking Negotiation Teaching (RNT) project have, from the beginning, emphasized that culture and context are integral and ongoing influences in negotiation. It can be presumptuous to use the predefined variables of Negotiation 1.0 when these very terms are themselves open to interpretation. For example, "interest" and "commitment" can vary in meaning and expression cross-culturally and situationally. In addition, what are explained as preparation tasks in the interest-based model may have to be renegotiated, in complex cases, not once beforehand, but throughout the negotiation. What first appears simple can quickly become also "wicked problems"[4] about what can be negotiated, who can negotiate (at the table or behind the scenes), how negotiations will unfold, the role and importance of time, and how to identify success and even outcomes. We should immediately disclaim any intent to provide here a thorough justification for the opinions which follow; that will have to await a more developed treatment, since we are just beginning on this subject. But we believe a brief review of some areas of particular importance would have to include at least the following:

Inter-cultural and cross-cultural dynamics

Culture may be an obvious factor in cross-cultural negotiation; that is, when negotiation parties come from two or more recognized "cultures." Culture as found in typical negotiation concepts is based on the idea that cultures derive from distinct cultural groups, typically identified as "traditional" tribes or "modern" nation states (see Knauft 1996). This concept of culture has been an important part of colonial and post-colonial global discourse and geopolitics. However, culture manifests itself more in social behavior like negotiation through patterned meanings of ideas, actions, and interpersonal dynamics that inform individual and collective understanding. In a postmodern, global world, culture is less a question of nation and more about other groupings; moreover, culture is always subject to change rather than timeless (see Crampton 2008). For example, a second-generation American with grandparents from Italy is likely to be somewhat culturally different from a second-generation American with Russian origins.

Culture is derived not only through nationality (or nationalities) but also family, neighborhood, workplace, religion, and occupation. Moreover, the *salience* of cultural traits or practices may vary among negotiations, such that what was a significant difference or point of conflict in one case is a superficial and even mundane aspect of another (see Docherty 2010). This variation is due in part to how each person internalizes cultural influences in their life, so that cultural differences can even be found among those who are nominally from the same cultural background. Cultural sensitivity then requires openness and curiosity about these differences, the variable significance of those differences, and the dynamics of cultural influence on negotiation processes. Negotiators must attune themselves to how culture informs the emotional *and* rational foundation of negotiations as brought in by each party, and how it affects the dynamics of group interaction over time. Acknowledgment of differences integral to the identity or understanding of parties can also be important.

Gender dynamics

Similar to culture, gender is a dimension largely lost in Negotiation 1.0 but found in advanced negotiation trainings. The style of the early days of approaching negotiation as a battlefield – a male tendency – has evolved into something beyond satisfaction with short-term achievements alone. As in other fields such as education, business and also entertainment, over the last thirty years more and more behavior that was once considered "feminine" is emerging as "mainstream" and is being embraced across the board. Factors such as listening, collaborating, and expressiveness are qualities becoming increasingly apparent and acceptable in the "male façade" and, of course, in "men's style" of negotiation. Yet this is all still true only up to a point (see Tinsley et al. 2009; Schneider, Cheldelin, and Kolb 2010).

Gender dynamics also include roles of women and men in negotiating. Sensitivity to the place and part that women are taking – or allowed to take (see, e.g., Kolb and Williams 2006) – in negotiation in different cultures is very important to consider. Where in some places in the world women will negotiate almost exclusively with women, such as in the Haredi community (an ultra-religious Jewish sect), in other places, merely raising the question of what is acceptable or unacceptable for women may seem out of place or strange.

This means that in some negotiation contexts, despite recent American gender-blind mores, a strategic choice of a male or female negotiator (or one of each) may be all but unavoidable. Depending on the content, a negotiation may proceed more effectively if done by a man, or a woman. Or, in some cases, the situation may call for men who easily display feminine characteristics without compromising their manliness, or vice versa, a woman who does not blink in the most hostile male environment, without losing her "feminine mystique." While varying from locale to locale, accepting the influence of gender in negotiation as fact, and being able to address it, is extremely important. It hardly needs emphasizing that this runs counter to the thrust of the typically American-influenced and (supposedly) gender-blind basic instruction in this field. There are also cultures where its full application is likely to contravene the law.

Role of emotions

Much has already been written about Negotiation 1.0 as a model that attempts to ignore or suppress emotion (see, e.g., Patera and Gamm 2010). However, emotions are an integral part of negotiation in at least five ways: emotions of the negotiators, emotions of parties as triggered through societal influences; emotions that emerge during negotiation; emotions of parties outside the direct negotiation who nevertheless can influence the process and outcomes; and emotions triggered by larger circumstances that may put pressure on negotiation parties, process, or outcomes. Clearly, in different places and cultures, dealing with emotions, and developing the *ability* to deal with them, may involve very different practical skills. The intensity and variability of emotional dynamics requires what Melissa Lewine-Boskovich, director of Peace Child Israel, calls the "triple A" facilitation approach: Aware, Allow, Address. This tool enables the negotiator to be aware of the emotional palette, to respect and allow the power and pertinence of emotions, and to acknowledge and address emotions as they emerge.

Emotions are an area that demands humility and mastery of the self. This includes willingness to be emotionally vulnerable, and an ability to retain composure in the face of strong emotional reactions of each and any party, as well as group dynamics.

Non-negotiables: Religion and values

Not every aspect of a conflict is negotiable. Religion and values, for example, are stronger than needs, stronger than emotions, and have no price tag. Religion can be defined as a cultural system that creates powerful and long-lasting meaning by establishing symbols that relate humanity to beliefs and values. Values are important and enduring beliefs or ideals shared by the members of a culture about what is good or desirable and what is not. Values exert a major influence on the behavior of an individual, and serve as broad guidelines in all situations.

Religious values and fundamentalism are sometimes embraced to help restore order and inner peace from the chaos of current times. They have an enormous impact on many negotiations. In a connected world, they can be the nemesis of even a brilliant negotiator. Raw edges are exposed; there is no perceived room for judgment; there is only right and wrong, as differently perceived by the parties. These are conditions of fragility and must be approached accordingly, especially when the parties' belief systems differ with those of others involved.

In some situations, there will be religious authority figures who are not directly involved but who can influence negotiations more than anyone else. Professional negotiators should help identify them and realize how they can be more than a source of information; they can also be a source of accessibility to negotiating parties. Humility in a negotiator is essential in addressing non-negotiables. The professional serves the process by honoring the religion and values of the partners to the negotiation. This is not an easy or immediate area of expertise, but rather rewards life experience.

Conflict transformation

Negotiation 1.0 provides "tips" for avoiding or reducing conflict by reframing disputes. What was conflict is now a misunderstanding, solvable through improved communication or adherence to common principles. However, conflict in negotiation cannot always be so easily dismissed. What Peter Coleman (2012) refers to as "the 5%" can become the Achilles heel of even top leaders, who then find a professional negotiator's contribution particularly critical. Advanced communication skills needed for this type of conflict resolution are derived, again, from a blend of confidence and humility, which allows transparency in conflict processing and management. Similarly, such a professional negotiator also must be able to assess when a third-party intervention is necessary for dispute resolution, and which type of third party would be most beneficial.

Multi-party negotiation

Multi-party negotiation is often taught in negotiation courses as an additional and optional means of advancing basic skills. However, multi-party negotiation is becoming more common and thus must become an expected part of negotiation training. This is partly a result of the increased level of connectedness in the world, with an increasing need to deal (often, without much time) with people very unlike yourself, and a consequently greater set of opportunities for fear and suspicion. The choice of a team rather than an individual negotiator offers valuable support in a world seen as threatening. Or, it may be a cultural habit to bring a team rather than appoint a lone negotiator. An inexperienced negotiator, who perceives a team approach as a "crutch" that is "unnecessary" may require guidance by a professional (see the Bosnia discussion by Calvin Chrustie in Gadlin, Matz, and Chrustie, *Playing the Percentages in Wicked Problems*, in this volume). Professional negotiators are also needed to advise on how to identify the potential for a coalition, and when and how to build or dissolve coalitions. Another area of expertise is understanding how group dynamics can be volatile and change from meeting to meeting. One vital skill is to help identify the roles parties assume, such as the leader, trouble-maker, joker, problem-solver, etc. Being sensitive to "groupthink" is also critical, even when that group has lots of past success stories.

Preparation for multi-party negotiations, especially when preparing a team, includes organizing data in order to influence the participants, timing, atmosphere, and place. This demands balancing empathy with assertiveness during negotiation, as well as sensitivity to direct and indirect communication within group dynamics – all of which reward long experience. More time is generally needed, also, than the parties may have budgeted for, if the negotiator is really to help limit misunderstanding and miscommunication. A negotiator who will have to play for that time, and therefore for more resources to be devoted to the effort, will find the sense of authority that comes from a long and successful previous career an advantage.

Section Two: Additional Issues

Leadership negotiation

Leadership negotiation (that is, negotiation about, by and among leaders) is distinct from that of directors and managers. A director focuses on goals and objectives, which often serve as functional models. A manager's focus is generally on overall systemic understanding of objectives. The leader, however, is charged with creativity and vision. The leader is required to see beyond the here and now. This creates a dynamic in which leaders of organizations are less likely to respond well to negotiators who are not seen as of comparable professional stature.

Particularly in light of the political considerations present in leadership negotiation, whatever the immediate topic, it is one of the most complex forms of negotiation. Professional negotiators become familiar with four different types of leaders, based on four styles of leadership:

1) Charismatic leadership, based on personality rather than credentials;
2) Status leadership, based on specific responsibilities;

3) Circumstantial leadership, based on context and immediate events; and

4) Enabling leadership, used to empower and support.

Professional negotiators in leadership negotiations clearly understand transparency, accountability, staff development, exposure impact, and awareness of internal and external politics. They provide this expertise in helping leaders improve negotiation outcomes. Again, this kind of expertise and the resulting credibility are difficult to acquire early in a career.

High-risk and crisis negotiation

Under stressful situations, external forces are at work and our control of reactions is limited. The quality of decision making is critical, because severe damage may be caused to the relationship and parties involved. When pressured, we tend to err and make decisions based on "optimistic overconfidence" (see Korobkin and Guthrie 2006), thinking that we have at our disposal all the necessary information and that we can rely on past experience and on our interpretation of the situation. However, this is often not the case, because stress tends to restrict abilities to accurately interpret complex situations. In particular, stress causes the physiological fight-flight-freeze reaction to take over, none of which are useful in negotiation. We cannot entirely control such basic reactions; but with training and experience, we can be aware of these reactions and of their influence on our train of thought. This then helps us to control impulses and avoid rash measures. Professional negotiators know that it is generally possible to negotiate for time[5] for constructive thinking and consulting. But do most ordinary negotiators have command of these skills? Probably not, we think.

There are ten components for negotiating crisis situations:

1) Team building experience relevant to the crisis situation;
2) Evaluation of risk in terms of what parties are capable of doing as evidenced through past behavior;
3) Assessment of advantages and disadvantages of time, such as time constraints;
4) Heightened need and intensity of communication, which includes collapsing physical distance between parties as emotional intensity rises;
5) "Second circle" influences from outside parties that may have a direct or indirect influence[6];
6) Leverage gained through attention to emotional, physical, or rational needs and dynamics;
7) Intermediaries who can be of assistance;

8) Interim agreements that help build trust;

9) Maintaining and monitoring progress by preserving achievements; and

10) Reducing stress by creating and announcing the final scene of negotiated outcomes.

How, we ask, is an early-career or part-time negotiator supposed to become competent at *that* list? And as noted above, in our chaotic reality of living in a "flat world," crisis and high-risk negotiations are more common than ever before. The abilities and sensibilities required will be increasingly relevant in business (Taylor and Donohue 2006) and in other environments well beyond the traditional crisis milieu.

Identifying Professional Negotiation Students: Not Everyone Can Negotiate, After All

Interest-based negotiation is an inspirational and powerful model for those who tend either to avoid conflict or to default into adversarial bargaining. Novice negotiators can indeed learn integrative bargaining alternatives through short courses, whether using classic simulations or the adventure learning and other tools developed in these volumes. The ideal students for professional negotiation programs, however, do not need this training now, if they ever did. (They may have identified inner traits and an inclination to negotiate from an early age.) Over time, either way, they have developed and internalized basic principles, interpersonal skills, and intuition about negotiation through personal and professional experience. This most likely means they are older and have demonstrated maturity through successfully meeting life challenges.[7]

While modern technology has introduced fabulous advances, YouTube and Facebook are not a replacement for life experience. Time, on the human relations level, is a force of nature that high tech has yet to alter. Simply put, a forty-year-old professional negotiator will have a greater repertoire to access than a negotiator twenty years his or her junior. The impact of interpersonal relations on negotiation is significant, and while there are those who are "wise beyond their years," most forty-year-olds will have explored and accrued more of this life-experience than almost any twenty-five-year-old fresh out of law or graduate school. Furthermore, a person's character is enriched by dealing with the challenges life throws his or her way, controversial or not. A more experienced negotiator may have richness of character proportionate to his or her time roaming the planet. Professional negotiation, with its extended parameters and demands, further reinforces the need to begin training, at the level we describe, with experienced professionals rather than novice negotiators.

A professional negotiation program, then, does not attempt to add information onto a blank slate,[8] but rather to *mentor* experienced students, in two ways. The first is by providing a framework and vocabulary of negotiation theory, practice, and ethics. The second is by cultivating the self-awareness and maturity that prove instrumental during difficult or challenging negotiations. Content for the first part consists of the analytic work already developed in the negotiation field, along with additional issues raised in this chapter. Each profession consists of theory, practice, and ethics, and certainly the groundwork of interest-based Negotiation 1.0, leading into the mass of knowledge that has been described for convenience in the RNT teaching series as Negotiation 2.0, is a logical starting point. The common denominator in professional negotiation remains that partners to the negotiation must be satisfied enough that they can live with the result; success means that neither the process nor outcome results in substantial negative fallout or residual hard feelings.[9]

In addition to teaching theory, practice, and ethics, however, professional education requires a second and parallel process of personal development. Much has been written about the former in our field, but insufficient attention has been given to the latter. Challenging negotiations, such as those that are more "wicked" than "tame,"[10] require not only explicit skills but also a maturity and ease of ego that are the outcome of time invested, hard-won experience (which is not the same thing), and a clear ethical code.

The Content of Professional Negotiation Training

Negotiation is not the only profession that requires specific training content, but also prior experience, demonstrated maturity and personal ethics, personal reflection, and ongoing practice opportunities. Professional graduate programs in other areas, such as business, often value prior work experience. Admissions committees in law, medicine, and social work evaluate ethics and maturity of each applicant. Helping professions, such as psychotherapy, require personal reflection and self-awareness in both educational and licensing credentialing. Ongoing practice opportunities are common in professional education, offered through clinics, field placements, internships, and apprenticeships. In the more "sink or swim" approach of cultural anthropology, students may be sent to a remote field site with little instruction, while in more technical professions, such as medicine and engineering, supervised placements are necessary. The exact structure may vary globally according to the national and regional contexts of graduate education, including norms about required hours of classroom versus practical experience, supervision and reflection, and the ability of a professional program to organize practice opportunities formally (such as clinics or short term contracts) rather than requiring students to be more entrepreneurial. But clearly what we are proposing differs more in degree than in kind from existing practice in a variety of fields.

In terms of procedure, professional negotiation programs could incorporate a combination of graduate seminar-type discussion and personal reflection with direct observation and practice. The purpose of the seminar would not be to present content as if negotiation were a topic new to the student, but rather to engage students in mastering and then dismantling and modifying negotiation frameworks and concepts. The dynamic would be similar to that described by Jayne Docherty (2010), presenting interest-based negotiation, and even some of the material developed in this project, more as a start to dialogue about how then to tailor these models to individual students and particular negotiation contexts. In such a model, the instructor is not the sole source of knowledge (and the outcome might help push further advances in negotiation theory and practice.)[11] Classroom discussion would also be used to debrief and share experiences following direct observation and participation in negotiation processes.

Although a student would be encouraged to share his or her past experiences based on memory, some form of clinic or field internship or residency would be ideal. In fact, practice experience should be the main part of training. This could also allow students who are expert in one field to develop familiarity with the terrain of others. For example, a student whose background was in a law firm might seek a placement with a police force, to learn the cultural context of a different profession, and how that impacts negotiation dynamics. An ideal program would attract students from a range of professional backgrounds to enrich understanding of variable negotiation dynamics, processes, and potential outcomes.

One of many logistical questions would be how many hours of direct observation and how many hours of supervised negotiation would be necessary to earn professional credentials. Significant time is needed not only to ensure quality of skill development, but also to allow students to develop their own personal style and mode of action through seminar discussion, practice debriefing, and personal reflection. Becoming a professional negotiator has quite a lot to do with the "self," and capacity for self-assessment is not as simple or natural as it may sound. Particularly in high-stakes situations, ego is a factor, demanding nurturing, but also development of advanced self-control, in such a way as to allow for a "day-after" that is sufficiently gratifying for all parties in the negotiation. (Any reader of a biographical description of a negotiator such as the late Richard Holbrooke – see, e.g., Cholett and Power 2011 – will recognize that this is not easy for a highly-talented practitioner to accomplish; indeed, above a certain level of quickness of mind and technical skill, it may become *more* difficult.)

What is the outcome of such an effort? As a profession, negotiation might follow the rituals and organizational forms of twentieth century professions, or pursue a more twenty-first century approach through social networking. These options are explored next.

Recognizing, Organizing, and Sustaining Negotiation as a Profession: Formalization or Networking?

Much has been written and discussed on the development and evaluation of formalizing practice into distinct professions. Early pioneers of alternative dispute resolution (ADR), for example, have both pointed to great success, evidenced by institutionalization, and lamented the loss of some originally hoped-for outcomes (Honeyman and Schneider 2004; Menkel-Meadow 2006). The professionalization process requires recognition and promotion of a distinct body of theory and knowledge, an area of practice, and a code of ethics. This chapter mainly addresses the "theory and practice" element, arguing for an integration of international negotiation expertise and cultural experience to develop a truly global profession. Ethics have been given less space here, as this discussion is preliminary, and have been addressed primarily in the context of non-negotiable values differences, along with the broad principle to "do no harm." One challenging question is how to develop a global code of ethics broad enough for diverse negotiation contexts, and whether the ethical principles of interest-based negotiation are simply too narrow a starting point for this task (see Docherty and Lira, *Adapting to the Adaptive*, in this volume; Pou 2003).

Another question is whether to follow twentieth century professionalization practices. This includes formation of a professional association supported by dues-paying members, conferences, and peer-reviewed journals, for purposes of networking and establishing authority over education and credentialing of those who carry professional titles. Once institutionalized, however, negotiation as a profession would face the same pressures that have led scholars to argue against such formalization, as resulting in a cycle of innovation, institutionalization, and capitulation "to the routine" (Honeyman, Ackerman, and Welsh 2003). (This concept includes both the dangers and the opportunities of routinization and bureaucracy.) Such a process could ironically lead negotiation to give up the hallmark of its own expertise – creative responses to ambiguity and conflict.

However, new social forms are emerging in the twenty-first century, as a result of new technologies. The internet and cell phones facilitate ongoing contact and easy access to information-sharing and publication. This means that global networks can be driven and sustained by the needs of members more than by the external control of a small group of leaders. Moreover, these technologies are changing relationships between producers and consumers, by inviting and sometimes requiring ongoing dialogue rather than singular production of an identified commodity. The news and entertainment *industries*, for example, no longer control news and entertainment as they did in the twentieth century, and adaptation has led to some creative results.[12] In the fields of international development and nonprofit work, social entrepreneurs are finding ways to succeed outside of formal institutions, in terms of both funding and organization (see Bornstein 2004). As a twenty-first century profession, global negotiation may be able to avoid the dangers of capitulation, given creative exploration of how technology can facilitate new forms of organization and sustainability. Sustaining global negotiation as a standalone practice then becomes itself another area of negotiation, rather than an obvious process of imitating existing professions.

Conclusion

Most of this chapter has been an argument for what should change in conceptualizing, teaching, and professionalizing negotiation. However, we do not propose a complete departure from the legacy of ADR and negotiation pioneers. Michael's proposal is for an evolution rather than revolution: this legacy began with recognizing negotiation as a distinct area of practice. Emphasis was placed on then teaching broad audiences how to improve this practice in both everyday and professional lives. The next step is in recognizing that negotiation as practiced by experts is also beneficial to broad audiences who might hire professionals for particularly important or challenging cases. This proposal, then, focuses not on how to bring the novice negotiator up to speed, but rather how to train professional negotiators who can then advise and guide others through the negotiation process. The role has something in common with Bernard Mayer's concept of a negotiation coach (Mayer 2004), though Mayer's version starts with a "professional neutral."

In keeping with the focus on context and culture in this series, Alexandra also notes that another need for this evolution lies in how the historical, political, and economic context that made interest-based negotiation so innovative and important in the world has changed. Roger Fisher often explained that he wrote *Getting to Yes* as a World War II veteran who wanted to teach an alternative to war. In the binary context of the Cold War, the global focus was on two nations whose approach to negotiation was underpinned by the rather simple concept of mutually assured destruction. In this context, interest-based negotiation, fleshed out by game theory, offered a necessary counter to adversarial bargaining that might result in nuclear war.

After about 1990, "Negotiation 1.0" thrived globally in U.S. foreign policy funding for democratic, civil society and anti-terrorism initiatives. The "Negotiation 1.0" legacy to some extent continues. However, the global context is also changing. As economic, technological, and demographic trends shape ever more complex international contexts, what were taught as basic negotiation variables such as "who are the parties," "what do they want," and "how should we evaluate success" may themselves require ongoing negotiation. The continuing need for innovation in and impact of negotiation as a field now requires bringing context and cultural variations at a high professional level into negotiation concepts, teaching, and practice. This proposal is one option. We welcome dialogue on it, and on others.

Notes

[1] While the success of Negotiation 1.0 may seem like manifest destiny today, Bruce Patton wrote a PON working paper about the struggle to convince the faculty of Harvard Law School that negotiation *could* be taught (Patton 1984). This struggle was won in part by inviting criticism and dialogue about the model as it developed.

[2] In other words, not everyone becomes a professional negotiator because not everyone responds to opportunities and challenges with a negotiation temperament or mindset.

[3] See Taylor and Donohue (2006) as to why, from a professional skills point of view, these situations occur quite often in business, not just in violent bank robberies or terrorist attacks and the like.

[4] See generally chapters 24-27 in *Venturing Beyond the Classroom* (Honeyman, Coben, and De Palo 2010: 439-528), where the authors used the term "wicked" to describe problems that exhibit some combination of the following features: the problem is ill-defined and resists clear definition as a technical issue; each problem contains an interconnected web of sub-problems; merely defining the problem can incite passionate conflict. Solutions to a wicked problem cannot be labeled good or bad; they can only be considered better or worse, good enough or not good enough; and every proposed solution to part or the whole of the wicked problem will affect other problems in the web.

[5] Jack Cambria, commanding officer of the hostage negotiation team of the New York City Police Department (NYPD) offers the following insight (Cambria et al. 2002: 338):

> Bob Louden [former chief hostage negotiator, NYPD] . . . was negotiating a rather difficult, very long and ongoing hostage situation. The chief of detectives said, 'Hey Louden, seems like you aren't

having any success here.' Bob said, 'I think we are.' The chief says 'What's your definition of success then?' Bob says 'Lack of failure.'

[6] As noted by Maria Volpe and colleagues (2006), hostage negotiation is far from the only circumstance in which the person responsible for a negotiation must somehow report to difficult supervisors, who may try to micromanage a job and too often do not appreciate the intricacies, the need for patience and the time inevitably involved in making talk work. But in a police department, the hierarchy is overt and often insistent. There could easily be a district commander in the offing, saying "I don't have any time for this, this guy is blocking traffic," or resenting the fact that the case happened on their watch, because there is a meeting to go to, or theater tickets to be considered. Hostage takers, however, cannot be told to come back tomorrow. The role of the coordinator is therefore to handle all of the *external* negotiations that threaten to disrupt the all-important negotiation "at the door." (When Hugh McGowan, one of the co-authors of the 2006 book chapter, was promoted to NYPD chief negotiator, he was informed that that did not mean that he got to negotiate any time he wanted. It meant he got to negotiate with the Chief – a significantly less desirable and more challenging honor.)

[7] This description is very similar to the "wise elder" described in anthropological research about dispute settlement in "traditional" societies (see, e.g., Gibbs 1963). Although this wise elder concept was part of the early ADR movement in the United States (Crampton 2005: 231-232), emphasis on identifying and training local leaders has generally been replaced by training professionals in other fields, or volunteers, who have no presumed prior experience or demonstrated expertise.

[8] Or to civilize Rousseau's "noble savage."

[9] This corresponds to common professional codes of ethics to "do no harm" as a first principle. For a longer treatment of hoped-for outcomes and some typical blockages, see Wade and Honeyman (2006).

[10] See supra endnote 4 for description of "wicked" problems. "Tame" problems, as summarized by Ritchey (2005-2008:1) have relatively well-defined stable problem statements that belong to a similar class of problems, which can be solved in a similar manner; a definite stopping point, so all know when a solution is reached; and a solution that can be objectively evaluated as right or wrong. See also chapters 24-26 in *Venturing Beyond the Classroom* (Honeyman, Coben, and De Palo 2010: 439-509), and chapters 17-21 in this volume.

[11] Jayne Docherty (2010) contrasts Paulo Freire's description of a "banking model," seen as typical in formal education, in which teachers deposit information directly into students as whole chunks of content, with the need for greater humility from the instructor and willingness to let students modify content according to their interests and expertise. This approach reflects changes in higher education pedagogy today known as "student-centered learning" – reflected in a number of writings in this series.

[12] Here we are thinking of the paradoxical success of allowing consumers to comment on, and even contribute to, creative direction – in the past, few could produce music or mass media publications without the resources of the entertainment or news publishing industry. Now, content creators often follow the lead from consumers – and still maintain a sense of originality (and still make a lot of money).

References

Bornstein, D. 2004. *How to change the world: Social entrepreneurs and the power of new ideas*. New York, NY: Oxford University Press.

Cambria, J., R. J. DeFilippo, R. J. Louden, and H. McGowan. 2002. Negotiation under extreme pressure: The "mouth marines" and the hostage takers. *Negotiation Journal* 18(4): 331-344.

Chollet, D. and S. Power. 2011. *The unquiet American: Richard Holbrooke in the world*. Philadelphia, PA: Perseus Book Group.

Coleman, P. 2011. *The five percent: Finding solutions to seemingly impossible conflicts*. New York: Public Affairs.

Coleman, P. 2012. Getting down to basics: A situated model of conflict in social relations. *Negotiation Journal* 28(1): 7-43.

Crampton, A. 2005. Addressing questions of culture and power in the globalization of ADR: Lessons from African influence on American mediation. *Hamline Journal of Public Law & Policy* 27(2): 229-242.

Crampton, A. 2008. Teaching negotiation as cross-cultural work: An anthropological view. *Teaching Negotiation* 1(2). Available at http://archive.constantcontact.com/fs079/1101638633053/archive/1102183104329.html (last accessed June 15, 2012).

Docherty, J. S. 2010. "Adaptive" negotiation: Practice and teaching. In *Venturing beyond the classroom: Volume 2 in the rethinking negotiation teaching series*, edited by C. Honeyman, J. Coben, and G. De Palo. St Paul, MN: DRI Press.

Fisher, R., W. Ury, and B. Patton. 1991. *Getting to yes. Negotiating agreement without giving in*, 2nd edn. New York: Penguin.

Gibbs, J. L. 1963. The Kpelle moot: A therapeutic model for the informal settlement of disputes. *Africa: Journal of the International African Institute* 33(1): 1-11.

Honeyman, C., R. Ackerman, and N. A. Welsh (eds). 2003. Compilation of 17 articles, responding to the Broad Field Project/Penn State Dickinson Law School 2003 conference on threats to the conflict resolution field. Special issue, *Penn State Law Review* 108(1): 1-348.

Honeyman, C., J. Coben, and G. De Palo (eds). 2010. *Venturing beyond the classroom: Volume 2 in the rethinking negotiation teaching series*. St. Paul, MN: DRI Press.

Honeyman, C. and A. K. Schneider. Catching up with the major-general: The need for a "canon of negotiation." *Marquette Law Review* 87: 637-647.

Knauft, B. 1996. *Genealogies for the present in cultural anthropology*. New York, NY: Routledge.

Kolb, D. and J. Williams. 2000. *The shadow negotiation: How women can master the hidden agendas that determine bargaining success*. New York: Simon & Schuster.

Korobkin, R. and C. Guthrie. 2006. Heuristics and biases at the bargaining table. In *The negotiator's fieldbook: The desk reference for the experienced negotiator*, edited by A. K. Schneider and C. Honeyman. Washington, DC: American Bar Association.

Mayer, B. 2004. *Beyond neutrality: Confronting the crisis in conflict resolution*. San Francisco: Jossey-Bass.

Menkel-Meadow, C. 2006. Why hasn't the world gotten to yes? An appreciation and some reflections. *Negotiation Journal* 22(4): 485-503.

Patera, M. and U. Gamm. 2010. Emotions – a blind spot in negotiation training? In *Venturing beyond the classroom: Volume 2 in the rethinking negotiation teaching series*, edited by C. Honeyman, J. Coben and G. De Palo. St Paul, MN: DRI Press.

Patton, B. 1984. On teaching negotiation. Program on Negotiation Working Paper, Harvard Law School (updated in 2000 with commentary and included in *Teaching negotiation: Ideas and innovations*, edited by M. Wheeler. Cambridge, MA: PON Books).

Pou, C. 2003. "Embracing limbo": Thinking about rethinking dispute resolution ethics. *Penn State Law Review* 108(1): 199-225.

Ritchey, T. 2005-2008. *Wicked problems: Structuring social messes with morphological analysis*. Swedish Morphological Society. Available at www.swemorph.com/wp.html (last accessed June 15, 2012).

Schneider, A. K., S. Cheldelin, and D. Kolb. 2010. What travels: Teaching gender in cross-cultural negotiation classrooms. In *Venturing beyond the classroom: Volume 2 in the rethinking negotiation teaching series*, edited by C. Honeyman, J. Coben, and G. De Palo. St Paul, MN: DRI Press.

Taylor, P. J. and W. Donohue. 2006. Hostage negotiation opens up. In *The negotiator's fieldbook: The desk reference for the experienced negotiator*, edited by A. K. Schneider and C. Honeyman. Washington, DC: American Bar Association.

Tinsley, C. H., S. I. Cheldelin, A. K. Schneider, and E. T. Amanatullah. 2009. Negotiating your public identity: Women's path to power. In *Rethinking negotiation teaching: Innovations for context and culture*, edited by C. Honeyman, J. Coben, and G. De Palo. St Paul, MN: DRI Press.

Volpe, M., J. J. Cambria, H. McGowan, and C. Honeyman. 2006. Negotiating with the unknown. In *The negotiator's fieldbook: The desk reference for the experienced negotiator*, edited by A. K. Schneider and C. Honeyman. Washington, DC: American Bar Association.

Wade, J. H. and C. Honeyman. 2006. A lasting agreement. In *The negotiator's fieldbook: The desk reference for the experienced negotiator*, edited by A. K. Schneider and C. Honeyman. Washington, DC: American Bar Association.

∽ 26 ∾

The Education of Non-Students

Eric Blanchot, Noam Ebner, Christopher Honeyman, Sanda Kaufman & Rachel Parish*

Editors' Note: Most people do not take courses – yet they learn new things and change their attitudes and behavior all the time. So far, with some exceptions, our field has taken little advantage of informal avenues for education. This concluding chapter explores how we might foster social change toward better attitudes in negotiation, using various media far outside the classroom setting (electronic games, film and other visual materials, and theater) that can serve as platforms for informal negotiation education. The authors believe our field needs not one or two, but an array of such approaches.

* **Eric Blanchot** is a mediator and a documentary filmmaker based in Paris; he also teaches negotiation and conflict management for the United Nations Institute for Training and Research (UNITAR) and at the Sorbonne, the Ecole Nationale d'Administration, and several other French universities. His email address is ericblanchot@gmail.com. **Noam Ebner** is assistant professor at Creighton University School of Law, where he chairs the online master's program in negotiation and dispute resolution. His email address is noamebner@ creighton.edu. **Christopher Honeyman** is managing partner of Convenor Conflict Management, a consulting firm based in Washington, DC and Madison, Wisconsin. He has directed a twenty-year series of major research-and-development projects in conflict management, including as co-director of the Rethinking Negotiation Teaching project. His email address is honeyman@convenor.com. **Sanda Kaufman** is a professor of planning, public policy and administration at Cleveland State University's Levin College of Urban Affairs. Her research spans negotiation, intervention, framing and intractability in public conflicts, participation in public decisions, decision analysis, risk communication, and program evaluation. Her email address is s.kaufman@csuohio.edu. **Rachel Parish** is artistic director of Firehouse Creative Productions, a London-based theater company which specializes in collaborative theater. Her email address is rachel.parish@ googlemail.com.

Introduction

The title of the second book in the *Rethinking Negotiation Teaching* series hinted at a reality which even the contributors were, perhaps, not yet prepared to address. For all its innovations, *Venturing Beyond the Classroom* (Honeyman, Coben, and De Palo 2010) was based almost without debate on an underlying assumption which, with an additional year or two of reflection, we now find rather limiting: that education takes place primarily *in* the classroom, whether literally or metaphorically. Admittedly, even for a project that has been described as ambitious, there had to be a limit to what was considered within its scope. We still think that focusing on formal teaching, and organized training of adults in executive-style courses has been productive. Yet the final works of this series would be incomplete if we did not at least attempt to explore what is missing.

Even while challenging traditional practice, the *Rethinking Negotiation Teaching* project has implicitly adopted a set of assumptions which might be summarized like this: everybody negotiates – for jobs, in jobs, for goods and services, within their family, and on and on – wherever joint decisions are necessary. People need to know how to do it, or they will do it badly (i.e., leaving resources on the table, harming relationships, missing opportunities and worse). We teach negotiation. Therefore, if we teach good courses – well-designed and well-executed to change attitudes about conflict and negotiation as well as to provide concrete technical skills – those who sign up will become better negotiators, and their own interests as well as society's will be advanced.

Of course, many of our project participants have questioned whether "good" courses can actually be delivered in the one- to five-day seminar structure typical of the contemporary executive-style training world. But the larger challenge we have barely begun to address is what to do if "students" *don't* sign up for any course, short or long. And, in fact, they mostly don't: what we consider a burgeoning student population in our field is but a small fraction of the total population. Based on the numbers we know, even in the United States – the home of organized teaching of negotiation and allied elements of conflict management – it appears highly unlikely that more than one percent of the working population has ever taken any such course.

Even the most classroom-bound teacher knows that human beings do not learn only in classrooms, or even in teacher-organized settings outside the classroom. Indeed, people learn new skills and change their perceptions all the time. And the vast majority of this attitudinal change and skill development occurs at some remove from formal "teachers" or "trainers." Examples of such learning are all around us.

An obvious example of informal learning is use of the Internet. Around 1994, for example, one of the chapter authors found himself tasked by his then employer, a government agency, with developing a strategy that would ensure effective adoption of new computer technology by his professional peers, a notoriously independent-minded bunch of mediator-arbitrators. He began by conducting a survey of his colleagues' attitudes towards new technology and of their willingness to engage with it. He discovered a phenomenon he had not previously encountered: a distribution of responses that looked like an inverted bell curve with one arm shorter than the other. This meant that attitudes towards technology among this particular professional group were sharply divided, with a few people willing to try anything once and use it again if it worked, a much larger group who would resist using any new technology until dragged into it kicking and screaming, and virtually no one in the middle. Yet only three years later, the entire group was using the Internet on a regular basis.

What happened? Did management threaten, with a directive laden with draconian penalties for noncompliance? Were courses organized, scheduled conveniently and taught by brilliant and enthusiastic trainers? Were those who took such courses rewarded with degrees or certificates? Not a bit. Instead, day-by-day, month-by-month, the culture changed,[1] both internally among a rather inward-focused group and externally.

Internet usage is largely a matter of adoption of technical innovation, and therefore might be expected to follow the Rogers bell-curve model of diffusion of innovation (see, e.g., Rogers and Shoemaker 1971); however,[2] there are other instances of rapid percolation of attitude change, such as some overtly political issues that go through a similar transformation. One example is the recent change in U.S. public attitudes toward gay rights. Strident opposition to gay rights held public attention for quite a while. It was front-and-center in several conservative strategies for winning state and federal office as recently as the mid-2000s. Yet in the last five years as of this writing, the public perception of this issue – even in its most controversial form, marriage – has gone through a startling transformation. By mid-2012, in a hotly political season in the United States, conservative campaign speeches have made only the most perfunctory mention of the issue. Even the most stalwart of the anti-gay rights candidates appear to have concluded that the issue is at best a distraction and at worst a vote-loser among the population at large. Meanwhile, the military, at one time the locus of much debate in this area, has adopted new policies with what amounts, in a huge bureaucracy, to crisp dispatch. In short, sentiment seems to have shifted in American society with surprising suddenness.

Neither of these examples of attitude change can be credited to public education, at least in any version of formal teaching and training. There are courses on gay rights in universities; but from casual observation, it is not a random cross-section of the student population that signs up for them. Many employers, as well as schools, offer training in the use of computers. But is that how you, the reader, actually came to use the Internet? We suspect not. In fact, for a while it was a standing joke of family life that the six-year-old child was better at using the Internet than the adults; but school computer courses in most schools do not start in kindergarten.

If formal education and training have only limited reach in the change of some social attitudes and widespread learning of some new technical skills alike, what is doing the main job? One answer, explicated below, is informal education – learning without obvious, direct intervention by a teacher. This approach to learning is something our field has rarely used strategically (with honorable exceptions, e.g., the community-based work John Paul Lederach (2005) describes in *The Moral Imagination*). A number of other fields and disciplines, however, have already recognized the potential influence of informal education in social change, and have invested significantly in research to establish what works and how. We do not need to reinvent this wheel.

What Can We Learn From Other Domains?

Making effective use of research in fields other than negotiation requires making some distinctions to which our field is not yet accustomed; for example, *informal* education is not the same thing as *nonformal* education, though in casual use even professionals often allow these terms to overlap (NAAEE 2004: 36). Education (away from school) can range from a closely-directed experience to one that allows the learner a great deal of choice. Either can be effective if good learning design is observed. Examples of this range might include shopping-mall displays vs. museum displays; public television vs. commercial television; or social marketing vs. commercial advertising. In each pair, either may have an educational effect; but one carries an explicit educational goal, while the other does not. When education *is* an explicit goal, it is more likely to be reached if it has clear and specific objectives and uses accurate information and effective teaching strategies.

Nonformal education refers to education that is not part of a formal certification or degree program. The term is also often used to refer to learning which takes place away from school facilities but that may address formal schooling requirements, or be part of an organized sequence of educational activities or resources designed to reach specified objectives.

Informal education or *free-choice learning* refers to the learning that occurs when people choose what, when, how and why to learn without any obvious intervention by a teacher.[3] People learn when they watch TV, visit a museum, read instructions for how to do something, talk with their neighbors, etc. According to the Institute for Learning Innovation,[4] free-choice learning is "the most common type of lifelong learning" and is "self-motivated and guided by the needs and interests of the learner."[5] Significantly, it is also often the result of an activity in which people engage without necessarily having a conscious desire to "learn" something, at least as they would describe the experience. Most people do not go to see *Macbeth* because they want to "learn" about ambition or murder.

In the context of this chapter, the *free choice* characterization is key to any strategy we might devise for delivering conflict management content. But learning goals can be incorporated into many life experiences when they are designed by a group/team that includes the necessary combination of expertise – a subject matter specialist, an educator, an audience representative.[6] Our means of delivery must reach people where they are, at least in terms of the delivery platforms – web, social media, TV, movies, theater, newspapers – they visit for information and entertainment. To reach its target, free choice information has to be meaningful to the learners; meet learners' needs; be at an appropriate skill and knowledge level; and challenge learners within the scope of their existing experience and skills.

As discussed in much of the writing in all four volumes of this project, we especially need to match the diversity of cultures, but different ages and to some extent genders may also demand specialized approaches. (It is not for naught that commercial broadcasting typically identifies the strongest market for a given TV show very specifically as, for instance, females between twenty-nine and forty-five years of age.) This means no single modality is apt to suffice or always succeed. If we are to see changes in the ways people relate to each other to resolve conflicts productively and nonviolently, we need a multiplicity of avenues and vehicles carrying consistent messages to that effect. Therefore, the design of an education experience for free-choice learning must consider many of the same criteria that are important to all education programs – from the point of view that the learner has the freedom to choose whether to participate or withdraw at any moment. Educators need to organize an experience that answers the question: What will attract and *keep on attracting* the learner to this opportunity sufficiently for the messages to be adopted (learned)?

It is worth noting that the research on free-choice learning is extensive: almost every noun in the preceding paragraphs is a term of art which has been defined rigorously, studied, and strategized in depth. Our field can only benefit from paying more attention to this existing research. In general, however, we propose that people absorb new information and change their attitudes by drawing upon a wide variety of "free-choice" sources, such as the popular press or entertainment industry, and therefore these are likely to become effective venues for broad transfer of negotiation knowledge and skills.[7]

The chapter authors have worked with particular forms of informal education in some depth. We have all noticed the power of electronic media, TV shows, films and theater to disseminate new ideas rapidly and broadly until they become mainstream, as well as to shape attitudes. We explore here what some of these media might contribute to the dissemination of wise negotiation practices. We will focus our analysis on the potential roles of electronic games, film, and theater, in that order. Is it possible that these, perhaps in combination with other media/venues not yet on our horizon, might be employed in some strategic way to improve skills and change attitudes about conflict and its management?

Games as a Vehicle for Informal Negotiation Education

One of the leading pedagogical methods used in formal negotiation education is *play*. Role-play, an imaginative childhood pursuit, is also a specific educational technique used among adults. In fact, simulation games and role-plays are the primary learning method negotiation teachers name when explaining how students come to acquire knowledge and skills in their classes (e.g., Alexander and LeBaron 2009; Druckman and Ebner 2010; Ebner and Kovach 2010). Role-play is only one form of play, however. As Johan Huizinga (1950: 1) put it in the opening to his seminal book *Homo Ludens*, "[p]lay is older than culture, for culture, however inadequately defined, always presupposes human society, and animals have not waited for man to teach them their playing." Huizinga goes on to say that:

> It (play) is a *significant* function – that is to say, there is some sense to it. In play there is something "at play" which transcends the immediate needs of life and imparts meaning to the action. All play means something (1950: 1).

What is play? It consists of a broad group of interactive experiences often incorporating some "serious" (life-like) elements: dominance, interdependence, strength, creativity and more. The presence of these elements allows players to focus on them perhaps more than is possible in real situations, to assess their own skills, and to become adept at assessing others' abilities. Through testing in play, we hone our real-life skills for dealing with these same elements, or for recognizing and getting around difficult situations where necessary. In that sense, play often provides training for real-life tasks.[8] For example, children play hide-and-seek, tag or other games that incorporate elements of stealth and speed, of chase and evasion. These games are similar to real preparation for the hunt, or for the battlefield, which is likely their evolutionary source. They serve valuable purposes for members of developed societies as well, for example by providing an opportunity for individuals and groups to build self-esteem – as do other, more complicated competitive games such as chess, or Go. Thus some kinds of play offer children and adults the opportunity to develop abilities needed to survive and overcome obstacles in interactions with others.

Games as a Type of Play

In this section we look at play involving *interactive* pursuits that allow for fairly direct learning of negotiation elements. We focus on games, because millions of people engage in games whose outcome hinges on two or more players' choices. Role-play and simulations fall in this category. Salen and Zimmerman (2003: 80) define such games as "…a system in which players engage in an artificial conflict, defined by rules, that results in a quantifiable outcome." Clark Abt's (1970) definition is even more germane to our purposes: "A game is an *activity* among two or more independent *decision-makers* seeking to achieve their *objectives* in some *limiting context*." Other authors note that a win/lose outcome is in the very nature of the activity. For instance, according to Elliot Avedon and Brian Sutton-Smith (1971: 405) games require *"a contest between powers, confined by rules in order to produce a disequilibrial outcome."* The game rules that lead to winner/loser dynamics are those allowing players to intervene in each other's actions, to interfere and to attack, as each tries to pursue individual goals. Interference is of the essence in differentiating games from other activities. As Chris Crawford put it, if the player can only out*perform* the opponents, but not attack them to interfere with their performance, the *conflict* is a *competition* rather than a *game* (2003: 8). Thus, a race, a spelling-bee or a hammer-toss are competitions, whereas wrestling, Monopoly or World of Warcraft are games. Therefore, most games are not only inherently competitive but extremely so, as each participant seeks both to maximize his own "take" and to downgrade the opponents' takes. Consequences for the use of games in informal negotiation education will be discussed next (see also Falçao 2012).

In determining which of these categories of play – competitions or games – might be more conducive to inclusion in negotiation education, games enjoy clear advantages over competitions. In the latter, the low level of interaction involved allows for only limited negotiation-type behavior – though competitors sometimes negotiate the rules of the competition, or rulings in the competition. Games provide a high level of interaction and a rich tapestry of elements incorporating, mimicking or reflecting negotiation kinds of behavior. At times, the explicit and implicit rules of the game have to be negotiated; parties are constantly trying, directly and indirectly, to achieve their own outcome even at the expense of others. Whether this is accomplished by brute force, dexterity, quick thinking or eloquent persuasion depends on the nature of the game and the characters involved – just as it does in real negotiation settings.

Thus games offer interesting opportunities for informal education. While they might reach anyone playing games, they especially get to those who play most – children and youth This seems promising for furthering the goals of our field.

Electronic Games

By far the newest of potential informal education vehicles, electronic games have a dubious record, with respect to our field. There is no getting around the fact that some electronic games have been so violent as to sicken adults with a sensitive disposition. Some researchers claim that the widespread use of such games by children and teenagers has created *negative* social capital. Others counter that children can tell the difference between games and reality, and that such games offer a harmless and necessary avenue for expending natural but violent impulses that would otherwise find expression in real contexts (for a helpful review of this literature, see Barlett, Anderson, and Swing 2009).[9] Either way, this debate supports our point: if it is possible to design electronic games either to cause adverse social consequences or to allow some people's violent tendencies to be safely expressed, then the proposition that people learn *something* from games is confirmed. Ironically, the technical learning that occurs when kids use a computer joystick to control fighters and spacecraft in games on the screen may have found a rather grim application in the drones that are replacing expensive fighter aircraft and are "piloted" from a distance, by young operators thoroughly trained on joysticks.[10]

Two kinds of games are being advanced for purposes consistent with ours. We owe the first kind to computer industry innovators such as Jane McGonigal (2011), who are designing games that, besides being exciting and therefore marketable, are also socially constructive. These games include elements encouraging environmental mindfulness and promoting in-game or real-world collaboration by fostering norms under which players, who are also creators of scenarios and designs, allow other players to use their creations. The second kind of game is discussed in Chapter 2, describing a current effort to introduce a complex new form of game that encourages stakeholders in major public disputes to base their arguments on ascertainable facts, rather than passing off bogus allegations as factual (Honeyman et al., The "Deliberation Engine," in this volume).

The game format for delivering informal education has some advantages particularly rooted in the current fascination with electronic technology, the platform for their broad dissemination. It is not just the young who covet the latest in electronic technology. Nor is this technology available only to the moneyed elite or to the Western world. Increasingly, the young in many places around the globe have never known a world without computers or other electronic devices, or even without social media.[11]

Since we can be reasonably confident that when using electronic devices we can hold the attention of our informal education targets, it is incumbent on us to produce or make use of material – whether short YouTube movies, games, or Second Life experiences – that is well-matched to electronic media, and to offer it in venues frequented by our desired audience. There is precedent for successful delivery of games through social media: Facebook has managed not only to engage numerous members in various games, but even to get them to pay for the experience. Similarly, smartphones and tablets offer game apps that can be played individually or with friends. For instance, Scrabble has gained a new lease on life as an app; new games of strategy with exciting graphics get the competitive juices flowing among young and old alike. Scrabble is not the only board game that has been adapted to social media: Carcassonne, for example, is a captivating strategy game played in a medieval context. Invented in 2000 as a board game, it has crossed successfully into the app world.

But there's the rub, not unlike in film and theater (described below): most games, in any medium, are fueled by the *competitive* spirit of players, and in turn fuel the culture of competitiveness. While competition is appropriate for many games, it has become a reflexive strategy, too often misapplied to real conflicts. We seek to promote some life skills that may not be as exciting, but are likely to affect our reality for the better. In fact we, the academics and professionals singing the virtues of cooperation, need to compete – yes, *compete* – with the prevailing competition messages so successfully disseminated electronically.

We are receiving some welcome technological assistance from the advances that enable people at different geographic locations to play multi-party games. We are left with the challenge of inventing or adapting some games where "winning" (doing as well for oneself as possible) can *only* be achieved through coalitions and by making sure other participants also do well – the very essence of integrative negotiations. One of the chapter authors, Eric Blanchot, uses such a game (*Diplomacy*) in courses he teaches. There are already other games encouraging integrative solutions, even if their underlying framework is not necessarily conducive to cooperation. (The few attempts at *purely* cooperative negotiation games that limit opportunities for competition have not had commercial success; one example is a project in France in the 1980s.)[12] The models that might present the most interest for our purposes may be certain board games, such as *Republic of Rome*,[13] and online role-playing games. In the former, the players (usually four or more) represent a senatorial family in ancient Rome attempting to accede to power at the expense of others; but if Rome is destroyed in the process, all lose. Players must therefore help each other to deal with any external challenges. Thus the game is based on the principle of "competitive associates."

The principle underlying certain online role-plays is that a "master of the game" is in charge of the universe within which players are immersed. The goal is not to win, but rather to survive, solve problems, and make progress. To that end, a player must necessarily associate with *and cooperate with* a group of other players, even if from time to time the player might give in to the temptation to compete. While as far as we know, it is unlikely that the game creators ever thought of their system as potentially conducive to the development of awareness of the benefits of integrative bargaining, we see a strong and as yet underexploited potential. This principle also underlies some multi-player games where cooperation in the selection of tasks can greatly facilitate the characters' survival. We discuss next some ways in which games could be used for informal negotiation education.

Improving Game-Playing for Negotiation Skills

What needs to be incorporated into play designed to enhance negotiation skills? We suggest that for learning to happen, games must include *at least one* of the following:[14]

- A *feedback loop* that gives players information about their negotiation-related actions, and about their effects. Feedback might come in the form of rewards and penalties built into the rules, of peer commentary, or of external input. The clearer the feedback, and the more fine-tuned and specific it can be, the more directly the connection can be made between the game and negotiation skills. In that sense, external input (such as by a watchful parent) might be the most effective. However, as any parent knows, interfering in players' entertainment risks backfiring, by decreasing their motivation to engage in the game.

- *An overt negotiation theme*: if players know that negotiation is a key part of the game, they might be better able to draw their own conclusions from their iterated experiences. One might imagine a game called *Plea Bargain!*, where players take on the roles of a criminal and the police, or of a convict and a prosecutor. Participants negotiate with each other for treatment and sentencing, within predetermined constraints (e.g., type of offense committed, degree and value of the accused convict's cooperation, maximum and minimum penalties). Such a game does not require a formalized feedback loop; rather, action and reaction might suffice. Players will intuitively try out different negotiation approaches with multiple counterparts, and figure out for themselves what works. The challenge is to design the game in such a way that players are intuitively able to understand the transferability to reality of what they learn by playing the game.

- *A clear negotiation element*: a game might require one player to receive another's permission in order to do something of importance in the game, with some ability to be punished or rewarded for compliance. For example, a player who lands on another player's territory must either negotiate for the owner's permission to continue, or be docked for three turns. (The player wishing to continue might offer points or other resources, or threaten retaliation, in order to secure the other's cooperation.)

- A *guide to implementing negotiation tools*: games' instructions often contain information on how to perform well in the game. These instructions might include explicit recommendations for negotiation behavior. Picture, for example, the possible effects of changing the instruction guide to *Monopoly* to include a section on "three recommended negotiation approaches."

The Future of Gaming

Before we explore the use of computer games for informal negotiation education, we need to address the following question: Do electronic games provide a suitable environment for developing negotiation skills, given the nature of human-computer, as opposed to human-human interactions?

At first glance, human-computer interactions seem to contain a limited set of negotiation-type interactions. Indeed, early hand-held electronic games in which players faced off against the machine provided no such opportunities (with the exception, of course, of the game's owner needing to deal with requests from friends to "have a game," allowing for patterns of bargaining, reciprocity and log-rolling). However, gamers did not wait long before sophisticated artificial intelligence provided them with a more life-like interaction partner with whom to play. Very quickly, two-player interactive hand-held games were developed (such as *Head-to-Head Football*, introduced by Coleco in 1980, or even *BLIP* – a 1977 two-player electronic game manufactured by TOMY in which two players play catch). These games reintroduced the interactive, social element so characteristic of traditional games, as players not only contested on the screen, but also used body language and words to affect the game, and even jockeyed physically for control of the console itself.

Early games designed for gaming consoles and computers continued with the single-player/multiple-players duality. In two-player mode, however, many games allowed for players to either take each other on, or team up and cooperate[15] against the active agent provided by the computer.

The social element of computer gaming received a boost with the advent of mass multiplayer online role-playing games (MMORPGs). The level of negotiation interaction went up. Gamers might be sitting alone in their separate rooms, but they operate together with their tribes, clans, squads or armies, whose other members are frequently available for real-time conversation by chat or by voice through the game platform. To give a sense for just how wide this pool of interactions might be, we note that the most popular MMORPG, *World of Warcraft*, has a "population" of eleven million players. In a game at this scale, introducing elements of negotiation education might have significant effects.

Looking ahead, we see several trends for the potential to create spaces into which negotiation pedagogy might make inroads. One such trend is the increasing sophistication of artificial intelligence engines. The more the computer can interact "humanly" with the player, the more opportunities there can be for negotiation-like interactions. As games develop to allow emotions and thoughts to be expressed and affect game play (see, for example, QuanticDream's *Heavy Rain*, developed for the Sony's PlayStation 3 system), and as they are programmed to recognize, and react to, a variety of player inputs, these interactions will become increasingly common. Then computer games can be used for negotiation education in some of the ways we have explored, especially when coupled with the trend for Internet-based games to include the option of playing with others, whether friends or strangers.

Another trend is to "gameify" an increasing number of Internet activities. The incorporation of games into social networks to create "social network games" – such as *CityVille* on Facebook, with over eighty million registered players – has made games into social activities where the interaction may be, for many, more important than the outcome (see Wohn 2011). This is a step in our direction as we seek to informally build negotiation skills. This trend can be coupled with the more recent addition of gaming (as a layer of excitement) to more serious-minded, large-scale online activities. One very recent example is *Empire Avenue* (www.empireavenue.com). Participants seek to increase their own "share price," which is determined by their social capital as measured by the level of their online activity in terms of posts, tweets, blogs, etc. As players' share value increases, they receive rewards in game currency, status symbols and advanced game capabilities.

Another example of adding gaming to attract and retain participants in otherwise "serious" activities is in the Khan Academy (www. khanacademy.org) materials, also mentioned in the film and visual media section below. The Khan Academy offers a wide array of educational YouTube videos, each explaining a discrete element of math, physics, history, etc., as well as a map for proceeding from one lesson to the next. K-12 students can engage actively with the educational materials. Teachers can follow (in real time) the students who are practicing the concepts they have learned, and can pay them individual attention, either by helping with a question with which they are struggling, or by asking a student who has successfully completed that question to assist others. Students can help learners at their own level or below, not only in their classroom but anywhere in the world. Gameifying this system increases motivation and participation: in addition to earning "energy points" and badges for efforts and success in completing study tasks, students can earn additional levels and status symbols by tutoring others (Khan 2011). In this example too, the nature of emerging interactions among students assisting each other while striving/competing for rewards lends itself to informal negotiation education.

These examples signal the potential inherent in gameifying serious endeavors, such as the Deliberation Engine discussed elsewhere in this volume (Honeyman et al., *The "Deliberation Engine"*). Games are likely to be more effective in informal education for players than for spectators. Yet there is an art form that has conveyed informal education on a mass scale without the active participation element. Film has shown that learning *is* possible even when relatively passive – at least in terms of attitude changes, if not necessarily in terms of skill development.

Film (and Other Visual Materials on Various Platforms)

We have just over a hundred years of experience with movies as an art form. Throughout its history, film has proven effective in reaching large audiences, even across cultures. When they have been able to cross censorship barriers, movies have communicated to closed and oppressed societies, such as the Eastern Bloc countries, images of a freedom the audience could not experience themselves at the time. It is widely believed that these images helped to foster resistance, creating in the public mind the all-important concepts and possibilities without which regime change would have been impossible to imagine.

Tracing an explicit cause-and-effect relationship between movies and attitude changes is nigh impossible. But paradoxically, the peril that leaders of communist countries clearly perceived in allowing their peoples to see how others lived lends support to this proposition. Thus they have often only allowed the screening of "safe" movies, such as historical movies, or those portraying popular revolts or Western misery.[16] For that matter, to this day Cuba, North Korea, and to some extent China persist in their perception of the risks of allowing a free market in Western movies.

Al Gore's film *An Inconvenient Truth* is another example of the effectiveness of movies in producing – at least for a while[17] – palpable attitudinal change, in this case with respect to climate change. While most of the public cannot follow or evaluate the contradictory scientific claims and political stances with which they were being bombarded, Gore's vivid images were persuasive to a considerable proportion of the public. People worried about consequences of unchecked climate change; schools and colleges incorporated lessons in their curricula; and the media offered support for the call to act urgently to combat climate change. Yet this "persuasion success" was followed by a perceptible weakening of the collective resolve to act and forestall climate change. It may be useful to understand what characteristics made *An Inconvenient Truth* as successful as it was, especially in a field that usually attracts only the attention of environmentalists, a small subset of movie viewership. However, the negotiation field needs to understand not only which arguments through what media can produce attitudinal changes, but also what *sustains* them in the face of competition from a large set of other issues requiring attention and resources – as well as what causes a significant section of the public to conclude after a while that the same movie is selling them "a bill of goods."

The rather short half-life of *An Inconvenient Truth* likely has multiple causes, but one equal in salience to the movie's dire predictions for the future was the current severe economic downturn, which overtook public attention. Thus one hypothesis to be explored is that to be persuasive (and therefore useful for informal education) movies need to propose messages that either tap into already salient concerns (content) or arrive when few other concerns would compete (timing).

Films are routinely used in formal education, in recognition of their potential – for better or worse – to deliver direct or indirect information about past and present, as well as messages that might, and do, affect contemporary outlooks and behaviors. For better, the popular knowledge base can be enriched, and positive attitudinal and behavioral changes can be addressed, with relatively little effort. For worse, some of the same considerations apply.

One example of "for worse" from the standpoint of negotiation education are films that can and do make violence look like the socially approved choice of the brave, with no downside other than red paint splashed over the screen. They can also communicate a view of history that corresponds less to the facts than to the filmmaker's special pleading. (*Triumph of the Will* and other Nazi films by Leni Riefenstahl are merely the most notorious among a long and deplorable list of propaganda movies in the service of various dictatorial regimes.) The same audience aspects that make films a convenient and effective way of promoting positive social change – such as people's thirst for being entertained, and their general lack of factual knowledge against which can be pitted safely a fabricated reality that appears deceptively real (nowadays in 3-D!) – can yield results that society as a whole might not have sought.

For all of these reasons, two of our main challenges in using film as a vehicle for informal education are: 1) to design materials that carry *our* messages and that work well with both old and new platforms, as they are used by different audiences, and 2) to find the appropriate avenues for disseminating effectively the kinds of conflict management behavior we as practitioners and teachers find most constructive. These are not simple matters.

In the classroom experience of a course that uses film, an instructor can select the movies and the messages to be brought out, and can use debriefing to ensure that the desired message has actually reached the students. In contrast, informal education through films offers neither control over the message nor the opportunity to mitigate through debriefing any unintended messages. Success is possible – for example, the TV mini-series *Roots* helped to change long-entrenched erroneous perceptions and understandings of history. The work of Jacques-Yves Cousteau (and more recently, Gore's documentary *An Inconvenient Truth*) are powerful examples of successful outreach, communicating rather complicated, science-laden notions to a broad audience. But for worse, conspiracy-peddling movies (such as those related to President Kennedy's assassination) influence views of even recent history based on scant or decontextualized evidence. Thus, we should keep in mind that the film vehicle for informal education is a two-edged sword, precisely due to its ability to persuade through images. The same effects – changes in knowledge, attitudes and behavior – can operate in directions we seek, but also in directions we might consider undesirable.

Unless we devise an alternative form of delivery, the films we would consider helpful in portraying useful conflict management patterns have to be good enough to compete with the avalanche of movies in the marketplace, a daunting number of which model exactly the behaviors we most want to discourage. Perhaps we should instead construe "movies" as merely one example of a broader category of visual media. From this larger perspective we might include, for example, the kinds of short videos that "go viral" on YouTube or Facebook. Lest skeptical readers think that videos teaching negotiation skills informally might never rise to the level of viral, we might argue that even a lower level of success could still make a meaningful contribution – and that some examples[18] already exist of successful teaching of skills on such platforms. One example already mentioned is the *KhanAcademy* on YouTube, which already has more than 3000 videos to teach math and science skills for all ages.[19] Its success can be credited not least to a perfect match between message and venue: if the public we are attempting to reach tends to frequent YouTube, the likelihood of reaching them is considerably increased if we actually use YouTube. At the less-than-viral level, there already exists a considerable collection of YouTube-based negotiation videos, including film clips, cartoons and real negotiations. However, unless one already knows that negotiation insights might be useful and searches for them, the likelihood of stumbling upon such videos is rather small. Reaching out to large audiences informally will clearly require something more.

But can film foster, specifically, the emergence of conflict management modes such as (integrative) negotiation and mediation? One factor favoring such a societal role for films is that in general they tend to have a mimetic power on the audience: people want to be like their heroes. The news constantly reminds us, however, that people do not necessarily establish a direct link between fiction (and more generally, the representations carried by the broadcast media) and the reality they experience every day. This observation can be extended to video games, despite the controversy arising after each case of a violent crime perpetrated by a supposedly compulsive player.

More generally, citizens of countries anchored in a Judeo-Christian culture tend to maintain a distance between the images they see reflected in the contemporary media and their reading of reality, perhaps partly because they have had a longer time span to adjust. In general, the nuances of the relationship between image and reality are specific to different cultures, and demand our attention. Charles Tesson, former editor of *Les Cahiers du Cinema* and a specialist in Asian cinema, has argued that in terms of how images are processed by viewers there is a strong distinction between Judeo-Christian cultures and Asian cultures, driven by significantly different religious traditions. Image representation in the latter, he states, is less reflexively questioned and more likely to be uncritically accepted. Tesson mentions several "Asian change blockbusters" in this context. For example, he describes *Madame Freedom*, a 1957 Korean film, as a commercial as well as attitude-change success in its home market. This film revolves around the liberties taken by men but also, and more importantly, by women in couples. The main female character emerges from her shyness to assert her freedom to work, to socialize, to earn money and retain control of it, and to have love affairs. This movie became a classic for a generation of women who found in it a representation of their desire for emancipation.

The behavioral mimetism that characterizes the relationship between spectator and the role played by an actor is even more striking in the case of Indian consumers of Indian films. Bollywood is a good illustration of a cinema that manages to maintain a conspicuous moral tone. And in India, the cinema still has a greater influence than TV.[20] Directors can become real gurus, and film companies aware of their roles and responsibilities develop audacious movies. The films they produce provide for the audience a code of permissiveness and a scale of acceptable transgressions. Indian cinema has thus inherited the traditions of both sacred and profane theater. Like theater, Indian cinema's implicit philosophical stance is no longer to disseminate religious texts, but rather to promote a change of mental models.

One example is *Dilwale Dulhania Le Jayenge* (in English, *The Big Hearted Will Take the Bride*), a 1995 Bollywood film about forced marriage and the need to allow young people to choose their spouses. The father of the heroine is an Indian native living in London. He rejects modern culture, and requires his daughter to return to India to marry the man he has chosen for her. During a journey in Switzerland the girl falls in love with a "modern" Indian young man, who also lives in London, but does not fit her father's image of the ideal husband – he is Europeanized, drinks beer, etc. The option of the girl being kidnapped by her lover is clearly entertained; but eventually the young man agrees to submit to the rules set by his intended's father. This gesture of submission, however, leads in turn to changes in the father's outlook. He ends up accepting the possibility of breaking with tradition, and allowing his daughter to choose the man she loves. For the filmmaker, the father represents the benevolent state. It has been argued that village Indian viewers watch movies like this one with a measure of naiveté: in their eyes, beyond embodying his role, the actor really *is* the character he represents.

Some films intended to carry a social message have had unforeseen uses and contradictory consequences. Consider *The Battle of Algiers*, the 1966 Italian-Algerian film by Gillo Pontecorvo. It chronicles the struggle of the Algerian National Liberation Front (FLN) and the military victory of French paratroopers, using methods of counterinsurgency – displacement, torture – that led to military victory being undermined by loss in the battle for "hearts and minds." This film has been used by intelligence services in Latin America to train their officers and prepare them for fight against rebel movements, and more recently by the Pentagon to show how a battle against terrorism can be won (in Iraq). Similarly, *Objective, Burma!*, a movie directed by Raoul Walsh (1945), served to train Israeli Haganah recruits. There are clearly risks in assuming that a film will be perceived, or used programmatically, in accordance with the maker's intentions.

Can negotiation and mediation processes provide suitable topics to make *good* movies, or to become part of a screenplay that captures the public's fancy? This question is the film version of the theatrical requirement of "a crackin' good show" (see the next section) and is just as essential to sustained ability to produce new works on behalf of or in relation to our field. Movies about police hostage negotiators, while often exciting, have had a tendency to elicit eye-rolling among actual police hostage negotiators, despite their frequent claim to have hired expert advisers (Honeyman 2001-2009). Their educational value is thus suspect. One of the pillars of a good script, meanwhile, is the personal journey that forms and transforms the main characters. The change they undergo is the result of their adventures and of their choices. This speaks to the audience, which also vicariously lives the characters' experiences. Some filmmakers believe that through mimicry, this vicarious experience can trigger positive (or negative) change in spectators' behavior. It was said that members of the Mafia – the real one – were so impressed by Francis Ford Coppola's movie *The Godfather* that the movie had a strong impact not only on the public at large, but also on the gangsters' culture.

Could the search for compromise through negotiation and the highlighting of integrative solutions provide useful motors for fiction and, more generally, for documentary or fiction movies? We would need to overcome some major difficulties:

- Competition and the ensuing conflict are clearly driving forces behind the vast majority of films, just as in theater. To excel, to discover oneself, to accept oneself, to win over a loved one, all this while overcoming difficulties through "personal challenges" – these ingredients drive many plots. Notions of cooperation or the search for integrative solutions are difficult for writers to exploit in an equally exciting way. Scenes of negotiations in recent films, such as *True Grit*, are notable for distributive tactics more apt to garner admiration for the characters' devious skills than to model integrative approaches. In fact, they confirm cultural beliefs about how to conduct negotiations (mostly using a host of distributive tactics, each more marginally ethical than the next).

- Negotiation and mediation are quintessentially joint rather than unilateral decision-making processes. But acting unilaterally is usually one of the keys to the success of a movie character. The hero is called upon to decide, to respond and react, often quickly. However, not only does it take time to achieve results through negotiation and mediation, the use of those processes presupposes that the hero recognizes interdependence with others, and is ready to accept that other people may have different approaches with logics of their own.

- We teach students to take the time to study the specifics of a context. This contravenes the typically Manichean perspective of movies. Thus it is unclear whether the complex reality of negotiations can provide fodder for even the most adroit screenwriter. Yet there are encouraging exceptions; the fact that they are few speaks to the difficulties they faced. Some of them – *Citizen Kane* comes to mind as to complexity, if not as to a "cooperative" hero – have been extremely well-received. In a lighter vein, the Billy Crystal/Robert De Niro partnership in *Analyze This* offers plenty of psychological complexity. On television, *The West Wing*, which has rapidly become a classic, is chock-full of complex negotiation behavior, including believable dilemmas, coalition-building and trade-offs.

Nevertheless, by nature long-drawn-out, more complicated and less dramatic than unilateral decision, negotiation and mediation are often either relegated to second place or entirely absent from television or movie plots. The quest for victory is an easier story line with which to inspire the public than the search for an acceptable compromise.

How might we incorporate into a documentary what we usually teach in negotiation courses? There are at least two ways to do this. One way is to do it non-explicitly. Another way is to make it the central or at least secondary subject of the movie. In the first alternative, we are presented with many options, as long as what we teach is diverse and can be exemplified by many situations. However, the principle of cooperation underlying "integrative bargaining" is difficult to surface or to illustrate without showing an actual negotiation. But except for some specific cases and particular subjects, it is rare to find integrative bargaining negotiation scenes or situations in a movie. On the other hand, the principles that guide interactions in communication, including those underlying active listening and those that aim to reduce perceptual asymmetries, can be illustrated. For example, it is possible to draw the viewer's attention to the need to consider multiple viewpoints.

One of the authors, Eric Blanchot, attempted to do just that in a film on the role of North-African sharpshooters in the victories of the French army in 1942-45. The avowed aim was to reconcile the memories of the French of Algeria – i.e., those who resettled in France after 1962 – with the memories of Algerian immigrants, and more broadly of immigrants from the Maghreb, regarding events they recall of the voluntary sacrifices their parents and grandparents made during World War II. People bring up these sacrifices as the basis for their claims to greater equality, in the spirit of a republican logic inherited from the French Revolution and inspired by the Athenian democracy (which expanded the rights of citizenship to the ship rowers who had participated in the naval victory over the Persians). On one side were the memories of a rather reactionary colonial army (in the spirit of Pétain), sometimes close to the extremists of French Algeria. On the other side, there was the movement behind the "march of the Beurs,"[21] considered to be politically to the left of the left. The perceptual asymmetries are extremely strong and polarized. The filmmaker's intention was to avoid offending against either of these two streams of memories, but rather to attempt to foster bilateral empathy, to help these two groups open communication between two closed universes by appealing to the "superordinate goal" of promoting a shared pride and solidarity among these former combatants.

Two immediate consequences followed for the movie participants and for the subject of the movie. In one, Eric was forced to exclude a great Algerian figure, Ahmed Ben Bella, who fought in 1940 and then in Italian and French campaigns of 1943-44. Although Ben Bella agreed to be interviewed, Eric did not include him in the movie, because his voice and his face would have reminded many French of the Algerian war and of the loss of this territory, which would have rekindled the passions around the war. Similarly, Eric had to abandon any mention of the Sétif massacres and of the brutal repression of the May 1945 riots in Algeria (resulting in tens of thousands of victims). Combatants in Europe at that time had not been apprised of this repression (many were to leave soon after for Vietnam). These choices, open to criticism by those representing the memories of the victims, seemed essential for any reconciliation to succeed. Thereafter, to allay the suspicions of "pieds-noirs"[22] veterans, the author had to reassure them about the movie, and avoid making it seem to argue against them.

In the body of the movie, this translates into superimposed claims that may seem contradictory, and lacking in any attempt to choose between the several logics and several interpretations of the shared lived events. For example, did the fighters have a political consciousness, and had *they* aspired to independence? Or were they simple "fellahs",[23] following their leaders with no other purpose than their individual survival? Both contentions are present in the film, one following the other. Two "original French" veterans – one from the Vosges and one from Alsace – contend with empathy that the fighters from the colonies should have been awarded French nationality. None of these direct witnesses have criticized these choices, although no one was fooled by them. It is never easy to reduce perceptual asymmetries, and to encourage empathy and mutual listening. This movie was rather successfully shown on many French TV channels, and has been seen in North Africa as well (where, however, it unsettled Algerian intellectuals present at debates that followed the screenings).

The other alternative mentioned is to make movies whose very subject deals with negotiations, and analyze, for example, the rules and/or the practices of actors. In 2006 Eric made two documentaries: *The Time for Debating* and *The Age of Negotiations*, both focused on French union-management negotiations. Several clips show how the actors should behave in a good negotiation (interspersed with the Quebec contract bargaining model). Negotiators discuss past experiences and several experts explain how this arena came to be, how it has evolved since the 1920s and with which participants. Several clips allow for a comparison of the views of management and of union representatives. The subject of the reduced workweek illustrates an integrative negotiation, with the zone of possible agreement, the importance of the relationship, principal-agent tensions, and the constructive use of ambiguity. The movie was appreciated by both union and management representatives as well as by the politicians who have watched it, including some close to the presidency of the Republic (but it has not been aired again since then, and has therefore not been a *commercial* success).

We are confronted here with an added difficulty. Like the 1995 film *Our Friends at the Bank*, showing two years of debt negotiations between the World Bank and Uganda, Eric's films necessarily tackle complex problems. Having tested them with uneducated audiences, Eric is certain they are very accessible, sufficiently clear, and quite understandable outside the circles of power. However, although these subjects – business negotiations, unemployment insurance, etc. – are part of current everyday life, television channels are hesitant to show them. They self-censor whenever the topics have the potential to be difficult and provoke anxiety, which might translate into poor ratings. This creates added obstacles for movies that would benefit the general public by showing the underpinnings of a system that affects all citizens.

Does this mean that we should not enter the "belly of the beast" and talk about such negotiations? It is probably more accurate to say that we must reassure broadcasters by broaching less politically controversial topics, less marked by confrontation than union-management contract negotiations. Avoiding overly technical subjects such as the national debt might also be advisable. For example, a film about mediators of rural agricultural conflicts in the United States would pose fewer challenges. An exotic touch is probably helpful. This amounts to teaching negotiations by using situations that are simpler and less politically laden. For example, this is the case of Jihan El Tahri's movies, on the Cubans in Africa,[24] the negotiations that led to the independence of Namibia, or on the ANC,[25] which showed the negotiations that led to the end of apartheid in South Africa.

The future of negotiation movies may lie with fiction, and with TV series, but the success of reality TV as well as of "stealth" negotiation scenes embedded in some kinds of documentaries gives us hope. For instance, TV wildlife conservation series have sometimes included relevant stories of negotiation, particularly when the subject was deforestation. And on a less elevated level, the very popular reality TV shows may offer special opportunities. We might imagine an entire genre of "reality negotiation" shows (similar to "Court TV"). One such show could be set at a used car dealership. Alternatively, there are negotiation sidebar possibilities (or mediation alternatives) to all of the Judge Judy/People's Court-type shows; it would be relatively inexpensive to film negotiations before or after the judge rules in a dispute. This could attain a suitable level of drama even while modeling some integrative negotiation strategies. On the fiction side, a first U.S. series with a mediator as heroine, the recently produced *Fairly Legal,* seems to have attracted a relatively large audience. However, it is too early to take stock of even this one explicit commercial foray into our field. Although we are unlikely to be able to persuade more scriptwriters and producers to see the dramatic possibilities of the world of negotiation and mediation, this does not mean we should give up. The very existence of such a series produced for a highly competitive television market should encourage us to persevere.

This brings us to the third platform for teaching negotiation informally (after electronic games and film) – theater. It is becoming apparent that for our purposes there are at least two different ways of looking at theater: as an art form observed from outside, similar to the movie-watching experience just discussed, or as an active experience close to what the *Rethinking Negotiation Teaching* project has been developing under the heading of "adventure learning." We will discuss these two alternatives in succession.

Theater as Observed Art

Readers of this chapter are likely to be familiar with some of the Greek tragedies; merely mentioning them may be enough to note that the history of this art form extends back more than two thousand years. From early on, theater plays served to explore in a public/communal way a variety of conflict situations, and ways – some rather brutal – of coping with them. Plays often mirrored their time, reflecting and reinforcing codes of conduct some of which (we are glad to say) are out of favor nowadays. Since violence is frowned upon at least theoretically, perhaps theater can now serve not merely to mirror this rather well-established societal attitude, but also to demonstrate some peaceful ways out of conflicts that would otherwise be tackled violently.

Some plays and artists give voice to a message at a critical time or place. They give us models for bravery or eloquence, or illustrate the capacity for endurance and hope of the human spirit. The present-day campaign of the Belarus Free Theatre and the 1993 production of *Hair* in Sarajevo are two such examples. Mark Fischer (2008) suggests:

> The work of Dublin's Abbey Theatre contributed to the cultural movement towards nationalism and the foundation of the Republic of Ireland [and] . . . Terence Rattigan's thinly disguised gay play *Table Number Seven*, written when homosexuality was illegal, (was identified) as a "milestone" in the "shifting nature of public tolerance [that] shows the capacity of art to anticipate legal reform."

Similarly, riots prompted by the production of *Behzti* in Birmingham (U.K.) in 2005 revealed issues around censorship and gender inequalities in the Sikh community. This revelation shook the community and generated a new public discourse on these and related issues.

In recent years formal theater has lost some of its currency, with broad audiences attracted to more accessible and affordable entertainment media, such as television, movies and Internet. Yet theater remains influential in cities where "opinion leaders" live; also, a number of films and TV productions continue to originate on the stage. Theater is, moreover, a regular component of nonformal education for schoolchildren (as a popular after-school activity) and for college students (who also view theater as an outlet for their creative aspirations). In many places, it also functions on a community level, partly through amateur theater groups.[26] Furthermore, although the number of Broadway or West End productions may be down, the social attitude change effects of the surviving productions seem undiminished. Commentators have cited *Angels in America*, for example, as having had an influence on U.S. public attitudes toward gay rights; similarly, a distinguished series of mid-twentieth-century theatrical works had a widely discussed role in changing white attitudes toward African-Americans.

Theater offers an immediacy and intimacy of contact, and a vividness that may contribute to the effectiveness of informal learning. However, using theater plays as a direct vehicle for informal education may be limited in reach, as this medium must now compete with so many other avenues and modes of entertainment. Therefore, we should explore ways to conserve the advantages and overcome the drawbacks of this medium by bringing theater elements onto newer platforms with large traffic, such as the Internet. For example, as proposed in the section on games, we might design short (YouTube-length) productions incorporating negotiation and conflict management aspects, to be disseminated not only through YouTube but also other portals such as TED,[27] whose motto is "Ideas worth spreading." Its 2011 project TED-ED has in fact called on educators to submit precisely this kind of educational material, and as of yet it has no section on negotiation.

Theater as Experiential Education

There is a second sense in which theater could be employed in the informal teaching of conflict management. The *making* of theater (and the making of films or electronic games, for that matter) is rife with conflict, yet the mantra of the field is "the show must go on." As a result, some theater companies (not all) may constitute a kind of crucible in which daily practice models some (not all) negotiation notions and practices our field hopes to teach. It is possible to imagine that instead of managing conflict in order to put on a show, the coin might be turned over by deliberately putting on a show in order to create an authentic and engaging form of adventure learning (see generally Alexander and LeBaron 2009, as well as numerous other discussions of adventure learning in volumes 2, 3 and 4 of this teaching series). The premise of such an endeavor is that working, living, and collaborating with people who are different from us might function as a kind of training camp for the management of conflict situations.

Theater is an inherently collaborative endeavor. Some theater groups, however, particularly seek to embrace this collaborative essence, and to develop each aspect of the creative process to be as rich and layered as possible. One of the authors, Rachel Parish, founded such a company. We describe next an example of that company's experience, which illustrates the kinds of issues it finds important to consider in producing a play.

Process

This group does not start with a script. Instead, it assembles a team of artists to *develop* an idea for a play. The idea is developed through joint research, discussion and brainstorming. The team then develops a method of engaging the public with creative activities surrounding the themes of the play, and gathers real-life stories around the subject, which are then used as source material for assembling the play. The artists develop the play, and eventually a script is created for a production that is then performed. Both artists and non-artists actively contribute (in different ways) to the play-making process. But a high level of professionalism, of theatrical craft, is an ongoing demand throughout.

Two ideas anchor this type of process: 1) The show is more important than any one person/group's ideas, and 2) *no one* knows what the show should or will be until it emerges from the joint efforts. The show is not a thing, or a "product"; it is a meeting of minds, and a new collaborative event between an audience and the players in a particular time and space. This is reminiscent of Ken Fox's (2009: 22) description of negotiation as a dialogic process "where new meaning

is made and remade." The group's actions and thinking throughout
the process are guided by active listening and consensus building.

Starting a New Production

One new production began with a week-long brainstorm with a group
of artists. The theme of the week was "The contemporary relationship
to belief." The group explored the theme by sharing personal stories,
anecdotes and targeted research, and also by creating improvisations,
writing and staging ideas. One of the stories shared during that week
was a childhood memory of a preschool classmate:

> There was a child named Superjohn, who always wore a Superman
> outfit, and seemed to have superpowers. He was bald, and had to go
> away often. When he went away, you felt scared, because you knew
> he was doing something dangerous, but you knew, in your 4 year-old
> logic, that if anyone could do it, Superjohn could, because he had su-
> perpowers.

This story sparked a number of questions and ideas, and became the
basis for the production "Superjohn, A Play for All the Family": an adventure story about how children use their imagination to cope with
adversity. It is told through the eyes of two children, John, a child
with leukemia, and his "savior sister," Star.

A creative team of director, writer, and designer developed the
story line further. At the outset, all three generated ideas for images
and narrative together. As months went by, each took on an increasingly specialized role. They identified additional stakeholders (below)
and brought them into the team in different ways that fit their respective needs and circumstances. As stakeholders became engaged, the
show evolved and adapted its direction to the new information and
feedback.

The group has the following core question and answers constantly
in mind:

- How do we arrive at a show, any show?
- *We listen (with all of our senses). We make "offers"* (in their term-
  of-art theater sense, and using a range of communications;
  see Johnstone 1979), *and then we listen some more. We adapt. We
  work laterally, making both direct and indirect offers. We keep contributing until we move closer to the show. The show is an event – it
  is a meeting between audience and players in a particular place and
  time. During that meeting, new meaning is made – and perhaps new
  attitudes are forged.*

Identifying Stakeholders

In addition to conducting research, the theater group contacted hospitals and charities that deal with childhood cancer. They set up a partnership with an oncology clinic in North London, and began working with medical professionals and sitting in on chemotherapy sessions. They met children with cancer and their families, and learned firsthand about the multiple aspects of treatment. Then they ran creative workshops, and held one-on-one interviews with people from across the sectors involved in childhood leukemia-related issues. At the same time, the theater group began involving family theaters in London, and established a partnership with a theater to support the group along its first stages of development.

The group drew up a list of stakeholders. These were numerous: local government councils where the activities are taking place, the Arts Council England, local schools/teachers/students, national childhood cancer charities, national theater venues, local families, medical charities, related interest and activist groups.

Essential questions in identifying stakeholders are similar to those asked by public policy mediators: *Who is this play for? Who is it about? How do we get in contact with them? Who needs to know about this project?* The group begins by engaging the immediately obvious stakeholders, and listening to what they say. They find out that there are certain issues of which they weren't aware before, or that were obscure even to those immediately involved. The group then engages with the people or groups thus discovered. This parallels (for obvious reasons) the "snowball" technique for convening a group of stakeholders when building consensus around an initiative or mediating a public dispute.

Defining the Objectives of the Play

Some of the objectives of our example production are specific to the situation; one is common to all theatrical ventures.

1) Make a play that explores an issue, such as, in our example, the role of *imagination* in dealing with adversity from a child's point of view.

2) Make a play that deals (in this instance) with issues surrounding childhood cancer, providing insight into
   a) the relevant science;
   b) the experience of the child's family;
   c) the relationships between the medical professionals.

3) Provide opportunities for members of the public, both with and without an experience of the issue, to *participate* in the creative process. In the given example, integration and cohesion between kids and families with and without cancer experiences are promoted.

4) Make a play that is "a crackin' good show," and one that will have wide appeal for a general family audience. The group is, after all, one of *theater* professionals.

Does this start to look relevant to negotiation and conflict management professionals, and their teachers? Like negotiators and conflict management professionals, the theater group must ask the right questions; identify all the stakeholders; find direct and indirect ways of bringing the stakeholders into the process at the earliest stage possible; develop means of communication between people with vastly differing needs; and still, remain subservient to the unifying goal (acknowledging here that the goals of a theater company differ from those of the conflict manager of a public conflict).

How has this process worked in the theatrical environment? As Rachel's company has found, the most important action by far is to identify the main *theatrical* goal, and to make sure that everyone commits to that goal before they begin the work: "we are going to make a really good show." Rachel admits she does not know at the outset how that will be achieved, and none of the other collaborators – artistic, medical, patients, producers – knows either. But they all share a unified objective.

At the outset, it is natural that everyone should have different views and wants. If anyone said "we're taking *x* position" early on, that might alienate some of the present stakeholders, not to mention those yet to be identified. The topic of childhood cancer in our example is a sensitive one, providing many opportunities for messing up in some way. However, the group articulates from the outset that "we're going to find something *together*." Group members resolve to travel down an exploratory path, and arrive at an event. This event is their unifying goal – and thus their greatest asset for collaboration. It yields a production that is bigger than the individual, larger than anyone's ownership of ideas, a clearly more attractive prospect than sticking intransigently to one's own viewpoint. Each group member has very different reasons for wanting to reach that goal. But everyone, especially Rachel as the "leader" of this process, must be committed to this subservience to the shared objective.

In putting together *Superjohn,* everyone involved in the process had to think and work in new ways. They had to learn new ways of communication, and practice active and multisensory listening. They had to adapt. They had, to put it in the terms of the *Rethinking Negotiation Teaching* project, to develop and practice their skills at negotiation, in a complex, iterated, and authentic way.[28]

And they never set foot in a classroom situation throughout.

Conclusion

"Conclusion" is, perhaps, an odd word to use at this juncture: we believe we are at the very beginning of a new direction. We will cheerfully admit that as of this moment, we have only the beginnings of an idea as to where this direction might lead us. To begin, it seems probable that we will need not a few, but many approaches and a variety of venues. Then, the strategy for each approach will need to take into account at least its *known or likely* strengths and limitations, for our purposes (such as age-based preferences among specific media such as YouTube, the risk of a film being subjected to a use or interpretation quite contrary to its makers' intent, or a game being found boring because it is designed with too much collaboration and not enough competition).

Beyond this, we could speculate that the collaborative theater process described above may be easier for, say, a local community or church group to imagine adapting to their own needs than is electronic game development, with its daunting level of investment by commercial players. But it will take significant further thinking and experimentation even to approach any conclusions as to what varieties of theater (observed or, particularly, participatory), film or YouTube-like media, and games (electronic or other) might provide for the general public some degree of what our roughly 100 colleagues have worked hard, these past years, to update for formal teaching and training. It will take still more work, no doubt by an expanded cast of characters, to begin to reap measurable results. Yet at the beginning of the past thirty years' formal teaching and training of negotiation and related fields there were many fewer committed players than are available today, and as a first generation's work goes, the results were not too shabby.

That said, it is time to recognize that one of the great strengths of our field – its numerous, committed and often ingenious teachers – has inadvertently kept our attention away from what may be an even more fruitful area of future inquiry. Simply put, our field has been highly dependent on the enrolled, organized teaching and training of new negotiators and mediators, to the point where even many of the better *practitioners* earn a significant part of their living from relatively formal teaching and training. In such an environment, it is only natural that the current project should have focused on the revamping of formal methods of education and training. There has been more than enough to do. The relatively little attention paid to the mechanisms by which most of humanity has actually learned most of what it knows and does has been not only a near-inevitable consequence, in the "short term" characterized by budgets, workloads and timetables, but a price well worth paying – for a while.

But no longer. This is an appropriate point to conclude the *Rethinking Negotiation Teaching* project, and to start to think about what our field might need next.

Notes

The authors thank Elaine L. Andrews, director emeritus of the University of Wisconsin's Environmental Resources Center, for her advice in the preparation of this chapter.

[1] Admittedly, one moment of this gradual progression may be viewed as "teaching," loosely construed. Having appreciated the depth of the resistance to the new technology, our protagonist sought some way of introducing doubt into the certainty of "this isn't for me." He discovered a website which, using reports from drivers throughout the United States, identified the locations of the favorite speed traps of every police force in the country. His colleagues, midnight mediators all with a geographic range of practice covering tens of thousands of square miles, were at unusually high risk from speed traps. He innocently sent them the link – which was well-received. The effect of this single gambit is not verifiable. It is a matter of record that behavioral change did occur; however, it seems doubtful that a single identifiable moment of "informal teaching" could have been the all-powerful key.

[2] There are other models that fit better with other kinds of situations, and that would reward study once our subject is fairly launched; but the differences are beyond the scope of this initial chapter.

[3] Note that indirect learning, from a peer who has been trained, is a mode that falls between the two poles described here, formal and informal. Two examples by Shmueli, Wallace, and Kaufman (2009) describe such teaching and learning in a Washington, DC gang environment, and in Bedouin villages in Israel. The teaching was tailored to each case but did not reach everyone. Instead, in both cases it was directed at leaders, who in turn taught conflict management skills through their own behavior and by instituting deliberation rules within their groups that amounted to teaching integrative negotiation.

[4] http://www.ilinet.org/display/ILI/Home (last accessed June 18, 2012).

[5] http://www.ilinet.org/display/ILI/Home (last accessed June 18, 2012).

[6] For example, conservation programs, which have been studied extensively are most likely to be effective when developed by a team that includes a natural resource expert and an educator, and when they are designed to enhance related goals of a network or organization.

[7] For an overview of free-choice learning, see Institute for Learning Innovation, http://www.ilinet.org/display/About/Free-Choice+Learning (last accessed June 18, 2012.) One application tailored to our field can be found at Honeyman 1999.

[8] Sometimes it is not so covert. "The playing-fields of Eton" have been famously influential – but in their relationship to British colonialism, and therefore the generation of conflict, have had a great deal to answer for.

[9] The arguments around the effects of violent games on youth mirror the debates surrounding traditionally gory childhood stories (including *Mother*

Goose and other favorites). In that case too, some argue that children have understood and enjoyed these stories for centuries without any ill effect, while others would "sanitize" or forbid them to avoid children's exposure to rather extreme depictions of violent acts (consider, for example, *The Old Woman Who Lived in a Shoe*, or *Hansel and Gretel*).

[10] While at this stage we were unable to find rigorous research results to support this notion, it seems widely accepted by the public, which is, in itself, a particularly telling indication of acknowledgement of the power of games (see, e.g., Singer 2009 and Gamepolitics.com (2010) at http://www.gamepolitics.com/2010/06/07/time-spent-playing-videogames-pays-drone-pilots (last accessed June 18, 2012).

[11] To get the measure of the information technology generation, consider Beloit College's Mindset List at http://www.beloit.edu/mindset/2015/ (last accessed June 18, 2012). It opens with:

> This year's entering college class of 2015 was born just as the Internet took everyone onto the information highway and as Amazon began its relentless flow of books and everything else into their lives. Members of this year's freshman class, most of them born in 1993, are the first generation to grow up taking the word "online" for granted and for whom crossing the digital divide has redefined research, original sources and access to information, changing the central experiences and methods in their lives.

[12] An excellent example of such a role-playing game, *Animonde,* was created by "croc," a French author, in 1988. *Animonde* is a game in which players are looking for internal peace and good relationships with others, as a way to create miracles(!) Unfortunately it was not a great success in the marketplace – unlike the same author's next game design, *In Nomine Satanis – Magna Veritas* (1989), which was very violent.

[13] *Republic of Rome* covers the period from 264 B.C. to 43 B.C. Three scenarios cover the Early Republic (roughly the era of the first and second Punic Wars), Mid Republic (the era of the Gracchi), and Late Republic (the time of the Roman civil wars and Julius Caesar). Each player represents a faction in the Roman Senate, with a collection of senators rated for their oratorical and military skills, popularity with the people of Rome, and most importantly, political influence. The goal of the game is to have one of one's senators amass enough influence to be declared "Consul for Life," or, barring that, have one's faction have most total influence when the maximum number of game turns has been played.

Within the game, Rome is threatened by foreign enemies and potential popular unrest. The heart of the game involves players managing the state's affairs in a series of mock Senate sessions, wherein proposals are made and voted on (with votes proportional to each player's total influence) to elect officers of the Senate (the Consuls and Censor, and in times of extreme emergency, a Dictator) and governors of provinces; to spend money to raise or disband legions and fleets; to appoint leaders to fight Rome's enemies with said military force; to enact land reforms to mollify the populace; and to prosecute Senators for putative ethical lapses, among other things. While pursuing their own individual goal of increasing their faction's influence, the players must co-operate to ensure that Rome is not overwhelmed by foreign threats, popular unrest, or bankruptcy, causing Rome to fall and all players to lose (although if a player's faction is in rebellion *against* Rome, they may win in such a situation). Within this framework, the players use diplomacy, alliances, persuasions, prosecutions, graft, bribery, murder and even conspiracies to advance their cause.

14 With these options in mind, we suggest some other practical channels through which negotiation education might be advanced, besides the electronic media on which we focus in the text:

- Creating a "negotiation play" variation of familiar and popular games, and including them in the instruction manual. For example, police procedural fiction has popularized the negotiations between local police and the FBI over cooperation in solving high-profile cases, with each seeking to maximize what they get and minimize what they give. This might be internalized into a new variation of the game of *Clue*, in which, as it is traditionally played, participants act individually, hoarding their information zealously, in pursuit of the murderer of Mr. Boddy.

- Providing guidance to parents: Game instruction manuals (such as that of *Monopoly* or *Risk*) could include information on how parents might develop their children's negotiation skills, utilizing opportunities presented by the game.

- Creating negotiation-themed games: These might be new board games (perhaps *Plea Bargain!* will become a reality, or the reality show *Shark Tank* might develop a home edition).

15 As technology became more sophisticated, this mix of individual gaming – allowing for limited or no "useful" interactions – and joint gaming has held, although one can see areas of overlap. For example, in *Age of Empires*, a series of strategy games in which players develop a civilization and aim to achieve regional domination through a mix of technological development, resource gathering and force, players can chat with each other – and can change their diplomatic status towards one another to neutral, ally or enemy, based on the outcome of their talks. They can even set up a tribute-paying mechanism. This negotiation element is not only integrated into the multiplayer version, but into the single-player mode as well (albeit in a limited fashion), with the computer playing the role of the other civilizations, changing diplomatic status, or demanding that tribute be paid.

16 The rare Western movie that made its way to the public (such as *Acapulco* or *The Young Ones* in Romania) managed in no time to overturn years of communist indoctrination about the wretched lives of people in the West! The pendulum swung in the opposite direction: not a few among the public came to believe that Westerners really lived as in these musicals. Movies cannot be credited with the social change that took place in the Eastern Bloc at the end of the twentieth century. It is likely, however, that they helped create an idealized image of Western societies that offered an alternative, though they may also have contributed to later disillusionment (and nostalgia for the old communist regimes) that some people experienced, as their new life in freedom failed to match this image. Analyses of the "Arab Spring" events have also mentioned dynamics of social change similar to those in the Eastern Bloc. Again, images of life in the West contrasted with life in Middle Eastern and North African countries are widely believed to have led to people's desire to enjoy the political freedoms they saw exercised in Western movies and television series. In both the Eastern Bloc and Arab Spring examples, the reality is so complex that no single factor can be convincingly linked causally

to a specific event or societal effect. However, it does seem that at least the leaders of totalitarian countries believe firmly in the negative effect movies have on their ability to control their subjects, or they would not expend the effort and treasure that they do in order to prevent the "corrupting" Western messages from breaking through. All current dictatorships are in firm control of the media to which their peoples have access, and prefer to produce mass entertainment "in-house." As added proof of the effectiveness of movies in persuading the masses to a certain point of view, polls indicate that large majorities in totalitarian countries hold firm views about people and places they have never seen – and broadly subscribe to conspiracy theories that were widely disseminated through regime-produced movies and television productions.

[17] The recent and surprisingly rapid decay of interest in environmental issues and particularly climate change seems primarily due to the competing economic worries that have engulfed people's attention in the United States and other countries. It is far from clear, however, that the young are equally distracted.

[18] See, e.g., http://www.youtube.com/watch?v=7rzq2Bq_EsA&feature=fvsr (last accessed June 18, 2012); http://www.youtube.com/watch?v=JwjAAgGi-90&feature=related (last accessed June 18, 2012).

[19] See http://www.ted.com/talks/salman_khan_let_s_use_video_to_reinvent_education.html (last accessed June 18, 2012).

[20] We lack confidence that readily available figures for India are authoritative, but as of 2007 a New York Times article (www.nytimes.com/2007/02/11/business/yourmoney/11india.html?_r=1&partner=rssnyt&emc=rss, last accessed June 18, 2012) calculated that about half of Indian households had a television, at 103,000,000. This figure seems at odds with a database maintained by www.nationmaster.com, which estimates 63,000,000 television sets in India (www.nationmaster.com/country/in-india/med-media, last accessed June 18, 2012.) But either way, it is widely understood that a huge number of Indian citizens do not have ready access to television, while even the higher TV figure compares with movie viewership figures of 2.86 billion – the highest in the world, by a large margin (see above nationmaster.com page, citing UNESCO Institute for Statistics.).

[21] The March for Equality and against Racism (*Marche pour l'égalité et contre le racisme*), labeled the Beurs March (*Marche des Beurs*) by French media, was an antiracist march that took place in France in 1983, beginning in Marseille on October 15 with thirty-two persons and arriving in Paris on December 3 with more than 60,000 marchers. It was the first national antiracist demonstration ever held in France, on the model of the nonviolent actions of Martin Luther King, Jr. and Gandhi. Its two main demands were a ten-year residence permit for foreigners and the right of foreigners to vote.

[22] Pied-Noir is a term referring to French citizens who lived in French Algeria before independence. Specifically, Pieds-Noirs include settlers of European descent, from France or other European countries, who were born in Algeria.

[23] A fellah is a peasant, farmer or agricultural laborer in North Africa.

[24] *Cuba, une Odyssée Africaine*, un documentaire de Jihan El Tahri, ARTE 2007.

[25] *Behind the Rainbow* un documentaire de Jihan El Tahri, ARTE (2009).

[26] See for example the discussion of the social and even conflict-management uses of theater which the city culture of Vancouver has developed, in LeBaron and Honeyman 2006.

²⁷ TED describes itself as follows:

TED is a nonprofit devoted to Ideas Worth Spreading. It started out (in 1984) as a conference bringing together people from three worlds: Technology, Entertainment, Design. Since then its scope has become ever broader. Along with two annual conferences – the TED Conference in Long Beach and Palm Springs each spring, and the TEDGlobal conference in Edinburgh UK each summer – TED includes the award-winning TEDTalks video site, the Open Translation Project and TED Conversations, the inspiring TED Fellows and TEDx programs, and the annual TED Prize. http://www.ted.com/ (last accessed June 18, 2012).

²⁸ For more on the sometimes unusual methods of "teaching" implicated in this setting, see Honeyman and Parish 2013.

References

Abt, C. C. 1970. *Serious games*. New York: Viking Press.

Alexander, N. and M. LeBaron. 2009. Death of the role-play. In *Rethinking negotiation teaching: Innovations for context and culture*, edited by C. Honeyman, J. Coben, and G. DePalo. St. Paul, MN: DRI Press.

Avedon, E. M. and B. Sutton-Smith. 1971. *The study of games*. New York: Wiley.

Barlett, C. P., C. A. Anderson, and E. L. Swing. 2009. Video game effects – confirmed, suspected, and speculative: A review of the evidence. *Simulation & Gaming* 40(3): 377.

Crawford, C. 2003. *On game design*. Indianapolis, IN: New Riders Publishing.

Docherty, J. S. 2010. "Adaptive" Negotiation: Practice and Teaching. In *Venturing beyond the classroom: Volume 2 in the rethinking negotiation teaching series*, edited by C. Honeyman, J. Coben, and G. De Palo. St Paul, MN: DRI Press.

Druckman, D. and N. Ebner. 2010. Enhancing concept learning: The simulation design experience. In *Venturing beyond the classroom: Volume 2 in the rethinking negotiation teaching series*, edited by C. Honeyman, J. Coben, and G. De Palo. St Paul, MN: DRI Press.

Ebner, N. and K. Kovach. 2010. Simulation 2.0: The resurrection. In *Venturing beyond the classroom: Volume 2 in the rethinking negotiation teaching series*, edited by C. Honeyman, J. Coben, and G. De Palo. St Paul, MN: DRI Press.

Falçao, H. 2012. A competition without losers. *Assessing our students, assessing ourselves: Volume 3 of the Rethinking Negotiation Teaching series*, edited by N. Ebner, J. Coben, and C. Honeyman. St. Paul, MN: DRI Press.

Fischer, M. 2008. The plays that change the world. *The Guardian*, September 16. Available at www.guardian.co.uk/stage/theatreblog/2008/sep/16/theatre (last accessed June 18, 2012).

Fox, K. H. 2009. Negotiation as a post-modern process. In *Rethinking negotiation teaching: Innovations for context and culture*, edited by C. Honeyman, J. Coben, and G. De Palo. St Paul, MN: DRI Press.

Honeyman, C. 1999. *The alternative court: Covering dispute resolution. IRE Journal* Jan/Feb 1999: 13-15. Columbia, MO: Investigative Reporters & Editors, Inc.

Honeyman, C. 2001-2009. Personal correspondence with three present and former chief hostage negotiators of the New York Police Department (copies on file with author).

Honeyman, C., J. Coben, and G. De Palo (eds). 2010. *Venturing beyond the classroom: Volume 2 in the rethinking negotiation teaching series.* St. Paul, MN: DRI Press.

Honeyman, C. and R. Parish. 2013 (forthcoming). Make a move. In *Make movement matter: Conflict, dance and neuroscience,* edited by M. LeBaron, C. MacLeod, and A. Acland. Chicago: American Bar Association.

Huizinga, J. 1950. Homo ludens: A study of the play-element in culture. Boston, MA: The Beacon Press.

Johnstone, K. 1979. *Impro: Improvisation and the theater.* London: Methuen.

Khan, S. 2011. *Let's use video to reinvent education.* TED Talk, March 2. Available at www.ted.com/talks/salman_khan_let_s_use_video_to_reinvent_education.html (last accessed June 18, 2012).

LeBaron, M. and C. Honeyman. 2006. Using the creative arts. In *The negotiator's fieldbook: The desk reference for the experienced negotiator,* edited by A. K. Schneider and C. Honeyman. Washington, DC: American Bar Association.

Lederach, J. P. 2005. *The moral imagination: The art and soul of building peace.* Oxford University Press.

McGonigal, J. 2011. *Reality Is broken: Why games make us better and how they can change the World.* New York: Penguin.

NAAEE, 2004 *Nonformal environmental education programs: Guidelines for excellence.* North American Association for Environmental Education. Available at http://eelinked.naaee.net/n/guidelines/posts/Nonformal-Environmental-Education-Programs-Guidelines-for-Excellence (last accessed June 18, 2012).

Rogers, E. M. and F. F. Shoemaker. 1971. *Communication of innovations: A cross-cultural approach.* New York: Free Press.

Salen, K. and E. Zimmerman. 2003. *Rules of play – Game design fundamentals.* London: MIT Press.

Shmueli, D., W. Warfield, and S. Kaufman. 2009. Enhancing community leadership negotiation skills. *Negotiation Journal* 25(2): 249-266.

Singer, P. W. 2009. *Wired for war: The robotics revolution and conflict in the 21st century.* New York: Penguin Books.

Wohn, D. Y. 2011. Reciprocity in social network games and generation of social capital. Available at http://src.acm.org/2011/D.YvetteWohn.pdf (last accessed June 18, 2012).

౮ Epilogue ౿

The Biz

Christopher Honeyman & James Coben*

Editors' Note: Collectively, the scholarship produced in the RNT project significantly "ups the ante" for what teachers ought to provide (and students and institutions ought to demand) in quality negotiation education. But can these higher aspirations be reconciled with the rapidly changing economics of higher education and the "entertrainment" tendencies of the executive training field?

Month after month, year after year they keep coming: the fresh-faced young hopefuls, the middle-aged characters, all in search of the glamour, the excitement, the prestige, the riches . . . . Well, maybe not the last of these. We are, after all, talking of the new arrivals not to Hollywood, but to negotiation and conflict management teaching.

Ambition runs up against limitations in every field. But the limitations are not the same in every field. This Epilogue closes out not just this volume, but a five-year, four-volume project, in which more than a hundred people have delved quite deeply, we think, into a wide variety of issues about the how, what, why, when and who of teaching. The scholarship produced has ranged from "big picture" theoretical pieces to detailed descriptions of innovative (and eminently practical) teaching and assessment tools. Rarely, though, have the project's contributors confronted the substantial *barriers* to change.

* **Christopher Honeyman** is managing partner of Convenor Conflict Management, a consulting firm based in Washington, DC and Madison, Wisconsin. He has directed a 20-year series of major research-and-development projects in conflict management, including as co-director of the Rethinking Negotiation Teaching project. His email address is honeyman@convenor.com. **James Coben** is a professor of law and senior fellow in the Dispute Resolution Institute at Hamline University School of Law, and co-director of the Rethinking Negotiation Teaching project. His email address is jcoben@hamline.edu.

The limitations that have not taken up much space in this series may have received less attention because they are generally perceived as not under the control of individuals; and they can be daunting. They arise, we think, from three different sources. At least one of these, in our brief discussion below, probably *is* beyond the capacity of anyone in our field to influence very much. If we collectively can attack the others, however, the next generation of teachers, not to mention their students, might find it easier to learn good work and do good work (see Gardner, Csikszentmihalyi, and Damon 2001).

The first set of limitations arises from the institutional economics of teaching and training environments. These come in several different varieties; the constraints on a private firm offering "executive" courses are not the same as those of a major research university. But in each case, they unfortunately militate against many of the strategies and tactics for better and more comprehensive teaching as compiled in this series.

Law schools, for example, typically offer only one course in negotiation, valued in academic terms at two to three credits. We can see little likelihood in the near term, despite the conspicuously increasing sophistication of the material which *might* be taught and *should* be taught, that many law schools will provide the time to teach it. This flies in the face of the continuing enthusiasm of the students for the subject; it also is illogical in light of steadily increasing evidence that negotiation and related tasks will actually consume a greater proportion of the post-graduate working lives of law students than almost anything else such students might learn. The reasons why are beyond the scope of this brief wrap-up; but, anecdotal as our information may be, our contacts in business schools, planning schools, schools of international relations and other formal teaching environments are numerous, and have given us no reason to suppose that the picture is much better in any of their settings.

Compounding the problem is the virtual arms race that is the contemporary world of distance education (Matz and Ebner 2010: 1 note 1). Institutional pressure, coming perhaps more frequently from the chief financial officer than the academic provost, forces more and more courses into economical distance formats. Certainly, there is much to be gained in this new teaching environment (see Matz and Ebner 2010, and Fox and Press, *Venturing Home*, in this volume, for descriptions of extremely effective uses of online tools). But in the brave new world of massive open online courses ("MOOCs"), an on-going challenge will be finding cost-effective ways for teachers to interact directly, and on an individual basis, with their students (Papano 2012).

Executive trainers, meanwhile, find themselves pressed by the demands of their clientele toward ever shorter and less substantial courses. As John Wade caustically observed near the beginning of this project:

> It is easy to ensure success. Just lower expectations (as in negotiations). For example, lower expectations to these goals: first, pay the bills for the course, and second, ensure that the majority of participants "feel good" for at least two hours after the course is over (2009: 172).

We have been nonplussed, in more than one country, to observe the avidity of program managers not only for every practitioner-student to be offered courses of as little as half a day's duration, but for mere attendance at such a course to be memorialized by a printed certificate, fully the equivalent in gilding and scrollwork to anything issued by Harvard or Yale. One of our colleagues in this project, inured to the economic realities of executive training, has described much of what she does all year as "entertrainment." We are more saddened than entertained that her undoubted talents must be thus directed.

The likelihood of new ideas for negotiation and conflict management keeping up the rates of development of the last thirty years, meanwhile, must face off against the decline in support for basic research: at the time of this writing it has been almost eight years since the last stalwart among the major U.S. foundations that initially funded "R&D" in negotiation (the Hewlett Foundation) closed its innovative program in our area of concern. Aside from the JAMS Foundation (which has graciously funded the RNT project from its inception, but which would be the first to acknowledge that it is not in the same financial league as Hewlett, Ford or MacArthur, the field's original three funders) there has been no sign that any other such institution is ready to pick up the slack; and meanwhile, government support for research (in many fields, not just our own) has been a victim of bitter and shortsighted politics. At the same time, we can see little prospect in the near to medium term for U.S.-based or European educational institutions to devote greater resources of their own to this field, though it is possible that in Asia and emerging economies elsewhere the picture may be somewhat brighter. (It is also possible that our composite field strikes so many sparks that the rate of new discovery will remain higher than the rate of funding would predict. We certainly hope so.)

The second set of limitations is also economic, but individual rather than institutional. We do not refer here to the prospect of lower earnings and benefits, and worse retirement arrangements, for full-time faculty in Europe and the United States. Even though many anticipate an adverse environment on these measures, it is far from clear that faculty will be worse off than practitioners who are competing for jobs requiring a related skill set. Instead, it is the low pay and academic status of *adjunct* teachers that is the likely key source of trouble for innovation in teaching in the future, even if all that is asked is adoption of innovations created by the dedicated professionals who have been our colleagues in this series.

Simply put, adjunct teachers typically add on, to something resembling a full-time workload (or beyond) in practice work, a significant number of class hours, which are paid so badly that a tendency to give short shrift to preparation is almost inevitable. And their numbers in relation to tenure-track faculty continue to grow.

The cynicism that drives higher education institutions to adopt and expand this model *is* institutional, if particularly risible in a field like ours, in which the rate of new discovery is high and professional self-respect therefore demands constant attention and response to change. But this becomes an *individual* issue when instead of struggling against this tide, adjunct teachers treat it as normal, or natural, or inevitable. One of the editors was privileged to give an account of this project's discoveries and propositions to an audience billed as "academic," approximately eighty percent of which turned out to be composed of adjunct faculty. Their predominant reaction, unhappily, was dismay at the amount of additional and uncompensated work they perceived the project to be laying on them.

Somewhere between the second set of limitations and the third is the relentless pressure on tenure-track faculty to "produce," but in terms that unfortunately do not look like constructive or innovative production to us. More than ten years ago, in a predecessor project, one of the editors and two colleagues compiled the results from a series of experiments, with academics and practitioners from a wide variety of backgrounds (Honeyman, McAdoo, and Welsh 2001). The central conclusion was that one of the most adverse trends affecting our field – a *composite* field, in which this series alone should demonstrate how the innovation and the excitement derive largely from combining ideas from other fields into new concepts – was the tendency of departments in each "home" discipline to demand that faculty publish within a constricted range of recognized journals, each of which was resolutely uninterested in material that did not hew closely to the already-established concerns of the home discipline.

It does us little good to surmise, as we do, that the first biochemists must have had this problem in their "home" department, of either biology or chemistry, since they presumably must have come from one discipline or the other. Perhaps there were many biologists and chemists who were unable to persuade their departments and journal editors to tolerate such deviant work, and good work was thus lost from the historical record, or never proposed at all. Self-evidently, *enough* biochemists withstood such pressures.

For our field, however, in which a predecessor of this project, *The Negotiator's Fieldbook* (Schneider and Honeyman 2006) compiled wisdom from nearly thirty disciplines and practice specialties, the promising combinations can be a lot stranger than a biologist working with a chemist. (See, for example, the authors of *Negotiating Wicked Problems: Five Stories* [Chrustie et al. 2010, chapter 25 in *Venturing Beyond the Classroom*], which included a key hostage negotiator for the Royal Canadian Mounted Police, a former President of Ecuador, a professor of peacebuilding, a Lieutenant Colonel in the U.S. Army, and the ombudsman of the U.S. National Institutes of Health.) So in our field, the likelihood of this kind of wooden-headedness having a seriously adverse effect on future productivity is proportionately greater. While a significant number of established scholars have successfully navigated the economic and competitive pressures and joined our multi-disciplinary effort, it is far from clear that most academics can or will do anything similar, especially newer faculty, who may have the most to offer in the long run, but also the most to risk.

The final set of limitations is clearly individual and psychological. A predecessor to this project (see Honeyman, Ackerman, and Welsh 2003) compiled a full issue of a law review, a series of 17 articles, analyzing the causes and circumstances of *routinization* in our profession, and historically in others. We cannot improve on the findings of that project and will merely refer the reader to them.

So far, so "pretty bad." And we see little prospect for individuals in our field, or even sizable groups such as the hundred-plus scholars who have contributed to this project, to have much effect on such "macro" elements of this picture as the poor funding for basic research, or the pay level for adjuncts.

But on some of the more individual elements, individual determination can have a significant effect. Certainly the initiation of our field within academia did not occur in an environment of plenitude or of a welcoming attitude from established disciplines. Rather, it was the impregnable professional position of a small cadre of very accomplished faculty, who had decided to work together in a new area across disciplines, which allowed the first notable program of our field, the Program on Negotiation at Harvard Law School, to begin: The program's other resources came later.

We can at least hope, again, that if the RNT project has done anything of note, it has "upped the ante" for what teachers and students might logically expect for the future. Such intellectual and moral ambition can help put steel in the spine. If the reader believes that continuous change and development have now been demonstrated to be the core of professional self-respect for the future, that alone becomes an asset for our field. Fighting the concept of "entertrainment," and pressing on every level for the field's more searching discoveries to be taken more seriously in teaching, may be an incremental rather than epochal approach to change; but incremental change in some other fields has had a notably positive effect, over time.

At least one field in which practice and teaching occur on a mass basis, and which impacts every human being at multiple points during life, has conspicuously succeeded at this process. In medicine, new research is followed avidly by at least many practitioners, though not by all; it is widely reported in the press; and the resources provided to researchers and teachers alike are, by the standards of our profession, awe-inspiring. Perhaps the last hundred years' progress in medicine can serve as inspiration and example at the end of our project, just as it did when we began (Honeyman, Coben, and De Palo 2009: 13-14).

Everyone needs good health; everyone except a hermit needs to deal with other people. There is even research showing how failures of the latter can lead to failure in the former (see, e.g., Lawler et al. 2005; Recine, Werener, and Recine 2009). We do not claim to be able to see, by ourselves, how an entire field gets from A to B. But we can at least see how the topic needs to be on the field's continuing agenda. That much, at least, we hope this four-volume series has accomplished.

References

Chrustie, C., J. S. Docherty, L. Lira, J. Mahuad, H. Gadlin, and C. Honeyman. 2010. Negotiating wicked problems: Five stories. In *Venturing beyond the classroom: Volume 2 in the rethinking negotiation teaching series*, edited by C. Honeyman, J. Coben, and G. De Palo. St. Paul, MN: DRI Press.

Gardner, H. E., M. Csikszentmihalyi, and W. Damon. 2001. *Good work: When excellence and ethics meet*. New York: Perseus.

Honeyman, C., R. Ackerman, and N. A. Welsh (eds). 2003. Special issue of 17 articles, responding to the Broad Field Project/Penn State Dickinson Law School 2003 conference on threats to the conflict resolution field. *Penn State Law Review* 108(1): 1- 348.

Honeyman, C., J. Coben, and G. De Palo (eds). 2009. *Rethinking negotiation teaching: Innovations for context and culture*. St. Paul, MN: DRI Press.

Honeyman, C., B. McAdoo, and N. Welsh. 2001. Here there be monsters: At the edge of the map of conflict resolution. *The Conflict Resolution Practitioner*. Atlanta, GA: Office of Dispute Resolution, Georgia Supreme Court. Available at www.convenor.com/madison/monsters.htm (last accessed December 3, 2012).

Lawler, K. A., J. W. Younger, R. L. Piferi, R. L. Jobe, K. A. Edmondson, and W. H. Jones. 2005. The unique effects of forgiveness on health: An exploration of pathways. *Journal of Behavioral Medicine* 28(2): 157-167.

Matz, D. and N. Ebner. 2010. Using role-play in online negotiation teaching. In *Venturing beyond the classroom: Volume 2 in the rethinking negotiation teaching series*, edited by C. Honeyman, J. Coben, and G. De Palo. St. Paul, MN: DRI Press.

Papano, L. 2012. Year of the MOOC. *New York Times* (November 2).

Recine, A. C., J. S. Werner, and L. Recine. 2009. Health promotion through forgiveness intervention. *Journal of Holistic Nursing* 27(2): 115-123.

Schneider, A. K. and C. Honeyman (eds). 2006. *The negotiator's fieldbook: The desk reference for the experienced negotiator*. Washington, DC: American Bar Association.

Wade, J. 2009. Defining success in negotiation and other dispute resolution training. *Negotiation Journal* 25(2): 171-180.

THE RETHINKING NEGOTIATION TEACHING SERIES

Rethinking Negotiation Teaching:
Innovations for Context and Culture (2009)
Christopher Honeyman, James Coben and Giuseppe De Palo, Editors

Venturing Beyond the Classroom:
Volume 2 in the Rethinking Negotiation Teaching Series (2010)
Christopher Honeyman, James Coben and Giuseppe De Palo, Editors

Assessing Our Students, Assessing Ourselves:
Volume 3 in the Rethinking Negotiation Teaching Series (2012)
Noam Ebner, James Coben and Christopher Honeyman, Editors

Educating Negotiators for a Connected World:
Volume 4 in the Rethinking Negotiation Teaching Series (2012)
Christopher Honeyman, James Coben and Andrew Wei-Min Lee, Editors

Christopher Honeyman is managing partner of Convenor Conflict Management (www.convenor.com), a consulting firm based in Washington, DC and Madison, Wisconsin. He is co-editor of *The Negotiator's Fieldbook* (with Andrea Schneider; ABA 2006), co-editor of all four volumes in the *Rethinking Negotiation Teaching Series*, a founding editor of 谈判 *Tán Pàn: The Chinese-English Journal on Negotiation,* and author or co-author of more than seventy published articles, book chapters and monographs on dispute resolution. Honeyman has directed a twenty-year series of major R&D projects in dispute resolution, and has served as a consultant to numerous academic and practical conflict resolution programs in the United States and elsewhere. He has also served as a mediator, arbitrator or in other neutral capacities in more than 2,000 disputes since the 1970s.

James Coben is a professor of law at Hamline University School of Law in St. Paul, Minnesota and former director of Hamline's Dispute Resolution Institute, consistently ranked by *U.S. News & World Report* in the top five among U.S. law school dispute resolution programs. He teaches civil procedure and a variety of alternative dispute resolution (ADR) courses, and created three Hamline foreign programs – an international commercial arbitration program in London, an international business transactions negotiation program in Rome, and a program in democratic dialogue and mediation in Budapest. He has published numerous ADR-related articles, is co-editor of all four volumes in the *Rethinking Negotiation Teaching Series*, a founding editor of 谈判 *Tán Pàn: The Chinese-English Journal on Negotiation,* and co-author of the third edition of *Mediation: Law, Policy & Practice* (West 2011).

Andrew Wei-Min Lee is the founder and president of the Leading Negotiation Institute, founded in 2007 and based in Shanghai. The Leading Negotiation Institute's mission is to develop dispute resolution pedagogy and practice in China. The Institute partners with leading universities and dispute resolution institutions both within China and around the world to provide opportunities to exchange personnel, ideas and opportunities in the field of negotiation and dispute resolution.

Made in the USA
San Bernardino, CA
15 November 2013